Encyclopedia of Popular Music

ENCYCLOPEDIA
of
POPULAR MUSIC

by Irwin Stambler

with special material by Vern Bushway,
W. P. Hopper, Jr., Hal Levy and Jean Majors

ILLUSTRATED WITH PHOTOGRAPHS & DRAWINGS BY
CONSTANCE STAMBLER

ST. MARTIN'S PRESS *New York*

Published in Canada by
THE MACMILLAN COMPANY OF CANADA LIMITED
70 Bond Street, Toronto 2

With love to
*Amy Ruth and Alice Joan, Lyndon Sidney
and Barrett Charles*

PICTURE CREDITS

Introduction and Acknowledgments

THE KALEIDOSCOPE that is popular music is a constantly shifting, always unpredictable fact of modern life. Because it is such a diverse medium, running the gamut from musical comedy to rock 'n' roll, it has usually been treated in book form one component at a time. The goal of this book is to present the full spectrum—to try to give the breadth and depth of popular music: the people responsible for it, its various forms, and its effects on modern life.

This is a tall order. To present every detail, list every person who deserves listing, define every term used in this field, or cover every successful musical of the past few decades would take not one book but dozens. This is a common difficulty of any encyclopedia, as a review of all of them, up to the most famous, amply demonstrates. It is possible, however, to distill the essence of any field, to present the most important highlights in careers and events that will, in turn, provide a meaningful panorama. Any encyclopedia must be such a distillation. This has been the basis of the encyclopedia concept, and its feasibility is illustrated by the importance of such volumes as references.

It is our belief that this book, despite its limitations, provides the most information on the overall field of popular music currently available between hard covers. But the goal has not been a dry recapping of facts and figures. Even a reference book can be entertaining, and this has been a major aim of this project. As much as possible, the attempt has been made to provide a series of vignettes of people or events that have affected the pulse of America and the world in recent years.

The Encyclopedia of Popular Music is not one book but is made up, to some extent, of books within a book. The various items can be read separately or, in some cases, as a group that can provide insight into certain areas.

The approximately seventy synopses of musicals also can be considered a book within a book. The goal here is not to include every hit musical of the last forty years but to cover the spectrum of musical form and content from 1925 to the present. The major types—revue, musical comedy, musical play, and operetta—are represented, and the shows described include efforts by most of the major writers of the period.

The list of song histories is also not intended to provide anything approaching coverage of all the successful songs of the past few decades. The objective is to show the many ways in which songs come to be written and the problems involved in getting them before the public. The songs discussed in the book were selected to include the different kinds of popular songs—romantic ballads, folk, instrumental, rock 'n' roll, etc.

To try to cover such a tremendous area as popular music by oneself is patently impossible. The successful completion of almost any book depends on the assistance given the author by people from many walks of life. I would like, therefore, to express my appreciation to the many individuals and organizations who have given so willingly and helpfully of their time.

I am grateful for the aid and encouragement of the professional organizations of the songwriting field—the American Society of Composers, Authors and Publishers (ASCAP), and Broadcast Music, Incorporated (BMI). Mr. Herbert Gottleib and Mr. Stanley Green of ASCAP were particularly helpful. I would like to thank Mr. Green not only for his personal advice and information but for the chance to refer to his excellent book on the musical theater, "The World of Musical Comedy." His book, Cecil Smith's "Musical Comedy in America," David Ewen's "Complete Book of the American Musical Theater," and Sigmund Spaeth's "History of Popular Music" are invaluable aids for any author working on the subject of popular music.

Thanks too are due the Record Industry Association of America and its executive secretary, Henry Brief; the National Academy of the Recording Arts and Sciences; and the Motion Picture Academy of Arts and Sciences. I am also indebted to the major broadcasting companies—CBS, NBC, and ABC—and record companies for supplying me with important background information. Among the latter are Columbia, RCA Victor, Capital, Dot, Liberty, Warner Brothers, Reprise, Kapp, and Imperial. I am also grateful for the assistance of such music publishers as Mills, Chappell, Robbins, Feist, Miller, and Ardmore.

I would also like to thank the many people who helped by providing information or granting interviews. These include Ray Evans, Harry Warren, Paul Mills, Jimmy Van Heusen, Sammy Fain, Boudleaux and Felice Bryant, Eddie Pola, Don Robertson, Leroy Anderson, Herbert Gottleib, Billy Bishop, and Ben Weisman. I would like to express my warmest appreciation to Grelun Landon for his many kindnesses. Others who have been of great help are Eliot Tiegel, Billy James, Herb Helman, Ron Tepper, Margit Zigre, Fuzz Pearson, and Fred Martin, Jr.

Finally, I would like to thank the following persons and organizations for permission to quote from their publications: Vernon Duke, "Passport to Paris"; Simon and Schuster: "Lyrics," by Oscar Hammerstein II; Doubleday: "Happy with the Blues," by Edward Jablonski; Alfred A. Knopf and Random House: "Lyrics on Several Occasions," by Ira Gershwin.

IRWIN STAMBLER
Beverly Hills, California
December, 1964

Contents

Popular Music: An Interpretation

"POPULAR MUSIC" is a term that is widely used but rarely defined. It can be used in many ways, depending on the prejudices of the speaker. To a teen-ager in the nineteen-sixties, popular music means rock 'n' roll. To older people, it means somewhat sweeter music—the music of the dance bands, the songs of Bing Crosby, Dinah Shore, Frank Sinatra—but includes the more hectic sounds of swing. To a jazz aficionado, it may mean Dixieland. To a Southerner, popular includes country-and-Western (what used to be known as "hillbilly" music).

It is difficult to pin down so flexible a term. Still, it is not possible to compile an *Encyclopedia of Popular Music* without some idea of what such a volume should embrace. For our purposes, we must define popular music as music of the past few decades (with some exceptions) which appeals to a mass audience rather than to a small one. The ballads and dance-band numbers of the thirties, forties, and fifties qualify, since these still provide the bulk of the adults' musical diet. Rock 'n' roll also qualifies, based on steady record sales to teen-agers. Our definition tends to exclude folk music, jazz, and classical music.

But it is impossible to be rigid. There are jazz and folk compositions and performers, for example, that go beyond their normally restricted appeal to become popular favorites. For the purposes of this book, these are treated as parts of popular music.

In record sales and total audience, country-and-Western has long accounted for a surprising percentage of the American music audience. Most of this has been in the South and Southwest, but country-and-Western has always had a large following in rural areas throughout the nation. To most of the American music audience, however, country-and-Western is not popular music. Nonetheless, many songs have crossed from country-and-Western into the general popular field, and vice versa.

The importance of country-and-Western has increased in recent years. This form of music is related to rock 'n' roll, folk music, and, to a lesser extent, jazz. While the mass of country-and-Western music is excluded from our definition of popular music, this genre must receive careful attention as a major source of much of what we call "popular."

Musical comedy has not yet been mentioned. In one sense, musical comedy is a minority choice. Probably no more people regularly attend musical comedies than follow Dixieland or folk music. But musical comedy is one of the major fruits of American popular-music activity. It has provided many of our standard songs. Important, too, is the increasing popularity with the American public of long-playing recordings of the more famous musical shows.

What makes popular music popular? Music expresses the moral and psychological tone of an age. Popular music must be in tune with the current cultural pattern. Some say that the public has no opinion and that popular taste is formed mainly by the artists and entrepreneurs of the music industry. But a close review of the field indicates that to be successful, a piece of music must strike a responsive chord in the mass audience and must reflect the culture at that point in history. The lachrymose ballads of the eighteen-nineties would fall on deaf ears today, just as the slick love songs of the thirties and forties would have made no sense to past generations.

The most respected and experienced artists-and-repertoire men of the music industry—men who have been listening to musical efforts for decades and who have produced many million-selling records—shake their heads over the unpredictable nature of the public. Again and again, songs that seem sure-fire to professionals fail to score sales of even a few thousand, while numbers put out mainly as fillers will become nationwide—even worldwide—sensations.

This is as true of performers as of material. It is hard to determine the combination of chances that takes an unknown to the heights of musical fame. Some excellent performers, such as Frankie Laine, may go unnoticed for ten or twenty years before reaching the top. Most popular singers, however, do not take this long, though a three- to five-year apprenticeship for those who become long-time favorites is not uncommon. Then there are those who catapult from complete obscurity to become worldwide household names (the Beatles, for example) in less than a year.

If it were true that all that was needed was a strong promotion campaign, there would be a lot more millionaire managers. There have always been very talented people who apparently had everything needed for stardom and plenty of chances to show their ability yet never caught on.

There must be something, in a performer or in a piece of music, *to ring a bell in the listener.* Scientists have set up computers to compose music, but they have yet to figure out how a computer can write sets of notes that will provoke just the right mood. The question of what the public will like next in music is still solved by experimentation. Take a dozen artists, turn out several dozen recordings of different songs in varied stylings, and wait until one or more of these catch the public fancy. When this happens, turn out close copies of the successes until the public loses interest in this style. If anyone could find a precise, scientific way to prejudge new music, any record company would beat a path to his door with drawn checkbook.

Ragtime was the rage at the beginning of the century, giving way to jazz around World War I, the Charleston and black bottom in the twenties, swing in the thirties and forties, and rock 'n' roll after World War II. Slow ballads showed far greater staying power over the years than did the more hectic musical styles. The faster-tempo types of music may dominate the market for a long time. Individual compositions in these styles, however, are short-lived, faddish items. The life of a rock-'n'-roll number is often measured in weeks. Some of these faster-tempo musical categories are popular because of their beat, not their words or melodies. Once one of this kind reaches a peak and then declines, it is rarely heard of again. There is nothing to distinguish it from dozens of new recordings that flood in after it, and therefore nothing to make it stick in people's memories.

When it comes to long-term popularity, a composition must have more than a beat. It must have a catchy lyric, a good melody, or a really unusual rhythm. So while ballads do not dominate the market over the short term, they do provide the items of long-time popularity, the standards that remain in vogue year after year (though even with a standard, changes in public taste demand changes in musical arrangements).

Partisanship is rampant in music. Jazz believers look down on classical and popular music; Dixieland-jazz fans are often aghast at progressive jazz, and vice versa; and all of them raise an eyebrow at rock 'n' roll and country-and-Western.

The point these partisans miss is that all art forms are continually evolving. Popular music is always changing to meet the mood of the times—that's what makes it popular. We can describe what has been or is popular now, but we cannot even begin to forecast what might become so in the future. It is this very unpredictability of popular music that makes it an exciting field to watch and survey.

A–Z of Popular Music

ACADEMY AWARDS: yearly awards for excellence in motion-picture arts.

The Academy Awards are administered by the Academy of Motion Picture Arts and Sciences in Los Angeles. The Academy is divided into twelve branches, each of which administers its own category. The Academy Music Branch gives awards for Best Score and Best Song. A list of winners of these awards through 1964 is given in the Appendix.

The Academy was founded in 1927, and the first awards (eleven Oscars) were made on May 6, 1929, for the 1927–28 season. There were no awards for music until 1934. The Best Score award originally was considered a music-department achievement, and the award was given to the department head. Beginning in 1938, the composer was given the Oscar.

Eligibility rules for the Best Song require that the song be used vocally in an eligible motion picture and "be sufficiently audible, both lyrically and musically, to be identified as such. A visual rendition of the song is not essential, and if the rendition is interrupted by dramatic action at any time, a significant portion of the song must be heard in the picture. The song must have both lyric and melody and both must be used professionally for the first time in the same picture." The rules also require that commercial recordings of the song be made only after the song is legally committed to the picture.

The award is in the form of a statuette. This was decided in 1927 at the first meeting of the Academy's first board of directors. It was suggested by Cedric Gibbons, later art director of MGM, as having more "dignity and individual character" than scrolls, plaques, or the like. The statuette was not given the name "Oscar" until several years later. In 1931, the new Academy librarian, Mrs. Margaret Herrick, on coming to work for the first time, looked at the statue and

The Oscar

said, "He reminds me of my Uncle Oscar." A newspaper columnist overheard this and wrote it in his column the next day. Since then, the name "Oscar" has always been associated with the statuette.

ADAMSON, HAROLD: lyricist. Born Greenville, New Jersey, December 10, 1906.

Most of Harold Adamson's childhood was spent in New York City, where he attended public elementary and high schools. After graduation, he attended the University of Kansas and then Harvard.

In high school, Adamson wrote poetry for school publications and sketches for shows. At Kansas, he wrote lyrics for several prize-winning songs. At Harvard, he composed sketches and lyrics for the "Hasty Pudding Shows." Adamson expanded his theatrical background by working in summer stock during vacations.

His contacts stood him in good stead when he decided to embark on a songwriting career. In the next few years, he met a number of people in the field, including a teen-age composer named Burton Lane. With Lane, he won his first major assignment in 1931 writing part of the score for the "Earl Carroll Vanities." Their work included the rousing "Heigh-Ho, the Gang's All Here." When Lane went to Hollywood two years later, Adamson was quick to follow. Their first movie standard, "Everything I Have Is Yours," appeared in "Dancing Lady" (1933).

In succeeding years, Adamson collaborated with many other top composers, including Jimmy McHugh, Walter Donaldson, and Victor Young. With Donaldson, Adamson wrote such songs as "Did I Remember" and "It's Been So Long" (1936), and with Young such numbers as "The Seven Hills of Rome" (1942).

Adamson's most successful collaboration was with McHugh. Their first efforts together began in 1936 with the score for the film "Banjo on My Knee." Over the next decade, the Adamson-McHugh team was to turn out many of the most played popular songs. A few of their major hits are "You're a Sweetheart" (1937), "I Couldn't Sleep a Wink Last Night" and "A Lovely Way To Spend an Evening" (1943), "Dig You Later" (1945), and "It's a Most Unusual Day" (1948).

In the fifties, Adamson continued to turn out important material, including the lyrics for "An Affair To Remember" and the score for the Academy Award-winning "Around the World in Eighty Days."

ADLER, RICHARD: composer-lyricist. Born New York, New York, August 23, 1923.

"It's impossible to say who does what and when. We've got rules. If I come in with what I think is a beautiful idea and he says, 'I don't like it,' I can scream, I can rave, but it's out. It obviates arguments. There has to be unanimity in our operation." That's the way the team of Richard Adler and Jerry Ross described their working relationship. It was a method that worked exceedingly well in the short time given them before Ross's untimely death in 1955.

Richard Adler's father was Clarence Adler, the concert pianist and teacher, but young Adler avoided music throughout his early years. After attending Columbia Grammar School in New York, he went on to study playwriting at the University of North Carolina. He came back to New York after graduation (and three years in the Navy) fully intending to make a career as a writer. His first job was as an advertising copywriter for a major firm.

Adler began to pick out songs on the piano and also to put words to them. When he began to work on his songs during the working day, he was fired. He decided to try to sell some of his material to publishers. He had no success until he met twenty-three-year-old Jerry Ross in 1950. Ross had also been composing unsalable songs during summers on the entertainment staffs of Catskill resorts.

They decided to collaborate, and the quality of their output increased immeasurably. Adler and Ross began to receive assignments to write special material for performers and then for the radio show "Stop the Music." In 1951, they were recommended to composer-publisher Frank Loesser, who hired them as staff writers for his publishing house. They wrote a number of minor successes, then hit the jackpot in 1953 with the million-selling "Rags to Riches."

That same year, they were signed to provide several songs for "John Murray Anderson's Almanac," which starred Hermione Gingold, Harry Belafonte, and Billy De Wolfe. Almost simultaneously, director-librettist George Abbott contracted them to write the score for his new musical "The Pajama Game." In May, 1954, "The Pajama Game" opened and critics hailed the new composing team as one of the brightest to hit Broadway in decades. The boys came right back with another great score for the 1955 "Damn Yankees."

At this point, a lung ailment struck down Ross at the age of twenty-nine. After Ross's death, Adler left music and returned to advertising.

ALL THE THINGS YOU ARE: song (1939). Words by Oscar Hammerstein II, music by Jerome Kern.

"Very Warm for May" was a flop as a stage

show, but it produced one of Jerome Kern's greatest numbers. It was also the last musical Kern wrote for Broadway. Critics gave the play an almost total thumbs down. In the New York *Herald Tribune*, Richard Watts said it was "Excessively tedious and humorless." New York *Times* reviewer Brooks Atkinson called it "a singularly haphazard invention that makes an appreciation of Mr. Kern's music almost a challenge."

Strange, then, that "All the Things You Are" turned out to be a standard. Kern wrote it because he liked the idea "artistically," not because he had any visions of its clicking with the audience.

"Very Warm for May" ended thirty-five years of Kern's work on Broadway, in which he provided music—in whole or part—for over eighty productions. Afterwards, he wrote music for movies, including the 1941 Academy Award-winning song "The Last Time I Saw Paris." "All the Things You Are," though, insured that Kern's farewell to Broadway was a memorable occasion in the annals of popular music.

ALLEN, STEVE: comedian, pianist, author. Born New York, New York, December 26, 1921.

Though Steve Allen is primarily known as a comedian, he is also an accomplished pianist, the author of several books, and the composer of many popular songs. He has also played the piano on several successful records, including the best-selling 1963 "Gravy Waltz" (one of the themes of Allen's 1962–1963 television show). Allen was co-composer of the song (with Ray Brown).

Allen's parents were vaudeville entertainers and were on tour in the East when Steve was born. His family continued to move from booking to booking as Allen grew up, with the result that he went to sixteen different schools, including five high schools and two colleges. The family's longest engagements were in Chicago, where Steve graduated from Chicago High School in 1941. Steve then enrolled in the journalism school of Drake University in Iowa. By 1942, he had transferred to Arizona State Teachers College. In Arizona, he began his professional career in radio as announcer with station KOY, Phoenix. Allen got a good all-around training at this station, for besides announcing he wrote commercials, played piano, and produced dramatic shows.

His stay in Arizona was cut short by World War II and a hitch in the Army. Steve was dis-

charged after five months because of asthma. He moved to Los Angeles, where, in 1944, he got a job as an announcer with station KFAC. From KFAC he went to station KMTR, then to a job as comedian on the Mutual Broadcasting Western-network show "Smile Time." In 1947, he moved to the Columbia Broadcasting System as a disc jockey on KNX, Hollywood. This six-night-a-week job started out as a record show, but the records soon gave way to ad-lib interviews, special guests, etc. During this period, Allen wrote a number of songs that were recorded by major stars, including "Let's Go to Church Next Sunday" (recorded by Perry Como and Margaret Whiting), which sold over three hundred thousand copies. Other songs were "Cotton Candy," "An Old Piano Plays the Blues," "Who Has To," and "Little Man."

Steve also wrote for and appeared in several movies, including "Down Memory Lane" and "I'll Get By." In 1955, he portrayed Benny Goodman in "The Benny Goodman Story." He also announced TV wrestling matches and wrote a book of verse, "Windfall."

In the summer of 1950, CBS moved Allen's midnight show to a nationwide hookup as a summer replacement for "Our Miss Brooks." In December of that year, the five-day-a-week Steve Allen television show was inaugurated. Though Steve gained many fans during his stay at CBS, it was not until he moved to NBC that he really won stardom. His late-evening five-day-a-week show "Tonight" was the freshest thing to hit TV

Steve Allen

since the first days of Milton Berle. Steve not only ad-libbed hilariously but also introduced many new faces, including actor-comedian Tom Poston and vocalists Eydie Gorme, Steve Lawrence, and Andy Williams. In 1956, he gave up the "Tonight" show to try his luck against such programs as "The Ed Sullivan Show" and "Maverick" on Sunday nights. In TV's most celebrated rating war, Allen took on both these attractions and more than held his own until 1960. After a vacation from TV, Steve failed in one comeback on ABC in 1961, but in mid-1962 he moved back into prominence with his late show for the Westinghouse TV network.

ANDERSON, LEROY: composer, arranger, conductor. Born Cambridge, Massachusetts, June 29, 1908.

In the mid-nineteen-fifties, when hillbilly music and the beginnings of rock 'n' roll were the rage, it hardly seemed possible that straight instrumental music could gain a wide audience. To everyone's surprise, including the composer's, a series of such compositions became best-selling records, including "Syncopated Clock," "Sleigh Ride," "Promenade," "Fiddle-Faddle," and "Blue Tango," all by Leroy Anderson.

Anderson's mother, a church organist, gave him lessons on the instrument when he was a small boy. Later, he also studied the bass violin. While attending Cambridge High and Latin School, he composed the graduation songs three years in a row. In 1925, Anderson entered Harvard, majoring in music. He graduated *magna cum laude* in 1929 and went on for his master's degree under the Elkan Naumburg fellowship grant. While getting his doctorate, Anderson helped pay his tuition by teaching at Radcliffe College.

He was director of the Harvard University Band from 1932 to 1935. Many of his arrangements for the band are still used. In 1935, having gained his doctorate, he decided to work as a freelance composer, arranger, and conductor. Anderson's services were soon in demand for major symphonic organizations in Boston and New York. Among his assignments was an appearance as guest conductor of the Boston Pops Orchestra. He conducted arrangements of Harvard songs. Pops leader Arthur Fiedler asked Anderson to become a regular arranger for the band as well as to conduct from time to time. In 1939, Anderson wrote "Jazz Pizzicato" for Pops performance and, in 1944, "Jazz Legato."

Anderson served in the Army in World War II, first in Iceland and later as a member of military intelligence in Washington. He is of Swedish descent, and his knowledge of Scandinavian languages helped.

After his discharge in 1946, Anderson returned to the Pops. Fiedler needed light after-intermission music for Pops concerts and asked Anderson to try his hand. The numbers were well received by the audiences, but the Pops considered them too much like popular music to record. The vice-president of Decca Records asked Anderson for permission to release the songs and offered him the chance to organize his own fifty-piece orchestra to record them.

Anderson was skeptical about his music catching on with the public, but finally agreed to turn out the records. He had hardly gotten underway on the project when, as a reserve officer, he was recalled to duty during the Korean conflict. By the time he returned to civilian life in 1952, his songs had become among the best-known in popular music. In 1952, "Blue Tango" became one of the most played songs in the United States and sold more than a million records. Anderson compositions have become standard fare for radio music listeners as well as themes for radio and television programs.

ANDREWS, JULIE: singer, actress. Born Walton-on-Thames, England, October 1, 1935.

Julia Elizabeth Wells's father taught metalcraft and woodworking, and her mother was a talented pianist. When Julie's parents were divorced, her mother married singer Edward Andrews. Little Julie accompanied her new family on tours throughout England. Her talents did not come to light until World War II. During air raids, Mr. Andrews tried to raise his neighbors' spirits by organizing choral singing in air-raid shelters. On one occasion, Julie's voice could be heard pure and clear above the others. Her parents soon started her on singing lessons.

Julie made her debut in London's West End at the age of twelve, singing an aria from "Mignon" in the Hippodrome. She performed with her parents for some years afterward. Julie also appeared in holiday pantomimes at the London Casino. During one of these shows, in December, 1953, she was playing the part of Cinderella when Vida Hope, director of the musical-comedy hit "The Boy Friend," spotted her. He offered her the lead in the troupe soon to depart for Broadway.

[6]

Julie Andrews, with Richard Burton in "Camelot."

As she wrote in the Beverly Hills *Citizen News:*

I'm the type of person who can never resist a challenge . . . My first real challenge came when I was appearing in a pantomime of "Cinderella" in London. An English producer . . . offered me the lead in the Broadway company of "The Boy Friend." I almost turned it down. I had never been away from home, my family or friends before and the thought of going to a strange country for an extended stay was frightening.

I finally talked myself into going, but rejected a two year contract in favor of a one year deal. I felt I could at least stick it out for that long, if worst came to worst. It turned out to be a lucky decision.

She was an immediate hit with the New York critics. When "The Boy Friend" opened on September 30, 1954, a typical reaction to the nineteen-year-old's performance was that of critic Walter Kerr, who called it "winsome and dazzling."

Just as her year's contract neared its end, she was offered the role of Eliza Doolittle in "My Fair Lady" (see separate listing). Her triumph in this show quickly moved her to the top of the musical-comedy profession. (Just before "My Fair Lady" opened, she also made her first mark on television, successfully debuting in "High Tor" with Bing Crosby on March 10, 1956. A few years later, she was Rodgers and Hammerstein's choice for the title role in their major television musical. Appropriately, the show was "Cinderella.") In 1961, Lerner and Loewe provided her with another great score, "Camelot" (see separate listing), and her favorite role to date, Guenevere.

She also continued to add to her audience with TV appearances. On January 31, 1960, she was one of many stars, including Rex Harrison, Jackie Gleason, and Henry Fonda, on a two-hour special, "The Fabulous Fifties." In early 1962, she teamed with another young star, Carol Burnett, in an hour-long show of comedy and song.

Having conquered Broadway and TV, Julie in 1963 turned to the movies. Walt Disney signed her to star in "Mary Poppins" with Dick Van Dyke. The show was released to excellent reviews in mid-1964. To prove her versatility still further, she chose as her next vehicle a nonsinging role in "The Americanization of Emily." To round out 1964, Julie played Maria von Trapp in the movie version of Rodgers and Hammerstein's "Sound of Music."

ANDREWS SISTERS: Patty, LaVerne and Maxene. All born Minneapolis, Minnesota. Vocal group.

The Andrews Sisters were the toast of the country during World War II. Their vocalizing helped many songs become standards. They also were featured in many hit musical films of the nineteen-forties and fifties.

The girls gave evidence of musical talent at early ages. LaVerne showed promise as a pianist, and Patty was the tap-dance champion of Minneapolis, their home town. Then Maxene decided that they should combine their abilities by singing as a trio. They began singing at school and local social affairs. In 1932, when Patty was twelve, LaVerne seventeen, and Maxene fourteen, their singing came to the attention of band leader Larry Rich, who hired them for a transcontinental tour with his orchestra. After this, they became well-known on the vaudeville circuit. But talking pictures soon killed vaudeville, and the girls were out of work.

The stage doors remained closed to them for six long years. Finally they made a successful appearance on a radio show, "Saturday Night Swing." An important booking in Boston was then offered them, but they were so broke that they couldn't afford the evening dresses needed for the show. Their agent managed to find three presentable evening dresses for four dollars each. From this 1937 engagement, the Andrews Sisters moved swiftly to the top. One engagement followed another, and soon their records were regularly among the national best sellers. From 1937 to the nineteen-fifties, they sold over fifty million records. They were featured in many films and for a time also teamed up with Bing Crosby on some of his radio shows. A few of the songs they made famous are "In Apple Blossom Time," "You Don't Have To Know the Language" (with Bing Crosby), "Beer Barrel Polka," "I Can Dream, Can't I?," "Bei Mir Bist Du Schön," "Drumboogie," and "Rum and Coca-Cola."

ANKA, PAUL: singer, composer. Born Ottawa, Canada, July 31, 1941.

The big popular hit of the 1957 season was the rock-'n'-roll recording of "Diana." The record, which was number one in the United States for thirteen weeks straight, was by the fifteen-year-old Canadian sensation Paul Anka. Besides singing the song, Anka also was its composer.

Anka is the oldest son of Ottawa restaurateur Andrew Anka and his wife Camy. From the time he was able to talk, Paul astonished his friends and family with his mimicry of them. He made his first public appearance, billed as an infant prodigy and impersonator, at the age of ten. At first, Anka's father was aghast at the idea of his son's eagerness for show business. Andrew was doing quite well since emigrating to the New World from his native Syria. He had worked his business up from a small sandwich shop into a sizable restaurant and had been elected vice-president of his city's Junior Chamber of Commerce. He wasn't impressed by Paul's debut at ten or by the fact that, at thirteen, his son had formed a trio of schoolmates that was earning as much as forty-five dollars a date. But he was coaxed to attend Paul's first Ottawa nightclub engagement, when Paul was fourteen. When Paul won the heart of the audience, his father's feelings began to change.

In March, 1957, one of rock and roll's royalty, the great Fats Domino, played Ottawa. Anka

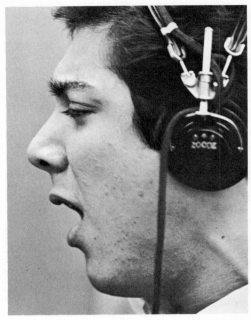

Paul Anka

fought his way into the theater to talk to Domino and give him some pointers. The show's manager, Irvin Feld, went into Domino's dressing room to escort the fifteen-year-old lumber-jacketed and blue-jeaned Paul out to the street. Two months later, "Diana" made Feld eagerly seek him out.

Meanwhile, Paul had rushed off to New York during the Easter vacation and talked his way into the inner sanctum of a record firm. An executive later remembered (*Life* magazine, August 29, 1960):

Can you imagine this 15-year-old kid bouncing into the office and playing 10 of his own songs? He leapt at the piano like it was a steak dinner and he hadn't eaten for months.

They liked "Diana" and called Anka's dad to fly to New York to sign the contracts.

Andy Anka became an ardent backer of his son's musical career, to the exclusion of his own restaurant business. By August, Paul had joined one of Feld's musical tours. Feld became Paul's personal manager soon after.

Paul followed with a series of hit records that made him a "global attraction of immense proportions." He became a favorite in Europe before he caught on in the United States. Paul attributes this to the fact that his song stylings, which partly reflected his Near Eastern ancestry, were more familiar to European ears. Such television shows as Dick Clark's "American Bandstand" and "The Ed Sullivan Show" vied for Anka's appearances. At sixteen and seventeen, Anka toured England, Australia, Hawaii, Japan, and Belgium and appeared in Paris and Monte Carlo. His enthusiastic reception everywhere bordered on idolatry. In Japan, where he had five songs at once on the Tokyo hit parade, two thousand fans waited all day in a typhoon to buy standing-room tickets. At the Olympia Music Hall in Paris, Paul outdrew Maurice Chevalier and Marlene Dietrich.

Columnist Art Buchwald, then writing from Paris, said:

A young Canadian of seventeen has been setting large parts of Europe and North Africa on fire for the past few months [in 1959]. His name is Paul Anka, and in the last year and a half he has become a million-dollar bobby-sox idol. On tour in North Africa . . . he had to have an escort of armed paratroopers to get from his hotel to the theatre. Mr. Anka sang at the Monte Carlo Casino last week and went over big with what is usually considered a very frigid audience.

Paul's list of gold records continued to grow, including such original compositions as "You Are My Destiny," "Lonely Boy," "Put Your Head on My Shoulder," "Puppy Love," "Crazy Love," "Don't Gamble on Love," and "My Home Town." Such singers as Connie Francis, Bobby Rydell, Annette, Johnny Nash, and Patti Page turned out hit records with Anka songs. Annette became a big-time vocalist with the help of Paul's "Train of Love."

Coming into the sixties, Anka began to make the transition from teen-age idol to all-around adult star. In 1960, Paul made his debut at New York's Copacabana, becoming the youngest performer ever to star on a stage which has held just about every famous name in show business. That same year, he also composed a musical production for the Copa which critics praised for its "charming sophistication" and "lilting melodies." Paul also appeared in several movies.

In 1963, Paul began recording for RCA Victor. His albums of the next few years included "Our Man Around the World," "21 Golden Hits,"

"Three Great Guys: Paul Anka, Sam Cooke and Neil Sedaka," "Songs I Wish I'd Written," and "Excitement on Park Avenue."

ANNETTE (FUNICELLO): singer, dancer, actress. Born Utica, New York, October 22, 1942.

The Funicellos moved to California when Annette was four. Her mother enrolled her at the age of five in the Margie Rix School of Dance in North Hollywood. When she was nine, Annette won a beauty contest as Miss Willow Lake. A number of amateur performances led to her playing the leading dance role in a youth show at Burbank Bowl, "Ballet vs. Jive," in 1955. Walt Disney saw the young dancer and signed her as one of the original twenty-four Mouseketeers for his new "Mickey Mouse Club." Annette was so successful on this and other television shows that Disney produced an entire series titled "Annette."

When "The Mickey Mouse Club" ended its long, successful run (it has since been revived), Annette started a new career in Disney movies and as a teen-age recording favorite. She was featured in the "Zorro" and "Elfego Baca" TV series on "Walt Disney Presents," and on Disney's "Golden Horseshoe Revue" series. She also made guest appearances on non-Disney shows. Annette played a featured role with Fred Mac-Murray in Disney's hit movie "Shaggy Dog," and costarred with Tommy Sands in Disney's re-creation of Victor Herbert's "Babes in Toyland." Several of her records reached the top-ten bracket in record polls.

ANNIE GET YOUR GUN: musical. Lyrics and music by Irving Berlin, book by Herbert and Dorothy Fields. New York opening: May 16, 1946, Imperial Theatre. 1,147 performances.

This hit marked the start of still a new cycle of Irving Berlin successes on Broadway. Up to this time, most of Berlin's compositions for the New York stage had been for revues. Now Berlin began writing the kind of closely integrated musical play pioneered by "Oklahoma!" Rodgers and Hammerstein, the producers of "Annie Get Your Gun" (and the writers of "Oklahoma!"), had originally signed Jerome Kern to do the score. It was to be his first Broadway musical in seven years. Kern's death caused them to turn to Irving Berlin as the one man who could do the job. Berlin demurred, feeling that he wasn't capable of working with this type of material. But Rodgers and Hammerstein persisted, resulting in the biggest stage hit of Berlin's career.

The play opens as Buffalo Bill's Wild West Show comes to a small town in Ohio. Charlie Davenport, the show's manager, argues with the proprietor of the town's small hotel, who doesn't want to rent rooms to show people. The show's star, sharpshooter Frank Butler, gets the hotel man to agree to a hundred-dollar bet that he can beat the local champion. The local rifle expert turns out to be a backwoods girl, Annie Oakley. She doesn't know how to read or write, but she gets along, as she sings, "Doin' What Comes Natur'lly."

When Annie sees Butler, she falls in love, not knowing that he's her opponent. Frank tells her that she's not feminine enough for him ("The Girl That I Marry"). Buffalo Bill comes to referee the contest. Frank is surprised to find that Annie is his competition and even more so when she outshoots him. Buffalo Bill wants her for the show, and Butler grudgingly agrees to let her assist him and hand him his guns, a job previously held by Charlie's sister, Dolly Tate. Annie knows nothing about show business, but Charlie enlightens her ("There's No Business Like Show Business").

As time goes on, Frank finds that he's falling in love with Annie. Annie secretly develops a shooting stunt using a motorcycle that she hopes will surprise Frank so much that he'll propose. An emergency arises as the show comes to Minneapolis. Rival showman Pawnee Bill is opening in the nearby city of St. Paul with Indian chief Sitting Bull as an attraction. Buffalo Bill and Charlie plead with Annie to do her stunt to draw the crowd. She agrees as Pawnee Bill and Sitting Bull come to watch. Annie's stunt is the hit of the show. Enraged, Frank leaves Buffalo Bill and joins Pawnee Bill, taking Dolly with him.

But Sitting Bull is so impressed with Annie that he joins Buffalo Bill and adopts Annie. When the adoption ceremony is over, Annie sings "I'm an Indian Too." The shows go their separate ways. Annie tours Europe, where she wins gold medals galore from European royalty. But both shows spend money as fast as it comes in. Buffalo Bill and his cast return to New York in a cattle boat to find Pawnee Bill playing Madison Square Garden. At a society party, each showman plans to trick the other into merging. Annie and Frank also plan to reunite, but fall to arguing again as each one sings that they can outdo the other ("Anything You Can Do"). A new contest is arranged. Charlie and Buffalo Bill fix Annie's guns so that she'll lose and Frank will regain his pride

and propose. The plan works, and Annie, Frank, and the two shows unite.

The original cast included Ethel Merman, as Annie; Ray Middleton, as Frank; William O'Neal, as Buffalo Bill; and George Lipton, as Pawnee Bill. The score included "You Can't Get a Man with a Gun," "They Say It's Wonderful," "My Defenses Are Down," "I Got Lost in His Arms," and "I Got the Sun in the Morning."

ANTHONY, RAY: band leader, trumpeter, actor, master of ceremonies. Born Cleveland, Ohio, January 22, 1922.

Aside from his success as a performer, there are two things which make Ray Anthony unique. One is his resemblance to Cary Grant. The other is being one of the few orchestra leaders to have continued success with a big band during the era of the small combo and rock 'n' roll.

Ray started studying trumpet at an early age. Before he was sixteen, Ray was playing with local Cleveland bands. Orchestra leader Al Donahue, a popular favorite in the Midwest be-

Ray Anthony

fore World War II, heard Ray and hired him as a featured performer just before Ray turned seventeen. Ray went on to Jimmy Dorsey. A year later, he was a member of perhaps the most fabulous organization of the big-band years, that headed by Glenn Miller. After a hitch with the Navy from 1942 to 1946, Ray started his own orchestra in the Midwest.

He was soon in demand at nightclubs and dance spots throughout that area, and his fame began to spread to both coasts. One of his records of those days, "Bunny Hop," started a national dance craze and sold over a million copies. Now a national favorite, Anthony went on to occasional television dates and, in 1953 and 1954, a show of his own as a replacement for Perry Como on the Columbia Broadcasting System. He was successful enough for ABC-TV to star the Anthony band in its own show during the winter season of 1954. The band appeared in such films as "Daddy Long Legs," "The Girl Can't Help It," and "This Could Be the Night." Anthony himself came across so well that he was cast as a featured actor in a number of films, including "Night of the Quarter Moon," "Beat Generation," and "The Five Pennies." The last was one of the major movies of 1959 and detailed the life of famous band leader Red Nichols. Anthony played the part of Jimmy Dorsey, in whose band Ray had once been a sideman.

During these years, the Anthony band turned out many extremely popular recordings. These included gold records of the themes from the TV shows "Dragnet" and "Peter Gunn," and, in 1962, a popular version of the country-and-Western standard "Worried Mind." Other best sellers included "Mr. Anthony's Boogie," "Tenderly," "Harlem Nocturne," "Slaughter on Tenth Avenue," and an album, "Dream Dancing." In 1960, Ray disbanded his orchestra to form a six-piece combination. In this act, Ray sang, played trumpet, and acted as master of ceremonies. In 1963, Ray once again was fronting a new TV show in Los Angeles.

ANYTHING GOES: Musical. Lyrics and music by Cole Porter, book by Guy Bolton, P. G. Wodehouse, Howard Lindsay, and Russel Crouse. New York opening: November 21, 1934, Alvin Theatre. 420 performances.

The burning of the luxury liner *Morro Castle* off New Jersey on September 8, 1934, came close to scuttling one of Cole Porter's brightest scores. The book for "Anything Goes" originally was

about a shipwreck, which seemed in poor taste after the disaster. With the opening only weeks away, authors Wodehouse and Bolton sent a hurry-up call to Howard Lindsay and Russel Crouse to help in the rewrite. The result was a plot which took place completely on board a ship traveling from the United States to Europe.

The show opens as the liner prepares to sail. On deck are American heiress Hope Harcourt; her mother, Mrs. Wadsworth T. Harcourt; and Hope's English fiancé, Sir Evelyn Oakleigh. Hope's mother has arranged the match to gain a title in the family. Playboy Billy Crocker, who is in love with Hope, decides at the last moment to stow away to try to win her away from Sir Evelyn. As the ship leaves the dock, all sing "Bon Voyage."

The passengers include Bishop Dobson and his two Chinese converts. It is rumored that Moonface Mantee, Public Enemy Number Thirteen, is on board. Reno Sweeney, an evangelist who is now a singer, meets her old friend Crocker. They salute each other with "You're the Top." Without a passport or ticket, Crocker has to use disguises. He meets the "Reverend Doctor Moon," who is really Moonface Mantee, and enlists his aid. In the meantime, Reverend Moon has seen that Bishop Dobson is put in the brig as the Public Enemy. Besides providing Crocker with a number of disguises, beginning with a sailor suit, Moon gives him a friend's passport. The friend is Snake Eyes Johnson, Public Enemy Number One, currently in an American jail.

Billy asks Reno to vamp Sir Evelyn to discredit him, with Reverend Moon breaking in to discover them. Moon breaks in too soon, however, and finds the two amiably chatting. Reno has discovered that Sir Evelyn really is quite charming, as she relates in "I Get a Kick out of You." Soon after, Billy is recognized by the purser as Snake Eyes. The passengers are excited to find such a celebrity aboard; as Reno sings, "Anything Goes." Crocker becomes the idol of the ship. Then someone suggests that Reverend Moon hold a revival meeting. Sir Evelyn admits a dalliance with a Chinese girl some years before, and Billy confesses that he isn't a public enemy. Billy is then thrown into the brig for impersonating a celebrity. Moonface joins him. Reno leads the company in a general confession of sins, "Blow, Gabriel, Blow."

In the brig, Billy sings of his love for Hope ("All through the Night"), and she joins in from the deck. But Mrs. Harcourt has talked the captain into performing the marriage before the boat docks. Moon and Billy find new cellmates in the Chinese converts. They win their costumes in a game of strip poker and, aided by Reno, arrive in time to break up the wedding ceremony. Billy wins Hope, and Mrs. Harcourt wins Sir Evelyn. A wire from Washington downgrades Moonface to Public Nuisance.

The original cast included Ethel Merman, as Reno; Victor Moore, as Moonface; William Gaxton, as Billy; Bettina Hall, as Hope; and Leslie Barrie, as Sir Evelyn. Other songs were "Be like the Bluebird," "The Gypsy in Me," and "There'll Always Be a Lady Fair."

APRIL IN PARIS: song (1932). Words by E. Y. Harburg, music by Vernon Duke.

"April in Paris," probably Vernon Duke's best-known song, was not composed in Paris, though Duke had once been a promising serious composer in that city, but in a restaurant on New York's West Side. The time was April, 1932, and Duke was working on the score for the musical "Walk a Little Faster."

As he recalls in his book "Passport to Paris" (Boston: Little, Brown, 1955): the song's birth occurred in a moment of relaxation after a day's work assembling the cast for the show.

After auditioning some particularly untalented girls, we all repaired to Tony's [Tony Soma's restaurant]; the "we" consisting of Dorothy Parker, Evelyn Hoey, Robert Benchley, Monty Wooley, Johnny McClain, Burr and myself.

Evelyn, whom I first heard singing a pseudo-Scottish air of Cole Porter's in the American revue at the Ambassadeurs in Paris in '28 or '29 (Cole put her in his Fifty Million Frenchman a year later and she scored a notable success), was to be entrusted with the singing chores in the new musical. After several double Scotches, we all got pretty sentimental, the Scotch reminding us of Miss Hoey's tartan skirt in her Paris number, and the mention of the number inevitably leading to Paris, how wonderful it was in the spring and how vile was Manhattan at that time of the year. I can't think whether it was Benchley or Wooley who cried out: "Oh, to be in Paris now that April's here!" The rest went off in true Class B musical-picture fashion. "April in Paris . . ." said I, melodramatically, "What

a title! My kingdom for a piano!" No sooner were these words uttered than the ever-obliging Tony [said] . . . that an old and wretched upright was at my disposal on the second floor. The piano was wretched indeed, but it made appropriate sounds when persuaded and, using the title "April in Paris" for what they call "the front phrase" in the trade, I soon completed the reasonably immortal refrain. I then proceeded to "ham it up," telling all . . . that I had just given birth to a masterpiece that was certain to "make the show." The lyrics were written a week later by Harburg.

Duke proved to be a poor near-term prophet. Far from "making the show," it received little or no attention, except that one columnist called the song "an unnecessary item." Few records of songs from the show were made at the time, and none at all of "April in Paris." As the years passed, first one and then another performer recorded the song, until suddenly Duke found that he had an all-time favorite. The song did not make the show, but it far outlived it, and if ever "Walk a Little Faster" is brought to mind, it's because of "April in Paris."

APRIL IN PORTUGAL: song (1947). Words by José Galhardo, music by Raul Ferrão, English words by Jimmy Kennedy.

"Coimbra E una Lição de Amor," a song written in honor of the University of Coimbra, in Portuguese East Africa, became popular far beyond the campus and finally reached Portugal itself. Sassetti, a Portuguese music firm, picked up the song, and it soon became very popular throughout Europe as "April in Portugal."

The song was sent to the American music-publishing company of Chappell for possible adaptation. An English lyric, titled "The Whispering Serenade," was written. Singer Georgia Carr recorded this version for Capitol, and the song had a minor success. Les Baxter and Freddy Martin became interested in the melody as an instrumental. Both of them preferred the European title. Soon two different records, one on Capitol and one on RCA Victor, were issued. "April in Portugal" became a hit as an instrumental.

Chappell commissioned Jimmy Kennedy to write a new lyric retaining the instrumental title. This too was successful, and instrumental and vocal recordings have both become highly popular.

ARLEN, HAROLD: composer. Born Buffalo, New York, February 15, 1905. Won Academy Award for Best Song of 1939 ("Over the Rainbow").

Harold Arlen (born Hyman Arluck) originally wanted to be a singer. He probably derived this desire from his father, who was a cantor in a Buffalo synagogue. His mother played the piano and made sure that her son learned the instrument. His parents hoped he would become a music teacher.

At fifteen, though, he organized a group known as the Snappy Trio and later put together a series of dance bands. One of these, the Buffalodians, was booked into the Silver Slipper nightclub in New York in 1927. Arlen not only played the piano but also did the band's arranging and some of its vocalizing. Arnold Johnson, New York band leader, liked Arlen's style enough to hire him for "George White's Scandals of 1928." Johnson let Arlen sing during intermission. This stint caused Vincent Youmans to hire Arlen for "Great Day." Arlen became rehearsal pianist for the show. One of the melodies he improvised had commercial possibilities, and he took it to a friend, Harry Warren, an already successful composer, at Remick Music. Warren introduced Arlen to lyricist Ted Koehler, and the result was the hit "Get Happy."

Koehler and Arlen were soon providing scores for the Cotton Club revues. By 1933, they had written such enduring numbers as "Between the Devil and the Deep Blue Sea," "I Love a Parade," "I've Got the World on a String," "Kickin' the Gong Around," and "Stormy Weather," which was introduced by Ethel Waters and Duke Ellington.

After writing three Broadway musicals—the 1930 "Earl Carroll Vanities," "You Said It" (1931), and "Life Begins at 8:40" (1934)—he went to Hollywood, where he quickly became one of the top writers of hit songs. With the exception of the score for the 1937 Broadway show "Hooray for What?" (written with lyricist E. Y. Harburg and starring Ed Wynn, it ran for two hundred performances), Arlen concentrated on motion pictures for close to a decade. With such collaborators as Harburg and Johnny Mercer, he wrote such songs as "It's Only a Paper Moon," "Let's Fall in Love," and "Happiness is a Thing Called Joe." With Harburg, in 1939, he provided the score for the movie classic "The Wizard of Oz," starring Judy Garland. The picture included their Oscar-winning "Over the Rainbow." In the early forties, Arlen and Mercer received Academy Award nominations for "Blues in the Night," "That Old Black Magic," and "My Shining Hour." Arlen teamed up with Ted Koehler again on the 1944 Oscar nominee "Now I Know."

In the meantime, Harburg had come up with the idea for a Civil War musical for Broadway. For the show, called "Bloomer Girl," Arlen and Harburg wrote such numbers as "Evelina" and "Right as the Rain." It opened on October 5, 1944, and had a hit run of six hundred and fifty-four performances. Arlen's next two Broadway shows did not fare as well. In 1946, with Johnny Mercer, he wrote "St. Louis Woman." Though the score was excellent, the show flopped. The same thing happened with the 1954 "House of Flowers," in which Arlen and author Truman Capote collaborated on the lyrics. Arlen's score was one of his finest, but the book was too weak to sustain it. Harburg came up with a new idea for a show set in the Caribbean, "Jamaica." This time, with Lena Horne as the star, the ingredients for a hit were all present. The show opened on October 31, 1957, and ran for five hundred and fifty-seven performances. It included such songs as "Take It Slow, Joe," "Ain't It de Truth," "Cocoanut Sweet," and "Push de Button."

Though concentrating on Broadway, Arlen didn't abandon Hollywood. During those years, the following songs received Academy Award nominations: "Ac-cent-tchu-ate the Positive" (1944), "For Every Man There's a Woman" (1948), and, with Ira Gershwin as lyricist, "The Man That Got Away" (1954).

ARMSTRONG, LOUIS (SATCHMO): band leader, trumpeter, singer. Born New Orleans, Louisiana, July 4, 1900.

Louis Armstrong's birthday, the fourth of July, seems appropriate, for Armstrong has been one of the best good-will ambassadors this country ever had. In addition, he has been one of the very few great innovators in jazz and popular music as well as one of the most talented trumpeters of all times.

At thirteen, Louis celebrated New Year's Eve by firing a gun in his home town of New Orleans. He was arrested for "carrying firearms within the city limits" and sent to a Waifs' Home for a year. Here he was given a bugle and a trumpet, which he began to play by ear. By the time he left, he was leader of the Home's band. He also had a new ambition—to become a great musician.

[13]

Louis Armstrong

He worked at many odd jobs between band work. The great trumpeter Joseph "King" Oliver coached the promising teen-ager. In 1918, when Oliver left the Kid Ory band to go to Chicago, Louis took his place. Armstrong went on to work for two years with the Fate Marable river-boat band. In 1922, Oliver brought Louis to Chicago as part of the great Oliver band. Armstrong made his first trip to New York in 1924, with Fletcher Henderson's band. Louis began to form his own bands, including the Hot Five and Hot Seven recording outfits. In 1929, he was featured in the "Hot Chocolates" revue at New York's Hudson Theatre.

Armstrong led a succession of bands and his fame spread throughout the world. His first visit to London's Palladium, in 1932, was a triumph, and he later spent several years touring Europe, not returning home until 1935. That same year, he signed a long-term contract with Decca Records, resulting in such hit records as "Rockin' Chair," "Ol' Man Mose," "Brother Bill," and "Sugar Foot Strut."

Armstrong won the *Esquire* poll from 1943 to 1947, the *Record Changer* All Time, All Star poll as trumpeter and singer in 1951, and the *Down Beat* critics' award in 1953 and 1954 as singer and in 1953 also as trumpeter. In January, 1944, he headed a group of *Esquire* poll winners in the first jazz concert held at New York's Metropolitan Opera House.

He was a major attraction from the forties through the sixties in movies and on radio and television. On radio and TV, he made a number of still remembered appearances on the Bing Crosby and Ed Sullivan shows. In 1947, he played a major acting role in the film "New Orleans." His other film credits include "Pennies from Heaven," "The Glenn Miller Story," "Artists and Models," "The Strip," and "A Song is Born." In 1954, the first volume of Louis's autobiography "Satchmo: My Life in New Orleans" was published by Prentice-Hall.

In the fifties and sixties, Armstrong and his band were featured at major jazz festivals throughout the world, including the 1948 one at Nice and the annual festivals at Newport, Rhode Island, and Monterey, California. On several occasions, Armstrong toured parts of the world, including Europe and Africa, under State Department sponsorship.

Louis continued to turn out great records, including his hit rendition of "Mack the Knife," and his own compositions, such as "Sugar Foot Stomp," "Satchel Mouth Swing," and "Struttin' with Some Barbeque."

In 1964, he had one of the top selling singles of the year with his version of "Hello, Dolly." His LP album of the same name also won acclaim. His tour of Eastern Europe in early '65 played to large, enthusiastic audiences in East Germany, Czechoslovakia, Rumania and Yugoslavia.

ARRANGEMENT, ARRANGER: a vocal and/or instrumental adaptation of a piece of music; the one who does the adaptation. A piece of popular music can be played in many different ways—in waltz time, as a fox trot, or as a jazz piece, for examples. The way in which a piece is thus shaped is called an arrangement. The man who writes the arrangement is called an arranger.

An arranger must know about rhythm, meter, harmony, phrasing, transposition, and all the other technical aspects of music. He must also have good musical imagination. Many composers of popular music know very little about

[14]

musical theory. They may come up with just the basic notes for a melody. Fleshing out these notes to something that can be used for, hopefully, a brilliant performance is the arranger's task. A good arrangement is as important to the success of a performer or a composition as is the composition itself.

ARTISTS-AND-REPERTOIRE MAN: record-industry term for the company executive in charge of artists and repertoire; that is, the man charged with selecting the material to be recorded by various artists. (The term "artists-and-repertoire man" is not universal. Some firms use such titles as "musical director" instead.)

Most A&R men are with record companies, though the term is sometimes used in other musical organizations. For instance, Broadcast Music, which publishes music but does not produce records, has an A&R man. The A&R man has overall charge of selecting music to be recorded (or, in some cases, promoted). He works with the artists and helps them choose the proper material for their particular style. The selection is also based on commercial factors.

The A&R man is an extremely important middleman. Songwriters and song publishers come to him with new material hoping that he will place it with one of his company's artists. His company will judge him on the commercial success of material he has selected. Obviously, too, a good A&R man is very important to a performer's career.

Most A&R men are musicians or have musical backgrounds. Some of the best ones are talented arrangers or composers. With performers on the way up, the A&R man's word on the material that is performed is usually law. Established performers can usually select their own material, but they too will listen very respectfully to the A&R man's advice.

Some of the leading A&R men of the nineteen-fifties and sixties were Mitch Miller, Ed Kleban, and Terry Melcher (Columbia), Hugo and Luigi (Roulette, later with RCA Victor), Billy Vaughn (Dot), Snuff Garrett (Liberty), Daryl Rice and Joe Reisman (RCA Victor), and Jim Econimedes and Nick Benet (Capitol).

ASCAP: American Society of Composers, Authors and Publishers; an organization founded in 1914 to protect performance rights of musical compositions.

ASCAP was established to protect the rights of composers, authors of musical material and song publishers from improper exploitation. The man given most credit in founding the Society was the great musical comedy composer, Victor Herbert. Many legends have grown up around the Society's founding. One story which has received wide circulation is that the idea for the organization came to Herbert after hearing one of his melodies played in 1913 in a New York restaurant. He then supposedly became infuriated at the fact that anyone could play a writer's copyrighted music for profit without paying anything for its use. But though Herbert more than anyone else breathed life into ASCAP, recent research clearly establishes that the idea was brought to him by others. Exactly where the concept originated is still open to question. One version is that the original restaurant incident occurred not to Herbert but to the Italian composer Giacomo Puccini. In 1910, Puccini, accompanied by his U.S. publishing representative, George Maxwell, reportedly heard his music played in several New York cafes. He was surprised to hear that no royalties would be paid and noted to Maxwell that this was not the case in Europe. Maxwell later repeated this statement to others in the field. A few years later, composer Raymond Hubbell had similar thoughts and with Maxwell and Herbert's friend and lawyer, Nathan Burkan, discussed a society to fight for performance rights. They enlisted Herbert's aid and, in October, 1913, planned a meeting at Lüchow's Restaurant in New York. Some 36 composers, authors and publishers promised to attend, but only nine showed up. The nine, however, with Herbert providing the most encouragement, laid plans for the organization. Besides Herbert, Burkan, Hubbell and Maxwell, the group included: Silvio Hein, Louis A. Hirsch, Gustave A. Kerker, Glen MacDonough and Jay Witmark. A second meeting attended by 35 people took place on January 14, 1914. This led to another, larger meeting, attended by over 100 people from the music field at the Claridge Hotel on February 13, 1914. On this date, ASCAP was formally organized and George Maxwell was elected first president. (Herbert was offered the post, but declined, preferring to serve as vice president.)

First goal of ASCAP was to gain enforcement of the copyright laws (first passed in 1897 and amended and repassed by Congress on July 1, 1909) covering performance rights. The laws permitted authors to collect damages for infringement of copyright in cases where their work was publicly performed for profit, but the principle had yet to be tested in the courts.

The court fight to force theaters, performers and other organizations to pay royalties to ASCAP, or any writer who could enforce the copyright laws, was a long and bitter one. Victory in court finally came in 1917. The case was based on unauthorized use of music from Herbert's "Sweethearts" at Shanley's Restaurant, New York, on April 1, 1915. Justice Oliver Wendell Holmes of the U.S. Supreme Court handed down the ruling which said, in part: "If music did not pay, it would be given up. If it pays, it pays out of the public's pocket. Whether it pays or not, the purpose of employing it is profit, and that is enough."

It took ASCAP some years to enforce compliance with this ruling across the U.S. But, by the mid-1920s, ASCAP's rights had been verified and accepted (including recording rights). From then on, as new areas of music dissemination came into prominence—radio, talking pictures, TV—ASCAP protected its members in all these new fields.

Probably the most famous battle over performing fees for authors erupted in the fall of 1940, when the radio industry turned down ASCAP demands for higher fees for renewal of a five year contract between ASCAP and the stations. This led ASCAP to bar playing of its members' music on the air. It also led to the formation, at the instigation of the stations, of a competing organization, BMI (Broadcast Music, Inc.). After a year long struggle, both sides compromised and a new contract was signed in late '41. But BMI continued as another strong force in the songwriting field.

ASCAP has continued to increase in strength over the years, growing to 250 members by 1921, 600 in '30 and over 6,700 in the early '60s.

AS THOUSANDS CHEER: revue. Lyrics and music by Irving Berlin, sketches by Moss Hart. New York opening: September 30, 1933, Music Box Theatre. 400 performances.

Irving Berlin and Moss Hart followed up their mild success in "Face the Music" with a brilliant triumph in "As Thousands Cheer." This was a topical revue which poked fun at everyone from newly elected President Franklin D. Roosevelt to Mahatma Gandhi and nonagenarian John D. Rockefeller. The score was one of Berlin's most

striking, giving birth to that perennial favorite, "Easter Parade." Many of the cast played several parts. Clifton Webb's roles ranged from a dapper Easter Parader of 1883 to Rockefeller and Gandhi. Helen Broderick played Mrs. Herbert Hoover in one scene and evangelist Aimée Semple McPherson in another.

The sketches and dances were presented in newspaper format. The curtain would blazon a dramatic headline, then open to display the scene behind the headlines. One was "FDR Inaugurated Tomorrow." The curtains parted to show Mrs. Hoover readying the White House for its new occupants and giving explicit vent to her feelings. Another title, "Metropolitan Opera Opens in Old Time Splendor," showed a brash radio sponsor taking the play away from the tuxedoed and bejeweled audience. "Heat Wave Hits N.Y." paved the way for Ethel Waters to rock the theater with "Heat Wave." The Act I close was "Easter Parade," sung by Clifton Webb to Marilyn Miller and Helen Broderick. Berlin had written the song in 1917 as "Smile and Show Your Dimple" but had put it aside because of the weak lyric.

In her final Broadway appearance, Marilyn Miller discarded her sweetness-and-light character in several scenes; in one, she did an acid portrayal of Joan Crawford. As Prince Mdivani, Clifton Webb paid court to Barbara Hutton (Marilyn Miller) ("How's Chances?"). Ethel Waters had two more great spots. In one she played Josephine Baker, in her lavish French chateau, singing "Harlem on My Mind." Miss Waters's favorite, and a major departure from the typical revue, was the song "Supper Time." The headline read, "Unknown Negro Lynched by Frenzied Mob." Miss Waters, as his widow, sets the evening table. Her anguished thoughts are of him and how she'll tell the children that their father won't come home any more.

AUTUMN IN NEW YORK: song (1934). Words and music by Vernon Duke.

In the summer of 1934, composer Vernon Duke was in Westport, Connecticut, working on the score for a musical, "America Dances." After spending all summer on this project and composing what everyone agreed was an excellent score, the play was postponed. Duke now had time on his hands, and the quietness of the country began to bore him. He felt a deep longing for the excitement of New York. (Though the city was close,

[16]

he had three weeks before his Westport lease ran out.) "Autumn in New York" was the result. Duke felt strongly enough about the subject to write the words himself.

Some weeks later, he was back in New York preparing to go to Chicago on an assignment when he got a phone call from showman John Murray Anderson, who was assembling a revue called "Thumbs Up" and needed music for some of the scenes. In particular he wanted a nostalgic song about Manhattan in the fall, a coincidence that Duke was quick to seize.

"Murray, I may have what you want," Duke replied, "only it's a crazy song; moves from key to key to key, and that makes it hard on a singer."

"Whose lyric?"

"Mine."

"What do you call it?"

"'Autumn in New York.'"

Murray let out a refined whoop, Duke recalls. "Get into a cab, you unfortunate Grand Duke; don't talk any more. Hurry!"

Within half an hour after the conversation, the song had been interpolated into the score.

AUTUMN LEAVES: song (1949). Music by Joseph Kosma, words by Jacques Prevert, English words by Johnny Mercer.

"Les Feuilles Mortes" was a poem by Jacques Prevert. Joseph Kosma wrote a melody to it, and the song was performed in French cafés in the late forties. There it was heard by a friend of Capitol Record executive Mickey Goldson, who sent the song to Goldson from Paris. Goldson liked it and contracted for it on a limited-time basis. He asked Johnny Mercer to write a lyric. A demonstration record was sent to Mercer, who lost it. Goldson had ten days before the option was up. He called Mercer, and Mercer asked for a new record. This was sent, but time was at a premium, and Mercer had to go to New York. Mercer said that perhaps if Goldson drove him to the station, he could work up something on the way. Goldson was late, and he found Mercer about to rush away. Johnny motioned to a paper stuck in the door. On the paper was the "Autumn Leaves" lyric.

Though twelve records of the song were made in 1950 by top artists, including Bing Crosby and Jo Stafford, the song failed to go over. Dave Kapp, then at Decca, liked it so much that he swore he would get a hit record if he had to make twenty different versions. Kapp left Decca for RCA Victor, then set up his own firm, Kapp Records. He kept trying to do something with "Autumn Leaves." In 1953, a then up-and-coming pianist, Roger Williams, recorded "Autumn Leaves" for Kapp and started the song and himself on the road to success.

BABES IN ARMS: musical. Lyrics by Lorenz Hart, music by Richard Rodgers, book by Rodgers and Hart. New York opening: April 14, 1937, Shubert Theatre. 289 performances.

For a youthful and talented cast, Rodgers and Hart provided a youthful and enduring score. Most of the cast were in their middle or early teens, and few productions have included such a phenomenal number of stars in the making. Among the principals were Mitzi Green, Ray Heatherton, Alfred Drake, and Wynn Murray, and in the chorus were Dan Dailey and Robert Rounseville. "Babes in Arms" was a rousing success with the critics and later, as a movie, with the public. The songs include some of Rodgers and Hart's greatest.

"Babes in Arms" is set on a farm in Eastport, Long Island. A group of teen-age boys and girls have been left there by their parents, a troupe of touring vaudevillians. The boys include Val Lamar, Marshall Blackstone, and Gus Fielding, and the girls include Baby Rose, Billie Smith, and Dolores Reynolds. The children don't have enough money to pay their bills, but they have, inherited talent from their elders, as shown by the duet between Val and Billie, "Where or When." They are, as Billie, Val, Marshall, and the chorus sing, "Babes in Arms," but they're determined to prevent Sheriff Reynolds from seizing their farm and sending them to a children's home.

They decide to put on a revue, "Lee Calhoun's Follies," to raise the needed funds. On the way to this, Billie sings "My Funny Valentine" and Baby Rose belts out "Johnny One Note." The show fails to provide the money, and it looks as though the sheriff will win. At this point, a French pilot, René Flambeau, crash lands on the farm. He provides the adult guidance needed to make the children's plans succeed.

The original cast included Mitzi Green, as Billie; Ray Heatherton, as Val; Alfred Drake, as Marshall; Rolly Pickett, as Gus; Wynn Murray, as Baby Rose; Grace McDonald, as Dolores; George Watts, as the sheriff; Dana Hardwick, as Lee Calhoun; and Aljan de Leville, as René.

[17]

Other numbers were "I Wish I Were in Love Again," "All Dark People," "Way out West," "Imagine," "All at Once," "Peter's Journey" (ballet), "The Lady Is a Tramp," and "You Are So Fair."

The movie opened at New York's Capitol Theatre on October 19, 1939. The plot and the names were altered, and new songs by Nacio Herb Brown and Arthur Freed were added. The stars were Mickey Rooney, as Mickey Moran, and Judy Garland, as Patsy Barton.

BABES IN TOYLAND: operetta. Lyrics and book by Glen MacDonough, music by Victor Herbert. New York opening: October 13, 1903, Majestic Theatre. 192 performances.

"Babes in Toyland" is an excellent example of the truly popular nature of Victor Herbert's music. Since the 1903 production, it has been often revived, on the stage and in several movies. The most recent movie version (1962) was made by Walt Disney, with Tommy Sands and Annette starring as the babes and Ray Bolger as Uncle Barnaby.

There have been so many adaptations over the years that there is some disagreement about the original plot. The following outline should be reasonably close to the original.

The villain of the piece is mean and miserly Uncle Barnaby. He wants to get rid of his niece and nephew, Jane and Alan, so that he can get their estate. A shipwreck attempt fails, and the babes wander into the story-book city of Mother Goose. Here they meet such nursery-rhyme characters as Mary Quite Contrary, Tom the Piper's Son, Jack and Jill, Peter Pumpkin Eater, and Simple Simon, and see the lively "Country Dance." In the town, their Uncle Barnaby is thrown into a pond as he tries to foreclose the mortgage on Mother Hubbard's house. Bo Peep rushes in crying, for her sheep are lost. Tom the Piper's Son and the others console her ("Never Mind, Bo Peep") and tell her that they'll be found. Uncle Barnaby gets his two ruffianly confederates, Roderigo and Gonzorgo, to lose Alan and Jane in the Forest of No Return. Later, lost in the forest, Alan sings the frightened Jane to sleep with the "Lullaby" ("Go to sleep, slumber deep"). But Alan and Jane, helped by gypsies, get out of the forest. They go to "Toyland," ruled by the Master Toymaker. The inhabitants are getting ready to make toys for Christmas ("Hail to Christmas"). Later, the toys parade ("March of the Toys"). The Master Toymaker brings toys to life and puts the spirit of evil into them. Retri-

bution occurs when the living toys turn on him and kill him.

Alan is accused of the murder and is tried in the Toyland Palace of Justice. He is sentenced to be hanged. But, at the last moment, Uncle Barnaby is unmasked as the true villain, and Alan is saved.

Other songs were "Mary, Mary, Quite Contrary," "With Downcast Eye," "Mignonette," "I Can't Do the Sum," "Song of the Poet," "He Won't Be Happy till He Gets It," and "We Are the Soldiers." The original cast included William Norris, as Alan; Mabel Barrison, as Jane; and George W. Denham, as Barnaby. One of the movie versions starred the comedy team of Laurel and Hardy.

BALLAD: defined by the dictionary as "a simple song; esp., a romantic song having the same melody for each stanza. . . ."

A popular-music ballad is usually a slow love song. Most "standards" are ballads. Despite this, it is much more difficult to persuade a publisher or an A&R man to publish a ballad or accept it for recording than it is to get him to take on a novelty or up-tempo number, because it takes a relatively long time for most ballads to catch on. A novelty or up-tempo number can become extremely popular very rapidly. The typical rock-'n'-roll hit, for instance, reaches the top of the charts and sells a million records or better in a few weeks. (Of course, it is probably never heard of again.) Another factor is the great number of ballads offered for publication every year. Many novelty hits are not composed but grow out of instrumental arrangements and improvisations. Most aspiring songwriters tend to write ballads, causing a surplus.

In spite of all this, ballads are published and recorded every season, and a few of these climb slowly into prominence and remain popular for many years.

BAND WAGON, THE: revue. Lyrics by Howard Dietz, music by Arthur Schwartz, sketches by George S. Kaufman and Dietz. New York opening: June 3, 1931, New Amsterdam Theatre. 260 performances.

One of the best revues to grace the American stage, "The Band Wagon" boasted a score (including "Dancing in the Dark," "High and Low," "New Sun in the Sky," and "I Love Louisa") that has echoed through the many years since the show opened. The show had a polish and swing that few revues achieved before or after. As Brooks Atkinson said in the New York Times:

George S. Kaufman and Howard Dietz have put the stigmata on stupid display by creating a thoroughly modern revue. It is both funny and lovely; it has wit, gaiety and splendor. The show was composed of incisive sketches poking malicious fun at many of the clichés of musical-comedy formula shows.

"The Band Wagon" was also notable for its mechanical aspects. It featured two revolving stages that were used in some of the dancing specialties of the show's stars, Fred and Adele Astaire.

In one scene, Helen Broderick, as a Westchester matron, was shown looking over bathroom appliances in a very high-toned salon. When she finally inquired about certain crucial fixtures, the salesman answered, "Heard melodies are sweet, but those unheard are sweeter." In another scene, "The Pride of the Claghornes," Frank Morgan played a Southern colonel who disowned his daughter because she violated Southern traditions by never going wrong. In a dance sequence, the Astaires, as young Parisians, frolicked to the music of "Hoops." The Act I finale took place in a Bavarian amusement park, where the cast sang "I Love Louisa" on a merry-go-round installed on one of the revolving stages. John Barker was given the pleasant task of introducing "Dancing in the Dark." Tilly Losch danced to the music on a slanted mirrored floor while a pattern of colored lights played over the stage.

Other songs were "Miserable with You," "Where Can He Be?," "The Beggar Waltz," and "White Heat."

BAXTER, LES: composer, conductor, arranger, pianist, singer. Born Mexio, Texas, March 14, 1922.

One of the most original of the young post-World War II conductor-composer-arrangers, Les Baxter leans musically in the direction of Latin America. He began as a concert pianist, starting serious studies while in his teens. After some time at the Detroit Conservatory of Music, he switched to Pepperdine College in Los Angeles. He started his professional career, as a vocalist in 1945 with the Mel Tones, who backed up Mel Torme, the singing sensation of the mid-forties.

Baxter began spending more and more time on conducting and arranging and became orchestral conductor or choral director for some of the important postwar radio shows, including "The Bob Hope Show," "Ronald Colman's Halls of Ivy," and the Abbott and Costello program. Those who used his arrangements included Nat "King" Cole, Margaret Whiting, and Frank DeVol.

In 1950, Baxter signed a long-term contract with Capitol Records. He produced many of Cole's greatest records for Capitol. In addition, he produced the records made by the unique Peruvian singer Yma Sumac, whose voice had an almost incredible range. Baxter is probably best-known for his albums featuring his own "jungle" compositions, such as "Le Sacre du Sauvage." Other Baxter recordings of note: "The Poor People of Paris," "The High and the Mighty," and "Unchained Melody."

BEATLES, THE: vocal group. All born Liverpool, England: Ringo Starr, July 7, 1940; John Lennon, October 9, 1940; Paul McCartney, June 18, 1942; and George Harrison, February 25, 1943.

Beatlemania was a main topic of conversation in the United States after February 9, 1964. On that date, the Beatles made the first of three

The Beatles: Ringo Starr (seated), standing (l. to r.) Paul McCartney, George Hamilton, John Lennon.

record-breaking appearances on the Ed Sullivan television show. By the end of February, they had repeated their conquest of Europe in the U.S. Not only were their merits hotly debated coast to coast, but they also had two American gold records, one for the album "Meet the Beatles," the other for the hit single "I Want To Hold Your Hand."

All four attended public schools in Liverpool. Perhaps because it was the port of entry for many transatlantic ships, Liverpool by the late fifties had become the rock-'n'-roll center of England. Sailors brought in the newest American recordings, and the sound was quickly picked up by teen-age musicians. Among those eagerly following these fashions were John Lennon and Paul McCartney. In 1956, the two met at a rock-'n'-roll café and decided to form a duo. George Harrison joined them soon after. The trio, all of whom played guitars, performed at many small clubs in the Liverpool area.

At first, they called themselves the Moon Dogs, then the Quarry Men, the Moonshiners, and the Silver Beatles. They finally arrived at plain "Beatles," a play on the musical term "beat." The trio made side trips to other towns in England. In 1960, they went to Hamburg, Germany, where they made their first record, accompanying singer Tony Sheridan. They added a fourth member, drummer Ringo Starr, in 1962.

The quartet was still little-known outside of Liverpool clubs. Soon after Starr joined them, they took another Hamburg booking, at the Indra Club, a strip joint, where they were heard by English promoter Brian Epstein. He felt that the Beatles had something to offer, and won them a contract with the major British recording firm, Electrical and Musical Industries. EMI issued the first Beatles record, "Love Me, Do," on the Parlophone label, in October, 1962. It sold about a hundred thousand copies. Their next disc, "She Loves You," issued in the spring of 1963, sold over a million copies. The Beatles followed up with a string of gold-record singles and albums as well as a series of personal appearances that made their name a household word in England. Their hit numbers included such songs as "P.S. I Love You," "Ask Me Why," "I'll Get You," "All My Loving," "Please Please Me," and "I Wanna Be Your Man." Most of their material was and is written by McCartney and Lennon.

By the end of 1963, the Beatles had extended their sway to most of Europe and were ready to try to make the grade in the United States. On December 30, 1963, the Baltimore *Evening Sun* warned,

> The Beatles are coming. These four words are said to be enough to jelly the spine of the most courageous police captain in Britain.... Since, in this case, the Beatles are coming to America, America had better take thought how it will deal with the invasion.... Indeed, a restrained 'Beatles, go home' might be just the thing.

The Beatles did go home, at the end of February, 1964, but not without laying serious claim to the title of new kings of rock 'n' roll.

In mid '64, the Beatles also made the extremely successful movie, "A Hard Day's Night," which won an Academy Award nomination for its score.

BEGUINE: a rumbalike dance rhythm of French-Spanish origin.

The beguine is a vigorous popular dance of St. Lucia and Martinique in the West Indies. The name derives from the French "*béguin*" (flirtation). There is little actual beguine material in popular music. The beguine is best-known in the United States through Cole Porter's "Begin the Beguine," from the Broadway show "Jubilee" (1935).

BELAFONTE, HARRY GEORGE: singer, actor. Born New York, New York, March 1, 1927.

The greatest practitioner of the West Indian folk song is a native New Yorker. Harry Belafonte came by his talents naturally, however. His parents were born in the West Indies, his mother on English-speaking Jamaica and his father on French-speaking Martinique. Harry spent his first eight years in New York. Then his mother decided that she preferred her home island and took him back to Jamaica. Here he could see and hear the sights and sounds that produced such haunting island songs as "Jamaica Farewell."

After five years in Jamaica, Harry and his mother returned to New York. He attended parochial school and then George Washington High School. He left high school before graduating to join the Navy during World War II. Back from the war, Harry went to work as an apartment-house handy man. One of the tenants gave him two tickets to the play "Home Is the Hunter." The show so impressed Harry that he decided to use the G.I. Bill to study acting.

Harry Belafonte

He enrolled at Erwin Piscator's Dramatic Worshop, where he tried out many roles, including one in which he sang. The owner of a Broadway club, the Royal Roost, was present at this performance. Harry used to visit the club for relaxation, and one night the club owner asked him if he'd take a two-week singing job. As Harry was earning his living pushing dress carts around the garment center, he accepted eagerly. The two-week engagement was such a success that it was twenty weeks before Harry left. His repertoire was the more usual nightclub fare. After the Royal Roost, Harry toured the country, appearing in nightclubs in many major cities, and signed a contract with Capitol Records. Harry suddenly decided this was not what he wanted and abruptly quit in late 1950.

He had fallen in love with the art of the folk song, and he studied folk song records for hours at a time in the Library of Congress. His friend, guitarist Millard Thomas, became his accompanist. Harry added his fund of West Indian material to his collection of American songs and soon opened at New York's Village Vanguard. The two-week engagement stretched to

fourteen weeks. After a stay at New York's Blue Angel supper club, Harry signed for a role in the Hollywood movie "Bright Road."

Then came a bid to join the cast of "John Murray Anderson's Almanac." The show opened in New York in December, 1953, and Harry's singing of "Hold 'Em, Joe" and "Acorn in the Meadow" won critical raves. Hollywood called once more, this time for Harry to play the lead role of Joe in "Carmen Jones." The title role was played by Dorothy Dandridge.

"Three for Tonight" (1954), in which he sang fourteen songs, was Harry's next project. The show toured most of the United States before opening in New York, and everywhere Belafonte's voice won new converts to folk singing. After the show closed, a television adaptation was presented CBS on June 23, 1955. Critic Jack Gould of the New York *Times* called him "The most compelling new artist of the TV year." From then on, Harry was a regular guest on the top shows of TV, including many appearances on "The Colgate Variety Hour," The Ed Sullivan Show," and a nonsinging role in "General Electric Theatre's" "Winner by Decision."

Belafonte recordings (*on RCA Victor*) and nightclub appearances were responsible for a calypso and West Indian folk-song craze that swept the United States in 1956 and 1957. His recordings of such songs as "Mathilda," "Day-O," "Jamaica Farewell," "I Do Adore Her," "Come Back, Liza," and "Brown-Skin Girl" have become standards. Harry has also proved himself adept at singing folk songs from almost every nation and culture.

BENNETT, TONY: singer. Born Queens, New York, August 3, 1926.

"Rags to Riches" was a tremendously popular song of the early fifties. Its title could stand for the ups and downs of the music profession. Tony Bennett made "Rags to Riches" a hit. At the time, his recordings were at the top of all the major surveys. Then Bennett's career was eclipsed by rock 'n' roll and rhythm and blues. In 1962, the pendulum swung back. Bennett's recording of "I Left My Heart in San Francisco," a slow ballad, sold over a million records and led to renewed demands for the singer's personal appearances. Bennett once more was one of the nation's popular-music favorites.

Tony was born Anthony Dominick Benedetto. He made his first public appearance at the age of seven in a neighborhood-parish

Tony Bennett

After a drought of several years in the late fifties, Bennett's return to glory was heralded by a one-man concert at New York's Carnegie Hall. The performance was sold out two weeks in advance, and almost two thousand persons were turned away, even after seats on the stage had been filled. This was followed by equally successful concerts across the country and a second Carnegie Hall appearance in 1963. In 1962 and 1963, the popularity of "San Francisco" was matched by another Bennett ballad, "I Wanna Be Around."

BERLIN, IRVING: composer, lyricist. Born Temun, Russia, May 11, 1888. Awarded gold medal by President Eisenhower in 1954 for "Gold Bless America." Won Academy Award for Best Song of 1942 ("White Christmas").

Jerome Kern once said, "Berlin has no *place* in American music; he *is* American music." Berlin has given this country far more than singable music; he has provided many of the near-essentials of American life—such classics as "White Christmas," "Easter Parade," "Always," and what has sometimes been called the second national anthem, "God Bless America."

A Cossack pogrom in 1892 drove the family of little Israel Baline to the United States. Baline grew up on New York's teeming East Side. His family was poor, but the environment was warm. When Baline was eight, his father died. Baline ran away from home several years later "to avoid being a burden" to his mother. He earned pennies by singing in New York Bowery saloons, and eventually became a song plugger for Harry Von Tilzer. In the back room of one saloon, he found an old piano on which he taught himself to pick out notes with one or two fingers. In 1906, Baline got a job as a singing waiter at the Pelham Café in Chinatown. The next year, when the waiters at a competing saloon wrote an original song, the Pelham owner urged his men to do the same. Baline supplied lyrics to music by the pianist, Nick Nicholson. The result was his first published song, "Marie from Sunny Italy." It bore his new name, I. Berlin.

He began writing more songs, meanwhile moving to other jobs further uptown, near the music-publishing industry. In a short time, he had his first success, "Sadie Salome, Go Home" (music by Edgar Leslie). His publisher, composer Ted Snyder, hired him as a staff writer.

minstrel show singing "Ida! Sweet as Apple Cider!" Later, he studied commercial art at Manhattan's High School of Industrial Arts and sang in a local club on weekends. When he graduated from high school, Tony concentrated on singing.

He sang with several Army bands while in the service. After the Army, Bennett entered the American Theater Wing's professional school for veterans, singing in clubs in his spare time. Comedian Bob Hope heard him in the Greenwich Village Inn and invited him to sing in a show at New York's Paramount Theatre. The audience liked Tony, and Bob decided to take him to six other cities as part of Hope's supporting cast.

Bennett's journey to stardom was rapid after this. In March, 1950, Mitch Miller, Columbia Records' popular-music director, heard an audition record and promptly issued a contract. By the autumn of 1951, a Bennett dual release of "Because of You" and "Cold, Cold Heart" had sold one million, three hundred thousand copies. Then came a string of successes, including "Candy Kisses," "Tender Is the Night," and "Rags to Riches."

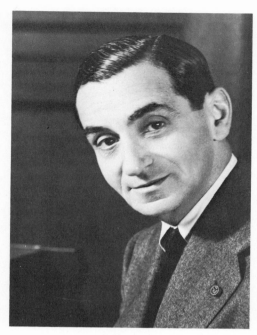

Irving Berlin

Soon Berlin was writing not only words, but music. In 1909, he wrote a ragtime version of Mendelssohn's "Spring Song," "That Mesmerizing Mendelssohn Tune." In 1911, he created a nationwide sensation with "Alexander's Ragtime Band," which quickly sold over a million copies of sheet music. Berlin followed up with such other hits as "That Mysterious Rag" (with Ted Snyder) and "Everybody's Doing It Now."

Then, just as he became a national celebrity, his young wife, Dorothy Goetz, died of typhus picked up during their honeymoon trip to Cuba. Berlin wrote his first real ballad, "When I Lost You." After some months, Berlin's natural talent and vitality reasserted themselves. In 1914, he composed his first complete Broadway show score, "Watch Your Step," which included "Play a Simple Melody," a song that Bing and Gary Crosby returned to hit status in 1950. Berlin entered the Army during World War I. In 1918, he wrote the music for Camp Upton's "Yip, Yip, Yaphank," including such memorable songs as "Oh! How I Hate To Get Up in the Morning" and "Mandy."

Back in civilian life, Berlin wrote many Broadway scores as well as individual songs.

In 1919, for "The Ziegfeld Follies," he wrote "A Pretty Girl Is Like a Melody." He also supplied star Eddie Cantor with the sprightly "You'd Be Surprised." For a series of "Music Box Revues" from 1921 to 1924, he provided such songs as "Say It with Music," "Lady of the Evening," "What'll I Do?," and "All Alone." In 1925, Berlin wrote the score for the Marx Brothers romp "The Cocoanuts." During the same period, Berlin's romance and marriage to heiress Ellin MacKay inspired him to write such standards as "Always" and "Remember."

For a time in the twenties and early thirties, Berlin felt himself written out. He disappeared from the popular-music scene, and some thought his career was over. But, in 1931, he received a bid to work on a new musical with Moss Hart. "Face the Music" opened on February 17, 1932, and was hailed as brilliant satire. "Let's Have Another Cup o' Coffee" became a Depression standard, and two nonshow songs, "Say It Isn't So" and "How Deep Is the Ocean?," were hits of the year. "As Thousands Cheer," which gave the world "Easter Parade," as well as "Heat Wave" and "How's Chances?," opened in 1933.

Berlin then took a sabbatical and began writing for the movies. Over the next few years, he provided scores for three Ginger Rogers and Fred Astaire movies. "Cheek to Cheek," from "Top Hat" (1935), was nominated for an Academy Award, as were "Change Partners," from "Carefree," and "Now It Can Be Told," from "Alexander's Ragtime Band" (both 1938). Kate Smith introduced "God Bless America" in 1938. In 1940, Berlin was again represented on Broadway with "Louisiana Purchase," starring Victor Moore, William Gaxton, and Vera Zorina. The show opened on May 28 at the Imperial Theatre and ran for four hundred and forty-four performances. The hit of the show was "It's a Lovely Day Tomorrow." Berlin won an Academy Award in 1942 for "White Christmas," written for the Bing Crosby movie "Holiday Inn."

During World War II, Berlin was again called on to write a service musical. He responded with "This Is the Army." "This Is the Army, Mr. Jones" was soon heard in all the juke boxes in the land.

"Annie Get Your Gun," "Call Me Madam," and "Mr. President" receive separate entries in this book. "Miss Liberty," which opened on

July 15, 1949, at the Imperial Theatre, ran for only three hundred and eight performances. But it included such Berlin gems as "Let's Take an Old-Fashioned Walk," "Paris Wakes Up and Smiles," and "A Little Fish in a Big Pond."

Composer Douglas Moore wrote in *Glamour* magazine (November, 1962):

> It is a rare gift which sets Irving Berlin apart from all other contemporary songwriters. It is a gift which qualifies him, along with Stephen Foster, Walt Whitman, Vachel Lindsay, and Carl Sandburg as a great American minstrel. He has caught and immortalized in his songs what we say, what we think about, and what we believe.

BERNSTEIN, LEONARD: composer, conductor, pianist. Born Lawrence, Massachusetts, August 25, 1918.

Leonard Bernstein

Versatility is not too unusual in music or in creative fields in general. But to straddle a whole range of very different interests—from classical to popular music and popular writing—and win honors in all of them is unlikely. Leonard Bernstein is generally conceded to have giant stature in classical orchestra conducting and in Broadway and serious composing, and to have impressive television stage presence. He does not come away from this diversity unscathed. A critic in one field may call Bernstein a dilettante because of his obvious popularity in another. The results, however, speak for themselves. Bernstein is the first American-born and -educated conductor of a major symphony orchestra, the New York Philharmonic, and at a very young age for such a post. He has composed such worldwide successes in the musical theater as "West Side Story" and the ballet "Fancy Free." He has written a best-selling book, "The Joy of Music."

Bernstein grew up in Boston. He graduated from Harvard University in 1939 after studying music with some of America's foremost teachers. From there he went to the Curtis Institute to study conducting with Fritz Reiner and orchestration with Randall Thompson. He also studied piano from an early age with illustrious teachers.

Conductor Serge Koussevitzky, founder of the Berkshire Music Center (Tanglewood), in Lenox, Massachusetts, was impressed with Bernstein's ability and took him as a student for the summers of 1940 and 1941. Artur Rodzinski, music director of the New York Philharmonic, met Bernstein at Tanglewood and engaged him as assistant conductor for the 1943–44 season. In November, 1943, guest conductor Bruno Walter became ill, and regular conductor Rodzinski was out of town. Bernstein had to go on. The challenge and Bernstein's response were summarized by the New York *Daily News:*

> Bernstein had one of those opportunities that are like a shoestring catch in center field. Make it, and you're a hero. Muff it, and you're a dope . . . he made it.

Bernstein was also making progress as a composer. In 1943, "Fancy Free" was presented by Ballet Theater. "On the Town," a musical-comedy version of the ballet, opened in December, 1944, and ran for well over a year. It starred Nancy Walker, had book and lyrics by Adolph Green and Betty Comden, and provided such song successes as "Lonely Town" and "Lucky To Be Me." Bernstein also wrote the "Jeremiah" Symphony, which won the New York Music Critics' Award for 1943–44.

From 1945 to 1948, Bernstein headed the New York City Symphony and also made many guest appearances with the Philharmonic. He was appointed one of two principal conductors of the Philharmonic in 1957. The next season, he assumed the music directorship. During all this, he wrote his second musical, "Wonderful Town" (1953), based on the book "My Sister Eileen." Edie Adams, wife of the late comedian Ernie Kovacs, sprang to prominence in this show as Eileen, and Rosalind Russell scored as sister Ruth. "Ohio" and "It's Love" are two songs from a score often heard on radio and TV.

In 1956, Bernstein wrote another musical, "Candide," which, while it did not succeed on Broadway, is considered by some to be a great step forward in musical theater. Then he topped all his popular-music efforts with "West Side Story," a contemporary version of "Romeo and Juliet." "Maria," "I Feel Pretty," "America," "Tonight," and the other songs have been heard around the world in the Academy Award-winning movie version.

In 1955, on the TV show "Omnibus," Bernstein began a series of lectures on the meaning of music. He has probably been more criticized for overpopularizing classical music on this program than for any other aspect of his career. But there can be no doubt that his efforts have brought millions of Americans to a much better understanding of music.

BEST FOOT FORWARD: musical. Lyrics by Ralph Blane, music by Hugh Martin, book by John Cecil Holm. New York opening: October 1, 1941, Ethel Barrymore Theatre. 326 performances.

Now and again, a show appears on Broadway that acts as a showcase for young, sparkling new talent. "Best Foot Forward" was a prime example of this. The production was both a great beginning—for many new stars, including June Allyson and Nancy Walker—and an ending. The ending was the brilliant partnership of Rodgers and Hart. As Hart became almost impossible to work with, Rodgers finally had to make plans to continue after the inevitable breakup. One such move was a secret alignment with George Abbott (Rodgers's name did not appear on the program) to coproduce "Best Foot Forward," which Abbott also directed.

John Anderson in the New York *Journal-American* echoed most of the critics when he wrote:

> . . . Abbott has met the juke box generation on its own footing and 'Best Foot Forward' . . . turned out to be quite a youth movement all by itself, bright, breezy and brash.

The show is set in a polite prep school, Winsocki, in the Pennsylvania Dutch country near Philadelphia. A student, Bud Hooper, egged on by friends Hunk Hoyt and Dutch Miller, writes a letter inviting Hollywood film star Gale Joy to the prom. Bud doesn't expect her to accept, and has also invited his girl friend, Helen Schlessinger.

The actress's first reaction is to turn it down. But her press agent, Jack Haggerty, points out that the publicity might help her now fading career.

The girls invited to the prom from nearby schools include one nicknamed "Blind Date" and her friends Ethel and Minerva. They sing that their favorite courses are "The Three B's" —barrelhouse, blues, and boogiewoogie. Later in the show, Blind Date sings the praises of her favorite hangout, "Just a Little Joint With a Juke Box."

As Bud, Hunk, and Dutch prepare to take Miss Joy to the dance, they sing "Three Men on a Date." But once they get to the school gymnasium, the jealous Helen sets the crowd to ripping off Miss Joy's clothes for souvenirs. Before the actress is through with her trying visit to the campus, she also plays hide and seek with the dean in the boys' dormitory. Meanwhile, Helen and Bud continue to have their arguments, interspersed with such songs sung by Helen as "Ev'ry Time" and "Shady Lady Bird." There's also a show-stopping interlude for Minerva and Hunk, "What Do You Think I Am?"

The climax is the big football game. School-boy Chuck Green leads the class and the old grads in the stirring fight song "Buckle Down, Winsocki." In the end, Gale Joy turns out to have a heart of gold as well as the ability to set everything right.

The original cast included Gil Stratton, Jr., as Bud; Kenneth Bowers, as Hunk; Jack Jordan, Jr., as Dutch; Rosemary Lane, as Gale; Nancy Walker, as Blind Date; June Allyson, as

Minerva; Victoria Schools, as Ethel; Maueen Cannon, as Helen; Marty May, as Haggerty; and Tommy Dix, as Chuck Green.

BIG BAND: a band having twelve or more members.

The term "big band," relative at best, refers to large dance or jazz bands as distinguished from small combos of perhaps four to six musicians. The era of the big band began in the early thirties and ended during World War II. Some of the most famous big bands were those of Benny Goodman, Glenn Miller, Duke Ellington, Tommy Dorsey, Jimmy Dorsey, Kay Kyser, Harry James, Gene Krupa, Bunny Berigan, and Lionel Hampton.

The heart of the big band is the rhythm section, which supplies the basic beat for each number. It usually includes bass, guitar, and drums, and sometimes piano. Against this background, the brass and reed instruments, plus the vocalist or vocalists, carry the melody and harmony. The big band includes trombones, trumpets, and saxophones, with the saxophonists usually doubling on clarinet.

The growth of the big band was spurred by the growth of the cities and the beginning of coast-to-coast radio in the early thirties. Ballroom dancing became increasingly popular, and soon major bands were traveling throughout the country for extended engagements and one-night stands at smaller cities and college campuses. World War II changed the pattern. Many musicians were called into service, and travel restrictions made it difficult to take large outfits all over the map. Wartime taxes on entertainment also discouraged hiring large bands for club dates. An additional factor, some experts feel, was the increasing tendency of many big bands to play for their own rather than the audience's pleasure, eventually for listening instead of dancing, thus eliminating one of the original reasons for big bands.

After World War II, most musical entrepreneurs concentrated on individual vocalists and performers and small combos, which required far less economic risk than the big band. Some big bands remained, and there are still some in vogue today. But instead of keeping the same musicians for all engagements, a leader today will hire enough local musicians to provide the size of band desired for a particular date.

BLACK BOTTOM: popular dance of the nineteen-twenties; also (capitalized), a song.

The black bottom was a precursor of the twist in that it involved shaking the hips. It was a sinuous, wiggling, decidedly indecorous dance, particularly in its original form. The black bottom began in Negro sections of the United States. In the mid-nineteen-twenties, showman George White decided to introduce a toned-down version to Broadway. The top songwriting team of Buddy de Sylva, Lew Brown, and Ray Henderson provided White with a song called "Black Bottom" to go with the dance. The 1926 edition of "George White's Scandals" opened at the Apollo Theatre in New York on June 14 and ran for four hundred and twenty-four performances. Both song and dance were hits, starting a national craze.

There are two main theories about the origin of the dance's name. One is anatomical. The other is that the dance originated in or got its name from Black Bottom, the tough, dissolute Negro section of Nashville, Tennessee.

BLUE MOON: song (1934). Words by Lorenz Hart, music by Richard Rodgers.

Rodgers and Hart went to Hollywood in early 1931, fresh from a string of Broadway triumphs. Supposedly it was to do one score for Paramount, but it stretched out to a three-year stint for several studios. In 1933, they were working on a Jean Harlow picture for Metro-Goldwyn-Mayer. They wrote several songs, including one for Jean called "Make Me a Star." Miss Harlow was dropped from the film, however, and so was the song. Rodgers and Hart loved the melody, so Hart wrote a new lyric titled "The Bad in Every Man." They resubmitted it to MGM for possible use in "Manhattan Melodrama," again unsuccessfully.

In the thirties, many movie companies, MGM among them, had their own music firms. One of MGM's affiliates was Robbins Music. Jack Robbins of that firm received the music for "The Bad in Every Man" and liked the melody but not the words. He asked Rodgers and Hart, by now back in New York, if they'd change it. The next day, they were ready with a new title and lyric. The title: "Blue Moon." Robbins released the song as a single—one of the few Rodgers and Hart numbers published independently of a show or movie. It was phenomenally successful. At a time when records had cut sheet-music sales to the bone, "Blue Moon" sold well over a million copies. It is one of the most performed Rodgers and Hart compositions.

BLUE NOTE: a musical note, usually a flatted third or seventh, which gives a blues feeling to a composition. (See *Blues*.)

BLUE TANGO: song (1952). Words by Mitchell Parish, music by Leroy Anderson.

Leroy Anderson had popular-music greatness thrust on him. For many years, he was arranger for the Boston Pops Orchestra. Then he wrote some light melodies for after-intermission music. The Pops played them, and the audience's reaction was enthusiastic. One of the numbers was "Blue Tango."

"In many numbers I have written," Anderson says, "the title came first, since it contained the idea for the music; for example, 'The Syncopated Clock,' 'A Trumpeter's Lullaby,' 'The Typewriter,' and 'Sandpaper Ballet.' With 'Blue Tango,' however, I made up the melody first, around 1947 and '48. I thought of calling it 'Tango Azul,' because I always liked the sound of the Spanish word for blue."

Word got around about Anderson's compositions. He signed a contract with Decca Records which arranged for him to have his own orchestra, the Leroy Anderson Pop Concert Orchestra.

Anderson continues, "In 1951, when I recorded my second album for Decca, we needed another number to fill out the record. The melodic tango I had written but not yet scored made a good contrast with the other numbers we were going to record.

"By this time, I had decided that it was better to have English titles, and, since the tango had a blues figure that ran throughout the piece, it was appropriate to call it 'Blue Tango.' As I said, it was just a melodic number to fill out the record, because the people at Decca felt that 'Belle of the Ball' would be the most popular, and I myself guessed that 'Plink, Plank, Plunk' would step out ahead of the others.

"We were all surprised when the record was played and radio stations all over the country began playing 'Blue Tango.' It started building up in January, 1952, and by the third week in June, my own recording had already sold one million copies." (This was even more surprising as country-and-Western music was the main vogue at the time.) " 'Blue Tango' was the first instrumental to reach number one on the Hit Parade. It was on the Hit Parade for fifteen weeks, and in the number-one position for seven weeks."

In the years following, "Blue Tango" was given almost every conceivable interpretation. It has been performed as a jazz number, and even as rock 'n' roll (by Bill Black's Combo). At the request of Anderson's publisher, Mills Music, lyrics were eventually added by Mitchell Parish. But the most popular style is Anderson's original instrumental arrangement.

BLUES: song characterized by a twelve-bar pattern with melancholy words and syncopated rhythm.

The blues are songs of man's troubles and weariness, his problems with love or the law or inhumanity. They arose spontaneously as folk music of the Negro slaves in the South, though the rhythms have roots in Africa. The blues spread from work gangs and guitar-playing slum troubadors to pianists in brothels or bars. As Abbe Niles, chronicler of W. C. Handy, has stated in "Blues" (New York: A. & C. Boni, 1926):

> In almost all blues, the essential element is the singer's own personality—his problems, opinions, etc. Melancholy is usually the theme. The words usually are in the form of an unusual three-line stanza instead of the two or four in conventional lyrics.

Niles also points out that the music generally has a pattern of twelve bars instead of the usual eight or sixteen.

W. C. Handy is known as "the Father of the Blues." This does not mean that he originated the style; the blues rhythms go back many years before Handy was born in 1873. But Handy did write some of the greatest formal blues and spread knowledge of this form of popular music far and wide.

Handy's approach to the blues was discussed by Niles in his introduction to "Treasury of the Blues," edited by Handy and first published in 1926. Niles wrote:

> When Handy wrote a blues, he sought to speak in the language of the folk singers— meaning not merely through words and turns of thought, but their musical language. For this last purpose, it was particularly necessary somehow to convey their typical slurring of the third note of the scale, which was a peculiarity of Negro folk singing generally, not merely the blues.
> One cannot reproduce on paper what a

Bessie Smith would do to this note; it is necessary to work out conventions. Handy's convention was the irregular introduction of the flatted third into his scripts. Thus the minor third might share a beat with the major, or appear as a grace note to the major or entirely replace the major. Handy's interpolated flat third caught and held popular attention even more than . . . the features that stemmed exclusively from the folk-blues. It has acquired a name of its own: "the blue note."

BLUES IN THE NIGHT: song (1941). Words by Johnny Mercer, music by Harold Arlen.

In 1941, composer Harold Arlen and lyricist Johnny Mercer were assigned to the Warner Brothers film "Hot Nocturne." The movie dealt with jazz and jazz musicians. In one scene, the hero is arrested and hears a Negro blues singer do a melody that exemplifies the kind of music he hopes someday to bring to the public. The singer was played by William Gillespie, a protégé of a good friend of Arlen's. Arlen wanted his song to be special and yet in the true blues idiom.

As Edward Jablonski related in "Harold Arlen: Happy With the Blues" (New York: Doubleday, 1961), Arlen locked himself in his study and carefully analyzed recordings of authentic blues. Jablonski wrote:

Because he wanted the jail blues to reflect the authentic folk blues he adapted the folk form's twelve-bar pattern. After two days at it Arlen emerged from his study confident that he had found the right melody. . . . He then played it for Mercer, who began inventing lyrical ideas, so many in fact that he had covered four pages with notations. In shuffling through them Arlen admired Mercer's work, suggested only one change—that a line appearing on the fourth page be placed at the beginning of the song. The line was "My mamma done tol' me . . ." and the song was, of course, "Blues in the Night."

The studio changed the name of the picture to "Blues in the Night." Band leader Jimmy Lunceford came out with a two-side instrumental version that became a best seller before the film was released. Later, Bing Crosby found an enthusiastic popular response for his vocal version.

The song was nominated for the 1941 Academy Award. Were it not for Hammerstein and Kern's sensational "The Last Time I Saw Paris," Arlen probably would have won his second Oscar in three years.

BMI: Broadcast Music, Incorporated.

BMI licenses performing rights of member songwriters and music publishers. It was founded in 1940 by the radio industry as the debate between stations and the American Society of Composers, Authors and Publishers over performing rights reached boiling point. The then current license agreement between the stations and ASCAP was due to expire, and the stations balked at ASCAP requests for sharply increased payments under a new contract. Their answer was to establish a rival performing-rights organization, BMI. On New Year's Day, 1941, the old contract expired and ASCAP forbade the radio performance of copyright material of its members. The matter was settled by arbitration after almost a year.

BMI, however, remained in existence and gradually became an independent and highly important part of the popular-music field. A great many of the younger songwriters during the late forties and fifties joined BMI, to some extent because of the stiff ASCAP qualifications for new members. (The ASCAP rules have since been modified.) Today, a great deal of popular music is performed under BMI license. BMI has been particularly strong in rock 'n' roll and country-and-Western. Like ASCAP, BMI does not publish music or make records but acts as an agent for its songwriters and independent music-publishing firms.

BOCK, JERRY: composer. Born New York, New York, November 23, 1928. Won Pulitzer Prize for "Fiorello!" (1959).

The 1959–60 season provided a bonanza of new writing talent for the musical theater. For decades, a handful of composers—Kern, Berlin, Rodgers, Styner, Loesser—had dominated the scene, and many had wondered if their passing might end the great days of American musical comedy. In the early fifties, a few bright lights appeared on the horizon: Richard Adler, Jerry Ross, and Bob Merrill. Then, in 1959–60, came a flood of new talent. Five extremely promising writers brought three hits to Broadway and off-Broadway within six months: Rick Besoyan ("Little Mary Sunshine"), Charles Strouse and Lee Adams ("Bye Bye Birdie"), and Jerry Bock and Sheldon Harnick ("Fiorello!").

Jerry Bock won his spurs as a composer at Camp Taminent, in Pennsylvania's Pocono Mountains. Bock, a native New Yorker, worked at Taminent under the supervision of director Max Liebman. Jerry had to write the score for a new one-act revue every week. After several seasons of this, Bock felt confident enough to tackle the New York musical world. He soon was writing special material for many top performers, including Carol Channing, Pat Carroll, Joel Gray, and Conrad Thibault. He had his eye on the musical theater, though, and placed three songs in the 1955 Broadway production "Catch a Star." Next came an assignment to do the score for a movie short, "Wonders of Manhattan," which won an award as the best short of the year. Three songs of his appeared in a second stage show, "The Ziegfeld Follies."

People were beginning to notice him, and he was able to collaborate with George Weiss and Larry Holofcener on the score for a new show called "Mister Wonderful." The numbers included the title song, "Ethel Baby," and "Too Close for Comfort." "Mister Wonderful," which starred Sammy Davis, Jr., opened on March 22, 1956, to unfavorable reviews. The public decided, however, that the show was better than its notices. It ran for three hundred and eighty-three performances.

Bock first began working with Sheldon Harnick in 1957. They both were under contract to music publisher Thomas Valando, and Valando suggested that they collaborate. Their first effort, "The Body Beautiful," folded in two months. The boys got the chance to work on a new show, "Fiorello!," under the watchful eye of veteran director-librettist George Abbott. "Fiorello!" dealt with New York's most beloved mayor, Fiorello LaGuardia. It was a sleeper. There had been little advance ballyhoo, but opening night (November 23, 1959) saw the critics enraptured. The first-night audiences applauded until their hands were sore for a score that included "Politics and Poker," "Little Tin Box," and "Till Tomorrow." "Fiorello!" was the third musical to win the Pulitzer Prize.

When Bock and Harnick's next effort, "Tenderloin," closed in 1961 after two hundred and sixteen performances (it opened on October 17, 1960), the critics shook their heads sadly. Then, on April 26, 1963, came "She Loves Me," Bock and Harnick's fourth Broadway show. This time they proved that they had the staying power of a possibly great team. United Press International critic Jack Gaver wrote:

This arrival at the Eugene O'Neill Theatre is a lovely, tuneful, intimate and enchanting musical that has about as much substance as a zephyr and is every bit as refreshing. . . . The songs are . . . soundly integrated into the script, but there are melodic standouts that will please you for years to come. . . .

On September 22, 1964, still another Bock and Harnick musical won raves from New York critics. This was "Fiddler on the Roof," based on stories by Yiddish author Sholom Aleichem, starring Zero Mostel as Tevye the dairyman. The score included: "Matchmaker, Matchmaker," "Sabbath Prayer," "To Life," "Miracle of Miracles," "Sunrise, Sunset," "Now I Have Everything," "Do You Love Me?" and "Anatevka."

BOOGIEWOOGIE: a percussive form of the blues, faster in tempo than the original blues; also, a dance developed to go with this music.

Boogiewoogie is a relatively late form of jazz based on the jazz riff. The riff is a short, constantly repeated phrase. The boogie riff was originally used as a base against which the other hand or the soloist would improvise. After a while, the base was used as a rhythmic background for ballads or specially written boogiewoogie compositions. Examples of some boogiewoogie popular songs which were popular in the early forties are "Cow Cow Boogie" (made famous by vocalist Ella Mae Morse) and "Beat Me, Daddy, Eight to the Bar." "Eight to the bar" refers to the rhythmic pattern of the base—eight counts to the bar.

Some musicians used to call boogiewoogie "galloping time." Paul Nettl ("The Story of Dance Music." New York: Philosophical Library, 1947) has written that the riff, or, as he calls it in musical terms, rhythmic ostinato, is

sharply dotted and reminds one strongly of the ostinato themes of the seventeenth and eighteenth centuries which likewise were based on the simplest melodic formulas. . . . They too were often strongly dotted in rhythm.

The origin of boogiewoogie is vague. It became very popular in the late twenties and throughout the thirties and early forties. Then it faded from popularity. In the sixties, however, some of the rhythms of rhythm and blues derived from boogiewoogie.

One of the innovators of boogiewoogie was pianist Pinetop Smith, who claimed that "Pinetop's Boogiewoogie" was the first boogie developed. Many top boogiewoogie pianists came to the fore during the twenties and thirties, including Meade Lux Lewis, Albert Ammons, and Pete Johnson.

The boogiewoogie dance was the forerunner of the Lindy hop, jitterbug, and rock 'n' roll forms.

BOOK: musical-theater term for the dialogue and stage directions of a musical production.

The book is a series of sketches (a revue) or, as has been mostly the case in recent years, a musical play. The man who writes the book is a playwright, except that he must keep the music in mind as he works.

The book may be original or it may be an adaptation of a play, a novel, a series of short stories, or a nonfiction work. In the last several decades, the trend has been away from original books. Examples of originals are "Finian's Rainbow," "Paint Your Wagon," and "Bye Bye Birdie." On the other hand, "South Pacific" was based on James Michener's short-story collection "Tales of the South Pacific," "My Fair Lady" on Shaw's play "Pygmalion," and "The Pajama Game" on the novel "7½ Cents." Shakespeare has been a rich source of inspiration. "West Side Story," based on "Romeo and Juliet"; "Kiss Me, Kate," on "The Taming of the Shrew"; and "The Boys from Syracuse," on "The Comedy of Errors," are examples.

The importance of the book was stressed by Alan Jay Lerner (who wrote book as well as lyrics for all the shows he collaborated on with Frederick Loewe) in a foreword to his "Paint Your Wagon" (New York: Coward-McCann, 1952):

The value of the basic story cannot be exaggerated. There is often a general tendency to regard the book of a musical as of little consequence. This is especially true when the musical is a success. But let the opening night be a two-and-a-half-hour wake and you will read the next morning how neither the music, the scenery, nor the dancing was able to overcome the inept plot. I can tell you the book is all-essential. It is the fountain from which all waters spring. . . .

BOONE, CHARLES EUGENE (PAT): vocalist, actor. Born Jacksonville, Florida, June 1, 1934.

A performer with a college degree is not too rare. But one who lets a potential million-dollar career mark time while he obtains his degree is. This Pat Boone did, even though he already was a regular on "The Arthur Godfrey Show" and one of the hottest vocalists on records. In 1957, at the peak of popularity, he turned down several lucrative jobs to earn his degree, *summa cum laude,* from Columbia University in June, 1958. Boone said at the time, "My parents always stressed the importance of education to us. They've often told us education is a great blessing, something that can never be lost or stolen. . . . Too many teen-agers want to quit school. I can't set a bad example."

Pat (his parents gave him his nickname) was descended on his father's side from frontiersman Daniel Boone. His father, a building contractor, was working in Jacksonville, Florida, when Pat was born. The family moved to Donelson, then, when Pat was six, to Nashville, Tennessee. At ten, Pat was singing in public. He was a member of the baseball, basketball, and track teams at David Lipscomb High School, was president of the student body, and was elected the school's most popular boy. By the time Pat met and proposed to Shirley Foley, daughter of radio and television Western star Red Foley, he had his own show, "Youth on Parade," on station WSIX, Nashville. He and Shirley eloped during Pat's freshman year at David Lipscomb College. They moved to Denton, Texas, where Pat ran a show for WBAP-TV for forty-four dollars and fifty cents a week plus groceries from his sponsors. In his off time, Pat continued his schooling at North Texas State College.

Denton TV fans began urging Pat to audition for "Arthur Godfrey's Talent Scouts." Pat tried out in 1954 and was one of the show's winners. (He had won the "Ted Mack Amateur Hour" while still living in Nashville.) Pat returned to Texas but was followed by Randy Wood, head of Dot Records. Wood signed Pat and arranged for his first commercial recording.

The first record, made in Chicago in February, 1955, rapidly reached the top ten in sales. Its title was "Two Hearts, Two Kisses." This was followed up with "Ain't That a Shame?"—a million-record seller and the first of over a dozen gold records Pat made by 1962. He also achieved a platinum record, for a single-record sale of over three million. Some of his other successes included "I Almost Lost My Mind," "Friendly Persuasion," "Love Letters in the Sand," and "Don't Forbid Me."

In the fall of 1955, Godfrey brought Pat back to New York as a regular on "The Arthur Godfrey Show"—and Pat promptly enrolled as a junior at Columbia. He had to interrupt his education temporarily to go to Hollywood for his first movie. The picture, the first of several for Twentieth Century-Fox, was "Bernadine." It was followed in 1957 by "April Love." Boone's record of the title song from the latter reached the million mark the same month the picture was released (November, 1957). The New York *Times'* appraisal of the picture was ". . . a batch of pleasant tunes. . . . But it's high time they gave such a nice lad a picture with a few teeth to it." As a result of these two pictures, though, Boone soon rated among the fifteen top-drawing stars. He also won a 1956 million-dollar contract with Twentieth Century for a picture a year for seven years. Pat insisted, however, on returning to Columbia for the 1957–58 school year. In the summer of 1958, he was back at work on his next movie, "Mardi Gras," followed a year later by "Journey to the Center of the Earth."

Pat found time to run his own TV show, "The Pat Boone Chevy Showroom." He also saw his book "Twixt Twelve and Twenty," completed in 1955, published by Prentice-Hall. It rapidly achieved best-seller status, with over four hundred thousand copies snapped up by his youthful fans. He became an executive of a radio company that bought station WKDA in Nashville and KWOK in Fort Worth, Texas. By the sixties, Boone had won almost every popularity or service award it would seem possible for a performer to win, from Most Popular Male Vocalist (*Cash Box* and *Billboard*) to 1959 Father of the Year (J. C. Penney).

BOSSA NOVA: a jazz samba; also, a dance performed to this music.

About the time when rock 'n' roll was beginning to catch on in the United States, another new rhythm—bossa nova—was becoming popular in Brazil. Bossa nova is a combination, developed by younger Brazilian musicians, of two musical strains, North American jazz and the South American samba. The term means "new flair" in Portuguese.

Stan Getz and Charlie Byrd's album "Jazz Samba" started the craze in the United States in the sixties. Getz did not bring the music to this country, however, nor is he one of the pioneers of bossa nova. In Brazil, composer and singer João Gilbert is generally regarded as the father of bossa nova. In 1953, Brazilian guitarist-composer Laurindo Almeida (living in this country at the time), saxophonist Bud Shank, bassist Harry Babasin, and drummer Roy Harte made one of the first bossa-nova recordings to be played in the United States. "Brazilliance" was released in 1963 by Pacific Jazz Records along with a new Almeida-Shank effort, "Viva Bossa Nova."

Originally, the music was made to be played and listened to rather than danced. When it became popular, dance steps were devised for it. The basic bossa-nova step (man's part; girl's opposite) is 1) forward step with left foot; 2) touch right big toe to right side without putting any weight on it; 3) step forward on right foot; 4) touch left big toe to left side without weight. This sequence is continued around the dance floor.

BOYS FROM SYRACUSE, THE: musical. Lyrics by Lorenz Hart, music by Richard Rodgers, book by George Abbott. Based on Shakespeare's "Comedy of Errors." New York opening: November 23, 1938, Alvin Theatre. 235 performances.

This musical version of a very old war-horse (Shakespeare, in turn, had adapted "The Comedy of Errors" from Plautus's play "Menaechmi") generally won rousing critical approval in 1938 and in a 1963 revival. Richard Watts, Jr., of the New York *Herald Tribune*, wrote about the 1938 production:

If you have been wondering all these years just what was wrong with 'The Comedy of Errors,' it . . . has been waiting for a score by Rodgers and Hart and direction by George Abbott.

Most of the comic action in the 1938 production was handled by Jimmy Savo and Lorenz Hart's brother Teddy Hart, who played long-separated twins. Rosamund Gilder in *Theatre Arts* wrote:

Jimmy Savo rolls frenzied eyes and tears about the stage in a crouching marathon, while Teddy Hart as the other Dromio seconds and sometimes excels him in dumbbell enthusiasm.

The plot turns upon the arrival of Antipholus of Syracuse and his servant Dromio in the city of Ephesus (preceded by Antipholus's father, who has been jailed by the Duke of Ephesus).

[31]

Each has a twin brother from whom he had been separated during a storm at sea while all were babies. Unknown to the boys from Syracuse (who sing their love for "Dear Old Syracuse"), their brothers, who are also named Antipholus and Dromio, are well-known residents of Ephesus. The Ephesus pair are also master and servant, and both are married, Antipholus to Adriana and Dromio to Luce. The Ephesus household also includes Adriana's pretty sister Luciana. As the play progresses, there is a constant round of mistaken identity, in which one Antipholus gives orders to the other, Adriana gives supper to the Syracuse Antipholus while locking out her husband, and the Syracuse Antipholus makes advances to Luciana, who is indignant at such attention from a man she thinks is married to her sister. The show stopper of 1938 was "Sing for Your Supper," sung by Adriana, Luciana, and Luce during the wild dinner-table maneuvering. Dromio's wife pursues both Dromios, "savoring to the full the bawdier cracks with which the occasion is generously sprinkled" (to quote Miss Gilder). The climax comes when Adriana has the Ephesus boys seized for being demented while the Syracuse team takes refuge in a priory. The boys' father and the Duke of Ephesus help straighten things out at the end.

The original cast included Eddie Albert, as the Syracuse Antipholus; Ronald Graham, as his brother; Muriel Angelus, as Adriana; Marcy Westcott, as Luciana; Wynn Murray, as Luce; and, in the small part of the tailor's apprentice, Burl Ives. The score included "This Can't Be Love," "Falling in Love with Love," "You Have Cast Your Shadow on the Sea," "What Can You do With a Man?," "The Shortest Day of the Year," "He and She," "Ladies of the Evening," and "Oh, Diogenes!" The successful 1963 revival starred Stuart Damon, as Antipholus of Syracuse; Rudy Tronto, as his Dromio; Clifford David and Danny Carroll, as the Ephesians; Ellen Hanley, as Adriana; Julienne Marie, as Luciana; and Karen Morrow, as Luce.

BREAK: a pause in the basic rhythm or an open passage in a performance, which may be filled by a short instrumental solo, a short vocal passage, or by the rhythm section marking time.

In folk blues, the singer usually performed two and a half bars of the four-measure phrase, and the accompanist filled the remaining bar and a half. This would occur three times in each statement of the normal twelve-bar blues. In popular songs, most of which use the thirty-two-measure chorus in an AABA form (see *Chorus* and *Release*), the break may come at the end of each eight-measure group. It may also come at the end of the release and at the end of each chorus. "Break" is also used to describe a phrase played by an instrument or instruments without the backing of the rhythm section.

Another definition of "break" is to change from one tone quality to another, or the point in the instrumental or vocal register where such a change occurs.

BREWER, TERESA: singer. Born Toledo, Ohio, May 7, 1931.

By the early nineteen-sixties, Teresa Brewer had packed several successful careers into a relatively few years. Though in her early thirties, she had voluntarily retired several times and come back each time to score even greater triumphs. Her first retirement came at twelve years of age, her first comeback at sixteen. She also was financially independent by the sixties, thanks to her singing, and the mother of six children.

Though a short girl, Teresa has a big voice with a soubrette sound suggestive of the Gay Nineties. She could carry a tune almost before she was able to talk. When she was two, she appeared on "Uncle August's Kiddie Show" on station WSPD, Toledo. At five, she was a sensation on "Major Bowes' Amateur Hour" and toured for seven years with the Major's road shows. At twelve, she became a regular member of one of the best-known network radio programs of the late thirties and early forties, "The Pick and Pat Show."

At this point came Teresa's first retirement. After four years, sixteen-year-old Teresa again made the rounds of the talent shows. She appeared on Eddie Dowling's "Big Break" and "The Talent Jackpot." The public went for her new style, and before long a major record company signed her. In a short while, she had her first million-record seller, her driving rendition of "Music, Music, Music." While still in her teens, she married Bill Monahan and, in 1950, gave birth to her first child, Kathleen. That same year also saw Teresa's first theater engagement, in which played to capacity crowds at New York's Roxy. As her family grew, Teresa cut down on her career to a great extent but still turned out a number of hit records, such as "Ricochet," during the fifties. Through the fifties and sixties, Teresa appeared as a featured guest on most major television shows, including those of Perry Como and Ed Sullivan.

BRIGADOON: musical. Lyrics and book by Alan Jay Lerner, music by Frederick Loewe. New York opening: March 13, 1947, Ziegfeld Theatre. 581 performances.

With the appearance of "Brigadoon," Broadway received notice that another great musical-theater team had come of age. After several false starts, Lerner and Loewe had found the path that was to lead to the musical miracle of "My Fair Lady." Critical appraisal was unanimously favorable. Despite the fantastic plot, it was agreed that Alan Lerner's original book was plausible, and Agnes de Mille's choreography was considered even one step beyond her work in "Oklahoma!"

"Brigadoon" is set in the Scottish Highlands. Tommy Albright and Jeff Douglas, young Americans on a hunting trip, stumble on a town not on their map. It is, as voices sing, "Brigadoon." A fair is in progress this morning, and Andrew MacLaren's daughter Jean is shopping for a jacket for her wedding to Charlie Dalrymple. The forthcoming marriage has enraged Jean's other suitor, Harry Beaton. Jean's pretty sister Fiona is still single ("Waitin' for My Dearie"). All are amazed when they see Tommy and Jeff, but they soon make them welcome. Fiona is impressed with Tommy, and a buxom girl named Meg makes eyes at Jeff. Charlie Dalrymple arrives and toasts his bride-to-be ("I'll Go Home with Bonnie Jean").

Tommy and Fiona walk to gather heather for the wedding and sing their growing affection ("The Heather on the Hill"). That afternoon, as Charlie comes to sign the family Bible, he tells his longing for Jean, who is secluded for the wedding that evening ("Come to Me, Bend to Me"). Back from their walk, Tommy exuberantly tells Jeff of his feelings ("Almost Like Being in Love"). But then Jeff looks at the Bible and shows Tommy that the entries are dated in the seventeen-hundreds. They ask the schoolmaster, Mr. Lundie, to explain. He tells them that the minister, to save the town from witches two hundred years before, made a miracle. Brigadoon would vanish from the map for a hundred years to reappear for one day. Though a hundred years had passed, the townsfolk would only be one day older. The spell wasn't affected by strangers, but if any of Brigadoon's inhabitants left, the town would disappear forever.

At Jean's wedding, Harry Beaton tries to kill Charlie but is driven off. Vowing vengeance, Harry announces that he is leaving Brigadoon. In a wild chase, Jeff trips Beaton, who dies in the fall. As night draws on, Tommy and Jeff leave reluctantly. Back in the United States, Tommy is unable to bear his longing for Fiona. Praying for another miracle, he makes Jeff fly back with him to Scotland. At Brigadoon's site, the schoolmaster wakens to welcome Tommy, while Jeff turns away.

The original cast included David Brooks, as Tommy; Marion Bell, as Fiona; George Keane, as Jeff; Lee Sullivan, as Charlie; and William Hansen, as Mr. Lundie. Other songs were "The Love of My Life," "There But for You Go I," "My Mother's Wedding Day," and "From This Day On."

BROWN, LEW: lyricist, composer, music publisher, producer. Born Odessa, Russia, December 10, 1893; died New York, New York, February 5, 1958.

During the early years of this century, the position of lifeguard had a strangely similar effect on the careers of two boys, one in California and one in New York. For while working on these jobs, both boys became interested in songwriting. Some years later, they met and formed two thirds of the fabulous team of de Sylva, Brown, and Henderson.

The California swimming enthusiast was Buddy de Sylva, the New York one (at Rockaway Beach) Lew Brown. Brown had been brought to the United States by his parents in 1898. They lived for a time in Connecticut, and Lew attended public schools in New Haven. When the family moved to New York, Lew went to De Witt Clinton High School in the Bronx. During one summer, he worked as a lifeguard and began to write parodies of popular songs. These met with such approval among his friends that he decided to try writing original lyrics.

He began to make the rounds of Tin Pan Alley. This led to his first major collaboration with one of the greatest songwriters of the time, Albert Von Tilzer. In 1912, they wrote a song that was a major hit then and is still heard today, "I'm the Lonesomest Gal in Town." From 1912 through 1921, they worked together on a series of hits, some of which became standards. These include "Kentucky Sue" and "Please Don't Take My Lovin' Man Away" (1912); "Give Me the Moonlight, Give Me the Girl" and "I May Be

Gone for a Long, Long Time" (1917); "Oh, by Jingo, Oh, by Gee" and "I Used To Love You but It's All Over Now" (1919); and "Dapper Dan, the Sheik of Alabam'" (1921).

In 1922, Brown began writing with a new partner, Ray Henderson. One of their first efforts was the song "Georgette" for "The Greenwich Village Follies." For the next two years, they wrote regularly together, though each worked with several other songwriters as well. Then, in 1925, they were called in to work on "George White's Scandals," which had just lost the services of George Gershwin. Already on hand was the man who had written Gershwin's lyrics for the 1924 "Scandals," Buddy de Sylva. The result was the most successful triumvirate in songwriting history. Though Henderson did most of the composing, de Sylva and Brown contributed ideas on melody as well as collaborating on the lyrics.

They worked on the "Scandals," those of 1925, 1926, and 1928. (Brown also worked on two other editions of the "Scandals.") Their first big success was the 1926 edition, which included "The Birth of the Blues," "Black Bottom," "Lucky Day," and "The Girl Is You and the Boy Is Me." They soon went on to write a series of scores for hit musicals, including "Good News" (1927), "Follow Thru" (1929), and "Flying High" (1930). (For other songs, see *de Sylva, George Gard (Buddy)*, and *Henderson, Ray*.)

The team also started its own publishing house, which was sold to a Hollywood studio in 1929. This helped lead to the breakup of the team, as de Sylva became more interested in producing films than songs. The team wrote songs for several pictures, including Jolson's "Sonny," before de Sylva left for California in the early thirties. In 1934, Brown also decided to work in Hollywood and collaborated with a number of top writers during the mid-thirties. One of his first efforts was with Jay Gorney on Shirley Temple's "Stand Up and Cheer." The score included "Baby, Take a Bow," with Brown working both as lyricist and co-composer. That same year (1934), he teamed with Gorney on the film "Carolina." Brown also worked with composer Harry Akst on such films as "Loud Speaker" (1934) and "The Music Goes Round" (1936). Another collaboration was with Louis Alter on the 1934 "Casino Varieties." In the late thirties, Brown returned to New York to continue songwriting, do some producing, and to reenter music publishing.

While best known for his lyrics, Brown was co-composer of a number of hit songs during the thirties and forties, including "Comes Love," "Beer Barrel Polka," "Don't Sit under the Apple Tree with Anyone Else but Me," and "I Came Here To Talk for Joe."

BROWN, NACIO HERB: composer. Born Deming, New Mexico, February 22, 1896; died San Francisco, California, September 28, 1964.

Nacio Herb Brown's family was musical: his father played the clarinet, his sister played the piano and cello, and his mother taught him beginning piano before he was five. Later, she also saw that her son learned the violin.

The Browns moved to Los Angeles in 1904. Nacio attended Manual Arts High School, from which he graduated in 1913. Then he went on a year's tour accompanying singer Alice Doll. The rigors of living out of a suitcase were too much for him, and he returned home. He decided to start his own business, a tailoring shop. It became one of the most popular in the movie colony and was patronized by such stars as Rudolph Valentino and Charlie Chaplin.

In 1920, Brown abandoned his booming tailor shop in favor of Beverly Hills real estate, in which he did even better. He fooled around with songwriting, and one of his first songs, "Coral Sea," came to Paul Whiteman's attention. Whiteman's band played it in Los Angeles, and it became a hit. Friends encouraged Brown to write more songs, and, while he did oblige with an occasional effort, such as the 1921 "When Buddha Smiles," he avoided making it a habit. In 1926, another of his numbers, "The Doll Dance," was the hit of the Hollywood "Music Box Revue."

Finally, the arrival of talking pictures caused Nacio's resistance to crumble. The instrument of his capitulation was the boy wonder of movies, Irving Thalberg, who talked Brown into taking a three-month leave of absence from real estate. The vehicle Thalberg had in mind was Metro-Goldwyn-Mayer's first musical, "Broadway Melody" (1929). He had lyricist Arthur Freed lined up to work with Brown, and the result was the nationwide song hit "The Wedding of the Painted Doll." Thalberg then got Brown to leave real estate for a year, and the die was cast. Freed and Brown provided a triumphal score for "Hollywood Revue," including "Singin' in the Rain" and "You Were Meant for Me." That same year, Brown wrote "Pagan Love Song" for the film "The Pagan."

Then film musicals died in the first stage of the Depression. Brown moved to New York, where he provided "You're an Old Smoothie" and "Eadie Was a Lady" for the revue "Take a Chance" and "Paradise" for the film "A Woman Commands." In 1933, Hollywood's revival led to his return to the Coast, where he spent most of the rest of his life. His song output for films during the thirties and forties included "We're Together Again" and "Temptation" (1933); "You Are My Lucky Star," "Broadway Rhythm," and "Alone" (1935); "Smoke Dreams" (1936); "You Stepped Out of a Dream" (1940); and "If I Steal a Kiss," "What's Wrong with Me?," and "Love is Where You Find It" (1948).

BRYANT, BOUDLEAX AND FELICE: songwriting team. Boudleax, born Shellman, Georgia, February 13, 1920; Felice, born Milwaukee, Wisconsin, August 7, 1925.

The names found on a great many major hit songs of the nineteen-fifties and sixties belong to the husband-and-wife team of Boudleax and Felice Bryant. They are among the best-known writers in the country-and-Western field, and have provided many gold-record songs for the popular-music field in general.

After Boudleaux's birth, his family moved to Moultrie, Georgia, where Bryant spent a good many of his formative years and started his excellent grounding in the classics. He began studying the violin when he was five and continued his studies until the age of eighteen, hoping to become a concert violinist. In 1938, he played a season with the Atlanta Philharmonic.

One day, Bryant was in a violin maker's shop in Atlanta when a man came in from station WSB. The man needed a fiddle player for a country band. Bryant was familiar with country music and took the job. Bryant continued in this field for a time. Then he joined a jazz band, touring such cities as Washington, Detroit, and Chicago during the mid-forties.

In 1945, Felice was working as an elevator starter at the Schrader Hotel in Milwaukee. Bryant's outfit was booked into the hotel, he met Felice, and two weeks later they were married.

She accompanied him to an engagement of several months at the Gibson Hotel in Cincinnati. The Bryants began writing songs for their own amusement. (He had previously had a few recorded by 'Texas swing' bands.) After a few years, they decided to write to publishers and musicians to see if they could place any. Nothing

happened, but on one tour they met a friend, Rome Johnson, who was a recording artist associated with Acuff-Rose music publishers in Nashville, one of the major country-and-Western publishers in the world. Johnson liked a song called "Country Boy" and sent it to Fred Rose, who quickly wired the Bryants some money to come see him. He took several songs. Country artist Jimmie Dickens recorded "Country Boy," and the record sold four hundred thousand copies.

In 1950, the Bryants moved to Nashville and began writing for many local stars. Fred Rose soon placed Bryant songs with many top country-and-Western and pop performers. Frankie Laine recorded "Hey, Joe" (which sold well over a million in several recordings), and Tony Bennett and Billy Eckstine recorded "Have a Good Time." Sue Thompson's 1962 recording of "Have a Good Time" made the top fifteen on popular-record charts.

In the mid-fifties, the Bryants met the Everly Brothers. These two youngsters were helped on the way to stardom by a long succession of Bryant numbers, such as "Bye Bye Love," "All I Have To Do Is Dream," "Wake Up, Little Susie," "Bird Dog," and "Devoted to You." All these sold well over a million records each. In all, the Everly Brothers sold some fifteen or sixteen million records of the Bryants' songs. In the sixties, "Devoted to You" was recorded by Dick Chamberlain, television's Dr. Kildare.

In 1961, Boudleaux wrote an instrumental, "Mexico," that made the top three in the United States and sold over a million in West Germany alone. Another song, recorded in the United States by Mitch Miller and later by Sue Thompson, was "Willie Can." Though doing fairly well in the United States, it was a sensation overseas, staying in the top ten in England for over seventeen weeks.

BURKE, JOHNNY: lyricist, composer, music publisher. Born Antioch, California, October 3, 1908; died New York, New York, February 25, 1964. Won Academy Award for Best Song of 1944 ("Swinging on a Star").

The team of Burke and Van Heusen probably had more successes to its credit than any other songwriting combination of the forties. The words half of the team, Johnny Burke, was brought up mainly in the Midwest. After graduating from Lindblom High School in Chicago, he attended Crane College in that city and later the University of Wisconsin. Burke played piano with college bands. He soon began writing words and music. After leaving school, he became a staff songwriter for music-publishing firms in Chicago and later in New York.

While still in his twenties, Burke began turning out hit songs with composer James V. Monaco. Their work won the attention of Bing Crosby, and Burke wrote regularly for Bing from 1935 on. Some of his songs of the thirties include "Pennies from Heaven," "That Sly Old Gentleman," "I've Got a Pocketful of Dreams," "My Heart Is Taking Lessons," "The Moon Got in My Eyes," and "On the Sentimental Side."

In 1939, during a trip to New York, Burke dropped into the music firm of Remick, where he met Jimmy Van Heusen, who also had quite a few hits to his credit. Burke asked Van Heusen if he had any tunes. The result was a collaboration that lasted a decade and a half. In one evening, they wrote three songs that are still often heard: "Oh! You Crazy Moon," "Imagination," and "Polka Dots and Moonbeams."

Paramount Pictures signed the team in June, 1940, for the score of "Love Thy Neighbor," which starred Jack Benny, Mary Martin, and Fred Allen. Bing Crosby, a Paramount star, also asked for the boys' services. Burke and Van Heusen spent a good part of the forties writing hit scores for Crosby vehicles, including most of the "Road" pictures. For the 1941 "Road to Zanzibar," they provided "It's Always You," "You Lucky People, You," "Birds of a Feather," and "You're Dangerous." After this picture, the team had offers from every major Hollywood studio and four Broadway shows. They preferred Hollywood and continued to turn out movie songs during World War II.

Their output included "Moonlight Becomes You" and "The Road to Morocco" (1942); "Sunday, Monday, or Always," "If You Please," and "Suddenly It's Spring" (1943); and perhaps their greatest collaboration, the score for the Academy Award-winning "Going My Way" (1944), which included "The Day after Forever," "Swinging on a Star," and the title song. In 1945, they wrote another of Bing Crosby's most famous numbers, "Aren't You Glad You're You?," for "The Bells of St. Mary's." They rounded out the forties with a steady stream of best sellers, including "My Heart Is a Hobo," "Country Style," "Smile Right Back at the Sun," "Apalachicola, Fla.," "But Beautiful," "Experience," and "You Don't Have to Know the Language" (1947); "If You Stub

Your Toe on the Moon" and "Once and for Always" (1948); and "Sunshine Cake" (1949).

While busy writing songs, Burke and Van Heusen started their own music-publishing house in 1944. They published not only their own work but many of the hits of such writers as Hoagy Carmichael.

The boys kept writing together during the early fifties, but they were not turning out hits as they once had. In 1954, they each began working with other partners, though occasionally they would get back together to write a song or two.

BUTTONS AND BOWS: song (1948). By Jay Livingston and Ray Evans. Won Academy Award for Best Song of 1948.

Letter writing doesn't usually open many doors for songwriters, but it did for Livingston and Evans. It was a letter written to Olsen and Johnson when the songwriters were unknown that led to their first break in show business. Later, another letter brought about a million-seller recording of "Buttons and Bows."

In the late nineteen-forties, Jay and Ray were on contract to Paramount. They were assigned to write a song for a Bob Hope picture called "The Paleface." The song was for a scene in which Hope was nervously approaching Indian country. They wrote a song called "Skookum," which the producer didn't particularly like. As they went back to their office, they analyzed the script situation. Hope was a tenderfoot about to go into an Indian ambush. They decided to try something in which he would long for the girls back east and a gentler way of life. The line "rings and things and buttons and bows" occurred to one of them. They selected for a working title "I Wish I Were Back East." As they walked along, Jay thought of the last four bars of the melody, but it took three weeks to figure out the first four. The dummy lyric was discarded and replaced with a new one called "Buttons and Bows." This was accepted for the picture.

The boys wanted to gain popular acceptance of the song as well. They had an extra sense of urgency as it was December, 1947, and a record-industry strike was to begin on December 31. Any songs not recorded before then would be dead if the strike turned out to be long.

The artist they most wanted to do the song was Dinah Shore. They had never met her, but they took a chance and wrote her a letter. (This was an even longer shot than they thought, for Dinah was to have a baby not too long after December.) She asked them to come out and play what they had for her. That was just before Christmas. Dinah recorded it the next week.

The record was not released until August, to wait for the picture's release. It won favor with disc jockeys and the public and became the biggest record of Dinah Shore's career.

BYE BYE BIRDIE: musical. Lyrics by Lee Adams, music by Charles Strouse, book by Michael Stewart. New York opening: April 14, 1960, Martin Beck Theatre. 607 performances.

Rock 'n' roll's contribution to American musical comedy was "Bye Bye Birdie." Not that there was very much rock-'n'-rollish about the music—most of it was polished show material. But the central character in the plot was a rock-'n'-roll singer, Conrad Birdie.

The show won rave notices from almost all the New York drama critics. It was the first book musical for the young team of Strouse and Adams. The book was by another newcomer to Broadway, Michael Stewart, who had written summer-resort revues with Strouse and Adams from 1954 to 1956.

The story revolves around the effects which Birdie's imminent induction into the Army has on the fortunes of his English-teacher-turned-music-publisher manager, Albert Peterson. Birdie is Albert's meal ticket, and his departure threatens Albert's financial ruin. Albert's secretary Rosie suggests that he write a new rock-'n'-roll number, "One Last Kiss," for Birdie to deliver while giving one of his fans a last civilian kiss. The song will tide Albert over until Birdie's return.

Kim MacAfee, the teen-age girl selected to receive the kiss, lives in the small Ohio town of Sweet Apple. She has just decided that she's too old for the Conrad Birdie Fan Club ("How Lovely To Be a Woman"). But she changes her mind when she learns that Birdie is to give her the kiss.

Birdie, Albert, and Rosie head for their Ohio train at New York's Pennsylvania Station. Albert cheers up an unhappy group of Birdie fans with "Put On a Happy Face." He and Rosie also save Birdie from a group of inquiring reporters, telling them that Conrad's just a "Normal American Boy." In Sweet Apple, the whole town turns out to greet Birdie. He tells them the secret of his success is that he's "Honestly Sincere." All goes

well in Sweet Apple until Rosie, who is also Albert's girl friend, gets miffed at his neglecting her, and Kim's teen-age boy friend Hugo gets jealous of Birdie. Rosie helps Hugo sneak into the theater as Conrad sings "One Last Kiss" to Kim. Enraged, Hugo starts a free-for-all just as Birdie is to deliver the kiss.

Rosie prepares to leave, and Birdie, tired of being watched over by his manager and pawed over by fans, runs off to have fun with the teen-agers. As he and they sing, they have "A Lot of Livin' to Do." The town's parents are soon out in force searching for their children. They state the perennial parents' lament that today's generation isn't like the polite, understanding children of their own youth ("Kids"). Finally, all the teen-agers are rounded up and sent to bed, and Albert gets Birdie on the way to camp. Though ruined by all this, Albert decides that he's best off marrying his girl ("Rosie"), and he abandons music publishing to return to teaching.

The original cast included Dick Van Dyke, as Albert; Chita Rivera, as Rosie; Dick Gautier, as Birdie; Michael J. Pollard, as Hugo; and Susan Watson, as Kim. Other songs were "An English Teacher," "The Telephone Hour," "One Boy," "Hymn for a Sunday Evening," "What Did I Ever See in Him?," "Baby, Talk to Me," and "Spanish Rose."

The movie version also starred Dick Van Dyke as Albert (but as a biochemist rather than an English teacher). The cast included Janet Leigh, as Rosie; Ann-Margret, as Kim; Jesse Pearson, as Birdie; and Bobby Rydell, as Hugo.

BYE BYE LOVE: song (1957). Words by Felice Bryant, music by Boudleaux Bryant.

From 1957 into the sixties, few could come close to the Everly Brothers in record popularity. With the teen-age fan they could do no wrong, and record after record of theirs sold well over a million copies. The song that started them on their way was "Bye Bye Love," by Boudleaux and Felice Bryant, who were major country-and-Western songwriters.

Artists-and-repertoire man Archie Blyer was in Nashville looking for material for two acts. He talked to Wesley Rose, of Acuff-Rose, publisher of most of the Bryants' material. Rose showed Blyer "Bye Bye Love," and Archie liked it for the better-known of the artists who were coming in the next morning to record. The other act was the Everly Brothers, then virtually unknown. The artist turned the song down, and Boudleaux

Bye Bye Birdie: This drawing represents two key songs in the score. In the foreground, Rock 'n Roll singer Conrad Birdie states that he's "Honestly Sincere." In the background, the teenagers of the town of Sweet Apple gossip about a new romance in their set in "The Telephone Hour."

demonstrated the song for the Everly Brothers on the guitar.

The Everlys recorded the number, and it quickly became number one on the popular charts throughout the country. It sold over a million records and became thoroughly identified with the brothers. They performed the song on most of the country's major television shows, including those of Dick Clark and Ed Sullivan. This was the start of a collaboration between the Bryants and the Everlys that lasted for several years.

CAHN, SAMMY: lyricist. Born New York, New York, June 18, 1913. Won Academy Award for Best Song of 1954 ("Three Coins in the Fountain"), 1957 ("All the Way"), 1959 ("High Hopes"), and 1963 ("Call Me Irresponsible").

Sammy Cahn grew up in New York, where he attended public schools and eventually teamed up with another struggling musician, Saul Chaplin. In the early thirties, they worked in pit orchestras at summer resorts in the Catskills. After much pounding on music publishers' doors, they finally began to move with the song "Rhythm in Our Nursery Rhymes." In 1936, they placed "Shoe Shine Boy" with Louis Armstrong, and, in 1938, scored their first major success with an English version of a Yiddish song, "Bei Mir Bist Du Schön," which was rocketed to success by the Andrews Sisters. They quickly supplied the girls with another hit, "Joseph, Joseph."

Cahn and Chaplin signed a contract with Warner Brothers. Once they reached Hollywood, though, they received no assignments. When their Warner Brothers contract ended, they wrote a score called "You'll Never Get Rich" for Republic. After this, the boys were out of work again, and finally went separate ways.

Sammy was about to give up when he got a phone call from a producer asking if he'd work with Jule Styne. "Would I!" he replied. "I'd do a score with Hitler!" he recalled in a *Saturday Evening Post* interview (December, 1959). When Styne came over, Cahn told the *Post*, Cahn said, "Shoot your best shot." Styne sat down at the piano and played a number.

"'I've heard that song before,'" said Cahn.

"What do you mean, you've heard it?" Styne snapped. "You a tune detective or something?"

"No! No!" Sammy cried, "I mean that's the title."

Frank Sinatra introduced it in a movie short, and the song won an Academy Award nomination for 1943.

For a number of years Styne and Cahn turned out a series of hits for movies, including such Academy Award nominees as "I'll Walk Alone" (1944), "Anywhere" and "I Fall in Love Too Easily" (1945), "It's Magic" (1948), and the 1954 Academy Award winner "Three Coins in the Fountain." Some of their other songs were "Let It Snow! Let It Snow! Let It Snow!," "Give Me Five Minutes More," "There Goes That Song Again," and "It's Been a Long, Long Time." In 1947, Styne and Cahn collaborated on a hit Broadway musical, "High Button Shoes," which starred Phil Silvers and Nanette Fabray. The score included "You're My Girl," "I Still Get Jealous," and "Papa, Won't You Dance with Me?."

After this, aside from an occasional song together, Styne concentrated on Broadway, and Cahn went back to Hollywood. For a time, Cahn wrote with Nicholas Brodszky. They won Academy nominations for "Be My Love" (1950), "Wonder Why" (1951), "Because You're Mine" (1952), and "I'll Never Stop Loving You" (1955).

In 1955, Cahn joined Jimmy Van Heusen. They too piled up nominations, as well as two Oscars. They were nominated for "The Tender Trap" in 1955, and in 1957 won an Oscar for "All the Way." In 1958, they were nominated for "To Love and Be Loved," and in 1959 won another Oscar for "High Hopes." Following this came nominations for "The Second Time Around" (1960) and "Pocketful of Miracles" (1961). Many of the Cahn and Van Heusen songs were either written for Frank Sinatra films or became Sinatra hits.

Besides their movie work, Cahn and Van Heusen also provided a score for the television version of Thornton Wilder's "Our Town" that won critical accolades. One of the songs, "Love and Marriage," besides being a nationwide hit, was given a special Emmy award for 1955. In 1962, Cahn and Van Heusen wrote the score for the Bing Crosby-Bob Hope-Dorothy Lamour "Road to Hong Kong." They also provided Frank Sinatra with the title number for "Come Blow Your Horn" (1962). In 1963, they won another Oscar with "Call Me Irresponsible" for Jackie Gleason's movie "Papa's Delicate Condition." When award time came around for 1964, Cahn and Van Heusen were once more represented by two Best Song nominations: "My Kind of Town" from "Robin and the 7 Hoods" and the title song from "Where Love Has Gone."

CALL ME MADAM: musical. Lyrics and music by Irving Berlin, book by Russel Crouse and Howard Lindsay. New York opening: October 12, 1950, Imperial Theatre. 644 performances.

Four years after the flamboyant Ethel Merman portrayed Annie Oakley on Broadway, Irving Berlin brought her up to date with a second smash hit, "Call Me Madam." The plot was a not too thinly disguised takeoff on the career of Mrs. Perle Mesta, appointed ambassador to Luxembourg by President Harry Truman. Berlin also may have had a hand in the career of Truman's successor. In one scene, a trio of United States lawmakers, led by Congressman Wilkins, give out with a rousing song in praise of General Eisenhower, "They Like Ike."

Critical comment was mostly complimentary. Brooks Atkinson wrote in the New York *Times:*

As you may have heard, [Ethel Merman] is cast as the American Ambassador to Lichtenburg. . . .[Not overawed by court decorum] She is still lighting up like an inspired pin-ball machine, and still blowing the music lustily throughout the theatre.

The curtain rises with famed Washington party giver Mrs. Sally Adams receiving her appointment as ambassador and falls as she is discharged. According to the program notes, "The play is laid in two mythical countries. One is called Lichtenburg, the other is the United States of America." It's only natural that Mrs. Adams get the job, for, as she sings, she's "The Hostess with the Mostes' on the Ball."

The scene shifts to Lichtenburg, whose virtues are outlined in a song bearing the country's name. Mrs. Adams presumes that her mission, besides giving some of her usual lavish parties, is to float a huge United States grant for the country. She outlines her policy in "Can You Use Any Money Today?" Unfortunately, Lichtenburg's prime minister, suave Cosmo Constantine, does not believe in giveaways and wants his country to make its way on its own. This results in many arguments between Mrs. Adams and Constantine, complicated when she finds herself in love with him.

Meanwhile, a young man on her staff, bookish Harvard graduate student Kenneth Gibson, meets the lovely Princess Maria, heir to the throne of Lichtenburg. They sing to each other, "It's a Lovely Day Today." Mrs. Adams continues alternately to argue with and woo Cosmo, singing her love in such songs as "The Best Thing for You." When not involved with the prime minister, she gives assistance and motherly advice to Gibson. When he tells her how strangely he feels, she points out the problem in the hit duet "You're Just in Love."

Mrs. Adams's mishaps with the Lichtenburg government result in her recall to Washington, where she is discharged. But all ends happily: Gibson wins his princess, and the affairs of Lichtenburg, the United States, Sally Adams, and Cosmo Constantine are straightened out.

Besides Miss Merman, the original cast included Paul Lukas, as Cosmo; Russell Nype, as Gibson; Galina Talva, as Princess Maria; and Pat Harrington, as Congressman Wilkins. Other songs were "Washington Square Dance," "Marrying for Love," "Something To Dance About," and "Once Upon a Time Today."

CALLOWAY, CABELL (CAB): band leader, singer, actor. Born Rochester, New York, December 24, 1907.

One of the more original of the big-band leaders, Cab Calloway developed his own style of scat singing, using the syllables "hi-de-hi" and "ho-de-ho." With his great stage presence, he was more than a singer or band leader—he was a performer. The success of his approach is seen in that for an almost unbroken period from the beginning of the nineteen-thirties to 1948, Calloway toured the country with his big band.

Cab's family moved to Baltimore soon after his birth. He attended public schools there and enrolled in law school when the Calloways moved to Chicago. He had shown signs of musical ability, however, and his sister Blanche urged him to make music his career. Cab soon began singing in local clubs on Chicago's South Side. He became leader of a band called "the Alabamians." He took the group to New York, but left them when he received a bid to appear in "Connie's Hot Chocolates," a hit Broadway revue. This led to star billing at the legendary Harlem night spot, the Cotton Club.

Cab was soon heading up a new band, the Missourians. By 1930, the band had taken its leader's name and begun recording some numbers that began to gain public recognition. Calloway recorded "Minnie the Moocher," the song that made him a national celebrity, in 1931. In

Cab Calloway

cording activities, and his Coral album "Blues Make Me Happy" won attention in the sixties. Over the years, Calloway's bands provided seasoning for many musicians who were to gain fame on their own, including Chu Berry, Dizzy Gillespie, and Cozy Cole.

CALYPSO: a form of folk music of the West Indies, particularly Trinidad; also, a folk dance performed to this music.

Calypso had its origin in rhythms brought to Trinidad by African slaves. As with most folk music, the rhythm is relatively simple, in two-four or four-four time. In calypso, the unique thing is not so much the music as the words and word patterns. The early slaves, the story goes, were not permitted to talk while working, but they could sing. They would sing in their tribal tongues, mocking their masters and passing along gossip, news of the day, or anything else that came to mind. Suspecting that their chattels were making fun of them, the Spanish overlords of Trinidad insisted that the slaves learn and use Spanish. Later colonizers—first French and then English—acted similarly.

The result was a special calypso language, a weird conglomeration of many languages. When the slaves were freed, they continued their custom of arguing or discussing by means of song. Eventually, local merchants sponsored calypso contests at carnival time (before Lent), with prizes for the winners. Calypso singers also developed the custom of taking picturesque names, such as Mighty Killer, Sir Lancelot, and Lord Kitchener.

There are two types of native calypso singers. At one time, the leader of a calypso festival sang in French and was called the "chantwelle." His present-day equivalents are called "calypsonians," singers who do not repeat others' rhymes but make up new lyrics on the spot. The less versatile singer, who repeats other performers' material, is called a "calypso singer."

The word "calypso" is of vague origin. In Greek mythology, there is a sea nymph of this name who kept Odysseus on her island for seven years. But this has nothing to do with the musical term. One interpretation has "calypso" derived from the African word *"kai-so,"* meaning "bravo." There also was an insecticide, long since out of production, by this name that might have supplied the word. Another suggestion is that the derivation is from the French word *"carrouseaux,"* meaning "carousal." A similar

later years, Calloway scored still more successes with his "hi-de-ho," notably with such numbers as "St. James Infirmary." By 1933, Calloway was a national star. He was featured in his first movie, "The Singing Kid," which starred Al Jolson. Through the nineteen-thirties and forties, Calloway led his band in countless engagements here and abroad on radio and in stage shows, nightclubs, and movies. Some of the other movies he appeared in were "Stormy Weather" and "Sensations of 1945."

Calloway broke up his band in 1948, working mainly with small groups from then on. In 1951, he re-established a big band for a year and made a brief tour of South America. In 1952, Cab opened a new chapter in a fabulous career by taking on the role of Sportin' Life in a revival of Gershwin's "Porgy and Bess." The show played to sellout audiences not only in the United States and Western Europe but, under State Department auspices, in the Soviet Union.

The year 1954 found Cab once again leading a small outfit, a quartet, on the nightclub circuit. Calloway continued his nightclub and television appearances into the sixties. He kept up his re-

[41]

word, "*carrisimeaux*," a formalized march, is also a possibility. Successive modifications of this word, such as "*cariseaux*" and "*caliso*," are said to have led to the present-day "calypso."

Calypso as usually heard in the United States is a far cry from the native version. It is much more stereotyped and lacks the nuances and suggestiveness of the original.

Though Calypso has developed for hundreds of years in the West Indies, its first success outside the Caribbean came in 1939. Then Wilmouth Houdini, Brooklyn-born but a long-time resident of Trinidad, created a brief flurry of interest in the United States. At the same time, Lord Kitchener was doing the same thing in England. In 1944, comedian Morey Amsterdam brought back material from the West Indies that he turned into "Rum and Coca-Cola." An Andrews Sisters recording of the song was soon number one on the Hit Parade.

In 1957, the longest-lived calypso reign in the United States was started by Harry Belafonte and picked up by many other singers, from both the West Indies and the United States. Since then, calypso has settled down to become an established, though relatively minor, part of popular music in this country.

CAMELOT: musical. Lyrics and book by Alan Jay Lerner, music by Frederick Loewe. Based on T. H. White's novel "The Once and Future King." New York opening: December 3, 1960, Majestic Theatre. 873 performances.

To try to top a modern musical classic such as "My Fair Lady" is a monumental task for even as great a team as Lerner and Loewe. They decided to tackle the saga of King Arthur and his knights of the Round Table. It was a grueling task and was probably partly responsible for director Moss Hart's fatal heart attack and Loewe's non-fatal attack. The show did not overly please the critics. But it contained a first-rate score, and this, plus the spectacular setting, led to audience acceptance.

As the curtain rises, the court prepares to meet Arthur's bride-to-be Guenevere. The king remains behind—from nervousness, as he explains in "I Wonder What the King Is Doing Tonight." Guenevere is equally ill at ease ("Where Are the Simple Joys of Maidenhood?"). Later, they meet unexpectedly, and Arthur relates the joys of "Camelot." A woodland sprite lures Arthur's mentor Merlin away. A young French knight, Sir Lancelot, arrives to join the court, singing of his valor in "C'Est Moi."

His egotism outrages the court, including the queen, who incites three knights to joust with him ("Then You May Take Me to the Fair"). Lancelot defeats all three at the fair. As time goes by, he finds that he's falling in love with Guenevere. Fearing to hurt his beloved king, he goes off on knightly adventures. Two years later, he returns and is made a Round Table member. But his love for the queen remains ("If Ever I Would Leave You"). By now, the queen, is silently enamored of Lancelot.

Arthur's illegitimate son Mordred schemes to gain the throne. His aunt, sorceress Morgan Le Fey, agrees to trap Arthur in the enchanted forest for a night. Arthur has troubles aplenty, for his knights long for war ("Fie on Goodness"). Mordred and some knights trap Lancelot talking to the queen in her chambers. She is sentenced to death, but Lancelot carries her off to France at the last moment. To uphold his honor, Arthur must pursue and fight Lancelot's army, though he forgives his former friend and the queen. In France, just before the battle in which he will die with most of his knights, he finds a stowaway. He knights the boy and sends him back to England to preserve the ideals of the Round Table.

The original cast included Richard Burton, as Arthur; Julie Andrews, as Guenevere; Robert Goulet, as Lancelot; Roddy McDowall, as Mordred; and M'el Dowd, as Morgan Le Fey. Other songs were "Follow Me," "The Lusty Month of May," "How To Handle a Woman," "Before I Gaze at You Again," "The Seven Deadly Virtues," "What Do the Simple Folk Do?," "I Loved You Once in Silence," and "Guenevere."

CANTOR, EDDIE: comedian, singer. Born New York, New York, January 31, 1892; died Beverly Hills, California, October 10, 1964.

Eddie Cantor was one of many greats in music and entertainment who fought their way up from a rugged childhood environment. Born Edward Israel Iskowitz in New York's East Side ghetto, he was orphaned at two and raised by his grandmother.

As he grew up, he earned pennies by singing and joking on street corners. He never completed grade school, and took a series of jobs that didn't last because he was always cutting up. Then, in 1908, his childhood sweetheart Ida Tobias got him to enter the amateur night at Miner's Bowery Theatre. He won five dollars and, changing his name to Eddie Cantor, plunged into show business.

In a scene from *Camelot*, Sir Launcelot (Robert Goulet, kneeling) bends over a knight he has defeated in a jousting tournament as King Arthur (Richard Burton) looks on.

He moved on to a fifteen-dollar-a-week job at a burlesque house. Soon after, he was a singing waiter at a Coney Island saloon. The pianist there was a young man named Jimmy Durante. A few years later, Eddie was hired by the team of Bedini and Arthur. In part of the act he appeared in blackface. In 1912, Gus Edwards signed Cantor to appear as a blackface butler in a "Kid Kabaret" revue. After another blackface role in London, Eddie came home and, in 1914, married his Ida. In 1916, Florenz Ziegfeld made Eddie a part of the "Midnight Frolic" on the New Amsterdam roof in New York. Eddie was featured in Ziegfeld's "Follies" from 1917 to 1919. In 1923, Eddie was the star of the hit Broadway musical "Kid Boots." He was called to Hollywood in 1926 to perform in the film version. One of the songs he introduced was the long-time standard "Dinah."

Cantor's next major Broadway stint was in "Whoopee" (1928). This show provided Eddie with two more major hits, "Makin' Whoopee" and "My Baby Just Cares for Me." He also began writing books and articles, mostly in collaboration with David Freeman. These included his autobiography "My Life Is in Your Hands" (1928), "Between the Acts" (1930), "Your Next President" (1932), and "Ziegfeld, the Great Glorifier" (1934).

In 1931, guest appearances on the Rudy Vallee and Chase and Sanborn radio shows started Cantor on a new career. He rapidly became a feature on radio as well as a movie star. He began his own series of shows every Sunday night on station WEAF. By 1936, Cantor was the highest-paid star on radio. During the course of his radio shows, he discovered much new talent, including Deanna Durbin, Bobby Breen, Dinah Shore, and Eddie Fisher. In 1939, he was taken off the air because of a speech in which he accused certain public figures of being fascists. Through the efforts of Jack Benny, he finally returned to radio during World War II, as star of NBC's "Time to Smile."

His films included "Palmy Days" (1931), "The Kid From Spain" (1932), "Roman Scandals" (1933), "Strike Me Pink" (1936), "Ali Baba Goes to Town" (1937), and "Forty Little Mothers" (1940). In September, 1950, Cantor made his television debut on NBC's Sunday-night "Colgate Comedy Hour." He appeared once a month, rotating with such stars as Dean Martin, Jerry Lewis, Fred Allen, and Jimmy Durante. A heart attack in 1952 slowed him down, though he did return to the "Comedy Hour", for a while after his recovery. In 1953, his film biography "The Eddie Cantor Story," with Keefe Brasselle, was released. Some other songs Cantor made famous are "If You Knew Susie," "Ain't She Sweet?," "Ma, He's Makin' Eyes at Me," and "Toot, Toot, Tootsie."

In the years following Cantor's first heart attack, his deteriorating health forced him to take a less and less active part in show business. During his last years, he was mainly confined to his Beverly Hills home, where he died of a coronary occlusion at the age of seventy-two.

CARMICHAEL, HOAGLAND (HOAGY): composer, pianist. Born Bloomington, Indiana, November 22, 1899. Won Academy Award for Best Song of 1951 ("In the Cool, Cool, Cool of the Evening").

The man who wrote what is perhaps the greatest popular-music standard, the immortal "Star Dust," was raised on music. Bloomington is the site of the University of Indiana. Carmichael's mother helped support the family by playing for school dances and other affairs. When Hoagy was very small, she used to make him a bed of two collapsible chairs while she would play for university dances. Later, when Hoagy was in public school, he sometimes used to get into the movies free to hear his mother play the piano accompaniment for silent movies.

As Hoagy neared his teens, he discovered that he had a musical ear. One rainy day, when he was trying to while away the time at home, he sat down at the piano and found that he could pick out the tune being played on the university carillon. As time went on, he taught himself to play the piano. When he was in his mid-teens, his family moved to Indianapolis. He quit school for a time and worked as a cement mixer on the night shift. During the day, he struck up a close friendship with nightclub pianist Reggie Duval,

Hoagy Carmichael

an association that provided new insights into popular music for young Carmichael.

World War I was on, and Hoagy was anxious to enlist. He finally did in November, 1918, but his military career was cut short by the Armistice. Back in Indiana in 1919, Hoagy decided to complete his education. He moved into his grandparents' home in Bloomington, finished high school, and, in 1922, enrolled at the university as a law student. Hoagy managed to get his law degree, despite the temptations of music. While he was at school, he played in jazz and popular bands for many local functions. One of his friends was the legendary jazzman Bix Beiderbecke. During his school years, Hoagy also wrote his first song, "Riverboat Shuffle," which was recorded by Beiderbecke and the Wolverines. In 1925, he got the idea for another hit, "Washboard Blues," from watching a colored woman scrubbing clothes.

Then came graduation day in 1926, and Hoagy

headed for Florida, where he expected to set up law practice. But he was delayed in Washington and took time out to go to New York to see if Mills Music would publish "Washboard Blues." Mills did and also offered him a job as staff composer. Hoagy hesitated but turned it down and went to Florida. In Florida, though, he soon heard the Red Nichols record of "Washboard Blues." That was enough for him. Hoagy went back to Indiana to try for a musical career. Once there, he came up with the melody for "Star Dust." After two years of plugging it while he played piano with such bands as Jean Goldkette's and Don Redmond's, "Star Dust" finally was picked up by Isham Jones.

From then on, it was a clear track. In 1930, he wrote "Georgia on My Mind," following it up in 1931 with "Lazy River" and, in 1932, with "In the Still of the Night" and "Daybreak." His 1930 composition, "Rockin' Chair," also was winning new attention each year. He continued to score with such songs as "Lazybones" (1933), "Little Old Lady" (1937), "I Get Along without You Very Well" (1939), "Skylark" (1942), and "Ole Buttermilk Sky," which won an Academy Award nomination in 1946. Hoagy also found himself in demand as a movie performer and later a television star. His film credits include "To Have and Have Not," "The Best Years of Our Lives," and "Copper Canyon."

CAROUSEL: musical. Lyrics and book by Oscar Hammerstein II, music by Richard Rodgers. Based on Ferenc Molnar's play "Liliom," as adapted by Benjamin F. Glazer. New York opening: April 19, 1945, Majestic Theatre. 890 performances.

Many consider "Carousel," Rodgers and Hammerstein's second collaboration, their finest score. The New York critical reception was generally enthusiastic, though some thought it a less effective repeat of the "Oklahoma!" "formula." Robert Garland of the New York *Journal-American* said,

Yes, yes, a thousand times yes . . . When somebody writes a better musical play than 'Carousel,' written by Richard Rodgers and Oscar Hammerstein, Richard Rodgers and Oscar Hammerstein will have to write it.

John Chapman in the New York *Daily News* wrote, " 'Carousel' is one of the finest musical plays I have seen and I shall remember it always." The other end of the scale was reflected at the London opening on June 7, 1950, when critics blasted it as everything from American whimsey and treacle to blasphemy.

The story begins in a carnival in a small New England seaport. Billy Bigelow, the young barker for the carousel, meets Julie Jordan and Carrie Pipperidge, two girls from Bascombe's knitting mills. Ne'er-do-well Billy has plenty of girls, but Julie is different. He gets into trouble on her account with Mrs. Mullins, the carousel owner, and loses his job. While he goes to get his things, Carrie tells Julie that she's marrying a fisherman, Enoch Snow. She dreams of her future ("When I Marry Mr. Snow"). Soon after, alone together, Billy and Julie sing "If I Loved You."

The scene shifts to the house of Julie's cousin Nettie, several months later. Now married, Billy and Julie live there, for neither has a job. A group has gathered to get ready for a clambake at a nearby island. It's early summer, and, as all sing, "June Is Bustin' Out All Over." Billy's friend Jigger wants him to help rob Mr. Bascombe while everyone is at the clambake. Billy hesitates and almost is lured away from Julie when Mrs. Mullins comes to offer his old job back. But Julie tells him that she's pregnant. Proudly, Billy dreams of helping his offspring ("Soliloquy"). He rejects Mrs. Mullins and accepts Jigger's offer.

Mr. Bascombe, though, fights them off. Billy kills himself to avoid capture. Julie is despondent, but Nettie raises her spirits ("You'll Never Walk Alone"). Billy reaches heaven and is given one chance to go back to earth. By now, his daughter Louise is in her teens. Because of her father, she is looked down on by the townspeople, including now rich Mr. Snow and most of the nine children born to him and Carrie. But, at Louise's graduation, Billy manages to reach both her and Julie and make them face the future with hope and courage.

The original cast included John Raitt, as Billy; Jan Clayton, as Julie; Jean Darling, as Carrie; Christine Johnson, as Nettie; Jean Casto, as Mrs. Mullins; Bambi Linn, as Louise; Murvyn Vye, as Jigger; and Eric Mattson, as Enoch Snow. The movie version starred Gordon MacRae, as Billy, and Shirley Jones, as Julie. Other songs were "You're a Queer One, Julie Jordan," "When the Children Are Asleep," "Blow High, Blow Low," "This Was a Real Nice Clambake," "Geraniums in the Winter," "There's Nothin' So Bad for a Woman," "What's the Use of Wond'rin?," and "The Highest Judge of All."

CAT AND THE FIDDLE, THE: musical. Lyrics and book by Otto Harbach, music by Jerome Kern. New York opening: October 15, 1931, Globe Theatre. 395 performances.

"The Cat and the Fiddle" was a reasonably different and well-crafted show, though far from the Kern-Hammerstein 1927 masterpiece "Show Boat." Kern worked again with Otto Harbach, with whom he had written "Sunny" in 1925 and "Criss Cross" in 1926. The critics were generally enthusiastic about the music. Gilbert Gabriel wrote: "Broadway had not heard lovelier music in all its life." But they were less rapturous about the book. Still, the book was original, and the close integration of plot and music represented a departure from conventional musical comedy.

The plot involves a musical girl-and-boy rivalry. Shirley Sheridan is an American girl who loves popular music and has written some successful songs. She comes to Brussels to further her musical education. Wandering along the bank of the city's river, she meets Victor Florescu, a young Romanian composer of more serious music ("The Night was Made for Love"). The scene shifts to Florescu's studio, where he is hard at work on an operetta, "The Passionate Pilgrim." He does not know that Shirley has rented a studio nearby or of her taste in music. As he works, he is annoyed by the sound of popular music coming from outside. His feelings are not soothed when a visitor, the producer Daudet, condemns his score as too heavy, then commends the music from across the way as just right. Victor gives vent to his anger on finding his competitor to be Shirley. But "The Passionate Pilgrim" goes into production, amid constant feuding among Victor, Shirley, and such members of the cast as the prima donna, Odette. Finally, the musical conflict is resolved and Shirley and Victor are reunited.

The score included "I Watch the Love Parade," "The Breeze Kissed Your Hair," "Try to Forget," "Poor Pierrot," "She Didn't Say Yes," "A New Love Is Old," "One Moment Alone," and "Ha! Cha! Cha!" The original cast included Bettina Hall, as Shirley; Georges Metaxa, as Victor; and Odette Myrtil, as Odette.

CHA CHA: dance of Latin American origin.

The cha cha is a modification of the mambo, which, in turn, is derived from the rumba. The count for the mambo is one, two, three, pause. For the cha cha it goes one, two, cha-cha cha. The dance gave rise to some new music—mainly reworkings of North and South American standards in the new rhythmic pattern—most of which proved of only passing interest.

CHARLES, RAY: singer, pianist, band leader. Born Albany, Georgia, 1932.

If anyone has a right to sing the blues, it's Ray Charles, the great singer of what he calls "soul music." His early life was a long succession of terrible blows, any one of which would have caused most people to give up in despair. Yet Charles overcame all of them to become one of the most popular record artists in the United States. In 1962 alone, his record sales totaled over eight million dollars.

Charles was born to a desperately poor family. At six years of age, he was struck with an illness that left him totally blind. He was orphaned at fifteen and the following year became a drug addict. His schooling was very limited, though he learned to read Braille in his teens. He had an innate love for music, however; he liked to sing and to play the piano.

At seventeen, he became part of a trio that found work in Seattle. Charles's idol was Nat "King" Cole, and he played a style of piano much like that of the great Cole. He made out well enough as a routine club artist with this style, but in the early fifties, he began to sing "race music," a mixture of white hillbilly and Negro rhythm-and-blues. Charles soon developed an approach uniquely his own, a blend of styles ranging from jazz and country-and-Western to "shoutin' gospel."

He soon began to make records. In 1955, he scored his first major hit with "I Got a Woman" and was on his way to nationwide fame. Charles blazed new trails in several directions. He could sing a low-down blues or play and sing first-rate jazz. He could also sing country-and-Western with a flavor that appealed to white fans of this music. For example, his records of "You Are My Sunshine" and "Born To Lose," in the country-and-Western idiom, appealed to all segments of the population, from the rural towns of the South to the big cities of the Eastern seaboard. In addition to numerous appearances throughout the nation in theaters, clubs, jazz festivals, etc., he also scored a tremendous success in New York's Carnegie Hall. His two concerts at Carnegie in May, 1963, played to standing-room-only audiences. Charles won the 1963 Grammy for best rhythm and blues recording for the song "Busted."

By the late fifties and throughout the sixties his record albums were consistent best sellers.

By 1965, he had several dozen LPs on dealers' shelves. A few of the titles are "Yes Indeed!" and "At Newport" (1958); " What'd I Say?" (1959); "In Person" (1960); "Dedicated to You" and "Genius + Soul = Jazz" (1961); "Modern Sounds," "The Ray Charles Story," and "Greatest Hits" (1962); "Great Ray Charles" and "Recipe for Soul" (1963); and "Sweet and Sour Tears" (1964).

CHARLESTON: dance of the nineteen-twenties; also, a song.

The Charleston is almost synonymous with the twenties. As with so many popular dances and rhythms, it originated among the Negroes. The count is *one*, two, *one*, two (*Charles*-ton, *Charles*-ton), with the rapid steps, alternating at times with a short kick, done in place.

The Charleston was introduced to the public by Cecil Mack and Jimmy Johnston in 1923 as part of a Negro revue. It rapidly became a ballroom-dance favorite, remaining in vogue in the twenties. Since then, it has been performed mainly in movies and plays and on television shows dealing with the period, though there have been brief flurries of interest in Charleston ballroom dancing from time to time.

CHECKER, CHUBBY: singer, dancer. Born Philadelphia, Pennsylvania, October 3, 1941.

From chicken plucking to twisting is perhaps an odd transition, but the move helped make the name of Chubby Checker one of the best-known in the entertainment world. Thanks to Checker, the hip gyrations of the twist took the United States (and later the rest of the world) by storm.

Checker was brought up in Philadelphia, where his father, Raymond Evans, worked as a stevedore. His parents named their son Ernest. He attended grade school and South Philadelphia High School (which also lists singer Fabian among it alumni). During his high-school years, Chubby worked in a neighborhood market. His main task was cutting up chickens, but he also regaled customers with singing and his own brand of humor. The owner of the market, Henry Colt, liked Chubby's style and introduced him to Kal Mann. Mann and Colt became Chubby's comanagers, and Mann wrote a song called "The Class" and arranged a recording date for his protégé. The teen-ager changed his last name to Checker in imitation of his favorite performer, Fats Domino.

"The Class" was a hit, and Chubby became a favorite among teen-agers. By January, 1961, he had five hit singles plus a skyrocketing album, "Twist with Chubby Checker." The idea for the twist was started by country-and-Western artist Hank Ballard, who wrote a song called "The Twist" in 1958. In 1960, Chubby began singing Ballard's song and also demonstrating the dance to the words. The twist craze swept through the high-school ranks and, by 1962, had spread to adults. Chubby was featured on such major television shows as "The American Bandstand" and also was a major nightclub attraction. In 1962, his salary on the nightclub circuit was twenty-five hundred dollars a performance, or ten thousand dollars a week. Through 1962 and 1963, his recordings remained high on the best-seller lists. In 1962, Chubby started still another dance sensation. This time, with such records as the "Limbo Rock," he popularized the dance long performed for tourists by the limbo bands of the West Indies. Besides his record and nightclub stints, Chubby also appeared in a film, "Twist around the Clock."

CHERRY PINK AND APPLE BLOSSOM WHITE: song (1950, 1957). French words by Jacques Larue, English words by Mack David, music by Louiguy.

The factors that make a song a hit are intangible enough to make people in the music business prematurely gray. A very slight change in emphasis or a change in the public's mood can change a song from a failure to a major success. For instance, a song may be a hit in one part of the world and fall completely flat in another, even though the cultural tastes of the areas are similar. Persistence, though, can often eventually achieve success, particularly if there is the chance to try different arrangements of the number.

An example of this is "Cherry Pink and Apple Blossom White," which was originally published in France in 1950 and became a European best seller. In 1951, Chappell and Company brought the song to the United States, added English lyrics, and gained major records—both instrumental and vocal—from five or six major performers, including Jimmy Dorsey. All this was to no avail, for none of the records won favor. The song was neglected for six years. Then, in 1957, band leader Perez Prado turned out an instrumental version. He added one unique touch, a trumpet solo at the beginning which held a long note before the band took up the melody. This held the attention of the listener, and "Cherry Pink" became as popular in the

United States as it had been six years before in Europe.

CHEVALIER, MAURICE: singer, actor, comedian. Born Paris, France, September 12, 1888.

American popular music has been quick to borrow from other countries and vice versa. American jazz, for example, has become a worldwide art form and so, conversely, have the rhythms of Latin America. In the same way, a truly great popular music performer is at home in any land. One of the most obvious examples of this is France's gift to the genre, Maurice Chevalier.

Chevalier was born in Ménilmontant, a working class district of Paris, in 1888, a year in which the Eiffel Tower was nearing completion. He was the youngest of nine children in his family. In his district, education was a luxury in which few children could indulge. This was particularly true in Chevalier's case after his father, a housepainter, deserted the family when Maurice was eight. At 10, Maurice was apprenticed to an engraver and then to an electrician. But he could sing and joke and this led to his successful debut at the age of 12 in an amateur show at the Café de Trois Lions. He soon performed there three times weekly for five francs a week.

By the time he was in his teens, he had developed a routine that won him considerable notice in Paris bistros. He wore a tramp outfit and sang such songs as "Ma Pomme" (My Mug). Achieving some success with this, he worked up another character part, that of a fighter, which he used in exhibition fights and in music hall skits. His appearances included a role in the 1904 revue, "Parisiana," and star billing, soon after, at the Eden Music Hall in Asinères and a part in the Folies-Bergère.

Then, in 1909, the great French dancer Mistinguette became interested in the handsome Maurice. They formed a dance team that was the toast of Paris from 1909 to 1913. Chevalier's rising star was momentarily dimmed by World War I. He was called into service, wounded in action, and captured by the Germans. In prison camp from 1915–18, Chevalier thought of new routines and, more important, learned English. He did this as an escape from boredom, but it helped him start a new career after the War.

In February, 1919, he was featured in "Hello America" in London. In France, he was a regular performer throughout the 1920s at such places as the Casino de Paris, Olympia and the Folies-Bergèrè. In 1921, his performance in the operetta "Dédé" brought raves from such American visitors as George Gershwin, Mary Pickford and Irving Berlin. As a result, producer Charles Dillingham brought the show to New York, initiating a long love affair between U. S. audiences and Chevalier. Back in Paris, Chevalier reigned at the Casino de Paris from 1926–28, during which time he introduced the song that became his theme, "Valentine."

Throughout the twenties he was a fixture on the continent and his records sold all over the world. He sang love songs, comic songs, modern ballads and folk songs. His repertoire included such numbers as "Donnez-moi la main" (Give Me Your Hand); "Dites-moi, ma mere" (Mother, Tell Me Why); "Quand un vicomte" (One Viscount to Another).

Late in the twenties, Hollywood called on Chevalier for a series of films, extending into the thirties, that made him a major U. S. star. These included: "Innocents of Paris," "The Love Parade," "Paramount on Parade," "The Playboy of Paris," "A Bedtime Story," "One Hour With You," "Love Me Tonight," "The Way to Love," "The Man from the Follies-Bergère," "The Beloved Vagabond," and "Break the News." During his film stint, Chevalier introduced a number of hit songs, including "Louise," "One Hour With You," and "Mimi," the latter written by the great song team of Rodgers and Hart. Later in the thirties, he concentrated once more on the Paris stage and also appeared in such French films as "With a Smile" ('39); "The Man of the Hours" ('40); and "Personal Column" ('41). Then World War II interfered. He remained in seclusion in France during the Nazi occupation, but, after the liberation, once again claimed his role as France's leading entertainer.

The first volume of his autobiography, *Ma Route et ma Chansons*, appeared in 1947. The same year, his role in the film Le Silence est d'or won him a statuette of Saint Michael, the Belgian equivalent of the Oscar. In 1958, at 70, he scored a new triumph with his acting and singing in the Lerner-Loewe Academy Award winning film, "Gigi." His song hits included "I Remember it Well," and "I'm Glad I'm not Young Anymore." The latter song reflected his philosophy in his later years. "When I was younger," he told one interviewer, "there were beautiful women I was crazy about, but I was strong enough to run away. I had to choose between my public and a love affair, and I always chose the public. I am always having an eternal affair with the public."

In his seventies, Chevalier continued his many activities, from films to personal tours, with vigor and in continuous rapport with audiences. In the 1960s, he went on several one man tours throughout Europe and the U.S., playing to capacity audiences in such places as Carnegie Hall in New York and the Greek Theatre in Los Angeles. He appeared on several special Chevalier TV shows and was starred on such programs as Ed Sullivan and the Bell Telephone Hour in the U.S. and most important TV shows in other nations of the world as well.

CHIPMUNKS' CHRISTMAS SONG, THE: song (1958). Words and music by David Seville.

Since 1958, whenever Christmas rolls around, children again delight in the squeaky rendition by Alvin and the Chipmunks of their "Christmas Song." The Chipmunks are the brain children of songwriter David Seville, who also provides the Chipmunk voices. (He does this by recording his own voice at half speed, then playing it back at normal speed. The final record requires superimposing four tape recordings on one: three Chipmunk voices plus Seville's normal-speed voice.)

The "Christmas Song" gave birth to the Chipmunk theme. As Seville recounts in a release he wrote for Liberty Records, this occurred in the fall of 1958.

In September of 1958, I decided to try for a Christmas novelty. I thought of a melody on the way to work. I went right to the studio and whistled the melody into a tape machine so I wouldn't forget it.

Then I wrote the words and decided that the singers should be animals or maybe even insects. I don't know why, but that's what I decided. I recorded the song with half speed little voices (my own) and sang an introduction in my normal speed voice. When I finished the first recording, the voices sounded like butterflies, or mice—or rabbits—but, most of all, they sounded like chipmunks.

Seville asked Liberty executives Simon Waronker and Al Bennett to listen. All agreed that something was missing.

Everyone liked the melody, so I wrote a new lyric and called the song, "In a Village Park." A quartet sang, "In a quiet village park, when the night is still and dark, I can hear this melody and it brings you back to me"—nothing! The more I listened to the new version, the more I could hear the chipmunks singing "Christmas, Christmas time is near, time for toys and time for cheer." I recorded it again, this time with no

David Seville and his chipmunks (l. to r.) Alvin, Theodore and Simon.

words, as an instrumental. This too was nowhere. I decided against doing anything further and gave up the whole project. But the project wouldn't give me up.

By the end of November, the chipmunks in my head were driving me crazy, so I tried it again, but this time decided to give the chipmunks some kind of identity. After discussing it with Si Waronker and Mark McIntyre, my long time friend and advisor, we felt that I should give the chipmunks names and that I should, as David Seville, have a conversation with them and perhaps even an argument. The idea for names came quickly: Simon, after Si Waronker; Theodore, for Ted Keep, the recording engineer; and Alvin, after Al Bennett.

The record was finished after three months and four separate versions.

CHORUS: the main body or theme of a popular song (see also *Measure, Release Verse*).

The components of a popular song usually include an introduction or verse followed by the chorus. At one time, there was almost as much emphasis on the verse as on the chorus, as a glance at the complete lyrics of some of the songs of the first few decades of the century will show. In recent times, the verse has been cut to a minimum. It has been eliminated entirely in many more recent songs.

Most popular-song choruses are in AABA form. The letter A denotes the main phrase or theme of the song. This main phrase is repeated three times, with a secondary theme inserted for interest. Most songwriters restrict the chorus to thirty-two measures. For an AABA chorus, this would mean an eight-measure A theme repeated for a total of sixteen measures, followed by an eight-measure B phrase and another eight-measure A phrase.

Though the AABA chorus has been the most common, there are variations. The secondary or B theme might come earlier in the chorus to make the form ABAA. Other combinations sometimes used are ABAB and AABAA. Occasionally there may be a third theme introduced, but this is extremely rare. Besides the thirty-two-measure chorus the most-used patterns are of twenty-eight, thirty-four, or thirty-six measures.

CLOONEY, ROSEMARY: singer. Born Maysville, Kentucky, May 23, 1928.

Rosemary Clooney started singing when she was only a few years old, to help her grandfather in his bid for mayor. With Rosemary's younger sister Betty helping out, grandfather won the mayoralty three times.

As the girls grew older, they entered and won almost every amateur contest in the area. When Rosemary was thirteen, the family moved to Cincinnati, where she attended Our Lady of Mercy High School. She sang at many social events. In her senior year, she and Betty auditioned for local station WLW. They were accepted and were soon on the air seven nights a week. Word got around about these talented sisters, and, when they graduated from high school, jobs as vocalists were soon available with Tony Pastor's orchestra. They toured the country with Pastor for two and a half years, singing to highly appreciative audiences in almost every ballroom, theater, and hotel in the United States and Canada.

In 1949, Rosemary decided to become a solo vocalist. Columbia Records signed her to a contract almost as soon as she left the band. In short order, she racked up a number of hits, from the sentimental ballad "Tenderly" to the wild novelty "Come On-a My House." Through the nineteen-fifties and sixties, she became a star not only on records but on television and radio and in the movies. Her major-network TV appearances included repeated visits to such programs as the Ed Sullivan, Bing Crosby, and Bob Hope shows. In addition, she gave what critics called a star dramatic performance on "The Dick Powell Theatre." Her movie credits include "White Christmas," "Deep in My Heart," "Red Garters," "Here Come the Girls," and "The Stars Are Singing." In the sixties, Rosemary had her own shows on TV and radio, and her radio program was rebroadcast to the armed services overseas.

Some of Rosemary's other hit records are "Hey There," "Beautiful Brown Eyes," "Sentimental Music," and "This Old House."

COHAN, GEORGE MICHAEL: composer, lyricist, librettist, actor. Born Providence, Rhode Island, July 3, 1878; died New York, New York, October 5, 1942. Awarded gold medal by special act of Congress in May, 1940, for contributions to the American theater.

George M. Cohan helped pioneer a true American musical theater. He was to the manner born—the manner, that is, of the stage. His parents, Jeremiah and Helen, were vaudeville performers, and his father introduced his infant son to the theater by carrying him on stage during a skit. When George was eight, be began playing the violin in the pit orchestra. At nine, he made his stage bow as Master Georgie with his parents in Haverstraw, New York. He was a regular from then on. In 1888, the act became the Four Cohans with the addition of his sister Josephine. By now, young George was contributing songs and sketches that rapidly made the act one of the most popular in the country. In 1899, he married singing comedienne Ethel Levey, and the team became the Five Cohans.

But George wanted to write for the Broadway stage. He worked up one of his sketches into a musical, "The Governor's Son" and won an agreement with the Hyde and Behman vaudeville circuit to follow a one-year tour of the Cohans with the Broadway opening of the show. The Broadway opening, on February 25, 1901, was a flop, but the show was successful on the road. The same thing happened with Cohan's next attempt, "Running for Office." Cohan was downcast, for, he said, Broadway was "the only bell I wanted to ring."

In 1904, he tried once more with "Little Johnny Jones." Again, the reviews were negative but audiences outside New York were delighted. This time, Cohan brought the show back to Broadway and, for the first time, sparked acclaim. The show, in which Cohan played an American jockey wrongly accused of throwing a race in England, included "The Yankee Doodle Boy" and "Give My Regards to Broadway." From then on, Cohan musical and nonmusical shows were staple features on Broadway for close to two decades.

On January 1, 1906, "Forty-Five Minutes from Broadway" opened with a new actor, Victor Moore, starring instead of Cohan who played the role in a 1912 revival. Besides the title song, the score included "Mary's a Grand Old Name" and "So Long, Mary." On February 12, 1906, another Cohan show, "George Washington, Jr.," opened on Broadway, this one starring the Five Cohans. It included "You're a Grand Old Flag" and "I Was Born in Virginia." In the years that followed, Cohan provided a number of musicals and revues that were generally successful though not as noteworthy as his earlier efforts. These included "The Honeymooners" (1907), "The Talk of New York" (1907), "Fifty Miles from Boston" (1908), "The Yankee Prince" (1908), "The Man Who Owns Broadway" (1909), "The

Little Millionaire" (1911), "Hello Broadway!" (1914), "The Cohan Revue" (1916 and 1918), "The Royal Vagabond" (1919), "Little Nellie Kelly" (1922), "The Merry Malones" (1927), and "Billie" (1928). Cohan scored with several nonmusical plays, including "Get-Rich-Quick Wallingford" (1910), "Broadway Jones" (1912), "Seven Keys to Baldpate" (1913), "The Tavern" (1920), and "The Song and Dance Man" (1923).

When the United States entered World War I in 1917, Cohan wrote one of his greatest songs. It was not connected with a musical but simply expressed the spirit of the nation in those days. The song, was "Over There."

In the nineteen-twenties, Cohan found that he had lost touch with the new movements of the American musical theater. This, plus Cohan's violent objections to the efforts of Actors Equity to organize theatrical performers, led to his near-retirement from composing. He still reached great heights as a performer in other writers' vehicles, most notably in Eugene O'Neill's "Ah, Wilderness!" in 1934 and the Rodgers, Hart (Lorenz and Moss), and Kaufman "I'd Rather Be Right" in 1937. Cohan's portrayal of President Franklin D. Roosevelt was one of the highlights of musical-theater history. Cohan died after disobeying doctor's orders to rest after an operation and going for a last taxi tour of his beloved Broadway.

COLE, NAT "KING": singer, pianist, band leader, composer. Born Montgomery, Alabama, March 17, 1917; died Santa Monica, California, February 15, 1965.

Few can point to as long an unbroken reign as one of the most listened-to performers in popular music. Times changed, the record audience changed, other performers became stars and were forgotten, but Nat "King" Cole continued steadily along. On August 5, 1962, over nine hundred people jammed the Embassy Room of the Ambassador Hotel in Los Angeles to applaud Nat's twenty-fifth anniversary in show business. Lieutenant Governor Glenn Anderson of California read congratulations from Governor Pat Brown and President Kennedy. The cofounder of Capitol Records, Glenn E. Wallichs, presented him with a gold-plated microphone—the one (without the gold) used by Nat to record his first Capitol number, "Straighten Up and Fly Right."

Nat's father, Edward James Cole, was a Baptist minister and his mother a choir singer in Montgomery, Alabama. They named their new

Nat "King" Cole

the treasury. Stranded, Nat spent many weary days looking for work. As he recalled, "I played in practically every beer joint in Los Angeles, never making more than five dollars a night." Along the way he wrote a song called "Straighten Up and Fly Right." When someone offered him fifty dollars for it, he was only too happy to sign it over.

Nat's wanderings brought him to a small Hollywood spot, the Swanee Club, where he was intermission pianist. One night, he was playing an impromptu jam session when he was joined by guitarist Oscar Moore and bass player Wes Prince. The audience reaction was good, and the owner offered Nat seventy-five dollars a week to form a quartet. On opening night, the drummer failed to show up; the Nat "King" Cole Trio came into being. They were hired for a month, but the engagement stretched to over a year.

In 1941, they decided to try the big time, and got an engagement in New York at Kelly's Stables. That was the only work they could get in New York, however. They headed back to Los Angeles for a job at the 331 Club, where they stayed for a year and a half. More important, they signed a contract with a brand-new company, Capitol Records. Soon after, the trio racked up its first nationwide success. Ironically, the number they chose was Nat's own "Straighten Up and Fly Right." As a result of their efforts, the man who had bought the song netted over twenty thousand dollars. The group's reputation continued to grow, particularly among jazz fans. Many of their recordings are among jazz followers' most prized collector's items. But, as World War II drew to a close, so did the trio. Capitol suggested and Nat agreed that a big band behind him would sell more records.

Not too long after, the point was proved. A songwriter named Eden Ahbez, wearing a beard and leopard skin, brought Capitol a song that was to become one of the most successful ever recorded, "Nature Boy." From here on, Nat's singing and inspired piano playing, with the orchestral background, produced hit after hit, such as "Embraceable You," "Sweet Lorraine," "Too Young," "A Fool Was I," "Gina," "Route 66," "Non Dimenticar," and "Mona Lisa."

In the spring of 1959, Nat made a sensational tour of South America. One million persons saw him in person and seven times that many on television. His tours of Europe in the early fifties and in spring of 1960 were equally impressive. The 1960 tour was climaxed by a command per-

son Nathaniel Adams Cole. When Nat was four, his father became pastor of a Chicago church, and the family, which included three other boys and a girl, moved north. Nat was already beginning to play the piano. At four, he could pick out "Yes! We Have No Bananas." Nat's first piano lessons were in the classics. He also sang in the choir and, by the time he was twelve, played the church organ. But Chicago was a hotbed of jazz, and soon young Cole was avidly following the careers of such favorites as Louis Armstrong, Earl "Fatha" Hines, and the great New Orleans clarinetist Jimmy Noone. Noone's theme song was "Sweet Lorraine," a number now more often associated with Cole.

Cole formed his first band in high school. This was a fourteen-piece organization, with Nat doubling as pianist and leader. Their nightly fee was a dollar fifty a man, but they often settled for left-over food and refreshments. Nat also found time to excel at baseball and football.

After completing high school, Nat decided to continue in the entertainment field. In 1937, he joined a road company of a revue called "Shuffle Along." The company reached California and then broke up when someone walked off with

[52]

formance in London for Queen Elizabeth. At home and abroad, there were few major TV shows, nightclubs and ballrooms that were not graced by Nat's presence sometime in his long career. In addition, Nat portrayed W. C. Handy in Paramount Pictures' biography of the father of the blues, "St. Louis Blues." Nineteen-sixty-three found Cole still bubbling along on the record charts with such new hits as "Dear Lonely Hearts," "All over the World," and "Hazy, Crazy, Lazy Days of Summer."

To many people in the sixties, Cole's jazz background had been all but forgotten. In an article written for Capitol Records, jazz critic Ralph Gleason noted:

We tend to forget the deep roots he has in jazz. But the roots are there, and every time he sits down at the piano for even just one number in a show, the jazz artist is there again for all to hear. Nat Cole . . . probably never even thinks about it, but talk to the jazz piano players today and they'll tell you: Nat Cole has been a great influence in jazz. Part of Nat's magic as a pianist lay in his ability to make the whole thing sound so easy and simple. But when he took hold with both hands and really went into full stride, it was as exciting jazz listening as I have ever known.

On December 8, 1964, Cole entered St. John's Hospital in Santa Monica, California, where his illness was diagnosed as lung cancer. On January 25, 1965, his left lung was removed, but to no avail. His illustrious career came to a close soon after on February 15, 1965.

COMBO: musical slang for a small musical group ("combination").

Most combos have from three to five musicians, plus possibly a vocalist. Usually, one of the musicians can double as vocalist. Though there is no limit to the number of musicians an organization can have to be classed as a combo, a group of seven or more would certainly be considered a full-fledged band.

COMDEN, BETTY: lyricist, librettist, actress. Born New York, New York, May 3, 1915.

Betty Comden, born and brought up in New York, attended New York University. A fellow classmate, born the same year, was Adolph Green. As members of the Washington Square Players, they worked up a nightclub act in which

they and another young actress, Judy Holliday, performed. Called "the Revuers," the act was warmly applauded at the Village Vanguard in the late thirties. Among the audience a good part of the time was Green's sometime roommate Leonard Bernstein.

The team of Comden and Green wrote the book and lyrics for Bernstein's first Broadway effort, "On the Town." The show, which opened on December 28, 1944, was a hit. Besides providing the words for such song as "Lonely Town," "New York, New York," "I Can Cook, Too," and "Lucky To Be Me," Comden and Green also played major roles in the show. This was the first of a string of major successes for the team.

In 1947, they began working with Jule Styne. Their first collaboration was another hit, "High Button Shoes." In 1951 came another Comden-Green-Styne success, "Two on the Aisle." The score included "Hold Me, Hold Me, Hold Me" and "Catch Our Act at the Met." Another hit, Bernstein's "Wonderful Town," appeared in 1953. Going back to Styne, Comden and Green kept up their pace by contributing to Mary Martin's version of "Peter Pan" (1954), "Bells Are Ringing" (1956), and "Say, Darling" (1958). They also appeared on many major television shows, including Ed Sullivan's.

In May, 1964, another Comden-Green-Styne effort opened at the Mark Hellinger Theatre on Broadway. Called "Fade Out-Fade In," it spoofed Hollywood of the nineteen thirties. While the book received little applause from the critics, the show's stars, Carol Burnett and Jack Cassidy, won raves. The show continued as a major Broadway attraction into 1965.

COMO, PERRY: singer, master of ceremonies. Born Canonsburg, Pennsylvania, May 18, 1912.

Perry Como ranks as probably the only one-time barber to have the street his store was on renamed for him. He was the seventh son of Italian immigrants Pietro and Lucia Como. He was earning pin money and learning a little of the barbering profession after school at a local barber shop by the time he was fourteen. At fifteen, he opened his own shop and prospered to the extent that, when he ran it full-time after graduating from high school, he was earning a hundred and twenty-five dollars a week—a sizable sum even today, and a small fortune in Depression days. When Perry started in music, it was many years before he came close to earning as much.

Perry Como

Perry was a singing barber, and friends urged him to audition with Freddy Carlone's local band. He did so in July, 1933, at Lorain, Ohio, and went home to Canonsburg to marry his home-town sweetheart Roselle Belline. Four days after the wedding, an urgent wire from Carlone brought Perry his first professional band job, at twenty-eight dollars a week. His reputation expanded through the Pennsylvania-Ohio area until Ted Weems, then one of the top big-band leaders, took notice. Weems hired Perry at fifty dollars a week in 1936. For six years, life was a series of one-night stands, hurried recording dates, and occasional radio shows. Roselle had gone back to live in Canonsburg with the arrival of their first child, and Perry was becoming homesick and weary of traveling.

In 1942, Weems's outfit disbanded, and Perry went back to Canonsburg, determined to reopen his barber shop. But General Artists Corporation phoned that they had lined up a CBS radio show to be run by Perry at a hundred dollars a week, plus an RCA Victor recording contract. This arrangement, they promised, would let Perry stay put—in New York. Perry's wife and family urged him to take it, and he did.

In 1943, Perry sang to packed houses at New York's Versailles and Copacabana nightclubs, and to crowds of high-school fans at the Paramount Theatre. In 1943, his first RCA solo record, "Goodbye, Sue," made a mild impression on record buyers, but by 1945, such records as "Till the End of Time" were selling in the millions; four million Como pressings were made in a single week in 1946. Some of the other great Como renditions of the forties and fifties were "Prisoner of Love," "Because," "Temptation," "Don't Let the Stars Get in Your Eyes," "Round and Round," "Catch a Falling Star," "When You Were Sweet Sixteen," and "I Believe." In 1963, he had a best seller in "I Love You and Don't You Forget it."

Starting with his first show, in 1943, Como set some sort of record for longevity and continuing popularity on radio and television. From 1944 to 1950, he had a weekly show—five nights a week at the start, later thrice weekly, and finally a single half hour. In 1950, he switched to three times a week for fifteen minutes. In May, 1955, he signed a twelve-year contract with NBC-TV to do an hour show on Saturday nights. The show premiered on September 17, 1955, and rapidly became one of the fixtures on night-time TV. In the sixties, the show switched to Wednesday evenings. Perry was now able to stay close to home (in Sands Point, Long Island) with Roselle, spend his time with his family, and make a relaxed tour of the golf course on occasion. Though he traveled hardly at all, his familiar face and singing voice went around the world by means of records and videotaped versions of his TV shows.

COMPOSER: a writer of music.

In popular music, composers range from those with a great amount of formal musical training to those who have little or none. Some popular composers can write out their compositions, while others whistle into tape recorders or dictate the melodies to arrangers.

In general, the popular composers with the greatest staying power over the years had excellent classical grounding, such as Richard Rodgers, Victor Herbert, George Gershwin, and Cole Porter. There are plenty of notable exceptions, such as Irving Berlin and George M. Cohan, who were self-taught and who provided a legacy of great songs.

Methods of composing vary. In some cases, a composer becomes inspired and just sits down and writes a melody. In others, he matches music to a set of lyrics. For a show score, a composer may study the libretto and decide where the songs should be, after which he may write the melodies to fit the mood of the story at that point. Or a composer may allot a certain amount of time each day for composing, with the idea that he will finish a certain number of new melodic ideas in that period.

Inspiration is where you find it. One example of a major composer's work habits is given in this anecdote told by Fred Astaire in "Steps in Time" (New York: Harper and Brothers, 1959):

> A couple of nights Irving Berlin came down and played gin rummy with me for hours. Irving is always thinking up new song ideas, and in the middle of our gin games he would often sing and throw lyric ideas and rhymes at me to test them out. At this time Irving was working on the picture ["Follow the Fleet"] and his mind was particularly occupied when he left me at about three. He got into a taxi and told the driver to take him to . . . Beverly Hills. . . . It happened that he got a driver who didn't know much about Beverly Hills and proceeded to drive Irv all over the place, out into Malibu or somewhere. Irving told me the next day, "I wasn't paying any attention to the driver—my mind was on a tune. When I looked at my watch I found I'd been riding around for two hours."

Some composers have fairly set patterns for writing, such as working only during certain hours of the day or only when they are at an instrument. (Piano is the most used instrument for composing, but not the only one. The guitar is often used, for instance, and Meredith Willson has composed many numbers on a piccolo.) Others may write under a wide variety of conditions. Duke Ellington is an example of this type.

As Paul Mills, of Mills Music, which published much of Ellington's work, notes: "Sometimes Duke sat down with the idea of writing music and he wrote it. Sometimes it just grew. For instance, many years ago there was no time limit on a recording session. Depending on circumstances, such as studio availability or band dates, Duke might call his band together to record at two, three or four in the morning. If the members were late getting there, the guys might start jamming while they were waiting. Duke might have part of a tune and not know where to go from there. So he'd just play this part until some-

thing happened. Usually he'd come up with the balance of the melody himself, but sometimes one of the other musicians would fill it out. If one man contributed enough to a song to be identified with it, his name would go on it as well as the Duke's. Many times the result would be melodies Duke would turn over to Mills and forget about. Weeks or months later, after a lyric had been put on it, it would be shown to him and he'd say, "Did I write this?"

To give a technical review of theory of composition is beyond the scope of this book. Some of the definitions of musical terms elsewhere in the book may be of help. For more detailed information on musical theory, some of the references given in the "Songwriting Methods" section of the Bibliography might be consulted.

CONGA: dance in four-four time, of Afro-Cuban origin.

The conga, which achieved a brief vogue in the United States in the nineteen-forties, is danced to a pattern of one, two, three, kick. The dance can be done by couples, in a conga line, or in a combination of the two. When danced by couples, the partners face each other, one partner moving in one direction, the other moving the other way. On completing the one measure, each partner reverses his direction. A conga line is formed by the dancers lining up one behind the other, with each dancer's outstretched hands resting on the shoulders of the dancer in front. The one-two-three-kick pattern is then performed by the entire line in unison as it moves around the dance floor.

CONNIFF, RAY: arranger, conductor. Born Attleboro, Massachusetts, November 6, 1916.

Some of the most danceable music coming from FM stations in recent years has been conducted by Ray Conniff. The music is also eminently listenable, thanks to Conniff's way of blending voices with instruments. Without using words, accordingly to *McCall's* magazine (April, 1962), "In effect, these singers 'play' their voices as though they were instruments . . . more like subtly fluted woodwinds than singing." Female voices, for example, double with trumpets, high saxophones, or clarinets; male voices with trombones, trumpets, or low saxophones. This combination was carefully arranged by Conniff to mellow harsh tones, intensify soft ones, and produce his characteristic blend.

Though Conniff achieved national recognition for his arranging and conducting, he also served

Ray Conniff

for many years as a sideman with many top bands. He became interested in music at an early age from listening to his father play the piano. He decided against becoming a pianist and took up the trombone. By his junior year in high school, he was recognized as a first-rate trombonist. About this time, he answered a mail-order advertisement for a "transposer," a device to transpose melodies. This started Conniff in the rudiments of musical arranging.

After graduation, Ray played trombone with a Boston society band. He went on to serve with such famous band leaders as the late Bunny Berigan, Bob Crosby, and finally for a four-year stint with Artie Shaw. With Shaw, Conniff came into his own as an arranger, providing the band with interpretations of such songs as " 'S Wonderful" and "Jumping on the Merry-Go-Round" and a popular version of the Rachmaninoff Prelude in C-sharp minor. In his spare time, Conniff continued his musical studies at New York's Juilliard School of Music.

After a tour of duty in the Army during World War II, during which time Ray worked with Meredith Willson and the late Walter Schuman, he was hired by Harry James. His arrangements for James included "Easy On," "The Beaumont Ride," and "September Song." After several years with James, Conniff signed an exclusive contract as arranger for Columbia Records. He was soon conducting his own orchestra in his own arrangements. In many instances, Conniff's arrangements for some of CBS's top vocalists helped the singer win gold records. Examples include Johnnie Ray's "Walking in the Rain," Guy Mitchell's "Singin' the Blues," and Johnny Mathis's "Wonderful, Wonderful," "It's Not for Me To Say," and "Chances Are."

Ray's break as conductor-arranger came with the release in 1956 of his album " 'S Wonderful," which rapidly became a best seller. It was soon followed with a string of other successful LP's, including " 'S Marvelous," " 'S Awful Nice," " 'S Continental," "Say It with Music," "Memories Are Made of This," and "So Much in Love." By the end of 1962, his album sales had gone well beyond the five-million mark.

CONRAD, CON: composer, pianist, producer, actor. Born New York, New York, June 18, 1891; died Van Nuys, California, September 28, 1938. Won Academy Award for Best Song of 1934 ("The Continental").

Con Conrad was always a man in a hurry, driven on, perhaps, by memories of the run-down tenements and the struggle for existence in his birthplace, New York's teeming lower East Side. The restless energy that kept him on the move to many places in the United States and Europe also provided much memorable popular music, including the winner of the first Academy Award competition for a movie song, "The Continental," from "The Gay Divorcee."

His parents had an old second-hand piano in their small flat on Grand Street. Conrad (he was born Conrad K. Dober) began to play almost as soon as he could talk. While he enjoyed improvising on the piano, he hated school, and the older he became, the more he played hookey. By the time he was in his teens, he was through with formal learning; instead, he helped pay his family's rent with a four-dollar-a-week job in a brokerage house.

After a short attempt at selling real estate, the sixteen-year-old Conrad won a job as a pianist at the Vanity Fair Theatre on One hundred and twenty-fifth street. He soon began making the rounds of music publishers in his spare time, trying to sell songs. Along the way, he met a stage-struck ex-boilermaker named Jay Whidden. They formed an act that played the Keith circuit and also was signed for a revue in London.

When the revue closed, Conrad returned to New York and songwriting. In 1912, he wrote his first hit with Whidden, "Down in Dear Old New Orleans." Using his income from this, Conrad financed a show starring Al Jolson, the 1913 "Honeymoon Express." He continued to write, play the piano, and travel during World War I, but he really hit his stride in 1920 when he formed a publishing firm with Henry Waterson, a former Irving Berlin partner. He soon had written two 1920 hits, "Margie" and "Palesteena." In the years that followed, he turned out a steady stream of popular hits with various lyricists, including "Ma, He's Making Eyes at Me" (1921), (words by Sidney Clare); "Barney Google" and "You've Got To See Mamma Every Night" (1923) (both with lyrics by a new name on Broadway, Billy Rose); and "Lonesome and Sorry" (1926) (lyrics by Benny Davis).

Conrad also wrote for musicals during the twenties, including "Bombo," "Moonlight," "Mercenary Mary," "The Comic Supplement," "Kitty's Kisses," and the first edition of "Americana."

The rise of sound movies led to a bid from Hollywood. Conrad accepted in 1929 and contributed regularly to movies for the rest of his life. He also had an eye for singing talent and, in California, found a prime protégé in crooner Russ Columbo.

One of his first movie scores was for the 1929 "Fox Movietone Follies." In later years, he worked on Eddie Cantor's "Palmy Days" (1931); "The Gift of Gab," "I Like It That Way," and "The Gay Divorcee" (1934); "Here's to Romance," "Reckless," and "King Solomon of Broadway" (1935); and "I'd Give My Life" (1936). His last film, "The Story of the Castles," was released in 1939, less than a year after his untimely death.

COOKF, SAM: singer. Born Chicago, Illinois, January 22, 1935; died Los Angles, California, December 11, 1964.

Many great popular-music performers began as gospel singers or church-choir members. In quite a few instances, one of the singer's parents was a religious leader. This was true for Sam Cooke, whose father, Reverend Charles Cooke, was minister of a Chicago church.

As Sam grew up, he performed in his father's church choir and later joined a gospel group, the Soul Stirrers. They appeared in a concert at the Shrine Auditorium in Los Angeles, and a record-company executive asked Sam to record some popular songs. Sam asked his father what to do. He was told, "It isn't what you sing that is so important, but rather the fact that God gave you a good voice to use. He must want you to make people happy by singing, so go ahead and do so."

Sam concentrated on blues and ballads. His first record, a bluesy ballad called "You Send Me," made him an overnight celebrity and sold over two-million copies. From then on, Sam turned out a string of hit songs that sold at least two hundred and fifty thousand records each. Most of these ended up on the national top-forty list, including "Sentimental Reasons," "Ol' Man River," "Win Your Love," "Only Sixteen," "Everybody Loves to Cha-Cha-Cha," "Chain Gang," "Cupid," "Love You Most of All," "Twistin' the Night Away," "That's It, I Quit," and "I'll Come Running Back to You." He also sang the theme song, "Almost in Your Arms," for the Cary Grant-Sophia Loren movie "Houseboat," and turned out such hit albums as "Sam Cooke" and "The Best of Sam Cooke."

Cooke wrote much of his own material and was also an excellent guitarist. Sam made many guest appearances on such major television shows as that of Ed Sullivan and "The American Bandstand" during the nineteen-sixties. During the 1959–1960 TV season, he essayed a straight dramatic role, costarring with Sammy Davis, Jr., on "The General Electric Theatre."

Cooke died at the age of twenty-nine as the result of a shooting in a Los Angeles motel.

CORINNE CORINNA: song (1932, 1950, 1960). By J. M. Williams and Bo Chatman, additional lyrics by Mitchell Parish.

"Corinne Corinna," a rock-'n'-roll hit in the early nineteen-sixties, was based on a Dixieland favorite of the early nineteen-thirties.

The song as originally written had "race" lyrics—for instance, such lines as "Corinne Corinna, tallest girl in town, no misbehavin' or I'll mow you down." Mills Music had Mitchell Parish write additional lyrics for general consumption. In the early nineteen-fifties, just before rock-'n'-roll became a dominant factor in popular music, "Corinne" was revived in a hit rendition by Bill Haley and the Comets. Haley's version was fast, but not rock 'n' roll. In 1961, another version became a major hit, this time as a rock-'n'-roll song by young singer Ray Petersen.

COUNTRY-AND-WESTERN: type of music, usually characterized by a simple, two-beat feeling.

The phrase refers to two related categories of music which are similar musically but different in subject matter. Country music embraces what used to be known as hillbilly music. It usually is very simple, without the altered harmonies of rock 'n' roll, jazz, or other popular-music styles, and often has a hymnlike quality (a major exception is the Blue Grass banjo style, a type of country music containing complicated chordal structures). Country music has its roots in the Elizabethan songs brought over by the settlers of the South.

In most country music there are four beats to the measure, with the first and third beats accented. Some country music, however, is in waltz time.

Most performers of country music include Western material in their repertoire, and most performers of Western music also play and sing country music. The difference is in lyric content. The country songs deal mainly with personal subjects (such as love and trouble) and the Western songs with narrative subjects (such as the trail and the landscape). There is much blurring of the edges, and many songs are hard to classify.

At one time, country-and-Western music was for the most part restricted to the South or Southwest and the rural areas of other parts of the country. After World War II, country-and-Western music expanded in scope, and much of today's most widely performed popular music comes from the country-and-Western field.

COVER RECORD: record-industry slang for a record by an artist of a number already recorded by another artist that looks like a possible hit.

Reflected glory from a song already recorded by another performer can pay off handsomely. If the first recording becomes highly popular, many people will buy a record of the same song by another artist. It is also usually to the advantage of the songwriter and his publisher to get as many records of the song as possible: the more records turned out on a song, the better the chance for higher sales. The records that follow the original version are called "cover records." In quite a few instances, the cover record has turned out to be the better seller.

In recent years, particularly in such areas as rock 'n' roll, this practice has been abandoned.

One reason for this is that with such recordings it is not the song itself that sells but rather the style of the recording artist.

COWARD, NOEL PIERCE: playwright, librettist, lyricist, composer, author, actor. Born London, England, December 16, 1899.

There's little in the creative field that Noel Coward hasn't attempted successfully. During a career stretching over more than fifty years, he has turned out hit plays, musicals, movies, ballet scores, popular songs, television scripts, and books. In many of these efforts, he played major stage roles as well, doing everything from drama and comedy to song-and-dance routines.

Coward was born into a fairly comfortable English family and received his early education at private schools and Croydon. During these years, he began his musical career as a choirboy in the local church. By the time he was twelve, his family's finances needed augmenting. This resulted in Coward's first stage appearance. He became a member of Charles Hawtrey's provincial repertory players and toured England with them. The troupe included two other juveniles, Gertrude Lawrence and Estelle Winwood, who were to become leading actresses in the English theater.

He received some dramatic training at the Italia Conti Academy, England's finest drama school, but left for service in World War I. He was already becoming interested in writing and, at eighteen, wrote his first play, "The Rat Trap." At the end of the war, he graced the London stage in Cosmo Hamilton's "Scandal." Soon after, he starred in his first musical, "London Calling." He not only played the lead song-and-dance role but also had written the book, lyrics, and music.

Most of his output during the twenties was plays, with his first hit coming in 1924, thanks to Alfred Lunt and Lynn Fontanne's performance in "Hay Fever." His 1925 play "The Vortex" gave him his first New York triumph, following a successful London run. Another success in London and New York was his 1928 revue "This Year of Grace." But his luck wasn't all good, for he had such failures as "I'll Leave It to You" (1920), "The Young Idea" (1924), and "Sirocco" (1927).

In the late twenties, a nervous breakdown made Coward retire to Hawaii for a much needed rest. While there, he wrote the operetta "Bitter Sweet." This was a hit in the 1929–30 season in London and New York, as was his revue "On with the Dance." Though he was not writing primarily for the Broadway stage, his influence could be felt in many areas by this time. Some of his songs were heard regularly on American radio, and the 1930 Ziegfeld musical "Smiles" was based on one of Coward's ideas.

In the years that followed, Coward turned out a steady stream of musicals and revues for the London stage. His musical efforts included the revues "Words and Music" (1932) and "Sigh No More" (1945); the musical plays "Pacific 1860" (1946), "Ace of Clubs" (1950), and "After the Ball" (1954); and the ballet "London Morning." His nonmusical dramatic hits included "Private Lives" (1931), in which he played the lead; "Conversation Piece" (1934); "Present Laughter" and "This Happy Breed" (1943); "Blithe Spirit" (1941); and "Nude with Violin" (1956). "Blithe Spirit" achieved success on the New York stage, in the movies (1945), and as the framework for a Broadway musical.

"Blithe Spirit" was one of many Coward film credits. His work includes "In Which We Serve" (1942), "This Happy Breed" (1944), "Brief Encounter" (1945), "The Astonished Heart" (1950), "Our Man in Havana" (1959), and "Surprise Package" (1960).

Many books too bear Coward's imprint. One of the first was the 1930 collection of some of his shorter works. In 1937, his first autobiography, "Present Indicative," was published. Some of his more recent volumes are "Australia Visited" (1941), "Star Quality" (1951), "Noel Coward's Songbook" (1953), and the autobiography "Future Indefinite" (1954).

In 1960, Coward decided to try to gain his first laurel for an original Broadway musical. Called "Sail Away," with score and book by him, it opened on Broadway on October 3, 1961. Though the score won approval, the critics considered the book too old-fashioned, and the show ran only one hundred and sixty-seven performances. Coward's songs included "Sail Away," "The Passenger's Always Right," "Later than Spring," "Something Very Strange," "When Do You Want Me?," and "Why Do the Wrong People Travel?"

Three years later, a Coward-based musical did become a major Broadway hit, starring Beatrice Lillie and Tammy Grimes. Called "High Spirits," it was a musical interpretation of "Blithe Spirit." The book adaptation and the score were not Coward's, however, but the work of Hugh Martin and Timothy Gray. Coward kept his hand in, though, by directing the show.

CROSBY, GEORGE ROBERT (BOB): band leader, singer, master of ceremonies. Born Spokane, Washington, August 23, 1914.

Bob Crosby, the youngest of the five male Crosby children, gained fame the hard way. He had to overcome not only the formidable shadow of older brother Bing but also, in his early attempts, a rugged case of first-night jitters. Bob made his first attempt at performing before an audience at the age of thirteen, on an amateur show in Spokane. When he got on stage and opened his mouth, nothing came out. The orchestra played the introduction five times, but finally young Crosby abandoned the effort and fled in terror.

He refused to give up, however. While going to school in Spokane, he snapped up every opportunity to sing and was soon helping supply musical backgrounds to the dancing and walking marathon contests of the early nineteen-thirties. He also sang on the local radio station. As did brother Bing, Bob enrolled at Gonzaga University as a law student and also became a first stringer on several of the school's athletic teams.

Band leader Anson Weeks heard Bob sing on the radio and hired him. A bad case of nerves kept Bob from making a success, and Anson sent him home for seasoning. In 1933, a much more relaxed Bob Crosby approached Weeks again, and this time he stayed hired. In 1935, Bob was working in New York when he accepted an offer to lead an eleven-piece band, which became "Bob Crosby's Bob Cats." In the next few years, the group built a reputation as a good Dixieland and dance band. In 1938, a long engagement at the Black Hawk in Chicago won the band nationwide attention. The Bob Cats soon had a steady stream of nightclub and ballroom dates and also appeared in many Hollywood musicals.

When war came, Crosby enlisted in the marines as a lieutenant and spent almost a year and a half organizing shows and bands to play in the Pacific. In the fall of 1945, Crosby was discharged and went back to Hollywood to organize a new band. The band toured and played on radio for several years. At the end of the big-band era, Bob broke up his organization to work once again as a singer and as a master of ceremonies. In the nineteen-fifties and sixties, Bob made television as well as radio guest appearances while continuing to record and to head up nightclub shows in some of the country's major cities.

In its heydey, the Bob Cats' roster boasted some top Dixieland musicians, including Ray Bauduc on drums and Bobby Haggart on bass. One of the most famous Crosby records featuring these two was "Big Wind From Winnetka." One of his better-known vocal records was "Yes, Indeed," sung with brother Bing and Connee Boswell. Some of Bob's other recordings are "Jazz Me Blues," "Washington and Lee Swing," "Dear Old Donegal," and "A Gay Ranchero."

CROSBY, HARRY LILLIS (BING): singer, actor, master of ceremonies. Born Tacoma, Washington, May 2, 1904.

Bing Crosby's career, much like his easy manner of performing, stayed remarkably free of violent ups and downs once he gained stardom in the early nineteen-thirties. Year after year, he remained one of the reigning popular-music favorites of the American public. He starred in whatever medium he tried—records, movies, radio, or television.

A few years after Bing's birth (he was the fourth of seven Crosby children), his family moved to Spokane. Harry, Jr., gained his nickname at an early age. One story is that it came from his playing cowboy and shooting his toy gun, "Bing! Bing!" In the February 21, 1953, *Saturday Evening Post,* however, the name was attributed to a comic strip called the "Bingville Bugle." Bing attended public grade school, Gonzaga High, and then, in 1921, Gonzaga University.

In high school he joined a band called "the Musicaladers" and played for school and local functions. In college he and a friend Al Rinker sang duets in addition to playing in a small band. Bing switched to studying law in 1922, but in 1925, he and Rinker left school to try their hand at music. In a forty-dollar jalopy, they worked their way south to Los Angeles, where Rinker's sister, Mildred Bailey, was already a featured singer.

They worked at various jobs around Los Angeles until, in 1927, Paul Whiteman heard them. Whiteman signed them, but they didn't go over as a duo, and he had to let them go. They formed a trio with Harry Barris and rejoined Whiteman as the Rhythm Boys. This time, they clicked. They made such successful records with the band as "Mississippi," "From Monday On," and "My Suppressed Desire." In 1930, they appeared with the band in the film "The King of Jazz." But soon after, Paul let them go as he felt that Crosby wasn't serious enough. Returning to Los Angeles, the trio worked with Gus Arnheim's orchestra in the Cocoanut Grove, and Bing's solo work started to attract attention. On September 29, 1930, Bing married singer Dixie Lee.

In 1932, his recording of "I Surrender, Dear" led CBS executives to star Bing on his first radio show. Then came a fabulously successful engagement at New York's Paramount Theatre that lasted twenty consecutive weeks. Hollywood now wanted Bing, and in 1933 he was featured in "College Humor," the first of over forty films he made for Paramount Pictures. In 1934, he appeared in such films as "We're Not Dressing," "She Loves Me Not," and "Here Is My Heart." He also signed a contract with Decca Records. In the years that followed, Bing turned out dozens of hit records, including "Sweet Leilani," "Pennies from Heaven," "When the Blue of the Night Meets the Gold of the Day," "Sunday, Monday, or Always," "Don't Fence Me In," "Blues in the Night," "Marcheta," "Three Caballeros" (with the Andrew Sisters), and "Yes, Indeed" (with Connee Boswell).

He starred for years on CBS radio; then, in 1936, he switched to NBC to become master of

Bing Crosby

ceremonies of "The Kraft Music Hall." Bing also became one of the top box-office attractions in film history. (He was listed as one of the ten top money makers in the *Motion Picture Herald's* Fame Poll in 1934, 1937, 1940, 1943, 1944, 1945, 1946, 1947, 1948, 1949, 1950, 1951, 1953, and 1954.) His film credits include "Anything Goes" and "Pennies from Heaven" in 1936, "Waikiki Wedding" in 1937, "Doctor Rhythm" and "Sing, You Sinners" in 1938, "Paris Honeymoon" in 1939, and "If I Had My Way" in 1940. In 1940, he made the first of the fabulously successful "Road" pictures with Bob Hope and Dorothy Lamour, "The Road to Singapore." Other "Roads" were "Zanzibar" (1941), "Morocco" (1944), "Utopia" (1946), "Rio" (1948), "Bali" (1952), and "Hong Kong" (1962).

In 1941, Crosby starred in "Birth of the Blues," and, in 1942, introduced Berlin's "White Christmas" in "Holiday Inn." In 1944, Bing won an Academy Award for his portrayal of a young priest in "Going My Way," in which he started the song "Swinging on a Star" on the way to standard rating. In 1945, Bing's four sons appeared with him in the movie "Duffy's Tavern."

Bing switched his radio work to ABC in 1946 so that he could do the first magnetically taped show on radio (NBC at the time would not use taped shows). Bing did not make his TV debut until June, 1952, and it was not until some years later that he would agree to appear regularly on television. In the meantime, he moved back to CBS radio and continued to star in more films. Other film successes were "Blue Skies" (1946), "A Connecticut Yankee" (1950), "Here Comes the Groom" (1951), and "Little Boy Lost" (1952). In 1950, Bing and his oldest son Gary combined talents to turn out two hit records, "Sam's Song" and "Play a Simple Melody."

During the 1964–65 television season, Crosby was featured on the ABC network in the unlikely role of an engineer in a situation comedy (The Bing Crosby Show).

CUGAT, XAVIER: band leader, arranger, composer, violinist. Born Gerona, Spain, January 1, 1900.

Xavier Cugat, the rumba king, first made the rhythms of Latin America a staple of the American popular-music diet. Before becoming a success as a band leader, however, has was a concert violinist, a movie producer, and a cartoonist for a major newspaper.

When Xavier was four, his father's political

Xavier Cugat

activities in Spain made it vital that they leave their homeland. They moved to Havana, where his father soon achieved mild success by introducing the first acetylene lights to Cuba. A neighborhood violin maker gave Xavier a violin, and it soon became apparent that Cugat was a prodigy on the instrument. Xavier was enrolled in the conservatory, and, at nine, got his first professional job, playing in a theater. By the time he was twelve, he was first violinist in Havana's National Theater Symphonic Orchestra. The Cugat family then moved to New York, so that Xavier could pursue his violin studies. His first concert at Carnegie Hall won only lukewarm notices, however, and it was decided to return to Spain, which now had a republican government.

Xavier continued his efforts as a concert violinist and, in 1925, gave another concert in Carnegie Hall. When this also won only fair notices, he got a job with the Vincent Lopez nightclub band. From here Cugat moved to Los Angeles, where, for a time, he was a caricaturist for the Los Angeles *Times*, a movie producer, and, in 1927,

[61]

a pioneer sound dubber for some of Charlie Chaplin's movies. Soon Cugat was much in demand as a musical director, composer, and arranger of Latin American music. In the late twenties, his wife, Carmen Castillo, talked him into forming a Latin American dance band. Their first engagement was at a small Hollywood club, the Montmartre. Soon after, Cugat's band was playing as relief orchestra at the famed Cocoanut Grove.

By the thirties, Cugat had moved his group cross country to become a fixture at New York's Waldorf-Astoria, starting as a relief band. His tangos, rumbas, and congas swept the East. He soon had a nightly coast-to-coast broadcast on the NBC network. In the mid-thirties, the Cugat band was one of three on the National Biscuit Company's three-hour dance show, "Let's Dance." (The other bands were Benny Goodman's and Ken Murray's.) Among the many young Cuban musicians who played for Cugat in those years was one who became one of the greatest names on television, Desi Arnez. Others who starred with Cugat at one time or another included Dinah Shore, Buddy Clark, and Miguelito Valdes. Cugat's band soon had a long-term contract with RCA Victor.

Cugat later recorded for Columbia and MGM before returning to Victor. Through the thirties, forties, and fifties, the Cugat organization made dozens of hit records and performed in nightclubs, on radio and TV, and in many Hollywood movies. Some of Cugat's pictures were "Two Girls and a Sailor," "Bathing Beauty," and "Weekend at the Waldorf." His better-known band renditions include "Rancho Grande," "Mama Inez," "Oye Negra," "Babalu," "The Peanut Vendor," "Rhumba Rhapsody," "Taboo," and "Cui-Cui."

Cugat's marriage to Carmen Castillo ended in the mid-forties. After one short-lived marriage in between, Cugat married Abbe Lane, a tall, vivacious, and talented singer who starred with his bands in the fifties and sixties.

DAMN YANKEES: musical. Lyrics and music by Richard Adler and Jerry Ross, book by Douglass Wallop and George Abbott. Based on Wallop's novel "The Year the Yankees Lost the Pennant." New York opening: May 5, 1955, Forty-sixth Street Theatre. 1,019 performances.

"Damn Yankees" is a takeoff on the Faust legend. In the opening scene, Joe Boyd, a middle-aged fan of the lowly Washington Senators, disgustedly watches his team lose again on television. As his wife Meg and other wives in town sing, their men are glued to the TV sets "Six Months out of Every Year." Joe swears that he'd give his soul for one long-ball hitter so that the Senators could beat the New York Yankees. The Devil, in the form of a man called Applegate, immediately appears, and offers to change Joe into a young superstar in return for his soul. Joe agrees, but talks Applegate into an escape clause —Joe can back out the night before the season ends. Joe writes a farewell note to Meg, promising to return one day ("Goodbye, Old Girl").

Applegate takes his new protégé, now a twenty-two-year-old Adonis called Joe Hardy, to Washington manager Van Buren. Van Buren is telling his hapless crew that they can win, but that they need "Heart." On hand also is Gloria, a newspaper reporter. All are dubious when Applegate introduces Joe Hardy as the answer to their problem. But Van Buren finally agrees to let Hardy hit a few. Hardy hits ball after ball out of the park and plays shortstop like greased lightening. Gloria is suspicious and tries to pin down Hardy's origins. Joe puts her off by naming his wife's home town, Hannibal, Missouri, as his birthplace. Since Hardy's old shoes no longer fit him, Gloria nicknames him "Shoeless Joe from Hannibal, Mo."

To everyone's amazement, the fired-up Senators, with Hardy leading the way, not only beat the Yankees but move up in the standings from last towards the top of the league. But Joe is homesick, and despite Applegate's order to stay away from his old place, Joe rents his old room. Meg doesn't realize that Hardy is really Joe Boyd. Alarmed that Hardy might use the escape clause, Applegate calls in his number-one siren, Lola. She tries to seduce Hardy in the dressing room ("Whatever Lola Wants"). But Hardy remains faithful to Meg, while Lola begins to fall in love with him. Meanwhile, Gloria digs into Joe's past. She finds no record of any Joe Hardy in Hannibal but does find evidence that Hardy might be a ballplayer who took a bribe in the Mexican League. The league hearing takes place the night before the final day of the season.

Applegate has maneuvered things so that the pennant-deciding game with the Yankees takes place the next day. Meg clears Joe's name by coming to the hearing with some friends from Hannibal who swear that they knew Joe Hardy there. But Meg's appearance also keeps Joe from telling Applegate he wants to quit. Dejectedly, he goes to a nightclub with Lola to forget ("Two Lost Souls"). Lola drugs Applegate so that Joe can beat the Yankees the next day. As Joe makes the winning catch, he turns back into Joe Boyd. In this shape, he has escaped Applegate, and he runs out of the ballpark and home to Meg.

The original cast included Gwen Verdon, as Lola; Stephen Douglass, as Joe Hardy; Robert Shafer, as Joe Boyd; Shannon Bolin, as Meg; Ray Walston, as Applegate; Russ Brown, as Van Buren; and Rae Allen, as Gloria. The movie version starred Gwen Verdon and Ray Walston in their original roles; Tab Hunter played Joe Hardy. Other songs were "A Man Doesn't Know," "A Little Brains, a Little Talent," "Who's Got the Pain?," "The Game," "Near to You," and "Those Were the Good Old Days."

DAMONE, VIC: singer. Born Brooklyn, New York, June 12, 1928.

Vic Damone's career followed the roller-coaster pattern so common to show business. He was a star at nineteen, then went into eclipse for several years before making a successful come-back in 1960. He was born Vito Farinola. His musical ability was evident early in life; he could sing "You're Driving Me Crazy" when he was barely two. Later, while attending P.S. 163, he began singing in the choir of St. Finbar's Church.

The favorite anecdote about the early part of his career deals with his rise from usher at New York's Paramount Theatre (he started at fourteen) to star status on the stage of the same theater; it is reported that he stopped an elevator between floors to sing for passenger Perry Como. It was not an overnight transition, though. After two years as an usher, Vic began taking voice lessons. In 1945, he auditioned for "Arthur Godfrey's Talent Scouts." He won the audition, and Milton Berle liked his work and arranged a two-week engagement at what was then a leading New York nightclub, La Martinique. Later that year, he was back at the Paramount as a featured singer and also on radio with his own sustaining radio show. In 1947, he got a sponsor, Pet Milk, for a show which ran for two years. He got his biggest boost from a sensational Hollywood debut at the Mocambo nightclub. This won him many top nightclub engagements throughout the country, a steady stream of record sessions, and a movie contract with Metro-Goldwyn-Mayer. Shortly thereafter, he made his first million-selling record, "You're Breaking My Heart."

Vic Damone

Then, in 1951, Vic entered the Army. When he was discharged, in 1953, he found that things had changed. He was no longer in demand for records, nightclub engagements, or movies. "I was to blame for everything," he later wrote for Capitol Records.

I used to get all tied up when I went out on stage to sing. Actually, I didn't like what I had become. But I've since learned—the hard way—that you've got to have respect for yourself and what you're doing. . . . When you're young, it's pretty easy to let all those superlatives go to your head. And when that happens, you're in trouble.

Damone's career took a turn upward at the same place it had originally begun to skyrocket. This was the successor to the Mocambo, known in 1960 as the Cloister. He began to get more bids for club dates, and eventually signed a new contract with Capitol Records. His LP albums sold well. One of these, "Linger Awhile," released in January, 1962, was soon being played on the air more than any of his albums since 1950. Though less flamboyant than his earlier success, Damone's new career promised to be more solid.

DARIN, BOBBY: singer, actor, instrumentalist, songwriter. Born Bronx, New York, May 14,

[63]

Bobby Darin

He quit school but was unable to find work as an actor. He began writing radio commercials for local stores with a young song publisher, Donnie Kirschner. Eventually, young Darin signed a contract with Decca Records. Though he made several records, none made any impression on the public. Darin left Decca and signed with the little-known Atco company. For the next year, Darin turned out several records for Atco, but still no luck.

Then, while he was at a friend's house one evening, the friend's mother suggested jokingly that Bobby use the title "Splish, Splash, Takin' a Bath." Everyone laughed and, as a joke, Darin sat down and wrote music to the title. As the days passed, the song seemed less and less like a joke to Bobby. Finally, he decided to record it. The result was a hit, and Bobby followed this up with four more successes, including two more gold records. Then Bobby turned his hard-driving style to "Mack the Knife," the prologue song from "The Threepenny Opera." The result was a record that is still played all over the world. It led Walter Winchell to call Darin "the best since Jolson."

By the time he was twenty-three Darin was a headliner at nightclubs and hotels throughout the United States, including New York's Copacabana, where he played to standing-room-only audiences. In January, 1961, he became the youngest performer ever to star in his own network-television spectacular. He also was approached by the movies, and began work on the five films that were released in 1962—reputedly a record for the number of starring vehicles screened by an actor in one calendar year. The films were "Too Late Blues" and "Hell Is for Heroes" (Paramount), "State Fair" (Twentieth Century-Fox), "Pressure Point" (Stanley Kramer), and "If a Man Answers" (Universal-International).

In January, 1962, Darin began recording for Capitol on a long-term contract and also ended a year-long absence from public appearances with a month's engagement at the Flamingo Hotel in Las Vegas. The audience couldn't get enough of Bobby. The Flamingo management was so impressed that Bobby was signed to a four-year contract worth over a million dollars. His first engagement under the new contract, in August, 1962, broke all Flamingo records. In four weeks, forty-two thousand, seven hundred and sixty-nine patrons paid to see him, with a thousand turned away nightly.

1936. Won Grammy awards for Best New Singer and Record of the Year for 1959.

The songs "Splish, Splash" and "Mack the Knife" seem worlds apart, but the first made young Bobby Darin a teen-age idol, and the second, not too long after, led such observers as Ed Sullivan to call Darin "the greatest rhythm singer in the world." Darin not only sang "Splish, Splash," but also wrote it. It gave him his first million-selling record.

Darin had to make his way to stardom the hard way. He was born Walden Robert Cassotto (he picked his professional name from the phone book) into a family so poor that his crib was a tomato-juice-can carton. His father died before Darin was born, and he was raised by his mother and older sister Nina. Bobby grew up with a driving urge to make good. He learned to play the piano, became proficient on guitar and drums, and taught himself to dance. He finished high school and enrolled as a drama student at Hunter College in New York. But he decided he didn't have time to go through college; he was too eager to make his name known on Broadway.

The same success accompanied the new recording contract. Bobby's first record, the title song from "If a Man Answers," was released in September, 1962, and quickly made the bestseller charts. Sales of his first Capitol album, "Oh! Look at Me Now," also were brisk. In late 1962 and into 1963, it was rare that there was not at least one Darin song in the top forty in record sales in the United States. His single releases included "You're the Reason I'm Living" and "Eighteen Yellow Roses."

DAVIS, SAMMY, JR.: singer, dancer, actor, mimic. Born New York, New York, December 8, 1925.

In 1963, Sammy Davis, Jr., celebrated his thirty-third year in show business—he began his career when he was four. He was born into a well-known vaudeville family. His parents, Sam and Elvira (Sanchez) Davis, were members of the Will Mastin vaudeville act "Holiday and Dixieland." (Mastin was an adopted uncle of the Davises'.) In fact, young Sammy spent his first birthday in the dressing room of the Hippodrome.

At four, Sammy became part of the act. In 1931, he was already in the movies in an Ethel Waters picture called "Rufus Jones for President." The Depression made Mastin cut his troupe to five, including Sammy and his father. As Sammy grew up, the group shrank to a trio—Mastin plus the older and younger Davis. The going was rough, and they were often stranded and broke, but somehow they stayed in show business. During this period, they played Michigan and were seen by the late great performer "Bojangles" Bill Robinson. Robinson realized Sammy's potential and took him under his wing for many months, teaching him all he knew.

The trio kept on playing small nightclubs and theaters across the country until 1943, when Sammy went into the service. He kept on learning about the theater by writing, producing, and directing camp shows. In late 1945, he was discharged and rejoined his father and Mastin. The group was still largely unknown, but an engagement at Slapsie Maxie's in Hollywood was to change that. They came in as almost total strangers, but the audience response was so great that they were signed for a return date as headliners. A 1947 two-week engagement with Mickey Rooney at a Los Angeles theater added to their luster. The Mastin Trio stayed on for six months. Now in demand, they starred with many famous

Sammy Davis, Jr.

performers, including Jimmy Dorsey in Columbus, Ohio, Frank Sinatra at the Capitol Theatre, New York, and, in 1950, with Jack Benny and Dennis Day.

In April, 1954, Sammy debuted at New York's Copacabana and was soon playing to turn-away crowds. Decca Records quickly signed him, and his first two albums became best sellers. These were "Starring Sammy Davis, Jr.," which included imitations of such stars as Bing Crosby, Frank Sinatra, Martin and Lewis, and Jimmy Durante. The other was a collection of ballads and rhythm songs, "Just for Lovers."

That year, while playing Las Vegas, Sammy was called to Hollywood for a recording session. On the way, he was in an automobile crash that cost him his left eye. But Sammy came back a few weeks later to score a major hit at Ciro's in Hollywood. When he appeared with his eye patch, he received a ten-minute standing ovation. From here he was wildly welcomed by enthusiastic audiences at such places as the Copa City in Miami Beach and again at the Copacabana. Television appearances became common-place on such shows as Ed Sullivan's, Milton Berle's, and "The Colgate Comedy Hour."

His first Broadway musical, "Mr. Wonderful," opened at the Broadway Theatre on March 22, 1956. The critics turned thumbs down, but through word of mouth and interviews on the Barry Gray radio show and Steve Allen's NBC network TV show, word got around that Davis's performance was worth watching, and the show became a hit. The score provided Sammy with some of his best-known songs, including "Mr. Wonderful," "Too Close for Comfort," and "Without You."

After this, besides the usual many nightclub engagements and TV guest appearances, Sammy once more became a movie performer. In 1959, he was in "Anna Lucasta," with Eartha Kitt; in 1960, "Ocean's 11," with Frank Sinatra and Dean Martin; and in 1962, Sammy played Sportin' Life in the movie version of Gershwin's "Porgy and Bess." In 1964, he appeared as the streetsinger (who sings "Mack the Knife") in the movie version of "The Threepenny Opera."

October, '64, saw Sammy return to Broadway playing the title role in the new musical "Golden Boy." In general, he won high critical praise for his work in this adaptation of the Clifford Odets play.

DAY, DORIS: singer, actress. Born Cincinnati, Ohio, April 3, 1924.

But for a childhood accident, Doris Day might have been a dancer. Her father, William Kapple-hoff, was a classical musician and voice teacher in Cincinnati. When Doris Kapplehoff was born, her father and mother, if they thought of a career for her at all, thought of that of a classical musician. But at Hessler Dancing School in Cincin-nati, she proved to be an extremely talented dancer. She took lessons continuously during her public-school years, and when she was twelve, toured with the professional Fanchon and Marco stage show.

In Hamilton, Ohio, young Doris was in a car that was hit by a train. Doris was in and out of hospitals for fourteen months as doctors strove to mend a severely broken leg. To keep her spirits up during the ordeal, she began to take singing lessons with Cincinnati teacher Grace Raine. After regaining her ability to walk, Doris decided that she wanted to concentrate on singing instead of dancing. Her teacher was impressed with her voice and suggested that the now seventeen-year-old Doris sing on a local station—without

Doris Day

pay—to gain experience and poise. Band leader Barney Rapp heard the program and asked Doris to appear for twenty-five dollars at a nightclub he owned. He didn't like the sound of the name Doris Kapplehoff. Her most popular singing number had been "Day after Day," and Rapp renamed her Doris Day.

Soon she began to perform on pickup dates with some of the major bands, including Bob Crosby's and Fred Waring's. Les Brown hired her on a full-time basis, and for three years Doris was his main vocalist. One of the best-selling records of those years was a Doris Day and Les Brown rendition of "Sentimental Journey."

During an appearance at the Little Club in New York, she was observed by film director Michael Curtiz. He liked her bearing as well as her singing, and asked her to take a screen test. The results confirmed his opinion. She was signed by Warner Brothers and appeared opposite Jack Carson in "Romance on the High Seas." Doris remained with Warner's for eight years. In early 1954, she left to do her first movie for Metro-Goldwyn-Mayer. The picture was "Love Me or Leave Me," a biography of Ruth Etting, a famous popular singer of the twenties. Next came Para-mount and such films as "Pillow Talk," "Midnight Lace," "Please Don't Eat the Daisies," "Lover Come Back," "Touch of Mink," and "Jumbo." Her work in "Pillow Talk" won her an Academy Award nomination for Best Actress of the Year for 1961. The previous year, she was voted Star of the Year by the Theatre owners of America and Most Popular Actress in the World by the Hollywood Foreign Press Association. The mid-sixties found her firmly established as one of the ten biggest box-office draws in movies.

Throughout her long film reign, Doris continued to turn out best-selling records, including a number of gold records, such as "Sentimental Journey," "Que Sera Sera," and "Mister Banjo."

DEMONSTRATION RECORD: record-industry term for a record made to demonstrate a new song to music publishers or record companies or both. (See also *Lead sheet*.)

It is very rare today for a songwriter to go to a music publisher or record company and play his new song. One reason is that some writers are one-finger performers. But more important, the publisher, performer, or record company may want time to consider the composition, play it over, perhaps ask other people's opinion. The solution, in most cases, is for the writer to make a demonstration record (and a lead sheet). The demonstration record gives what the writer feels is as close as possible to a finished, professional performance.

To do this, the writer hires a vocalist (unless the piece is an instrumental) and some musicians to make a record. At one time, these demonstration records were fairly simple affairs; there was little emphasis on involved arrangements or special effects, such as echo chambers. Now, though, the demonstration record may call for as much effort as a final record for public distribution once did. Even the professional songwriter must compete with a great many other writers for the ear of the performer, publisher, or recording-company artists-and-repertoire man; it requires something special to attract their attention.

DENNIS, MATT: composer, pianist. Born Seattle, Washington, February 11, 1914.

A performer is only as good as his material. In the great days of the big bands, such vocalists as Frank Sinatra, Connie Haines, and Jo Stafford were able to score heavily with such songs as "Everything Happens to Me," "Let's Get Away From It All," "Violets for Your Furs," and "The Night We Called It a Day," all of which have become standards. Their composer, a performer in his own right, is Matt Dennis.

Dennis was born into a famous vaudeville family. His mother was part of the Five Musical Lovelands. His family later settled in San Rafael, California, where Matt attended public elementary and high schools. As he grew up, Dennis studied piano with his family and with professional musicians. He played the piano in high school and led school dance bands. He also began writing his own songs. Once out of high school, Matt moved to Hollywood. In the period just before World War II, he was vocal coach and arranger for many national favorites, including Martha Tilton, Jo Stafford, the Pied Pipers, and Margaret Whiting, and wrote arrangements for Tommy Dorsey's band. Matt moved to New York, where he composed songs for Frank Sinatra and Connie Haines, as well as for Jo Stafford. Dennis's first published songs were "Love Turns Winter to Spring" and "Relax."

World War II found Dennis in the Army Air Force. During his three-year tour of duty, he spent most of his time in the Radio Production Unit, arranging material, recording service programs, and entertaining at base hospitals. For the last six months of his service career, Matt was a member of the Glenn Miller Air Force Orchestra.

After the war, Dennis started his own solo-piano act. He appeared at many major night spots and on television shows. In the nineteen-fifties, Dennis appeared several times on the Steve Allen and Patti Page shows and on NBC's "Today." For one season, Dennis had his own television show on NBC. He continued to compose and also to turn out albums of his top hits for several major record companies, including RCA Victor, Capitol, and Kapp. In 1954, he wrote the official song, "The Spirit of Christmas," for the National Tuberculosis Association's Christmas Seal campaign. Dennis also appeared in films, including two movies with Ida Lupino, and played dramatic parts in the "Johnny Ringo" TV series.

Dennis's credits include such songs as "Angel Eyes," "Show Me the Way To Get Out of This World," "It's Over, It's Over, It's Over," and "Will You Still Be Mine?"

DENNY, MARTIN: band leader, pianist, composer, arranger. Born New York, New York, April 10, 1915.

The exotic sounds of the Pacific islands awoke the wanderlust in millions of radio listeners in

Martin Denny

the late nineteen-fifties and the sixties. These effects, which included bird calls, the pounding of the surf, and weird ringing or tinkling noises, were the result of the marriage of some aspects of jazz with the rhythmic music of Hawaii.

The man responsible for this music, first featured in his album "Exotica I," was Martin Denny. By the time he was ten, Denny was studying classical piano and was thought to be something of a prodigy. When Martin reached high-school age, his family moved to Los Angeles. Denny completed high school there, and enrolled as a premedical student at the University of Southern California. While attending college, he and five other boys formed a jazz group to play local school dates.

In 1931, after two years at USC, Martin and the group quit to tour South America. For four years after this, the group played American jazz in most major South American cities. In the mid-thirties, Martin returned to the United States, where he worked as a pianist with West Coast bands.

World War II interrupted Denny's routine for four years. He returned to the Coast to study music with Wesley La Violette and to play the piano in local nightclubs. After a few years, Denny played a six-month engagement as solo pianist at Don the Beachcomber's, a Hawaiian restaurant and cocktail lounge. Denny fell in love with Hawaii, and the six-month engagement grew to a long-range proposition. He formed a jazz trio that soon had an islandwide reputation. They became a permanent attraction at the Shell Bar in the new Hawaiian Village.

Denny added a fourth musician, and the new group began using the exotic sounds that became the Denny trademark. Such instruments as special glasses, small cymbals, and bamboo sticks were used in the new arrangements. Just when Denny felt that he was a fixture in Hawaii, a stateside visitor, Arnold Mills, heard the music and persuaded Denny to return to the West Coast for a tour under his management. The tour was extremely successful, and Liberty Records signed Denny to an exclusive contract.

Denny insisted that any contract leave him free to spend at least half of every year in Hawaii. He was also appointed Liberty's artists-and-repertoire representative in Hawaii. By the end of 1962, he had made sixteen record albums. As of 1963, his group consisted of himself (who played the piano and celesta in addition to composing and arranging), Hagood Hardy (vibraharp, marimba, and other percussion), Buddy Fo (bird calls, bongo, congas, and other percussion), Harvey Ragsdale (bass and marimbula), and Frank Kim (congas and other percussion).

DE ROSE, PETER: composer, author, radio artist. Born New York, New York, March 10, 1900; died April 24, 1953.

Peter De Rose attended New York City public schools. He showed a great interest in music from an early age and was encouraged by an older sister who was a professional singer. De Rose became an accomplished pianist, but his first entry into the music field was as a publisher's stockroom clerk. After working for several publishing houses, he became a staff pianist and composer. As a staff composer and later as a freelance artist, he turned out a wide range of music, including Broadway scores, popular songs, and piano works. Some of the shows to which he contributed music were the "Earl Carroll Vanities," "Burlesque," and "Yes, Yes, Yvette."

In 1923, De Rose and his wife, a talented

young singer named May Singhi Breen, began a career on radio that was to last until 1939. During this period, De Rose wrote many successful songs, including "When Your Hair Has Turned to Silver," "Muddy Water," "Somebody Loves You," "Have You Ever Been Lonely?," "Wagon Wheels," "Lilacs in the Rain," "I Hear America Singing," and "Deep Purple."

"Deep Purple" originally was the theme of a piano solo composed in 1934. In 1939, Mitchell Parish added words, and the song became a best seller. De Rose wrote many other notable piano works, including "The Starlit Hour," "Moonlight Mood," "Maytime in Vienna," "Royal Blue," and "The American Waltz." During World War II, he wrote several songs on service themes, including "God of Battles" and "Song of the Seabees."

DE SYLVA, GEORGE GARD (BUDDY): lyricist, composer, librettist, producer. Born New York, New York, January 27, 1895; died Los Angeles, California, July 11, 1950.

There's nothing unusual about a two-man songwriting team, but a trio is a rarity. In 1956, in "The Best Things in Life Are Free," the movies celebrated one of the few successful three-man collaborations. The title song was one of the many hits of this team, well known to playgoers of the late nineteen-twenties as de Sylva, Brown, and Henderson. Buddy de Sylva, the hub of the trio, was a man of many talents. After the team dissolved in 1930, he went on to make his mark as a producer and writer in movies and on Broadway.

Most of Buddy's formative years were spent in California. He came close to becoming a professional performer before he reached public-school age after he appeared in a song-and-dance act at the Los Angeles Grand Opera House. His grandfather stepped in to prevent it, however, and make sure Buddy had a normal upbringing. While Buddy attended Citrus Union High School in Azusa, his interest in show business awakened and he was active in school plays. He entered the University of Southern California in 1915. Buddy became interested in songwriting, and when some of his lyrics came to the attention of Al Jolson, his college career came to an end.

Jolson introduced his protégé's first song, "'N' Everything." He also sang de Sylva's first big hit, "Avalon," in the New York show "Sinbad." With royalties rolling in, de Sylva moved to New York and became a staff writer for Remick's music house, which employed some of the best young talent in Tin Pan Alley. He served his apprenticeship writing with many of the most famous names in popular music. In 1919, he wrote lyrics for some of George Gershwin's music for the show "La La Lucille." He worked on many other songs with Gershwin, including "Somebody Loves Me" and the scores for several "George White's Scandals." Some of de Sylva's other lyrics of the early twenties were "Look for the Silver Lining" for Jerome Kern, "A Kiss in the Dark" for Victor Herbert, and "April Showers" for Louis Silvers. De Sylva also worked on such other Jolson hits as "California, Here I Come."

When Gershwin withdrew from the "Scandals" after the 1924 edition, composer Ray Henderson was called in. Henderson had worked with lyricist Lew Brown. As de Sylva was already under contract for the show, it was decided to have the three men work together. They found that they had something as a trio that was far better than any two of them had. They soon started their own publishing house. For the rest of the twenties, shows featuring their songs were regular Broadway occurrences. Besides providing scores for the "Scandals" of 1924, 1925, and 1928, they worked on such hit musicals as "Good News" (1927), "Hold Everything" (1928), "Follow Thru" (1929), and "Flying High" (1930). Their hit songs for these included "The Birth of the Blues," "Black Bottom," "The Varsity Drag," "The Best Things in Life Are Free," "Good News," "You're the Cream in My Coffee," "Button Up Your Overcoat," and "Red Hot Chicago." The boys also worked on some film scores, including the songs "Sonny Boy" and "It All Depends on You."

In 1929, the sale of the team's publishing firm to a movie company led to de Sylva's increasing interest in film work. He produced many of Hollywood's most famous products, including such Shirley Temple classics as "The Little Colonel," "Poor Little Rich Girl," and "The Littlest Rebel." Some of the other de Sylva productions were "Captain January," "Rage of Paris," "Bachelor Mother," "Sunny Side Up," and "Just Imagine."

De Sylva still found time to work as a producer and librettist on major Broadway shows. In 1932, he worked on the book and helped produce the Ethel Merman-Jack Haley success "Take a Chance." Later, he capped his Broadway career by producing and in some cases providing part of the book for three of the theater's brightest musical hits. Two featured scores by Cole Porter: "Du Barry Was a Lady" (1939) and "Panama Hattie" (1940); and the third, "Louisiana Purchase," a score by Irving Berlin.

DIETZ, HOWARD: lyricist, librettist, author, producer. Born New York, New York, September 8, 1896.

In his long and varied career, Howard Dietz tried his hand successfully at writing everything from advertising copy to lyrics to juvenile books. But probably his most notable achievement was to aid in the rebirth of the revue by means of his collaboration with Arthur Schwartz in the late twenties and early thirties.

Dietz was raised in New York, attending Townsend Harris Hall and Columbia University. While attending Columbia just before the United States entered World War I, he contributed light verse to such well-known newspaper columns as Franklin P. Adams's "Conning Tower" and Don Marquis's "Sun Dial." He also won a five-hundred-dollar prize in an advertising-copy contest sponsored by Fatima cigarettes. This led to his gaining an ad-agency job. The agency handled Goldwyn Pictures Corporation, and Dietz was assigned to the account. He devised the company symbol, Leo the Lion, and its slogan, "Ars Gratia Artis."

Dietz served in the Navy during World War I. Afterwards, he returned to advertising, doing ad and publicity work for several movie firms. In 1924, he became director of advertising and publicity for Metro-Goldwyn-Mayer, a position he held for more than thirty years, rising to vice-president. In 1923, Dietz had added a new string to his bow by writing lyrics for an Arthur Samuels melody. Called "Alibi Baby," it was a hit in W. C. Fields's stage success "Poppy." In the next few years, Dietz collaborated on several Broadway shows, including "Dear Sir" with Jerome Kern (1924) and the revue "Merry-Go-Round" (1927). After the latter, Arthur Schwartz wanted to collaborate with Dietz, but Dietz preferred to work with more experienced composers. In 1929, they agreed to work together on the revue "The Little Show." With such performers as Clifton Webb, Fred Allen, and Libby Holman and such songs as "I Guess I'll Have To Change My Plan" and "Moanin' Low" (music by Ralph Rainger), the show was a major hit. A "Second Little Show" in 1930 failed. That same year, Schwartz and Dietz worked on another successful revue, "Three's a Crowd," for

which they provided "Something To Remember You By." In 1931, they turned out a far more memorable score for "The Band Wagon." (See separate listing.) Their next revue, "Flying Colors," was a step down, but it included "Alone Together," "A Shine on Your Shoes," and "Louisiana Hayride."

In 1934, the team tried its hand at a book musical, "Revenge with Music." The show included "You and the Night and the Music" and "If There Is Someone Lovelier than You." In 1935, they turned out the revue "At Home Abroad" (which contained "Love Is a Dancing Thing") and in 1937 the musical "Between the Devil" (which contained "By Myself," "Triplets," and "I See Your Face before Me"). Neither was too well received, and Dietz and Schwartz dissolved their partnership for over a decade.

Dietz concentrated on his work for MGM and also wrote material for radio programs and later for television. In 1944, Dietz provided book and lyrics for "Sadie Thompson" (music by Vernon Duke), which included "The Love I Long For." In 1948, Schwartz and Dietz once more teamed up to provide the score for "Inside U. S. A.," which starred Beatrice Lillie and Jack Haley and included the songs "Haunted Heart," "Rhode Island Is Famous for You," and "Blue Grass." Dietz turned his hand successfully to another field in 1950, providing English books and lyrics (with Garson Kanin) for the Metropolitan Opera production of "Der Fledermaus." In the sixties, Schwartz and Dietz wrote the scores for "The Gay Life" and "Jenny."

DISC JOCKEY: radio announcer who plays records and comments between them.

Sometimes the disc jockey actually places the record on the turntable and puts the needle down to play it; other times the DJ just provides commentary, and it's the studio engineer who actually plays the record (or, in some cases, the magnetic tape).

The DJ became a nationwide phenomenon after World War II, though disc-jockey shows had been pioneered in the early nineteen-thirties by such people as Martin Bloch with his "Make Believe Ballroom" in New York and Al Jarvis and Joe Yocum with a similarly named show in Los Angeles. Instead of records, many late-evening shows of the thirties and early forties broadcast nightclub dance bands.

The advent of nationwide television after World War II changed this. TV became the major medium for dramatic, comedy, and variety shows. Dance bands faded out, due to such factors as excise taxes on entertainment and higher costs of traveling with large organizations. As a result, radio turned to playing musical recordings. Disc-jockey shows, along with some new programs, took over day and night radio programing across the country. Some of this even spread to TV, with such shows as Dick Clark's "American Bandstand" combining records with teen-age dancing.

DIXIELAND: the original style of jazz. (See *Jazz, Ragtime.*)

Dixieland jazz began in New Orleans, the product of the many small brass marching bands favored by the Negroes for special events, such as holidays and funerals. After a time, the bands also performed indoors at nightclubs and brothels. By 1916 or so, Dixieland moved out of New Orleans to become popular in such cities as Chicago and Kansas City and eventually in most major cities of the Western world. After achieving great popularity during the nineteen-twenties, Dixieland yielded to other forms of jazz, such as boogiewoogie, swing, and progressive jazz. Many of the greatest Dixieland musicians had to find nonmusical jobs during the nineteen-thirties. By the forties, Dixieland had begun something of a comeback, and is still popular.

Dixieland music has four beats to the measure. The original Dixieland was improvised—a theme would be selected, and the band would play around it; the number never sounded the same twice. Much of today's Dixieland is arranged to sound improvised.

DOMINO, ANTOINE (FATS), JR.: pianist, composer. Born New Orleans, Louisiana, February 26, 1928.

Fats Domino is one of the most successful of all rock-'n'-roll artists. In eleven years, he sold some fifty million single records, three million albums, and won seventeen gold records. At the time, only two other performers, Bing Crosby and Elvis Presley, could show a greater total of gold records.

An accident in a bedspring factory where Fats worked during his teens almost ended his career before it began. A heavy spring gashed his hand, and doctors despaired of his ever playing the piano again. But Domino exercised his fingers day after day, until finally he was able to use the hand once more.

Domino's father liked to play the violin, but Fats was the only one of nine children who was musically inclined. A cousin left an old piano with the Dominos, and at the age of five, Fats could pick out tunes with one finger. Later, an uncle who had played with local bands taught him to play chords. The rest of Domino's musical education was his own. When Fats reached his teens, he began playing for pennies in "honky-tonks" (the Southern slang term for cheap roadside nightclubs) on weekends. At nineteen, he got a band job (and also got married). The job lasted two weeks. Fats quit and started his own band, earning himself three dollars a week for a three-night week at the Hideaway Club in New Orleans. Fats began to work days at a lumber mill to support his family, but Lew Chudd, the head of Imperial Records, at that time a new company, heard that there was a great pianist and composer in this small club. Chudd listened to him, and signed him to a contract on the spot.

Domino's first record for Imperial was a gold one, "Fat Man." He soon came up with many more, most of which he wrote himself. In a short time, Domino was in demand for appearances at nightclubs, on radio and television, and finally in the movies.

Of his own rock-'n'-roll compositions, he reported that most of them were based on everyday occurrences in his life. The idea for "I'm Walkin'" came after his car broke down, "Poor Me" from a particularly blue afternoon, and "Ain't That a Shame" from a remark made by a woman at seeing another woman slap her child.

DONALDSON, WALTER: composer, lyricist. Born Brooklyn, New York, February 15, 1893; died Santa Monica, California, July 15, 1947.

Though his name is little-known today, Walter Donaldson was one of the most prolific and successful composers in popular-music history. He grew up in Brooklyn. His mother was a pianist and music teacher and saw that Walter learned to play the piano. By the time he was in high school, he had begun to compose. After leaving school, however, he worked in a Wall Street brokerage. It wasn't long before he had gotten a more congenial position as pianist for a music-publishing firm. By 1915, he had written his first hits, "Back Home in Tennessee," "You'd Never Know That Old Home Town of Mine," and "We'll Have a Jubilee in My Old Kentucky Home." In 1918, he wrote "The Daughter of Rosie O'Grady."

With the onset of World War I, Donaldson devoted the better part of nineteen months to entertaining soldiers. During his visits to various camps, he became friendly with another composer of note, Irving Berlin. After the war, Donaldson became a staff writer for Berlin's music-publishing company, where he remained for a decade. Two of his early hits with Berlin were "How Ya Gonna Keep 'Em Down on the Farm?" (1919) and the Al Jolson favorite "My Mammy" (1921). In 1922, Donaldson met Gus Kahn, a young lyricist from Chicago who had made a name for himself in the Midwest. They celebrated their partnership with two hits of 1922, "My Buddy" and "Carolina in the Morning." The two worked together off and on for close to twenty years. Some of Donaldson's other songs with Kahn were "Yes, Sir, That's My Baby" and "That Certain Party" (both in 1925). Donaldson wrote with other lyricists as well and also began to write his own lyrics, turning out such numbers as "My Blue Heaven" and "At Sundown" (1927), "Makin' Whoopee" and "Love Me or Leave Me" (1928), and "You're Driving Me Crazy" (1930).

In 1928, Donaldson left Berlin to become a partner in a new publishing firm, Donaldson, Douglas and Gumble. In the early thirties, Donaldson went to Hollywood to do the score for "Whoopee." From then until his death, he was a regular worker in movies. His sometime collaborator in some of the films of the late thirties was Gus Kahn. Over the years, he also worked with many other top Hollywood lyricists. With Harold Adamson, for example, he wrote "It's Been So Long" and "Did I Remember" (both in 1936). With Johnny Mercer, he provided such film hits as "Could Be" (1938) and "Mister Meadowlark" (1940).

Among the films Donaldson scored or wrote songs for were "The Prize Fighter and the Lady" (1933); "Kid Millions" and "Hollywood Party" (1934); "Reckless" (1935); "Piccadilly Jim," "Suzy," and "The Great Ziegfeld" (1936); "Broadway Serenade" (1940); "Panama Hattie" (1942); and "Follow the Boys" (1944).

DORSEY, JAMES (JIMMY): band leader, instrumentalist. Born Shenandoah, Pennsylvania, February 29, 1904; died June 12, 1957.

Jimmy Dorsey's band leader father taught Jimmy to play the cornet at eight and the alto saxophone at ten. Jimmy taught himself to play the clarinet. As he grew up, Jimmy often took part in his father's brass-band concerts and parades. The band would provide music for holiday celebrations or for the local grudge baseball rivalry between Mount Carmel, Mahanoy City, and surrounding towns.

Off and on, as they passed through their teens, Jimmy and his brother Tommy joined forces to assemble local dance bands. In 1920, they formed the Dorsey Novelty Band, which disbanded after a lukewarm reception in Baltimore in 1922. While in Baltimore, they made one of the first radio broadcasts in that area. Soon after, Jimmy played clarinet and saxophone with one of the better-known hot dance bands of the day, the Scranton Sirens. Tommy joined the band as well. From 1922 to 1934, Jimmy played with one after another of the most famous orchestra leaders in the nation. His credits read like a *Who's Who* of popular music of the twenties—including the California Ramblers, Paul Whiteman, Jean Goldkette, Rudy Vallee, and Victor Young.

The facet of his career for which he is best known—his work as a first-rate band leader—began in 1933. Jimmy and Tommy joined once more as the Dorsey Brothers Orchestra. The era of the big dance band—of swing (and the Depression)—was on, and the Dorseys were musically right in line with popular taste. Though their band was successful, the brothers had different ideas of what kind of music they should play (Jimmy preferred to play it sweeter), as well as other personality clashes. They separated in 1934, and two all-time great orchestras—instead of one—was the result.

Throughout the thirties and forties, Jimmy Dorsey's band was featured coast to coast in nightclubs and movies and on radio. Jimmy popularized some of the most famous ballads of those years, such as "Maria Elena," "Amapola," "A New Shade of Blue," and "I Hear a Rhapsody." With the decline of the dance band after World War II, Jimmy drifted away from one-night stands and regular bands, preferring to use pickup sidemen. In 1953, though, Jimmy and Tommy joined forces for a time in a new band, the Fabulous Dorseys.

The death within a year of both the Dorseys signified the beginning of the end of an era.

DORSEY, THOMAS (TOMMY): band leader, instrumentalist. Born Mahanoy Plain, Pennsylvania, November 10, 1905; died November 26, 1956.

Before World War I, the local German band was an important part of American small-town life. In Shenandoah, Pennsylvania, such a band could be seen marching up and down Main Street on many special occasions. The band, led

Tommy Dorsey

before dissension broke out between the brothers. Besides the Dorseys, it included such famous names as drummer Ray McKinley, trombonist Glenn Miller, and vocalist Bob Crosby. When the split occurred, Jimmy and most of the band headed for California. Tommy stayed in New York and formed a new band in 1935.

The band opened at the French Casino in New York. This was followed by five months of highly successful one-night stands. Then Tommy filled in as summer replacement for Fred Waring on network radio. The country found a new band favorite. All during the swing era, Tommy's trombone and a steady succession of singers and bandsmen who were soon to become famous were heard on records and radio and at local dances from one end of the nation to the other. Among his vocalists were Frank Sinatra, Jo Stafford, Connie Haines, and the Pied Pipers. Tommy pushed many songs, such as "Marie" and "I'll Never Smile Again," to the top of the national song parade. But the one always associated with him was the song that became his theme, "I'm Getting Sentimental over You."

Before his death, Tommy had shifted away from a fixed band organization to working as a disc jockey and playing occasional pickup dates in some major cities. (In 1953, though, he joined brother Jimmy for a time in a new band, the Fabulous Dorseys.) Tommy was a success as a disc jockey. In the fifties, his transcribed program was popular not just in the United States but in Europe, Australia, and South America.

by Thomas Dorsey, Sr., had two very special horn players—Dorsey's sons Jimmy and Tommy. Dorsey, Sr., showed his namesake how to play just about every instrument in the band. But there was one that Tommy balked at. When he was twelve, his father gave him a trombone. Tommy didn't like the instrument at first. His dad insisted, and the trombone eventually became Tommy Dorsey's trademark.

By 1918, Tommy and Jimmy were leading bands at local dances and affairs. After leaving high school, Tommy worked for a while as a delivery boy for a meat market at sixteen dollars a week. While he was doing this, Jimmy worked in a coal mine. After the Dorsey Brothers Novelty Band, formed in 1920, folded in 1922, their father suggested that the boys take time off and polish their musical skills to a more professional degree. This they did—and it paid off in a long series of jobs with the most famous bandsmen in the country.

In 1933, they assembled the Dorsey Brothers Orchestra, which lasted for less than two years

DUBIN, AL: lyricist. Born Zurich, Switzerland, June 10, 1891; died New York, New York, February 11, 1945. Won Academy Award for Best Song of 1935 ("Lullaby of Broadway").

Al Dubin was brought to the United States when he was two years old. He went to public school and then to Perkiomen Seminary in Pennsylvania. At Perkiomen, he began to write song lyrics, which led him to become a staff writer for various New York music publishers after leaving school. In the years before World War I, he also gained a reputation with performers as a good source of vaudeville material. In 1916, he wrote his first song hit with composer Rennie Carmack, "Twas Only an Irishman's Dream." Dubin found his immediate ideas of glory to be a dream, however, for he soon was reduced to working as a singing waiter in a bar. He left this atmosphere by enlisting in the Seventy-seventh Division, with which he went overseas (and for which he wrote several songs).

[73]

When the war was over, Dubin came back and began his songwriting career in earnest. In the twenties, he wrote with many composers, turning out such hits as "Just a Girl That Men Forget" with Joe Garren, "A Cup of Coffee, A Sandwich and You" with Joseph Meyer, "The Lonesomest Girl in Town" and "My Dream of the Big Parade" with Jimmy McHugh, and "Memories of France" and "Halfway to Heaven" with J. Russell Robinson.

In the late twenties, Dubin was one of the first writers hired by the new talking pictures. With Joe Burke, he turned out such early film successes as "Tip-Toe Through the Tulips," "Painting the Clouds with Sunshine," and "The Kiss Waltz." In the early thirties, he was teamed with a new partner, Harry Warren, with whom he achieved the closest collaboration of his career. Throughout the thirties, they were one of the most prolific teams in Hollywood, turning out as many as sixty songs a year. Their efforts for 1932 and 1933 included "Keep Young and Beautiful," "The Gold Diggers Song—We're in the Money," "Forty-Second Street," "Shuffle Off to Buffalo," "You're Getting To Be a Habit with Me," and "The Boulevard of Broken Dreams." In 1934 and 1935, a few of their hits were "I Only Have Eyes for You," "About a Quarter to Nine," "The Little Things You Used To Do," and the 1935 Oscar winner, "Lullaby of Broadway." Some of their songs from 1936 to 1939 were "I'll Sing You a Thousand Love Songs," "With Plenty of Money and You," "Remember Me?," "Love Is Where You Find It" (with an assist from Johnny Mercer on the lyrics), and "September in the Rain."

In 1939, Dubin and Warren went their separate ways. Dubin wrote with many other top composers over the next five years. With Jimmy McHugh, for example, he worked on the film "Streets of Paris," which included "South American Way." Dubin achieved his last hit after his death. This was "Feudin' and Fightin'," written with Burton Lane for the 1944 show "Laffing Room Only." Thanks to singer Dorothy Shay, the song became a hit in 1947, two years after Dubin's death.

ELLINGTON, EDWIN KENNEDY (DUKE): composer, band leader, pianist. Born Washington, D.C., April 29, 1899.

Few in contemporary musical history have contributed more than Duke Ellington. Richard O. Boyer wrote in *The New Yorker* magazine for June 24, 1944:

Duke Ellington

Sometimes writing a song in no more than fifteen minutes and sometimes finishing concert pieces only a few hours before their performance, he has composed around twelve hundred pieces, many of them of such worth that Stokowski, Grainger, Stravinsky, and Milhaud have called him one of the greatest modern composers.

Duke took to the piano at an early age. He composed his first song, a version of a Carolina shout, when he was fifteen. After graduating from high school in 1917, Duke gave up a scholarship to study commercial art at Pratt Institute in Brooklyn to go into the band business. His band was soon playing at many Washington night spots.

In 1923, the band went to New York. The going was rough, and the outfit disbanded, Duke returning to Washington. But then word came of a job at New York's Hollywood Club. Duke hurriedly rounded up his crew and headed back to New York. The band stayed in the Hollywood Club (which became the Kentucky Club) for almost four years. Here Duke began composing in earnest. In 1927, his output included "East St. Louis Toodle-oo," "Black and Tan Fantasy," and "Birmingham Breakdown." In 1927, too, Duke met Irving Mills, who became manager of the Ellington organization and also provided the lyrics for some of Duke's great compositions. Mills was one of the owners of Mills Music, and much of Ellington's output was published by the firm.

Mills booked Ellington into the Cotton Club in Harlem. While there, Duke wrote such all-time standards as "Mood Indigo," "Creole Rhapsody," and "Sophisticated Lady." In the years that followed, Ellington became an institution in the United States and overseas. He made several triumphal European tours, the first in 1933. During this period, he wrote such songs as "Solitude," "Prelude to a Kiss," "I'm Beginnin' To See the Light," "Caravan," "Concerto for Cootie" (popularized in 1943 as "Do Nothin' Till You Hear from Me"), and "New York City Blues."

Ellington became a legend early in his lifetime. His music ranges over a variety of styles. He has been called a jazz composer, but, he says, "I don't write jazz, I write Negro folk music." His work in jazz and popular music has already achieved lasting fame. It's not unlikely that, in the future, his larger works—such as "New World A-comin'," "Echoes of Harlem," "Harlem Suite," and "Such Sweet Thunder"—may become part of the concert-hall repertoire as well.

EMBRACEABLE YOU: song (1930). Words by Ira Gershwin, music by George Gershwin.

This most durable of great standards was introduced in the show "Girl Crazy" in 1930. It was written, however, for an earlier, unproduced musical. The earlier production was to have been called "East is West" and was to star Marilyn Miller and the comedy team of Clark and McCullough. It was to have been a major undertaking of Florenz Ziegfeld, the legendary impresario of musical comedy.

The Gershwins were hard at work on the score for "East Is West" in the summer of 1928, and one of the numbers they had written was "Embraceable You." But then the volatile Ziegfeld read a J. P. McEvoy novel called "Show Girl" and decided to do this first. As Ira Gershwin wrote in "Lyrics on Several Occasions" (New York: Alfred A. Knopf, 1959): "In his hypnotically persuasive manner (always great charm until a contract was signed) Ziegfeld managed to have us postpone the operetta and start on *Show Girl*." But "Show Girl" was a costly flop, and "East Is West" was also shelved.

"Girl Crazy" marked the rise to prominence of Ginger Rogers. In the show she played Molly Gray, the postmistress of Custerville, an Arizona hamlet. Allen Kearns played a New York playboy who wants to marry her. "Embraceable You," as a duet, marked his success with the previously

intractable Molly. It was a hit in the show and has since become a universal favorite.

Commenting on the lyrics, Ira Gershwin noted that it is unusual for a popular song "in that some of its rhymes are four-syllable ones: "embraceable you—irreplaceable you," and (in a reprise) "silk and laceable you"; 'tipsy in me—gypsy in me.'" Also there is a trick four-syllable one in: "glorify love—'Encore!' if I love."[*]

EMMY: award given by the National Academy of Television Arts and Sciences for television excellence.

The awards were begun in the late nineteen-forties by the Academy of Television Arts and Sciences. In 1957, this group was superceded by the newly organized National Academy, which continued the award policy. The awards are basically for such categories as performance and program excellence, though there have been musical awards from time to time. In the early years, awards were given for best male and best female singer, but these were eliminated in the late nineteen-fifties. Other awards have been given under such headings as "Outstanding Achievement in the Field of Music" and "Outstanding Achievement in Original Music Composed for TV."

EVANS, RAY: lyricist. Born Salamanca, New York, February 4, 1915. Won Academy Award for Best Song of 1948 ("Buttons and Bows"), 1950 ("Mona Lisa"), and 1956 ("Whatever Will Be, Will Be"). (See also *Livingston, Jay*.)

There are coincidences in the lives of the members of one of Hollywood's most successful songwriting teams. Lyricist Ray Evans and composer Ray Evans were born the same year, have rhyming first names, and were at the top of their classes in high school and college.

Ray was brought up in a small town in upstate New York, midway between Buffalo and Jamestown. He played saxophone and clarinet in his high-school band. On graduation, Ray went to the University of Pennsylvania's Wharton School and majored in banking and finance. Though he kept playing, in college dance bands, his first thoughts were of a career in business. But he soon became friends with another young student, Jay Livingston. Jay, who was an accomplished pianist, thought he would try for journalism. They teamed up, and Evans became the

[*]*Lyrics on Several Occasions.* Knopf, 1959.

[75]

lyricist for a collaboration that provided songs for over a hundred motion pictures.

After graduation and a sixty-day job playing in a band on an ocean liner, Jay and Ray settled down in New York to try to crack the songwriting field. Ray's business training came in handy. While they were receiving a steady stream of rejections, he worked at such jobs as office boy, statistician, and accountant. In 1939, a letter Ray wrote to the comedy team of Olsen and Johnson led to an interview and evenutally the chance to write some material for the zany stage success "Hellzapoppin." Despite the success of their song "G'bye Now," which reached the Hit Parade in 1940, Ray still had to keep working as an accountant—by this time in an aircraft plant. Ray kept at it during the war, while Jay was in the service. By the time Livingston was discharged in 1944, Ray had moved to full-time show-business work as a gag writer for CBS radio.

Back as a team again, the boys went to Hollywood at the invitation of Ole Olsen. But the picture Olsen was planning failed to materialize. Ray and Jay decided to stay in California and try writing for the movies. A minor hit for Betty Hutton led to the chance to audition several songs for a Paramount movie she was to star in. This was a critical meeting with producer Buddy de Sylva.

As Evans recalls, "We got a call on Friday from Paramount Studios asking if we would be willing to write a song for Monday on speculation. Over the weekend, we wrote not one but three songs, for this was a door we couldn't afford to see closed. On Monday, we presented ourselves to music-department head Louis Lipstone and played two of these for him. He liked one, didn't care for the other.

"He agreed to call de Sylva over, saying 'Only play the one I like. We don't want to waste his time.' We played that one for de Sylva and he didn't like it. Dejectedly, we collected our music and started out of the office. We were out in the anteroom when Lipstone yelled for us to come back. He'd told de Sylva that perhaps we should play the other song. We did, and de Sylva loved it ('A Square in the Social Circle'). It was plain luck—if not for our guardian angel, we might be back in industry."

In short order, the boys won more assignments from Paramount and finally a contract that was to last from 1946 to 1956. The boys turned out song after song for such stars as Bob Hope, Jerry Lewis and Dean Martin, Bing Crosby, Rosemary

Clooney, Pearl Bailey, Nat "King" Cole, and even Roy Rogers. Besides the three Oscar winners, their credits include "To Each His Own," "Silver Bells," "Copper Canyon," "Marshmallow Moon," "Golden Earrings" (lyrics to melody by Victor Young), and "Home Cookin'." After 1956, the team began freelancing for various studios, writing such songs as "Tammy," "Almost in Your Arms," and the title song for Jerry Lewis's 1963 movie "Who's Minding the Store?" They wrote the theme song for the television shows "Bonanza" and "Mister Ed" and the score for the Broadway show "Oh, Captain!" "Oh, Captain!" won generally favorable reviews in 1958, but their next Broadway attempt, "Let It Ride," did not fare well.

Ray and Jay meet regularly three or four times a week to go over material. "Almost always," says Ray, "we start with a dummy title and lyric. Usually we discard both by the time we have the finished song. Jay writes the music from this— sometimes just taking one line he likes and going from there, sometimes writing the whole melody on the lyric pattern. Jay generally likes to work on the musical ideas after midnight, while I like to work up new lyric ideas in the morning. When Jay finishes a melody, we get together in one room and collaborate on the finished lyric. The process usually takes about three or four days. Some songs take longer. 'To Each His Own' took three or four weeks.

"Deciding what idea to work on is a case of your own taste, judgment and ear. It's based on 'color,' interesting thoughts, images. It must be a song you can feel. You can't be taught that. There are no rules. Anything can go. To succeed it must just have that intangible something that catches the public fancy."

EVERLY BROTHERS: vocal duo. Both born Brownie, Kentucky. Don, February 1, 1937. Phil, January 19, 1939.

From the late nineteen-fifties through the sixties, the young Everly Brothers remained one of the world's most successful popular-music teams. Accompanying themselves on the guitar, they played to standing-room-only crowds in all corners of the United States and in Australia, Canada, New Zealand, and the major nations of Europe.

The boys were born to a show-business family. Their parents, Ike and Margaret Everly, were well-known country-music artists. When Don was six and Phil eight, they made their first public appearance, on radio station KMA in Shenandoah, Iowa. For several years afterward, the family spent the summers performing on radio and in local shows throughout the country.

When the boys graduated from high school, their parents retired. Phil and Don decided to chance it alone as a vocal team. They moved to Nashville, Tennessee, the country-music capital. As they began to become better-known throughout that area, they signed their first recording contract. One day, looking for song material, they dropped in at the major Nashville music publishing firm of Acuff-Rose. There they met Boudleaux Bryant, one of the top popular songwriters. Bryant, whose songs were published by Acuff-Rose, had just finished a new number. He demonstrated it on the guitar for the brothers. They liked it and recorded it, and it rapidly developed into a million-record seller. One of the major hits of 1957, its title was "Bye Bye Love."

A close relationship developed between the Bryants (Boudleaux and his wife Felice write as a team) and the brothers. The Everly Brothers scored again and again with songs by the Bryants. They also wrote songs themselves, several of which also were hits.

Among the Everly Brothers' record successes were "Cathy's Clown," "Wake Up, Little Susie," "Bird Dog," "All I Have To Do Is Dream," "Devoted to You," and "When Will I Be Loved?" As their popularity climbed, the Everly Brothers appeared on just about every major television show, including those of Ed Sullivan, Bob Hope, Perry Como, Arthur Murray, Dick Clark, and Patti Page. Through 1963, their total record sales exceeded eighteen million.

FAIN, SAMMY: composer, singer. Born New York, New York, June 17, 1902. Won Academy Award for Best Song of 1953 ("Secret Love") and 1955 ("Love Is a Many-Splendored Thing").

Sammy Fain, one of the greatest popular-music composers, is not as well known as he should be. His songwriting career, which began professionally in 1925, was still going strong in the nineteen-sixties. A few examples of his many hits indicate his tremendous talent: "Wedding Bells Are Breaking Up That Old Gang of Mine," "I'll Be Seeing You," "April Love," "Dear Hearts and Gentle People," and "That Old Feeling."

Fain attended public and high school in New York State's Sullivan County, where his father was a cantor. Sammy taught himself to play the piano and began to compose popular songs. As

he grew up, he sent his songs to New York publishers. Publishers shy away from unsolicited manuscripts, and Fain received only rejections.

After graduating from high school, Sammy decided that the only way to succeed was to go to New York. His first job in the field was a stockroom boy for a music publisher. He used to sneak down and play his songs in the audition room. One day, his boss caught him. This would have been cause for dismissal, but the publisher felt that the boy might have something. Fain was given a job as song plugger. He became adept at it and worked for several major publishers in succeeding years. Along the way, he met singer Artie Dunn, and the two formed a singing team that became a major attraction in the early days of radio.

But Sammy's eye still was on composing. In 1925, a song of his was published (by Mills Music) for the first time. Titled "Nobody Knows What a Red-Headed Mama Can Do," it had lyrics by Irving Mills and Al Dubin. About this time, Sammy met Irving Kahal, who became his lyricist for seventeen years, until Kahal's death. Their first song, on which Francis Wheeler collaborated on the words, was "Let a Smile Be Your Umbrella" (1927). Fain and Kahal turned out hundreds of songs for Broadway and Hollywood, many of which have become standards, including "Wedding Bells Are Breaking Up That Old Gang of Mine" and "When I Take My Sugar to Tea."

In 1930, Paramount Pictures signed the team to write a song for the Maurice Chevalier movie "The Big Pond." They came to Los Angeles, wrote "You Brought a New Kind of Love to Me," and stayed mainly on the Coast from then on. In the nineteen-thirties and early forties, they worked for several studios, turning out such hits as "By a Waterfall," "Every Day," and "How Do I Know It's Sunday?" Two of their greatest collaborations, "I Can Dream Can't I?" and "I'll Be Seeing You," did not become hits until after Kahal's death (February 7, 1942). Both were written for an unsuccessful Broadway show called "Right This Way."

Though devoting much time to Hollywood, Fain continued to write for Broadway. He and Kahal had written material for "Manhattan Mary" in 1927 and "Everybody's Welcome" in 1931. In 1938, they provided numbers for Olsen and Johnson's "Hellzapoppin" and, in 1941, for their "Sons o' Fun." Later, Fain worked with George Marion, Jr., on "Toplitsky of Notre

Dame" (1946) and with E. Y. Harburg on "Flahooley" (1951).

After Kahal's death, Fain collaborated with several lyricists on material for motion pictures. He had a fruitful arrangement with lyricist Paul Francis Webster. Song after song of theirs was nominated for Academy Awards in the nineteen-fifties and sixties. In 1953, they won an Oscar for "Secret Love," written for Warner Brothers' "Calamity Jane." In 1955, they won another Oscar for the title song from "Love Is a Many-Splendored Thing" (Twentieth Century-Fox). In 1956, the song won the grand prize in an Italian film festival.

Several other Fain and Webster songs received nominations for Oscars: "April Love" (1957), "A Certain Smile" and "A Very Precious Love" (1958), and "Tender Is the Night" (1962).

FAITH, PERCY: composer, arranger, conductor, pianist. Born Toronto, Canada, April 7, 1908.

Percy Faith started studying violin when he was seven. At ten, he decided that he preferred piano. At eleven, he played piano for silent movies, earning three dollars a night plus carfare. Soon after, he enrolled at the Toronto Conservatory. He made a well-received concert debut at Toronto's Massey Hall when he was fifteen. Three years later, an accident in which he severely burned his hands made him turn away from concert work. He was soon arranging music for leading bands in the Toronto area. At the same time, he formed his own string ensemble and conducted it on local radio.

In 1933, the Canadian Broadcasting Company hired him as staff arranger and conductor. He soon had his own program, "Music by Faith," which was the CBC's most popular program for the seven years of the show's existence. In 1938, the show was relayed to the United States by the Mutual Broadcasting Company network. The 1939 *Variety* poll showed that Faith, who still lived in Canada, was the fourth most popular conductor in the United States.

He stayed in Canada until 1940, when a rush call came for him to take over the "Carnation Contented Hour" for a three-week guest engagement due to the sudden death of conductor Joseph Pasternak. By 1947, Faith had become musical director of the Coca-Cola and Woolworth shows.

Soon after Percy's arrival in New York, Columbia Records signed him as an arranger. Three of Tony Bennett's gold records—"Because of You,"

"Cold, Cold Heart," and "Rags to Riches"—owe much of their success to Faith arrangements. He also arranged for many other singers, including Rosemary Clooney, Johnny Mathis, and Doris Day. Faith's ability as a composer showed in such songs as "My Heart Cries for You," which helped win a gold record for Guy Mitchell and launch him as a highly successful artist.

Faith also worked for Hollywood. In 1953, his arrangement of "The Song from 'Moulin Rouge'" won the *Cash Box* award as the "best-selling single of the year." Another gold record came Faith's way for "Theme From 'A Summer Place.'" In 1955, Faith was nominated for an Academy Award for conducting and scoring the music for the movie "Love Me or Leave Me."

FANNY: musical. Lyrics and music by Harold Rome, book by S. N. Behrman and Joshua Logan. New York opening: November 4, 1954, Majestic Theatre. 888 performances.

One of the finest products of the French movie industry was Marcel Pagnol's sensitive and loving trilogy—"Marius," "César," and "Fanny"—about life in Marseilles. Playwrights Behrman and Logan and songwriter Rome blended elements from all three films into a warm and tuneful musical. Brooks Atkinson wrote in the New York *Times:*

> The story is so genuine and rueful, the writing is so tender . . . that it results in a thoroughly absorbing theatre experience. . . . The story is a simple one that involves appealing characters and the style is sentimental with a tart, worldly flavor.

"Fanny" is set in a small waterfront neighborhood. Marius is the son of the dapper César. César, a widower, is the proprietor of a small café that he hopes to turn over to his son. He also hopes that Marius will settle down and marry young Fanny, the daughter of Honorine, a fishstall keeper. But a strange waterfront character, the Admiral, has filled Marius with a love of the sea. As the story opens, a square-rigger has come to port, and the Admiral wants Marius to sign on for a five-year hitch. Marius has the wanderlust ("Restless Heart"), but he also loves Fanny. Meanwhile, César's friend Panisse, who has recently become a widower, comes to ask for Fanny's hand. He is in his fifties but feels that it's "Never Too Late for Love."

Marius signs to ship out. That night, as he closes the café and plans to pack his bags, César comes in from an evening with his ladylove. Though he likes to go out, he tells Marius, he always likes getting back to the café ("Welcome Home"). César goes to bed as Fanny, fearful that Marius's coldness may be because of another girl, comes in. She is the only one, he sings ("Fanny"). In an effort to keep Marius from going, she sleeps with him. But the lure of the sea is too much, and Marius goes. Weeks later, Fanny finds she is pregnant. Panisse agrees to marry her anyway, as he has always wanted a child. ("Panisse and Son," he sings exultantly.)

César is told. At first indignant, he realizes it is the only solution. The child is a boy, named Césario. On his first birthday, Marius returns and tells his love in "The Thought of You." But César finds them and tells Marius he must leave for the child's sake. He sings of the wonders of a baby ("Love Is a Very Light Thing"). Time passes, and Césario is twelve. Fanny explains "parents" to him ("Be Kind to Your Parents"). On Césario's birthday, the Admiral takes him off to see Marius. Panisse has a heart attack when he finds out. Marius returns the boy and goes off to America. On his deathbed, Panisse dictates a letter to César asking Marius to come home and take care of Fanny and Césario.

The original cast included Ezio Pinza, as César; William Tabbert, as Marius; Florence Henderson, as Fanny; Edna Preston, as Honorine; Walter Slezak, as Panisse; and Gerald Price, as the Admiral. The score included "Why Be Afraid To Dance?" "Cold-Cream Jar Song," "Octopus Song," "I Like You," "I Have To Tell You," "Birthday Song," "To My Wife," and "Other Hands, Other Hearts."

FASCINATING RHYTHM: song (1924). Words by Ira Gershwin, music by George Gershwin.

When George Gershwin was a young rehearsal pianist in New York, one of his occasional visitors was Fred Astaire. Astaire, in his early twenties— a few years older than George—was already an established performer, while Gershwin was still an unknown. On one visit, Fred told George how much he and his sister Adele longed to do a major Broadway show. Gershwin replied enthusiastically, "Wouldn't it be great if I could write a musical show and you could be in it?" A few years later, it happened. The show, one of the major musical hits of the nineteen-twenties, was "Lady, Be Good." It opened in 1924, and one of the main numbers performed by Fred and Adele Astaire was "Fascinating Rhythm."

In "George Gershwin" (New York: Simon and Schuster, 1931), Isaac Goldberg quotes brother Ira:

When George was in London doing *Primrose* . . . he wrote the first eight bars of what afterwards became Fascinating Rhythm. Alex Aarons, who was with him, and who is one of the keenest judges of a smart tune among the managers, told him to develop it for the next show. George didn't finish the tune until weeks later in New York. It was a tricky rhythm for those days, and it took me several days to decide on the rhyme scheme. I didn't think I had *the* brilliant title in Fascinating Rhythm but A) it *did* sing smoothly, and B)—I couldn't think of a better. The rhyme scheme was a, b, a, c—a, b, a, c. When I got to the 8th line I showed the lyric to George. His comment was that the 4th and 8th lines should have a double (or two-syllable) rhyme where I had rhymed them with single syllables. I protested and, by singing, showed him the last note in both lines had the same strength as the note preceding. To me the last two notes in these lines formed a spondee; the easiest way out was arbitrarily to put the accent on the last note. But George couldn't see, and so, on and off, we argued for days. Finally I had to capitulate and write the lines as they are today:

> 4th line   I'm all a-*quiv*er.
> 8th line   —Just like a *flivver*,

After George proved to me that I had better use the double rhyme; because, whereas in singing, the notes might be considered even, in conducting the music, the downbeat came on the penultimate note.

FIELDS, DOROTHY: lyricist, librettist. Born Allenhurst, New Jersey, July 15, 1905. Won Academy Award for Best Song of 1936 ("The Way You Look Tonight").

Only a small percentage of successful songwriters have been women. It takes a brave woman indeed to brave the rough-and-tumble songwriting trade. Still, women can succeed in music, and there is no finer example than the versatile Dorothy Fields.

Her father was the redoubtable Lew Fields, member of the comedy team of Weber and Fields and later a major Broadway producer. Dorothy was the youngest of the talented Fields brood, which included librettist-producer Herbert and playwright-librettist Joseph ("My Sister Eileen," "Junior Miss," etc.). After attending New York public schools, supplemented by private tutors, Dorothy began teaching art in a high school. She also began contributing poetry to magazines and writing lyrics.

For a while, her lyric efforts were unsuccessful, but in 1928 she teamed up with composer Jimmy McHugh. Their songs for the revue "Blackbirds of 1928" included two all-time hits, "Diga, Diga, Doo" and "I Can't Give You Anything but Love." They collaborated on Broadway shows and Hollywood movies for several years. Their output included such songs as "Dinner at Eight" (1933), "Thank You for a Lovely Evening" (1934), "I Feel a Song Comin' On" and "I'm in the Mood for Love" (both in 1935). Dorothy and Jimmy combined talents with Jerome Kern in 1935 to write a near-Academy Award winner, "Lovely To Look At."

This started a Fields-Kern song cycle that continued for several years. Dorothy's work with Kern included "I Dream Too Much" (1935) and the Academy Award-winning "The Way You Look Tonight" (1936).

As time went on, Dorothy showed a new facet of her talent by collaborating with her brother Herbert, first on screenplays and later on a series of hit Broadway musicals. Their first major stage efforts were for Cole Porter. Dorothy and Herbert turned out the book for "Let's Face It" (1941), "Something for the Boys" (1943), and "Mexican Hayride" (1944). The Fields then became interested in writing a musical with Jerome Kern about Annie Oakley. When Kern died, they gained a new coworker in Irving Berlin. The result was "Annie Get Your Gun."

Dorothy worked on both libretto and lyrics for such other composers as Sigmund Romberg and Arthur Schwartz. A year before "Annie" arrived, she worked on the 1945 Romberg success "Up in Central Park." With Schwartz she provided some highly singable songs for Shirley Booth in "A Tree Grows in Brooklyn" (1951) and "By the Beautiful Sea" (1954).

FINIAN'S RAINBOW: musical. Lyrics by E. Y. Harburg; music by Burton Lane, book by Harburg and Fred Saidy. New York opening: January 10, 1947, Forty-sixth Street Theatre. 725 performances.

The elderly Finian McLonergan and his daughter Sharon arrive in the United States from Glocca Morra, a mythical Irish town. Finian has stolen a pot of gold from the Leprechaun Og. He wants to bury it at Fort Knox, hoping that it will multiply. On his way, he comes upon Rainbow Valley, Missitucky. He falls in love with the country and buys land from sharecroppers. The anti-Negro Senator Billboard Rawkins plots to steal the land, which has magically become very valuable, from Finian and the Negroes. The valley folk don't take the threatened auction and dispossession seriously ("This Time of the Year").

Og arrives in search of his gold. Sharon asks him, "How Are Things in Glocca Morra?" She is in love with Woody Mahoney, the handsome young leader of the sharecroppers. Og is attracted to Woody's sister Susan, a deaf mute who speaks by dancing. He is torn between love for Susan and the fearful awareness that he is turning into a mortal. Finian has three wishes on his crock of gold. He changes the Senator's color so that he will know what it's like to be the underdog, gives Susan back her voice through Og's magic, and saves Sharon from the Senator's anger by turning him into a likeable person.

The score included "If This Isn't Love," "Look to the Rainbow," "Old Devil Moon," "Something Sort of Grandish," "That Great Come and Get It Day," "When I'm Not Near the Girl I Love," "Necessity," and "When the Idle Poor Become the Idle Rich." The original cast included Ella Logan, as Sharon; David Wayne, as Og; Donald Richards, as Woody; Anita Alvarez, as Susan; and Albert Sharpe, as Finian. The 1960 revival included Jeannie Carson as Sharon, Howard Morris as Og and Bill McGuire as Woody.

FIORELLO: musical. Lyrics by Sheldon Harnick, music by Jerry Bock, book by George Abbott and Jerome Weidman. New York opening: November 23, 1959, Broadhurst Theatre. 796 performances.

"Fiorello!" blazed new ground as well as walking off with most of the honors of the 1959–60 season, including the Pulitzer Prize, the New York Drama Critics' Award, and the Antoinette Perry Award. It was a showcase for the new songwriting team of Jerry Bock and Sheldon Harnick, and the first Broadway engagement for Tom Bosley, who played the title role.

Mayor Fiorello La Guardia, New York's "Little Flower," was one of the most flamboyant and best-loved politicians ever to hold office. More than that, he was a crusader who believed his own speeches. La Guardia probably achieved more lasting reforms than any other New York mayor. The play deals with the period from La Guardia's decision to enter politics just before our entrance into World War I to the eve of his successful election fight for former mayor Jimmy Walker's post in 1934.

La Guardia is first shown as a lawyer dedicated to defending the rights of poor and downtrodden clients. His office manager Morris, young law clerk Neil, and secretary Marie extol his virtues ("On the Side of the Angels"). La Guardia tells Marie that the corruption of Democratically controlled Tammany Hall has made him decide to run for Congress on the Republican ticket. Meanwhile, at Republican headquarters, doleful Republican boss Ben Marino and his aides sit trying to select a candidate for what seems a hopeless cause. They review the mores of campaigns ("Politics and Poker"). La Guardia rushes in and shocks them into nominating him by his cocksure statement that if they do so he will give them a Congressman. Soon Fiorello is in the thick of a fight to help a group of striking female garment workers win better working conditions. He frees their leader Thea from jail, where she had been taken on false charges.

He then wins popular support in soapbox speeches using the languages of New York's major minority groups. To the amazement of Marino and his friends, La Guardia is elected ("The Bum Won"). Marie secretly loves La Guardia, but he is always breaking dates to do his political good deeds. Such conduct toward her should be illegal, she sings ("Marie's Law"). In Congress, La Guardia urges the unpopular course of United States support of the Allies. He backs up his beliefs by enlisting as a captain. He proposes to Thea, and she accepts at his farewell party. They dance to the waltz "Till Tomorrow."

Fiorello returns from the war, and the scene shifts to the late nineteen-twenties. He is running for mayor against popular Jimmy Walker, whose campaign is plugged by Marie's friend Dora ("Gentleman Jimmy"). Fiorello loses by a landslide. His beloved wife dies, and La Guardia quits politics. But the next few years see the corruption of the Walker administration become a statewide scandal, a situation gleefully reviewed by Marino and the Republicans in the comic "Little Tin Box." Marino appeals to La Guardia to run again, and Fiorello agrees. The long-suffering Marie is rewarded as La Guardia fires her—for he cannot court an employee.

Besides Bosley, the original cast included Patricia Wilson, as Marie; Ellen Hanley, as Thea; Pat Stanley, as Dora; Howard da Silva, as Ben Marino; Nathaniel Frey, as Morris, and Bob Hilday, as Neil.

FITZGERALD, ELLA: singer. Born Newport News, Virginia, April 25, 1918.

Ella Fitzgerald's ear is said to be so exact that musicians can tune their instruments by her voice. Her phrasing is close to perfection, and her voice has extreme clarity of tone. Her style is so cogent that she has been called "the Hemingway of singers."

Ella's parents died soon after her birth, and she was raised by an aunt. They moved to Harlem, where Ella entertained her neighborhood friends with singing and dancing. They persuaded her to perform at the weekly talent auditions at the Harlem Opera House.

The sixteen-year-old Ella went on not as a singer but as a dancer. She was gripped with such stage fright that her legs refused to function, and she sang instead. The song was called "Judy," and it won her first prize, twenty-five dollars. Band leader Chick Webb was in the audience, and he rushed backstage to offer her a job singing with his band. In 1936, at the age of eighteen, Ella was one of Webb's stellar attractions, mainly as a scat singer. Then she became nationally famous with a song she wrote herself, a version of the old children's rhyme "A-Tisket A-Tasket." Webb died, and Ella took over as the band's leader. When World War II broke up the organization, Ella went out as a solo vocalist. In her twenties, she was already a legend with jazz fans. Her name was well-known outside jazz circles but most people did not consider her a popular-music singer.

Still, she had the ability to sing any type of song well. In 1956, she made her first album of show music, "Ella Fitzgerald Sings the Cole Porter Song Book." The album reached the top brackets of LP sellers soon after its release and is still being played. Ella was soon appearing on most of the major television shows, from Dinah Shore's to Pat Boone's. Records of other song books followed—those of Duke Ellington, Irving Berlin, Harold Arlen, Rodgers and Hart, and George and Ira Gershwin. Ella also turned out such jazz items as "Ella and Louis," "Ella and Louis Again," and "Jazz at the Hollywood Bowl."

In the late fifties and the sixties Ella's concert tours took her to Sweden, Germany, Japan,

Australia, South America, and Canada. During the same period, she also made three movie appearances: singing roles in "Pete Kelly's Blues" and "St. Louis Blues: The W. C. Handy Story," and a dramatic role in "Let No Man Write My Epitaph."

Ella Fitzgerald has won many jazz and popular-music polls as best female vocalist. And in the first two years of the newly established record-industry Grammy awards, Ella walked off with three honors. In all, a fitting tribute to a singer of whom Bing Crosby said, "Man, woman, or child, Ella's the greatest."

FOLK SONG: a song of the people. (See also *Ballad, Blues, Country-and-Western, Rhythm and Blues.*)

There is some argument over what is a folk song. Purists claim that a folk song has no specific author but grows out of the people. Others believe that a folk song is any song that is taken up as an expression of the feeling of some part of the population. Most folk songs have evolved over many years, changed here and there by generations of singers. But there are some composed songs that are accepted as expressing true folk feeling. One recent example is "Scarlet Ribbons"; some songs of Stephen Foster are older examples. Most folk songs are ballads in the classic sense: they tell a story. Many derive from the days of the minstrels or from rural balladeers.

FORD, ERNEST JENNINGS (TENNESSEE ERNIE): singer. Born Bristol, Tennessee, February 13, 1919.

In 1961, Tennessee Ernie Ford achieved the rare distinction of singing a song to the accompaniment of a joint session of the legislature of his home state. The song was "Sixteen Tons," one of the highlights of a career that has made Ford's name a household word to millions of television and radio fans.

Ford began singing lessons while in high school, and spent much of his spare time at the local radio station. In 1937, the station hired him as a staff announcer for ten dollars a week. Ernie continued his singing studies, going on to a term at the Cincinnati Conservatory of Music. He then returned to announcing, serving at stations

The mid-1960's found the modern folk song (i.e., a song of folk origin with a new arrangement or, more often, newly-composed) growing in popularity. Especially in vogue was the audience-participation folk-song show known as the Hootenanny. One of the most successful of the groups taking part in such shows is the New Christy Minstrels, above.

[82]

Tennessee Ernie Ford

out six albums from 1956 to 1962 that each sold over a million dollars worth of copies. In late 1962, Prentice-Hall published a book of sheet music and notes on fifty of Ernie's best-liked hymns. Ford's biography, "This Is My Song, This Is My Story," was published by Doubleday in 1963.

FOX TROT: a form of ballroom dance. Also, the music to which the dance is performed.

The fox trot, which began its vogue in the decade before World War I, is one of the oldest forms of ballroom dancing still current, and is still one of the most popular. One reason for its continued popularity is its simplicity. The dance derives from the two-step, and is in four-four time. Usually the first and third beats are accented. A typical fox trot is made up of combinations of quick and slow steps, including a slow walk, in which the dancers glide forward or backward to a two-beat pattern; the box step, which includes forward and side steps; and a quick step, in which three steps forward or backward are taken, one on each beat.

FRANCIS, CONNIE: singer. Born Newark, New Jersey, December 12, 1938.

Connie Francis won a major share of top-female-vocalist awards from 1958 on into the sixties. She won her first popularity poll when she was under twenty. Rock 'n' roll was the rage with the younger set, but the song with which she made it to the top had been famous when her parents were just approaching high-school age. The song was "Who's Sorry Now?," written in 1923 by Bert Kalmar, Harry Ruby, and Ted Snyder. Connie sang the song with a rock-'n'-roll beat, an approach suggested by her father, who also suggested the song to his daughter.

She was born Constance Franconero. Her father loved to play the concertina. When Connie was four, her parents bought her an accordion, and she soon started taking lessons. Before long, she sang and accompanied herself at church benefits and family affairs. The accordion won Connie her first professional work, at the age of eleven. She auditioned as a singer for George Scheck's "Startime," a juvenile variety show in New York. Scheck had too many singers, so Connie auditioned on the accordion. She won the audition. Later, she impressed Scheck with her singing, and he became her manager. At twelve, Connie won on "Arthur Godfrey's Talent Scouts" show. It was Godfery who suggested she change her name. All through high

in Atlanta, Georgia, and Knoxville, Tennessee. In 1942, he enlisted in the Air Force. He met his wife-to-be while stationed in California. After his discharge in 1945, he went home to Bristol. There was no work, and he and his wife used their savings to buy a 1941 car and head to California.

He landed a job with a San Bernardino station, then did a short stint in Reno, Nevada. He became a hillbilly disc jockey for station KXLA in Pasadena. On Ford's first day in the studio, he joined band leader Cliffie Stone's show just for fun. Ford became a regular on Cliffie's Saturday-night show. Stone was under contract to Capitol Records. In 1947, when Capitol artists-and-repertoire man Lee Gillette heard Ernie singing along with the records during an early-morning show, he asked to meet him.

Among other things, Ernie recorded a song he had composed, "Shotgun Boogie." The record sold close to a million copies and gained international popularity. Ernie then turned in another major performance, "I'll Never Be Free," with Kay Starr. This was followed by "The Cry of the Wild Goose," "Farewell," and "The Ballad of Davy Crockett." In 1955, Merle Travis, originally from the Kentucky coal fields and a well-known hillbilly performer and songwriter, brought to Ford's attention a new composition, "Sixteen Tons." Ford's recording sold over three million copies within nine weeks after its release.

Ernie was soon appearing regularly on radio and TV. From 1957 to 1961, his TV show was one of the most popular in the nation. Ernie turned school, Connie made records—some twenty single sides—but none was very successful. At eighteen, with a four-year scholarship to New York University in the offing, she thought of limiting her show-business activities. In a reversal of the usual way of things, her father urged her to make just one more record try. "Take something different," he said. "Maybe an old song like 'Who's Sorry Now?' You could do it with a beat," and he demonstrated a little on his concertina.

Connie wasn't impressed; the song still sounded square. But she had an arrangement made, and in November, 1957, made the record. After a slow start, the disc began to move. By mid-1958, the record had sold a million copies. From then through 1962, she sold twenty-three million records throughout the world. She turned out seven other gold records: "My Happiness," "Everybody's Somebody's Fool," "My Heart Has a Mind of Its Own," "Lipstick on Your Collar," "Frankie," "Mama," and "Where the Boys Are"—the last to go with her first movie role, in the picture of the same name.

Connie drew record crowds at nightclubs from the New York Copacabana to the Las Vegas Sahara. Her life story was reviewed in such magazines as the *Saturday Evening Post* (September 23, 1961) and *Newsweek* (February 5, 1962), and by Ralph Edwards on television's "This Is Your Life." From a teen-age favorite she has become an established performer.

By the mid '60s, she had appeared on most major TV shows. On March 21, '65, she made her twenty third appearance on the Ed Sullivan Show. (Her first Sullivan spot was in 1958.)

FRIML, RUDOLF: composer, pianist. Born Prague, Bohemia (now Czechoslovakia), December 7, 1879.

The American musical theater evolved from the European operetta. At first, American impresarios imported European operettas and adapted them. Eventually, several composers, among them Rudolf Friml, wrote new American operettas. Finally, other composers, such as Gershwin, Youmans, and Rodgers, pioneered the uniquely American musical play. Friml provided an important bridge between the old and the new, but his heart always belonged to the classical operetta. Thus, though a power on the musical stage from 1912 to the late twenties, he did little after 1930.

Friml showed signs of musical ability early in life, and his family and friends pooled their resources so that he could attend the Prague Conservatory. He was fourteen when he enrolled, and completed the six-year course in three years. For ten years after, he was piano accompanist to his fellow student, the great violinist Jan Kubelik. In 1901, Kubelik was signed for an engagement in the United States. Friml had not intended to go, but when Kubelik's scheduled accompanist fell ill, Friml took his place. In 1906, Friml again toured the United States with Kubelik. This time he decided to stay. He gave recitals and appeared as soloist with many symphony orchestras, and wrote a good deal of music.

An argument between composer Victor Herbert and singer Emma Trentini led to Herbert's refusing to write a new operetta for her. Friml, who had not worked in the popular theater, was called in. His score for the 1912 hit "The Firefly" included such songs as "Giannina Mia," "Love Is Like a Firefly," and "Sympathy." Friml concentrated on the Broadway stage from then on. He turned out a succession of hit shows, including "High Jinks" (1913), "The Peasant Girl" and "Katinka" (1915), "Sometime" (in which Mae West made her Broadway debut) (1918), "Tumble In" (1919), and "The Blue Kitten" (1922).

In 1924, in collaboration with Oscar Hammerstein II and Otto Harbach, Friml scored his greatest success with "Rose Marie." The show ran for five hundred and fifty-seven performances. It featured such songs as "Rose Marie," "Indian Love Call," "Totem Tom-Tom," and "The Mounties." The next year, Friml wrote another major success, "The Vagabond King." "Song of the Vagabonds," "Only a Rose," and "Waltz Huguette" were in the score. In 1928, Friml hit the jackpot once more with "The Three Musketeers," which ran for three hundred and nineteen performances. After two failures— "Luana" (1930) and "Music Hath Charms" (1934)—Friml faded from the Broadway scene.

His operettas, though, continued to be performed by touring companies and turned into motion pictures. After 1934, Friml's output consisted of songs for the movies, in particular for movie versions of his Broadway successes. In 1937, for instance, Friml provided a new hit, "The Donkey Serenade," for the movie of "The Firefly." For a post-World War II movie of "The Vagabond King," Friml wrote "Bon Jour" and "This Same Heart" with Johnny Burke.

FRUG: In-place dance; modification of the twist.

Funny Girl: In this hit musical of 1964 Barbra Streisand portrays the late, great Fanny Brice. Above, Miss Streisand, aided by jazz musicians, sings the ragtime song, "Cornet Man."

FUNNY GIRL: musical. Lyrics by Bob Merrill, music by Jule Styne, book by Isobel Lennart. Based on a story by Miss Lennart. New York opening: March 26, 1964, Winter Garden.

A musical based on the life of singer-comedienne Fanny Brice would seem a natural for the Broadway stage, and so it proved out in the 1964 hit "Funny Girl." The critics loved the show, but they were even more enthusiastic about the sensational young singer Barbra Streisand. In this, her first Broadway role, she gave every promise of achieving all-time fame, as did the young Fanny Brice, whom she portrayed.

The story, told in a series of flashbacks, is based on Fanny Brice's unhappy marriage to gambler Nick Arnstein. As the show opens, Fanny, a Ziegfeld star, sits in her dressing room looking back on her rise to fame and her life with Nick, who is soon to return from prision.

The scene changes, and Fanny is a stage-struck teen-ager in the year before World War I. She plans to audition at Keeney's Music Hall that night. Her mother and her card-playing women friends warn Fanny that there's not much chance "If a Girl Isn't Pretty." Sure enough, Fanny is turned down. She meets vaudeville performer

Eddie Ryan, however, and talks him into coaching her by singing "I'm the Greatest Star."

After many nights' training, she makes the grade at Keeney's and sings the lead in the ragtime number "Cornet Man." After the show, dapper Nick Arnstein comes backstage to meet and praise her. For Fanny, it's love at first sight. But even more exciting is a wire from Florenz Ziegfeld offering her a job in the "Follies." Her mother and Eddie feel she might forget them now, although they're the ones "Who Taught Her Everything." After Fanny's "Follies" debut, Nick Arnstein again appears and is invited to a neighborhood celebration for Fanny. As Nick proudly tells Fanny, "I Want To Be Seen with You Tonight." When the party on "Henry Street" is over, Fanny expresses her feeling for Nick ("People"). The glow is short-lived, for Nick has to go to Kentucky to look after a newly purchased horse farm.

Months go by. Then Fanny, on tour in Baltimore, meets Nick once more. She decides to quit the show and marry him. She yearns for happiness ("Don't Rain on my Parade"). On going to their new home, a Long Island mansion, after the wedding, they are greeted by a surprise party. Fanny happily praises marriage to their friends ("Sadie, Sadie"). Mrs. Brice feels left out of things, and Eddie and her friend Mrs. Strakosh suggest she remarry ("Find Yourself a Man").

Nick has grandiose plans for a Florida gambling casino. He tries to get funds from Ziegfeld. When he is refused, Fanny gives him the money. She returns to the "Follies" and stars in a World War I military number called "Rat-Tat-Tat-Tat." But she is disturbed on opening night that Nick does not come to wish her luck. After the show, he does arrive, to tell her the casino venture has failed. Soon after, his pride makes him reject a new offer of help from his wife, and he tries his hand at a bond deal. The project fails, and he's jailed for embezzlement. Mrs. Brice gives Fanny the courage she needs to go on that night and sing "The Music That Makes Me Dance," a song that suggests Fanny's troubles with Nick.

The memories fade, and the scene returns to Fanny's dressing room. Nick comes back but soon understands that their love is not enough to make their marriage work. Sadly they part, but Fanny squares her shoulders to go on with her career.

Besides Miss Streisand, the original cast included Sydney Chaplin, as Nick; Danny Meehan, as Eddie; Kay Medford, as Mrs. Brice; and Jean Stapleton, as Mrs. Strakosh. Other songs are "His Love Makes Me Beautiful," "You Are Woman," and "Who Are You Now?"

GARLAND, JUDY: singer, actress. Born Grand Rapids, Michigan, June 10, 1922.

Judy Garland was born Frances Ethel Gumm into a vaudeville family. When she was two and a half, she joined her two older sisters on stage and sang two choruses of "Jingle Bells." She had to do seven encores. From then on, she was a member of the act. When she was twelve, the Gumm Sisters scored a major success at the Oriental Theatre in Chicago. George Jessel, who was on the bill, suggested they drop the name of Gumm, and Frances Gumm became Judy Garland. That same year, a talent scout heard Judy do a show-stopping number at Lake Tahoe, California, and signed her to a Metro-Goldwyn-Mayer contract.

She was lent to Twentieth Century-Fox for her first movie, "One Sunday Afternoon." After that, she did a number of movies for MGM, including several with Mickey Rooney in the "Andy Hardy" series. Then she was cast as the heroine of the "Wizard of Oz." The movie, released in 1939, became a classic. In it Judy sang

Judy Garland

the song that became her theme, "Over the Rainbow."

She then appeared in a procession of major movies, including "Life Begins for Andy Hardy," "For Me and My Gal," "Girl Crazy," "Strike Up the Band," "Meet Me in St. Louis," "Easter Parade," and "The Pirate." From the late thirties to 1949, Judy made some thirty major movies. This breakneck pace began to show. Judy became sick while making "Annie Get Your Gun" and was released from her contract in 1950. She was unable to work for many months, and it looked as though she might be through. In 1951, however, she struggled back to health and accepted an engagement at the Palladium in London, where she scored a tremendous success. She returned to the United States for an even greater triumph at the Palace Theatre in New York. She set a vaudeville record with nineteen weeks and a hundred and eighty-four performances.

One reason for her resurgence was Sid Luft, who was first her manager, later her husband. In 1954, she and Luft made their own movie, "A Star Is Born," which won much critical praise. Still, Judy sometimes found herself exhausted in the following years. Each time, she came back; but in 1958 and 1959, her resiliency began to disappear and her voice to lose its power. By the fall of 1959, she couldn't work at all. It was partly overwork, partly hepatitis. The Lufts moved to England, and Judy's health improved. On August 28, 1960, she again was a great success at the Palladium. Early in 1961, she started a fourteen-week tour in Dallas with a two-and-a-quarter-hour performance that brought two standing ovations. On April 23, 1961, she reached the high spot of the tour with a great performance at New York's Carnegie Hall. The Capitol record of this concert is considered one of the major events in record history. That same year, Judy also played a dramatic role in "Judgment at Nuremberg."

In 1962 and 1963, her career continued at its new pinnacle. Besides concert appearances, she turned out several top-rated television specials. In 1963, she made another movie, "I Could Go On Singing." In the 1963–64 season, she did her own television series. In November 1964 she once again scored a major triumph at the London Palladium, this time in a joint concert with a new young singing star, her 19 year old daughter, Liza Minnelli.

GENTLEMEN PREFER BLONDES: musical. Lyrics by Leo Robin, music by Jule Styne, book by Joseph Fields and Anita Loos. Based on Miss Loos's novel. New York opening: December 8, 1949, Ziegfeld Theatre. 740 performances.

The twenties were nowhere better captured than in Anita Loos's best-selling 1925 novel "Gentlemen Prefer Blondes." In 1926, it scored again as a play, and, in 1949, as a musical. The plot of the musical differed somewhat from that of the novel (Lorelei originally abandoned her elderly button manufacturer and married Henry Spofford), but heroine Lorelei Lee was as coyly avaricious as ever. As New York *Times* critic Brooks Atkinson wrote: Lorelei is "husky enough to kick in the teeth of any gentleman on the stage, but mincing coyly in high-heel shoes and looking out on a confused world through big, wide, starry eyes." His summation of the show was echoed by just about all his colleagues: "Happy days are here again. . . . 'Gentlemen Prefer Blondes' is a vastly enjoyable song-and-dance antic put on with humorous perfection."

Lorelei and her friend Dorothy Shaw, on leave from "The Ziegfeld Follies," are sailing for Paris on the Ile de France. The year is 1924, and Dorothy is eager to leave Prohibition behind ("It's High Time"). Lorelei's hobby is collecting jewels—real ones, and as expensive as possible. One of her best sources is her sugar daddy Gus

Esmond, a rich button manufacturer. She is sad at leaving him ("Bye Bye Baby"). Once at sea, though, she quickly decides that a new protector is required. She is, as she tells Dorothy, just "A Little Girl from Little Rock" (who also just happened to shoot a man).

On board is Henry Spofford, a rich Philadelphia bachelor who shuns girls who are not nice. He has in tow his mother, a teetering old lady looking for a drink. Lorelei brings Dorothy and Henry together by playing Henry's favorite song, "Just a Kiss Apart." Later, in Lorelei's empty suite, dancer Gloria Stark practices a routine.

Also on board is an English couple, Sir Francis and Lady Beekman. Lorelei is entranced with Lady Beekman's diamond tiara, for her collection doesn't contain one. She vamps the normally miserly Sir Francis into lending her the money to buy the tiara.

The girls arrive in Paris. Henry and Dorothy express their love in "You Say You Care." Lorelei finds a new daddy in zipper manufacturer Josephus Gage. The indecently healthy Mr. Gage sings "I'm Atingle, I'm Aglow." Lady Beekman has discovered the source of the tiara money. She sends a father-and-son team of French lawyers to pursue Lorelei. Gus Esmond arrives to find Lorelei entertaining Gage. Enraged, he stalks off to sponsor Gloria Stark's nightclub debut. Commenting on all this, Lorelei concludes that "Diamonds Are a Girl's Best Friend." The debut is a success. Lorelei makes up with Gus and repays Sir Francis. Now all are longing for home ("Homesick Blues"). Some days later, back in New York's Central Park Casino, Lorelei and Gus, and Dorothy and Henry, decide to marry. Dorothy sings that all will "Keep Cool with Coolidge."

The original cast included Carol Channing, as Lorelei; Yvonne Adair, as Dorothy; Jack McCauley, as Gus; Eric Brotherson, as Henry; Alice Pearce, as Mrs. Spofford; George S. Irving, as Gage; Rex Evans, as Sir Francis; and Anita Alvarez, as Gloria Stark. Other songs were "I Love What I'm Doing," "Scherzo," "It's Delightful Down in Chile," "Sunshine," "Mamie Is Mimi," and "Gentlemen Prefer Blondes."

GERSHWIN, GEORGE: composer, pianist. Born Brooklyn, New York, September 26, 1898; died Hollywood, California, July 11, 1937. Won Pulitzer Prize for "Of Thee I Sing" (1931)

"When [they] tell me that now and then I betray a structural weakness, they are not telling me anything that I don't know. I don't claim to

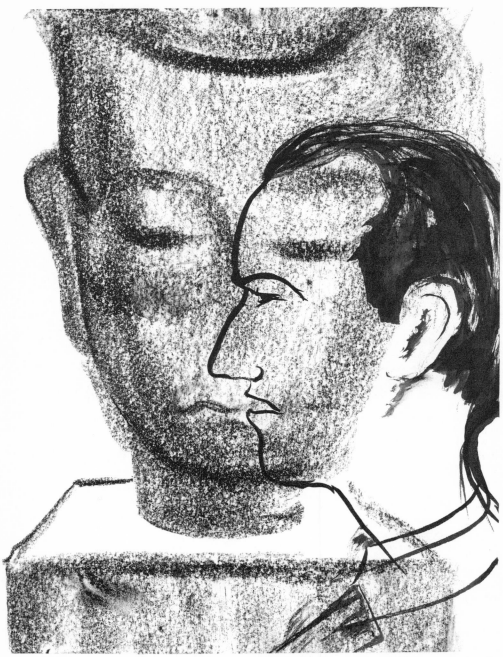

George Gershwin left a legacy of great music, both popular and in the classical vein. Here a profile sketch of the composer is superimposed on a drawing of the bronze head of Gershwin made by Isamu Noguchi.

be perfect; I hope I have too great a sense of humor for that. But I know where I'm going and I'm on my way." Thus spoke young George Gershwin (as quoted by Edward Jablonski in *Musical America*, July, 1962), who took up music at thirteen, was a professional pianist at fifteen, and had his first hit musical, "La La Lucille," on Broadway at twenty. Into the seventeen years remaining to him he crowded enough triumphs in popular and concert music for two men.

During his early years, Gershwin was not interested in music but only wanted to play ball and have fun. Music suddenly became his whole life when his mother bought a piano (originally intended for his older brother Ira). He left New York's High School of Commerce at the age of fifteen for a job as a pianist with Remick Music. His first published song, "When You Want 'Em You Can't Get 'Em" (lyrics by Murray Roth), soon appeared.

He left Remick for a job as a vaudeville accompanist, and later became a rehearsal pianist for the show "Miss 1917." Some of his songs were performed at a Sunday-night variety concert sponsored by the show's producers. Publisher Max Dreyfus was impressed and signed Gershwin as a staff composer for Harms. Gershwin arrived with the score for "La La Lucille" in 1919. The same year, Al Jolson made Gershwin's "Swanee" a nationwide favorite. Gershwin wrote most of the music for "George White's Scandals" from 1920 to 1924. His most famous song for this series was "Somebody Loves Me" (1924).

Several of his tries at Broadway musicals in the early twenties failed. Then, in 1924, he teamed up with his brother Ira for their first complete score together. The show, a major hit, was "Lady, Be Good," which included "Fascinating Rhythm" and "Oh, Lady Be Good." (The first song of George's for which Ira provided words was "The Real American Folk Song" in 1918.) With a few exceptions, Ira provided the lyrics for George's songs from then on. Also in 1924, George wrote the "Rhapsody in Blue" at Paul Whiteman's request. Gershwin later wrote other major orchestral works, including the Concerto in F and "An American in Paris."

The Gershwins' score for 1925 was a miss ("Tell Me More") and a hit ("Tip-Toes"). The latter contained "That Certain Feeling," "Looking for a Boy," and "Sweet and Low-Down." Then came a string of three successes: "Oh, Kay!" (1926), "Funny Face" (1927), and "Rosalie" (1928). These included such songs as

"Maybe," "Clap Yo' Hands," "Do Do Do" (from "Oh, Kay!"), "'S Wonderful," "Funny Face," "He Loves and She Loves" (from "Funny Face"), and "How Long Has This Been Going On?" (from "Rosalie"). "Treasure Girl" (1928) was a flop, but it contained "I've Got a Crush on You" and "I Don't Think I'll Fall in Love Today." In 1930, Gershwin came up with two triumphs, "Strike Up the Band" and "Girl Crazy" (see separate listings.) The latter marked the stage debut of Ethel Merman, who stopped the show with her sparkling, driving performance of "I Got Rhythm."

"Of Thee I Sing" (1931) marked the high point of Gershwin's efforts in musical comedy. It was the first musical to win a Pulitzer Prize. The score included the title song, "Wintergreen for President," "Love Is Sweeping the Country," and "Who Cares?"

Gershwin first became interested in writing an opera in 1926, after reading DuBose Heyward's short novel "Porgy," about the Negro slum of Catfish Row in Charleston, South Carolina. He became even more convinced of the rightness of his idea after "Porgy" was turned into a hit play in 1927. He corresponded with Heyward about the project for some years, but other committments kept getting in the way. After two unsuccessful musicals ("Pardon My English" and "Let 'Em Eat Cake"—both in 1933), Gershwin finally signed Theatre Guild contracts with Heyward for what was to become "Porgy and Bess." The opera opened in New York on October 10, 1935, to mixed reviews. Since then it has become recognized as one of America's greatest contributions to the world's stage.

After "Porgy and Bess," Gershwin went to Hollywood to work on movie musicals. While there, he collapsed from a brain tumor and was rushed to Cedars of Lebanon Hospital. He died after an emergency operation.

Gershwin believed in America and in its popular-music heritage, which he called "the most vital of contemporary popular music. . . .I am not ashamed of writing songs, so long as they are good songs!"

About composing: "My work is done almost exclusively at night, and my best is achieved in the fall and winter months. A beautiful spring or summer day is least conducive to making music, for I always prefer the outdoors to work. . . .[But] when other people are asleep or out for a good time, I can get absolute quiet for my composing."

As noted by Jablonski (see above), Gershwin

believed that feelings and ideas were the most important things in music. "The various tonalities and sounds mean nothing," Gershwin stated, "unless they grow out of ideas. Not many composers have ideas." And "To me feeling counts more than knowledge. Of course, feeling by itself, without certain other attributes, is not enough, but it is the supreme essential."

GERSHWIN, IRA: lyricist. Born New York, New York, December 6, 1896.

One of the very greatest manipulators of words in the history of popular music, Ira Gershwin was long overshadowed by his younger brother and long-time collaborator George. Ira had proved his worth as a lyricist with Vincent Youmans before working on musicals with his brother. Later, after George's death, Ira's words shone as brightly with other great popular-music composers as they had during George's glory years.

The first piano in the Gershwin household was bought for Ira. It soon turned out, however, that George had the greater musical talent, and the lessons went to him. Ira attended New York's Townsend Harris Hall and the City College of New York. He wrote a column for the college paper and provided material for one of the college magazines.

He earned his first dollar as a writer in 1917, for a humorous paragraph sold to *The Smart Set.* As George began gaining ground in music, Ira began thinking about writing lyrics. In 1918, he wrote his first professional song with George, "The Real American Folk Song," which was introduced by Nora Bayes in "Ladies First."

One of George's coworkers at Harms, the music publishers, was Vincent Youmans. Gershwin suggested to producer Alex Aarons that Youmans do Aarons's next musical. The show, "Two Little Girls in Blue" (1921), featured lyrics by Arthur Francis, a pseudonym for Ira Gershwin. For this, his first Broadway musical, Ira wrote the words for such songs as "Oh Me! Oh My! Oh You!," "Dolly," and "Who's Who with You?"

In 1921, Ira worked with brother George on a show called "A Dangerous Maid," which folded before reaching Broadway. Their first hit collaboration, "Lady, Be Good," appeared in 1924. Such lyrics as "Oh, Lady Be Good," "The Half of It, Dearie, Blues," and "Fascinating Rhythm" marked Ira as a future master of the art. For "Tip-Toes" (1925), Ira provided "That Certain

Feeling" and "Sweet and Low-Down." His work for "Oh, Kay!" (1926) included "Maybe," "Clap Yo' Hands," "Do Do Do," and "Someone To Watch Over Me." The score of "Funny Face" (1927) contained "'S Wonderful," "He Loves and She Loves," and "The Babbitt and the Bromide." "Treasure Girl" (1928) introduced "I've Got a Crush on You." The show flopped and the song was used in "Strike Up the Band" (1930), which included "Soon" and the stirring title song. "Girl Crazy" (1930) contained "Bidin' My Time," "Could You Use Me?" "Embraceable You," "But Not for Me," and "I Got Rhythm." Among the notable songs in "Of Thee I Sing" (1931) were "Love Is Sweeping the Country," "Who Cares?," and the title song.

The last major project on which Ira worked with George was "Porgy and Bess" (1935). Ira and the play's author, DuBose Heyward, were colyricists. When Heyward would give them some written scenes from the show, "after their extraordinary fashion, [they] would get at the piano, pound, wrangle, swear, burst into weird snatches of song, and eventually emerge with a polished lyric" (Isaac Goldberg: "George Gershwin." New York: Simon and Schuster, 1931).

After George's death in 1937, Ira wrote with many leading composers, mostly for the movies but occasionally for Broadway. In 1941, he collaborated with Kurt Weill on the hit show "Lady in the Dark." One of his feats of lyric virtuosity propelled Danny Kaye to stardom. This was Ira's tongue-twisting catalogue of famous Russian composers, "Tschaikowsky." Other hit songs from the show were "My Ship," "This Is New," and "The Saga of Jenny." In 1944, Ira worked with Jerome Kern on the score for the movie "Cover Girl." One of their numbers, "Long Ago and Far Away," besides being a nationwide hit, was an Academy Award nominee. A Weill-Gershwin collaboration in 1945, "The Firebrand of Florence," lasted only forty-three performances.

Ira wrote for a number of successful musical films with Harold Arlen. Perhaps their best score was for the Judy Garland version of "A Star Is Born." This included "The Man That Got Away," which was an Oscar nominee for 1954.

GETZ, STAN: band leader, saxophonist. Born Philadelphia, Pennsylvania, February 2, 1927. (See also *Bossa nova.*)

Bossa nova, moved musicians famous in other areas, such as progressive jazz, to the foreground.

This was the case with tenor saxophonist Stan Getz. His album "Jazz Samba" (with Charlie Byrd) is credited with touching off the bossanova boom in the United States. (Getz was not the first to bring bossa nova to this country, but this was the first highly successful record.)

Getz had been a professional musician for twenty years but was known only to a relatively small segment of the music public. Still, he was only in his thirties when his bossa-nova break occurred, for he started in the band business at fifteen in the saxophone section of the Dick Rogers Orchestra. Soon after Stan was born, his family moved to New York, where he studied bass and bassoon before switching to saxophone. After breaking in with Rogers, Getz played with the bands of Jack Teagarden, Bob Chester, Stan Kenton, Jimmy Dorsey, Benny Goodman, Randy Brooks, Herbie Fields, and others before he reached the age of twenty.

He was one of the Four Brothers with Woody Herman's Herd of 1947–49, with whom he recorded a famous saxophone solo in "Early Autumn." Stan soon started his own quartet. Though not widely known outside jazz circles in the United States, he was a major attraction in Europe. After an overseas stay in the fifties, he returned to the United States for nightclub dates and a part in the movie "The Benny Goodman Story," and toured with Jazz at the Philharmonic in 1957 and 1958. He then moved to Copenhagen, Denmark, which remained his base until the beginning of 1961.

As a jazz saxophonist and leader he has had no peer, winning the *Metronome* magazine jazz poll for eleven straight years from the beginning of the fifties. He also captured *Playboy's* jazz poll four years running and the *Down Beat* Critics' Poll from 1953 to 1958. His album "Focus" (with Eddie Sauter) was one of the major jazz LPs turned out in the fifties. Then came the sixties and "Jazz Samba," which started a new cycle of popularity for Latin American dance rhythms in the United States.

GIRL CRAZY: musical. Lyrics by Ira Gershwin, music by George Gershwin, book by Guy Bolton and John McGowan, New York opening: October 14, 1930, Alvin Theatre. 272 performances.

"Girl Crazy" was a major event for the Broadway stage for several reasons. The hackneyed, uninspiring plot was not one. But the show contained one of the Gershwin brothers' greatest scores, and it marked the Broadway debut of two all-time musical stars, Ethel Merman and Ginger Rogers. Critic Newman Levy wrote in *The Nation:*

. . . to those of us who would rather listen to a song by Gershwin than a symphony by Mahler a new Gershwin show is an event. As in most of their other shows, the brothers Gershwin have had to carry the burden of a libretto that does not measure up to their splendid talents. . . .But in a Gershwin show the important thing is, of course, the songs. I use the word "songs" advisedly. The acclaim of George Gershwin as a composer has been so great that it has somewhat overshadowed the achievement of his brother Ira as . . . the most skilful versifier writing for the American stage.

"Girl Crazy" is set in a dude ranch in the small town of Custerville, Arizona. Eastern playboy Danny Churchill has been sent there by his father to keep him out of girl trouble. Danny makes the trip in a taxi operated by Gieber Goldfarb, who becomes the sheriff of Custerville. Danny opens a dude ranch and sponsors a gambling room in the bar of Custerville's only hotel. The wife of the bar and gambling-room operator is Kate Fothergill ("Frisco Kate"). Ethel Merman, as Kate, electrified the audience when she appeared in a sultry costume in the bar to sing "Sam and Delilah." Later in the show, she reviewed the problems of being the wife of a petty gambler in her sorrowful rendition of "Boy! What Love Has Done to Me!" But most impressive of all was Kate's red-hot number "I Got Rhythm," sung as part of the show at Churchill's nightclub.

Churchill continues his irresponsible ways, but his downfall is forecast when he meets Molly Gray, the pretty postmistress of Custerville. The usual combined attraction and repulsion of the romantic leads of a musical comedy when they meet was expressed in the duet "Could You Use Me?" Danny and Molly slowly draw closer, but then comes the also usual lovers' quarrel. Molly sings of her loneliness after this parting in "But Not for Me." Finally, Danny shows Molly that he has seen the error of his ways and wins her as he sings "Embraceable You." Another great song from "Girl Crazy" is "Bidin' My Time," which was sung during scene changes by a group of cowboys.

Besides Miss Merman, the original cast included Ginger Rogers, as Molly Gray, Allen Kearns, as Danny and Wille Howard as Goldfarb. The pit orchestra was one of the most illustrious ever assembled for a Broadway show. It included Benny Goodman, Glenn Miller, Gene Krupa, Jack Teagarden, and Jimmy Dorsey.

GIRL FRIEND, THE: musical. Lyrics by Lorenz Hart, music by Richard Rodgers, book by Herbert Fields. New York opening: March 17, 1926, Vanderbilt Theatre. 409 performances.

In 1926, Rodgers and Hart began to pick up steam on Broadway after their first big success in the 1925 "Garrick Gaieties." In collaboration with Herbert Fields, they came up with two hits in one year. The first was "The Girl Friend," the second "Peggy-Ann." Alan Dale of the New York *American* called "The Girl Friend"

> . . . a show with gumption. . . .What I liked best . . . was its music. This WAS music, instead of molasses. . . .'The Blue Room' . . . should be sung to exhaustion. . . .

The opening scene takes place on a Long Island dairy farm. The chorus sings "Hey! Hey!" and then extols the virtues of "The Simple Life." The hero is young Long Island dairyman Leonard Silver, who hopes to become a great six-day bicycle racer and practices on a bike he has attached to a butter churn. He is supported in his endeavors by Mollie Farrell, daughter of a professional cyclist. She is, as she and Leonard sing, "The Girl Fried" and acts as his trainer, manager, and promoter. She propels him into professional competition by forging letters from famous sports personalities. Arthur Spencer, a professional manager, takes Leonard in tow, however, for "He's a Winner!" The manager's sister Wynn is romantically interested in the dairyman. Leonard is entered in a six-day bike race which, unknown to him, has been fixed. A crew of gamblers is involved, and they try to make sure their man wins. But Leonard wins the race and Mollie.

The original cast included Sam White, as Leonard; Eva Puck, as Mollie; Frank Doane, as Arthur Spencer; and Evelyn Cavanaugh, as Wynn Spencer. Other songs were "Good-bye, Lenny!," "Cabarets," "Why Do I?" "The Damsel Who Done All the Dirt," "Town Hall Tonight," "Good Fellow, Mine," "Creole Crooning Song," "I'd Like To Take You Home," and "What Is It?"

GOLD RECORD: record-industry term for a million-seller record.

Gold Records and other awards for their hits are displayed by the Beatles.

In 1958, the Record Industry Association of America decided to award gold records for million-seller records to those firms that would agree to proper certification procedures. The criteria for the award are: single records, sales of one million copies; long-playing record albums, factory sales of one million dollars. A list of certified RIAA awards since 1958 is given in the Appendix.

GOODMAN, BENJAMIN DAVID (BENNY): band leader, clarinetist. Born Chicago, Illinois, May 30, 1909.

The period of the big bands is dominated by the towering figure of Benny Goodman. He won the title of King of Swing and held it, unopposed, from the mid-nineteen-thirties into the sixties. Even when swing faded out, a Benny Goodman performance always commanded capacity audiences, whether at Carnegie Hall or at major entertainment centers in this country and overseas.

Goodman was born near the Chicago stockyards, the eighth of eleven children. His father, a tailor, was poor but worked hard to educate his family. This included exposure to music. In 1918, the Keheleh Jacob Synagogue distributed instru-

[92]

Benny Goodman

ments to children of the congregation. Benny's older brothers Freddy and Harry received a tuba and a trumpet, and Benny was given a clarinet. He received a few lessons then, but mostly he taught himself. In later years, whenever he could, he studied with famous instructors, including, in the fifties, the great classical clarinetists Reginald Kell and Simon Bellison.

By the time he was fourteen, Goodman was playing with local bands in the Chicago area. He took part in many jam sessions that featured such musicians as Louis Armstrong, King Oliver, Bix Beiderbecke, and Frank Teschemacher. In 1925, Benny joined Ben Pollack's band and remained with it for the better part of three years.

In 1928, Benny decided to stay in New York for a while. He organized at pit band for the Broadway show "Hello Daddy." After the show closed, he stayed in New York playing with local outfits and making records with pickup bands. In 1933, he met young jazz impresario John Hammond, who helped Benny organize his first big band. In the summer of 1934, Benny and his band were booked into Billy Rose's Music Hall in New York. Then came a series of one-nighters across the country, followed by Benny's being signed to play on the "Let's Dance" radio pro-

gram. The program, plus a tremendous reception at the Palomar Ballroom in Los Angeles, made swing popular with the country's popular-music audience. In November, 1935, the word "swing" was first used in publicity, and Benny's orchestra was billed as a "swing band." In early 1936, during a series of three jazz concerts sponsored by the Chicago Rhythm Club, Benny first introduced the Benny Goodman Trio. In the following months and years, the other Goodman combos—trios, quartets, quintets, and sextets—came into being.

Hit engagement after hit engagement followed, climaxed by two 1938 milestones. One was the first of many Carnegie Hall jazz concerts. The other was the famous stay at New York's Paramount Theatre, where swing fans literally danced in the aisles. In 1938 as well, Benny was named King of Swing in the *Down Beat* poll. In the years that followed, Goodman kept busy with his band work and also made many appearances as a classical clarinet soloist. In 1941 and 1942, for instance, he appeared with the Rochester and New York Philharmonics.

Over the years, the Goodman band included some of the most famous names in popular music, such as drummer Gene Krupa, pianists Jess Stacey and Teddy Wilson, vibraharpist Lionel Hampton, trombonist Glenn Miller, trumpeter Harry James, and vocalists Peggy Lee, Patti Page, Dick Haymes, and Art Lund. Some of the more famous of his many recordings are "Let's Dance" (his theme), "Avalon," "Whispering," "Tiger Rag," "Pagan Love Song," and perhaps the most legendary, "Sing, Sing, Sing," which was the high spot of the famous 1938 Carnegie Hall concert. It featured great solos by such musicians as Stacey, Krupa, James, and Goodman himself.

In 1955, a movie was made of his life, "The Benny Goodman Story." Steve Allen played Goodman, and Goodman provided the music for the sound track.

In the nineteen-fifties and sixties, Goodman made several major European tours. In 1961, his tour of Russia reportedly made one of the greatest impressions on the Russians ever made by a foreign musical organization.

GORDON, MACK: lyricist, actor. Born Warsaw, Poland, June 21, 1904; died February 27, 1959. Won Academy Award for Best Song of 1943 ("You'll Never Know").

Mack Gordon is probably best known as half of the famous nineteen-thirties team of Revel and Gordon. He wrote with a number of other composers, however, including James V. Monaco, Jimmy Van Heusen, Ray Henderson, and Harry Warren. His collaboration with Warren, in fact, resulted in a level of creativity that often exceeded any of his earlier efforts.

Gordon came to the United States at a very early age. He was educated in public schools in Brooklyn and the Bronx. His interests ran towards show business rather than school. He began his career as a boy soprano with a minstrel show. Later, he made his mark as vaudeville comedian, though he did some singing as well. In the late twenties, the advent of talking pictures gave him a new vocation, writing special material for films.

Between collecting songs for his stage career and writing lyrics, Gordon spent a lot of time in music-publishing houses. On one occasion, he met Harry Revel, a composer newly arrived from England. Revel needed a lyricist and tried to induce Gordon to take the job. Gordon turned down the offer and went on tour. Revel followed, and his persistence finally won Gordon over.

From 1929 to 1933, they turned out many hit songs and worked together on several Broadway shows. Their output included "A Boy and a Girl Were Dancing," "Underneath the Harlem Moon," "It's within Your Power," "Listen to the German Band," and "An Orchid to You." In 1933, they moved to Hollywood and for the next six years collaborated on many important film scores. Their first year's efforts included the standard "Did You Ever See a Dream Walking?" Some of their other major hits from 1933 to 1939 were "Love Thy Neighbor," "With My Eyes Wide Open I'm Dreaming," "Stay as Sweet as You Are," "Paris in the Spring," and "My Lucky Star."

In 1940, the partnership dissolved, and Gordon soon started a new collaboration with composer Harry Warren. Their first film assignment was "Young People," which included "Fifth Avenue" and "Tra-La-La-La." The same year, for "Argentine Nights," they wrote "Two Dreams Met" and "Down Argentine Way." In 1941, they provided Carmen Miranda with several hits, such as "Chica Chica Boom Chic" and "I Yi-Yi-Yi-Yi-Yi Like You Very Much." Another Warren-Gordon success was the score for Glenn Miller's "Sun Valley Serenade," which included "Chattanooga Choo Choo" and "I Know Why and So Do You." The following year, Miller played more of their hits in "Orchestra

Wives," which featured "Kalamazoo" and "Serenade in Blue." Another 1942 song hit was "I Had the Craziest Dream," from "Springtime in the Rockies." In 1943, they turned out the song which brought Gordon his first Oscar, "You'll Never Know," from "Hello, Frisco, Hello." In the later forties, Gordon began to work more and more with other composers, including James V. Monaco, with whom he wrote "I Can't Begin To Tell You" and "I'm Making Believe." He and Warren still found time to collaborate, however, turning out such hits as "My Heart Tells Me," "The More I See You," and "Friendly Star."

GORME, EYDIE: singer. Born Bronx, New York, August 16, 1931.

Eydie Gorme made her first appearance at the age of three on a children's radio show, after she wandered onto a line of performers while her parents were shopping at a New York department store. While attending William Taft High School, she was featured vocalist of the high-school band and star of many school musicals. She attended night classes in economics and foreign trade at City College after graduating from Taft. During the day, she put her knowledge of Spanish to work as an interpreter for a theatrical-supply export company.

She might have remained a practical breadwinner had not a former City College classmate, band leader Ken Greenglass, asked her to sing with his band on weekends. Soon after, Ken gave up the band and Eydie her job so that Ken could manage her career as a professional vocalist. Band leader Tommy Tucker heard one of Eydie's demonstration records at a music publisher's office and hired her for a two-month tour. Greenglass learned that Tex Beneke, successor to the great Glenn Miller, was looking for a singer. Eydie auditioned at the close of the Tucker tour, and won the job. After a successful stay with Beneke, Eydie went out as a solo performer in the early fifties. Besides nightclub, radio, and television guest appearances, she also had her own Voice of America program, "Cita con Eydie" ("A Date with Eydie"). Then came her biggest step toward stardom, Steve Allen's 1953 invitation to become a regular on his "Tonight" show. While starring on "Tonight," Eydie made her New York nightclub debut in February, 1956, at the Copacabana (as a hurried replacement for an indisposed Billy Daniels). She won a standing ovation and was booked for a return engagement as the star of her own show. In January, 1957, Eydie appeared at New York's Palace Theatre as the premiere vocalist of the Jerry Lewis show. The same year was even more eventful for her; in December, she married "Tonight" coperformer Steve Lawrence in Las Vegas.

Eydie continued to star in nightclub engagements and on TV shows during Steve's stint in the Army from 1958 to 1960. After Steve's discharge, the Lawrences began highly successful appearances as a team at such clubs as the Copacabana, Los Angeles's Cocoanut Grove, and Miami's Eden Roc, and at the Sands and Sahara Hotels in Las Vegas. In 1962, Eydie signed with Columbia Records and turned out her 1963 hit single of "Blame It on the Bossa Nova," which also provided the title for a best-selling long-play album. In 1963, she also scored with the single "Don't Try To Fight It, Baby" and the album "Let the Good Times Roll." That same year, she and Steve also turned out the hit LP "Steve and Eydie at the Movies."

GOSPEL SONG: religious song developed by the Negro during slavery days in the southern United States.

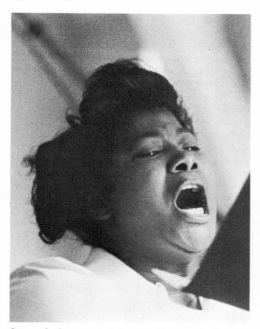

One of the most famous of gospel singers, Mahalia Jackson.

The terms "gospel song" and "spiritual" are synonymous. Though religious in origin, the gospel song and its rhythms have had a great effect on many areas of popular music. Many country-and-Western and jazz standards, for instance, are derived from gospel music.

In slavery times, gospel songs were often pleas for freedom in a language the whites couldn't understand. Examples of gospel songs are "Joshua Fit the Battle of Jericho," "Go Down, Moses," "When the Saints Go Marchin' In," and "Ezekiel Saw the Wheel." The tremendous demand for this type of music is seen in the fact that Mahalia Jackson's first single gospel record, "Move Up a Little Higher," sold over eight million copies after its release in 1953.

Most folk singers have at least a few gospel songs in their repertoires. In recent years, there has been a trend for gospel singers to appear in coffeehouses and nightclubs. This pop gospel singing is often souped up. Miss Jackson decries this approach: "The word of God is too precious to be degraded by presenting it in a nightclub." She has also stressed the difference of gospel rhythm from other Negro melodic patterns: "The blues taught me all I know and I respect it deeply, but too often gospels are confused with blues or jazz. They are not the same. They are from the same source, but the tempo and, even more important, the internal emphasis are quite different."

GOULD, MORTON: composer, arranger, conductor. Born Richmond Hill, New York, December 10, 1913.

Gould played the piano and wrote music at the age of four. His first piece was published when he was six and was titled, aptly, "Just Six." While attending public schools in Richmond Hill, he also appeared widely in vaudeville and on the concert stage and radio. By the time he was seventeen, he was a staff arranger for New York's Radio City Music Hall. At twenty-one, he conducted and arranged a series of programs for radio station WOR. Later, Gould was a staff arranger for the National Broadcasting Company network.

As he grew older, Gould turned out many ambitious popular and serious works. His music was played by major conductors, including Toscanini, Stokowski, Monteux, and Rodzinski. In 1952, he wrote and conducted a Symphony for Band as part of the West Point sesquicentennial celebration. Some of his other orchestral works are "Fall River Legend," "Tap Dance Concerto," "Lincoln Legend," "Composer Inventions," "Showpiece," "Latin American Symphonette," "Declaration," "Jekyll and Hyde Variations," and "St. Lawrence Suite."

Gould also wrote for movies and Broadway shows. His Broadway output includes the scores for "Billion Dollar Baby" and "Arms and the Girl." He provided the score and also appeared in the film "Delightfully Dangerous," and wrote the scores for "Windjammer" and "Cinerama Holiday."

The Gould touch also has won favor with record fans. His output for RCA Victor includes "Jungle Drums," "Moonlight Sonata," "Kern and Porter Favorites," "Beyond the Blue Horizon," "Piano Favorites," "Love Walked In," and "Good Night, Sweetheart" and "More Jungle Drums."

GOULET, ROBERT: singer, actor. Born Lawrence, Massachusetts, November 26, 1933.

One of the most promising newcomers on the popular-music scene in the nineteen-sixties,

Robert Goulet

handsome Robert Goulet reached Broadway stardom by way of Canada. He attended high school in Canada, then tried to storm New York, but finally had to make his mark by going north of the border again. In a CBS release he noted:

I was not an overnight success. New York City, which has been so warm, so responsive, so wonderful for me, was a cold, lonely place indeed in the winter of 1955, when I couldn't even get someone to listen to me do vocal exercises.

Goulet, who is of French extraction, with a trace of Irish, was born and partly raised in New England. When he was fourteen, his father died, and the family moved to Canada. After graduating from high school, Goulet got his first show-business job as a disc jockey with station CKCA, Edmonton. Soon after, he won a vocal scholarship to Toronto's Royal Conservatory of Music. Goulet made his first ill-fated try for New York success in 1954. The only work he could get was selling stationery in Gimbel's.

He gave up and returned to Toronto, where his luck changed. He won a leading role in the Canadian Broadcasting Corporation's production of "Little Women." This led to his gaining a role in the annual Canadian topical revue "Spring Thaw." He also became a regular member, for three years, of the top-rated Canadian television program "Showtime."

A theatrical agent recommended Goulet for a major role in the Lerner and Loewe "Camelot," and when the show began its pre-Broadway try-out in Toronto on October 1, 1960, Goulet appeared as Sir Lancelot. On December 3, 1960, "Camelot" opened at New York's Majestic Theatre. The reviews were mixed as far as the show was concerned, but Goulet received unanimous raves.

On October 6, 1962, when Goulet left "Camelot," he was a national favorite. While still with "Camelot," he had become known to TV fans everywhere with a series of stellar guest spots on Ed Sullivan's and Gary Moore's shows and in an NBC-TV special "The Broadway of Lerner and Loewe." Besides this, Goulet and Judy Garland provided the voices for a movie comedy about cats, "Gay Purr-ee." In November, 1962, Goulet scored a success with his singing debut at New York's Persian Room. He also established himself as a major recording artist; his LP albums include "World of Love" ('63), "Without You" ('64), and "My Love Forgive Me" ('65).

The Grammy Award

GRAMMY: award given by the National Academy of the Recording Arts and Sciences (NARAS) for achievements in phonograph recordings. (See also *National Academy of the Recording Arts and Sciences.*)

As of 1963, there were thirty-nine different categories for Grammy awards. Typical categories are Record of the Year, Album of the Year, and Best Instrumental Theme. NARAS competition covers all major music forms.

The Academy was founded in 1957, a surprise outgrowth of a promotion campaign by the Hollywood Chamber of Commerce. The Chamber's request for record-industry executives to provide names for sidewalk plaques in the Hollywood and Vine area led to the idea of an organization to provide yearly awards to deserving record-industry artists. An organizing committee was set up, and NARAS was incorporated soon after. The awards are in the form of miniature replicas of an old-time gramophone, with a large horn-shaped speaker and a winding crank, and are called Grammys. (See Appendix for award listings.)

GRANT, EARL: singer, instrumentalist. Born Oklahoma City, Oklahoma, January 20, 1933.

Earl Grant originally planned to be a schoolteacher. His father was teaching at Texas South-ern University, Houston, when Earl was born. Earl's family moved to Kansas City soon after. Earl grew up with music, studying a wide range of instruments, including piano, organ, drums, and trumpet.

The most likely profession with this background was teaching music. Grant entered the University of Southern California as a music major in the late forties. After winning his degree, he taught for a time and also took additional courses in music at the Kansas City Conservatory of Music, New Rochelle Conservatory, and DePaul Conservatory in Chicago. After a hitch in the Army, he returned to USC for graduate work.

Earl played at small Los Angeles nightclubs to help pay his tuition. He developed an intimate vocal style to go along with his piano and organ playing. His following at the Pigalle grew so great that the club had to expand three times. Earl soon had his own informal show on Los Angeles television.

In 1959, Grant's recording of "Fever" won national attention. Soon he was appearing on the Ed Sullivan and other shows. He began making nightclub appearances throughout the country and recording for Decca. Earl's tours of Japan, Australia, Canada, and Mexico made him an international favorite.

Though Grant made a number of hit single records ("Fever" and "Swingin' Gently" among them), his albums were far more popular. Some of the most successful of these were "Ebb Tide," "At Basin Street East," and "Beyond the Reef."

GREEN, ADOLPH: lyricist, librettist, actor. Born New York, New York, December 2, 1915.

Some of the most brilliant moments in the musical theater of the nineteen-forties and later were provided by the team of Adolph Green and Betty Comden. Both attended New York University, and became members of the Washington Square Players. Before long, they wrote and appeared in their own nightclub act, the Revuers, with Judy Holliday. Between college and the Revuers, Green had played a pirate king in a 1937 summer-camp production of "The Pirates of Penzance." The music counselor at the camp was Leonard Bernstein, and thus began a friendship that was to bring Comden and Green into the ranks of major Broadway writers.

In 1939, when the Revuers were booked into New York's Village Vanguard, Green shared an apartment with Bernstein, whose visits to the Vanguard further impressed him with Adolph and Betty's way with words. Comden and Green wrote the book and lyrics for Bernstein's first musical, "On the Town" (1944). Green also played one of the three sailors on leave in New York. Because of Bernstein's committments in the classical field, eight years passed before they worked on another show with him. When they were asked to contribute to "Wonderful Town," the musical version of "My Sister Eileen," Comden and Green were dubious. As Stanley Green notes in "The World of Musical Comedy" (New York: Ziff-Davis, 1960) Adolph thought the play "so awfully Thirties-bound, sort of a post-Depression play, full of overexploited plot lines and passé references." Bernstein's enthusiasm was transmitted to them, however, and once more they turned out a sparkling set of lyrics.

Before this show, Betty and Adolph had begun working with Jule Styne, with whom they did most of their work for Broadway up to the sixties. They provided the lyrics and, in most cases, the book for five straight hits: "High Button Shoes" (1947), "Two on the Aisle" (1951), "Peter Pan" (1954), "Bells Are Ringing" (1956), and "Say, Darling" (1958). In "Bells Are Ringing," Comden and Green once more worked with their old teammate Judy Holliday. In the 1964–65 season, Green and Comden were represented on Broadway by "Fade Out-Fade In," which starred Carol Burnett.

GREEN, JOHN W. (JOHNNY): composer, conductor, arranger, band leader, motion-picture musical director. Born New York, New York, October 10, 1908. Won Academy Award for Best Scoring of a Musical Picture in 1948 ("Easter Parade"), 1951 ("An American in Paris"), and 1961 ("West Side Story"), and for Best Scoring of a Short Subject in 1953 ("The Merry Wives of Windsor").

Johnny Green is one child prodigy who made good, not just in one field but in a wide number of areas, from popular songwriting to symphony-orchestra conducting. He received his early education at Horace Mann School in New York and New York Military Academy, and graduated with an economics degree from Harvard at nineteen. He quickly received a job in Wall Street and might have been a successful banker or stock-broker. Music had already attracted his attention, however; in 1927, he had begun his musical career as an arranger for Guy Lombardo. By the time he had finished college, he was an accom-

plished pianist and a talented composer of popular music.

In 1928, he wrote his first song hit, "Coquette," following this up in the next few years with such other all-time standards as "I'm Yours" and "Body and Soul" (1930), "Out of Nowhere" (1931), and "I Cover the Waterfront" and "You're Mine, You" (1933). During these same years, Green was also in demand as a conductor and accompanist. From 1931 to 1933, he accompanied Gertrude Lawrence, Ethel Merman, and James Melton. He also worked as arranger, composer, and conductor for Paramount Pictures Eastern studios from 1930 to 1932. In 1932, Paul Whiteman commissioned him to write the "Night Club Suite," which was performed at Carnegie Hall in New York, Symphony Hall in Boston, and by the British Broadcasting Corporation Symphony in London.

From 1933 to 1941, Green was the leader of nationally known dance bands that played engagements across the country and also for network radio shows. Some of the shows on which Green was featured were those of Ruth Etting, Jack Benny, and Fred Astaire. During 1939–40, Green was star of the Philip Morris network program.

In 1942, a brand-new phase of Green's career began when he was invited to Hollywood. From 1942, on, he made his mark on the Coast with his musical work for films and as a leader in the cultural life of southern California. In the latter capacity, he was featured at many symphony and light-classic programs at the Hollywood Bowl and Greek Theatre. Beginning in 1949, he conducted the Hollywood Bowl Symphony. During 1947–48, he had his own highly popular musical program on local radio, "The Man Called X."

During the mid-forties, Green scored the films "Broadway Rhythm," "Bathing Beauty," "Weekend at the Waldorf," "The Sailor Takes a Wife," "Easy To Wed," "Fiesta," and "Easter Parade." The last two were nominated for Academy Awards, and "Easter Parade" won Green the Oscar for the best scoring of 1948. In 1949, he became musical director at Metro-Goldwyn-Mayer, and from 1949 on he scored or directed many more important movies, including "The Inspector General," "Rhapsody," "Brigadoon," "An American in Paris," and "The Merry Wives of Windsor."

In 1958, for "Bernadette," he provided the first original dramatic score for film television.

He also produced many TV films for Desilu studios.

GUYS AND DOLLS: musical. Lyrics and music by Frank Loesser, book by Abe Burrows and Jo Swerling. New York opening: November 24, 1950, Forty-Sixth Street Theatre. 1,200 performances.

The world of Damon Runyon—with its offbeat horse-race addicts, gamblers, and Broadway hangers-on—was turned into the funniest, most tuneful musical show of the 1950–51 season. The book for "Guys and Dolls" was mainly based on Runyon's short story "The Idyll of Miss Sarah Brown," but some of the characters were taken from other Runyon stories. This marked the transition to Broadway of a highly talented radio script writer, Abe Burrows, who went on to do the book for such shows as "Can-Can," "Silk Stockings," and "Happy Hunting." The score for "Guys and Dolls" was one of Frank Loesser's finest.

The play opens with a glimpse of the hustle and bustle of Broadway. The spotlight then focuses on three horse players, Nicely-Nicely Johnson, Benny Southstreet, and Rusty Charlie, who sing of their betting choices in "Fugue for Tinhorns." As they stand there, Sister Sarah Brown of the Save-A-Soul Mission comes by and exhorts the sinners of Broadway to repent. But Sarah, pretty as she is, has little success. As she goes away, the show's central character, Nathan Detroit, arrives. He is the proprietor of "the oldest established permanent floating crap game in New York." Nicely and friends want to know the site of the next game, but Nathan is having trouble finding a new location that Police Lieutenant Brannigan doesn't know about.

His last resort, the Biltmore Garage, requires a thousand-dollar "rent," and Nathan is broke. To get the money, he decides to set up a sure bet with gambler Sky Masterson. He finds Sky and bets a thousand dollars that Sky won't be able to get Sarah to go to Havana with him. Sky finds Sarah and woos her ("I'll Know"), but she snubs him. Nathan visits his girl Adelaide, a nightclub performer. As he arrives at the club, the girls sing "A Bushel and a Peck." Adelaide tries to talk Nathan into turning their fourteen-year engagement into a marriage, and he runs off. To Detroit's woe, Sarah has gone to Havana—for Sky has promised to deliver her twelve or more sinners the next night. It's Sarah's last chance, for her superior has threatened to close the mission.

In Havana, Sarah realizes she loves Sky ("If I Were a Bell").

They return to New York and find the crap game, which Nathan installed in the mission during their absence, fleeing from Brannigan. The game is going on in a sewer when Sky catches up with it. He won't welsh on his word to Sarah, and he shoots each man a thousand dollars against an appearance at the mission ("Luck Be a Lady Tonight"). Masterson triumphs, and all show up the next night to "give testimony." The reformed Broadway denizens go straight; Sky marries Sarah and joins the mission band; and the new proprietor of Nathan Detroit's Newsstand marries Adelaide.

The original Broadway cast included Sam Levene, as Nathan; Robert Alda, as Sky; Isabel Bigley, as Sarah; Vivian Blaine, as Adelaide; Stubby Kaye, as Nicely-Nicely, and Pat Rooney, Sr., as the mission drummer. Other songs were "The Oldest Established," "Adelaide's Lament," "Guys and Dolls," "My Time of Day," "I've Never Been in Love Before," "Take Back Your Mink," "More I Cannot Wish You," "Sue Me," "Sit Down, You're Rockin' the Boat," and "Marry the Man Today." The movie version had Frank Sinatra, as Nathan; Marlon Brando, as Sky; Jean Simmons, as Sarah; and Vivian Blaine, as Adelaide. Added to the movie score was a new Loesser song, "A Woman in Love."

GYPSY: musical. Lyrics by Stephen Sondheim, music by Jule Styne, book by Arthur Laurents. Based on Gypsy Rose Lee's autobiography. New York opening: May 21, 1959, Broadway Theatre. 702 performances.

For many years, Gypsy Rose Lee reigned supreme as queen of burlesque and did it in such regal fashion that she is remembered more as a performer than as a stripper. But "Gypsy," based on Miss Lee's memoirs, deals with burlesque only in passing. The story—at least on the stage—is more that of Gypsy's mother Rose, a strong, determined, and domineering yet lovable person. The show was written to taken advantage of the dynamism of Ethel Merman, who played Rose.

The story begins in Seattle in the early twenties. Rose is training her two young daughters, Louise (Gypsy) and June for their first attempt at vaudeville in a local children's show. They sing "May We Entertain You," the reprise to which ("Let Me Entertain You") later serves as Gypsy's strip tease theme music. Rose's whole world is wrapped up in her children's life in show business. She can't see how anyone could enjoy a commonplace, everyday life ("Some People").

Rose is partial to June and adds some boys to the act, which becomes "Baby June and Her Newsboys," with Louise as one of the newsboys. The act meets with indifference until Rose meets a likable candy salesman ("Small World") and talks him into managing the group. Under Herbie's wing, the group succeeds in getting bookings in many minor parts of the vaudeville circuit. The girls grow older and fashions change, but Rose still makes the girls wear children's clothes and perform the same routines. Herbie then gets them a contract on the Orpheum circuit. He asks Rose to retire and marry him, but she refuses, for show business is all the world to her.

June runs away and gets married. Rose is shocked for a time but recovers with the thought that Louise can take over the role ("Everything's Coming Up Roses"). But vaudeville is on its last legs, and Herbie accidentally books the act into a burlesque theater. Rose wants to cancel, but Louise, knowing how hard-pressed they are, learns the striptease routine from three girls in the show ("You Gotta Have a Gimmick"). Rose drops her scruples and, when the top stripteaser is arrested, has Louise go on. This causes Herbie to leave for good. Louise goes on to success. For a time, she shrugs off her mother, who is still trying to dominate her life. At the end, both gain more understanding of each other and are reunited.

Other numbers in the score were "Baby June and Her Newsboys," "Mr. Goldstone," "Little Lamb," "You'll Never Get Away from Me," "Dainty June and her Farm Boys," "If Mama Was Married," "All I Need Is the Girl," "Together Wherever We Go," and "Rose's Turn." Gypsy Rose Lee was played in the show by Sandra Church and in the movie by Natalie Wood. In the movie, Rose was portrayed by Rosalind Russell. Other members of the original cast were Jack Klugman, as Herbie; Lane Bradbury, as June; and Paul Wallace, as the "newsboy" Tulsa, whom June marries.

HAMMERSTEIN, OSCAR, II: lyricist, librettist. Born New York, New York, July 12, 1895; died New York, New York, August 23, 1960. Won Pulitzer Prize Special Award for "Oklahoma!" (1943), Pulitzer Prize Drama Award for "South Pacific" (1949), Academy Award for

Best Song of 1941 ("The Last Time I Saw Paris") and 1945 ("It Might as Well Be Spring").

Around World War I, New York's Columbia University was the alma mater of a group of young men who were to revolutionize the American musical theater—Lorenz Hart, Richard Rodgers, Morrie Ryskind, Howard Dietz, and Oscar Hammerstein. Hammerstein's grandfather Oscar had been a power in grand opera and had built the Manhattan Opera House in New York. His father William managed the Victoria, an important vaudeville theater. His uncle Arthur was a great Broadway producer.

Oscar's parents, though, were aware of the difficulties of earning a living in the field. When Oscar reached college age, they suggested he study law. At Columbia, Oscar soon became involved in the Varsity Show. He appeared in its productions and wrote some of the material, including a 1916 scene in which he and Lorenz Hart appeared. He went on to enter Columbia Law School, but soon quit to work as a stage manager on some of his uncle Arthur's shows. The first three were Rudolf Friml operettas, "You're in Love," "Sometimes," and "Tumble In." Oscar also kept active in Columbia Varsity Show work and helped pick Rodgers and Hart's show "Fly With Me" one year.

He began writing plays. His uncle produced two of these, but they were failures. Then Arthur suggested that Oscar work with the more experienced Otto Harbach. Their first collaboration, "Tickle Me," with music by Herbert Stothart, opened on August 17, 1920, and ran for two hundred and seven performances. Their next endeavor, "Jimmie," closed after seventy-one performances. After several more false starts, Hammerstein and Harbach provided the words for Vincent Youmans's success "Wildflower." The show opened on February 7, 1923, and ran for five hundred and eighty-six performances. In 1924, Harbach and Hammerstein provided Rudolf Friml with book and lyrics for the immortal "Rose Marie." Besides the title song, the show included such standards as "Indian Love Call" and "Totem Tom-Tom."

In 1924, Harbach, Hammerstein, and Jerome Kern wrote the Marilyn Miller hit "Sunny." Out of this grew the Hammerstein-Kern interest in Edna Ferber's novel "Show Boat." Before this show materialized, Hammerstein collaborated with Sigmund Romberg on the 1926 hit "The Desert Song." Then, on December 27, 1927,

Oscar Hammerstein II listens intently as Richard Rodgers, his most famous collaborator, picks out a tune on the piano.

"Show Boat" blazed forth to start a new era in musical theater. Hammerstein wrote the book and the lyrics (except for "Bill"). The score included such all-time favorites as "Ol' Man River," "Make Believe," "Can't Help Lovin' Dat Man," and "Why Do I Love You?"

Working with Kern and such other famous composers as Romberg and Friml, Hammerstein provided book and lyrics for many hit shows in the late twenties and early thirties, including "The New Moon," "Music in the Air," "Sweet Adeline," and "May Wine." During the middle and late thirties, Hammerstein worked on a series of unsuccessful shows. In the meantime, long-time friend Richard Rodgers was helplessly watching his collaborator Lorenz Hart become increasing ill. Shortly before Hart died in 1943, Rodgers and Hammerstein agreed to work to-

gether. Rodgers was interested in adapting Lynn Riggs's play "Green Grow the Lilacs" to the musical stage. Hammerstein immediately grew enthusiastic about the project. The show, named "Oklahoma!," brought to a fever pitch the musical revolution begun sixteen years before by "Show Boat." As Burns Mantle wrote in the New York *Daily News:*

> "Oklahoma" seems to me to be the most thoroughly and attractively American musical comedy . . . since "Show Boat". . . . (It) really is different—beautifully different.

For a brief time, Rodgers and Hammerstein went in different directions. Rodgers worked on the new version of "A Connecticut Yankee." Hammerstein completed work on his modern-dress adaptation of Bizet's "Carmen." With an

[101]

all-Negro cast and called "Carmen Jones," it opened on December 2, 1943, to a hit run of five hundred and two performances.

Soon Rodgers and Hammerstein were together again, a team that continued to provide new landmarks in the American musical theater up to Hammerstein's death. The year 1945 brought their movie "State Fair" and musical play "Carousel." Included in "State Fair" was the Academy Award-winning "It Might as Well Be Spring." "Carousel" provided another great score, including "If I Loved You," "When I Marry Mister Snow," "June Is Bustin' Out All Over," "What's the Use of Wond'rin'," and "Soliloquy." After stumbling slightly with "Allegro" in 1947, Rodgers and Hammerstein wrote "South Pacific" in 1949 and "The King and I" in 1951. Of their four remaining efforts, three were successful but not quite up to the standards they themselves set earlier. The three were "Me and Juliet" (1953), "Flower Drum Song" (1958), and "The Sound of Music" (1958). "Pipe Dream" (1955) ran for only two hundred and forty-six performances and was the least impressive of all their work. Many of their shows scored equally great successes as motion pictures. In addition, Rodgers and Hammerstein provided one of the classics of television, "Cinderella." Julie Andrews played the title role in the original version.

After one of the most productive careers in theater history, Oscar Hammerstein died of cancer at the age of sixty-five.

HAMPTON, LIONEL: band leader, instrumentalist. Born Louisville, Kentucky, April 20, 1913.

Lionel Hampton continued successfully to lead a big band long after many other famous organizations had faded away with the end of World War II. A five-week tour of Japan by Hampton's band in April and May, 1963, reportedly set off a whole new era of music in that country.

Soon after Hampton was born, his family moved to Birmingham, Alabama. By the time he was of high-school age, they had moved again, to Chicago. When Hampton was sixteen, another move landed him in Los Angeles. Lionel entered the University of Southern California. To help pay his tuition, he worked nights as a soda jerk. He began to get interested in playing drums. At night, he worked out some of his rhythmic patterns by drumming on the counter with spoons.

When he began tapping the glasses, his boss had enough and fired him.

Lionel decided to try making his living in music and quit school. He got a job as drummer with Les Hite's Orchestra. His fame as a jazz drummer spread rapidly. But Hampton also played the piano with a special two-finger method and also mastered the vibraharp. Louis Armstrong sat in with Hite's band for a recording session and was particularly impressed with Hampton's vibraharp work. He suggested Lionel concentrate on this instrument. Hampton never regretted following Satchmo's advice, for the great Benny Goodman heard Hampton in 1936 and promptly hired him. Lionel became part of the famous quartet with Benny on clarinet, Teddy Wilson on piano, and Gene Krupa on drums. Besides playing as soloists on band dates, the quartet gave concerts on its own and made many records that are now collectors' items.

The Goodman band provided solid schooling for many band leaders of the forties. Hampton went out on his own after several years with Benny. The Hampton band was an almost immediate success, with Lionel playing not only his vibraharp but occasional drum and even piano solos. From the band's beginning through the fifties and sixties, Hampton experimented with many styles, from swing to boogiewoogie and be-bop. Some of his recordings are "Flyin' Home," "Six Appeal" (with Benny Goodman), "Hamp's Salty Blues," "Hamp's Boogiewoogie," "Flyin Home #2," "Chord-a-Re-Bop," "New Central Avenue Breakdown," "Pink Champagne," "Air Mail Special," and "Mingus Fingers."

HARBACH, OTTO: lyricist, librettist. Born Salt Lake City, Utah, August 16, 1873; died New York, New York, January 24, 1963.

In a career lasting over fifty years, Otto Harbach compiled one of the most distinguished records in American musical history. His diverse talents helped create a body of works that still grace the stages of the world and the repertoires of leading singers and major recording organizations. In addition, he had a hand in the development of another great lyricist, the late Oscar Hammerstein II. A few of the famous songs which feature his lyrics (some of them in collaboration with Hammerstein) are "Giannina Mia," "Bambalina," "Indian Love Call," "Romance," "Rose Marie," "The Desert Song,"

"One Alone," "Who?," "The Night Was Made for Love," "She Didn't Say Yes," "You're Devastating," "The Touch of Your Hand," "Yesterdays," and "Smoke Gets in Your Eyes."

Harbach's parents were Danish immigrants named Hauerbach who crossed the country on foot and by ox cart to settle in Utah. His family was poor but hard working, and they saw that their children had the proper respect for education. Otto attended the Collegiate Institute in Salt Lake. He then worked his way through Knox College in Galesburg, Illinois, to gain his bachelor's degree. After graduation, he worked as an English teacher in Walla Walla, Washington, for six years. He had a great desire to go to New York, however, to sample the learning and culture of the city. His chance came in 1901 when he received a sabbatical leave to study for an advanced degree at Columbia University.

Once in the big city, he was entranced with all its aspects, but particularly its theater. He decided to abandon schooling to try to make his way as a playwright. The going was not easy. Harbach had to work during the day and write at night. After a short stint as a newspaperman, he switched to advertising as a copywriter with the George Batten Company, a forerunner of the great B.B.D. & O. agency of today. He wrote serious plays and operettas, including one in 1902 with the then unknown composer Karl Hoschna.

Harbach kept writing and trying to place his work, but with little success. Luckily he had learned the meaning of hard work and determination, and he kept trying even as his stay in New York extended to seven years. It was his work with Hoschna that finally paid off. They tried to sell their original play, "The Daughter of the Desert," for six years without success. But they became known in the field and were asked to work on an operetta, "The Three Twins." The score for the 1908 production included "Cuddle Up a Little Closer." Though the show was a success, however, Harbach got little more than prestige as a reward. He had to keep his job as copywriter while he and Hoschna tried to come up with a second success. In 1910, they made the grade with the highly successful "Madame Sherry," which featured "Every Little Movement."

Hoschna's death in 1911 threatened Harbach's hard-won achievements. But Harbach had gained enough notice for him to gain a contract with Victor Herbert to write "The Firefly." A disagreement between Herbert and the show's singing star, Emma Trentini, led to Herbert's withdrawal. He was replaced by Rudolf Friml. Harbach's book and lyrics blended perfectly with Firml's melodies, resulting in one of the theater's great operettas. It led to a close collaboration that included such shows as "High Jinks" (1913), "Katinka" (1915), "Kitty Darlin'" (1917), "Tumble In" and "The Little Whopper" (1919), "June Love" (1921), "Rose Marie" (1924), and "The Wild Rose" (1926).

Harbach turned out librettos and lyrics with seeming ease. During the twenties and thirties, he worked with such other major composers as Louis Hirsch, Harry Tierney, George Gershwin, Sigmund Romberg, Vincent Youmans, and Jerome Kern. He also worked with a lesser-known composer, Herbert Stothart. In 1920, he was asked to collaborate with a young and promising new writer on a show called "Tickle Me," for which Stothart provided the music. The new writer was Oscar Hammerstein II, and the result was Hammerstein's first stage hit. In the years thereafter, Harbach and Hammerstein often worked together on major shows, including "Rose Marie" and "The Desert Song."

With Vincent Youmans, Harbach turned out such major hits as "Wildflower" (1923) and "No, No Nanette" (1925). The latter was one of five successful shows of Harbach's that appeared on Broadway at the same time. With Gershwin he worked on the 1925 show "Song of the Flame." With Tierney, he wrote the 1923 Eddie Cantor hit "Kid Boots" to order for the star at the request of Florenz Ziegfeld.

Harbach's most significant collaborations after Friml were with Romberg and Kern. His main work with Romberg was the immortal "Desert Song." With Kern, Harbach turned out such successes as "Sunny" (1925), "The Cat and the Fiddle" (1931), and "Roberta" (1933).

Harbach's accomplishments were recognized by his fellow writers when he was named president of ASCAP from 1948 to 1953.

HARBURG, E. Y. (YIP): lyricist, librettist. Born New York, New York, April 8, 1898. Won Academy Award for Best Song of 1939 ("Over the Rainbow").

One of the most versatile lyricists for the movies and Broadway, Yip Harburg didn't start his musical career until over the age of thirty.

He came from New York's lower-East Side ghetto. Through hard work at many jobs, from selling newspapers to lighting street lamps, Harburg persevered through public school, high school, and the City College of New York. His high school was Townsend Harris Hall, an experimental school for talented children. He contributed poetry to his high-school and college papers.

After finishing school, Harburg worked at a variety of jobs, eventually going into business for himself. In the late twenties, he set up an electrical shop. But it was a dismal failure, and he decided to look elsewhere for a livelihood. At an age when most people have settled down to their life's work, he began writing lyrics with Jay Gorney, a lawyer turned composer. They wrote six songs for Earl Carroll's 1929 "Sketch Book," and Harburg's future was assured when Paramount Pictures offered contracts to both him and Gorney.

In the early thirties, Harburg collaborated on several shows with Vernon Duke. His lyrics included the immortal "April in Paris" for the 1932 revue "Walk a Little Faster." He also provided the words for a Gorney melody that was called "the anthem of the Depression," "Brother, Can You Spare a Dime?" In Hollywood, Harburg worked closely with composer Harold Arlen. Their output included the 1933 "It's Only a Paper Moon" and the score for the 1939 movie classic "The Wizard of Oz." A few years later, Arlen and Harburg collaborated on a hit musical, the 1944 "Bloomer Girl," which included "Evalina," "Right as the Rain," "I Got a Song," and "When the Boys Come Home."

In 1957, Harburg and Arlen turned out another Broadway bell ringer, "Jamaica," which starred Lena Horne and for which Harburg also worked on the book. Between "Bloomer Girl" and "Jamaica," Harburg provided what has been the high point of his career, the lyrics and, with Fred Saidy, the book for "Finian's Rainbow" (1947). His partner for this was composer Burton Lane. They met when both were working for Paramount. In 1940, they collaborated on an Al Jolson Broadway vehicle, "Hold On to Your Hats" (which included "There's a Great Day Coming Mañana"). This led to "Finian's Rainbow," with its ever-fresh score that includes "Old Devil Moon," "If This Isn't Love," "How Are Things in Glocca Morra?," "When I'm Not Near the Girl I Love," and "Look to the Rainbow."

HARMONY: the combination of tones into a chord; also, the structure of a piece of music according to the composition, progression, and modulation of its chords.

Harmony is a blending of musical notes to give body to a piece and to achieve a desired musical effect. Harmony, melody, and rhythm are the integral parts of a musical composition.

Harmony is usually provided by playing three or four notes together to form a chord. On the piano, the chords are usually played with the left hand and the melody with the right.

HARNICK, SHELDON: lyricist, composer. Born Chicago, Illinois, December 27, 1924. Won Pulitzer Prize for "Fiorello!" (1959).

Sheldon Harnick originally seemed destined to be a musician rather than a words man. He studied violin while growing up in the Midwest, and continued as a violinist during his years as a music major at Northwestern University. After graduating, he decided to concentrate on songwriting rather than playing an instrument.

At first, Harnick thought of himself as a composer more than a lyricist. But in 1950, he began putting words to some of his own as well as others' music. He went on to New York to try to make the grade as a Broadway composer. Before too long, he had won the ear of Leonard Sillman, producer of the "New Faces" series. Harnick supplied a show stopper for "New Faces of 1952" called "Boston Beguine," a wildly funny lament of a wallflower. The next year, Harnick supplied another satirical song for the John Murray Anderson "Almanac." The song, "Merry Minuet," reviews such things as rioting in Africa and nuclear bombs to an all-is-well type of music.

Harnick began to get more assignments, and he provided material for a number of shows, mostly off Broadway. Some of those for which he supplied lyrics or music or both were "Two's Company," "Kaleidoscope," the first and second "Shoestring Revues," the Phoenix Theatre's "Littlest Revue," and Julius Monk's nightclub revue "Take Five." He also collaborated on a musical called "Fair Haired Boy," which was presented at the Dallas theater of Margo Jones. Harnick also wrote special material for a variety of performers, including Ray Bolger, Giselle MacKenzie, Eddie Fisher, and Hermione Gingold.

When veteran lyricist E. Y. Harburg suggested that Harnick should concentrate on words alone, he accepted the advice. In 1957, this suggestion was taken up by Harnick's music publisher, Thomas Valando, who also had on his roster a very talented composer, Jerry Bock. Valando felt that Harnick and Bock should try working together. At first, this did not seem too promising an idea. Bock and Harnick provided the score for the Broadway musical "The Body Beautiful," which closed in two months. But Bock and Harnick felt they worked well together.

They got the chance to write a musical about New York mayor Fiorello La Guardia. "Fiorello!," with a book by George Abbott and Jerome Weidman, came into New York unheralded on November 23, 1959, and won just about unanimous praise from the critics. It became the third Broadway musical to win the Pulitzer Prize.

Bock and Harnick then wrote the score for "Tenderloin," an ambitious musical which lasted only a few months. After the first weeks of disappointment, Bock and Harnick bounced back to concentrate on a new venture, a musical based on a play by Miklos Laszlo which had been turned into a movie called "The Shop Around the Corner" a few years before. Playwright Joe Masteroff rewrote it as a musical called "She Loves Me." This time the magic of "Fiorello!" returned, and Bock and Harnick produced a score for a tightly knit production that starred Barbara Cook, Daniel Massey, Barbara Baxley, and Jack Cassidy. A New York critic quoted but not named by the Hollywood *Citizen News* wrote:

This is one of those shows that appears on the surface to be so effortless and uncomplicated that, once free of the enchantment of the performance, you think back and wonder how it could possibly have worked. But it does, and if that is magic, then it is all the more to be praised because the theatre has known too little magic in recent years.

In 1964, Bock and Harnick received even more ringing praise from New York reviewers for a new hit, "Fiddler on the Roof," starring Zero Mostel.

HART, LORENZ MILTON: lyricist. Born New York, New York, May 2, 1895; died New York, New York, November 22, 1943.

A man of exceptional talent, certainly one of the all-time great popular-music lyricists, Lorenz Hart was often a victim of his own self-doubts. His anxieties eventually led to excesses that cut his life short, but he left a legacy that has bright-

Lorenz Hart

ened the lives of millions of people the world over.

On his father's side, Lorenz was descended from the great German poet Heinrich Heine. His family was wealthy, and most of Hart's education was at private schools. He studied at Weingart's Institute and Columbia Grammar School (except for a short time at the public De Witt Clinton High School). In 1913, after a tour of Europe with his family, he entered New York's Columbia University, where he attended the School of Journalism and performed and wrote material for the 1915 and 1916 Varsity Shows. In 1917, he left school before gaining his degree and put on summer shows at a boys' camp while working as a translator of German operettas during the other months.

In 1918, a mutual friend, Philip Leavitt, introduced Hart to a high-school student with aspirations for composing. The student, seven years Hart's junior, was Richard Rodgers. Referring to the meeting some time later in *Theatre Arts* magazine, Rodgers said:

He was violent on the subject of rhyming in songs, feeling that the public was capable of understanding better things than the current monosyllabic juxtaposition of "slush" and "mush." . . . I was enchanted by this little man and his ideas. Neither of us mentioned it, but we evidently knew we'd work together, and I left Hart's house having acquired in one afternoon a career, a partner, a best friend, and a source of permanent irritation.

Rodgers and Hart were soon turning out their first songs. In 1919, Leavitt was instrumental in placing their first song in a Broadway musical, "Any Old Place with You," inserted by Lew Fields into "A Lonely Romeo." That fall, Rodgers entered Columbia, and he and Hart wrote the score for a Varsity Show musical, "Fly With Me." After attending a performance, Lew Fields commissioned the team to write a number of songs for "Poor Little Ritz Girl." Only four out of twelve were used in the show, which opened on July 27, 1920.

For the next five years, Rodgers and Hart pounded on doors of Broadway producers with very little success. In 1925, they were close to giving up when they were invited to write the score for "The Garrick Gaieties." The show, for which they provided such songs as "Manhattan" and "Sentimental Me," was an immediate success. From then through 1931, they worked on one show after another, many of them major hits.

In 1925, they wrote such songs as "Here in My Arms" and "I Beg Your Pardon" for "Dearest Enemy." The 1926 success "The Girl Friend" included "The Blue Room," and the 1926 "Garrick Gaieties" contained "Mountain Greenery" and "What's the Use of Talking." For "A Connecticut Yankee" in 1927, Rodgers and Hart provided "My Heart Stood Still," "Thou Swell," and "I Feel at Home with You." "Spring Is Here" in 1929 included "With a Song in My Heart," and "America's Sweetheart" in 1931 was notable for "I've Got Five Dollars." Rodgers and Hart wrote dozens of other popular songs for these and other shows during this period.

In 1930, they began a four-year stint in Hollywood. The pace and method of movie musicals weren't too much to their liking. Oddly, the greatest success from this period was a song turned down for several movies. It was "Blue Moon," one of the few Rodgers and Hart songs to be released apart from a show.

In 1934, they accepted Billy Rose's offer to write the score for his extravaganza "Jumbo." In the years that followed, they sent the musical theater to new heights with a series of sparkling scores for such shows as "On Your Toes" (1936), "Babes in Arms" (1937), "I'd Rather Be Right" (1937), "I Married an Angel" (1938), "The Boys from Syracuse" (1938), and "Pal Joey" (1940). (See individual listings.) Just a few of the standards from these shows are "Where or When," "My Funny Valentine," "There's a Small Hotel," "Spring Is Here," "This Can't Be Love," "I Could Write a Book," and "Bewitched."

By the end of the thirties, Hart was becoming ever more moody and unpredictable. He would disappear for weeks, and it took a great deal of effort for Rodgers and his other friends to help him keep going. He and Rodgers turned out one more hit musical "By Jupiter," starring Ray Bolger, which opened on June 2, 1942, and ran for four hundred and twenty-seven performances.

In 1943, Hart worked on a new production of "A Connecticut Yankee." On opening night, he wandered up and down for a time at the back of the theater, then disappeared. After a two-day search, he was found unconscious in a hotel room. He was rushed to Doctors Hospital with acute pneumonia. Rodgers and his wife remained at Hart's bedside for three days, but on November 22, Hart died at the age of forty-eight.

HELLO, DOLLY!: musical. Lyrics and music by Jerry Herman, book by Michael Stewart. Adapted from Thornton Wilder's play "The Matchmaker." New York opening: January 16, 1964, St. James Theatre.

In the years following World War II, producer David Merrick compiled a record of hits to rival that of the greatest of Broadway showmen. From the mid-fifties to 1964, he produced thirty-five Broadway shows, of which twenty-seven were runaway successes. The twenty-seventh was "Hello, Dolly!," which won the New York Drama Critics' Award as the best musical of the 1963–64 season and a record 10 Antoinette Perry (Tony) awards.

The show featured the creative efforts of two relatively new names on Broadway. The book was provided by Michael Stewart, who had won his spurs with "Bye Bye Birdie." Music and lyrics were the work of thirty-year-old Jerry Herman, who served his Broadway apprenticeship by writing the score for the 1961 hit "Milk and Honey."

The show opens on a summer day in 1898. The heroine, Dolly Gallagher Levi, widow of Ephraim Levi, is on her way to Yonkers. She is a matchmaker ("I Put My Hand In"). Her mis-

Carol Channing, shown here recording the best-selling LP of *Hello, Dolly!*, helped make the show one of the most popular of the mid-60s.

sion is to arrange a second marriage for wealthy merchant Horace Vandergelder. She secretly intends to claim him herself. In Yonkers, the egotistical Vandergelder is busy ordering about his two clerks, Cornelius Hackl and Barnaby Tucker, and his timid niece Ermengarde. He tells them of his reasons for marrying in "It Takes a Woman."

Dolly's first chore is to wean Horace away from the young widow Irene Molloy, to whom she had previously introduced him. Horace is planning to go to New York to march in a parade. Dolly tells him she knows a new, wealthy prospect in New York whom he can meet after the parade, but Horace intends to see Mrs. Molloy. After he leaves, his clerks decide to seize the chance to enjoy the big city ("Put On Your Sunday Clothes"). They join with Dolly in trying to get Ermengarde also to defy Horace.

In New York, when the young clerks accidentally see Horace coming, they hide in Mrs. Molloy's shop. Dolly, Mrs. Molloy, and her clerk, Minnie Fay, try to prevent Horace from catching his errant help by singing "Motherhood." But he finds out that Mrs. Molloy is hiding two men (but

not who the two are) and breaks with her. Dolly soothes Mrs. Molloy by arranging for the clerks to take the widow and Minnie dancing at the Harmonia Gardens Restaurant. Dolly tells Horace he can meet his new ladylove that evening after the parade.

As the clerks' finances are shaky, they talk Mrs. Molloy and Minnie into walking to the Harmonia rather than going by cab, singing that walking is the height of "Elegance." The Harmonia staff is elated to hear that Mrs. Levi, an old favorite of theirs, is coming. The staff greets her ("Hello, Dolly!"), and she returns the compliment. Dolly attempts to woo Horace, but her efforts are stymied when he discovers his clerks and Ermengarde in the middle of the floor show. A riot ensues in which Horace fires Cornelius and is arrested for creating a disturbance. Cornelius tells Horace off and proposes to Mrs. Molloy. At the station house, Dolly says goodbye to Vandergelder ("So Long, Dearie"). But soon after, a chastened Horace begs her hand and forgiveness in a reprise of "Hello, Dolly!"

The original cast included Carol Channing, as Dolly; David Burns, as Horace; Charles Nelson

Reilly, as Cornelius; Jerry Dodge, as Barnaby; Eileen Brennan, as Mrs. Molloy; Sondra Lee, as Minnie; and Igors Gavon, as Ermengarde. Other songs were "Ribbons Down My Back," "Dancing," "Before the Parade Passes By," and "It Only Takes a Moment."

One of the most successful in Broadway's history, "Hello Dolly" by early 1965 has grossed over $14.5 million and sales of the original cast album (RCA Victor) passed the 2,000,000 mark. Rights to the movie version were sold to 20th Century Fox in '65.

HENDERSON, RAY: composer. Born Buffalo, New York, December 1, 1896.

The songwriting trio of de Sylva, Brown, and Henderson was one of the popular-music phenomena of the late nineteen-twenties. They were among the most sought-after writers on Broadway for several years, turning out many hit shows and many songs that are still popular.

Henderson was the composer of the team (de Sylva and Brown were lyricists and librettists). His mother taught piano, and Ray learned to play before he began grade school. When he was a little older, he played the organ and sang in the choir of the local Episcopal church. By the time he reached high school, he had already begun composing serious music. He went on to study at the Chicago Conservatory of Music.

To help pay his way, however, he played piano in local jazz bands and worked in a vaudeville comedy act. When he finished at the conservatory, he decided to try his lot in popular rather than serious music. His next step was to try for work in New York. He gained a job as a song plugger for the music firm of Leo Feist. He soon moved to Fred Fisher as staff pianist, and, before long, moved again to the house of Shapiro, Bernstein. One of the firm's owners, Louis Bernstein, decided to team Henderson with lyricist Lew Brown. The result was two hit songs, "Humming" and "Georgette." From then on, Henderson's reputation grew, helped by such other hits as "Alabamy Bound" and "Five Foot Two, Eyes of Blue." In 1925, George White was faced with the task of replacing George Gershwin as composer for his "Scandals." He asked Henderson to take the job. Henderson already had a lyricist in Brown, but he also agreed to work with Bud de Sylva, who had provided lyrics for some of Gershwin's "Scandals" material. The amalgam of the three took hold, and the result was such hits as "Black Bottom," "The Birth of the Blues,"

and "The Girl Is You and the Boy Is Me" for the 1926 "Scandals," and "An Old-Fashioned Girl" and "I'm on the Crest of a Wave" for the 1928 edition.

Between "Scandals" work, the team began to work on material for Broadway book musicals. Their first effort, "Good News," was a major hit of 1927. Its score included "Lucky in Love," "The Best Things in Life Are Free," and the title song. For the 1928 success "Hold Everything," they provided "You're the Cream in My Coffee," and for the 1929 "Follow Thru," the team wrote "Button Up Your Overcoat," "I Could Give Up Anything but You," and "My Lucky Star." The team rounded out the decade with the musical "Flying High" in 1930.

De Sylva had become interested in producing shows and movies, and the team broke up. They had written several movie scores, including "Sonny," "The Singing Fool" and "Sunny Side Up." De Sylva concentrated on the movies in the thirties and forties, and Brown also eventually moved to Hollywood. Henderson did some work for films, but his heart mainly remained with Broadway. He worked on such shows as "George White's Scandals" of 1931 and 1935 and the 1943 "Ziegfeld Follies."

In 1956, the screen biography of de Sylva, Brown, and Henderson was presented under the title "The Best Things in Life Are Free."

HERBERT, VICTOR: composer, cellist, conductor. Born Dublin, Ireland, February 1, 1859; died New York, New York, May 26, 1924.

Victor Herbert's engagement to be married was a great stroke of luck for American popular music. This event led to his coming to the United States, where he became not only a giant in the American musical theater but one of the leaders in the establishment of the American Society of Composers, Authors and Publishers.

His father died when Victor was a very young child. Later, his mother married a German physician and moved to Stuttgart, where, at fifteen, Victor began to study the cello. Before long, he was touring Europe with leading orchestras. He spent five years with the court orchestra of Stuttgart and published his first composition, the Suite for Cello and Orchestra. At twenty-six, he met and soon proposed to Therese Förster, a soprano with the court opera, in Vienna. Then Frank Damrosch appeared in Stuttgart, seeking talent for New York's Metropolitan Opera. He came to hear a young tenor, but Miss Förster impressed him more. But she refused to go to the United States unless a place was found in the orchestra for her fiancé. Thus, at twenty-seven Herbert came to New York.

For some years, Herbert appeared as a leading soloist with several orchestras. His interests began to turn toward popular music. In 1893, he wrote his first comic opera, "La Vivandière," for Lillian Russell, but it was never produced. In 1894, he wrote his first Broadway production, "Prince Ananias." This got a halfhearted reception, but his 1895 effort, "The Wizard of the Nile," was a hit.

His next major success came some eight years later. In between, he had written eight operettas, most of them long-forgotten, and served three years as conductor of the Pittsburgh Symphony. In 1903, he and Glen MacDonough turned out the ever-popular "Babes in Toyland." From then until his death, it was a rare year that didn't see a Herbert hit on Broadway. In 1904, "It Happened in Nordland" appeared, in 1905 "Mlle. Modiste," and in 1906 the great "The Red Mill." The last included "The Isle of Our Dreams," "Every Day Is Ladies' Day with Me," and "Moonbeams." After several undistinguished productions, another of Herbert's gems, "Naughty Marietta," appeared in 1910. For this Herbert composed "Italian Street Song," "Tramp, Tramp, Tramp," "I'm Falling in Love with Someone," and "Ah! Sweet Mystery of Life." In 1912, he had another hit with "The Lady of the Slipper;" and in 1913, "Sweethearts" was a major success. "Sweethearts" also was instrumental in the establishment of ASCAP (See *ASCAP*).

Some of Herbert's other successes were "The Princess Pat" (1915), "The Century Girl" (1916), and "The Velvet Lady" (1919). For "Eileen" (1917) he wrote "Thine Alone" and "The Irish Have a Great Day Tonight." Besides his operettas, Herbert also wrote operas (none successful) and such individual songs as "Indian Summer." In the last years of his life, Herbert began contributing to "The Ziegfeld Follies." He was working on the 1924 edition when he was stricken with a fatal heart attack.

HERE'S LOVE: musical. Lyrics, music, and book by Meredith Willson. Book adapted from the movie "Miracle on 34th Street," story by Valentine Davies, screenplay by George Seaton. New York opening: October 3, 1963, Shubert Theatre.

"Here's Love" was Meredith Willson's third Broadway success in a row ("Music Man" and "The Unsinkable Molly Brown" were the first two). The adaptation of the movie classic about a Macy's Santa Claus caught the spirit of the original, though the score did not have the high spots of Willson's earlier work.

The show opens on the morning of Macy's Thanksgiving Day parade. Kris Kringle, who looks like Santa Claus in street clothes, is seen correcting the order of the reindeer in a toy vendor's stall. Meanwhile, a young lawyer, Fred Gaily, meets a little girl, Susan Walker, on the steps of his brownstone. She tells him her mother's divorced and that they live next door. Fred takes Susan to the parade.

Susan's mother Doris is promotion director for Macy's. With her somewhat addled assistant, Marvin Sheilhammer, she is handling parade details. When the regular Santa Claus gets sick, she spots Kris and hires him on the spot. That night, she and Susan compare their day ("Arm in Arm"). Told that Fred thought Susan should believe in Santa Claus, career girl Doris warns her daughter not to believe in illusion ("You Don't Know").

The next day, Kris proves to be Macy's most popular Santa Claus. Susan happens by, and Kris tries to convince her of the spirit of Christmas ("Here's Love"). Kris soon panics store executives by sending people to other stores for some types of toys. Marvin fires Kris, but Doris rehires him when she gets the idea of calling Macy's "The Friendly Store." All three cheer the brighter outlook ("Pine Cones and Holly Berries"). R. H. Macy himself comes in to say that the store is even more packed with customers, thanks to the new policy.

But Kris's insistence that he's really Santa Claus leads to a hectic interview with sullen store psychologist Mr. Sawyer. Sawyer gets Kris arrested for observation. Doris up to now has been sparring with Fred for filling her daughter's head with nonsense. She turns to Fred for help in defending Kris at the sanity hearing, however. The judge has been warned by his adviser, Tammany O'Halloran, not to preside at the trial. It's political suicide, says Tammany, to say whether or not there's a Santa Claus. In a wild case in which R. H. Macy testifies that he believes Kris is Santa Claus ("That Man Over There"), Fred wins the decision. And, as Kris once promised Doris, she and Fred are destined to form a new family in her dream house in Connecticut.

The original cast included Janis Paige, as Doris; Valerie Lee, as Susan; Laurence Naismith, as Kris; Fred Gwynne, as Marvin; Craig Stevens, as Fred; David Doyle, as Sawyer; Paul Reed, as Macy; Cliff Hall, as the judge; and Arthur Rubin, as Tammany. The score included "The Big Clown Ballons," "The Bugle," "My Wish," "Look, Little Girl," "Expect Things To Happen," "She Hadda Go Back," and "My State."

HERMAN, WOODROW WILSON (WOODY): band leader, instrumentalist, singer. Born Milwaukee, Wisconsin, May 16, 1913.

A great name in jazz and the big-band era, Woody Herman started in show business at the age of nine. He was billed then as "Boy Wonder of the Clarinet," and also sang, danced, and played the alto saxophone. By the time he was fourteen, he had joined his first orchestra and was avidly following the careers of such great jazz musicians as Duke Ellington and Red Nichols. Though he kept working as a musician all through his teens, he got through high school in Milwaukee and even enrolled in an advanced music course at Marquette University.

In 1931, he made the move toward the big time with Tom Gerun's band as an instrumentalist and singer. (Two other singers with the band were Ginny Simms and Tony Martin.) By 1932, Herman had moved to the Harry Sosnick outfit, and soon he joined the Isham Jones Orchestra. When Jones disbanded, Woody and many of the other musicians formed their own band. Their first engagement was at Brooklyn's Roseland dance hall.

For six years, the band played all over the United States but made little headway. Their music had a Dixieland flavor that didn't jibe with the era of swing. But in 1939, they played an engagement at New York's Famous Door club that had the audience stomping and applauding for more. Radio dates and motion-picture roles quickly came the way of the Herman organization. Up to 1941, the band was more or less cooperative. With the war and the many changes in the band's makeup, a reorganization was called for, and Herman became the leader. The Herman Herd, as it was nicknamed, changed its style closer to that of the current musical fashion. The band became even more in demand, and its records sold better each year. Five major popularity polls showed the Herman Herd in number-one spot. Woody also headed a network radio show. The upheaval in the band business after World War II led to the breakup of the group,

and, for a time, Herman freelanced. In 1947, he formed a new organization that opened at the Hollywood Palladium and went on to make records for Capitol and MGM. The nineteen-sixties found Herman still going strong leading his band on television spectaculars. Some of the recordings by the Herman Herds over the years were "The Woodchoppers' Ball," "Bijou," "Baby, Baby, All the Time," "Time Changes Everything," and "Oh, Look at Me Now."

HERMAN'S HERMITS: Vocal-instrumental group, all born Manchester, England; Peter (Herman) Noone, November 5, 1947; Karl Green, July 31, 1947; Derek Leckenby, May 14, 1943; Barry Whitwam, July 21, 1946; Keith Hopwood, October 26, 1946.

The success of the Beatles started a trend of rock 'n' roll prominence for English groups. One group that seemed likely to challenge the Beatles for long term popularity is the quaintly titled Herman's Hermits. The Hermits' leader, vocalist Peter Noone, gained this name when he joined a group called the Heartbeats. The other members of the band thought Peter looked like a character in the American TV cartoon show "Rocky and His Friends" called Sherman. They got the name confused, though, hence the Herman designation. When the group reorganized with Noone as the lead singer, they chose his nickname as their title and added Hermits because the words had an interesting sound.

Noone started out as a child actor on English TV programs. His father sent him to Manchester School of Music when Peter was 14 for a two year course in voice (mainly classical) and drama. At 16, Noone often went to a Manchester youth club to listen to the rock 'n' roll combos. One evening the group called the Heartbeats needed a fill-in singer and Noone offered to help out. The audience reaction was so favorable that Noone became a regular with the Heartbeats.

Now the group began to get bids to play all over the north of England. This led to a reorganization as Herman's Hermits in August of 1964. Of the original Heartbeats, only Karl Green remained—as bass guitarist. The Hermits now had Derek Leckenby as lead and rhythm guitarist, Keith Hopwood who alternated as lead and rhythm guitarist, and Barry Whitwam on drums.

The new combination rose rapidly to even greater prominence than the old. By late '64, they had their first major hit, "Baby, Baby, Can't You Hear My Heart Beat." In early '65, they hit the top brackets world wide with "Mrs. Brown,

You Have a Lovely Daughter." Following this came "The End of the World" and "I'm Henry the VIII." In mid '65, their albums "Herman's Hermits on Tour" and "Introducing Herman's Hermits" were high on the best selling charts. The Hermits appeared on major U.S. TV shows, including Hullaballoo and Ed Sullivan and travelled to Los Angeles for their first film roles in MGM's "When the Boys Meet the Girls."

HEYWOOD, EDDIE, JR.: composer, pianist. Born Atlanta, Georgia, December 4, 1915.

The year 1956 was a big one for a man whom illness had seemed to rule out of the music field close to a decade before. This year saw the publication of two of Eddie Heywood's most popular compositions: "Canadian Sunset," which placed Andy Williams on the gold-record road, and "Soft Summer Breeze."

Heywood's father was a pianist of some note as well as the leader of his own small band. When Eddie was eight, his father began teaching him piano. Eddie was an apt pupil, and by the time he was fifteen, he was playing with local organizations. In 1935, he joined the more widely known band of Clarence Love. A few years later, Eddie decided he was ready for New York. By 1938, he was playing piano with bands in Harlem nightclubs. The following year, big-band leader Benny Carter, fresh from several successful years in Europe, asked Heywood to join his new American organization. The band included such sidemen as trombonists Tyree Glenn and Vic Dickenson. In 1941, Carter switched to a small combo, and Heywood began playing for shows at the Village Vanguard in New York. In 1943, Heywood formed his own sextet. Besides playing piano, he wrote the group's arrangements as well as some original compositions, such as "Taint Me" (1944). His popular arrangement of "Begin the Beguine" in particular resulted in the Heywood group becoming more widely known throughout the country. Some of their other records were "The Man I Love" and "On the Sunny Side of the Street." In 1945, Eddie won *Esquire* magazine's award for the new star of the year.

In 1947, he suffered a partial paralysis of his hands and had to give up his band. After four years of exercise and work, Eddie was able to resume piano playing, appearing as a soloist or heading his own trio. Though the best-selling record of his "Canadian Sunset" was a vocal arrangement, Eddie's own instrumental version also achieved some popularity. The main records

of "Soft Summer Breeze" have been instrumental. Besides these, some of Heywood's other compositions are "Sleep," "Fish Fry," and "I'm Saving Myself for You."

HIGH BUTTON SHOES: musical. Lyrics by Sammy Cahn, music by Jule Styne, book by Stephen Longstreet. Based on Longstreet's stories. New York opening: October 9, 1947, Century Theatre. 727 performances.

For many years, Jule Styne was one of Hollywood's leading arrangers and composers. He longed for more than the monetary rewards of movie land, however. As he put it (quoted by Stanley Green in "The World of Musical Comedy." New York: Ziff-Davis, 1960), "In Hollywood, you're a song-writer; in New York, you're a composer." In 1947, he made the break and, with Sammy Cahn, worked on his first Broadway musical, "High Button Shoes." The book was based on Stephen Longstreet's *Gourmet* magazine stories of his grandfather's life in pre-World War I New Jersey. The setting proved a perfect foil for comedian Phil Silvers's wild slapstick routines. This plus a pleasant Styne-Cahn score insured a long run. Cahn settled for one Broadway hit and returned to the more leisurely ways of California. Styne went on to have a hand in many major musical successes of the fifties and sixties.

Confidence man Harrison Floy (Phil Silvers) is heading east from Kokomo, Indiana, with his accomplice, Mr. Pontdue. Their journey takes them to the quiet streets of New Brunswick, New Jersey, home of Rutgers University as well as the distinguished Longstreet family. The year is 1913, and such Latin dances as the tango are beginning to invade the United States. In one scene, Uncle Willie Longstreet and a girl named Nancy are shown gritting their teeth to learn the tango from a mail-order booklet. Floy gets to meet the Longstreets, who include Henry Longstreet, his lovely wife Sara, and their daughter Fran. Fran is being ardently wooed by Hubert Ogglethorpe, a Texan football star, who sings to her, "Next to Texas, I Love You." As the show proceeds, however, he expresses his feelings more romantically in such songs as "Can't You Just See Yourself in Love with Me?" and "You're My Girl."

As Floy and Pontdue make themselves at home, Floy gets the chance to lecture the lady bird-watcher's society and to go on a picnic. As the group moves off to the picnic grounds, the ensemble sings how fine it is to "Get Away for a

Day in the Country." Floy by now has found his angle. He starts a real-estate boom based on some marsh land owned by the Longstreets.

Once Floy has collected from the townspeople, he and Pontdue decamp to Atlantic City with the money. Here they are pursued in a wildly funny ballet takeoff on Mack Sennett silent films. The show-stopping sequence was choreographed by Jerome Robbins. Said William Hawkins in the New York *World-Telegram:*

. . . bathing beauties chill their toes in the waves and skitter about in the most outrageously girlish pantomine. The seedy cops fly trembling into the air at the slightest surprise, and the depraved villians look as if they had crawled out from under an ancient sun dial.

When the chase is over and Floy's scheme defeated, the scene shifts back to New Brunswick and the Longstreets. Their warm family ties and good nature are shown during the evening as Henry and Sara sing and dance to such songs as "Papa, Won't You Dance With Me?" and "I Still Get Jealous." Though taken over the hurdles by Floy, they are still fascinated by him. Floy tries to recoup by betting on Princeton to beat Rutgers. At half time, with Rutgers leading forty to zero, Floy enters Rutgers's dressing room and tries vainly to cripple the whole team. Though his plans fall through once more, Floy is finally saved when it turns out that the mud from the Longstreet's marsh can be sold to beauty shops across the nation.

The original cast included Phil Silvers, as Harrison Floy; Joey Faye, as Pontdue; Nanette Fabray, as Sara; Jack McCauley, as Henry; Lois Lee, as Fran; Mark Dawson, as Hubert; Helen Gallagher, as Nancy; and Paul Godkin, as Uncle Willie. The score included "You're My Boy," "There's Nothing Like a Model T," "Bird Watcher's Song," and "Security."

HIGH HOPES: song (1959). Words by Sammy Cahn, music by Jimmy Van Heusen.

It often happens that songs that win Academy Award nominations are last-minute additions, as was the victor for 1959, Jimmy Van Heusen and Sammy Cahn's "High Hopes." The song was performed in the picture "Hole in the Head," which was adapted from the Broadway comedy.

The play had no music. The script was purchased, and the cast was to include Frank Sinatra, as a bumbling but warm man idolized by his son;

Eddie Hodges, as his son; and Edward G. Robinson, in a supporting role. With Sinatra playing the main role, there was now reason to add music. Still, the movie was not a musical, and any music had to be used sparingly. Toward the end of the film, there was one episode that seemed strained. This was a scene where Sinatra was down on his luck and his son was depressed. The original screenplay called for Sinatra to try to cheer up the boy by talking to him. But the scene lacked life. The directors thought that perhaps a song at this point would solve the problem.

Cahn and Van Heusen were given the assignment. Cahn analyzed the plot sequence and came up with the title idea of "High Hopes." Van Heusen put together a melody, and Cahn completed the words.

Sinatra's record of "High Hopes" is probably better remembered today than the movie. Since then, many other artists have recorded the song. It was also used by the Democratic party during John F. Kennedy's Presidential campaign.

HILLBILLY: slang term for a type of music popular in rural and southern areas of the United States, more properly called "country-and-Western." (See *Country-and-Western*.)

HOLD EVERYTHING: musical. Lyrics by Buddy de Sylva and Lew Brown, music by Ray Henderson, book by de Sylva and John McGowan. New York opening: October 10, 1928, Broadhurst Theatre. 413 performances.

Satire (not too thickly laid on) came into its own on Broadway with the rise to prominence in the late nineteen-twenties of the team of de Sylva, Brown, and Henderson. Starting out as successful Tin Pan Alley songwriters, they teamed up to write the scores for the 1925–28 versions of "George White's Scandals." In 1927, they turned out the first of six straight musical-comedy hits. Called "Good News," it was a satire on college football. This served as a pattern for succeeding takeoffs on prizefighting ("Hold Everything"), golfing ("Follow Thru"—1929), flying ("Flying High"—1930), and bullfighting ("Hot-Cha!"—1932). Their other success was not a satire but a George White extravaganza, "Manhattan Mary," in 1927.

Welterweight champion Sonny Jim Brooks is the hero of "Hold Everything." His girl is Sue Burke, but a society girl, Norine Lloyd, wants to take Sonny Jim away from Sue. The burden of most of the humor falls on Gink Schiner, who was played by Bert Lahr in the original production. It was Lahr's first major success on Broadway. His girl friend was played by Nina Olivette.

An example of the repartee is her angry remark to Schiner, "For two cents I'd knock you out."

"You're mercenary! You're mercenary!" was the reply.

Schiner puts on a wild sparring performance in Jim's dressing room, but his usual position in the ring is flat on his back.

Jim has a big championship fight coming up, but Sue, jealous of Norine, spurns him. He is so despondent that is seems likely he'll lose the fight. At the last moment, Sue tells Sonney she loves him and raises him to fever pitch by telling him that the challenger insulted her.

The hit song, still a favorite, was sung by Jim: "You're the Cream in My Coffee." Other songs were "Don't Hold Everything," "Too Good To Be True," and "To Know You Is To Love You." The original cast included Jack Whiting, as Sonny Jim; Ona Munson, as Sue; and Betty Compton, as Norine.

HORNE, LENA: singer. Born Brooklyn, New York, June 30, 1917.

Lena Horne's mother, who had been an actress with the Lafayette Stock Company, encouraged her beautiful young daughter to try for the stage. Through friends, she was influential in getting Lena a job in the Cotton Club chorus in Harlem when Lena was still in her teens. Orchestra leader Noble Sissle was impressed with Lena's work and hired her to sing and dance with his band. Then came a six-month tour with Charlie Barnet's band (during which time she made her first major recording for Victor, "Haunted Town"). Lena left in 1939 to appear on Broadway in Lew Leslie's "Blackbirds." The show was unsuccessful, but the critics singled out Lena for special praise.

On the strength of this came a seven-month Café Society engagement. Then Lena went to the Little Trocadero in Los Angeles, where a Metro-Goldwyn-Mayer scout saw her act. She signed with MGM and appeared in many movies, including "Cabin in the Sky," "Stormy Weather," "Broadway Rhythm," "Till the Clouds Roll By," and "Words and Music."

During the war, Lena performed widely for the United Service Organizations. She also appeared at such night spots as New York's Copaca-

bana, Chicago's Chez Paree, San Francisco's Fairmount Hotel, Miami's Eden Roc, and the Sands in Las Vegas, and on the "Lower Basin Street" radio show with Duke Ellington.

Miss Horne's first European tour, in 1947, was so well received that she returned in 1950, when her itinerary included the London Palladium, the Lido in Paris, and Stockholm's China Theatre. Her third tour, in 1952, won her the title of Number One Variety Star at the Palladium. The mutual fascination continued with engagements in 1954, 1955, 1956, and 1959. The gap from 1956 to 1959 was partly caused by Lena's return to the Broadway stage to star in "Jamaica," which ran for a year and a half.

Following her success in "Jamaica," Lena returned to the international nightclub circuit, adding highly successful work at New York's Waldorf-Astoria to her laurels. Television offers also poured in, including a series of spectaculars taped in England and New York.

Some of Lena's better-known record albums are "Give the Lady What She Wants," "It's Love," "Jamaica," "Lena Horne at the Waldorf-Astoria," "Stormy Weather," "Porgy and Bess," "Lena at the Sands," and "Lena on the Blue Side."

HOW TO SUCCEED IN BUSINESS WITHOUT REALLY TRYING: musical. Lyrics and music by Frank Loesser, book by Abe Burrows, Jack Weinstock, and Willie Gilbert. Based on Shepherd Mead's novel. New York opening: October 14, 1961, Forty-sixth Street Theatre.

Shepherd Mead's 1952 best-seller proved an excellent vehicle for two very different artists. One was a veteran performer and vocal idol of the nineteen-twenties and thirties, Rudy Vallee, the other a brash newcomer, thirty-year-old Robert Morse. Vallee, as J. B. Biggley, business tycoon, and Morse, as J. Pierrepoint Finch, enterprising young man on the rise, provided a perfect one-two punch for a hilarious Pulitzer Prize-winning spoof of the present-day corporate scene.

The saga of J. Pierrepoint Finch opens with him working as a window washer on the building that houses the World Wide Wicket Company. His prized possession is a new book, "How To Succeed in Business without Really Trying." Following the rules in the book, he wangles a job in the mail room of World Wide Wickets from Mr. Bratt, the personnel manager. Bratt introduces Finch to secretaries Rosemary and Smitty, and to Biggley's nephew, Bud Frump. Frump, who also works in the mail room, hopes to use his mother's relationship to J. B. to move up to head of the mail room. Rosemary falls for Finch, and she doesn't mind his preoccupation with getting ahead ("Happy To Keep His Dinner Warm").

A week later, during that event described in the song "Coffee Break," Finch starts his move upward. He meets Biggley's secretary, Miss Jones, and deftly sets things up for a move to junior executive in Plans and Systems, headed by Mr. Gatch. Meanwhile, Biggley tells Bratt to hire a young lady named Hedy La Rue. Her effect on male employees makes Bratt warn all that "A Secretary Is Not a Toy."

Finch learns that Biggley likes to knit and play golf and is an ardent old grad of Old Ivy College. Just happening to be working on a Saturday when he knows that Biggley is in town to play golf, Finch meets the big boss. Giving Biggley the impression that he too is an Old Ivy graduate, Finch joins J. B. in singing the merits of "Grand Old Ivy." When Biggley later finds Finch knitting, the young man's position is assured. Finch gets Gatch to make a pass at Hedy, resulting in Biggley's replacing Gatch with Finch.

A reception is held in honor of the new advertising vice-president, B. B. D. Ovington. Bud Frump tries to frame his rival, Finch, by getting him alone with Hedy and telling J. B. But Rosemary comes along to save the day. Biggley finds Finch kissing her instead of Hedy. Finch finds that he loves her ("Rosemary"). He achieves his goal of vice-president of advertising when he lets Biggley find out that Ovington graduated from Old Ivy's greatest rival, Northern State.

Frump has one more card to play. He tells Finch the idea for a television giveaway show he knows his uncle turned down. But Finch gets Hedy on the show. He feels confident that he will get J. B.'s approval as he sings in the washroom, "I Believe in You," to a background of other company executives singing "Gotta Stop That Man." J. B. buys the show, but Hedy's miscues turn it into a debacle for the company. All seems lost when the chairman of the board comes to fix the blame. Finch and he both turn out to have started as window washers. Biggley is saved as president, but his new superior is now chairman of the board Finch.

The original cast included Bonnie Scott, as Rosemary; Charles Nelson Reilly, as Frump;

Ruth Kobart, as Miss Jones; Paul Reed, as Bratt; Claudette Sutherland, as Smitty; and Virginia Martin, as Hedy. Other songs were "How To," "The Company Way," "Been a Long Day," "Paris Original," "Cinderella, Darling," "Love from a Heart of Gold," "The Yo Ho Ho," and "The Brotherhood of Man."

HUMMINGBIRD: song (1955). Words and music by Don Robertson.

"Hummingbird" was one of the major songs of 1955. The song presented little trouble as far as placing it was concerned, and it took relatively few weeks for Les Paul and Mary Ford's recording to move to the top of the polls. But writing it was another matter. It took a year and a half from conception to completion.

Robertson had taken a small studio in Los Angeles to give him the peace and quiet he needed for composing. He was looking out the window one day when a hummingbird came into view and hung suspended for a moment before darting off toward the shrubbery. He was fascinated by the bird and thought of the analogy of it with a real-life Don Juan. He set to work immediately and thought up a musical pattern that called for a second line in which the lyric pattern reverses that of the first. This determined the lyric pattern as a set of couplets. (Robertson often writes the words as well as the music for his songs.) He just couldn't seem to find the right series of couplets, however. Day after day, he devised new couplets and rearranged old ones, but the pattern just didn't seem right. After working on it for almost a year, he put it aside. By this time, he had an inch-thick file of some two hundred couplets.

After six months or so, a friend happened by who had been shown some of the early material on "Hummingbird." When told that the song had been put aside, he suggested it was too good to let go and that Don take another look. Robertson took out his file and looked it over. He immediately had a different feeling; having been away from it for so long, it was as though he was criticizing someone else's work. The song seemed to go together almost by itself. Within ten minutes, the final version was ready.

I CAN'T GIVE YOU ANYTHING BUT LOVE: song (1928). Words by Dorothy Fields, music by Jimmy McHugh.

Two of the great names in popular-music history are those of lyricist-librettist Dorothy Fields and composer Jimmy McHugh. Both scored many of their greatest triumphs with other collaborators, but it was their work together in the late twenties that gained them nationwide reputations. And their first great effort was the score for the memorable Broadway revue "Blackbirds of 1928."

Their output for this included "Diga Diga Doo," "Doin' the New Low-Down," and, most notable of all, "I Can't Give You Anything but Love." The last did not come easily. When they had finished most of their numbers for the show, they still lacked one really good production number. Day after day, Fields and McHugh worked on all sorts of fast-paced combinations of words and music, but nothing seemed right.

After one more unsuccessful effort, they decided to take some time off and relax. It was evening, and they took a walk down New York's Fifth Avenue in the upper Fifties. This section featured many fine shops, including Tiffany's. As they walked towards the store, they saw a man and woman windowshopping. Drawing abreast of the couple, Fields and McHugh heard the man turn to his girl and say, "Gee, honey, I'd like to get you a sparkler like that, but right now, I can't give you nothin' but love."

The last line struck home. The songwriting team looked at each other, then quickly decided to head for a piano. Once seated at the keyboard, they wrote the song in less than an hour.

I'D RATHER BE RIGHT: musical. Lyrics by Lorenz Hart, music by Richard Rodgers, book by George S. Kaufman and Moss Hart. New York opening: November 2, 1937, Alvin Theatre. 290 performances.

"I'd Rather Be Right" was to President Franklin D. Roosevelt what Vaughn Meader was to President John F. Kennedy. The Meader version was not musical, but its satire was no more severe than the Kaufman and Hart portrait of Kennedy's distinguished predecessor.

The book for "I'd Rather Be Right" was topical, as were the closely integrated music and lyrics. As a result, the play is dated for today's audience. A person who lived under the New Deal may still get a laugh from rereading the script, but to one who has grown to maturity since World War II, much of the material is unintelligible. The show, though, was a landmark in its time. George M. Cohan topped off a long and distinguished musical-comedy career with his portrayal of F.D.R.

The plot was almost nonexistent and served mainly as an excuse for many topical gibes at Democrats, Republicans, organized labor, management, government-controlled jobs, and politics in general.

On a balmy summer evening in New York's Central Park, young Phil Barker, his head cradled in the lap of his fiancée, Peggy Jones, tells her that they can't get married as his boss won't give him a raise because of the unsettled economy.

He falls asleep on her lap and dreams that F.D.R. is passing by. He stops the President, explains his plight, and begs him to balance the budget. F.D.R. summons his cabinet (Farley and Perkins and Perkins and Farley) on the spot. A great amount of badinage between F.D.R. and the cabinet follows. Secretary of the Treasury Morgenthau, for instance, tells Roosevelt he's running out of money again.

F.D.R. asks, "Now, Henry—what happened to that money I gave you last week?"

"I spent it," Morgenthau replies.

"Three hundred million dollars?" says the President. "That ought to last more than a week, Henry."

F.D.R. then introduces Phil and Peggy and their problem ("Have You Met Miss Jones?"). The rest of the book deals with the many ideas proposed for balancing the budget and how each one fails. Interspersed with this are asides on everything from President Roosevelt's grandchildren, Sistie and Buzzie, to a wild (but still valid) skit about labor-management relations. As a last resort, F.D.R. tries a superspecial fireside chat. Postmaster General Jim Farley is master of ceremonies: ". . . our new program—WHITE HOUSE HOTEL, featuring FRANKLIN D. ROOSEVELT and all the lads." When this fails too, the President gives up trying to balance the budget. He advises Phil and Peggy to take a chance on their country and marry anyway. Waking up, Phil does just that.

Besides Cohan, the cast included Joy Hodges, as Peggy; Austin Marshall, as Phil Barker; Paul Parks, as Farley; Taylor Holmes, as Morgenthau; Marion Green, as Cordell Hull; Bijou Fernandez, as Frances Perkins; Evelyn and Warren Mills, as Sistie and Buzzie; John Cherry, as the Chief Justice of the Supreme Court; and Marie Louise Dana, as F.D.R.'s mother. Other songs were "Spring in Vienna," "Song of the Supreme Court," "We're Going To Balance the Budget," "Song of the P.W.A.," "Off the Record," and "A Baby Bond for Baby."

IDA: song (1903). Words by Eddie Leonard, music by Eddie Munson.

The man most closely associated with "Ida" is Eddie Cantor: his wife was named Ida, and the song was his trademark from his first glory days in "The Ziegfeld Follies." Indeed, many people believe that Cantor wrote the song.

But the lyricist of "Ida" was a great performer in his own right. When Eddie Leonard wrote the song, Eddie Cantor was a child, soon to become one of the boys in Gus Edwards's newsboy act. Leonard (originally Eddie Toomey), from Richmond, Virgina, was discovered by songwriter and publisher Edward B. Marks, who got him a job with the then nationally famous minstrel show of Primrose and West. Though Leonard was a singer and dancer, company manager Jim Decker started him off as a cymbal player in the band and general handy man. Leonard worked his way up to a member of the singing ensemble. He eventually was given the song "Don't Do Nothing for Nobody That Won't Do Nothing for You." Eddie decided he could write a better song himself, and one night got the idea for "Ida." He wrote the words, and Eddie Munson wrote the music. It was published on August 3, 1903, by Joseph W. Stern and Company, in which Marks was a partner.

Leonard bothered Decker and other members of the Primrose and West Company for the chance to sing "Ida" instead of "Don't Do Nothin', etc." It was decided to fire him. In his book "They All Sang" (New York: Viking Press, 1934), Marks recalls the evening when Leonard was supposed to give his last performance.

. . . But Decker stood out against the change. I spoke up for Eddie—we were publishing his song . . . and said, "Jim, why don't you let him try out his new song?" Jim was letting Eddie out anyway, so he answered, "He's through—his trunk's out in the alley." Leonard asked me what to do and I advised him to go on anyway and take a chance on his new song, "Ida." After all, he had nothing to lose. He sang it, and it was a sensation —encore. Jim Decker came rushing backstage and yelled at Eddie, "Bring your trunk in out of the alley."

IT AIN'T NECESSARILY SO: song (1935). Words by Ira Gershwin, music by George Gershwin.

The brothers Gershwin contributed much to the American popular-music heritage. Not the least of their achievements was the opera "Porgy and Bess." Ira, who brought new refinement and poetic ingenuity to lyric writing, recalled the writing of a key number from "Porgy and Bess" in his book "Lyrics on Several Occasions" (New York: Alfred A. Knopf, 1959):

After my brother played me a sixteen-bar tune which might be the start of something for Sportin' Life in the Picnic Scene, I asked for a lead sheet (the simple vocal line); and to remember the rhythm and accents better, I wrote across the top a dummy title—the first words that came to my mind: "It ain't necessarily so." (I could just as easily have written "An order of bacon and eggs," "Tomorrow's the 4th of July," "Don't ever sell Telephone short"—anything—the sense didn't matter. All I required was a phrase which accented the second, fifth, and eighth syllables to help me remember the rhythm.)

For two days, Ira tried all sorts of new word combinations, but nothing seemed right. Then he recalled a time a few years back when he had collaborated with composer Vincent Youmans. Youmans had looked at Ira's dummy title and insisted it be the final song title.

So I began to explore the possibilities of *this* dummy title. At one point I decided that trouble maker Sportin' Life, being among a group of religious Sons-and-Daughters-of-Repent-Ye-Saith-the-Lord picknickers, might try to startle them with a cynical and irreligious attitude. And what would certainly horrify his auditors would be his saying that some accounts in the Bible weren't necessarily so. Once I had the rhymes "Bible—li'ble" and "Goliath—dieth," I felt I was probably on the right track. George agreed. He then improvised the scat sounds, "Wa-doo, Zim bam boddle-oo." Together, in a week or so, we worked out the rather unusual construction of this piece, with its limerick musical theme, the crowd responses, the lush melodic middle, and the "ain't nessa, ain't nessa" coda. Happily, in all the years that the song has been around, I have received only one letter remarking on its possible irreverence.

IVES, BURL: folk singer, actor. Born Huntington Township, Illinois, June 14, 1909.

Burl Ives is a rare performer who has made his

[116]

mark in a great many widely divergent entertainment areas. A great folk singer, he also scored with popular ballads and show music. At the height of rock 'n' roll's popularity, Ives also won the ear of the teen-age audience with his gold-record rendition of "A Little Bitty Tear." As an actor, Ives won a motion-picture Oscar and the New York Drama Critics' Award.

Ives seems to symbolize the American folk-music heritage. His ancestors arrived in the New World in the seventeenth century, and produced a hardy line of ministers and farmers. Burl Icle Ivanhoe Ives's parents were tenant farmers. Singing was a family tradition, and Ives early learned many traditional folk songs from his grandmother. By the time Burl was four, he was performing in public with his brothers and sisters.

Ives's broad shoulders and weight suggest the build of a fullback, which indeed he was at Newton High School. Despite his interest in music, Burl decided to become a football coach and enrolled in Eastern Illinois State Teachers College. But in 1930, he left school to hitchhike and ride the rods all over the United States, Canada, and Mexico. He earned his keep by playing his banjo, singing, and doing odd jobs. As he roamed the land, he found many folk songs to add to his already impressive repertoire.

Then he enrolled in Indiana State Teachers College in Terre Haute. To pay his way through school, he worked in a drugstore and sang on the local radio. He also began taking voice lessons. His teacher liked his work and strongly urged him to go to New York and continue his studies. In New York, Ives tried to get bookings, but theatrical agents told him they "weren't interested in hillbilly acts." He decided that some formal musical training might help, and enrolled at New York University in 1937.

The summer of 1938 finally saw Ives's luck take a turn for the better. He played in summer stock at Rockridge Theatre, Carmel, New York, in several plays. Librettist-director-producer George Abbott became interested in Ives and wrote a small, nonsinging part for him into "The Boys from Syracuse." Soon after, Burl was singing to appreciative audiences at New York's Village Vanguard.

In 1940, he performed on several NBC and CBS radio shows. CBS gave him his own show, "The Wayfarin' Stranger." After an Army hitch, in which he played in Irving Berlin's "This Is the Army," Ives returned to civilian life and a fea-

tured spot at New York's Café Society Uptown in 1944. Later that year, Ives appeared in the folk-song cavalcade "Sing Out, Sweet Land." The show was not too popular with the critics, but Ives was singled out for praise, particularly for his singing of "The Blue-Tail Fly," and won the Donaldson Award as the best supporting actor in the 1944–45 Broadway season.

Burl made his movie debut in "Smoky" in 1946 and was featured in six other pictures by 1955. His autobiography, "Wayfarin' Stranger," was published by McGraw-Hill in 1948. He later collected and wrote the notes for a number of books of and about folk songs.

Ives played Cap'n Andy in the 1954 Broadway revival of Jerome Kern's "Show Boat." The following year, he won raves in Tennessee Williams's "Cat on a Hot Tin Roof," and in 1958 in the film. He played a series of well-received film roles in O'Neill's "Desire under the Elms" and "The Big Country" (1958), and "Our Man in Havana" (1960). Ives won an Oscar for his work in "The Big Country."

JAMES, HARRY: band leader, trumpeter, composer. Born Albany, Georgia, March 15, 1916.

One of the greatest popular-music trumpeters and a major band leader in the big-band era, Harry James started in show business at the age of four—not as a musician but a contortionist. In the Mighty Haag Circus tour of the South in 1920, he was part of the act billed as "The Youngest and Oldest Contortionists in the World." His partner, who had started coaching James at the age of two, was seventy years old.

Harry was born in a run-down hotel next to a jail. His mother was a trapeze artist, and his father led the circus band. When Harry was six, he gave up acrobatics and began taking cornet lessons from his father. At nine, Harry was playing trumpet in Christy Brothers Circus Band, and by the time he was twelve, he was leading the band. When Harry was fifteen, his family settled in Beaumont, Texas. Harry kept up his trumpet work while going to high school. At sixteen, he tried for a job with Lawrence Welk, whose band had a Beaumont date, but was turned down because he played too loud for Welk's style.

At twenty, Harry had his own orchestra and played dates throughout the Southwest. Big-time band leader Ben Pollack, whose organization boasted such famous alumni as Glenn Miller and Benny Goodman, heard James and immediately signed him. James spent several years with the

Pollack band. Benny Goodman heard a Pollack record featuring James, and soon James was helping record some of the Goodman swing classics.

After two years with Goodman, and with some financial help from Goodman, James started a new organization. For several years, the band plodded along, playing dance and nightclub engagements but gaining little major attention. Harry concentrated on the brass section, often with his own lightninglike trumpet carrying the lead, and it took the public a while to get used to this powerhouse style. Harry had to disband and start anew several times. In one case, James lost a promising young singer, Frank Sinatra, to the Tommy Dorsey band.

In 1942, important radio, nightclub and stageshow dates began to come James's way. His great swing renditions of "Two O'Clock Jump," "Music Makers," "Ciribiribin," and "The Flight of the Bumblebee" were eagerly snapped up by record fanciers across the nation. Harry could play it sweet as well, as shown by such records as "September in the Rain," "Lullaby of Broadway" (with Doris Day as vocalist), and "You'll Never Know" (with Rosemary Clooney).

The fadeout of the big band after World War II saw James, still a great name in music, cut down on his activities. He still was in demand, but instead of a formal band, Harry for a time put together whatever combination he needed for an engagement. In 1963, James's new band, the Music Makers, was a feature attraction at Disneyland and on the Jerry Lewis television show.

JAZZ: a syncopated, originally improvised, type of popular music.

There are dozens of theories about the origin of the word "Jazz." The most likely derivation is from a sexual term commonly used in Negro brothels in New Orleans. Originally the word was not "Jazz" but "jass," and the first bands to use the term called themselves "jass bands." Other theories are that the word comes from a Creole word meaning "to speed up." It's also been attributed to a French word *jaser*, "to prattle," and to the use of the word "jasbo" in minstrel shows. Still another report has it that there once was an early jazz musician named Charles or James whose name was shortened to a nickname such as Jas or Jass.

Jazz originated in New Orleans, particularly in its fabled colored brothel-ghetto section of Storyville. The word "jazz" is thought by some

to have been coined later, when the music spread to Chicago. Jazz has always been primarily brass music. The original New Orleans jazz outfits were descended from brass bands that played at all kinds of occasions, from holidays to funerals. The classic jazz bands had from five to seven instruments, four or five of which were trombones, clarinets, cornets, or another wind instrument, plus piano, bass, and/or guitar. The cornet was particularly important; Buddy Bolden, one of the pioneers of New Orleans jazz, was a great cornettist.

The music began flowing out of New Orleans to the rest of the nation around World War I, partly because of government orders closing the Storyville sporting houses but also because jazz was new, interesting, and dynamic. About this time, the original Dixieland Band in Chicago provided a new style of jazz in which the white idiom was fused with the more abandoned playing of New Orleans. The Original Dixieland Band was made up of white musicians—Larry Shields, clarinet; Dominique LaRocca, cornet; Eddie Edwards, trombone; Henry Ragas, piano; and Tony Sharbaro, drums—as were most of the 1917–1920 Chicago bands. In addition to Bolden, some of the most famous Negro greats were Bunk Johnson, Kid Ory, Johnny and Baby Dodds, Freddie Keppard, Jelly Roll Morton, and Louis Armstrong.

Jazz is characterized by breaks, or improvised changes in the musical pattern by soloists. Originally the improvisations were unrehearsed, though this is not the case with much of modern jazz. Besides Dixieland, jazz covers a multitude of forms, such as boogiewoogie and progressive jazz.

JERK: in-place dance, derived from the Twist, characterized by abrupt motions of the arms and upper torso.

JITTERBUG: one of several dances performed to jazz. Also, a devotee of these dances.

Most of these dances originated in the Negro sections of the United States to be performed to forms of jazz. Included in this category are the black bottom, shag, Lindy hop, and rock 'n' roll.

JOLSON, AL: singer, actor, comedian. Born Srednicke, Russia, May 26, 1886; died San Francisco, California, October 23, 1950.

The name of Al Jolson blazed brightly for over forty years at the pinnacle of show-business fame. Though he suffered moments of eclipse over these years, at his death his popularity was probably as great as it had ever been. As one critic, quoted in *Current Biography* (November, 1940), said, "Jolson is a great, great man. He is one of the greatest dominators in the theatre. . . ."

Asa Yoelson came to this country with his family when he was seven. They settled in Washington, D.C. His father was a learned rabbi, and Asa's first ambition was to become a cantor. As he became acclimated to America, Asa's aims changed. He decided to become an actor instead, and caused his parents much travail by constantly running away to sing in cafés and saloons.

His first stage appearance was a member of a mob in a scene from Israel Zangwill's "Children of the Ghetto." After this, having changed his name to Al Jolson, he traveled with vaudeville and minstrel shows. He became a regular member of Lew Dockstader's minstrel troupe, performing mainly as an end man. In 1909, when the show was playing San Francisco, Jolson filled in for a star and scored a major success singing his first "mammy" song. His reputation grew, and he was hired by the Shuberts for their Winter Garden productions in New York.

Jolson proved one of the most vibrant personalities to hit the New York stage. He was a headliner in a long series of Winter Garden shows, appearing mostly in blackface as a stock character named Gus. These shows included "Vera Violetta" (1911), "The Whirl of Society" (1912), "The Honeymoon Express" (1913), "Dancing Around" (1914), "Robinson Crusoe, Jr." (1916), and "Sinbad" (1918). In 1921, he appeared in "Bombo" in a theater named for him. In 1925, he scored again in "Big Boy."

Hollywood signed him for the first feature talking picture. "The Jazz Singer" (1927) marked the end of the silent-film era and became a classic that it still shown all over the world on television. In succeeding years, Jolson starred in several more films, including "The Singing Fool" and "Say It with Songs."

In 1932, Jolson's popularity in the movies declined, and he turned his attention to the newly important medium of radio. In the thirties, he starred with Parkyakakus and Martha Raye in his own weekly show on the Columbia network. Jolson's career waned later in the thirties, but in 1940, he made a successful return to Broadway in "Hold On to Your Hats." After this, his career seemed to fade again, but Jolson wasn't through. He made a sensational comeback when his voice was featured on the soundtrack of the movie of his life, "The Jolson Story." Larry Parks became a star overnight portraying Jolson. And Jolson's recording of "The Anniversary Song" became one of the best-selling records ever made.

Albums of some of the all-time Jolson hits were soon on the best-seller lists. These songs included "Sonny Boy," "April Showers," "Mammy," "California, Here I Come," "Toot, Toot, Tootsie!," "Swanee," and "Rock-A-Bye Your Baby with a Dixie Melody." Jolson also had his own radio show in the late forties and was a television star until his death.

JONES, JACK: singer. Born Los Angeles, California, January 14, 1938.

When Frank Sinatra calls a young singer "the next major singing star of show business," that's praise no observer of the music scene can ignore. It's also a prediction that's hard to live up to. But so far Jack Jones has taken it in stride and seems well on the way to making it come true.

Jones comes by his talent naturally; his father is Alan Jones, who made many hit records in the nineteen-thirties and forties, and his mother is actress Irene Hervey. At University High School in Los Angeles, Jack was a top-flight athlete as well as a lead actor in many school productions. After graduation, Jones decided to concentrate on show business, taking courses in voice, dramatics, and dance.

Jack teamed with his father in an act that won notice in an Elko, Nevada, nightclub. From there they went to an extended booking at the Thunderbird Hotel in Las Vegas. A little later, the father and son were starred at the Statler-Hilton Hotel in Los Angeles.

Jack wanted to make his own way, however. He submitted some demonstration records to Capitol Records without indicating his family background. Capitol quickly signed him to a contract and soon released several singles and Jack's first album, "This Love of Mine." Jack switched to Kapp Records in 1961 and scored his first hit in 1962 with "Lollipops and Roses." This record won him the record-industry Grammy award for the best single record of 1962. Jack's star rose rapidly after this, and his face became familiar on television during 1963 and 1964. Some of the shows he was featured on were those of Steve Allen, Dick Clark, Peter Lind Hayes, Dinah Shore, Garry Moore, and Jerry Lewis, and a Bob Hope spectacular. He was selected the Most Promising Male Vocalist of the year in the 1962 and 1963 *Cash Box* Magazine disc-jockey polls.

Jones's popularity continued to increase with many appearances at important night spots, including New York's Plaza Hotel, the Slate Brothers Club in Los Angeles, and the Fairmont in San Francisco. In the first four months of 1964, he was a guest star on fifteen major TV shows. He won another Grammy as best male vocalist of 1963 for his hit recording of "Wives and Lovers." His single records and albums regularly appeared high up on the top-hundred-record-sales charts. He started off 1965 with a best selling single, "The Race Is On." His Kapp albums include "Shall We Dance" and "I've Got a Lot of Living to Do" (1961), "Gift of Love" and "This Was My Love" (1962), and "She Loves Me" (1963).

Jones's appeal ranges from high-school to adult audiences. He told Los Angeles *Times* columnist Art Seidenbaum (May 4, 1964):

I've been lucky to find audiences for more or less straight music. That's what opened television to me. The important shows are more likely to buy the sort of singing I do; they don't really know what to do with Rock and Roll.

JUMBO: musical. Lyrics by Lorenz Hart, music by Richard Rodgers, book by Ben Hecht and Charles MacArthur. New York opening: November 16, 1935, Hippodrome. 233 performances.

Any showman worth his salt longs for the chance to stage an extravaganza. Billy Rose achieved this goal in 1935, combining a circus, folk drama, and extravaganza with a top musical score by Rodgers and Hart. Taking over and remodeling the Hippodrome Theatre in New York, he provided an evening's entertainment still recalled with awe by older theatergoers. Besides the usual death-defying stunts of the big top he threw in such tidbits as a balancing act in which acrobats walked a plank over an open lions' cage. In another feat, a plane circled the auditorium while acrobats hung from it by their toes. Though seemingly made to order for Hollywood treatment, it was not until 1962 that "Jumbo" was turned into a movie spectacular.

As the festivities get under way, the John A. Considine circus is preparing to play a Midwestern city. The clown, animals, brass band (led by Paul Whiteman), and the rest arrive to the strident rhythms of "The Circus Is on Parade." One of the circus stars is Considine's daughter Mickey, a bareback rider. But the main attraction is the extraordinarily talented elephant Jumbo. Considine is engaged in a running feud with rival circus owner Matt Mulligan, who wants to take over Jumbo and eliminate Considine's circus. Mulligan gets his son Matt, Jr., to join Considine's outfit under an alias to help in the plot.

Considine gets deeper and deeper into debt because of his craving for liquor. His press agent, Claudius B. Bowers, comes up with all sorts of odd schemes to thwart the bill collectors. One of these is to pay off the creditors by burning down Considine's house and collecting the insurance.

As the tour continues, Matt, Jr., and Mickey fall in love. While they perform on horseback, Matt sings "The Most Beautiful Girl in the World." Mickey warmly tells her feelings in "My Romance." But the lovers quarrel and part when Mickey learns Matt's identity. Sad and lonely, Mickey finds she is "Little Girl Blue." At the end, Bowers reconciles the families and Matt and Mickey are married in a gala "Circus Wedding."

The original cast included Jimmy Durante, as Bowers; Gloria Grafton, as Mickey; Donald Novis, as Matt, Jr.; Arthur Sinclair, as Considine; and W. J. McCarthy, as Mulligan. The movie changed the lineup of characters. Jumbo was now part of the Wonder Circus, with Jimmy Durante playing Pop Wonder and Doris Day his daughter Kitty. The movie eliminates Bowers and introduces a new character, Pop Wonder's long-suffering fiancée Lulu, played by Martha Raye. The rival circus is now run by John Noble (played by Dean Jagger), with Stephen Boyd appearing as Noble's son Sam.

KAHN, GUS: lyricist. Born Coblenz, Germany, November 6, 1886; died Beverly Hills, California, October 8, 1941.

For a great lyricist, variety has often been the spice of life. A good example is Gus Kahn, certainly one of the greatest. The composers with whom he worked include Harry Akst, Louis Alter, Nacio Herb Brown, Con Conrad, Walter Donaldson, Ted Fiorito, George Gershwin, Jay Gorney, Arthur Johnston, Isham Jones, Jimmy McHugh, George W. Meyer, Sigmund Romberg, Egbert Van Alstyne, Harry Warren, Richard Whiting, Harry M. Woods, and Vincent Youmans. The result has been one of the most impressive list of standards in the popular-music repertoire.

Kahn came to the United States at the age of five. His father, a cattle dealer, settled in Chicago, and young Gus was educated in that city's public schools. In the years after the turn of the century, Chicago was second only to New York as a popular-music center. The city's night spots featured some of the greatest bands in ragtime and, during World War I, jazz. It had a thriving music-publishing industry, and many songwriters and performers frequented the demonstration halls of these firms. Gus Kahn could feel the underlying rhythms of Chicago during his years in school and began to write his first amateurish songs.

After finishing school, he nursed a desire to make songwriting his profession, but at first he had to settle for jobs in hotel-supply firms and mail-order houses. He made the rounds of the publishers when he could, gaining his first published song, "I Wish I Had a Girl," in 1907. With this success, he began to concentrate on songwriting, adding to his small income by writing special material for vaudeville performers.

His first break came just before World War I. Composer Egbert Van Alstyne, who sometimes frequented Chicago, had just lost his partner, Harry Williams, to Hollywood. He heard of Kahn, and the result was a collaboration that lasted for several years. Their first hit was the 1913 "Sunshine and Roses." In 1915, they hit again with "Memories," and the following year turned out the ever-popular "Pretty Baby." (Tony Jackson collaborated on the music for "Pretty Baby.") In 1917, they wrote "Sailing Away on the Henry Clay" and, in 1919, "Your Eyes Have Told Me So." Though they went separate ways in the twenties, they still turned out an occasional song, such as "Old Pal" (1924) and "You're in Style When You're Wearing a Smile" (1928).

By the start of the twenties, Kahn had moved to New York. His main collaborator during the decade was Walter Donaldson, but Kahn also worked with many other composers. In 1922, Donaldson and Kahn got off to a roaring start with "My Buddy" and "Carolina in the Morning." Some of their other efforts included "Beside a Babbling Brook" (1923); "My Sweetie Turned Me Down," "That Certain Party," "Yes Sir, That's My Baby," "I Wonder Where My Baby is Tonight," and "The Midnight Waltz" (1925); "For My Sweetheart" and "Let's Talk About My Sweetie" (1926); and "She's Wonderful" (1928). In addition, Donaldson and Kahn provided the

score for Eddie Cantor's 1928 Broadway hit "Whoopee," including "Makin' Whoopee," "My Baby Just Cares for Me," and "Love Me or Leave Me." The last was introduced in the show by Ruth Etting.

In the early twenties, Kahn also turned out several hits with band leader Isham Jones, including "Swingin' Down the Lane" (1923); "It Had To Be You," "I'll See You in My Dreams," "Spain," and "The One I Love Belongs to Somebody Else" (1924); and "Ida I Do" (1925). Some of Kahn's other efforts of the twenties include "Sittin in a Corner" (1923) with George W. Meyer, "You Said Good Night" (1927) with Jay Gorney, and collaboration with the Gershwins on the 1929 musical "Show Girl."

In the early thirties, Donaldson went to Hollywood, but Kahn stayed in New York. In 1931, Kahn worked with Richard Whiting and Harry Akst on the hit song "Guilty." He succumbed to Hollywood's lure in 1933. For a time, he teamed with his old partner Donaldson. From 1933 to 1935, they turned out scores for a number of films, including "The Prize Fighter and the Lady," "Kid Millions," "Operator 13," "Hollywood Party," and "Reckless."

In 1936, Kahn worked with Jimmy McHugh on the two films, "His Master's Voice" and "Let's Sing Again." Among his other Hollywood collaborators was Sigmund Romberg. Beginning in 1937, Kahn worked with Romberg on three Nelson Eddy films: "Maytime," "Girl of the Golden West," and "Let Freedom Ring."

After Kahn's death, his career was reviewed in the movie "I'll See You in My Dreams," featuring Danny Thomas, as Kahn, and Doris Day, as his wife.

KALMAR, BERT: lyricist, librettist, actor. Born New York, New York, February 16, 1884, died Los Angeles, California, September 18, 1947.

A knee injury helped put Bert Kalmar on the road to popular-music fame. The accident, which occurred while Kalmar was performing as a dancing comic, sidelined him for several months just before this country's entry into World War I. His friend, composer Harry Ruby, suggested they use the time to work up some special material for singer Belle Baker. The result was a collaboration that became one of the most notable in songwriting history.

By the time Kalmar met Ruby, he was a show-business veteran, having run away from home at ten to join a tent show. By the time he was in his teens, he was working as a vaudeville comedian as well as writing special material in his spare time. After a while, he began to write parodies of popular songs and from this switched to doing songs of his own. In 1911, he added words to music by Ted Snyder to produce his first hit, "In the Land of Harmony." While continuing the rounds as a vaudeville comic, he met many other hopeful composers, including Harry Ruby, who was working as a pianist with a trio.

After Kalmar's accident, his work with Ruby provided Belle Baker with a hit, "He Sits Around." Though Kalmar went back to the stage, he and Ruby collaborated on a series of sit songs, including "So Long! Oo-Long" in 1920, "My Sunny Tennessee" and "She's Mine, All Mine" in 1921, and, with an assist from Ted Snyder on the music, the great standard "Who's Sorry Now?" in 1923.

Kalmar and Ruby also started to turn their attention to the Broadway stage. Here Kalmar not only worked on lyrics but often provided all or part of the book for major shows. His output included material for "No Other Girl" (1924); "The Ramblers (1926) (with Guy Bolton and Ruby); "Lucky" (1927); "Five O'Clock Girl" (1927), which included "Thinking of You"; and lyrics for "Good Boy" (1928), including "I Wanna Be Loved by You."

The year 1928 was eventful for Kalmar and Ruby in many ways. Not only did they write several nationwide song favorites, they also worked on the stage show "Animal Crackers," which starred a new comedy team called the Marx Brothers. The result was a close working partnership that resulted in Kalmar and Ruby's moving to Hollywood in 1930. That year, they wrote their first film hit for the movie "Check and Double Check." The song was "Three Little Words," which served as the title for the 1950 film biography of Ruby and Kalmar. For the film version of "Animal Crackers" in 1930, they turned out "Why Am I So Romantic?" To make the year still more memorable, Kalmar and Ruby helped speed another comedy team on the way to stardom by providing material for the Wheeler and Woolsey hit "The Cuckoos."

In succeeding years, they worked on several other Marx Brothers films, including "Duck Soup" and "Horse Feathers." This, however, represented only a small part of their film output, which included scores for "The Kid from Spain," "Hips, Hips Hooray," "Happiness Ahead," "Bright Lights," "Walking on Air," and "Everybody Sing."

KENTON, STANLEY NEWCOMB (STAN): band leader, arranger, pianist. Born Wichita, Kansas, February 19, 1912.

One of the prime movers in progressive jazz, Stan Kenton was one of the few in the field also to achieve any degree of widespread popular success. Stan was brought to California at a young age and spent most of his formative years in Los Angeles. He was also exposed to music at an early age as his mother was a music teacher. She taught him for a time and later brought in private teachers. Stan was an apt pupil and by the time he was sixteen had written his first arrangement.

By 1930, he was playing piano with various local bands and was beginning to receive attention from more widely known leaders. He soon joined the Everett Hoagland organization as pianist and arranger. In the years that followed, he worked with the bands of Vido Musso and Johnny Davis. Stan became eager to go out on

Stan Kenton

his own. In 1941, he assembled a band for a date at Balboa Beach, California. From then on, Kenton was his own man. The Kenton bands were the proving grounds for many top-flight musicians and vocalists of the forties, fifties, and sixties.

During 1941 and 1942, the band made some records but won little national attention. In 1943, Kenton signed with Capitol, a new West Coast record company. The first recording session, in November, 1943, provided a hit in the band's theme, "Artistry in Rhythm." Since then, Kenton has been a name to reckon with in popular music and jazz. The band won the *Down Beat* magazine poll in 1947 and then held the title from 1950 to 1954. Kenton won the same accolade from *Metronome* magazine from 1947 to 1949 and again in 1954.

During the mid-forties, Kenton featured such great vocalists as Anita O'Day and Gene Howard. Anita left in 1945, and Stan signed a new singer who made his fans almost forget his former star. The new girl was June Christy, and by the end of 1945, one of the top hits in the country was her version of "Tampico." Over the years, Stan also brought in some of the country's top arrangers, including Pete Ruggulo, Gerry Mulligan, and Shorty Rogers.

Kenton continued in musical prominence during the fifties and sixties, though for much of this time he did not keep a band on a steady basis. Instead he would organize a new band for part of a season, disband it, and start again some time later. He continued to experiment and in 1950 toured the United States with a forty-piece outfit, including a string section, in "Innovations in Modern Music."

Kenton albums of the late fifties and early sixties include "Back to Balboa" (1958), "Kenton Touch," and "Lush Interlude" (1959), "Road Show," and "Standards in Silhouette" (1960), "West Side Story" and "Romantic Approach" (1961), "Adventures in Jazz" and "Sophisticated Approach" (1962), and "Artistry in Bossa Nova," "Adventures in Blues," and "Adventures in Time" (1963).

KERN, JEROME DAVID: composer. Born New York, New York, January 27, 1885, died New York, New York, November 11, 1945. Won Pulitzer Prize for "Show Boat" (1927), Academy Award for Best Song of 1936 ("The Way You Look Tonight") and 1941 ("The Last Time I Saw Paris").

If Jerome Kern had written nothing but "Show Boat," it would have been enough to assure his undying musical fame. As Cecil Smith wrote in "Musical Comedy in America" (New York: Theatre Arts Books, 1950): "No other American piece of its vintage left so large a permanent musical legacy, and certainly no other surpassed it in quality." But Kern wrote not only "Show Boat" but dozens of scores besides—scores which included such standards as "Smoke Gets in Your Eyes," "They Didn't Believe Me," "All the Things You Are," and "The Way You Look Tonight."

Kern was born into a comfortable New York family. His father held the water-sprinkling contract for Manhattan. His mother, who liked to play the piano, gave her son his first lessons at an early age. When Jerome was ten, his father took over a merchandising house in Newark, New Jersey, and moved his family there. In Newark High School, Jerome often played the piano and organ in assembly and wrote music for school plays. He wanted to take up music as a career, but his father insisted his son enter the business. When Jerome was seventeen, his father sent him on an errand to buy two pianos. Instead, Jerome contracted for two hundred. Though Mr. Kern managed to sell the pianos, he reluctantly agreed that his son might better pursue music than business.

Jerome studied at the New York College of Music for a year. In 1902, he went to Europe for further studies. In London he got a songwriting job with producer Charles Frohman. Kern returned to the United States in 1904 to try to crack Tin Pan Alley. He started as a song plugger for Lyceum Publishing Company, then moved over to T. B. Harms as a salesman and rehearsal pianist. This led to his first musical assignment, revising the score of an English show, "Mr. Wix of Wickham" (1904). In 1905, Kern scored his first song hit with "How'd You Like To Spoon with Me?" Kern was soon providing one or several interpolated songs for many Broadway shows, most of which were European imports. In 1912, he wrote his first complete score for an American original, "The Red Petticoat." His 1914 contribution to the English import "The Girl from Utah" included "They Didn't Believe Me."

But Kern wanted to concentrate on writing complete scores for more American-oriented books. In 1915, he achieved his first breakthrough in this direction by providing the music to "Very Good, Eddie" (book by Guy Bolton and Philip Bartholomae). A major hit, it was one of the first musicals to try to closely integrate music, lyrics, and plot. Kern had found an excellent teammate in Guy Bolton. With lyricist P. G. Wodehouse, they turned out a series of shows including "Oh, Boy!" (1917), "Leave It to Jane" (1917), and "Oh, Lady! Lady!!" (1918).

With the exception of 1928, every year of the twenties saw a Kern show or two on Broadway. For "Sally" (1920), Kern wrote such songs as the title song and "Look for the Silver Lining." "Good Morning, Dearie" (1921) included "Ka-lu-a" and "Blue Danube Blues." After "The Bunch and Judy" (1922), "Stepping Stones" (1923), and "Sitting Pretty" and "Dear Sir" (1924), Kern moved on to a new high in 1925 with "Sunny." Working for the first time with Otto Harbach and Oscar Hammerstein II, he wrote such songs as "Sunny," "Who?," and "D'Ye Love Me?" In Oscar Hammerstein he found a kindred soul who also believed in the close relationship of all facets of a musical play. They soon began work on adapting Edna Ferber's novel "Show Boat" to the stage. Though Miss Ferber was at first dubious, they succeeded so brilliantly that the show is still in fashion. Such songs as "Ol' Man River," "Make Believe," "Why Do I Love You?," and "Bill" have become part of America's musical heritage.

Alternating between Harbach and Hammerstein in the years following, Kern wrote "Sweet Adeline" (1929), "The Cat and the Fiddle" (1931), "Music in the Air" (1932), and "Roberta" (1933). Some of the songs from these are "She Didn't Say Yes," "The Night Was Made for Love," "I've Told Ev'ry Little Star," "You're Devastating," "Smoke Gets In Your Eyes," and "Yesterdays."

Except for a brief excursion to Broadway in 1939, Kern wrote mainly for films from 1933 on. The 1939 show "Very Warm for May" was a failure but provided "All the Things You Are." Kern continued to write his songs in Hollywood. In 1935, "Lovely to Look At" was nominated for an Academy Award. Kern won an Oscar in 1936 for "The Way You Look Tonight" and again in 1941 for "The Last Time I Saw Paris." In 1945, after completing the score for the film "Centennial Summer," he returned to New York to write "Annie Get Your Gun." Shortly after arriving, Kern suffered a heart attack. He died six days later.

KING AND I, THE: musical. Lyrics and book by Oscar Hammerstein II, music by Richard Rodgers. Adapted from Margaret Landon's novel "Anna and the King of Siam." New York opening: March 29, 1951, St. James Theatre. 1,246 performances.

Rodgers and Hammerstein followed their wildly successful "South Pacific" with the almost equally well received "King and I." The setting was still exotic, this time Siam. Margaret Landon's novel was a fictionalized version of the trials and travails of Anna Leonowens, a widowed English schoolteacher who was hired by the king of Siam in the eighteen-sixties to bring Western culture to his country.

Said Brooks Atkinson of the New York *Times:* "The King and I is a beautiful and lovable musical play."

As Anna and her son prepare to disembark at Bangkok, they are seized with some trepidation at the thought of living in a strange land. Anna calms her boy by singing "I Whistle a Happy Tune." The prime minister, who is unsympathetic to alien ideas, meets them and after several weeks brings her to the king. The king introduces her to his many wives, and she agrees to teach them as well as their many children. The king goes back on his promise to provide her with her own home and installs her in the palace. The wives tell her of a present from the king of Burma of a new wife, a young Burmese girl, Tuptim, who loves another man. Anna expresses her approval (to the queens' surprise) of romance ("Hello, Young Lovers"). The audience ends with the introduction of the royal offspring ("March of the Siamese Children"). Anna begins to teach and continues to demand a home of her own. She comes to love the Siamese pupils, as she tells them in "Getting To Know You." The balance of the play deals with the duel of wits and growing mutual respect between the king and Anna as each tries to make the other see his principles.

Tuptim and her beloved, the Burmese ambassador, meet secretly ("We Kiss in a Shadow"). A British gunboat approaches, looking for a pretext to take over Siam as "uncivilized." To prevent this, the king asks Anna to help him show how civilized Siam is. If she will, he vows to give her the promised house. Anna knows the British ambassador arriving on the ship and arranges a dinner that saves the day. Tuptim prepares a show for the guests, a Siamese version of "Uncle Tom's Cabin" (a ballet called "The Small House of Uncle Thomas"). After the party, the king hesitatingly expresses his thanks to Anna. They talk of the strange custom of ballroom dancing.

In the movie version of the Rodgers and Hammerstein success, *The King and I*, English schoolteacher Anna Leonowens (Deborah Kerr) prepares to lecture the many children of the King of Siam.

Anna teaches him the polka ("Shall We Dance"). Tuptim is caught trying to run away. The king wants to whip Tuptim, but Anna intervenes. In a battle of wills, Anna wins, and the king falls fatally ill from shame. On his deathbed, the king begs Anna, about to leave for England, to stay on to train his people in the new ways of the world, and she finally agrees.

The original cast included Gertrude Lawrence, as Anna; Sandy Kennedy, as her son Louis; Yul Brynner, as the king; John Juliano, as the prime minister; Doretta Morrow, as Tuptim; Larry Douglas, as the Burmese ambassador; and Dorothy Sarnoff, as Lady Thiang, the king's favorite wife. The film version also starred Brynner, with Deborah Kerr, as Anna, and Rita Moreno, as Tuptim. Other songs were "My Lord and Master," "A Puzzlement," "Shall I Tell You What I Think of You?," "Something Wonderful," "Western People Funny," and "I Have Dreamed."

KING, WAYNE: band leader, composer. Born Savannah, Illinois, February 16, 1901.

At the height of the era of big bands and swing, the Wayne King organization, known mainly for its waltzes, remained consistently popular with a large part of the American population. Even more surprising, King's style remained in favor long after the demise of most big bands. In 1965, his band was in demand for engagements throughout the United States, including an appearance at Disneyland's "Big Band Summer."

King spent his childhood in many places, including Texas and Oklahoma; his father was a railroad man and constantly on the move. By the time he was fifteen, Wayne had worked in a doctor's office, an Iowa bank, and a garage. At fifteen, his father gave him a clarinet, and Wayne's perspective changed. In 1920, while at Valparaiso University in Indiana, Wayne played in a band to help pay his tuition. After graduation, he went to Chicago to try for a career in music.

At first, he had to settle for clerking in an insurance company. He learned a second instrument, the saxophone, in his spare time. After six months, Wayne's extra skill won him a job with the pit orchestra in the Tivoli Theatre, where he eventually became assistant conductor.

In 1927, he started his own outfit and won an engagement as relief band at Chicago's Aragon Ballroom. He favored waltzes and other slow-tempo numbers. By 1930, King had established a nationwide reputation as "The Waltz King." He did this mainly through his coast-to-coast radio show, "The Lady Esther Serenade," which was a network fixture for eight years.

King stayed at the Aragon until 1935, when he left to fulfill major engagements throughout the country. In World War II, he served as a major in the Special Service Command. After the war, he once more organized a band and made a steady series of appearances playing for dances, at concerts, and on the radio. His byline remained the song he had composed as his band's theme, "The Waltz You Saved for Me." Some of King's other compositions are "Goofus," "Corn-silk," "Blue Hours," "So Close to Me," and "I'd Give My Kingdom for a Smile."

KINGSTON TRIO: vocal group. Original group: Bob Shane, born Hawaii, February 1, 1934; Nick Reynolds, born Coronado, California, July 27, 1933; and Dave Guard, born near San Francisco, California, October 19, 1934. Guard later was replaced by John Stewart, born San Diego, California.

Coffeehouses and basement clubs have had marked effects on the pattern of American entertainment since 1950. These off-beat (and, until they became well known, inexpensive) spots have spawned a new generation of folk singers. Most folk singers stay within their own tightly knit circle, playing small night spots, civic auditoriums, and college campuses. They are well supported by their fans—college students and followers of folk music. Rarely, though, do they break through to national prominence, as did the Kingston Trio.

The hungry i and Purple Onion, in San Francisco, were the two most famous cellar clubs of the fifties. In 1957, the hungry i offered a new act—three guitar-playing ivy-league types wearing the striped-shirt campus uniform. The boys were not ivy leaguers but were from local colleges. A few months before, the trio had been playing at a small college hangout, the Cracked Pot, in Palo Alto. San Francisco publicist Frank Werber heard them and signed them to a contract written

The Kingston Trio

[126]

on a table napkin. They chose the name Kingston Trio because calypso was in great demand, and "Kingston" sounded both collegiate and calypso.

After months of polishing up, they had been booked into the hungry i. The trio was received well but not sensationally. They moved across the street to the Purple Onion, where they began to catch on. A one-week stay stretched to two, then to a month, and finally seven months. The trio's fame began to spread out from San Francisco. The group left the Purple Onion and moved eastward. First came Mr. Kelly's in Chicago, then the Blue Angel and Village Vanguard in New York. The crowds turned out in record numbers. Television and records followed.

Initially they appeared on TV in acting as well as singing roles on "Playhouse 90" ("Rumors of Evening"). In June, 1958, Capitol Records put out their first album. The record sold well enough, but the important part was one song in the package: "Tom Dooley." This old ballad from the hills of Carolina shot to million-record status in a few months, the first of a long series of such successes, including "MTA," "Raspberries, Strawberries," and "Where Have All the Flowers Gone?"

John Stewart, who had arranged many of the trio's numbers and composed such songs as "Molly Dee" and "Green Grasses," joined the group when Dave Guard left.

The trio continued as national favorites. Such songs as "Tiajuana Jail," "Worried Man," and, in 1963, "Greenback Dollar" and "Reverend Mr. Black" proved that the Kingston Trio was more than three folk singers—it was an institution.

KISMET: musical. Lyrics by Robert Wright and George Forrest. Music adapted by Wright and Forrest from themes of Alexander Borodin. Book by Charles Lederer and Luther Davis. Adapted from Edward Knoblock's play. New York opening: December 3, 1953, Ziegfeld Theatre. 583 performances.

"Kismet" revolves around the miraculous acts of Hajj, a poet-beggar of Baghdad. All these acts take place in a twenty-four-hour period, in which Hajj becomes Emir of Baghdad for a day. In this day, Hajj must match wits with a wicked Wazir of Policer, who is also married to—and has wronged—Hajj's daughter Marsinah. In typical "Arabian Nights" fashion, Hajj fights off adversaries, performs numerous amazing feats, and schemes his way to victory over the Wazir. At the end of the day, Hajj gains wealth and fame and also avenges Marsinah by drowning the Wazir

in a fountain. In a subplot, the Caliph of Baghdad, who, disguised as a gardener, is observing the workaday life of his subjects, meets Hajj's daughter and, at the end of the play, marries her. Along the way, Hajj also wins a duel of verses with Omar the Tentmaker.

In the original cast were Alfred Drake, as Hajj; Doretta Morrow, as Marsinah; Henry Calvin, as the Wazir; Richard Kiley, as the Caliph; and Philip Coolidge, as Omar.

Among "Kismet's" best-known songs are "Baubles, Bangles and Beads," "Stranger in Paradise," adapted from the "Polovtsian Dances" from the opera "Prince Igor" (as were "Not Since Nineveh" and "He's in Love"), and "This Is My Beloved," from the third movement of the D-major String Quartet. Other adaptations include "Night of My Nights," from the Serenade for Piano; "Rhymes Have I," from the last act of "Prince Igor;" and "Gesticulate," from symphony No. 1. "Kismet's" finale was based on these as well as "In the Steppes of Central Asia." The score also included "Fate," "Bazaar of the Caravans," "Was I Wazir?," "Rahadlakum," and "Zubbediya."

KISS ME, KATE: musical. Lyrics and music by Cole Porter, book by Sam and Bella Spewack. Based on Shakespeare's "Taming of the Shrew." New York opening: December 30, 1948, Century Theatre. 1,077 performances.

The play within a play is nothing new. But applying the music and lyrics of Cole Porter to such a device is something else again. As the New York *Times* critic noted after the premiere, it was raining too hard that night for dancing in the streets—but the show certainly merited it.

"Kiss Me, Kate" opens with a Baltimore cast preparing for a revival of "The Taming of the Shrew" ("Another Op'nin', Another Show"). Producer-director Fred Graham is enamored of singer Lois Lane, who is interested in another performer, Bill Calhoun. The cast also includes Fred's former wife, Lilli Vanessi. Bill, who loves to gamble, tells Lois he signed Graham's name to a ten-thousand-dollar IOU in "the most respectable floating crap game in town." She begs him to change ("Why Can't You Behave?"). Lilli and Fred become nostalgic over past shows ("Wunderbar"). Fred leaves, and Lilli is mistakenly handed some flowers he intended for Lois.

"The Taming of the Shrew" begins ("We Open in Venice"). Katharina, the shrew, is played by Lilli. Lois plays her younger sister Bianca, who must wait until the older Katharina marries before she can marry Lucentio (Bill). The hero, Petruchio (Fred), arrives looking for a rich wife ("I've Come To Wive It Wealthily in Padua"). He agrees to marry Katharina, though he would like it better, he says unconcernedly, if she were the wife of whom he dreamed ("Were Thine That Special Face").

As the action of Shakespeare's play unfolds, the backdrop play continues. Lilli learns that her flowers were intended for Lois and starts to walk out. But some gangsters have come to collect the IOU and won't let anyone leave. Bill unhappily finds Lois flirting with someone else. Her retort to this is the tongue-in-cheek "Always True to You in My Fashion." The gangsters must wait until "The Taming of the Shrew" is finished to seize their man. But, while Petruchio wears down the spirited Katharina to be a proper wife, the gangsters find that their gang leaders have changed and that the IOU is now worthless. Before they leave, they sing a song in praise of the bard ("Brush Up Your Shakespeare"). With Katharina settled down, Lilli comes back after the curtain falls on "The Taming of the Shrew" to rejoin Fred, while Bill and Lois also join hands.

The one thousand and seventy-seven performances of "Kiss Me, Kate" is a record for any Porter musical, and few musicals ever had longer runs. Eight years after its premiere, the show became one of the biggest hits ever performed in Europe. After opening at the Volksoper in Vienna on February 14, 1956, it broke all records in that theater's fifty-eight-year history. Subsequently, it was a smash with Polish audiences as well.

The original cast included Alfred Drake, as Fred and Petruchio; Patricia Morison, as Lilli and Katharina; Lisa Kirk, as Lois and Bianca; and Harold Lang, as Bill and Lucentio. Other numbers were "So in Love," "Tom, Dick or Harry," "I Hate Men," "Where Is the Life That Late I Led?," "Bianca," "I Am Ashamed That Women Are So Simple," and "Too Darn Hot."

KNICKERBOCKER HOLIDAY: musical. Lyrics and book by Maxwell Anderson, music by Kurt Weill. New York opening: October 19, 1938, Ethel Barrymore Theatre. 168 performances.

This takeoff on Washington Irving's history of Dutch New York is a plea for individualism. Maxwell Anderson's book satirizes dictatorship of both the left and right, and big government

in general. According to Anderson, taxes, social security, and all the other appurtenances of the welfare state militate as much against true freedom of the individual as some of the worst facets of fascism and communism.

The play opens in Washington Irving's study as he works on his history. As he looks in on Nieuw Amsterdam, the bumbling city council (whose members sport such names as Roosevelt, Vanderbilt, and de Peyster) prepares to meet the new governor, Pieter Stuyvesant. They are worried, for it is hanging day and they have no one to hang. Finally they find a prospect, young Brom Broeck, who is incapable of taking orders. (He is, as a Broeck-Irving duet, "How Can You Tell An American?," discloses, the "first American.") Broeck loves Tina Tienhoven, daughter of another council member. Her father doesn't like Brom's defiance, and talks the council into hanging him. Stuyvesant arrives just in time to pardon Broeck.

The governor soon turns out to be worse than the council, for he is efficient—efficiently vicious and corrupt. All will go well, he tells the people, as long as all "Do As You Are Told." He appoints Tienhoven his payoff man. This makes the councilor, sings Stuyvesant, "The One Indispensable Man." Stuyvesant demands Tina in marriage. The wedding must take place the next day. The reason is expressed in the governor's lament about the darkening shadows of old age, "September Song." Brom is soon jailed. Tina steals into Brom's cell and is found by her father. As the lovers part, they sing "Desperate Our Need."

Stuyvesant regiments industry, wages, and prices so that soon the government will own everything. He also organizes an army ("To War, to War, to War"). The governor prepares to marry, but his plans are disrupted when the Indians, drunk on liquor sold them by Stuyvesant, attack. They burn the jail, freeing Brom. He promptly runs away from them, as does the army. Stuyvesant orders Brom to retreat to the fort. Brom, who can't obey an order, turns and fights. With Stuyvesant's aid, the Indians are routed. Brom still must be hanged for disobeying. But he rouses the council to stand "For Our Ancient Liberties" and drop the rope. Stuyvesant has one trump card, his cannon. Before he can fire, Irving intervenes to remind him of posterity. Stuyvesant decides that the applause of future generations is worth changing his ways, and all ends happily.

In the original cast, veteran Walter Huston,

as Stuyvesant, gave one of his greatest performances. Richard Kollmar was Brom; Jeanne Madden, Tina; Mark Smith, her father; George Watts, Roosevelt; and Ray Middleton, Washington Irving. Other songs were "There's Nowhere To Go but Up," "It Never Was You," "The Scars," "Hush, Hush to You," "Young People Think about Love," and "Dirge for a Soldier."

KOEHLER, TED: lyricist. Born Washington, D.C., July 18, 1894.

One of the important men in the music business is what might be called the "journeyman lyricist." He is a professional writer who can provide lyrics to order. He has the ability, which some lyricists do not, of accommodating his output to meet the style of any composer. Among this breed of craftsman are such famous names as Mitchell Parish, Ned Washington, and Ted Koehler.

Koehler was raised mainly in the New York area. His parents were musically inclined and encouraged his interest in music. He attended public schools in New York and Newark and also learned to play the piano. But though his father wanted his son to take an interest in music, he felt that Ted should earn a living working in his photoengraving plant. He taught his son the trade, and, for a time, young Koehler worked at it.

Then Ted left to work as pianist in silent-movie theaters. A little later, he worked for music publishers, helping to plug new songs by playing them in the theaters. The association with the publishing field gave Koehler an opportunity to meet songwriters and vaudeville and musical-comedy performers. Soon he was turning out special material to be used in vaudeville acts and stage shows. Eventually, he also worked at producing cabaret floor shows.

By the late twenties, he was becoming more interested in songwriting. He met a young writer named Harold Arlen, and they formed a close collaboration. This lasted only a few years but resulted in some of the greatest songs in popular-music history. In 1930, they wrote "Get Happy," following up with such other hits as "Kicking the Gong Around" and "I Love a Parade" (1931), "I've Got the World on a String" (1932), and "Happy as the Day Is Long" and "Stormy Weather" (1933). They also worked on the 1930 and 1932 "Earl Carroll Vanities"; one of their songs for these was "I Gotta Right To Sing the Blues."

After 1933, Arlen and Koehler both went to Hollywood, though each worked mainly with other collaborators. They did work on an occasional song together, such as the 1936 "Last Night When We Were Young." Some of the other composers with whom Koehler worked were Sammy Fain, Ray Henderson, Burton Lane, and Jimmy McHugh. His efforts with Fain included the title song for the 1933 film "Let's Fall in Love" and "And There You Are" for the 1945 movie "Weekend at the Waldorf." With McHugh, Koehler provided the score for "King of Burlesque" (1935) and "Dimples" (1936). In 1935, he also collaborated with Ray Henderson and lyricist Irving Caesar on the score for Shirley Temple's "Curly Top." The Koehler-Lane collaboration included such movies as "Artists and Models" (1937) and "Rainbow Island" (1944).

KOSTELANETZ, ANDRE: conductor, arranger, pianist, composer. Born St. Petersburg, Russia, December 22, 1901.

The Bolshevik revolution of 1917 drove many talented people from Russia. Not the least of these was Andre Kostelanetz, who up to that time was one of the most promising pianists and conductors in Russia. He had shown an interest in piano from his earliest years, and gave his first private recital at the age of five. He made his professional debut at eight. He continued his musical education at the St. Petersburg Academy of Music. In the midst of the revolution, Kostelanetz, then only in his teens, applied for the position of assistant conductor and chorus master with the Petrograd Grand Opera. He received the appointment in 1920. Though increasingly disenchanted with political events in Russia, he remained in this post and also continued his studies at the Petrograd Conservatory of Music for two years more.

In 1922, Kostelanetz made his way to the United States and was hired as accompanist and coach for singers of the Metropolitan and Grand Operas. He toured the country with them for several years. In 1928, he joined the music staff of Atlantic Broadcasting Company, which soon became part of the Columbia Broadcasting Company.

Kostelanetz conducted his first commercial broadcast in 1931. From then on, his name was familiar to audiences across the country. His broadcasts consisted mainly of light classical or popular music. Kostelanetz continually experimented with different arrangements for his large orchestra. He did some of his early broadcasts and recordings with echo-chamber effects. Another of his trademarks was the use of massed strings.

During World War II, Kostelanetz conducted service orchestras throughout the world, including advanced theaters of operation. He also made many tours of the armed forces with his wife, soprano Lily Pons. He won the Asiatic-Pacific Campaign Service Ribbon for his efforts. After the war, he resumed his concert, radio, and recording work, and added television appearances.

Kostelanetz's recordings have been among the top sellers over the years. From 1940 to the sixties alone, he sold over twenty-five million records on Columbia. Typical of his albums are "Carnival Tropicana," "Music of Chopin," "Kostelanetz Strings," "Repeat Performance" (with Lily Pons), "Music of Victor Herbert," "Music of Jerome Kern," "Music of Cole Porter," "Album of Rodgers," "Fire and Jealousy," "Kostelanetz Festival," and "Wonderland of Hits." He has continued to conduct symphony orchestras as well as to compose. His compositions include "Music for Tomorrow," written for the 1939 New York World's Fair.

LADY IN THE DARK: musical. Lyrics by Ira Gershwin, music by Kurt Weill, book by Moss Hart. New York opening: January 23, 1941, Alvin Theatre. 388 performances.

Psychoanalysis provided the basis for this major musical of the forties, which was the work of three of the greatest talents of the theater. The idea for the book, written by Pulitzer Prize-winner Hart, reputedly grew out of his own experiences with analysis. Gershwin and Weill provided the perfect blend of music and subtle lyrics to meet the needs of the script, which was outwardly lighthearted but had serious overtones. Besides blazing a new trail in musical-theater subject matter, the show also moved a new, talented performer into the public eye, Danny Kaye.

The central character is famous fashion-magazine editor Liza Elliott. In her late thirties, the tough, masculine-seeming Miss Elliott has created the magazine, *Allure,* and made it a symbol of feminine charm throughout the nation. Suddenly, after years of being in apparently complete control of her emotions, Liza becomes deeply depressed and unable to function properly. She enlists the aid of a psychiatrist, Dr. Alexander Brooks. He helps her interpret her strange dreams, in which people from her everyday life appear in odd new roles.

In one dream, instead of being her usual severely dressed self, Liza appears as a glamorous, seductive woman courted by many men ("Girl of the Moment"). When the scene shifts to her office, the characters of the dream appear as their real selves. These include Kendall Nesbitt, who backed Liza financially, photographer Russell Paxton, and advertising manager Charley Johnson. Liza has been Kendall's mistress for many years because his wife won't divorce him. Liza also meets Hollywood movie star Randy Curtis, a real hunk of man, who asks her for a date. Worried by Liza's illness, Kendall tells her that his wife has agreed to a divorce and that he and Liza can marry. Instead of making Liza happy, this triggers another dream sequence in which she is marrying Kendall with Charley Johnson as the minister. Dr. Brooks also comes into her dream, and she sings him a song from her childhood, "The Princess of Pure Delight."

The next day, she has another of a long series of arguments with Charley Johnson. He tells her that he is quitting soon to become publisher of another magazine. He wants the Easter cover to be about the circus, but Liza is undecided. In a dream sequence in which Paxton is ringmaster and Johnson a trapeze artist, Paxton rattles off dozens of Russian composers' names in Gershwin's famed tongue twister "Tschaikowsky." The theme of the sequence is Liza's inability to make up her mind. She points out the dangers of making up one's mind in "The Saga of Jenny."

Finally, flashbacks to her early childhood show that Liza's too beautiful mother, plus some chance remarks of her father and, later on, her schoolmates, made Liza feel that she was an ugly duckling who could never compete with other women. She realizes that Curtis, who now also wants to marry her, and Nesbitt are as weak as she had been. They want her as a crutch. She concludes that Charley Johnson is the one for her. The curtain falls as they plot the magazine's future together.

The original cast included Gertrude Lawrence, as Liza; MacDonald Carey, as Charley; Danny Kaye, as Paxton; Victor Mature, as Randy Curtis; and Bert Lytell, as Kendall. Other songs were "My Ship," "One Life To Live," and "This Is New."

LAINE, FRANKIE: singer. Born Chicago, Illinois, March 30, 1913.

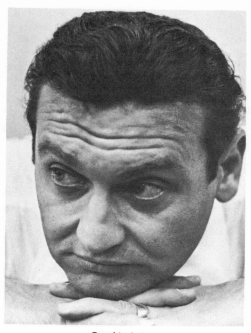

Frankie Laine

Frankie Laine was born in Chicago in the heart of Little Italy. His parents, John and Anna Lo Vecchio, had emigrated to the United States from Monreale, Sicily. While in grammar school, Frank sang in the choir of Immaculate Conception Church. By the time he went on to Chicago's Lane Technical High School, he had decided to become a singer. At the age of fifteen, he began spending as much time as he could watching performers at the Merry Garden Ballroom. He didn't have too many minutes to use in this way, for he had to help out at home. Frank's after-school jobs included working in a drugstore and as an office boy. In following years, he added to his list of nonsinging jobs such diverse occupations as dancing teacher, shipping clerk, auto salesman, machinist, and songwriter.

Merry Garden band leader Joe Kayser liked the voice of the seventeen-year-old Frankie and got him an eight-month stint singing for a marathon-dance contest. After this, Frankie was at loose ends. The Depression arrived in full force, and it was hard to find a job of any kind. The marathon dance had by now developed into a national craze. Frankie decided to try his luck as a dancer. He won his first contest after one

hundred and five days, during ninety of which he danced solo. For a time, Laine managed to earn a living of sorts this way. But in 1935, the craze faded out.

Frankie got a singing job on a Stamford, Connecticut, radio station, only to see it end after three weeks. Then came a shipping-clerk job until he saved enough money to go to New York. Nothing happened there, and he went back to Chicago. In 1937, he met Perry Como, who got him a job with Fred Croyole's band. Frankie didn't take to being a band vocalist, and went it. alone soon after. A few jobs later, he was back in New York, so broke this time that he spent four days sleeping on benches in Central Park and eating candy bars. He finally got a booking on station WINS, followed by a number of other odd jobs and a contract to be master of ceremonies on a South American cruise boat.

During these wanderings, Frankie auditioned for a radio job. The program manager suggested that Lo Vecchio was too difficult for people to remember. "Why not call yourself Frankie Lane?" the manager asked. Frankie took the advice, adding an "i" to differentiate it from female vocalist Frances Lane.

While waiting for the South American boat to leave, he went to Chicago in May, 1940 for his brother's wedding. An accident resulted in a knee injury which laid him up for eight months. When he was walking again, Frank decided to give up singing. He got a job on the midnight shift in a defense plant. But he couldn't keep away from music. He started composing songs, some of which won the approval of a girl trio, who asked Frank to manage them. One of the songs came to the attention of Nat "King" Cole. Cole decided to sing it on a transcription date, and Frankie went to Hollywood for the occasion.

He decided to remain in Hollywood for a time. Things turned up for a while, then nose-dived again. One day in March, 1946, he was down to his last forty dollars. Two holdup men took this last reserve away. Thoroughly discouraged, Laine wandered into Billy Berg's, a Vine Street nightclub, where the regular patrons often sang just for fun. Frankie sang "Ol' Rockin' Chair." Though Frankie didn't know it, Hoagy Carmichael, the song's composer, was in the audience. Hoagy urged Billy Berg to hire Laine, and Berg agreed. A few nights later, Mercury Records executives heard him sing "That's My Desire." The result was a contract and a hit recording of the song. Mitch Miller was artists-

and-repertoire man for Mercury, and his next selection for Laine was the all-time Laine favorite, "The Cry of the Wild Goose." (Laine later switched to Columbia Records when Miller did.)

Such songs as "Mule Train," "Ghost Riders in the Sky," "I Believe," and "Black and Blue" not only topped record-popularity lists but also set off trends in American popular music. As of 1963, Laine had sold over sixty million records.

Among Laine's credits are major-nightclub appearances, star billing in six movies, his own television show, "Frankie Laine Time," on CBS during 1955 and 1956, and a record-breaking tour of England in 1954. In the sixties, he made his debut as a TV dramatic performer in a "Rawhide" episode.

LANE, BURTON: composer. Born New York, New York, February 2, 1912.

"Finian's Rainbow" provided a pot of pure gold in the form of one of the brightest, best-integrated musical scores in modern theater history. It also paid off handsomely for Burton Lane, bringing his great ability, long obscured by the anonymity that is the fate of most movie songwriters, to the public's attention.

Lane was raised in New York City. His father had done well in real estate and could afford to send his son to the best schools. He was, therefore, a little unhappy as the years passed and Burton seemed more interested in music than in schooling. Young Lane learned to play the piano and began composing while still in grade school. When he was fourteen, some of his work came to the attention of showman J. J. Shubert. This led to a request for material for a proposed edition of "The Greenwich Village Follies." Lane presented some twenty songs, but star James Barton fell ill and the show was canceled.

Lane decided, though, to concentrate on music and soon obtained a job as a pianist at Remick's music firm. Here he met many other young writers, including Howard Dietz, who collaborated with Lane on two songs interpolated into the 1930 hit revue "Three's a Crowd": "Forget All Your Books" and "Out in the Open Air." (Earlier that year, he had collaborated with Samuel Lerner on material for "Artists and Models.") Lane then worked with lyricist Harold Adamson on several songs for the 1931 "Earl Carroll Vanities" and "The Third Little Show."

In 1933, Lane accepted a bid from Metro-Goldwyn-Mayer to move to Hollywood. After a short time with MGM, followed by several years of work for other studios, Lane signed a contract with Paramount in 1936, becoming one of that company's main composers. From 1933 through 1954, Lane concentrated most of his songwriting effort on movie scores. His film songs include "Everything I Have Is Yours" (1933), "Trocadero" and "You're My Thrill" (1935), "Stop! You're Breaking My Heart" (1938), "Says My Heart" (1938), "The Lady's in Love with You" and "Here's to Love" (1939), "I Hear Music" and "How about You?" (1941), "I'll Take Tallulah" (1942), and "Too Late Now" (1951).

Offers came for Broadway assignments from time to time. One of these was from E. Y. Harburg, a lyricist with whom Lane had worked on several films. The result was the score for the 1940 Al Jolson-Martha Raye musical "Hold On to Your Hats." The show's run was brief because of Jolson's ill health, but the score included "There's a Great Day Coming Mañana" and "Don't Let It Get You Down." In 1944, Lane collaborated with Al Dubin on material for the Olsen and Johnson extravaganza "Laffing Room Only." One song from this, "Feudin' and Fightin'," became a hit several years later when Dorothy Shay sang it on Bing Crosby's radio show.

Harburg had been working with librettist Fred Saidy on a favorite idea of his for a nonmusical Broadway vehicle. The idea had grown out of two thoughts. One dealt with a bigoted Southern Senator who turns black and suffers under segregation laws, the other with a leprechaun with three wishes. Neither idea seemed to jell until Harburg hit on combining them and adding music. When the libretto was finished, Harburg asked Lane to write the score. Lane was unsure about his ability to do something as wide in scope as this, but Harburg convinced him he could do it. The result was "Finian's Rainbow," a landmark in musical comedy. (See separate listing.)

After this, Lane returned to his movie writing chores, including a collaboration with Alan Jay Lerner on the 1951 Fred Astaire film, "Royal Wedding." In 1965, after a long absence from Broadway, Lane began work on a new musical with Lerner.

LAST TIME I SAW PARIS, THE: song (1940). Words by Oscar Hammerstein II, music by Jerome Kern.

The 1941 Metro-Goldwyn-Mayer movie "Lady, Be Good" was based on George Gershwin's success of the twenties. It contained many of Gershwin's greatest songs, but the song from it which won the Academy Award for that year was new. It was a deserved winner, for there could be no doubt of the deeply felt meaning of Hammerstein's words and Kern's inspired music.

Normally, Kern wrote the melody and asked the lyricist to provide words. In this case, the words were written a continent away, without any awareness on Kern's part that he would set them to music. The writer, Oscar Hammerstein II, wasn't even working with Kern at the time; he was collaborating with Sigmund Romberg on a new musical comedy, "Sunny River."

Hammerstein had spent much time in France —Paris in particular—and deeply loved the country. When Paris fell in June, 1940, Hammerstein felt he had to say something. He wrote the words in New York and put them aside for a forthcoming trip to Beverly Hills, California, to see Romberg. He felt that Kern, also living in Beverly Hills at the time, was the one to write the music for this lyric.

When he arrived in California, Hammerstein showed Kern his words. The next day, Kern wrote the music.

The song did not first appear in the movie but was originally performed by Kate Smith on her radio program. It is a measure of Kern's integrity that he felt it was not fair that the song was not performed in the picture first. He therefore influenced the changes made in the Academy rules that songs must be first performed in a movie to be considered.

LATOUCHE, JOHN: lyricist, librettist. Born Richmond, Virginia, November 13, 1917; died Calais, Vermont, August 7, 1956.

In his short life, John Latouche never quite realized the great promise he demonstrated when he was barely in his twenties. When he was twenty-two, his "Ballad for Americans" was extremely popular in the United States. At twenty-three, he had his first Broadway stage hit, "Cabin in the Sky." From then on, fate did not smile on him.

Latouche was raised in Richmond, Virginia, where he attended the Richmond Academy of Arts and Sciences. At fifteen, he moved to New York, attending first the Riverside Preparatory School and later Columbia. He showed marked talent while in college, winning the Columbia Award for prose and poetry while still a freshman. He also worked on the score for the varsity show during his sophomore year. He got his first chance in the professional theater providing some of the material used in the 1937 hit labor revue "Pins and Needles" (sponsored by the In-

ternational Ladies' Garment Workers' Union). Most of the music was by Harold Rome, with additional music by Earl Robinson.

In 1939, Latouche and Robinson wrote "Ballad for Uncle Sam" for a WPA revue, "Sing for Your Supper." The show failed, but "Ballad for Uncle Sam" did not. Under the new title "Ballad for Americans," it became a major patriotic hit of World War II.

In 1940, Vernon Duke was asked to write the music for a fantasy about Negro life called "Cabin in the Sky." He was turned down by several top lyricists. Some one suggested the twenty-three-year-old Latouche. The result was one of Broadway's great musicals. The show opened on October 25, 1940, and ran for one hundred and fifty-six performances. Such songs as "Taking a Chance on Love," "Honey in the Honeycomb," and the title song are still heard today.

In the years that followed, Latouche never had the chance to work on a vehicle that had the depth of "Cabin in the Sky." In 1941, with Harold Adamson, he wrote the lyrics to Duke's score for Eddie Cantor's "Banjo Eyes." He also worked on the 1942 Duke show "The Lady Comes Across." A few years later, he wrote the book and lyrics (the music was by Jerome Moross) for "The Golden Apple." He tried for years to get it produced, but it was not until 1954 that it reached the stage. It was hailed by most critics and won the New York Drama Critics' Circle Award as best musical of the season. His 1955 effort, "The Vamp," was a failure, as was "Candide," the more ambitious 1956 Leonard Bernstein musical on which Latouche worked.

LAWRENCE, STEVE: singer. Born Brooklyn, New York, July 8, 1935.

One of the happy discoveries of the old Steve Allen "Tonight" television show was Steve Lawrence. Though barely twenty at the time, Lawrence had the poise and vocal ability of a veteran combined with youthful exuberance. Lawrence was originally signed for a single performance, but Allen was impressed enough with Lawrence's talent to make him a permanent member of the cast.

Lawrence began singing in local Brooklyn choirs at the age of eight. When he entered Thomas Jefferson High School, he joined the glee club. The praise he received for his vocal ability from his high-school teachers helped Steve decide to try for a musical career. He also studied

The Lawrence family, otherwise known as popular singing stars Steve Lawrence and Eydie Gormé.

piano and saxophone, and tried his hand at composing and arranging.

By his late teens, Steve was auditioning for singing dates on New York radio and TV stations. Persistent calls finally paid off with appearances on a number of shows, capped by Steve's success on "Tonight." In the course of several years as a regular on the Allen show, Lawrence also courted and married cast comember Eydie Gorme. They were married in December, 1957, setting the stage for a top-ranking husband-and-wife singing team. Their plans were interrupted by Steve's induction into the Army in September, 1958. Steve performed as official vocalist for the United States Army Band-Orchestra at Fort Myer, Virginia. As a result of his work in Army recruiting programs and savings-bond drives, Steve won the Army Medal of Commendation.

In 1960, Steve was discharged and set about renewing his career. He found his popularity with audiences at an all-time high. He was soon in demand for a wide range of TV shows, including appearances as a panel member on "What's My Line" and guest shots on "The Bell Telephone Hour" and "The Gary Moore Show." In addition, he was signed for numerous supperclub engagements across the country as a solo performer and with his wife.

In 1962, Steve signed with Columbia Records. His first album, "Come Dance with Me," won wide critical approval. That same year, he played the title role in "Pal Joey" on the summertheater circuit. During 1963 and 1964, he made some of his most popular records including the major hit single "Go Away, Little Girl" and such albums as "Steve Lawrence Winners," "Academy Award Losers," and "Steve and Eydie."

In 1964–65, Lawrence added a new dimension to his career by heading up the cast of the hit Broadway musical, "What Makes Sammy Run?" The show, which opened Feb. 27, '64, was an adaptation by Budd and Stuart Schulberg of Budd Schulberg's novel of the same title.

LEAD SHEET: sheet of music giving, as simply as possible, the melody of a song. (See also *Demonstration Record.*)

In the early days of Tin Pan Alley, presenting a new song to a publisher was a fairly straightforward affair. Most songwriters could play the piano at least well enough to give the outline of the song, and, in most cases, the music publisher was the all-important man to sell on the song's merits. If the publisher liked the song, he took care of most of the work from then on, including placing the song with a performer. The arrival on the scene of radio, television, and particularly records changed all this. The prime importance of the publisher gradually faded, and the record-company artists-and-repertoire man and in many cases the performers became the final arbiters.

Now a songwriter had to give publisher, performer, or record company something they could go over in their leisure. Until recently, these were usually a lead sheet and a demonstration record (or, more lately, a magnetic tape). A publisher today would not commit himself to publishing a new song until he felt reasonably assured a performer would use it. The lead sheet and record give him the tools to feel out the opinions of vocalists or other musicians.

A lead sheet may also be used in other ways; for instance, in a collaboration where the music is composed first, the composer might draw up a lead sheet for the lyricist to work to.

If the lyrics are already written, they may be included on the lead sheet. Sometimes the sheet may include symbols indicating the song's chords.

Typically, the function of the lead sheet is to give the publisher, A&R man, or performer the chance to scan quickly the words and music to see if the blend seems attractive. If so, the demonstration record is played to see how the music sounds in performance.

LEE, BRENDA: vocalist. Born Atlanta, Georgia, December 18, 1944.

Brenda Lee, a little girl (under five feet) with a big voice, swept into the teen-age spotlight in 1956 at the age of twelve. Even then, she was amazing listeners with the maturity of her vocal delivery. Four years later, she was still a headliner, and *Time* magazine (January 2, 1961) was saying:

. . . she can transform herself with a clap of her chubby hands from a comics-reading teen-ager into a tortured woman. But her

career suggests a peculiar problem: if she sounds 32 at 16, how will she sound at 20?

She was born Brenda Lee Tapley. At the age of six, she won top honors in a local children's talent contest, which led to her having her own fifteen-minute television show. Before long, Brenda was performing all over the South at country shows and jamborees. Offers came in for more engagements and finally a regular spot on a TV show of some prominence in Springfield, Missouri. Here she was observed by Dub Albritten, an important agent in the country-and-Western and popular fields. He became her manager and began grooming his new protégé for bigger things. Brenda soon signed a long-term contract with Decca Records. In 1956, she had her first nationwide hit, a rousing rendition of "Jambalaya," a song that had been made famous a few years earlier by Jo Stafford.

At the same time, Brenda began appearing on the most popular shows on network television. Starting with her first network date in March, 1956, she was seen on the shows of Perry Como, Ed Sullivan, Danny Thomas, Steve Allen, Tennesse Ernie Ford, and Dick Clark. From 1956 into the sixties, she made one best-selling record after another. Her numbers covered a wide range, from spirituals to rock 'n' roll. Some of her better-known records of these years were "Sweet Nothin's," "I'm Sorry," "Emotions," "Dynamite," "When the Saints Go Marchin' In," "Dum-Dum," "Fool Number One," "Bill Bailey," and "Break It to Me Gently." Brenda's career reached a high mark in 1960. Her record sales for that year were around three million, three hundred thousand, second only to Connie Francis's. At the end of the year, she had two best-selling single sides, "I Want To Be Wanted" and "Rockin' around the Christmas Tree." In addition, she had two albums that had scored over a quarter million sales each, "Brenda Lee" and "This Is Brenda Lee."

By then, she had moved with her family to Nashville, Tennessee. She didn't see too much of the new home her earnings had bought, however, for she was off on singing engagements all over the world. She played to packed houses in Paris and other major European cities. In another tour, this time of South America, she won compliments not only from turnaway crowds in such Brazilian cities as Santos and Rio de Janeiro, but from the Brazilian president as well.

In 1961, Brenda's star flickered a little, and

there were some who felt that her career might end with her teens. During 1962, though, Brenda came back with a rush, with two LPs on the best-seller lists and such single records as "All Alone Am I." She won a *Billboard* magazine nod for one of the comebacks of the year.

LEE, PEGGY: singer, songwriter, actress. Born Jamestown, North Dakota, May 26, 1920.

Besides being a top popular singer, Peggy Lee is a renowned jazz vocalist, a songwriter, sculptor, painter, and writer. As an actress, she won an Academy Award nomination for her part in "Pete Kelly's Blues" (1955).

Peggy was born Norma Jean Engstrom in a small plains town. Her family was a large one of Swedish origin, and all the children had to help with the household chores. It often fell to young Norma Jean's lot to wash the dishes. Whenever she did, she liked to have the radio on full blast. After a while, she began to sing along. She was an excellent student in high school, breezing through to finish at sixteen with honors. By now, she had decided that she wanted a singing career. She went to the North Dakota city of Fargo, where she got a job singing on a local station. The pay was so low that she had to work as a waitress to make ends meet.

Undaunted, Peggy decided to strike out for

Peggy Lee

Hollywood. She arrived there with eighteen dollars in her pocket and took a series of jobs, from waiting on tables to barker for an amusement concession, while persistently trying to get work as a singer. This paid off with a job at a place called the Jade Club. Though she received only two dollars a night, she was sure she was on the right road at last. Then Peggy was hit with a throat infection. She returned to Jamestown. Her home-town doctor operated on her throat, and Peggy joyfully went back to work, singing at small hotels and clubs throughout the Midwest, starting with a stint at a Fargo hotel. After two years of this, she found a better job in Minneapolis including the chance to sing on various radio programs. She soon auditioned for band leader Will Osborne. Peggy toured with the band for a year, but then her throat began acting up again.

This time she went to Palm Springs, California, to recuperate. After several months, she was able to sing at the Doll's House in that city. A guest from Chicago caught her act and got her a job with the Buttery Room of that city's Ambassador West Hotel. One night, Benny Goodman heard her. A few months later, when Helen Forrest left his band, he sent a hurry-up call for Peggy. Her first recording for Goodman, still occasionally heard on radio, was "Elmer's Tune." The following year, Peggy and Goodman recorded a now classic swing number, "Why Don't You Do Right?" More important, Peggy married band guitarist Dave Barbour. In 1943, she retired from show business to await the arrival of a daughter, Nicki.

But Peggy found she just couldn't stay away. In 1944, she signed with newly formed Capitol Records. Except for three years with Decca (1952–55), she turned out a steady series of great single records and albums with Capitol. Her numbers ranged from blues and jazz to pseudo-Spanish. In the last category was one of her greatest successes, "Mañana," which she wrote herself. Some other songs Peggy wrote are "It's a Good Day" and "I Don't Know Enough about You." Peggy also collaborated on the score for Walt Disney's full-length cartoon "Lady and the Tramp." Some of her major albums are "Latin à la Lee!," "Beauty and the Beat" (with George Shearing), "Sugar 'n' Spice," and "Basin Street East."

Besides her recording, film, and writing work, Peggy also continued to be a top favorite in personal appearances. Her four-week standing-room-only-performance at New York's Basin Street East nightclub in May 1961 caused *Journal-American* critic Nick Lapole to write:

> . . . the audience rose as a group, cheered, stomped, whistled and cried for more. Never was a performer more worthy of this tribute. Peggy Lee's return was a triumph. They came to see, to hear and to be conquered. Conquered they were.

And Bob Rolontz of *Billboard* magazine added:

> Superlatives are no longer enough for Peggy Lee. The gal is so outstanding . . . that to say she is superb is almost faint praise. She is one of the great performers of the era.

LERNER, ALAN JAY: lyricist, librettist. Born New York, New York, August 31, 1918. Won Pulitzer Prize for "My Fair Lady" (1956), Academy Award for Best Song of 1958 ("Gigi").

Alan Jay Lerner's father founded the very successful Lerner Shops, a chain of women's clothing stores which today has branches throughout the United States. Alan learned to play the piano when very young and later studied at New York's Juilliard School of Music. He attended exclusive schools in the United States and Europe and won his bachelor-of-science degree from Harvard University in 1940. At Harvard he wrote words and music for two Hasty Pudding shows. Two of these songs were published: "Chance To Dream" (1938) and "From Me to You" (1939).

Lerner returned to New York after graduating. His writing ability helped him get started in show business, as a radio script writer. He is said to have turned out some five hundred scripts from 1940 to 1942.

One day in 1942, Lerner was playing cards in New York's Lambs Club when he was approached by composer Frederick Loewe, who wanted someone to work with him on a musical comedy in Detroit. Lerner accepted, and thus was born one of the great teams of Broadway history.

The show, "Life of the Party," duly opened in Detroit. There was nothing exceptional about it, but the two seemed to like working together and went on to another project. This provided Lerner with his first Broadway vehicle. Called "What's Up?," it lasted only sixty-three performances in 1943. Two years later, they were again represented on Broadway, this time with a near hit, "The Day before Spring." Besides the title song, it included "A Jug of Wine," "I Love You This Morning," and "You Haven't Changed at All."

In their next try, Lerner and Loewe entered the winner's circle. The show was "Brigadoon" (1947), which ran for five hundred and eighty-one performances. (See separate listing.)

Even with this success, Lerner and Loewe worked apart for a time. In 1948, Lerner worked with Kurt Weill on "Love Life," which ran for two hundred and fifty-two performances. The show dealt with a marriage that lasts from 1791 to 1948. The couple remains young, but their marriage withers and dies. The score included such songs as "Green-Up Time," "Here I'll Stay," "Love Song," and "Economics." Lerner also worked for a time on motion-picture scores. In 1951, he won an Academy Award nomination for the song "Too Late Now" (music by Burton Lane), from "Royal Wedding."

Lerner and Loewe had not abandoned each other, though. After much thought, Lerner proposed a show based on the California Gold Rush. The result was "Paint Your Wagon." (See separate listing.) While not quite the success "Brigadoon" was, it still provided a great score, including "I Talk to the Trees," "They Call the Wind Maria," "Another Autumn," and "I Still See Elisa."

In 1952, they were approached by Hungarian movie producer Gabriel Pascal, who had secured the musical rights to Shaw's "Pygmalion." Pascal had already been turned down by many great Broadway names, who felt the task of adapting the play as a musical to be almost insurmountable. Lerner and Loewe, too, for a time gave up. But they were attracted to the assignment and in 1955 completed the first draft. On March 15, 1956, the show opened to one of the greatest choruses of acclaim ever to greet a Broadway show. "My Fair Lady" established a new Broadway record, running for two thousand, seven hundred and seventeen performances, and provided an almost legendary score. (See separate listing.)

Lerner and Loewe followed up with a smash score for the 1958 Hollywood film "Gigi." The title song won them the Academy Award for Best Song of 1958. They then turned to King Arthur and his knights of the Round Table for inspiration. Loewe said that "Camelot" was to be his last show. The critics were less enthusiastic about "Camelot" than about "My Fair Lady," but it was a hit nevertheless.

LIMBO: trick dance of West Indian origin.

The limbo is more a contest or demonstration of skill than a dance. The object is to move under a thin, simply supported bar without knocking it off its supports. The bar is moved progressively lower until it is either knocked off or is barely above floor level. Professional limbo dancers can go under a bar only eight inches off the floor.

The dancer leans far back while folding his legs back under his torso. In this position, his upper body is roughly parallel to the floor. The position of his legs is such that he is delicately balanced and won't fall back onto the ground. He then carefully moves his feet to propel his body forward under the bar.

The dance was introduced into the United States by touring steel-band troupes. In 1962, the limbo was picked up by such popular-music performers as Chubby Checker. Limbo-type songs with a touch of rock'n'roll were composed. Conventional instruments, rather than steel drums, were used. Such records as "Limbo Rock" became nationwide hits, and the limbo was soon a popular dance throughout the United States.

LINDY, LINDY HOP: dance popular during the nineteen-thirties and forties.

Charles A. Lindbergh's pioneer flight across the Atlantic to Paris in 1927 gave rise to over a hundred songs in his honor, plus a version of the jitterbug called the Lindy hop. The songs faded quickly, but the Lindy in modified form was the dance most performed to the swing music of the big bands of the thirties and forties. The dance is fast-moving, often violent, usually to four-four time, with many breaks in which the male dancer may throw his partner out, spin her around, sometimes toss her in the air. The successors to the Lindy are the rock-'n'-roll dances and their many offshoots, such as the hully-gully and mashed potato.

LITTLE MARY SUNSHINE: musical. Lyrics, music, and book by Rick Besoyan. New York opening: November 18, 1959, Orpheum Theatre.

The surprise hit of 1959 was the off-Broadway satire on old-time operetta "Little Mary Sunshine." The show introduced a new name to the musical stage, Rick Besoyan, who not only wrote the score and book but also directed the show. Besoyan, born in California, won a scholarship to Trinity Music College in London, and later toured the United States, Canada, and England with the Savoy Light Opera Company. During his four years with the Savoy, he came up with the idea of writing "a new musical about an old operetta."

The critics were overjoyed with the product. Said Brook Atkinson in the New York *Times:* "'Little Mary Sunshine' is a merry and sprightly spoof." Besides setting new standards for off-Broadway theater, "Little Mary Sunshine" was the first non-Broadway show selected by Capitol Records for an original-cast recording.

As "Little Mary Sunshine" opens, it is the early nineteen-hundreds at the Colorado Inn, high in the Rockies. Chief Brown Bear reports the approach of the Forest Rangers, soon heard singing "The Forest Rangers." The inn is owned by Little Mary Sunshine, who was rescued by Brown Bear's Kadota Indians when, as a little girl, she got lost while berry picking. Little Mary has advised the chief, her foster father, to ask Washington, D.C., to settle his land claims. As Mary appears, the Forest Rangers greet her with the title song. Because she defaulted on her mortgage, the government is forced to foreclose —but she believes all will turn out well ("Look for a Sky of Blue").

Ranger Captain Big Jim Warington tells Mary that his mission is to capture a band of renegade Indians. Fleet Foot (who is actually old and infirm and who originally rescued Mary) is to guide him.

Into the middle of all this comes a European opera star, Mme. Ernestine Liebedich. She recalls her romantic youth in "In Izzenschnooken on the Lovely Essenzook Zee." A lively group of young Eastern girls on vacation also arrives. They are happy to cut loose with such daring innovations as "Swinging" (on a garden swing) and eying the handsome rangers. The rangers return the compliment ("How Do You Do?"). Captain Jim tells Mary that he is after Yellow Feather. Aghast, she tells him that Yellow Feather is Brown Bear's bad son, believed dead, who has threatened to have his way with her. As Jim departs, he and Mary sing the "Colorado Love Call." Soon after, General Oscar Fairfax (retired) arrives to take over in Jim's absence. Desiring to woo the girls with favors from his goodie box, he sends the rest of the rangers to bring back Jim. Later, he and Mme. Ernestine find that they both were gay young things in Vienna ("Do You Ever Dream of Vienna?").

Mary searches for Jim at night in the garden and is attacked by Yellow Feather. But, at the last minute, Jim arrives to save her. Then the general announces that Washington has agreed to Brown Bear's claim—something like a quarter of Colorado. The chief gives Mary her land and makes the rest of the property a national park for the rangers. Mary and Jim, the general and Mme. Ernestine, and the others pair off. Repentant, Yellow Feather comes back to his father, waving an American flag as the curtain descends.

The original cast included Eileen Brennan, as Mary; William Graham, as Jim; Elizabeth Parrish, as Mme. Ernestine; John Aniston, as Brown Bear; Robert Chambers, as Fleet Foot; and Mario Siletti, as the general. Other songs were "You're the Fairest Flower," "Playing Croquet," "Tell a Handsome Stranger," "Once in a Blue Moon," "Every Little Nothing," "Such a Merry Party," "Naughty, Naughty Nancy," "Mata Hari," and "Coo Coo."

LIVINGSTON, JAY: composer. Born McDonald, Pennsylvania, March 28, 1915. Won Academy Award for Best Song of 1948 ("Buttons and Bows"), 1950 ("Mona Lisa"), and 1956 ("Whatever Will Be, Will Be"). (See also *Evans, Ray*.)

The desire to make his career in music came early to Jay Livingston, the musical half of the team of Livingston and Evans. Jay had his first inkling of this when his mother took him and his brother on trips to such cities as New York from their home in the Pittsburgh suburbs. For ten years, from public school into high school, Jay concentrated on his piano lessons. In high school, he played piano with all the school orchestras plus dance-band engagements at local night spots on Saturday nights. He didn't neglect his school studies, though, and graduated from high school as first honor student.

He entered the University of Pennsylvania in 1933. By now, he thought he might become a writer instead, and majored in journalism. But in his freshman year, he met Ray Evans, who played saxophone and clarinet in a dance orchestra. Soon after, Ray's band needed a pianist for a trip to Europe, and Ray suggested Jay. The two became fast friends and, after graduating from college, decided to write songs together. The market proved too rough to crack then, so the boys re-formed their orchestra.

Coming back to New York in 1938, they made the rounds of the music publishers, who gave them no encouragement. But in 1939, Ray read in the paper that Olsen and Johnson were looking for new songs for their hit stage show "Hellzapoppin" and wrote a letter to them. Normally, a team as busy as Olsen and Johnson would not ask total unknowns in to play new material. But a new secretary sent Ray and Jay an invitation to come in, and Olsen agreed to listen. He liked what he heard and, while not taking anything for the show, gave them free run of the theater. Eventually, Olsen and Johnson began to use their material. In 1940, Livingston and Evans wrote their first hit, "G'Bye Now," which was played on "The Lucky Strike Hit Parade" for five weeks.

Still, the boys couldn't live on their income from music. Livingston worked as an accompanist and arranger for NBC singing stars and musical groups. After a two-year hitch in the Army, Jay rejoined Evans in 1944 for what was to be the turning point in their careers. Olsen and Johnson had some picture plans in the works in Hollywood and asked Livingston and Evans to come out. Then Olsen's plans fell through. But Jay's aunt got them a job writing songs for a Martha Tilton picture. Soon after, some work for Johnny Mercer led to a chance to provide material for Capitol vocalist Betty Hutton. The song, "Stuff Like That There," was four years old, but it fit Betty perfectly. Producer Buddy de Sylva had cast Betty Hutton in a new Paramount picture, "Stork Club," and Mercer suggested that Livingston and Evans provide the songs for this too. The meeting with de Sylva came within a hair of being another disaster. De Sylva turned down one song but bought the second, "A Square in the Social Circle," immediately.

Livingston and Evans soon became contract writers for Paramount. They started work in 1945 and remained at Paramount for ten years. They soon had written their first all-time standard, "To Each His Own," one of very few songs to have sold over a million copies of sheet music. In 1946, Livingston and Evans did one of their rare collaborations with another writer, creating the words for Victor Young's theme melody for "Golden Earrings." In 1948, the assignment to write a song for Bob Hope's picture "Paleface" led to the Academy Award for "Buttons and Bows." In the years that followed, they wrote such classics for Paramount as "Mona Lisa," "Silver Bells," "I'll Always Love You," and "Que Sera Sera" (Whatever Will Be, Will Be). In all, their work included songs for twelve Bob Hope pictures, plus material for just about every Paramount star.

In 1956, they left Paramount to freelance. In 1957, they provided a song for Debbie Reynolds called "Tammy" that won an Academy Award nomination. "Almost in Your Arms," for Cary Grant and Sophia Loren's picture "Houseboat" (1958), won another nomination. The boys wrote title songs for many movies, including "Saddle the Wind" and "Another Time, Another Place," and "Let Me Be Loved," the theme song for "The James Dean Story."

The year 1958 saw the first Livingston and Evans Broadway show, "Oh, Captain!" A few years later, in another departure, they wrote the theme song for the television show "Mr. Ed." Livingston himself sang the song now heard on each "Mr. Ed" program.

In 1964, Livingston and Evans collaborated on the lyrics to go with Henry Mancini's music for the title song for the movie "Dear Heart." The song reached hit status and also won an Academy Award nomination.

LOESSER, FRANK HENRY: composer, lyricist, librettist, producer, publisher. Born New York, New York, June 29, 1910.

Frank Loesser has had a great impact on American musical theater for many reasons. As a lyricist, he wrote the words for many of the movies' most memorable songs. As a composer, lyricist, and sometime librettist, he wrote some of Broadway's most enduring musicals. As a producer and music publisher, he was instrumental in bringing such new talent to the musical stage as Meredith Willson, Richard Adler, and Jerry Ross.

Loesser attended public schools and City College in New York. His schoolwork was poor, and he flunked out of college after a year. Frank's father, a piano teacher, disliked popular music, and Frank had to teach himself how to play this kind of music. At the age of six, Loesser had indicated where his talents lay with his first composition, "The May Party."

After leaving school, Loesser took a succession of odd jobs. He was a process server, a reporter for a newspaper that failed, a restaurant inspector, a resort-hotel waiter and pianist, a trade-journal editor, and a publicist. Along the way, he began writing lyrics. In 1931, he teamed with composer William Schuman on his first published song, "In Love with a Memory of You." In 1934, he scored his first song hit, writing the words to Joseph Meyer's music for "I Wish I Were Twins." Then, with Irving Actman, he provided five songs for the 1936 "Illustrators' Show." These numbers were enough to bring a Universal Pictures contract for Actman and Loesser. Frank went

to the West Coast, soon moved to Paramount Pictures, and over the next ten years worked with many of Hollywood's top composers. In 1937, he collaborated with Alfred Newman on his first film hit (for Paramount). The song, "The Moon of Manakoora," was sung by Dorothy Lamour in "The Hurricane." Some of his other film songs were "Says My Heart," with Burton Lane; "Jingle, Jangle, Jingle," with Joseph Lilley; and "Small Fry" and "Two Sleepy People," with Hoagy Carmichael. During World War II, he began writing music as well as lyrics. As a civilian and later an Army private, Loesser wrote some of the best songs of the war. The first, "Praise the Lord and Pass the Ammunition" (1942), sold over two million records, and a million copies of sheet music. Later he added "The Ballad of Roger Young" and the official infantry song, "What Do You Do in the Infantry?" After his discharge, Loesser concentrated mainly on the Broadway stage, but in 1949 he won an Academy Award for "Baby, It's Cold Outside," from Metro-Goldwyn-Mayer's "Neptune's Daughter."

In 1946, he was approached by former movie and television executives Cy Feuer and Ernest Martin to write the score for a musical adaptation of "Charley's Aunt." When "Where's Charley?," starring Ray Bolger, opened in New York in 1948, the critics agreed that a new composing star had risen over Broadway. The show included such hits as "Once in Love with Amy," "The New Ashmolean Marching Society and Students Conservatory Band," "My Darling, My Darling," and "Make a Miracle." Two years later, Loesser followed up with the even more impressive "Guys and Dolls," which contained "A Bushel and a Peck," "If I Were a Bell," "Guys and Dolls," "I'll Know," and "I've Never Been in Love Before."

The perfectionist nature of Loesser is shown by the time he took to complete his next Broadway hit. For four years, he worked on not only the score but the complete book for "The Most Happy Fella." The final product was again a hit and one of the finest combinations of music and words to reach Broadway. (See separate listing.) Continuously experimenting, Loesser next did a rural drama laid in a small English town on the banks of the imaginary Meander River. Called "Greenwillow" and starring Anthony Perkins, it opened on Broadway on March 8, 1960, and ran for ninety-five performances. A box-office failure, the critics generally agreed that it showed another interesting facet of Loesser's ability. His score included "Summertime Love," "The Music of Home," "Never Will I Marry," and "Faraway Boy."

In the meantime, Loesser was instrumental in bringing to Broadway such successes of other writers as Meredith Willson's "Music Man" and Adler and Ross's "Pajama Game" and "Damn Yankees."

In 1961, Loesser provided the score for the fabulously successful "How to Succeed in Business Without Really Trying," which was a fixture on Broadway until March 1965. (See separate item.)

LOEWE, FREDERICK: composer, pianist. Born Vienna, Austria, June 10, 1904.

The man who wrote the music for "My Fair Lady" reached his goal after a strange odyssey. Beginning as a child prodigy, he abandoned music for many years and drifted from one odd job to another. Then, after "twenty-one years of starving," he hit pay dirt in collaboration with the much younger Alan Jay Lerner. In 1959, at the height of his fame, Loewe again did the unexpected by retiring to "enjoy life."

Loewe was born into a famous theatrical family. His father, a well-known tenor, played Prince Danilo in the original cast of Lehar's "Merry Widow." At five, Loewe already played the piano, and at nine, he composed a forty-five-minute musical play for his father. The elder Loewe performed his son's composition throughout Europe. In Berlin, some of the most famous music teachers were happy to tutor this impressive new talent. At thirteen, he appeared as a soloist with the Berlin Symphony, the youngest ever to do this.

Though occupied with the classics, Loewe already gave hints of his future calling. At fifteen, he wrote a popular song that swept Europe. Called "Katrina," it sold over a million copies of sheet music. After World War I, though Loewe won the Hollander Medal for excellence as a pianist, the going was becoming difficult in inflation-ridden Germany. Loewe decided in 1924 to pursue his fortunes in the United States. But his musical compositions sounded strange to American ears, and his foreign accent made things more difficult. He began to drift away from music. First he took a job as a pianist in a Greenwich Village night spot, then as a bus boy in a cafeteria.

Discouraged, he decided to forget about music altogether. Loewe knocked about for the rest of the twenties. He was a riding instructor at a New Hampshire resort for a while. Then his quick reflexes and muscular build made him seem a natural for the prize ring. He fought nine professional fights as a bantamweight and did fairly well at first. But in the ninth fight he came up against Tough Tony Canzoneri, one of the great champions of the Golden Age of boxing. Said Loewe some years later, "Canzoneri ended *that* career in the eighth round!"

Loewe decided to go west. He worked at such tasks as cowpuncher, gold miner, and horseback mail deliverer. Just as he had drifted away, Loewe began to drift back into music as the thirties approached. He got a job playing piano on ships carrying thirsty Americans from Miami to Havana. This lasted until the repeal of Prohibition. Loewe went back to New York and worked as a pianist in Yorkville, the German section of the city.

Then he met a radio and movie writer Earle Crooker, and in 1935, they put together some songs. Loewe and Crooker won some success with an original musical for the St. Louis Opera Association. This led to a Broadway assignment for a show titled "Great Lady." The show closed after only twenty performances, and Loewe went back to work as a pianist.

In 1942, he got a bid to redo his St. Louis Opera work for a Detroit producer. He needed someone to update the lyrics. Not too long before, he had heard sketches for a Lambs Club play that had impressed him. The writer was a young club member named Alan Jay Lerner. Loewe introduced himself to Lerner at the club one day while Lerner was playing cards and asked if he'd be interested in working on the lyrics. They rewrote the material for Detroit, under the title "Life of the Party." Both felt that they could do better in the future if they continued to collaborate.

Their first effort, "What's Up?," opened on Broadway in November, 1943. "Obviously," Loewe said later, "nothing was up. It was awful." But their next show, "The Day before Spring," opened in 1945 to critical acclaim, though it flopped at the box office. Now Loewe and Lerner felt that they were getting close to what they really were capable of. On March 13, 1947, they proved it to everybody's satisfaction. That was the date "Brigadoon" came to life at the Ziegfeld Theatre in New York. (See separate listing.)

In November, 1951, their next effort, "Paint

Your Wagon," seemed a step backward. (See separate listing.) It won much critical applause but failed commercially. Still, it had a great score, and its book, about California Gold Rush days, blazed new trails.

Lerner and Loewe searched for a new project. The one they finally settled on was one they had tried briefly two years earlier, then abandoned. This was a musical adaptation of George Bernard Shaw's "Pygmalion." Hungarian film producer Gabriel Pascal had obtained stage rights for this from the Shaw estate. He had approached and been turned down by just about every famous writer of Broadway musicals. Lerner and Loewe had been among those who had looked at it and decided it couldn't be done. After having temporarily dissolved their partnership to try other things, they decided to have one more go at "Pygmalion"—ironically, just when the persistent Pascal died. The result was "My Fair Lady," which premiered on March 15, 1956, at the Mark Hellinger Theatre and ran for over six years on Broadway.

Loewe and Lerner had come up with the only American musical to sweep not only all American awards but to become a true worldwide favorite. Loewe evaluated it for Los Angeles Times critic Cecil Smith:

In 100 years, there have been four musical shows that swept the world. The first was the first operetta—really "silly opera"— "Orpheus." The whole world danced to it. That was in the 1860s. In the 70s, there was "Fledermaus" which also enchanted the world. Then, in 1904, there was "The Merry Widow." And in 1956, "My Fair Lady."

Everywhere, in every language, the success of the "Lady" is the same. In Australia, two companies play her; in West Germany, there are three companies. She plays every city in South America. I had a card from a friend the other day saying she is opening in July in Tokyo in Japanese.

Lerner and Loewe went on to another complex play, a musical about King Arthur and the knights of the Round Table called "Camelot." The show was said to be the most expensive staged to that time, costing six hundred and thirty-five thousand dollars. The director, Moss Hart, suffered a heart attack, a recurrence of which claimed his life a year later; the costume designer died in the middle of the production; Lerner fell ill with ulcers; and Loewe suffered a

mild heart attack. Reversing the earlier case when their work won critical praise but failed, this time Lerner and Loewe received cool reviews but sensational audience response. "Camelot" ran for close to two years on Broadway, then went on a highly successful tour.

While "Camelot" was not as great as the once-in-a-lifetime "My Fair Lady," it was still a high point for Loewe to bow out on. Talking about his new life of ease to Cecil Smith, Loewe said:

Do you think now that I can have all this, I'd give it up to go back to sleepless nights, cold coffee and stale cheese sandwiches? . . . I starved for 21 years. Now that I have the wherewithal, I am going to live. . . . I had one warning. . . . Should I wait for another. . . . like poor Moss?

But when asked about finding an "irresistible" new idea, he replied, "Irresistible? I would be a very stupid little boy to try and resist that, wouldn't I?"

LOMBARDO, GUY ALBERT: band leader. Born London, Canada, June 19, 1902.

Guy Lombardo successfully perservered with sweet, danceable music from the nineteen-twenties into the sixties, despite the Roaring Twenties, jazz, swing, and rock 'n' roll. Through these years, the Lombardo band sold well over twenty-five million records and topped many dance-band polls in many sections of the country. In 1946, the New York World-Telegram said that it was one of the five biggest-money-making bands of all time.

Guy and his four brothers attended public schools in Canada. All were interested in music at an early age, and Guy formed his first band when he was eleven. After finishing high school, he worked for a time as a bank clerk. In 1921, he formed the Lombardo Brothers and Their Orchestra. He refused outside engagements for three years and kept his band playing local dates. Then, in 1924, the band took a week's booking at the Hippodrome Theatre in Cleveland, Ohio. They soon took other dates in Akron and Cleveland, settling down to a two-year engagement at the Music Box Café in Cleveland. Their next move, to the Granada Café in Chicago, which included a nationwide radio hookup, gained Lombardo a prominent spot in the music spectrum that he never lost. In 1929, the band accepted an invitation to play at the Roosevelt Hotel in New York, and for many years used this as home base.

Playing such songs as "Managua, Nicaragua," "Who Wouldn't Love You?," "The Wedding Samba," and "Come to the Mardi Gras," the band seemed to live up to Lombardo's goal of playing "the sweetest music this side of heaven." The band had many hit records over the years, starting with "Give Me a Little Kiss, Will Ya, Hon?" and including "Mairzy Doats," "The Peanut Vendor," "Boo Hoo," and "Coquette."

LONDON, JULIE: singer, actress. Born Santa Rosa, California, September 26, 1926.

Julie London was born into show business. Her parents were a song-and-dance team, and Julie made her first radio appearance at the age of three, singing "Falling in Love Again" on a local California station. Still, in her early years, she didn't really think that she might someday make the theater her career.

Her family moved to San Bernardino, where Julie attended Arrowview Junior High. School was not to her liking. In 1941, when her family moved to Los Angeles, the fifteen-year-old Julie quit school to work as an elevator operator. While she was on the job, Sue Carol, an actor's agent and wife of Alan Ladd, saw her and was impressed with her beauty. At first, Julie thought Miss Carol's offer was some sort of joke. She found that it was legitimate when she received a movie contract. Beginning with "The Red House," she appeared in a series of B movies throughout the forties.

Along the way, she met a struggling actor named Jack Webb, and they married in 1947. When Webb's television show "Dragnet" became a national favorite in 1950, Julie decided to retire. In 1953, the Webb's separated. A year later, aided by instrumentalist-songwriter Bobby Troup, Julie returned to show business. Now her career took off like a rocket. An appearance at Johnny Walsh's nightclub in Los Angeles led to a recording of "Cry Me a River," a song which was one of the top hits of 1956. Her sultry style graced one song after another that year, and *Theme* magazine voted her the most exciting new vocalist of 1956.

From then on, Julie was in demand for coast-to-coast nightclub engagements, guest appearances on most of the top TV shows, and movies. After her Walsh engagement, she starred in rapid succession at New York's Cameo Room and on the Perry Como, Steve Allen, and Ed Sullivan TV shows. Her new movie career started with the critically acclaimed "The Great Man," in which she costarred with Jose Ferrer. Since then,

she has appeared in over a dozen more films, including "Saddle the Wind" (1957), "Wonderful Country" (1959), "The Third Voice" (1960), and "The George Raft Story" (1961).

Many of her long-play albums on the Liberty label have been top sellers. The titles include "Julie Is Her Name," "Lonely Girl," "Calendar Girl," "About the Blues," "London by Night," "The 90's Jazz," "Sing Me an Old Song," "Make Love to Me," "Your Number, Please," "Around Midnight," "Julie at Home," "Whatever Julie Wants," "Love on the Rocks," and "Latin in a Satin Mood."

LONG-PLAY (LP) RECORD: a record that can play for an extended time, at a speed slower than seventy-eight revolutions per minute.

A major drawback to the old-style seventy-eight-revolution-per-minute record was its short playing time, three minutes or so for each side. In addition, albums of seventy-eight-r.p.m. records were bulky and heavy. Scientists and engineers at major record companies worked for many years to develop new types of records that would play longer.

An answer was to make the record grooves narrower, so that there could be more grooves on a record, and to have the record revolve at a slower speed, to permit compressing the length of the groove needed for each sound. The last step is needed since with smaller groove length per sound, if the record revolves at seventy-eight revolutions per minute, the needle may skip over some of these fine indentations.

The long-play record did not become practical until special materials, such as very strong plastics, became available. Strong plastics were needed because narrowing the grooves called for very thin walls between adjacent grooves. These walls had to be made of material much stronger than those used for the old-style seventy-eight-r.p.m. record. These plastics, which also made nearly unbreakable records possible, became available in volume during World War II. Engineers also had to devise new, very fine needles to fit the thinner grooves, improved lightweight phonograph pickup arms, and internal phonograph electrical-electronic systems compatible with the new approach.

The most common long-play speed selected for development was thirty-three and a third revolutions per minute. Methods for making and playing thirty-three-and-a-third-speed records were devised in 1926. The reason for the choice of this speed was given by inventor J. P. Maxfield in his 1927 patent application. Tests showed that there was a minimum satisfactory linear speed at which the record moves past the stylus for each size of stylus. There are various possible minimum speeds, depending on groove width and diameters, but for the optimum record diameter, thirty-three and a third seemed best.

As early as 1931, RCA Victor offered thirty-three-and-a-third-r.p.m. records for special uses (movies and radio, for instance) that were twelve inches in diameter, with a playing time of about fifteen minutes a side. In the mid-forties, it became practicable to produce long-play records in volume, and Columbia Records offered these for sale, starting a revolution in the record industry. In 1949, RCA Victor, besides making thirty-three-and-a-third-speed records, introduced a new forty-five-r.p.m. disc requiring a one-and-a-half-inch hole in the center of the record and a new type of phonograph.

Continuing research may provide records with even longer playing capability. Some sixteen-r.p.m. records are available now, and this speed may receive wider circulation in the future.

LOVE AND MARRIAGE: song (1955). Words by Sammy Cahn, music by Jimmy Van Heusen.

Few songs have been written directly for television. A fairly high percentage of such songs, however, have turned into national favorites. "Love and Marriage" was one of these, besides winning an Emmy for an original musical work. As of 1964, it was the only popular song ever to win a TV award.

Sammy Cahn and Jimmy Van Heusen were assigned to write the music for an hour-and-a-half performance of Thornton Wilder's "Our Town." The show starred Frank Sinatra and Eva Marie Saint. The first act dealt with daily life, the second with love and marriage, the third with death. As Van Heusen notes: "The third act, which took place in a cemetery, gave us the most trouble. The second-act song was fairly easy because we had Thornton Wilder's line, 'Love and Marriage,' to work from. Actually, we wrote it tongue-in-cheek as a 'cute' song, but it had something about it that made people take it very seriously. In recent years, almost every wedding I've gone to the band is asked to play 'Love and marriage—go together like a horse and carriage.'"

LOVE IS A MANY-SPLENDORED THING: song (1955). Words by Paul Francis Webster, music by Sammy Fain.

In 1954, Sammy Fain and Paul Francis Webster were asked to provide the title song for a Twentieth Century-Fox movie titled "A Many-Splendored Thing." The song was accepted, and a top artist recorded it. Then the studio decided to change the picture's title to "Love Is a Many-Splendored Thing." This meant scrapping the original song and writing a new one.

"I rushed back to my hotel," Fain recalls, "and wrote a new melody in a couple of hours. I turned it over to Paul Francis Webster, and he soon wrote new words." The new approach pleased the writers and the studio, but there were other complications. This time, the writers could find no top performer willing to record it. The singers they talked to felt that this was not the type of ballad the public wanted at that time. Finally, the Four Aces agreed to do it. When the record was released, it became one of the fastest selling numbers of the fifties.

With the picture almost ready for release by the time the new song was written, there was a question of how much footage could be devoted to the song. To be eligible for an Academy Award, a song has to be performed vocally. Luckily, the producers decided to have the song performed by a vocal group at the end of the picture. As a result, the song was eligible and won the Oscar for 1955. Since then, many other records of "Love Is a Many-Splendored Thing" have been made, and sales have totaled well into the millions.

LULLABY OF BROADWAY: song (1935). Words by Al Dubin, music by Harry Warren.

In 1932, Harry Warren had scarcely been west of New Jersey. Within three years, he not only was established in the Golden West but had won an Academy Award for a song in honor of his old home town. The song was "Lullaby of Broadway," written for "Gold Diggers of 1935."

Warren had been called to Hollywood because of a book titled "Forty-Second Street." Darryl Zanuck, then with Warner Brothers, wanted to do it as a musical. His studio had a top-notch lyricist in Al Dubin but had no composer to work with him. Zanuck asked Edwin H. Morris of a New York music-publishing firm controlled by Warner Brothers for suggestions. Morris said that Warren, then a staff writer with part of the Warner combine, was the best there was. "They gave me a ticket on the Chief," Warren remembers, "and four days later I was in Hollywood."

Warren had written dozens of hit songs and was used to writing to order. Soon he and Dubin were taking on assignments in acceptable Hollywood production-line fashion. Their next assignment after "Forty-Second Street" was "Gold Diggers of 1933." A year later, they were picked to do the score for "Gold Diggers of 1935."

"How did I come to write 'Lullaby of Broadway'? They came to Dubin and me and said they needed a production number, so we wrote one. The only unusual twist was that, in those days, I was mighty homesick; I loved New York. But Dubin, though he came from there, was a confirmed Californian, wouldn't even go back on a trip if he could help it. Still, he was always coming to me with nostalgic lyrics about New York all the years we worked together: 'Meet me at Lindy's,' 'I miss Coney Island,' or something like that."

"Lullaby of Broadway" won the 1935 Oscar for Best Song of the year. It was the second ever awarded in Academy Award competition for this category, and the first of three won by Warren.

LYRIC; LYRICIST: the words of a popular song; the writer of such words.

"Lyrical poetry" is a general term for poetry which is capable of being sung. Except in a few instances, however, popular-music lyrics are not poetry. They must instead conform to the patterns of popular music, which are quite different from poetic forms.

Many of today's song lyrics are written to order. A composer or music publisher will commission a lyricist to write the words to a song or words to fit a certain pattern. In many cases, a song will become popular as an instrumental. Months or even years later, the publisher or composer may decide to have a lyricist add words. Sometimes words are written to order for a song in a foreign language, when the foreign lyric cannot be translated to fit the melody.

There are three ways in which a song may be created. The lyric may be written first and the music composed to it; the music may be composed first and the lyric added; or the music and lyric may be written more or less simultaneously.

The ways in which lyricists work vary widely. Johnny Mercer likes to lie on a couch and listen to the music over and over, either by having the composer play it or by using a demonstration record. As ideas strike him, he writes them down. Some lyricists work more as poets do. Oscar Hammerstein II often used to read and reread the script for a new musical to get the feel of it. Then he would write the lyric, polishing and repolishing it until it seemed complete. He would

then take it to the composer for the music. Ray Evans thinks up a title and works with the composer until they arrive at some melodic phrases. Evans then likes to write a dummy lyric around which the final music is composed. The dummy lyric is then worked and reworked until it seems to express the feeling of the music. Stephen Sondheim was quoted by John Wilson in *Theatre Arts* (June, 1962) as saying:

> Not enough songwriters understand the function of a song in a play. They write songs in which a character explains himself. This is self-defeating. A song should reveal the character to the audience but the character does not have enough self-knowledge to describe himself in these terms.

Some insight into the mechanics of lyric writing were once given by Lorenz Hart:

> If I am trying to write a melodic song hit, I let Richard Rodgers get his tune first. Then I take the most distinctive melodic phrase in his tune and work on that. What I choose is not necessarily the theme or first line, but the phrase which stands out. Next I try to find the meaning of that phrase and develop a euphonic set of words to fit it. For example, in one of our songs, the first line runs like this: "Here in my arms, it's adorable," The distinct melodic phrase came on the word "adorable," and "adorable" is the first word that occurred to me, so I used it as my pivotal musical idea. And, as the melodic phrase recurs so often in the chorus, it determined my rhyme scheme. Of course, in a song of this sort, the melody and the euphonics of the words themselves are really more important than the sense.

The degree of formal musical training possessed by lyricists ranges from none to a complete musical grounding. Many lyricists can write words only; others, such as Cole Porter, Irving Berlin, Frank Loesser, and Meredith Willson, write the music as well.

MAMBO: dance and dance rhythm of Latin American origin.

If the bossa nova can be called the jazz samba, the mambo can be called the jazz rumba. Basically, the mambo is a considerably faster rumba. It has been described as "swinging the rumba." It has the same step sequence as the rumba—one, two, three, pause. But the mambo is danced with a forward and backward motion rather than the in-place or sideward movement of the rumba.

The mambo is generally agreed to have been evolved by Mexican and Cuban musicians. It is a mixture of the Cuban (not the American) rumba and American jazz. The mambo is said to have been started in Mexico by such band leaders as Anselmo Sacasas and Julio Gutierrez and spread to other parts of Latin America, particularly Cuba.

Perez Prado is credited with bringing it to the attention of the United States. Prado began working on mambo rhythms in 1943 while he was serving as pianist and arranger for the Orquesta Casino de la Playa in Havana. In 1947, Prado toured South America, Panama, Puerto Rico, and Mexico, playing mambos, many of which he wrote himself, to wildly excited crowds. Soon many of his mambo records were being distributed throughout Latin America on RCA Victor's International label. One of these, "Que Rico el Mambo" created a sensation both outside the United States and initially among Spanish-speaking citizens of this country. Before long, the mambo spread beyond the Latin American segment of the United States to become accepted by the public in general. By the early fifties, many bands, including those of Noro Morales, Machito, and even North American leaders, were vying for mambo popularity in the United States. Today, though the initial fervor has died down, the mambo is still popular on the dance floor.

MAN THAT GOT AWAY, THE: song (1954). Words by Ira Gershwin, music by Harold Arlen.

A mark of a great lyricist is his ability to work with many top-notch composers in a wide variety of styles. Ira Gershwin meets this requirement many times over, with such lyrics as "Long Ago and Far Away" with Jerome Kern and "I Can't Get Started" with Vernon Duke, and the scores for the musical play "Lady in the Dark" with Kurt Weill and the musical film "A Star Is Born" with Harold Arlen. The last contained "The Man That Got Away," which was made famous by Judy Garland, who sang it in the film. (A male version was later recorded by Frank Sinatra.)

Judy played a band vocalist named Esther Blodgett. In a musicians' hangout after working hours, Esther is supposed to sing a torch song. Ira thought of the fisherman's lament, "You should have seen the one that got away," which he quickly transformed into the song title.

In Ira's book "Lyrics on Several Occasions" (New York: Alfred A. Knopf, 1959), Arlen recalls his decision to take a short rest in Palm Springs after finishing this number. Also there were Judy, Sid Luft (her husband and the movie's producer), and script writer Moss Hart. Meeting the Lufts on the golf course, Arlen teasingly whistled the main theme of "The Man That Got Away." After much prodding, he finally admitted that it was a new song for the picture. He played the song for them in the clubhouse and later for Moss Hart and his wife, Kitty Carlisle. All thought the song was wonderful; Judy "went wild with joy."

Their verdict was correct, for the song has become a standard, as closely associated with Judy Garland as "Over the Rainbow" (also an Arlen composition).

MANCINI, HENRY: composer, arranger, instrumentalist. Born Cleveland, Ohio, April 16, 1924. Won Academy Award for Best Song of 1961 ("Moon River") and 1962 ("Days of Wine and Roses").

Like Meredith Willson, Henry Mancini is a piccolo player turned composer. His father, Quinto Mancini, was a steel worker with a great love of music. Quinto would come home from his hours at the mill and relax by playing the flute. His son Henry followed his father by learning first the piccolo, then the flute, and finally the piano. Quinto encouraged his boy to continue music professionally. At thirteen, Henry won an

Henry Mancini

award as first flutist in the Pennsylvania All-State Band of 1937. After graduating from high school, Henry studied first at the music school of Carnegie Institute of Technology in Pittsburgh and later at New York's Juilliard School of Music. He continued his studies with composers Mario Castelnuovo-Tedesco and Ernest Krenek.

All the while, Mancini worked in his spare time with local dance bands to help pay his tuition. As piccolo players aren't too much in demand in dance bands, he served mostly as a pianist. Then Henry spent several years in the service in World War II. When he returned to civilian life, he decided to pursue popular rather than classical music. Tex Beneke was forming his successor to the late Glenn Miller's organization. Mancini won a place in it and stayed with Beneke for several years.

In 1951, Universal Pictures invited Mancini to serve as staff composer. He was assigned to collaborate on the score of "The Glenn Miller Story." The picture was reasonably well received, but much of the critics' enthusiasm was for the score rather than the movie. Mancini was nominated for an Oscar. With this impressive showing, he was asked to write the score for UI's next band-leader biography, "The Benny Goodman Story."

Mancini also turned his talents to television. One of his first efforts was the theme for the "Peter Gunn" series. This instrumental swept rapidly to the top of the best-seller lists. It won the *Down Beat* magazine annual disc-jockey survey as best jazz album of the year (1956). The National Academy of Recording Arts and Sciences called it the "Best Arranged LP of the Year" and the "Album of the Year." Mancini then composed the music for another private-detective series, "Mr. Lucky," and once more his album hit the top of the charts.

He won two Oscars for the 1961 "Breakfast at Tiffany's," one for the score, the other for the song "Moon River," with lyrics by Johnny Mercer. The following year, Mancini won his third Oscar with the title song from "Days of Wine and Roses," also with lyrics by Mercer. In 1963, Mancini and Mercer won still another nomination for "Charade," but failed to win the Oscar. Mancini's Academy nominations in 1964 included the score for the movie "The Pink Panther," plus a fourth straight nomination for best song with "Dear Heart" from the picture of the same name. His lyricists for the latter were Jay Livingston and Ray Evans.

MARTIN, DEAN: singer, comedian, actor. Born Steubenville, Ohio, June 7, 1917.

When Dean Martin and Jerry Lewis broke up their comedy act, both demonstrated more talent and versatility than they probably would have if they'd stayed together. For Martin, it was the chance to make the grade as a major popular vocalist and also to try his hand at acting.

Dean's family moved to Long Beach, California, in 1937. Martin (original name, Dino Crocetti) worked as a mill hand and gas-station attendant, was a good amateur boxer for a time, and, when jobs were scarce, even served as a croupier in a gambling casino.

Dean began to do vocal imitations of such popular radio singers as Bing Crosby. He developed a style of his own at the same time, and started to take the idea of becoming a singer seriously. His style, he says, "wasn't too good, but it seemed to pay better than cleaning windshields and I took fewer punches than I took in the ring, so I devoted more time to it." Dean started his singing career in 1943. By 1946, he was working at the 500 Club in Atlantic City. On the same bill was a young comedian, Jerry Lewis. Their paths had crossed a few times before, and when the nightclub owner needed a comedy act, they volunteered. Their first attempt was far from auspicious. The audience was bored and sat on its hands. Martin and Lewis begged for one more chance.

The boys tried to write an outline for their act, but nothing seemed to jell. Finally, they decided to ad-lib. The next night, as Dean sang, Lewis smashed dishes and threw unrehearsed lines at Martin to which Dean returned the first thought that came into his head. This time, the audience went wild. Within a few years, their act had become one of the most talked-about on the nightclub circuit. They played to sell-out crowds at such major spots as New York's Copacabana, Chicago's Chez Paree, and Hollywood's Slapsie Maxie's. At Slapsie Maxie's, Paramount producer Hal Wallis saw their act and quickly signed them to a contract for their first picture, "My Friend Irma." For eight years, Martin and Lewis turned out one box-office hit after another—sixteen in all—including "At War with the Army," "Jumping Jacks," "That's My Boy," and "The Caddy."

In 1957, they announced their breakup as a team. Though there were almost as many reasons given as there are gossip columnists, Martin emphasizes that the true reason was that the best of associations can wear thin. Both of them had reached the point where there were things they wanted to do separately. Martin appeared alone, shortly thereafter, in a farce called "10,000 Bedrooms." He then surprised everyone by doing a dramatic role with Marlon Brando and Montgomery Clift in "The Young Lions." In the years following, Dean played a wide range of movie roles. These included a dramatic performance in "Toys in the Attic," a comedy role in "Who's Been Sleeping in My Bed?," and a combination of the two in "4 for Texas." He also appeared in several pictures in the late fifties and early sixties with his close friends Frank Sinatra and Sammy Davis, Jr., including "Sergeants 3," "Some Came Running," and "Ocean's 11."

Martin also made a series of highly successful records and albums. He had three gold records between 1957 and 1963, plus one song, "That's Amore," that sold over three million copies. He has also been in demand for such television attractions as "The Dinah Shore Show," Judy Garland specials (with Frank Sinatra), and Bob Hope's 1963 *TV Guide* Award Show. In 1965, Dean won an RIAA Gold Record for the album "Everybody Loves Somebody."

MARTIN, FREDDY: band leader. Born Springfield, Ohio, December 9, 1906.

In the years after World War II, there were few top stars in music that did not play the famed Cocoanut Grove in Los Angeles's Ambassador Hotel. They were usually welcomed by an enthusiastic audience but, equally important, they had excellent musical backing from one of the best orchestras in the country. This band, which attracted many people who just liked to dance to its music, was that of Freddy Martin.

The road to success had not been easy for Martin. Both his parents died when he was four. He was placed in an orphanage in Springfield, Ohio, where he remained until he was sixteen. One bright spot for him was the music training the orphans received from a Professor Schultz. Freddy was assigned the drums, though he soon gained a secret liking for the saxophone. This longing stayed with him after he left the home to attend high school in Cleveland, supporting himself by working evenings in a grocery store. He bought a saxophone from some of his earnings and taught himself to play it. He then organized a small dance band at his school.

Soon after his grocery-store stint, he got a job selling saxophones. This led to a meeting with band leader Guy Lombardo. Lombardo didn't buy any instruments, but he did become inter-

ested in Martin's band. He got the management of the Music Box Restaurant, where he was then playing, to hire Martin's group as a substitute on Lombardo's days off.

Freddy was not quite ready for the big time, however. After his Music Box engagement, he spent some years as a sideman with various orchestras. This included a trip to Finland as a member of a military band. The tour started poorly, and the leader switched to a hot-jazz band featuring Freddy. This too was a failure, and Freddy returned to the United States six months later. The Depression was in full swing, but Martin managed to win a job with Eddy Hodges and his Band of Pirates. This served as a jumping-off point for a position as tenor saxophonist and part-time vocalist with the Jack Albin band at Brooklyn's then fashionable Hotel Bossert.

Freddy had the urge to go out on his own once more. On January 2, 1932, he started a new band, which soon was engaged for New York's Roosevelt Grill. Martin's highly danceable style quickly won him a wide following, and his name became known in other large cities. In the years preceding World War II, he played many engagements at well-known hotels and nightclubs throughout the country.

In 1941, he scored his first major West Coast success at San Francisco's St. Francis Hotel. By now he had developed his specialty of making modern arrangements of classical concertos. At the St. Francis, he introduced "Tonight We Love," a new arrangement of the Tchaikovsky Piano Concerto No. 1. This soon became a nationwide record hit. Throughout the forties and fifties, Martin turned out many other best-selling records, including "The Hut Sut Song," "Warsaw Concerto," "Santa Catalina," "Why Don't We Do This More Often?," "Cumana," "Blue Champagne," "Grieg Piano Concerto in A minor," and "I've Got a Lovely Bunch of Cocoanuts."

Not long after the St. Francis engagement, Martin's orchestra took up regular quarters at the Cocoanut Grove, where it was still going strong in 1965.

MARTIN, MARY: singer, actress. Born Weatherford, Texas, December 1, 1914.

Mary Martin, one of the reigning ladies of the Broadway musical theater in the nineteen-fifties and sixties, started out with a burning desire to conquer Hollywood. But once she did, she found that what she really wanted all along was the

Mary Martin and some of her classic roles: (from top left) in *The Sound of Music;* singing "My Heart Belongs to Daddy," the song that first made her famous; and in *Peter Pan.*

New York stage. It was a fortunate decision for Broadway, providing New York audiences with stirring performances in such hits as "One Touch of Venus," "South Pacific," and "The Sound of Music."

She was born into a comfortable family. Her father was an attorney and her mother a violin teacher. When Mary reached high-school age, she was sent to the fashionable Ward-Belmont School in Nashville, Tennessee. She took voice lessons while in Nashville. But the 1929 crash affected her family's finances, and Mary had to return home. When she finished high school, she entered the University of Texas to continue her vocal studies. She left after a year for a short-lived marriage, which ended in divorce after the birth of a son, Larry Hagman.

Then Mary and a friend, Mildred Woods, undertook to run a dancing school in Weatherford. Business boomed, and Mary had to spend a summer in Hollywood brushing up her dancing at the Fanchon and Marco studio. While she was there, some of the glamour of the movie town rubbed off on her. Some time after, when the building which housed the dancing school burned down, Mary told Mildred: "It's a sign. Let's go to Hollywood." Once there, the going was rough. Mildred acted as Mary's agent, but for many months could find only minor radio and nightclub jobs. Finally, she got Mary one, then several, screen tests. Mary, who failed them all, got the nickname "Audition Mary." Then she ran into her former Nashville voice teacher, who suggested six more months of study.

Mildred then got Mary to try out at the Trocadero nightclub's "Opportunity Night." After a poor start with an operatic aria, Mary swung into a blues number and rocked the house. Producer Lawrence Schwab was there and signed her for a New York show. The show was canceled, but Schwab placed her in a minor role in a new Cole Porter show, "Leave It to Me." Her rendition of "My Heart Belongs to Daddy" stopped the show and was one of the high spots of the 1938 season. In 1939, she made her first major nightclub appearance and took New York's Rainbow Room by storm.

Now Hollywood offers came in droves, but Mary no longer wanted them. It took much urging by Mildred and a Paramount talent scout to get her to return to the West Coast. There Mary was featured in many films, beginning with "The Great Victor Herbert" (1939) and including "Rhythm on the River" and "Love Thy Neigh-

bor" (1940), "New York Town," "Birth of the Blues," and "Kiss the Boys Goodbye" (1941), and "Star-Spangled Rhythm" (1943). In 1940, she married Richard Halliday, who became her manager. (Their daughter, Mary Heller Halliday, later appeared with her mother in the television classic "Peter Pan.")

Mary longed to go back to Broadway, however. When an offer came to appear in a new Kurt Weill musical, she snapped it up. The show, "One Touch of Venus," was one of the hits of the 1943–44 season. She sang such songs as "Speak Low," "How Much I Love You," "That's Him," and "I'm a Stranger Here Myself."

An established star, Mary now was offered many stage and film roles. One of her stage performances was as the touching heroine of the Chinese fantasy "Lute Song." In the late nineteen-forties, she took over Ethel Merman's role in the transcontinental tour of Irving Berlin's "Annie Get Your Gun." She later portrayed Annie in the TV version. In 1949, Mary reached the heights as one of the stars of Rodgers and Hammerstein's sensational "South Pacific." As Navy nurse Nellie Forbush, she introduced "A Cockeyed Optimist," "I'm Gonna Wash That Man Right outa My Hair," and "A Wonderful Guy."

Besides her stage career, Mary starred in many TV specials and was a featured guest on many major network shows. Her most famous TV role was Peter Pan, which she first did in the 1954 musical. In 1959, Mary once more graced a Rodgers and Hammerstein production, this time as Maria in "The Sound of Music." Some of the songs she presented were "My Favorite Things," "Do-Re-Mi," "The Lonely Goatherd," and the title song. In 1964, even her prodigious talents could not make a hit out of the musical "Jenny."

MARTIN, TONY: singer. Born San Francisco, California, December 25, 1913.

Tony Martin was born Alvin Morris, Jr., and grew up in the San Francisco area. By the time he was twelve, he could play saxophone and clarinet with considerable skill. By the time he reached sixteen, he was playing sax and singing with a band at San Francisco's Palace Hotel. In 1932, he made his debut on coast-to-coast radio singing on "The Lucky Strike Hour," which featured Walter Winchell plus dance bands from around the country. Tony worked at night; during the day, he attended St. Mary's College. His college career ended abruptly, however, when one of the fathers heard him playing jazz on the college organ. After leaving school, he went to play at the Chicago World's Fair of 1933. There he met Frances Langford, who suggested he try for the movies.

In Hollywood one of his first acts was to change his name. For a time, he made no headway. His closest opportunity was a role opposite Joan Crawford that he lost to Gene Raymond. After months of trying, Tony finally was hired by Twentieth Century-Fox and was soon playing in the first of some twenty pictures. Among the stars with whom he appeared were Rita Hayworth, Lana Turner, and the Marx Brothers. Tony became well known to movie fans, but his recordings didn't sell well. In 1942, he entered the Army for a four-year tour of duty that included a long period as an Air Force technical sergeant in the China-Burma-India theater. He returned to Hollywood with the Bronze Star and a Presidential citation.

Once Martin re-entered the movies, he found himself in demand for nightclub, radio, and later television appearances. His records began to sell. Martin turned out gold record after gold record in the forties and fifties. These included such songs as "I Get Ideas," "To Each His Own," "There's No Tomorrow," "Begin the Beguine," "Comme Ci, Comme Ça," "Night and Day," and "Domino." Besides being popular in the United States, he broke many attendance records at nightclubs in foreign countries and played command performances for European royalty.

Some of the movies Martin appeared in are "Casbah," "Show Boat," "Till the Clouds Roll By," "Here Come the Girls," "Easy To Love," "Hit the Deck," and "Ziegfeld Girl."

Beginning in 1963, Martin won new applause coast-to-coast when he started a new act with his wife, dancer-actress Cyd Charisse. Their 1965 version, "A Two-Act Revue," opened to rave notices at the Riviera Hotel in Las Vegas. Show stopper was the "Hong Kong Ballet."

MATHIS, JOHNNY: singer. Born San Francisco, California, September 30, 1935.

Athletics' loss is music's gain. Johnny Mathis became a millionaire long before he reached thirty, thanks to an almost continuous series of best-selling single records and LP albums. Yet he originally intended to become an athletic coach. He won six letters in high school and a number of sports awards at San Francisco State College. A particular forte was the high jump, in which he

Johnny Mathis

achieved the then record-breaking mark of six feet, five and a half inches.

Mathis was the fourth of seven children. In his preteen years, he sang in his church choir and school glee club. At thirteen, he began six years of singing lessons with San Francisco teacher Connie Cox. Still, though Johnny loved singing, coaching seemed a much more likely—and secure—goal.

To support himself at college, Mathis sang at small clubs in the area. During a Sunday-afternoon jam session at the Black Hawk in San Francisco, Mathis joined the group and was overheard by club co-owner Helen Noga. She asked if he would sing professionally, and this led, in 1955, to a long-term contract with Columbia Records. Within a year, Mathis had turned out a hit in "Wonderful, Wonderful." This was soon followed by such others as "Chances Are" and "It's Not for Me To Say."

Guest appearances on coast-to-coast television shows—including Ed Sullivan's and Perry Como's—were followed by one-man shows across the country, from Forest Hills Stadium in Queens, New York, to the famous Greek Theatre in Los Angeles. In the sixties, Mathis's tours of Europe—from London to the Italian Riviera—

were equally successful. He also sang the title songs of such Hollywood pictures as "Wild Is the Wind" and "That Certain Smile." His albums also were extremely successful and many won him RIAA Gold Record awards: "Faithfully," "Swing Softly," "Open Fire, Two Guitars," "Johnny's Greatest Hits," "Heavenly," "Warm," "Merry Christmas," and "More Johnny's Greatest Hits." In 1963, Mathis came up with a hit record titled "What Will Mary Say?"

In liner notes on a Mathis album, New York *Times* writer Gilbert Millstein discussed the qualities of the singer's voice:

> It is a voice that is at once luxuriant and incisive; its quality is an oddly engaging combination of seductiveness and innocence. Mathis can lend it the sense of being lingering, insouciant or teasing at will, as well as compressed, hopelessly involved or mortally serious when the mood is upon him or the lyrics of a song demand it. He is capable of making it wily, coaxing and gentle, or straightforward, urgent and growing. His enunciation is impeccable, so that it is possible not merely to hear what he is singing, but to understand him.

McHUGH, JAMES (JIMMY): composer. Born Boston, Massachusetts, July 10, 1894.

Jimmy McHugh is one of many great popular-music composers who started out in the classics and then found their niche in the popular field. His mother taught him to play the piano, and his father, a plumber, gave him some pointers on piping systems. After he graduated from St. Paul's Preparatory School, he worked for a time as his father's apprentice. Then he found a job as office boy and rehearsal pianist to the managing director of the Boston Opera House. He was offered a scholarship to the New England Conservatory but turned it down to stay with the opera. He eventually decided that this wasn't for him and got a job as a song plugger for the Boston office of the Irving Berlin Music Corporation.

As time went on, he felt that he would rather write his own music than plug somebody else's. He moved to New York and by the early nineteen-twenties was on his way to composing greatness. During this period, he wrote such songs as "Emaline" (1921), "When My Sugar Walks Down the Street" (1924), "The Lonesomest Girl in Town" (1925), and "I Can't Believe That You're in Love with Me." Besides writing

many individual songs, McHugh composed for the stage. This included working for seven years on the Cotton Club revues and providing a major Broadway hit, "Blackbirds of 1928." With Dorothy Fields, one of his main collaborators, providing the lyrics, "Blackbirds" included such hits as "I Can't Give You Anything but Love," "Diga Diga Doo," and "Doin' the New Low-Down."

In 1930, McHugh wrote the standards "On the Sunny Side of the Street" and "Exactly Like You" for "Lew Leslie's International Revue."

He then accepted a summons from the film industry and became one of Hollywood's most important songwriters. A few of his songs for Hollywood are "Cuban Love Song" (1931), "Don't Blame Me" (1933), "I Feel a Song Comin' On" and "I'm in the Mood for Love" (1935), "Can't Get Out of This Mood" (1942), "Comin' in on a Wing and a Prayer," "A Lovely Way To Spend an Evening," and "I Couldn't Sleep a Wink Last Night" (1943), and "It's a Most Unusual Day" (1948).

McHugh also had several of his songs nominated for Academy Awards, including "Lovely To Look At" in 1935, for which McHugh and Dorothy Fields provided lyrics to a Jerome Kern melody. Other nominees were "My Own" (1938), "I'd Know You Anywhere" (1940), and "Say a Prayer for the Boys Over There" and "I Couldn't Sleep a Wink Last Night" (1943).

MEASURE: the group of beats made by the regular recurrence of primary, or heavy, accents, the position of which is marked on the staff by bars just before them. (See also *Chorus, Rhythm, Time, Verse.*)

A measure consists of the notes and/or rests between two adjacent bars. The bar is the vertical line that divides one measure from another. Thus another word for measure is "bar."

The usual form for a popular-music composition is a short verse of perhaps eight or sixteen measures followed by a chorus of thirty-two measures. This is not an absolute rule, since there are many songs or compositions with choruses of 28, 36 or other numbers of measures. (See *Chorus.*)

MERCER, JOHN H. (JOHNNY): lyricist, composer, singer, author, publisher. Born Savannah, Georgia, November 18, 1909. Won Academy Award for Best Song of 1946 ("On the Atchison, Topeka and the Santa Fe"), 1951 ("In the Cool, Cool, Cool of the Evening"), 1961 ("Moon

[152]

Johnny Mercer

River"), and 1962 ("Days of Wine and Roses").

Johnny Mercer started out with a driving ambition to be an actor. But he early showed talent in writing, composing his first song, "Sister Susie, Strut Your Stuff," when he was fifteen. His parents wanted him to go to college and sent him to Woodbury Forest Preparatory School in Orange, Virginia. But John concentrated on little-theater work, which eventually led to his group's winning a national contest in the Belasco Cup Tournament.

At nineteen, Johnny worked his way to New York on a steamship to try for the Broadway stage. Jobs in theater were difficult to find, so he supported himself by working as a runner, delivering papers and securities in Wall Street. In 1929, Mercer attended an audition for a new show called "Garrick Gaieties." Backstage, he heard that they needed a song for Sterling Hollo-way. He found another fellow at the audition, Everett Miller, who had some songwriting experience, and they wrote a song called "Out of Breath and Scared to Death of You." This was

Mercer's first published song. It led to a job as contract writer for Miller Music in New York, an arrangement that lasted four years.

In 1935, Jerome Robbins, of Robbins Music, sent Mercer to London to do one of Lew Leslie's "Blackbirds." When Johnny returned in 1936, he was offered a contract with Warner Brothers in California. After a year of this, Johnny decided to freelance so that he could write with a variety of collaborators and organizations. In the years preceding World War II, Johnny proved to be a man of many talents, serving several years as a master of ceremonies and vocalist with Paul Whiteman and later (1938–39) with Benny Goodman. During this time, Johnny kept turn-ing out song lyrics, such as "Jeepers Creepers," "Love of My Life," and "I'd Know You Any-where," all of which received Academy Award nominations.

By 1940, Johnny had abandoned band work to concentrate on Hollywood. He turned out some of his greatest songs in rapid succession. In 1941, with Harold Arlen, came "Blues in the Night"; in 1942, with Jerome Kern, "Dearly Beloved"; and, with Arlen again, "That Old Black Magic" (1942), "My Shining Hour" (1945), and "Ac-cent-tchu-ate the Positive (1945). All of these were nominated for Oscars but lost. Finally, Johnny and Harry Warren won the award in 1946 for "On the Atchison, Topeka and Santa Fe." Johnny also found time to help found Capitol Records. For a time, he served as the president of the company and helped further the careers of such performers as Nat "King" Cole and Peggy Lee. During these years, Mercer also was a frequent performer and guest star on many top network radio shows.

After World War II, Johnny wrote several Broadway shows. In 1951, he wrote words and music for the hit musical "Top Banana," which starred comedian Phil Silvers. Other shows were "Texas, Li'l Darlin'," which he wrote with Robert Emmett Dolan, and "St. Louis Woman," which he wrote with Arlen. In 1963, Mercer worked with Dolan on "Foxy," which starred Bert Lahr. The show opened in New York in February, 1964, to fairly complimentary re-views, but closed in two months time.

Besides the songs previously mentioned, there are dozens of other hits to Mercer's credit as a lyricist. Among these are "Lazybones," "Laura," "And the Angels Sing," "Skylark," "Autumn Leaves," "One for My Baby," "Come Rain or Come Shine," "If I Had My Druthers," and

"Mister Meadowlark." Though known primarily as a lyricist, Mercer is also a talented composer. His music credits include "Something's Gotta Give," "Dream," "I'm an Old Cowhand," and "I Wanna Be Around."

In the nineteen-sixties, Mercer began collaborating with composer Henry Mancini. The result was Academy Awards for the best songs of 1961 and 1962. The 1961 award was for "Moon River," from "Breakfast at Tiffany's," the 1962 one for "Days of Wine and Roses," from the film of that name. The Mercer-Mancini 1963 effort, "Charade" won an Academy Award nomination, but failed to win the Oscar.

MERMAN, ETHEL: singer, actress. Born Queens, New York, January 16, 1909.

There are few singers in the history of the musical theater to compare with Ethel Merman as a show stopper. No one who has ever seen her perform can forget the almost tangible vibrancy of her movements or the way she belts out a song with her amazingly strong, throaty voice. As critic Wolcott Gibbs remarked, "[her] voice might easily have tumbled the walls of Jericho." She also serves as inspiration to the office working girl, for she's a prime example of a secretary who made good.

Ethel Agnes Zimmerman was born on the top floor of her grandmother's house on Fourth Avenue in the Astoria section of Queens, New York. Her father was an accountant for a dry-goods store. While in grade school, Ethel sang Sunday nights at her family's Lutheran church and at her father's Masonic lodge. At eight, she entertained World War I soldiers with such songs as "How Ya Gonna Keep 'Em Down on the Farm?" Ethel attended William Cullen Bryant High School in Long Island City, where she studied shorthand and typing. After graduation, she got a job as secretary to the president of a large corporation in Queens. But she wanted to become a singer and kept performing at social affairs, company get-togethers, and eventually at local clubs. Her boss knew producer George White. Finally she got the courage to ask him to write White; he dictated a letter, which she typed. White offered her work in the chorus, but Ethel wanted only a singing job and returned to typing.

Then a freelance agent got her a two-week engagement at the Little Russia restaurant in New York. Another agent, Lou Irwin, heard her and got her a number of small bookings, including a short stint with Warner Brothers. In one short movie, she ran across the stage in a leopard skin.

In 1929, she auditioned for and was accepted by a new trio, Clayton, Jackson, and Durante. She appeared with them at Les Ambassadeurs Club on Broadway, but had to leave because of tonsillitis. When she recovered, she teamed with pianist Al Siegel at the Ritz Theatre in Elizabeth, New Jersey, on weekends. During the week she played at the Brooklyn Paramount, where producer Vinton Freedley heard her and decided that she was just what was needed for a new Gershwin show, "Girl Crazy."

Gershwin auditioned her in his penthouse apartment. She was so awed that she was tongue-tied when he spoke to her. He mistook this for dissatisfaction with the song he'd played, "I Got Rhythm," and asked if she thought he should change something in it. She finally replied, "That will do very nicely, Mr. Gershwin." And very nicely it did. Ethel stopped the show with it in 1930.

In 1932, she triumphed in a Vincent Youmans-Richard Whiting-Nacio Herb Brown-Buddy de Sylva effort, "Take a Chance," stopping the show with such songs as "Rise 'n' Shine," "Eadie Was a Lady," and "Should I Be Sweet?" The show opened on November 26, 1932, and ran for two hundred and forty-three performances. In 1934, she appeared in Cole Porter's "Anything Goes," in which she sang the title song, "I Get a Kick Out of You," and "Blow, Gabriel, Blow." Hollywood was quick to bid for her services. She made such films as "Kid Millions," with Eddie Cantor, and "Alexander's Ragtime Band." In the latter, she became well acquainted with Irving Berlin, a composer who was to provide some of her major roles.

In 1936, Ethel was back on Broadway in Cole Porter's "Red, Hot and Blue!," costarring with Jimmy Durante. The show, with book by Howard Lindsay and Russel Crouse, opened on October 29 and ran for one hundred and eighty-three performances. It included such songs as "Down in the Depths," "It's De-Lovely," and "Ridin' High." She then worked with Bert Lahr in Porter's "Du Barry Was a Lady," which opened on December 6, 1939, and ran for four hundred and eight performances. The book for this show and the next Porter hit, "Panama Hattie," were by Herbert Fields and Buddy de Sylva. In "Panama Hattie," which opened on October 30, 1940, and ran for five hundred and one performances, Ethel sang "I've Still Got My Health," "Make it Another Old-Fashioned, Please," and "Let's Be Buddies." She concluded her Cole Porter cycle by starring in the 1943–44 hit "Something for the Boys."

In 1946, Irving Berlin was called in to write the score for "Annie Get Your Gun." Miss Merman was asked to play the title role, and Berlin provided her with such standards as "Doin' What Comes Naturally," "There's No Business Like Show Business," and "They Say It's Wonderful." Ethel then appeared in Berlin's 1950 hit "Call Me Madam." She scored once again with her renditions of "You're Just in Love," "The Hostess with the Mostes' on the Ball," and "Something To Dance About."

After taking time out from Broadway to do a movie, "There's No Business Like Show Business," Ethel went back to her first love in 1959. The show was the Jule Styne-Stephen Sondheim-Arthur Laurents adaptation of Gypsy Rose Lee's autobiography "Gypsy." On Broadway and later on a nationwide tour, Ethel, playing Gypsy's ambitious mother Rose, thrilled audiences with her interpretations of "Some People," "You'll Never Get Away from Me," "Everything's Coming Up Roses," and "Together Wherever We Go."

MERRILL, BOB: composer, television and movie producer, radio writer, author, actor. Born Atlantic City, New Jersey, May 17, 1922.

There are very few things Bob Merrill didn't try in the creative arts on the road to popular-music fame. He compressed more successful careers of this type into ten or fifteen years than most people would go through if they had nine lives. He grew up in Philadelphia, where he went to public schools and soon showed an interest in the theater. At sixteen, he was considered a promising actor and was a protégé of producer Richard Bennett. For a time, young Merrill went to Hollywood and appeared in several motion pictures. For four years, he worked as a motion-picture director, but slowly his attention shifted to writing popular music.

Merrill started composing in a sophisticated vein, concentrating on ballads, and won only rejections from music publishers. He then switched to writing novelty numbers, with phenomenal results. From the late forties to 1952, there was hardly a record poll that didn't show at least one Merrill novelty number near the top of the list. In at least two instances, Merrill compositions

helped make stars out of vocalists. One was Eileen Barton, who recorded the hit version of Merrill's "If I Knew You Were Comin' I'd've Baked a Cake." Guy Mitchell also sold many millions of records with Merrill material, including "My Truly, Truly Fair," "Belle, Belle, My Liberty Belle," and "Pittsburgh, Pennsylvania." Other Merrill novelty successes were "Sparrow in the Tree Top" and "Candy and Cake." His most sensational novelty song was "How Much Is that Doggie in the Window?," made famous by Patti Page.

In the mid-fifties, Merrill began looking for new musical worlds to conquer. In one of his movie endeavors, he was under contract to Metro-Goldwyn-Mayer to both produce and write musicals. His first chore was a musical adaptation of "Anna Christie," Eugene O'Neill's play about a prostitute. The movie was never made, but later Merrill suggested a stage show on the same theme to veteran producer-director-librettist George Abbott. The result was Merrill's first Broadway stage show, "New Girl in Town." Merrill wrote the lyrics and music and Abbott the book. Though the critics had some reservations, "New Girl in Town" was a mild hit. It opened at the Forty-sixth Street Theatre in New York on May 14, 1957, and ran for 431 performances. Star performers Gwen Verdon and Thelma Ritter won accolades for their work in the show. Merrill's songs include "Sunshine Girl," "Flings," "It's Good To Be Alive," "Did You Close Your Eyes?," and "Look at 'Er."

Merrill soon was working on another musical adaptation of an O'Neill work, "Ah, Wilderness," which received the musical title of "Take Me Along." The show opened on September 9, 1959 to generally good reviews and ran for four hundred and forty-eight performances. Its cast included Jackie Gleason, Walter Pidgeon, Eileen Herlie, Susan Luckey, Una Merkel, and a young actor who has since made a blazing name for himself on Broadway, Robert Morse. Merrill's score included the title song, "Sid, Ol' Kid," "Staying Young," "We're Home," "Promise Me a Rose," and "But Yours."

In 1961, Merrill wrote still another major success, "Carnival!," which starred Anna Maria Alberghetti. The most played number from the show is "Love Makes the World Go Round."

MILLER, GLENN: band leader, trombonist, arranger. Born Clarinda, Iowa, March 1, 1909; died over the English Channel, December, 1944.

Glenn Miller

The most important single loss suffered by popular music due to World War II was that of Glenn Miller. The Glenn Miller organization dominates much of the memories of the big-band era; it's hard to realize it was only in existence for about five years. And some two years of this were taken up in the struggle for recognition. In the roughly three years of its heyday, the group turned out a fabulous number of standard recordings. It was estimated, for instance, that in 1940, one out of every three juke-box plays was a Miller record.

Soon after Glenn's birth, his family moved to North Platte, Nebraska. After some years there, they moved once more, to Grant City, Oklahoma. Here, at thirteen, Glenn became interested in the trombone. He earned the money to buy his first instrument by milking cows at two dollars a week. Miller finished high school at Fort Morgan, Colorado, and then entered the University of Colorado. In 1926, he quit school and went to the West Coast to work as an arranger and trombone player for local bands. Not too long afterward, leader Ben Pollack asked Glenn to join his band. Glenn stayed with Pollack until the band reached New York.

Here they parted, with Glenn staying in the city to work as trombonist and arranger for such bands as those of Red Nichols, Victor Young, and

Freddy Rich. In his spare time, Glenn studied arranging with Joseph Schillinger. In 1930, Glenn helped the English leader Ray Noble form a new American band. All through the early thirties, Glenn saved his money and thought about the day he could form his own outfit. He finally did this in 1937, with the help of Charlie Spivak and saxophonist Toots Mondello.

After some months, he felt that this band just wasn't what he was looking for. He disbanded it, and, in early 1938, reorganized and started over. For a year, the band struggled through a string of one-nighters and got little notice. But in 1939, they opened at a New York theater and soon had lines waiting outside for each performance. The next stop was an engagement at the Meadowbrook, where they were heard on radio ten times a week. That summer, the band moved to the Glen Island Casino and broke all previous attendance records. In 1940, the band was signed by Chesterfield Cigarettes for a three-times-a-week major-network show. Other engagements in cities coast-to-coast plus movie contracts rolled in.

Song after song by the Miller crew, which featured such singers as Ray Eberle, Marion Hutton, and Tex Beneke, moved to the top of the surveys. A few of the titles are "Moonlight Serenade" (the band's theme song), "Little Brown Jug," "Johnson Rag," "In the Mood," "I Got a Gal in Kalamazoo," "Chatanooga Choo Choo," and "Tuxedo Junction." In 1941, the band and Glenn were featured with Sonja Henie in the Twentieth Century-Fox movie "Sun Valley Serenade." Songwriter Harry Warren provided Miller with "Serenade in Blue" for the picture. Another film which featured the band was "Orchestra Wives."

In late 1942, Miller broke up his band to enlist as a captain in the Army Air Force. He was lost when the transport plane he was in disappeared over the English Channel in December, 1944.

MILLER, MITCH: conductor, vocal-group leader, television master of ceremonies, oboist, arranger. Born Rochester, New York, on July 4, 1911.

Some of the greats in popular music got their start with relatively obscure instruments. Meredith Willson was a piccolo player, and Mitch Miller, who brought close harmony in the home back in vogue with his sing-along records, started with the oboe. When Miller was a twelve-year-old in high school, he was stuck with the oboe because it was the last instrument left for prospective orchestra members. As years passed, Miller became one of the best classical oboists in the field.

Mitch took piano lessons from six to high-school age. His success with the oboe, though, led him to transfer to Rochester's Eastman School of Music, where he held down three top oboe assignments at one time—with the East-man Symphony, the Syracuse Symphony, and the Rochester Philharmonic. At the height of the Depression, Miller headed for New York. He played with the Works Progress Orchestra for a time, toured with Gershwin's "Porgy and Bess," and, in 1936, joined the CBS Orchestra.

For eleven years, he played with a series of famous conductors, including Andre Kostela-netz, and concert ensembles, such as the Buda-pest Quartet. But he began to long for something with a little more potential than the position of first oboist. His first move in this direction was to supervise some chamber-music recording ses-sions for a small company, Keynote Records, which was bought in the late forties by Mercury Records (which in turn was eventually absorbed by another firm). At Mercury, Mitch found the chance to do artists-and-repertoire work. It soon was apparent that Miller was an extremely wise hand at talent and popular-music selection. At Mercury, he was responsible for such suc-cesses as Frankie Laine's "Cry of the Wild Goose" and Vic Damone's "You're Breaking My Heart."

The result was that Mitch's old firm, CBS, approached him to take over A&R work at Columbia Records. In 1950, Mitch moved to Columbia and soon was responsible for a series of million-selling single records. These included Guy Mitchell's "My Heart Cries for You," Tony Bennett's "Rags to Riches," Doris Day's "Que Sera Sera," Marty Robbins's "White Sport Coat," and Johnny Mathis's "Chances Are." More important from a personal standpoint, Miller began to experiment with his own vocal and band arrangements. In the mid-fifties, he decided to try his own version of a song that had long been a regional favorite, "The Yellow Rose of Texas." This was an immediate success. In May, 1958, came "Sing Along with Mitch," sixteen old-time songs ranging from "Down by the Old Mill Stream" to "I've Got Sixpence." By 1959, he had turned out four more albums, and all five were among the best sellers of that year. Coming into the sixties, Mitch transposed

his sing-along ideas to his equally successful television program. The show started as a tem-porary network replacement, but soon it was a year-round feature. Not only did it induce more singing by the public, it also provided a new showcase for young singers such as Leslie Uggams.

In September '64, after a three year TV run, NBC failed to renew his program. The decision stuck, even though the network was deluged with over 15,000 letters of complaint from Miller fans.

MILLS BROTHERS: vocal group. John, born Bellefonte, Pennsylvania, February 11, 1889; Herbert, Harry F., and Donald F., born Piqua, Ohio, April 2, 1912, August 9, 1913, and April 29, 1915.

The Mills Brothers was one of the consistently great vocal groups in recent popular-music history. From their first success in the early thirties to the sixties, they were always in de-mand and steadily turned out many great standards.

The group originally consisted of four brothers —John, Jr., Herbert, Harry, and Donald—all living in Piqua, Ohio. From the beginning, they were encouraged in their harmonizing by their father, who, though then a barber, had at one time been a concert singer. They were always being asked to sing at local functions. While they were still in their teens, a band leader whose orchestra was about to audition for a spot on station WSAI, Cincinnati, heard them and de-cided to take them along. At the audition, the station signed the boys instead of the band.

They were unsponsored for ten months but gained in popularity, particularly in Piqua. They finally won their first stage appearance in their home town for ten dollars a night. They were billed as Four Boys and a Kazoo. But one night they found themselves on stage without the kazoo. John filled the breach by imitating one. This was so popular with the audience that the boys developed imitations of a whole range of instruments. Anyone familiar with many of the Mills Brothers' hit records of the thirties and forties remembers the self-provided musical background. The boys needed just one actual instrument from there on—a guitar for rhythm.

A year later, the Mills Brothers gained star billing at New York's Palace Theatre on Broad-way. They stayed for fourteen weeks and moved on to a steady string of radio, nightclub, and movie appearances. Just about every major radio —and later television—variety show eventually had the Mills Brothers as honored guests.

In 1935, the boys considered disbanding after the sudden death of John, but their father volunteered to join them. The group continued to make nationwide hits of both old-time and brand-new songs. During the forties, they recorded "Paper Doll," the song that is most often identified with them. The record sold more than a million copies. Some of the other hits of those years were "Lazy River," "Georgia on My Mind," "I'll Be Around," "Guess I'll Get the Papers and Go Home," and "I Love You So Much It Hurts." They were still at it in the fifties and sixties. One of their outstanding renditions of this period was a swinging version of the old operetta favorite "Glowworm."

MR. PRESIDENT: musical. Lyrics and music by Irving Berlin, book by Howard Lindsay and Russel Crouse. New York opening: October 20, 1962, St. James Theatre. 265 performances.

"Mr. President" deals with a young, vigorous President nearing the end of his last term of office and faced with "retirement." The main theme of the show is the heavy pressures weighing on the office of President due to the cold war. Though he is soon to be free of these burdens, President Stephen Decatur Henderson still would like somehow to be of service to his nation. His wife Nell shares his cares and, while understanding them, longs for the simpler life outside officialdom. The subplot deals with the desires of his young son and daughter Larry and Leslie to date whom they want, away from the watchful eyes of the Secret Service.

The opening scene shows a white-tie-and-evening-dress party in progress at the White House. The President has not yet arrived, and the guests are twisting. Henderson and his wife come in, and the twist gives way to a waltz as Nell sings, "Let's Go Back to the Waltz." Nell and Stephen leave, and the twist resumes.

The usual cat-and-mouse game with the Russians is going on. The President must decide whether or not to cancel a world trip including a visit to Moscow. Leslie complains about agents covering her dates with neutral diplomat Youssein Davair ("The Secret Service"). Larry is unhappy about interference with his date with dancer Kyra and about not being able to drive fast.

The President and his family finally make the trip. On a stopover in Youssein's country, the diplomat makes love to Leslie in his palace ("Don't Be Afraid of Romance"). The President lands in Moscow, despite last-minute orders from the Kremlin not to. He makes an impromptu speech, translated by Larry, to Russian bystanders. The aftermath of the trip causes the candidate of Henderson's party to lose the election, and this lessens Henderson's chances to make his experience available to the United States. He goes disconsolately off to his home town of Mansfield. But his family is happy (Nell sings "Glad To Be Home"). Leslie learns that Youssein has been double dealing and finds that she really loves her Secret Service bodyguard Pat Gregory ("The Only Man in the World"). Leslie vows, "I'm Gonna Get Him." Larry satisfies his love of speed by becoming a motorcycle cop. Finally, the new President, Chandler, asks Henderson to assist him at a forthcoming overseas conference. The curtain falls to "It's a Great Country."

Opening notices were mixed, but the advance sale was phenomenal—two million, six hundred thousand dollars, including three hundred and ninety-five theater parties. Typical of the early reviews was *Time* magazine's

> *Mr. President* is still the worst musical on Broadway, despite the fact that Robert Ryan [President Henderson] and Nanette Fabray [First Lady] are thrashing about on stage as valiantly as goldfish in a dry bowl.

That was on December 7, 1962. By January 11, 1963, *Life* was saying:

> Forget what you may have heard about this Irving Berlin musical tale of an average American family in the White House. After being pruned and pummeled into shape, it shapes up as an enjoyable old-fashioned show. . . . Berlin has written the kind of songs to sing around the piano.

Besides the principals, the cast included Anita Gillette, as Leslie; Jerry Strickler, as Larry; Jack Washburn, as Youssein; Jack Haskell, as Pat Gregory; and Wisa D'Orso, as Kyra. The score included "In Our Hideaway," "The First Lady," "Meat and Potatoes," "It Gets Lonely in the White House," "They Love Me," "Empty Pockets Filled with Love," and "The Washington Twist."

[158]

MONA LISA: song (1950). Words by Ray Evans, music by Jay Livingston.

There were many ironies associated with the success of this Academy Award-winning song. Its writers provided it as a small side assignment amid their major movie-studio chores. It was never performed in its entirety in the movie it was written for, and it was thought to have so little potential that it was released as the "B" side of a Nat "King" Cole record.

The assignment came when Evans and Livingston were pretty solidly established as Paramount Pictures staff songwriters, with lots of major projects to work on. As Evans recalls, "We were up to our necks in a Martin and Lewis effort. A relatively minor picture starring Alan Ladd was also being filmed. This film, 'Captain Carey, USA,' dealt with a group of Italian partisans fighting the Nazis during World War II. A key part in the Ladd script was the use of a particular melody as a warning by the lookout that the enemy had arrived and the partisans should leave."

The music department asked Evans and Livingston to try to find a spare moment to write this song. One suggestion was to use either an adaptation of an old Italian melody or something that had this flavor. "We started to think about it and thought that instead of going *misterioso* we would do something sweet. I thought of the working title 'Prima Donna,'" said Evans. "We had to consider it in our off time. Jay lived in the San Fernando Valley and had a fairly good drive to work. The next day, coming into work, Jay used the phrase 'Prima Donna' and wrote the whole main theme around it. He came into the studio and played it for me. I said, 'That's pretty,' and later put words to it using that title, but somehow it sounded awfully phony. I kept thinking about it, and a few days later, the words 'Mona Lisa' just came to me. I guess it was a natural association—Italy and one of its most famous works of art. At any rate, the lyric just seemed to write itself, and I finished it in a day."

The film's producer liked it and used it throughout the picture—but in bits and pieces. The song was begun and quickly broken off as the partisans fled. Also, in the picture, the song is always sung in Italian.

Jay and Ray wanted to get wider coverage. "We got the wild idea of giving the song to Nat Cole. We and the publisher chased him all over the country for three months. When Nat heard it, he liked it very much but was afraid to do it because it was very different from anything he'd done before. When he finally recorded it, Capitol Records put it out as the 'B' side. The 'A' side, everyone told us, would be Nat's greatest hit. It was a song called 'Greatest Inventor of Them All.' "

Everything seemed against "Mona Lisa": lack of enthusiasm, a picture no one remembers, "B" side. But when the record came out, everyone began playing it.

There was some confusion at Academy Award time because the song was never sung in English in the picture. This led to a clarification of rules. If a song is just translated into the foreign language, only the American writers are eligible. If major changes are made by another lyricist, he too is eligible for the award.

MOON RIVER: song (1961). Words by Johnny Mercer, music by Henry Mancini.

The sixties saw the beginning of a new and highly successful collaboration betweeen composer-arranger Henry Mancini and lyricist Johnny Mercer. Mancini and Mercer had known each other for years but had not worked together. Then Paramount asked Mancini to do the score for the Audrey Hepburn vehicle "Breakfast at Tiffany's." Mancini came up with what seemed to be a good theme melody and asked Mercer if he would write the lyric for it. Mercer agreed and asked for a demonstration record of the melody.

After listening to the record many times and looking over the script, Mercer chose an important plot point as a basis for his lyric. The heroine is a confirmed New York City dweller whose past is a mystery. At one point, she thinks back for a moment to her earlier life in the country. Since the rural scene included a river, Mercer and Mancini decided to pattern the lyric after this, contrasting the actual river with the way her life had flowed away from this to a new and very different environment. They considered such titles as "June River," "Red River," and "Blue River," before settling on "Moon River."

Some thought was given during the filming to having the heroine look out at the East River while doing the song. In the final version, however, no direct relation of the lyric to a river is given. As a result, during editing, the vocal version was almost dropped from the picture. But it was decided that the song stood so well on its own that it was worth including, even if the meaning might be hard for the audience to grasp. In fact, "Moon River" was chosen as the overall theme for the movie.

Mancini is a recording artist as well as an arranger. He often uses a background chorus that doesn't try to sell the lyric too much. The first thing that enters the public's mind and stays there in the case of a ballad, he feels, is the melody. Once the melody is sold, then there is much more interest in the lyric. In the case of "Moon River" and the Mercer-Mancini 1962 Academy Award winner "Days of Wine and Roses," the first Mancini RCA Victor record was basically instrumental. Both records were and are very popular. "Moon River" was shown as well to singer Andy Williams, who came out with a vocal version on Columbia Records. Williams's effort was an immediate hit, reaching the million-sales mark.

MOST HAPPY FELLA, THE: musical. Lyrics, music, and book by Frank Loesser. Adapted from Sidney Howard's 1924 Pulitzer Prize play "They Knew What They Wanted." New York opening: May 3, 1956, Imperial Theatre. 678 performances.

Frank Loesser's version of Sidney Howard's play was four years in the making. Loesser was so discouraged at times as to almost give up the project. Luckily, he persevered, and the result was his third Broadway hit in three tries. (The first two were "Where's Charley?" and "Guys and Dolls." Some considered "The Most Happy Fella" closer to opera than to musical comedy. It contained over thirty separate numbers, with dialogue used only for developments that were "not emotional in content, such as exposition." Loesser called the show an "extended musical comedy." Critical comment was highly favorable. Said Brooks Atkinson of the New York *Times:* "[Loesser] told something of vital importance in terms of dramatic music."

"The Most Happy Fella" deals with a mail-order romance between a middle-aged Italian winegrower and a young waitress. The show opens in a run-down San Francisco café, where Tony sees Amy (or, as he calls her, Rosabella) and falls in love with her on sight. Amy tells her friend and fellow worker Cleo that she's lonely ("Somebody, Somewhere"). Tony is too shy to propose to Amy in person, so he begins a correspondence with her. Self-conscious about his looks, he sends her a picture of Joey, the young, handsome foreman of his vineyard, as his own.

When the mailman brings Tony a letter from Amy in which she agrees to come and marry him, he exults as "The Most Happy Fella" in California's Napa Valley. Tony is greatly loved by his workers and neighbors, including a gentle young man named Herman. Herman and his friends tell what they do in their time off. With no money for dates, they gain their enjoyment from "Standing on the Corner" watching the girls go by. Joey is different from the others. He is a good worker but has the wanderlust and after a few years always moves on to a new part of the country ("Joey, Joey, Joey").

When Rosabella arrives, she soon finds out about Tony's deception. She wants to go but is comforted by Joey ("Don't Cry") and has an affair with him. Tony breaks his leg and invites Cleo to come down to keep Amy from being lonely. He's unsure of proper manners and is coached in the way to greet the visitor ("Happy To Make Your Acquaintance"). Cleo and Herman meet and find that they're both from Dallas ("Big D"). As the days pass, Amy begins to realize Tony's essential goodness, and they pledge their love ("My Heart Is So Full of You"). But then she finds that she's carrying Joey's child. When Tony gets the news, he is overwrought, and Amy plans to leave. Joey has meanwhile gone away. Tony accepts the idea of having a new heir, and he and Rosabella are reconciled. Cleo and Herman also decide to marry.

The original cast included Robert Weede, as Tony; Jo Sullivan, as Amy; Susan Johnson, as Cleo; Shorty Long, as Herman; and Art Lund, as Joey. Some other major numbers were "Ooh, My Feet," "Rosabella," "Abbandanza," "Benvenuto," "How Beautiful the Days," "Warm All Over," "Song of a Summer Night," and "I Made a Fist."

MUSIC IN THE AIR: musical. Lyrics and book by Oscar Hammerstein II, music by Jerome Kern. New York opening: November 8, 1932, Alvin Theatre. 342 performances.

Jerome Kern could do no wrong on Broadway in the beginning of the Depression. For three years in a row—1931, 1932, and 1933, he had hit musicals: "The Cat and the Fiddle," "Music in the Air," and "Roberta." "Music in the Air" was a direct stepping stone to the modern era of the musical play. Oscar Hammerstein's book, even more so than Otto Harbach's "Cat and the Fiddle" libretto, thoroughly integrated plot and lyrics. Still, by current standards the book is pretty trite, but the music is among Kern's best. New York *Times* critic Brooks Atkinson declared:

At last the musical drama has been emancipated. . . . Without falling back into the clichés of the trade [Hammerstein] has written sentiment and comedy that are tender and touching.

A week or so later, he added,

. . . Mr. Kern and Mr. Hammerstein have discovered how musical plays, which used to be assembled, can now be written as organic works of art."

The show opens in the small Bavarian mountain village of Edendorf in the singing school of town music teacher Dr. Walter Lessing. He leads the village choir in the chorale "Melodies of May." His daughter Sieglinde is part of the choir and has a pleasant but not great voice. Lessing has written a melody, and village schoolteacher Karl Reder has provided lyrics for it. During the early part of the play, Karl introduces "I've Told Every Little Star," which recurs several times in the play. Reder is Sieglinde's sweetheart. Sieglinde and Karl decide to take a long walk to Munich to try to get the song published. In Munich they meet a musical playwright, Bruno Mahler (who performs his Letter Song, "I'm Coming Home") and a famous and temperamental opera star, Frieda Hartzfeld. Frieda sets her cap for Karl, while Bruno woos Sieglinde by promising to write a new operetta for her talents. The stage-struck Sieglinde leaves Karl. But she finds that she really isn't good enough to be a professional singer, while Frieda soon tires of Karl. Sieglinde and Karl are reunited and go contentedly back to village life to a finale which features the show's theme, "I've Told Every Little Star."

The original cast included Walter Slezak, as Karl; Al Shean, as Dr. Lessing; Katherine Carrington, as Sieglinde; Tullio Carminati, as Bruno; and Natalie Hall, as Frieda. Also in the score were "There's a Hill beyond a Hill," "And Love Was Born," "I'm Alone," "One More Dance," "Night Flies By," "When Spring Is in the Air," "In Egern on the Tegern See," and "The Song Is You." An attempted revival in 1951 failed when most critics found the book badly dated, though the music was hailed as just as fresh as ever.

MUSIC MAN, THE: Lyrics, music, and book by Meredith Willson. New York opening: December 19, 1957, Majestic Theatre. 1,375 performances.

Meredith Willson's warm recollections of his Iowa boyhood re-created an era—the peaceful American-small-town scene in the years before World War I. He did this, however, in tune with the modern theater, and the result was the runaway best musical of the 1957–58 season and certainly a classic of the American musical scene for many years to come.

The setting of the show is River City, Iowa, in 1912. Slick-talking con man "Professor" Harold Hill comes to town. His gimmick is to sell a town the idea of outfitting a band with uniforms and with instruments he will teach them to play. As soon as he would make the sale, he would skip with the money. In River City he finds an old coworker and enlists his aid.

Hill's usual plan is to woo the town's female piano teacher so that she won't have time to point out his lack of musical training. In this case, the teacher is also the town's beautiful librarian, Marian Paroo. The arrival of a new pool table in town gives him his opening. He suggests to the people that a new brass band is the answer to the pool-hall problems ("Seventy-six Trombones"). The townspeople fall for this, but the mayor, who brought in the pool table, and Marian are unimpressed. The mayor orders the four-man school board to get Hill's credentials, but Hill takes their minds off this by forming them into a barbershop quartet.

Hill collects deposits for instruments and uniforms, including some from Marian's mother for Marian's little brother. The brother, Winthrop, is tongue-tied because of the shock of his father's death a few years before. Marian gains proof that Hill never attended his claimed music school. Before she can turn him in, the express wagon brings in the instruments ("Wells Fargo Wagon"). Her brother excitedly starts talking again, and Marian's attitude toward Hill softens. To stall exposure for two weeks until the uniforms come in, Hill tells his band members to think the Minuet in G and soon they will be able to play it.

The denouemont comes on the night of the big summer "sociable." An irate traveling salesman comes to town determined to expose Hill to the mayor and save the sales profession. Meanwhile, Hill's friend is busy collecting the money for the uniforms, which have arrived. After staving off the school board by giving them a new song, "Lida Rose," Hill asks Marian to meet him in lovers' lane during the sociable. As they find that they're in love ("Till There Was You"), Hill's friend warns him that the town is aroused and that he should leave quickly. But Hill, now in love, stays and is dragged to a meeting at the schoolhouse. The town argues what to do with him when the band, in its ill-fitting uniforms, bursts in. Miraculously, they manage to play a recognizable version of Minuet in G, and Hill is saved.

The original cast included Robert Preston, as Professor Hill, in perhaps his greatest performance. Barbara Cook was Marian; Pert Kelton, her mother; Iggie Wolfington, Hill's friend; and Eddie Hodges, Winthrop. Preston also starred in the movie version (1962), with Shirley Jones, as Marian; Pert Kelton, as her mother; and Buddy Hackett, as Hill's friend. The Buffalo Bills quartet was the school board in the stage and screen versions. The score included "Goodnight, My Someone," "Trouble," "Rock Island," "Piano Lesson," "Marian the Librarian," "Shipoopi," "My White Knight," and "Gary, Indiana."

MUSICAL, MUSICAL COMEDY, MUSICAL PLAY: type of theatrical performance, usually light in tone, consisting of musical numbers and dialogue with a definite (though often slender) plot.

The phrase "musical comedy" has been used to describe all the theatrical presentations that fall into the peculiarly American type of musical stage shows. This type of show is distinguished from revues, burlesque, variety, and such in that it has a plot. For most of its history, the word "comedy" was an apt description for the American musical. In recent years, however, the American musical theater has treated of more serious matters. In these shows, the music and lyrics are closely integrated with the story, unlike the rather loose relationship in conventional musical comedy. These newer examples are more aptly described by the phrase "musical play."

The American musical evolved from the earlier European opera and operetta. The operetta diverged from the opera in that, whereas the latter was almost completely sung and was usually tragic in tone, the operetta was generally light, often humorous, with spoken dialogue combined with musical numbers. It was not until after the middle of the nineteenth century that any great interest in the lighter forms of musical drama developed in the United States. It is generally agreed that the first major step towards an American musical theater was "The Black Crook," which opened in New York on September 12, 1866. This was a combination of French romantic ballet and German romantic melodrama. It was a great hit and was often revived over the next forty years.

Now that it had been shown that combined music with dialogue could succeed in this country, there were many productions of various kinds staged for American audiences. Most of these were based on European traditions. There were exceptions, such as "Evangeline" in 1874 and "The Brook" in 1879. ("The Brook" is considered the first full-length musical to approach what was later known as musical comedy. That is, whereas light or comic opera is highly stylized, based on fairy-tale stories with handsome heroes, damsels in distress, etc., the musical comedy is based on everyday life, with songs, dances, and dialogue related to the way people really act and appear.) In the main, however, it was the European operetta that dominated American theater. The Gilbert and Sullivan comic operas and English versions of French opéras bouffes, for instance, were great favorites during the late nineteenth century. Most of the other musical offerings from 1880 to World War I were imports or adaptations of European operettas.

Just past the turn of the century, there were two notable harbingers of change. One was the rise to prominence of the first great American musical showman, George M. Cohan, who turned out a series of topical musicals based on the American scene. The other trend was the development of a made-in-America genre of operettas by such composers as Victor Herbert, Rudolf Friml, and Sigmund Romberg.

In the background, though, were murmurings of a radical departure from operetta to a new type of show based on the American cultural heritage, now quite different from its European antecedents. During World War I, Jerome Kern came to the fore with such shows as "Very Good, Eddie" in 1915 and "Leave It to Jane" in 1917. Very soon there were other names—Gershwin, Porter, Youmans, Rodgers, Hart, and Hammerstein. Though the operetta still had much life in it, its days as a major feature of the current American theater were numbered.

The twenties saw the musical comedy come into vogue, first in the United States and later in other countries. The intimate nature of the plot and the relation of the songs to real life were basically American contributions. The era was exemplified by such shows as "No, No, Nanette," "Oh, Kay!," "The Girl Friend," "Good News," and "Strike Up the Band." In 1927, the first glimmerings of still another shift in musical development appeared. This was Jerome Kern and Oscar Hammerstein's "Show Boat," still a classic and the forerunner of the long series of hit musical plays that reached fruition from the forties on.

The second major turning point towards this goal was Rodgers and Hammerstein's "Oklahoma!" in 1943. By the sixties, the dominating theme of the American musical stage was the musical play or drama. Perhaps the most perfect blending of plot and music in this style up to the mid-sixties was Lerner and Loewe's "My Fair Lady" of 1956.

MUTE: device used to deaden the sound of a musical instrument.

Mutes are used with brass instruments to produce a wide range of sound effects. The original mute was probably not a special accessory but rather the hand of the musician or, perhaps, a hat, which he placed over, then removed from, the bell of the instrument. One of the first specially made mutes was called a "plunger." Several different types of mutes are in use today, including the straight mute, which is a cone with a flat base, and the plunger and "wa-wa" mutes, which have a movable base. Early mutes were made of wood or copper; current types are made of plastic or aluminum.

A song in which the texture is almost completely based on the use of the mute is "Sugar Blues," as played by Clyde McCoy.

MY FAIR LADY: musical. Lyrics and book by Alan Jay Lerner, music by Frederick Loewe. Based on George Bernard Shaw's play "Pygmalion." New York opening: March 15, 1956, Mark Hellinger Theatre. 2,717 performances.

"I absolutely forbid such outrage. If *Pygmalion* is not good enough for your friends with its own verbal music, their talent must be altogether extraordinary. Let them try Mozart's *Cosi fan tutti*, or at least Offenbach's *Grand Duchess*." The words are those of Bernard Shaw (quoted in Stanley Green: "The World of Musical Comedy." New York: Ziff-Davis, 1960) in reply to a friend's suggestion that "Pygmalion" be set to music.

Shaw had once been as adamant on letting his plays be made into movies. Luckily, there were men of equally strong purpose to argue and persuade even Shaw to bend a little. Such a one was Hungarian producer Gabriel Pascal, who had once gained the rights to film Shaw's works, the only man ever to do so. As time went on, Pascal became enthralled with the idea of turning "Pygmalion," which he filmed in the thirties, into a musical. He tried unsuccessfully to get Shaw's approval. Perhaps Pascal's persistence might have won again, but Shaw died in 1950 without having changed his mind.

But Pascal was obsessed with his idea. Without the rights, he started looking for a major Broadway team to do the adaptation. No one would attempt it. Finally, Lerner and Loewe, then somewhat lesser lights on Broadway, agreed to try. Meanwhile, Pascal got a two-year option from Shaw's estate. But even Lerner and Loewe couldn't see how to do the job. They decided to part, and each turned to separate new projects.

A few years later, Lerner and Loewe came together again for one more try at "Pygmalion." This time, all the pieces went together. Said Lerner to a New York *Times* interviewer:

For years Fritz and I floundered around, trying to find our natural way of writing. "My Fair Lady" revealed it to us. The property dictates it, the characters in the story. We are the means by which they express themselves, not vice versa. When we felt we really knew them, then we began to work on the score. We try to find some thought of a character that motivates him and, in turn, the story.

By now, Pascal had died. But Lerner and Loewe, on the basis of the finished script, gained the rights from the Pascal estate. On March 15, 1956, the show opened to a rapturous reception. The critics reported that something momentous had occurred. By December, 1958, about half way through its New York run, the show had grossed ten million dollars, smashing the old record held by "South Pacific." Since its opening, "My Fair Lady" has been shown, month in and month out, somewhere in the world. In 1963, a national touring company played to capacity audiences in major cities throughout the United States.

As the show opens, it is a cold March night in front of the Opera House in Covent Garden, London. Poor street performers and flower sell-

My Fair Lady: The closing scene of the Lerner and Loewe musical version of Shaw's *Pygmalion.* As professor Higgins mourns the loss of his supposed protégée, Eliza, she steals softly back to his arms.

ers are trying to make a few pennies from crowds leaving the opera. Among the flower sellers is the cockney Eliza Doolittle. Wealthy Professor Henry Higgins is taking notes on British dialects. He meets a distinguished fellow language expert, Colonel Pickering, and comments sadly on English usage ("Why Can't the English?"). As he tells Eliza, if she learned to speak properly from him and Pickering, she could move higher in the world, perhaps have her own flower shop. As she and her fellow cockneys later sing, "Wouldn't It Be Loverly?"

Her father, Alfred P. Doolittle, is an amiable ne'er-do-well who lives mostly off Eliza's earnings. He is seen outside a London pub, expounding his carefree beliefs ("With a Little Bit of Luck").

Eliza decides to go to Professor Higgins at his fashionable home and take up his offer. He finally agrees that she can live there while he and Pickering tutor her. At times, though, her slum accents and mannerisms get under Higgins's skin, as he tells Pickering ("I'm an Ordinary Man"). His unbending way of teaching also rubs Eliza the wrong way. She tells herself she'll get even someday ("Just You Wait"). Alfred Doolittle gets wind of Eliza's whereabouts, and he appears, not to ask her return, but to pleasantly request some money from Higgins. Higgins gives him some and, fascinated by Doolittle's odd cockney philosophy, sends him to a friend who runs lecture tours.

The lessons proceed, and Eliza at last achieves correct pronunciation. The event leads to a wildly happy song and dance among Eliza, Higgins, and Pickering ("The Rain in Spain"). Later, unable to fall asleep from the excitement, Eliza tells the housekeeper, "I Could Have Danced All Night."

Higgins takes her to the Ascot races, where Eliza meets Henry's mother and the handsome dilettante Freddy Eynsford-Hill. Attracted to Eliza, Freddy finds out where she lives and spends his days outside trying for a chance meeting ("On the Street Where You Live"). Higgins and Pickering now are set for the crucial test, taking their protégé to the Embassy Ball. Despite a former student of Higgins who is adept at finding frauds, Eliza makes a brilliant debut. Later, back in his study, Higgins's success is toasted by Pickering and the servants ("You Did It"). But Eliza feels left out, for Higgins seems to treat her more as a guinea pig than a girl. She leaves with Freddy, whom she enjoins not just to talk of his love but to "Show Me." She and Freddy go to Soho to visit her father. They find him in fancy clothes for his wedding. Higgins tricked him, he moans, into becoming a rich, successful lecturer who now must marry the woman he's lived with for many years. But he will have one last fling ("Get Me to the Church on Time").

Higgins finds that he can't get along without Eliza and frantically seeks her. She has left Freddy, and he finds her at his mother's. They argue once more, and Higgins heads for home. But, he ruefully notes, "I've Grown Accustomed to Her Face." He goes home to listen to records of her voice. As he listens, Eliza slips softly back into the room.

The original cast included Rex Harrison, as Higgins; Julie Andrews, as Eliza; Robert Coote, as Pickering; Stanley Holloway, as Mr. Doolittle; Michael King, as Freddy; and Margery Maude, as Mrs. Higgins. Other numbers were "Ascot Gavotte," "The Embassy Waltz," "A Hymn to Him," and "Without You." In 1964, the movie version created just as much of a stir as the original stage play. Starred in the film were Rex Harrison and, in the roll of Eliza, Audrey Hepburn.

MY HEART STOOD STILL: song (1927). Words by Lorenz Hart, music by Richard Rodgers.

In January, 1927, Richard Rodgers and Lorenz Hart went to London to see their show "Lido Lady." They had written it the year before, but returned to the United States before it opened. In the meantime, it had premiered and was on the way to being a hit. In London they met English musical producer Charles B. Cochran, who hired them to write the score for a new review, "One Damn Thing after Another." Opening day was May 20. A few weeks before this, Rodgers and Hart took some time off and went to Paris. While on a date with two girls, the taxi they were in missed a collision by a hairbreadth. One of the girls gasped, "My heart stood still!" Hart calmly said, "That would make a nice title for a song." Rodgers extracted a pencil and notebook from his pocket and noted the phrase; then both promptly forgot it.

Back in London, Rodgers worked late one evening while Hart slept. Coming across the Paris note, Rodgers sat down at the piano and wrote a melody for it. When given the music for a lyric, Hart admitted that he'd forgotten the whole taxi scene, which inspired one of the most successful numbers of Rodgers and Hart's long years of collaboration.

The Prince of Wales (who became King Edward VII, then the Duke of Windsor) liked the song. It became the hit of the review, and Rodgers himself taught it to the prince. One night at the Café de Paris in London, Prince Edward asked the band leader to play it. The leader didn't know it, so the Prince sang the whole song until the band picked it up. The resultant publicity made most of London start humming the song.

Rodgers and Hart bought back the song rights from Cochran for five thousand dollars. When they returned to the United States, they decided to spot the song in a new show they were working on. The show was "A Connecticut Yankee," based on Mark Twain's comic novel "A Connecticut Yankee in King Arthur's Court." The show turned out to be one of their most successful, playing four hundred and eighteen performances on Broadway. "My Heart Stood Still" was the most popular song in a sparkling score.

NASHVILLE; NASHVILLE STYLE: the country-and-Western-music capital; a style of country-and-Western music.

Nashville, Tennessee, is one of the three music capitals of the United States, the other two being New York (see *Tin Pan Alley*) and Hollywood. For country-and-Western music, Nashville is *the* capital. Most country-music-publishing firms have home offices in Nashville, and all major publishers and record companies have important, fully staffed divisional offices there. Most country-and-Western artists, as well as a great many rock-'n'-roll or rhythm-and-blues artists (often the same people), make their homes in Nashville.

After World War II, Nashville expanded from a regional music center for country-and-Western to a combined regional and national center. This was due to the rise of rock 'n' roll and associated musical styles, which were at least in part directly related to country-and-Western. As time went on, Nashville became a center for other types of popular music, though still not as important as New York and Hollywood in these areas. (Tennessee was once the center for much of the blues-publishing industry. W. C. Handy, for instance, wrote "St. Louis Blues" in Memphis and published this and other blues in that city.)

Much popular music after World War II came from Nashville and was generally referred to as "Nashville style." Arranger Bob Mersey and guitarist George Barnes describe this in their album on guitar-playing methods:°

> The Nashville rhythms and sounds are the result of musicians getting together in a recording studio and "fooling around." Written music is rarely used and would be of little use because the rhythms are practically impossible to notate and many of the players, though highly skilled, do not read music. The material to be recorded is played over and over again, with various ideas contributed by the players which are tried, discarded or accepted, until finally a desirable result is obtained. These sessions go on all day, every day, in Nashville and produce the greatest amount of records of this type. It is often said in the record business, "If you want the Nashville sound—go to Nashville."

In discussing country-style music, they noted:

> In Nashville, the drummer will often play with "closed brushes" on a battered suitcase while a couple of "round hole" guitars are strummed in the background along with a jew's harp and bass fiddle. In country records, you can note the occasional resemblance to sounds heard in a country barnyard: chickens flapping and squawking, and so on. And not surprisingly, for that is where the music was born.

NATIONAL ACADEMY OF THE RECORDING ARTS AND SCIENCES (NARAS): nonprofit organization of the record industry to foster recognition of creative ability in the field and assist in further development of such ability by grants, membership meetings, etc.

The Academy was founded in 1957 as an outgrowth of a campaign by the Hollywood Chamber of Commerce to improve the Hollywood and Vine area. A Hollywood Beautification Committee was set up to imbed star plaques in the sidewalks of this section of the city. On each star was to be the name of a famous personality in some area of the performing arts, such as movies, television, radio, or records. The committee asked five record-industry executives—Sonny Burke (Decca), Lloyd Dunn (Capitol), Dennis Farnon (RCA Victor), Jesse Kaye (MGM), and Paul Weston (Columbia)—to provide the names of industry artists.

° "George Barnes' Living Guitar Method," copyright, '61, by Pamela Music, Inc.

As Weston told the Los Angeles *Times* in 1963:

Five of us sat around and had to pick people on the basis of sales. There was no other criticism. We wound up with a lot of people who had sold a lot of records, but many great performers were left out. That was when we decided we needed some way to recognize quality.

As a result, the five asked recently retired Columbia Records president Jim Conkling to organize what was to become NARAS. In June, 1957, top industry figures met to appoint a steering committee and nominate governors. Later that year, the Hollywood chapter elected Paul Weston its first president and the New York chapter chose Guy Lombardo.

Today, NARAS membership totals over two thousand, all of whom vote in the Grammy competition. (See *Grammy*.) NARAS rules are that active memberships are open to anyone "making a direct, creative contribution to at least six recorded and released sides or albums."

NELSON, ERIC HILLIARD (RICK): singer, guitarist, actor. Born Teaneck, New Jersey, May 8, 1940.

One of the most successful younger performers of the nineteen-fifties and sixties, Rick Nelson began with a heritage of show-business success. Before beginning the perenially successful "Adventures of Ozzie and Harriet," his parents had long been stars in music. During the big-band era, Ozzie Nelson's orchestra, featuring the vocals of his wife Harriet, was a major attraction at nightclubs and theaters across the nation.

The two Nelson boys literally grew up in the sight of millions on the television version of "Ozzie and Harriet." The show, which began on radio, marked its twentieth consecutive year on the air (twelve of these on TV) in the fall of 1963. Rick made his appearance on the show at the age of eight and soon was accepted by the public as the typical younger brother.

In 1957, Rick blossomed out as a singing star, accompanying himself on the guitar. He rapidly became one of the most admired performers among teen-agers, and by 1963, he had marked up eight gold records. Another release, "String Along," in the spring of 1963 promised to provide a ninth gold record. The eight were "Be-Bop Baby," "My Bucket's Got a Hole in It," "I Got a Feelin'," "Never Be Anyone Else but You," "Sweeter than You," "Stood Up," "Poor Little

Fool," and "Travelin' Man." Nelson began recording for Imperial Records and, in 1963, switched to Decca.

Besides his single records, Nelson also turned out seven straight albums from 1957 to 1963 that became number-one sellers in the country. These were "Ricky," "Ricky Nelson," "Ricky Sings Again," "Songs by Ricky," "More Songs by Ricky," "Rick Is 21," and "Album Seven by Rick."

Through the years, Rick continued to star on his parents' TV show. As his singing career progressed, he became a major attraction at theaters and auditoriums throughout the United States and abroad. He began his film career portraying himself in Universal International's "Here Come the Nelsons." He also appeared with Ethel Barrymore and Leslie Caron in Metro-Goldwyn-Mayer's "Story of Three Loves" and with Jack Lemmon in "The Wackiest Ship in the Army." Rick also played a western role in Warner Brothers' "Rio Bravo."

Besides "String Along," Rick released a number of records of note in 1963. These included the album "For Your Sweet Love" and an extended-play record featuring "I Will Follow You," "One Boy Too Late," "Pick Up the Pieces," and "Let's Talk the Whole Thing Over, Baby."

NERO, PETER: pianist. Born Brooklyn, New York, May 24, 1934.

Peter Nero, born Bernard Nierow, began playing the piano at seven and was called a prodigy by his teachers. By the time he was fourteen, Nero had appeared in symphony concerts, won several contests, and been awarded a scholarship to New York's Juilliard School of Music. Nero concentrated on the classics for three years but maintained a lively interest in popular music and jazz. He studied composition at Brooklyn College and auditioned for the "Arthur Godfrey's Talent Scouts" program with his own arrangement of music from the film "The Brave Bulls."

He did not make the grade this time but, two years later, at nineteen, auditioned again with the same material. This time, he got on the program and later won first prize. Soon after, he performed on "Chance of a Lifetime," "Paul Whiteman's TV Teen Club," and Kathy Godfrey's "On Your Way." Whiteman took Nero on a cross-country tour in which Nero played George Gershwin's "Rhapsody in Blue."

He began appearing as a solo performer at major night spots—the Embers, Village Vanguard, and Blue Angel in New York and the Sands in Las Vegas. His TV appearances on "The Dave Garroway Show," "Revlon Revue," and "Big Party" helped widen his audience. By the sixties, Nero's first album, "Piano Forte" (including a piece of his own called "Scratch my Bach"), had been released and very well received. He followed up with such albums as "New Piano in Town," "Young and Warm and Wonderful," and "For the Nero-Minded."

NEW MOON, THE: operetta. Book and lyrics by Oscar Hammerstein II, Frank Mandel, and Laurence Schwab, music by Sigmund Romberg. New York opening: September 19, 1928, Imperial Theatre. 509 performances.

The score of "The New Moon" is generally agreed to be Sigmund Romberg's greatest. The show did not have quite as long a run as "The Student Prince," but it has stood the test of time far better. Many of "The New Moon's" songs are still popular favorites, and the movie version was highly successful.

"The New Moon" opens in the grand salon of Monsieur Beaunoir's mansion in New Orleans. The year is 1792, and the once French city has been part of the Spanish empire for close to twenty-five years. Beaunoir is a wealthy ship owner. The ship *New Moon*, commanded by Captain Paul Duval, has just arrived from France. On board is famed detective Vicomte Ribaud with secret orders from the French king to seize a Chevalier Robert Misson, a man of noble birth but a revolutionary. Beaunoir has a number of bond servants of French origin, including Robert and Alexander. Robert, who is in love with Beanoir's beautiful daughter Marianne, is really Robert Misson. Alexander is having amours with Marianne's maid Julie and another girl, Clotilde. Julie and the girls joke about his fickleness ("Gorgeous Alexander"). Duval tries to express his love for Marianne, but Robert, as a servant, keeps getting in his way.

The scene shifts to a tavern, where some of the *New Moon's* crew and some of the bond servants gather. Robert is met by his friend Phillipe, who warns him of the dangers of love ("Softly, as in a Morning Sunrise"). Robert and Phillipe urge the sailors to join them in the fight for liberty ("Stouthearted Men"). Robert must gain a kiss from Marianne. He decides to go to a masked ball that night. Marianne discloses to some friends that she too is saving "One Kiss" for the right man. Robert sees her, and they sing of love ("Wanting You"). Then Duval and Ribaud

break in, rip off Robert's mask, and take him away, while Ribaud makes Robert believe that Marianne betrayed him.

On board the *New Moon*, the sailors pledge to sail to Martinique, not France. Marianne gets on board by saying that she loves Duval and must go with him. The sailors sing of woman's treachery ("Funny Little Sailor Men"). Marianne sends a note to Robert ("Lover, Come Back to Me"). Another boat overtakes the *New Moon*. Its crew, with the bond servants and their girls, are under Phillipe. Robert and the crew take over the *New Moon*. They sail to a small island, building a stockade and proclaiming a government based on equality for all. A year passes. Marianne has been against the mutiny. Robert finally agrees to let her go, but she finds that she loves him too much. Ribaud plots revenge, and his hopes rise as two French ships are sighted. The admiral, DeJean, however, informs them of the revolution at home, praises Misson's enterprise, and takes Ribaud back to face the guillotine.

The original cast included Robert Halliday, as Robert; Evelyn Herbert, as Marianne; William O'Neal, as Phillipe; Max Figman, as Ribaud; and Edward Nell, Jr., as Duval. Other songs were "The Girl on the Prow," "Interrupted Trio," "The Trial," "Try Her Out at Dances," "Love Is Quite a Simple Thing," and "Never for You."

NIGHT AND DAY: song (1932). Words and music by Cole Porter.

Cole Porter spent many years abroad traveling or at his various homes in Europe. During a trip to Morocco, he heard a Mohammedan muezzin chanting the weird "Allah-Il-Allah" used to call the faithful to worship. This was the inspiration for "Night and Day," Porter reports in "Men and Melodies," by Leonard A. Paris (New York: Thomas Y. Crowell, 1954).

The song was written for the musical comedy "The Gay Divorce," which premiered in New York on November 29, 1932, and ran for two hundred and forty-eight performances. Making his first solo appearance in musical comedy in this show was Fred Astaire. (His former partner, his sister Adele, had just retired.) Astaire introduced "Night and Day," perhaps Porter's best-known all-time standard.

In "Musical Comedy in America" (New York: Theatre Arts Books, 1950), Cecil Smith says:

... many consider [it] if not the best, at least the archetypal, example of Porter's gift for extending a long-lined, dusky melody far beyond the usual confines of the standard thirty-two-bar structure. Porter showed the expertness and individuality of his musical style in its bitter-sweet harmonies and well prepared climax, and his impatience with convention in . . . the text. . . .

In 1946, the song became the title of the screen biography of Cole Porter, starring Cary Grant.

NO, NO, NANETTE: musical. Lyrics by Irving Caesar and Otto Harbach, music by Vincent Youmans, book by Harbach and Frank Mandel. New York opening: September 16, 1925, Globe Theatre. 321 performances.

This more or less stock musical comedy of the twenties was tried out in Detroit in 1924 to such a cool audience reception that producer H. H. Frazee called for complete overhaul. Not only did Harbach and Mandel rewrite the script but a new lyricist, Irving Caesar, was called in to work with Vincent Youmans. Five of the original songs were thrown out and four new ones added. Of these new ones were two that changed it from a routine show to a truly memorable one. The songs, to which Caesar wrote the words, were "I Want To Be Happy" and "Tea for Two."

The rewritten show was so well liked on the road that it stayed a year in Chicago before being brought to New York. Eventually, some seventeen touring companies brought "No, No, Nanette" before audiences in Europe, China, South America, New Zealand, and the Philippines. In London alone, the show rang up six hundred and sixty-five performances.

The curtain rises on the reception room in the home of Jimmy Smith, a wealthy publisher of Bibles. The twenties feeling is quickly established by the young people calling on Smith's ward Nanette. As they sing, they are "flippant and fly and free," going on "petting parties with the smarties." Smith, who is married to a domineering wife, has an eye for sweet young things. He is soon embroiled with the problems of three of them, Betty from Boston, Flora from Frisco, and Winnie from Washington. The plot winds around Mrs. Smith eventually becoming suspicious of her husband (with some mistaken identity thrown in). Jimmy seems headed for trouble, but he is saved by the machinations of a lawyer friend, Billy Early.

The original cast starred Louise Groody, as Nanette, and Charles Winninger, as Jimmy. These two introduced "I Want To Be Happy."

Others in the cast were Wellington Cross, as Billy Early; Beatrice Lee, as Betty; Edna Whistler, as Flora; and Mary Lawlor, as Winnie. The score included the title song, "Too Many Rings around Rosie," and "You Can Dance with Any Girl at All."

NO STRINGS: musical. Lyrics and music by Richard Rodgers, book by Samuel Taylor. New York opening: March 15, 1962, Fifty-fourth Street Theatre. 580 performances.

In 1960, after the death of Oscar Hammerstein II, many wondered where Richard Rodgers could turn after years of collaboration with such unparalleled lyrical geniuses as Hammerstein and Lorenz Hart. The answer came when Rodgers wrote both lyrics and music for "No Strings." Critics agreed that if Rodgers's words to such songs as "The Sweetest Sounds" and "La La La" did not have the perfection of his former partners' work, they showed far more ability than those of most professional lyricists.

The show received mixed notices. The music and lyrics were generally praised, but there were reservations about Samuel Taylor's book. Howard Taubman of the New York *Times* said:

> Richard Rodgers is . . . still a magician of the musical theatre. . . . he has dipped into the freshest sources of his lyric gift. . . . he has composed a score full of romance and vivacity. . . . Taylor's book is at best a fragile sentimental fable . . . but styled in gay, inventive stage garb it has been wafted into a shimmering and delightful never-never land.

Robert Coleman of the New York *Daily Mirror* said:

> . . . it pioneers new paths in musical comedy. . . . It has a libretto that's on the dull side. But it also has some of Dick Rodgers' best tunes.

The plot dealt with a Parisian romance between a Negro high-fashion model and a white novelist from New England. One of the show's unique features was the coupling of specific musical instruments to each main character. There was no pit orchestra; all music was supplied on stage. There were no strings in the orchestra, which was partly responsible for the show's title. The play opens with the sound of a flute. The model, Barbara Woodruff, appears and sings "The Sweetest Sounds" as she walks to-

No Strings: Diahann Carroll (l.) played the feminine lead in Samuel Taylor's story of an ill-starred romance in Paris. Miss Carroll portrayed an American high fashion model, here about to be photographed by Luc Delbert (Alvin Epstein) and his assistant, Jeanette (Noelle Adam).

wards the flutist seated on the stage edge. A clarinet signals the appearance of Pulitzer Prize-winner David Jordan. (The two have not yet met.) Jordan won the honor eight years before, but the easy life of sponging off rich American tourists in Europe has stifled his writing. Barbara and David meet at the studio of photographer Luc Delbert. Present for the picture session are Delbert's assistant Jeanette Valery and *Vogue* editor Mollie Plummer. Barbara and David fall in love and wander off through the streets of Paris ("Loads of Love"). The scene switches to the entrance of rich middle-aged Frenchman Louis De Pourtal, who hopes to buy Barbara's love with fabulous presents. Accompanied by an oboe, he sings "The Man Who Has Everything." Barbara and David pursue their love through the sights and sounds of France, a country which proves, as Mollie and madcap oil heiress Comfort O'Conner sing, that "Love Makes the World Go."

As they draw closer together, Barbara tries to get David interested in writing again. They go off for inspiration to the Riviera, where David recalls his home ("Maine"). But the gay life of Europe provides too many temptations exemplified by the raucous jazz nightclub scene ("Eager Beaver"). They finally realize that David must go back to Maine if he is to write. But with the color bar this means separation. Barbara sends him off, and they part with "No Strings" attached.

The original cast included Diahann Carroll, as Barbara; Richard Kiley, as David; Noelle Adam, as Jeanette; Alvin Epstein, as Luc; Polly Rowles, as Mollie; Mitchell Gregg, as Louis De Pourtal; and Bernice Massi, as Comfort O'Connell.

OF THEE I SING: musical. Lyrics by Ira Gershwin, music by George Gershwin, book by Morrie Ryskind and George S. Kaufman. New York opening: December 26, 1931, Music Box Theatre. 441 performances.

In the depths of the Depression, "Of Thee I Sing" mercilessly lampooned all the sacred cows of the American political system. It brightened a

[170]

dark period, and it also threw light on some of the things in the political life of those times that needed improvement. The show's opening was the cause for general rejoicing by the critics. This judgment was borne out by the subsequent award of the 1932 Pulitzer Prize for Drama to the show.

The play opens with the campaign for President of John P. Wintergreen, a fast-talking, unethical man ("Wintergreen for President"). His running mate is a sad-faced, meek nonentity, Alexander P. Throttlebottom. The stage directions for the opening read, in part:

> The marchers, with their torchlights and banners, move against a shadowy background of skyscrapers, churches, and—almost certainly—speakeasies. . . . [Huge banners proclaim] "FOR PRESIDENT: JOHN P. WINTERGREEN." The name of the vice-presidential candidate, however, is lost in shadow. As for the countenances of the candidates, it is a little hard to pick them out in the general blur, and the chances are that that's a break for the party.

The campaign is based on love. The scene shifts to Atlantic City, where a beauty contest is being held to select a bride for the President-to-be. Diana Devereaux, who is the eventual winner, and the girls sing "Who Is the Lucky Girl to Be?" "Love Is Sweeping the Country" proves true, and Wintergreen is elected. But he wants not Diana but his secretary, plain Mary Turner, who "can really make corn muffins." Diana threatens to sue for breach of promise. Act I closes with "Of Thee I Sing" sung by Mary and the chorus as the Supreme Court marches in to swear in the President.

Once elected, Wintergreen has to cope with very serious affairs of state, mainly caused by Diana. The French ambassador has taken up her cause, creating an international incident, because he has found that Diana is "an illegitimate daughter of an illegitimate son of an illegitimate nephew of Napoleon." Wintergreen is urged to leave Mary, now his wife, or resign. When he refuses, the Senate meets to impeach him. But the day is saved when Mary enters and cries, "Stop! My husband is in a delicate condition. He is about to become a father!" As Throttlebottom notes, no expectant President has ever been impeached, and the Senate drops the charges. Mary then gives birth to twins, posing the knotty problem for the Supreme Court of

determining the children's sex, which they achieve on a strict party vote.

The score included "Posterity Is Just around the Corner," "Trumpeter, Blow Your Horn," "I'm About To Be a Mother," and "Who Cares?" The original cast included William Gaxton, as Wintergreen; his long-time teammate Victor Moore, as Throttlebottom; Lois Moran, as Mary; and Grace Brinkley, as Diana.

The Pulitzer Prize won by "Of Thee I Sing" was the first ever given a musical comedy, but, as the citation stated:

> This award may seem unusual, but the play is unusual. . . . Its effect on the stage promises to be considerable, because musical plays are always popular and by injecting satire and point into them, a very large public is reached.

OH, KAY!: musical. Lyrics by Ira Gershwin, music by George Gershwin, book by Guy Bolton and P. G. Wodehouse. New York opening: November 8, 1926, Imperial Theatre. 256 performances.

"Oh, Kay!," which contained one of George Gershwin's most brilliant scores, moved him unquestionably into the front rank of popular composers. Most of the songs he wrote for it are still highly popular. The original cast of "Oh, Kay!" also included Gertrude Lawrence in her first musical-comedy role on Broadway.

The show opens at the Long Island estate of playboy Jimmy Winter. A group of pretty girls informs the audience that Jimmy, who loves attractive young things, is returning from a trip, and all are looking forward to a gay party ("The Woman's Touch"). It soon turns out that someone else had been using the house during Jimmy's absence. A titled Englishman, helped by his sister Kay, has become a bootlegger to try to repair his family's finances. Assisting them is a wistful American rumrunner, Shorty McGee. They've been using the Winter estate as a cache for the booze.

Jimmy returns and toasts all his many loves ("Dear Little Girl"). His love life is tangled indeed. On a bet, he married an already married woman. He is also engaged to the daughter of a judge. And when Kay arrives, he recognizes her as a girl who saved him from drowning in Long Island Sound. In gratitude, he proposes to her as well. Shorty and Kay move in on Jimmy to keep an eye on the liquor. Shorty poses as the Winters' butler. Kay poses at times as Winter's wife, and at other times as Shorty's. Into all this comes a revenue agent trying to catch the bootlegging mob. Jimmy helps Kay outwit the agent and also finds that he's in love with her, as developed in such duets as "Maybe," "Bride and Groom," and "Do, Do, Do."

The original cast included Gertrude Lawrence, as Kay; Oscar Shaw, as Jimmy; Victor Moore, as Shorty McGee; and Gerald Oliver Smith, as Kay's brother the duke. Other songs were the title song, "Someone To Watch over Me," "Don't Ask," "Clap Yo' Hands," "Fidgety Feet," and "Heaven on Earth" (in which Howard Dietz collaborated with Ira Gershwin on the words).

OH, WHAT A BEAUTIFUL MORNIN': song (1943). Words by Oscar Hammerstein II, music by Richard Rodgers.

"Oklahoma!" was more than a milestone in American musical history; it was a revolution. It was not a musical comedy or a play with music added; it was a completely integrated whole, a musical play in which every line of the lyrics was intended to advance the action of the play. Rodgers and Hammerstein collaborated in a much different way from Rodgers and Hart. Rodgers had almost always written the music first and then Hart the words. But now the words almost always came first.

In the preface to his book "Lyrics" (New York: Simon and Schuster, 1949), Oscar Hammerstein II has described how this worked out for several of the song hits of "Oklahoma!" Here is his description of the composition of "Oh, What a Beautiful Mornin'."

Searching for a subject for Curly to sing about (in the opening scene), I recalled how deeply I had been impressed by Lynn Riggs' description at the start of his play. "It is a radiant summer morning several years ago, the kind of morning which, enveloping the shapes of earth—men, cattle in the meadow, blades of the young corn, streams—makes them seem to exist now for the first time, their images giving off a visible golden emanation that is partly true and partly a trick of the imagination, focusing to keep alive a loveliness that may pass away."

On first reading these words, I had thought what a pity it was to waste them on stage directions. Only readers could enjoy them. An audience would never hear them. Yet, if they did, how quickly they would slip into the mood of the story. Remembering this reaction, I reread the description and determined to put it into song. "Oh, What A Beautiful Mornin'" opens the play and creates an atmosphere of relaxation and tenderness. It introduces the lighthearted young man who is the center of the story. My indebtedness to Mr. Riggs' description is obvious. The cattle and the corn and the golden haze on the meadow are all there. I added some observations of my own based on my experience with beautiful mornings, and I brought the words down to the more primitive level of Curly's character. He is, after all, just a cowboy, not a playwright.

"The corn is as high as an elephant's eye" —I first wrote "cow pony's eye." Then I walked over to my neighbor's cornfield and found that, although it was only the end of August, the corn had grown much higher than that. "Cow pony" was more indigenous to the western background, but I had reservations about it even before I gauged the height of the corn. It reads better than it sounds.

"All the cattle are standin' like statues." This picture had come into my brain several years before I wrote the song, and it had stayed there quietly waiting to be used. When I came to the second verse of "Oh, What a Beautiful Mornin'," I remembered.

The writing of this lyric, Hammerstein notes, took three weeks. This kind of writing and refining is more in the order of playwrighting or story writing than the usual lyric writing. After he completed the lyric, Hammerstein conveyed it to Rodgers's home in Connecticut. Rodgers wrote the music in under ten minutes, he has said, for "When you're given words like 'the corn is as high as an elephant's eye,' you get something to say musically."

OKLAHOMA!: musical. Lyrics and book by Oscar Hammerstein II, music by Richard Rodgers. Adapted from Lynn Riggs's play "Green Grow the Lilacs." New York opening: March 31, 1943, St. James Theatre. 2,248 performances.

The evening of March 31, 1943, was a momentous occasion in the American musical theater. The musical came of age, providing the world with a uniquely American art form. "Oklahoma!'s" New York premiere was more than that of a hit musical; it was a landmark, sharply dividing the history of the musical theater. Before this, American librettists, lyricists, and composers knew that they were groping toward something new. They were aware that the revue and the operetta were outmoded, but it was not until Rodgers and Hammerstein made the breakthrough with "Oklahoma!" that their fellow craftsmen could see plainly what the goal had been. From then on, one great musical play after another graced the Broadway stage: "Carousel," "Guys and Dolls," "South Pacific," "Paint Your Wagon," "The King and I," and "My Fair Lady." The groundwork had been laid for an American musical repertoire theater that could rival the grandest periods of opera.

The work that went into the book and music— the careful polishing and matching of every word of lyrics to every note and every song to every action of Oscar Hammerstein's book—is evident. (See *Oh, What a Beautiful Mornin'*.) Rodgers had lost one great partner in Lorenz Hart and amazingly replaced him with a coworker as great —or greater. Strangely, too, just as "Oklahoma!" represented a complete break with the past, so did Rodgers in his collaboration with Hammerstein seem like a completely different composer from the Rodgers of "By Jupiter" and before.

The show opened its tryout run at New Haven's Shubert Theatre on March 11, 1943, under the title "Away We Go." On March 15, it started another short run at the Colonial Theatre in Boston. The enthusiasm of the Boston audiences for the song "Oklahoma" caused the title to be changed before the New York opening. The show ran for more than five years on Broadway before closing on May 29, 1948. The New York cast toured the country for fifty-one more weeks, and other nationwide road companies played the show until May 2, 1953.

"Oklahoma!" takes place in the Oklahoma Territory in the years just before Oklahoma became a state. The still reigning cowboy is slowly giving way to the fences and plows of the farmer. The play opens with Curly, a young cowboy, coming to visit the farm owned by his girl Laurey and her aunt Eller. As he approaches, he sings gaily, "Oh, What a Beautiful Mornin'." He wants to ask Laurey to go with him to the box social that night ("The Surrey with the Fringe on Top"). But they quarrel, and Laurey says that she'll go with Jud Fry, the farm handy man. She soon has second thoughts, though, for Jud is a gruff, burly, and very odd man.

Laurey's friend Ado Annie arrives with an itinerant peddler, Ali Hakim. Annie is engaged to cowboy Will Parker, who is away on a trip to Kansas City, but, she sings, "I Caint Say No." Will is supposed to return with fifty dollars, for Annie's father says that Will can marry her if he has that sum. But Will has splurged on presents, and Annie's father uses a shotgun to persuade Ali Hakim to marry her instead. Curly goes away and returns soon after with the crowd of girls and boys on their way to the social. They all have been asked by Aunt Eller to freshen up at the farm before going on. Laurey jealously observes that another girl, Gertie, is setting her cap for Curly. Still, when Curly tries to get her to change her mind and go with him, she turns him away ("People Will Say We're in Love"). Curly angrily goes off to visit the hovel where Jud lives and sings a mock funeral song, "Pore Jud." Laurey wanders off to a grove and dreams. (The dream is shown in the form of a ballet, one of several striking ones by Agnes de Mille.) In her dream, Curly and Jud fight over her, and she gives herself to Jud to save Curly.

At the party, the group sings "The Farmer and the Cowman." Ali Hakim manages to see that Will gains fifty dollars so that Will can take Annie off his hands. Attention centers on the box-lunch auction, run by Aunt Eller. When Laurey's basket comes up for bids, a hot contest ensues between Curly and Jud, with Curly finally winning by selling all his cowboy gear, including his horse. Jud swears revenge. Now Will gets Annie to set the date, as does Curly with Laurey. Curly vows he'll run the farm.

The scene shifts to Laurey and Curly's wedding night. While waiting to do a shivaree (a form of frontier hazing), the wedding guests sing the praises of "Oklahoma." Jud bursts in on the party and tries to knife Curly. In the fight, Jud falls on his own knife and is killed. In a rump court, Curly is adjudged to have acted in self-defense, and he and Laurey go off on their honeymoon.

The original cast included Alfred Drake, as Curly; Joan Roberts, as Laurey; Betty Garde, as Aunt Eller; Celeste Holm, as Ado Annie; Howard da Silva, as Jud; Lee Dixon, as Will Parker; and Joseph Buloff, as Ali Hakim. The film version, which premiered in New York on October 13, 1955, had Gordon MacRae, as Curly; Shirley Jones, as Laurey; Charlotte Greenwood, as Aunt Eller; Gloria Grahame, as Ado Annie; Eddie Albert, as Ali Hakim; and Rod Steiger, as Jud. Other songs were "Kansas City," "Many a New

[173]

Day," "It's a Scandal! It's a Outrage!," "Lonely Room," "Out of My Dreams," and "All er Nothin'."

OLIVER! musical. Lyrics, music, and book by Lionel Bart. Based on Charles Dickens's novel "Oliver Twist." New York opening: January 6, 1963, Imperial Theatre.

This great musical was a turnabout in many ways for the musical theater. From World War I on, the musical theater was dominated by the new type of show developed in America. In "Oliver!" there finally was a fresh, vital show devised by a highly talented Englishman, Lionel Bart, that began in London (June 30, 1960) and crossed the Atlantic to make its mark in the United States. To carry the reversal one step further, the show premiered not on Broadway but in Los Angeles (August 6, 1962). By 1964, "Oliver!" was still a hit in London and had already finished the first year of a successful run on Broadway.

Freely adapted from the Dickens classic (the main criticism was it was much less grim than the original), the show opens in the boys' home, where Oliver and the other young unfortunates wait for "Food." Oliver makes the mistake of asking wicked Mr. Bumble, the parish beadle, and Widow Corney, who runs the workhouse, for more. Instantly Bumble, Mrs. Corney, and the other boys ridicule him ("Oliver"). After making passes at the widow (who coyly sings "I Shall Scream"), Bumble takes Oliver out and sells him to an undertaking firm. Alone among the coffins, Oliver wonders, "Where Is Love?"

He runs away and, in the streets of London, meets a group of boy pickpockets. They like him ("Consider Yourself at Home") and take him to Fagin, their mentor. Fagin runs a school for thieves ("You've Got To Pick a Pocket or Two"). The brutish criminal Bill Sikes and his girl friend Nancy are close friends of Fagin's. Nancy tells Oliver and the boys, "It's a Fine Life." Fagin sends Oliver out with the Artful Dodger and the rest of the boys to pick pockets, but Oliver is caught.

At a London tavern, where Nancy is entertaining with "Oom-Pah-Pah," word comes to Sikes and Fagin of Oliver's fall. Afraid that Oliver will squeal to the police, they send Nancy to bring him back. Oliver, though, has found a friend, a rich old gentleman. In fine clothes and in a pleasant house, Oliver hopes that his luck will hold ("Who Will Buy?"). But soon Nancy finds him and drags him back to Fagin, who had

thought for a moment of earning an honest living ("Reviewing the Situation") but quickly discarded the idea.

Finding out about Oliver's luck, Bumble and the widow, whom he has since married, try to take him away and get his money. Their scheme is thwarted, but Nancy feels sorry for Oliver and frees him. For her pains, she is brutally murdered by Sikes, who, in turn, is shot as he tries to recapture Oliver. The boys leave too, and Fagin is left alone and penniless.

The Los Angeles cast included Bruce Prochnik (replaced in New York by Paul O'Keefe), as Oliver; Georgia Brown (from the original London cast), as Nancy; Clive Revill, as Fagin; Danny Sewell, as Sikes; Willoughby Goddard, as Bumble; and Hope Jackman, as Mrs. Corney. Other songs were "Boy for Sale," "Be Back Soon," "My Name," "As Long as He Needs Me," and "I'd Do Anything."

OL' MAN RIVER: song (1927). Words by Oscar Hammerstein II, music by Jerome Kern.

When producer Florenz Ziegfeld delayed the opening of "Show Boat" for almost a year, it seemed like a major blow to the composer and lyricist. It turned out to be a stroke of good fortune. Kern and Hammerstein kept examining the show to see if it could be improved. Originally, the score had no "Ol' Man River." But then Hammerstein decided it would be a good idea to include a song giving the feel of the great Mississippi, the river on which the showboat *Cotton Blossom* operated. Kern agreed, and they wrote "Ol' Man River." Said Hammerstein, "It is a song of resignation with a protest implied, sung by a character who is a rugged and untutored philosopher." More than that, it became the hub around which the whole show turned.

When the song was completed, Kern played it for Edna Ferber, author of the novel on which the musical was based. As she recalls in her autobiography "Peculiar Treasure" (New York: Doubleday, Doran, 1939):

As the writing of the musical play proceeded ... I heard bits and pieces of the score. Once or twice everything was seemingly abandoned because Ziegfeld said he couldn't produce the play. Almost a year went by. I had heard Can't Help Lovin' Dat Man ... had melted under the bewitching strains of Make Believe and Why Do I Love You? ... And then Jerome Kern appeared at my apartment late one afternoon with a strange

Oliver!: Fagin fondly supervises the students of his school for pickpockets in the 1963 musical adaptation of Dicken's *Oliver Twist*.

look of quiet exultation in his eyes. He sat down at the piano. He doesn't play the piano particularly well and his singing voice, though true, is negligible. He played and sang Ol' Man River. The music mounted, mounted, and I give you my word my hair stood on end, the tears came to my eyes, I breathed like a heroine in a melodrama. This was great music. This was music that would outlast Jerome Kern's day and mine. I have never heard it since without that emotional surge.

ON THE ATCHISON, TOPEKA AND THE SANTA FE: song (1945). Words by Johnny Mercer, music by Harry Warren.

This song provided composer Harry Warren with his third Academy Award with as many partners. The first was with Al Dubin, the second with Mack Gordon, and, in 1946, the third with Johnny Mercer. The song was one of fourteen written for Judy Garland to sing in "The Harvey Girls." "Usually, when you write a score for a picture," Warren says, "you like to latch onto the title. Johnny and I couldn't figure out anything worthwhile to go with 'Harvey Girls.' But we examined the script and noticed it opened with the girls coming out west on the train. We decided to write a railroad song."

Mercer provided the title, Warren wrote the tune, and Mercer then completed the lyrics. The title came to Mercer as he was taking a trip on the Union Pacific. A freight train passed by with Santa Fe markings, and the rhythmic sound of the wheels seemed to say "Atchison, Topeka, and Santa Fe" over and over.

"The most important part of a song," says Warren, "is how it's launched. In this instance, we had two important records. One was done by Johnny Mercer himself for Capitol Records; the other was Bing Crosby's."

Warren placed the second record himself. Normally he left the task of getting his songs recorded to his publisher's song pluggers. However, Dave Kapp, then with Decca and later founder of Kapp Records, was a good friend of Warren's. "When he came to the Coast, he always visited my house. This trip, he asked if I had anything new. I played 'Atchison, Topeka,' and he loved it and wanted to show it to Bing. 'But you can't do anything with it until the picture is released,' I reminded him. Kapp said he'd do it anyway and wait. He waited six months, but Crosby's record still was a best seller for Decca."

ON YOUR TOES: musical. Lyrics by Lorenz Hart, music by Richard Rodgers, book by Rodgers, Hart, and George Abbott. New York opening: April 11, 1936, Imperial Theatre. 315 performances.

Rodgers and Hart's spoof on ballet was one of the bright spots of the 1936 theater season. The show included two ballet sequences by George Balanchine. One was a ballet satire, "Princesse Zenobia"; the other, "Slaughter on Tenth Avenue," was performed to Rodgers's most memorable instrumental music. The critics were highly complimentary. Said Robert Coleman in the New York *Daily Mirror*, ". . . . one of the seven wonders of 1936. . . . It's great!"

The score retained its freshness over the years. As for the rest of the show, Brooks Atkinson's comments in the *Times* on the 1954 revival were: "Eighteen years is a trifle old for 'On Your Toes.' Most of us had mercifully forgotten that it also had a book. . . ."

The hero is Phil Dolan III, who with his parents forms the vaudeville team of the Three Dolans ("Two a Day for Keith"). His parents want more for him than hoofing, and he leaves to become a classical-music teacher ("The Three B's"). One of his students, a girl named Frankie Frayne, shows him a jazz ballet called "Slaughter on Tenth Avenue." Phil tries to interest famous ballerina Vera Barnova in getting her Russian ballet troupe to perform it. Ballet master Sergei Alexandrovitch is not overly impressed with the ballet or Phil's attempts to be a ballet dancer.

Phil's love life becomes a triangle. On the one hand is Frankie (with whom he sings "There's a Small Hotel"). On the other is seductive Vera. As Vera comes to love Phil, she agrees to help him try to get the ballet performed. The company has not been doing well, and its backer, Peggy Porterfield, is thinking of withdrawing her support. The jazz ballet is accepted as a last resort. Vera's partner, however, finds the style of the new ballet too difficult. In the nick of time, Phil draws on his vaudeville background to take over the part. The show reaches a climax with the great success of "Slaughter on Tenth Avenue." In the ballet, a vaudeville hoofer and his girl are being pursued by gangsters. They are trapped in a Tenth Avenue café. The girl is killed, but the hoofer is saved by the arrival of the police. The show closes with Phil deciding that his true love is Frankie, not Vera.

The original cast included Ray Bolger, as Phil; Doris Carson, as Frankie; Tamara Geva, as Vera; Luella Gear, as Peggy; and Monty Woolley, as

Sergei. Other songs were "It's Got To Be Love," "Too Good for the Average Man," "The Heart Is Quicker than the Eye," "Quiet Night," "On Your Toes," and "Glad To Be Unhappy." In Warner Brothers' 1939 movie, Eddie Albert played Phil and Vera Zorina was Vera. The 1954 revival opened on October 11 at the Forty-sixth Street Theatre and ran for sixty-four performances. The plot was somewhat revised. In the cast were Bobby Van, as Junior (the hero); Vera Zorina, as Vera; Kay Coulter, as Frankie; Elaine Stritch, as Peggy; and Ben Astar, as Sergei.

110 IN THE SHADE: musical. Lyrics by Tom Jones, music by Harvey Schmidt, book by N. Richard Nash. Based on Nash's play "The Rainmaker." New York opening: October 24, 1963, Broadhurst Theatre. Ran 331 performances.

This ingratiating though uneven musical chalked up another hit in the amazing career of producer David Merrick. His successful Broadway productions in the musical field alone include such shows as "Oliver!," "Carnival!," "Irma la Douce," "Take Me Along," "Gypsy," "Jamaica," and "Fanny." Many of these introduced new writing talent to Broadway, and this was true of "110 in the Shade." The score was provided by the young team of Tom Jones and Harvey Schmidt, who had written the off-Broadway phenomenon "The Fantasticks."

The show's locale is a small Western farm town early in this century. The town is in the grip of a murderous drought, as Sheriff File and the townspeople relate in "Gonna Be Another Hot Day." At the railroad station, the Curry family—father H. C. and his sons Noah and Jim—is waiting for the boys' sister Lizzie ("Lizzie's Comin' Home"). They hope the inhibited, shy Lizzie has found a husband on her trip. She arrives to tell them their plans failed. The brothers get a new idea. Perhaps the bachelor sheriff can be snared if he samples Lizzie's food at the forthcoming annual picnic. Lizzie, who longs for marriage, sings her hopes ("Love, Don't Turn Away"). The Currys invite File to the affair ("Poker Polka"), but File isn't in the mood to go.

At the park, the women are busy preparing food ("Hungry Men"). In the middle of the festivities, a dark, handsome stranger named Starbuck appears and announces that he's a rainmaker ("Rain Song"). For a hundred dollars he'll break the drought, he tells the farmers. Lizzie, already hurt by File's failure to appear, takes out some of her resentment on Starbuck. Find-

ing him alone, she calls him a fake. Starbuck responds by telling her she's too scared to be a woman. Later, comforted by her father, she imagines herself a woman of the world ("Raunchy").

Unexpectedly, File comes to the picnic. He tells Lizzie he isn't really a bachelor but a divorced man. She unconvincingly tries to make it seem that this would not bother her, and File stalks away. Now even Noah tells her she'll never marry; for a plain girl, she's too choosy. Sadly she contemplates her life as an "Old Maid." That night, as the townspeople dance and relax at the picnic pavilion, Lizzie seeks out Starbuck in his rainmaker's wagon. He tells her to live a dream and change her name to "Melisande." But she does not want a wild, adventurous life ("Simple Little Things"). Starbuck and Lizzie embrace, and she wonders, "Is It Really Me?" Admitting he is a fraud, he tells Lizzie that if she'll have him, he'll marry and settle down. File breaks in with a warrant for Starbuck's arrest. Lizzie talks him into letting Starbuck go, and Starbuck begs her to go with him. File realizes that he too loves Lizzie. Both men now bid for her hand, and each promises that life with him would be "Wonderful Music." Lizzie chooses File, and then, miraculously, Starbuck's attempts do bring rain to break the drought.

The original cast included Inga Swenson, as Lizzie; Robert Horton, as Starbuck; Stephen Douglass, as File; Scooter Teague, as Jim; Steve Roland, as Noah; and Will Geer, as H. C. The score includes "You're Not Foolin' Me," "A Man and a Woman," "Everything Beautiful Happens at Night," and "Little Red Hat."

ONE O'CLOCK JUMP: instrumental (1937). Music by Count Basie and Otho Lee Gaines.

A popular favorite of the swing era and still a jazz classic, "One O'Clock Jump" was composed by Count Basie in 1937. As with so many jazz instrumentals, it can be said more to have happened than to have been composed. Basie could compose a song or could strike an interesting passage on the piano and work it up into a full-scale number.

English critic Raymond Horricks, discussing the band of the thirties in his book "Count Basie and His Band" (London: Victor Gollancz, 1957), talks about this:

trombonist Eddie Durham had contributed several arrangements of a more complex nature, yet the blues riff remained the stock

[177]

item of material, the greatest source of inspiration for soloists and for the ensemble. Harry Edison's "Jive at Five," Earl Warren's "Rocking the Blues" and Basie's own . . . "One O'Clock Jump" are typical examples of where slight melodic phrases occurring in the course of solos by these men were picked up by the entire band and moulded immediately into riff tunes.

Basie came up with an interesting bit of melody and with his band composed the song. When a band member contributed a substantial part of the new rendition, that member usually was put down as cocomposer. Otho Lee Gaines's name appears on "One O'Clock Jump" along with Basie's.

OPERETTA: musical play in the general form of an opera, but lighter in tone and with spoken dialogue.

An operetta is a play set to music, with much of the action carried forward by songs. The operetta uses spoken dialogue, whereas in opera all dialogue is set to music. Operetta music is generally lighter, and the plot usually is a romance or comedy with a happy ending, rather than the drama and tragedy of most opera.

Operetta originated in Europe and is particularly connected with the Viennese musical theater and the French *opéra bouffe*. Typical works of the former school are the operettas of Johann Strauss, such as "Die Fledermaus," or those of Franz Lehár, such as "Gypsy Love" and "The Merry Widow." The French theater gave birth to such works as Offenbach's "Tales of Hoffmann" and "Orpheus in the Underworld." Operetta dominated American musical theater for many years. Pillars of American operetta were such composers as Rudolf Friml ("The Firefly"), Karl Hoschna ("Madame Sherry," "Wall Street Girl"), Sigmund Romberg ("Maytime," "Blossom Time," "The Student Prince," etc.), and Victor Herbert ("Babes in Toyland," "The Red Mill," "Naughty Marietta," etc.). By the twenties, the traditional operetta had given way in the United States to the peculiarly American form of musical known as "musical comedy."

The dividing line between operetta and musical comedy is hard to define. For a time, it could be said that operettas were whimsical plays set to music, whereas musical comedy was an outgrowth of vaudeville, with loosely connected sketches or a vague plot into which musical numbers were interpolated. As time went on, the American musical stage began to feature what really were musical plays, such as "Show Boat" and "Oklahoma!" The difference from operetta in this case is mainly in style. The traditional operetta was based on European light music—waltzes in particular—and used highly stylized characters. The American musical play, on the other hand, to a great extent is based on dialogue and characters from everyday life. It makes wide use of this country's many types of popular music, from the ballads of Irving Berlin or Rodgers and Hammerstein to jazz and blues.

OSCAR: statuette awarded yearly for excellence in motion-picture arts by the Academy of Motion Picture Arts and Sciences. (See *Academy Awards*.)

OVER THE RAINBOW: song (1939). Words by E. Y. Harburg, music by Harold Arlen.

This great song is so identified with the classic motion picture "The Wizard of Oz" that it seems almost unbelievable that it was almost cut from the picture—not once but three times.

Harold Arlen and E. Y. Harburg had been working on the score for the picture for Metro-Goldwyn-Mayer for some time. They had finished the lighter numbers, such as "We're Off To See the Wizard" and "Ding-Dong! The Witch Is Dead." It was felt that a ballad "with a broad, long, line" was needed to provide balance to the score.

In Edward Jablonski's book "Happy With the Blues" (Garden City, New York: Doubleday, 1961), Arlen relates how the song came to him as his wife drove them to a movie at Grauman's Chinese Theater. They reached the spot on Sunset Boulevard where the original Schwab's drugstore was located. "When the 'broad, long-lined, melody' came to Arlen; he jotted it down in the car. 'It was as if the Lord said, "Well, here it is, now stop worrying about it." ' "

Arlen wrote the middle of the song the following day. But when he saw the completed piece, Harburg did not care for it. "That's for Nelson Eddy, not a little girl in Kansas." He felt that the tune was too involved melodically, that it might clash with the simplicity of the rest of the music for the picture. They played the song for Ira Gershwin. Gershwin liked it, which was enough to persuade Harburg to write a title and lyric.

The performers—including star Judy Garland—liked the song immediately, as did associate producer Arthur Freed. But others in the organization did not. Even the song's publishers opposed it. According to Jablonski: "... the publisher ... objected to the difficult-to-sing octave leap in the melody on the word "some-where," and to the simple middle, '... why it's like a child's piano exercise.'" The song was deleted from the print of the movie three different times, but Freed and Arlen argued and cajoled and finally it was left in.

Judy Garland recalls in the book:

"I wasn't aware until the first preview of *The Wizard of Oz*, that they were thinking of cutting 'Over The Rainbow' out of the picture. I couldn't understand it because it was a beautiful song. However, in those days I had very little to say about anything.

"['Over The Rainbow'] has become a part of my life. It is so symbolic of everybody's dream and wish that I am sure that's why people sometimes get tears in their eyes when they hear it. I have sung it dozens of times and it's still the song that's closest to my heart. It is very gratifying to have a song that is more or less known as my song, or my theme song, and to have had it written by the fantastic Harold Arlen."

The 1940 Academy Award competition found "Over the Rainbow" the overwhelming choice for Best Song of 1939.

PAGE, PATTI: singer. Born Claremore, Oklahoma, November 8, 1927.

One of the most consistently successful vocalists of the fifties and sixties, Patti Page broke into music thanks to her ability in art. The Page family consisted of eight girls and three boys. Perhaps because it takes special talent to stand out in such a crowd, Patti started singing.

A few years after she was born, the family moved to Tulsa, where she attended grammar and high school. In her free time, Patti sang and acted in civic and school plays. She tried to further her singing career by trying out for a local station. The program director called her in for an interview, but he wanted a staff artist, not a singer. Patti had studied art in high school. She decided that a job's a job and went to work at the drawing board.

Her first break came when the station's regular singer quit and Patti took over. Soon she had her own afternoon show. One October day, a band leader named Jack Rael was in Tulsa on a band date. Whiling away the time in his hotel room, he

Patti Page

turned on the radio and heard Patti sing. Excitedly he called the station to find out who it was. On finding that she was a local girl, he immediately contacted her and offered to become her manager.

Rael gave up his band to further his new protégé's career. First he got her a job with a name band. Then he gained an audition with "The Breakfast Club." Though in her teens, Patti impressed the show's talent scouts with her poise and ability. She was soon heard five times a week on the show, which originated from Chicago. Not too long after this, Mercury Record offered Patti a contract. She began to receive requests for personal appearances at nightclubs and on other radio shows and television. Patti could sing every type of song, but, thanks to her Tulsa upbringing, she had a way with numbers with a country-and-Western flavor. She scored mild successes with such songs as "Sentimental Music," "Detour," and "Money, Marbles and Chalk."

Instead of having her own pianist-arranger, Patti works out her own arrangements on a pitch pipe. One of the songs that got the pitch-pipe treatment was a country-and-Western-style waltz. She and Rael liked the song and decided it would make a good "B"-side number to back up a song they thought had hit possibilities. But the "B" side turned out to be Patti's biggest hit. The song was "Tennessee Waltz," and it sold over three million copies. Through the fifties and sixties, Patti showed that she also had a way with novelty numbers, scoring gold-record sales with such songs as "How Much Is That Doggie in the Window?" Patti appeared as a guest star on most of the major TV shows of the fifties and sixties and had a major-network show of her own for several years, beginning in 1955. In mid-1963, she scored a major hit with her record of "Say Wonderful Things."

PAINT YOUR WAGON: musical. Lyrics and book by Alan Jay Lerner, music by Frederick Loewe. New York opening: November 12, 1951, Shubert Theater. 289 performances.

"Paint Your Wagon" points up some of the significant facts of life about the post-World War II musical theater. At one time, a run of half its two hundred and eighty-nine performances would have been a rousing success, but "Paint Your Wagon" lost money. This highlights the astronomical rise in production costs for major shows from the nineteen-forties on. The other significant point is that this was one of the very few original shows, in terms of plot, to appear in this period. Most other post-World War II Broadway musicals have been adapted from a novel, play, or some other previous work.

Despite its initial financial failure, "Paint Your Wagon" will probably be among those shows regularly revived in years to come. For, besides Lerner's book and lyrics, it features some of Loewe's best music, including "They Call the Wind Maria" and "I Talk to the Trees."

"Paint Your Wagon" is set in California during the Gold Rush. When sixteen-year-old Jennifer Rumson and her father Ben find gold at Rumson Creek, it starts an onrush of hundreds of prospectors from all points of the compass ("I'm on My Way"). Soon the once empty land has become the town of Rumson, with seven hundred men and one girl—Jennifer. The men are hard put to keep away from her, but she falls in love with a young Mexican miner, Julio Valveras. When they meet, Julio tells of his hopes ("I Talk to the Trees"). In their loneliness, the other miners sing of the wives or sweethearts left behind and call on the wind, Maria, to "blow my love to me." Ben learns of the romance and wants to send Jennifer away to school in the East. She

refuses to go. He thinks of his late wife ("I Still See Elisa"). Shortly after, Jennifer leaves for school because of disgust at her father's buying a new wife from a Mormon. Julio promises to wait, sure that his claim is a good one. Just at that time, the gold begins to run out. Julio is persuaded to accompany a miner north to look for a fabled lake of gold. Rumson becomes close to a ghost town, and Ben's new wife runs off with another man. Home after a year in school, Jennifer is now a grown-up lady. She refuses to go back and waits for Julio. As the play ends, Julio returns, dispirited and without gold. The area is becoming good farmland, though, promising eventual rewards for Ben, who now owns most of the town. Finding Jennifer waiting, Julio is heartened to start anew.

The original cast included Olga San Juan, as Jennifer; James Barton, as Ben Rumson; and Tony Bavaar, as Julio. The score included "Another Autumn," "Wand'rin' Star," and "All for Him."

PAJAMA GAME, THE: musical. Lyrics and music by Richard Adler and Jerry Ross, book by George Abbott and Richard Bissell. Based on Bissell's novel "7½¢." New York opening: May 13, 1954, St. James Theatre. 1,063 performances.

A wage strike in a Midwest pajama factory was the subject of a best-selling novel by Richard Bissell. The novel became the basis for a hit show which featured the first complete score by the young and talented team of Richard Adler and Jerry Ross. They had only been working together since 1950 when this assignment came along, and they were both only in their late twenties. As a team (they collaborated on both words and music) they had written special material for performers and for such radio programs as "Stop the Music." Then Frank Loesser placed them under contract and got them a series of assignments, including "John Murray Anderson's Almanac" and then "The Pajama Game." This show and its successor, "Damn Yankees," seemed to mark the team for greatness, but their work was cut short by Ross's death in 1955.

We are introduced to the Sleep-Tite pajama plant by its efficiency expert, time-study man Hines, who sings "The Pajama Game." He urges the girls to work faster; they sing that they're "Racing with the Clock." The union president, Prez, has promised to ask for a seven-and-a-half-cent-an-hour raise, but he wants to wait until the factory owner, Mr. Hasler, has a large number of orders on hand before striking. Meanwhile, a good-looking new plant superintendent, Sid Sorokin, has been hired. Hines accuses his girl friend, Hasler's secretary Gladys, of making eyes at Sid. Then, ashamed, he promises, "I'll Never Be Jealous Again." Sid is attracted to Babe Williams, the beautiful chairman of the union grievance committee. He asks her for a date, but she refuses, for he is management and she is union. Sid sings of his lovelorn condition ("Hey There"). But soon after, at the union picnic, he gets a kiss from her and happily sings that this is his "Once-a-Year-Day." As the days pass, Sid and Babe find that they're in love ("There Once Was a Man").

The union presses Hasler for a raise. When he says he can't afford it, the workers start a slow-down. Sid catches Babe damaging plant machinery and has to fire her. Despite the slowdown and the return of pajamas with buttons coming off, Hasler won't give in. Sid suspects that Hasler's business is better than he claims and tries to get Gladys to give him the key to the carefully guarded ledger. To do this, he finally asks her for a date. She wants to go, she sings, to "Hernando's Hideaway." Babe finds them there and angrily tells them that Hines is looking for them with a knife. But Sid gets to look at the books and finds that Hasler added the seven and a half cents to his prices six months ago. Hasler comes to terms, Sid is reunited with Babe, and all, presumably, happily make pajamas forever after.

Other songs were "A New Town Is a Blue Town," "I'm Not at All in Love," "Her Is," "Sleep Tite," "Small Talk," "Steam Heat," "Think of the Time I Save," "Jealousy Ballet," and "Seven and a Half Cents." The original cast included John Raitt, as Sid; Janis Paige, as Babe; Carol Haney, as Gladys; Eddie Foy, Jr., as Hines; Stanley Prager, as Prez; and Ralph Farnsworth, as Hasler. The show was revived at New York City Center in May, 1957. The movie starred most of the original cast, except that Doris Day played Babe. Bissell used the experience gained from turning his novel into a show as the basis for a new novel, "Say, Darling," which also was made into a show.

PAL JOEY: musical. Lyrics by Lorenz Hart, music by Richard Rodgers, book by John O'Hara. Based on O'Hara's short stories. New York opening: December 25, 1940, Ethel Barrymore Theatre. 374 performances.

"Pal Joey" opened to mixed notices and had only lukewarm success. The objections were not to the score—it contained some of Rodgers's best music and Hart's wittiest lyrics—but to the "hero." The book revolves around Joey, an amoral and unprincipled dancer and singer, who cheats his way to brief success. Though he loses out at the end, he is just as unprincipled and unremorseful as ever.

Said New York *Times* critic Brooks Atkinson in 1940:

If it is possible to make an entertaining musical comedy out of an odious story, "Pal Joey" is it. . . . the ugly topic that is up for discussion stands between this theatregoer and real enjoyment of a well-staged show. . . . Rodgers and Hart have written the score with wit and skill.

The show lay dormant for a decade. Then Jule Styne and Leonard Key revived it on January 3, 1952, at the Broadhurst Theatre. Whether the level of audience sophistication was higher or the production was more tightly put together, this time "Pal Joey" was a smashing success. It ran for five hundred and forty-two performances, followed by a national tour.

Atkinson wrote of the revival:

. . . no one is likely now to be impervious to the tight organization of the production, the terseness of the writing, the liveliness and versatility of the score, and the easy perfection of the lyrics. . . . Brimming over with good music and fast on its toes, "Pal Joey" renews confidence in the professionalism of the theatre.

The other critics vied in finding superlatives to describe the show.

The play opens with Joey winning a job as performer and master of ceremonies in a small Chicago nightclub. The manager catches Joey in boasting about imaginary successes in New York, but hires him anyway. Joey soft-soaps the girls in the chorus, beginning with Gladys. He is an artist at handing women a line, which he proves again in the next scene with Linda, a girl who works in a pet shop. After winning her confidence with tales of a lost family fortune, he woos her ("I Could Write a Book").

Back at the nightclub, he bypasses Linda, who has come to see him perform, when Mrs. Vera Simpson comes in. Joey insults her and she leaves. The manager is ready to fire him, but Joey turns the tables by pursuing and winning the wealthy Vera. Wise in the ways of the world though she is, Vera falls in love with Joey ("Bewitched").

Soon Vera is keeping Joey ("In Our Little Den of Iniquity") as well as sponsoring him as manager of his own nightclub, Chez Joey. But Gladys and Joey's agent Ludlow Lowell blackmail Vera by threatening to tell her husband of Joey. She thwarts them but in the process realizes that she's now bored with Joey. Joey is out in the cold again, and though Linda still waits for him, he throws her over and goes on his way.

The original cast included Gene Kelly, as Joey; June Havoc, as Gladys; Leila Ernst, as Linda; and Jack Durant, as Lowell. In the original and the revival, Vivienne Segal's portrayal of Vera was hailed as one of musical theater's greatest characterizations. The revival starred Harold Lang, as Joey; Helen Gallagher, as Gladys; Pat Northrop, as Linda; and Lionel Stander, as Lowell. Other songs were "You Mustn't Kick It Around," "That Terrific Rainbow," "What Is a Man?," "Happy Hunting Horn," "Zip," and "Take Him."

PARISH, MITCHELL: lyricist. Born Shreveport, Louisiana, July 10, 1900.

Mitchell Parish grew up mainly in New York City, where he attended public schools and Columbia and New York Universities. He wrote poetry and short stories for school publications and also was a school-magazine editor. He wanted to become a doctor, and worked in his spare time as an admitting clerk at a hospital. One of the doctors became interested in his poetry and showed it to a music publisher, who offered Parish a job as a staff writer. The year was 1919, and, though he did obtain his bachelor-of-arts degree, Parish concentrated from then on at writing lyrics.

Rather than collaborate with a composer, he mainly wrote lyrics to order for a piece of music, often years after the melody had been written. For example, one of his most famous lyrics was for the all-time standard "Deep Purple." Peter De Rose wrote the music in 1934 as a piano piece, and the words were added by Parish in 1939.

From 1919 through the sixties, Parish provided lyrics for over a thousand songs. Some of his most famous include "Star Dust," "Sophisticated Lady," "Stars Fell on Alabama," "One Morning in May," "Don't Be That Way," "Moonlight Serenade," "Tzena, Tzena, Tzena," "Riverboat Shuffle," "Take Me in Your Arms," and "Volare."

PETER, PAUL AND MARY: vocal group. Peter Yarrow, born New York, New York, May 31, 1938; Paul Stookey, born December 30, 1937; Mary Ellin Travers, born Louisville, Kentucky, November 9, 1936.

Peter, Paul and Mary all grew up in large towns. Peter Yarrow, a native New Yorker, says, "We are a cosmopolitan group. It would be dishonest for us to imitate the folk-singing style of any particular ethnic group. But our urban background is an asset. We can present in a modern musical form the feelings of many ethnic groups and do it with integrity."

During his high-school and college days, Paul Stookey played electric guitar in a rock-'n'-roll band and earned money for tuition at the University of Michigan by working as a master of ceremonies. When he graduated, he moved with his family to Pennsylvania. After various odd jobs, he decided to brave New York with four hundred dollars in his pocket. Soon he was broke "I lived for a week on $1.48—peanut butter, soup and crackers." Then he got a job with a chemical firm and started working as a comic on the side. By 1960, he had progressed to where he was a top standup comedian in Greenwich Village night spots.

He met Mary in 1961. She had gone to a number of private schools in New York after her family moved there from Louisville. She started learning folk music in kindergarten, for one of her teachers was folk artist Charity Bailey. In high school, she sang with several teen-age folk groups, twice in Carnegie Hall. After graduating, she was in the chorus of a Broadway flop, then worked at a series of literary and advertising jobs before meeting Stookey. Soon the two were working together on folk music.

Peter Yarrow had been a painting prodigy. He sold his first painting when he was seven. While going to school, he first learned the violin, later the guitar. He majored in psychology at Cornell University. After graduating, he returned to New York and considered a psychology-oriented job with a television-research firm, but turned it down to try folk singing with various New York groups. In May, 1960, he appeared on the CBS spectacular "Folk Sound, U.S.A." His performance won him a contract with the Newport 1960 Folk Festival. He then toured coast to coast in the coffeehouses and folk-singing clubs that sprang up in the fifties.

Paul and Mary's manager spotted Peter as a natural third, and for seven months the three rehearsed together before trying their wings. In 1962, they were ready, and in an amazingly short

[182]

Peter, Paul and Mary

time they had made a string of successful TV and coffeehouse appearances, as well as record albums and singles. By 1965, their hits included such songs as "Big Boat," "Stranger in the Town," "Puff, the Magic Dragon," and "Blowin' in the Wind." The last named won the 1963 National Academy of Recording Arts and Sciences Grammy for the best performance by a vocal group.

PHONOGRAPH: instrument for reproducing sound through a mechanically vibrating stylus or needle in the groove of a moving record. (See also *Record, Recording.*)

PIAF, EDITH: singer, actress. Born Edith Giovanna Gassion, in Paris, France, December 19, 1915; died Paris, France, October 11, 1963.

In Parisian streets during the early 1930s, a small, pugnacious teen-age girl won notice from passers-by with a poignant voice that had a powerful, strangely penetrating quality. Literally singing for her supper, this waif took the songs of the back alleys of Montmarte and the Paris music

halls and gave them a new vibrancy that haunted listeners long after they had hurried by her. Those who thought there was something different about her were right, for Edith Piaf had started her march from poverty to recognition as one of the greatest international favorites in popular music history.

She had much to overcome. She was an illegitimate child, born in a doorway in the Rue Belleville section of Paris. Her mother was an Italian café singer and her father a French acrobat. Neither parent wanted her, and she spent her first two years with her maternal grandmother who ran a house of prostitution.

Finally, her father's mother took Edith to a new home in the country. Fate was no kinder here. Shortly after, at three, a series of illnesses plus emotional disturbance blinded little Edith. She lived in a world of darkness and loneliness for four years. Her grandmother prayed at the shrine of St. Terese of Lisieux for her granddaughter's recovery. Miraculously, Edith's sight returned.

Her father, who returned home from time to

time, decided she might make a good addition to his act. He took her with him on his next carnival tour. From then on, Edith's life was a succession of dingy rooming houses and circus tents all over Europe.

At 15, far wiser in the ways of the world than most adults, she left her father for the Paris streets. However, as she stressed, "I never begged. If passers-by offered me pennies, I pretended not to see them, and my girl friend collected the money." Her street songs led to wider fame and soon she was singing at some of the local clubs and music halls. In 1935, her big chance came when Louis Leplée, the owner of the well known cabaret, Gerny's, gave her a featured spot in his show. He asked her to wear the shabby sweater and skirt in which he'd first seen her and suggested she change her name to Piaf (which means Sparrow in French).

Paris show business stars and members of society soon were wildly applauding the new singer. Once again, though, her life took a dark twist. Leplée was murdered during a burglary. Edith was arrested for questioning. She was released shortly after. Though she apparently was not involved in any way, the police never officially verified her innocence. The murder was never solved, but the notoriety made the singer's name a household word. From this time on, Piaf's rise to stardom was almost uninterrupted, although in her private life happiness continued to elude her. It may have been this pattern that accounted for the rapport between Piaf and her audiences. The tone of her voice, each movement of her facial muscles told too well of the fleeting joy and vast unhappiness that man is heir to.

In 1939, she scored a major success at the Bobino Music Hall in Paris. Her performance was the talk of France and her records were in demand at every record store. In 1940, she starred in a hit play, "Le Bel Indifferent," by Jean Cocteau. During the German occupation, Piaf continued to perform, but avoided command appearances for such hated conquerors as Nazi propaganda minister Goebbels.

When the war ended, Piaf's career glowed brighter than ever, in films as well as on the stage. In 1945, she starred in the movie, "Montmartre sur Seine" and also discovered the new singing group, Les Compagnons de la Chanson. They appeared with her in the '47 film, "Neuf Garçons—Un Coeur." The year 1947 was an

eventful one for Edith. She was featured in another film, "Etoile sans Lumière," found a great love in boxer Marcel Gerdan, and made the first of many successful visits to the U.S. Her debut in October, '47, at New York's Playhouse caused a small stir, but her next engagement, at the Versailles in January, '48, was a triumph. From then on, she was a regular visitor to America, starring at night clubs and appearing many times on major TV shows. Her recordings preceded her into almost all the countries of the globe.

Her song hits during the forties and fifties included "La Foule" (The Crowd); "L'Accordeoniste" (The Accordionist); "No, Je Ne Regrette Rien" (No Regrets); "Boulevard Du Crime" (Boulevard of the Crimea); "T'es Beau, Tu Sais" (You're Handsome, You Know), and "Milord" (Mister). American audiences associated her with "La Vie En Rose" (Life Through Rose Colored Glasses). Some of her other record hits, which became popular in other renditions in most of the tongues of the world, were "La Goulante de Pauvre Jean" (The Poor People of Paris); "Vallee" (Suddenly There's a Valley); and "Les Trois Cloches" (The Three Bells).

In 1949, Piaf suffered another tragedy when Marcel Cerdan died in a plane crash. In 1952, she married singer-composer Jacques Pils in New York, but this too did not last. In the mid fifties, injuries and illnesses plagued her. She was in four automobile crashes during her remaining years, the first of which resulted in severe injuries from which she never completely recovered. She suffered, too, from ulcers, arthritis and physical exhaustion. Still she continued to perform for her beloved public. "I must sing!" she said, "Singing is all I have. If I stop singing I will die!"

In 1957, she and Pils were amicably divorced. A few years later, she met the young Greek singer, Theo Sarapo. They formed a singing act and, not long after, on October 9, 1962, were married in Paris. There were many who said that Piaf, a physical wreck, was past her peak. Yet in March '63, she and Sarapo scored a sensational hit at the Bobino in Paris. Critics were amazed by her apparent new strength and vitality and predicted many more years of stardom.

But illness, overwork and the auto injuries had taken their toll. By summer, she had to retire to her home, tended by Sarapo. Finally, in October '63, she died. She was buried in the Pere Lachaise cemetery in Paris in a ceremony attended by an estimated 40,000 people and with tributes from all over the world.

PORGY AND BESS: opera. Lyrics by DuBose Heyward and Ira Gershwin, music by George Gershwin, book by Heyward. Based on Heyward's novel and DuBose and Dorothy Heyward's play. New York opening: October 10, 1935, Alvin Theatre. 124 performances.

From an inauspicious beginning of a run of only one hundred and twenty-four performances, "Porgy and Bess" has gone on to gather increasing glory and affection all over the world. It has been revived twice and made into a hit movie. After a successful run on Broadway, the 1952 revival made a sensational tour of Europe climaxed by an ecstatic welcome behind the Iron Curtain.

The opera opens on a summer evening in Catfish Row, a rundown Negro section of Charleston, South Carolina, fronting on the ocean. The inhabitants are itinerant workers, beggars, and fishermen. A crap game is in progress while a young mother, Clara, sings her baby to sleep ("Summertime"). Jake, Clara's husband and leader of the fishermen, takes the baby and sings "A Woman Is a Sometime Thing." The crippled beggar Porgy enters in his goat-drawn cart to play and soon is winning heavily.

As the game progresses, the brutish Crown gets into an argument with a man named Robbins. Crown kills Robbins and runs away. After Robbins is buried, his widow Serena mourns ("My Man's Gone Now"). Left alone, Crown's girl Bess takes refuge with Porgy. Porgy can give her love, but otherwise, he sings, "I Got Plenty o' Nuttin'." As time goes on, Bess grows to love the warm, kindly Porgy. She slowly gains the esteem of the women of the Row. Porgy and Bess sing their love ("Bess, You Is My Woman").

Then comes an all-day picnic at nearby Kittiwah Island. Here the wily dope peddler Sportin' Life appears and pokes fun at the God-fearing people ("It Ain't Necessarily So"). Returning from the picnic, Bess is waylaid by Crown, who has been hiding on the island. She finally escapes and several days later returns, sick and delirious, to Porgy. They reavow their love ("I Loves You, Porgy").

A great storm arises. Jake's boat is caught at sea as the frightened people on shore sing "Oh, de Lawd Shake de Heaven" and "Oh, Dear Jesus." Crown returns, makes fun of their fears, and goes out to try to rescue the crew, whose boat has been wrecked by the storm. The scene shifts to the day after the storm. While the people mourn their dead, Crown tries to kill Porgy, but Porgy slays Crown instead. The police come and though they can prove nothing, take Porgy away as a witness. Sportin' Life tempts the despairing Bess with "happy dust" and the bright lights up north ("There's a Boat That's Leavin' Soon for New York"). Porgy returns to find her gone and, as the play ends, sets out in his goat cart to bring her back ("I'm on My Way").

The original cast included Todd Duncan, as Porgy; Anne Brown, as Bess; Warren Coleman, as Crown; John W. Bubbles, as Sportin' Life; Abbie Mitchell, as Clara; Ruby Elzy, as Serena; Henry Davis, as Robbins; and Edward Matthews, as Jake. The movie version starred Sidney Poitier, as Porgy; Dorothy Dandridge, as Bess; and Sammy Davis, Jr., as Sportin' Life. Another famous Sportin' Life was Cab Calloway, who played it in the 1952 revival and on the world tour. Other songs were "They Pass By Singing," "Gone, Gone, Gone!," "It Takes a Long Pull To Get There," "Clara, Clara," and "Where's My Bess?"

PORTER, COLE: composer, lyricist. Born Peru, Indiana, June 9, 1893; died Santa Monica, California, October 15, 1964.

In many ways, Cole Porter's life reads like that of a musical-comedy hero. Born to wealth, educated in the finest schools, he disobeyed family wishes by turning from a "respectable" career to that of popular-music composer. After a tour of duty in the French Foreign Legion, he succeeded in popular music, was reinstated in his grandfather's affections, and, with his wife, the beautiful Linda Lee, became a world traveler and renowned party giver. But beyond this façade there was Porter the artist, who later overcame a crippling accident to continue to supply some of Broadway's most memorable evenings.

Porter's family was wealthy, thanks to his grandfather's success in West Virginia coal and timber speculation. Cole's mother saw to it that he began studying violin at six and piano at eight. By 1903, he had composed two songs, one of which—"The Bobolink Waltz"—his mother had published. His grandfather, though, felt that Cole must become a lawyer. Porter attended Worcester Academy in Massachusetts, then Yale.

Porgy and Bess, George and Ira Gershwin's memorable folk opera about southern Negro life, takes place in the run-down waterfront ghetto of Catfish Bend, near Charleston, South Carolina. Porgy, a kindly, crippled beggar, strives to protect his beloved Bess from her former boy friend, the dissolute Crown.

He soon had one song ("Bridget") published by Remick Music and wrote two of Yale's great fight songs, "Bingo Eli Yale" and "Yale Bulldog Song." In 1913, after graduating from Yale, he entered Harvard Law School. Despite his grandfather's objections, he soon switched to the School of Music. There he turned out his first Broadway score, "See America First" (1916), in collaboration with T. Lawrason Riggs. When the show flopped, Porter took off for North Africa and joined the French Foreign Legion. He took along a portable piano with which he entertained his comrades. During World War I, he helped teach gunnery to American soldiers in France.

After the war, Porter sailed for the United States to ask his grandfather for a larger allowance. On shipboard he met producer Raymond Hitchcock, who commissioned him to write the score for the third of Hitchcock's "Hitchy-Koo" revues. One of Porter's songs, "An Old-Fashioned Garden," paid off so well that Cole was able to set up regal residence in Europe. His income was soon augmented by a million-dollar bequest from his grandfather's will. Porter and his wife then toured the world and gave lavish parties. During most of the twenties, Porter's musical output was slight. He provided the score to another "Hitchy-Koo" revue and, in 1924, wrote the music, including "I'm in Love Again," for the "Greenwich Village Follies."

Then producer E. Ray Goetz made a special trip to the Riviera and persuaded Porter to do the score to the 1928 musical "Paris." The Porter numbers included the great standard "Let's Do It." Almost every year after 1928 saw at least one, sometimes two, Porter musicals on Broadway or European stages. His first major hit, "Fifty Million Frenchmen" (1929), included "You Do Something to Me" and "You Don't Know Paree." The same year saw the opening of "Wake Up and Dream," which included "What Is This Thing Called Love?"

In 1930, Cole wrote "The New Yorkers," and in 1932, "The Gay Divorce." The former contained "Love for Sale," and the latter included "Night and Day" and "After You." Over the next few years, he wrote the scores for "Anything Goes" (1934), "Jubilee" (1935), and "Red, Hot and Blue!" (1936). But in 1937, while riding a horse at a friend's estate in Long Island, the horse fell on Porter and crushed his legs. For a time, doctors thought amputation of both would be necessary. But Porter underwent dozens of

Cole Porter

operations to save them until 1958, when the right leg had to be removed.

Despite this, Porter went back to writing and also continued his worldwide travels. Besides writing a steady stream of stage shows, he also wrote such movie songs as "I've Got You under My Skin," "You'd Be So Nice To Come Home To," and "Don't Fence Me In." His first shows after his accident were "You Never Know" and "Leave It to Me" (both in 1938). In 1939, he gained a major success with "Du Barry Was a Lady," and in 1940, he wrote "Panama Hattie." For "Let's Face It" (1941), he wrote such songs as "Farming," "Ace in the Hole," and "Let's Not Talk about Love." Then came "Something for the Boys" (1943), "Mexican Hayride" (1944), and two relative failures, "The Seven Lively Arts" (1944) and "Around the World in Eighty Days" (1946). In 1948 came Porter's most brilliant triumph, "Kiss Me, Kate" (see separate listing). After a setback in 1950 with "Out of This World," Porter came up with two more hits, "Can-Can" (1953) and "Silk Stockings" (1955).

The former included "C'est Magnifique," "Allez-vous En," "It's All Right with Me," and "I Love Paris." The latter contained "Paris Loves Lovers," "All of You," "Siberia," and the title song. In 1946, Porter's motion-picture biography, "Night and Day," starred Cary Grant.

Porter died after a kidney operation in a Santa Monica, California, hospital at the age of seventy-one.

PRADO, PEREZ: band leader, arranger, composer. Born Matanzas, Cuba, December 11, 1922.

El Rey del Mambo is the title given the man most responsible for the worldwide popularity of that Latin American rhythm. Prado began taking piano lessons at an early age. As he grew older, he concentrated more and more on music. By the time he was twenty-one, he was pianist and arranger for one of the best-known outfits in Cuba, the Orquesta Casino de la Playa in Havana. He became interested in the mambo, which had its roots in Mexican music, and began working up his own arrangements for it. The Prado compositions won more and more adherents in Cuba, and the mambo's fame spread throughout Latin America. In 1947, Prado cemented this interest with a triumphal tour of Argentina, Mexico, Panama, Puerto Rico, and Venezuela.

It wasn't long before the mambo craze spread throughout the United States. By the fifties, Prado had moved his home base to Mexico City, whence his recordings were sent north and south of the Mexican borders by means of RCA Victor International. Some of Prado's recordings were "Mambo à la Kenton," "Que Rico el Mambo," "Guajiro," "Cuban Mambo," "Broadway Mambo," and "Mambo de Paris."

Prado's bands are famous for soaring trumpets. In 1957, Prado turned them loose on a song that had been popular in France some seven years before to score one of his greatest successes. Originally it had been a ballad, and efforts to introduce it as such in the United States had failed. Prado added some Latin American rhythm, and the result was his hit "Cherry Pink and Apple Blossom White." Though his output of records released in the United States in the fifties and sixties was relatively small, Prado continued to provide numbers that looked as though they were likely to become standards. In 1958, "Patricia," which was written by Prado, was a major hit.

PRESLEY, ELVIS AARON: singer, guitarist, actor. Born Tupelo, Mississippi, January 8, 1935.

Elvis Presley has confounded many of the experts. Some thought he was a passing fad, a teen-age idol who would lose favor as his audience grew older. But they reckoned without Presley's tremendous personal magnitude and real talent. Long before he became a national favorite, Elvis had tremendous prestige in the South as a country-and-Western artist. As time went on, far from diminishing in popularity, Presley continued to mature and gain new audiences in every age bracket all over the world.

Elvis began singing in the First Assembly of God church in Tupelo when he was only a few years old. His mother recalls, "When Elvis was just a little fellow, not more than two years old, he would slide off my lap, run down the aisle, and scramble up to the platform. He would stand there looking up at the choir and try to sing with them. He was too little to know the words, of course, but he could carry the tune." As Elvis reached grade-school age, he and his parents often sang at camp meetings, revivals, and

Elvis Presley

church conventions. One day, his father bought him his first guitar, and before long, Elvis knew how to play it.

When Elvis was thirteen, his family moved to Memphis, Tennessee, where he attended L. C. Humes High School. Elvis sang in school programs and, in his spare time, worked at many jobs, including usher at Loew's State Theatre in Memphis. In 1953, Presley graduated from high school and got a thirty-five-dollar-a-week job driving a truck for the Crown Electric Company. He kept up his interest in music, and one day that summer walked into the Sun Record Company in Memphis, counted out four dollars, and asked to cut a record. The record helped him gain several local jobs, and a year later, the record company recorded a new Presley side, "That's Alright Mama," and released it. The record had a new sound that created a local flurry. Though the record was not a best seller, it was highly important for Elvis. It brought him to the attention of Colonel Tom Parker, who became Presley's manager, bringing together Elvis, guitarist Scotty Moore, and bass player Bill Black.

Elvis toured the country areas as "The Hillbilly Cat." That fall, he appeared at the annual convention of the Country and Western Disk Jockeys Association in Nashville, Tennessee. Among the record-company executives attending the convention was Steve Sholes, head of RCA Victor's Specialties Division. Sholes, who had previously heard Elvis's record of "That's Alright Mama," was even more taken with the style Elvis displayed at the convention. He sought out Sam Phillips, of Sun Records, who had Elvis under contract, and paid thirty-five thousand dollars for the contract plus five masters of unreleased Presley recordings. Victor pressed the five under its own label and released them at once. The response wasn't long in coming; Victor knew it had made one of the greatest recording finds of the decade.

Soon after, this was confirmed by Elvis's first national television appearance, in the Jackie Gleason production "Stage Show." Presley appeared with Tommy and Jimmy Dorsey, singing "Heartbreak Hotel." He sang it three times on the show, and it rapidly became number-one record across the country. After six weekly appearances on the show, Presley flew to Hollywood for a screen test and also was booked for "The Milton Berle Show." His screen test led to a seven-year, one-picture-a-year contract with Hal Wallis. Soon after, Elvis was signed for "The Steve Allen Show" and for three appearances with Ed Sullivan. He turned out record after record that swept the polls. By 1959, he had rolled up nineteen consecutive gold records. These included such songs as "Love Me Tender," "All Shook Up," "Don't Be Cruel," "You Ain't Nothin' but a Hound Dog," and "Jailhouse Rock." His first four movies—"Love Me Tender," "Loving You," "Jailhouse Rock," and "King Creole"—were not only highly successful, but songs in them also became major hits. In "King Creole," for instance, Presley sang eleven songs, resulting in record sales of over two million.

Elvis won just about every popularity poll, both in this country and overseas. He was voted most popular singer in England, Norway, and Germany. He also won the American Bandstand Poll in 1956, 1957, and 1958 as most popular male singer, and won the same title three years in a row from trade magazine *Cash Box.* Despite all this sustained success, some thought that Elvis's entrance into the Army in 1958 would hurt his career. But, even though he was overseas in late 1958, his record sales in the United States for 1958 totaled over ten million. After Presley's discharge, he came home to as much public acclaim as ever. His records continued to sell throughout the world, and record audiences watched such films as "In Blue Hawaii" and, in 1963, "It Happened at the World's Fair."

PREVIN, ANDRE: composer, arranger, pianist. Born Berlin, Germany, April 6, 1929.

The years after World War II show the rise to prominence of a group of young composers and arrangers who are also highly talented instrumentalists, such as Henry Mancini, Ray Coniff, Warren Covington, and Andre Previn. Previn performed the rare feat of succeeding in three widely different areas of music: jazz, popular, and classical.

Andre gave early signs of musical ability. Before he was ten, he studied at the Berlin and Paris conservatories. The events of 1939 caused his family to move to the United States. They settled in California, where Andre attended Beverly Hills High School. Soon after he graduated from high school, he became an arranger for Metro-Goldwyn-Mayer. In those early days, Andre served his popular-music apprenticeship by working Sundays for six dollars a day at Billy Berg's club in Hollywood.

From 1947 on, Previn steadily arranged or wrote scores for dozens of movies. As of 1962,

Andre Previn

the total was over forty, including "Three Little Words," "Elmer Gantry," "Bells Are Ringing," "Long Day's Journey into Night," "Gigi," "Porgy and Bess," "The Four Horsemen of the Apocalypse," "Irma la Douce," and "Kiss Me, Kate."

At the same time, he was appearing cross-country as a classical and popular musician. As a concert pianist and conductor, he played with symphony orchestras in New York, Boston, St. Louis, Cleveland, and Los Angeles. He was soloist for nine years in a row with the Los Angeles Philharmonic at Hollywood Bowl. In a series of concerts in twenty-one cities of the western United States, he devoted half of the program to modern classical compositions and the other half to jazz.

On the popular side, Previn by the late fifties and sixties was in demand as a guest star on just about every major television program. From 1959 on, he also turned out many top popular albums, including his own original-sound-track recording of "Porgy and Bess," "Like Love" (which was a best seller for many months), "Give My Regards to Broadway," "Selections from 'Camelot,'" and "A Touch of Elegance," a tribute to Duke Ellington. His jazz records also were favorites. A series of these, in which Previn

fronted his own small jazz group, provided jazz versions of important Broadway shows, including "My Fair Lady," "Pal Joey," "Gigi," and "Bells Are Ringing."

Through 1963, Previn scores and compositions were nominated for Oscars nine times. He won top honors twice, for his scoring of "Gigi" and "Porgy and Bess." His 1963 nomination was for "Second Chance," from "Two for the Seesaw," for which his talented wife Dory Langdon provided the words. The husband-and-wife team was signed by the New York Theatre Guild to write music and lyrics for "The Street of the Laughing Camel." Previn won the Berlin Film Festival Award for his scoring of "Bad Day at Black Rock" and the Screen Composers Association Award for his ballet in "Invitation to the Dance."

PRIMA, LOUIS: band leader, trumpeter, singer. Born New Orleans, Louisiana, December 7, 1911.

As might be expected of a boy born on the corner of Peter and Basin Streets in New Orleans, Louis Prima early became an adherent of Dixieland and jazz in general. His parents were not musical, but a grandfather had been an expert on the mandolin. Louis and his older brother Leon were given music lessons when they were about public-school age. Though Louis eventually became a jazz trumpeter, he started on the violin. By the time he was ten, he and his brother, who played the piano, had won many amateur contests in their neighborhood. At the age of twelve, Louis organized a dance band that played at local theaters for three dollars a member for each performance.

Louis listened whenever he could to the jazz greats then holding forth in many parts of the city. In particular, he was fascinated by the trumpet work of King Oliver and decided to learn the instrument himself. Soon he was playing with many well-known bands and also doing some singing. His gravel voice wasn't beautiful, but it fitted in well with jazz and blues.

From 1930 to 1933, he was much in demand, playing from New Orleans to New York with such bands as Red Nichols and his Five Pennies. In 1933, Guy Lombardo heard Prima in New Orleans and suggested that he go out on his own. From then on, Prima was a headliner. He first organized a Dixieland band that, by 1935, was featured at the then famous New York jazz club the Famous Door. His female vocalist was Martha Raye. Before long, she and Louis were signed to appear on Rudy Vallee's variety show "The Fleischmann Hour" on radio.

By 1938, Prima had moved into the big-band field, in which he held a unique spot for years. Some of the novelty songs he made famous include "Robin Hood," "Civilization," "For Mari-Yootch I Walka da Pooch," "The River St. Lawrence," and "Angelina the Waitress at the Pizzeria."

In 1953, Louis married the young and beautiful Keely Smith. They developed a new style dealing with a wide range of songs, from jazz to pop ballads, that brought them and the Prima orchestra to a new height of popularity in the country. Besides Keely, the Prima entourage also featured Sam Butera and the Witnesses, a group that made many records that ranked high on the teen-age lists in the fifties and sixties. The Primas were an institution in Las Vegas until their parting in 1961. Afterwards, Keely went out as a solo singing star and Louis continued as one of the foremost bandsmen in popular music.

RAGTIME: music characterized by a strongly syncopated melody against a regularly accented accompaniment.

Ragtime was the rage from the late eighteen-nineties to the end of World War I. It did not die, though, but gave birth to jazz. Ragtime itself is still with us with periodic revivals of some of the original ragtime compositions. Examples of ragtime are Cole and Johnson's "Under the Bamboo Tree," Scott Joplin's "Maple Leaf Rag," and Shelton Brooks's "Darktown Strutters' Ball."

Ragtime is based on a melodic distortion of conventional harmony (as is jazz, though jazz carries the distortions somewhat further). Instead of appearing in the natural places, the melodic accents are shifted to off beats. This is known as syncopation.

Ragtime descended from Negro folk music, and some of the first ragtime to reach national recognition was performed by 19th-century minstrels in their version, for instance, of the Negro cakewalk. Ragtime on the popular level did not reach full bloom until the late eighteen-nineties. By this time, it was based on a number of influences, including "authentic" ragtime, which came from the Negro bands, piano players, and vocalists, particularly in New Orleans. The minstrel material and the coon song were other main factors in the white-Negro ragtime composed in the early nineteen-hundreds.

Probably the first published rag was Kerry Mill's "Georgia Camp Meeting (1897). In 1899,

pianist Scott Joplin, of St. Louis honky-tonk background, wrote the "Maple Leaf Rag." This started him on the way to the title of King of Ragtime.

The origin of the word "ragtime" is not clear. It may come from the French word "raguér," meaning "scraped." It is certain that in the late nineteenth century, the Negroes used "ragging" to refer to their clog dance. The rag dance was described by Rupert Hughes in the *Musical Courier* in 1899 as

a sort of frenzy interrupted with frequent yelps of delight from the dancer and spectators and accompanied by the latter with banjo strumming and clapping of hands and stamping of feet. The banjo-figuration is very noticeable in the rag-music and the division of one of the beats into two short notes is perhaps traceable to the hand clapping; [each person] pats his hands with two quick slaps alternating with the time-beating of the foot.

RECORDING: system for reproducing sound by transmitting to the air the mechanical vibrations of a phonograph needle in contact with a groove in a moving record. (See also *Tape Recording*.)

The minute changes in groove depth or width in a record represent changes in sound pattern. As the phonograph needle moves along this groove path, it causes vibrations in a sensitive crystal (or a special magnetic device), and these vibrations are converted back into the original sound pattern.

Making a record begins with making a master of the original performance. This may be done in a studio in a recording session or live at performances or special events. Usually the original recording is made on magnetic tape, which is then used to cut a master disc. Before tape became available, the disc was usually cut directly from the performance. This master disc is made of a special material, such as lacquer or a form of wax known as metallic soap. Present-day recording practice often involves combining several tapes on one tape, thus allowing the recording engineer much leeway in the final version. This tape is then used to make the master.

After the master has been engraved, it is given an electrical-conducting coating so that it can be electroplated. A metal, such as copper or zinc, is then plated onto the master. The metal plate, when it is removed, forms a negative of the rec-

ord. This metal die is then used in stamping machines to make pressings of the recording.

Thomas Edison produced the first audible sound with a phonograph device in 1877. Sound had been reproduced in nonaudible form years earlier, however. (Devices were used to plot the shape of sound waves on paper, for instance.) One of the first known instances of sound recording was the work of Leon Scott. In 1857, he invented a phonograph that traced a lateral wavy spiral line on a rotating cylinder. Edison used a similar system to produce the first true phonograph record. He used the "hill-and-dale" method of embossing grooves of varying depth on a rotating cylinder covered by thin tin foil. In 1887, Emile Berliner invented an instrument

The making of a record begins in a recording studio (l.), like this huge, specially-designed one at RCA Victor's Los Angeles headquarters. The musical performance is first recorded on magnetic tape. Below, a sound engineer at Capitol Records monitors the taping of a recording session.

After the initial recording, engineers transfer the music from the magnetic tape to a special acetate disc (above). This disc is used to make a "master." The disc is covered with a series of metal coatings, beginning with the application of a fine, silver spray as shown below, and followed by heavier deposits of nickel and copper. The acetate is then stripped away, leaving its impression in the metal master. The master is used as a mold from which a solid nickel "stamper" is made.

using lateral grooves—instead of Edison's vertical ones—which he called a "gramophone." (In the lateral method, the sound patterns are cut into the sides of the groove walls rather than on the base of the groove, as in Edison's approach.) Berliner's early devices used cylindrical records, but he later devised a form of gramophone using a flat record, which was the direct ancestor of today's records. For many years, however, records were made on the Edison type of cylindrical disc.

One of the problems with the early phonographs was that the vibrations from the crystal were transmitted directly to the air, making a

Two stampers, one for each side of the record, are then fixed in a stamping press. At left, a press operator at Capitol inserts a plastic wafer into the press. When the press is closed the stampers force the plastic into the final record shape. Finally an inspector (below) tests a record from each batch to make sure proper musical quality is being achieved.

very weak signal. To improve the sound, the early phonographs added large horns to provide a megaphone effect. The situation improved with the birth of electronics in 1907 with Lee De Forest's invention of the triode vacuum tube. The new electronic devices permitted incorporating amplifier tubes into the phonograph circuit. Now the sound vibrations could be sent to these tubes and amplified before being released to the air through a speaker. The speaker was slowly brought down in size from the bulky horn devices of the early systems. In the mid-twenties, scientists and engineers began working on the next major improvement in recording systems, development of extended-play records. (See *Long-Play [LP] Record.*)

REESE, DELLA: singer. Born Detroit, Michigan, July 6, 1932.

Della Reese was one of five children. Her original name was Dellareese Taliaferro. Like so many popular singers, Della got her start as a gospel performer. Her very religious mother had Della singing in local church choirs at the age of six. She continued to perform at many local churches until she was thirteen. The first turning point in her life occurred then, when Mahalia Jackson passed through Detroit and heard Della. Mahalia asked Della to join her troupe. Della sang with them for five summers. She worked only in the summer because she hoped to gain a college degree. When she finished high school and was accepted at Wayne University in Detroit as a psychology major, Della gave up her summer chores. She kept her hand in, however, by forming her own college gospel group, the Meditation Singers.

But Della's hopes for a college degree were thwarted when her father fell ill and her mother died. Della had to do clerical work to help support the family. After a short time, Della landed a job as manager of a Detroit nightclub—with the proviso that she double as a popular singer. Soon word got around the city that this small club had a much better than average singing star. The owners of the Flame Club lured her away. The Flame Club featured many of the greatest vocalists in the field—Ella Fitzgerald, Al Hibbler, Johnny Ray, Sarah Vaughan—and Della had the chance to see them in action and also to get to know them. Her name began to be known beyond the Detroit area. One of her local recordings was heard by talent manager Lee Magid, who signed Della and brought her to New York.

Here he soon placed her with Erskine Hawkins's great band. In band date after band date, audiences asked for more encores from the dynamic and beautiful young vocalist. In 1957, she won a rash of awards as most promising girl singer from the Disk Jockey's Association and several trade publications.

Then Magid arranged a contract with Jubilee Records. Della's records of "In the Still of the Night," "Time after Time," and an album called "Story of the Blues" stirred a great deal of interest. Along with these came such hits as "And That Reminds Me." In 1959, Della signed a long-term exclusive contract with RCA Victor. Her first Victor recording, "Don't You Know?," was a best seller.

From the late fifties on, Della made many television and nightclub appearances. On "The Ed Sullivan Show," the audience called her back fifteen times. She also starred on the shows of Perry Como, Patti Page, and Jackie Gleason. Her nightclub engagements took her to the Caribe Hilton in Puerto Rico, the Flamingo in Las Vegas, and spots in Chile, Uruguay, Israel, Australia, England, Germany, and Scandinavia. In 1958, she made her movie debut in "Let's Rock."

At her '63 Cocoanut Grove appearance, one of the great favorites with the crowd—an old song that Della had revived with her own touch—was "Bill Bailey (Won't You Please Come Home)." Said Della about the song, which was also a record hit for her, "I like Bill Bailey. He's a sweet man. He's been good to me."

RELEASE (also called "bridge," "channel," or "middle"): the secondary theme of the chorus (see *chorus*).

The main melodic theme and the song title are repeated several times in most popular songs. Some relief is needed and this is provided by the release.

The typical chorus is made up of thirty-two measures divided into four phrases. These phrases usually are divided into three main A phrases and one secondary B phrase (the release). The most common arrangement is two A's, then the release, and a final A (AABA form). Some other combinations include ABAB and AABAA.

The release lyric may have a different rhyme pattern from the main phrase. The song title is rarely mentioned in the release. On the other hand, the title is mentioned at least once, and usually several times, in the A phrases.

REVEL, HARRY: composer, pianist. Born London, England, December 21, 1905; died November 3, 1958.

If Harry Revel's music has an international flavor, it's not surprising; he was born in London and got his start in a Hawaiian band in Paris. After many years as a Continental favorite, he became a major contributor to Broadway and Hollywood.

Revel was brought up in London, where he took his first piano lessons at nine. Though he did attend the Guild Hall of Music in London, he was mostly self-taught. His Hawaiian-band engagement came in 1920, when he was fifteen. He toured Europe with the band and, started to compose songs. His first was "Oriental Eyes," which was published in Rome. After the tour, Revel settled in Berlin for a time and wrote his first show, "Was Frauen Traumen." For most of the twenties, Revel was well-known throughout Europe as a composer and pianist. He provided music for shows in all the major cities, including Berlin, Rome, Copenhagen, Vienna, and Paris. In 1925, he played the piano for the Italian royal family in Rome. In 1928, he provided the score for "Charlot's Review" in London.

In 1929, he moved to New York. To his surprise, he found that little of his European reputation had crossed the ocean. He also realized that he needed an American lyricist. In his rounds of the publishers, he met Mack Gordon and induced Gordon to collaborate with him. From 1929 through the early thirties, they wrote many hits, including "Underneath the Harlem Moon," "An Orchid to You," "Listen to the German Band," and "A Boy and a Girl Were Dancing." Revel also began to work on Broadway shows. His work included material for "The Ziegfeld Follies" and "Fast and Furious" (1931), and "Marching By" and "Smiling Faces" (1932).

In 1933, Revel and Gordon went to Hollywood and, through the rest of the thirties, were prolific producers of movie song hits. In 1935 alone, they were awarded nine bonus prizes by ASCAP for best-selling songs. They started right off in 1933 with "Did You Ever See a Dream Walking?" for "Sitting Pretty." In 1934, they provided "Love Thy Neighbor" for "We're Not Dressing," "With My Eyes Wide Open I'm Dreaming" for "Shoot the Works," and "Stay as Sweet as You Are" for "College Rhythm." In 1935, they wrote the title song for "Paris in the Spring." The Shirley Temple vehicle "Stowaway" in 1936 included still another standard, "Good Night, My Love." Some of the other films they worked on in the late thirties were "This Is My Affair," "Wake Up and Live," and "Ali Baba Goes to Town" (1937); "In Old Chicago," "Josette," "My Lucky Star," and "Love Finds Andy Hardy" (1938); and "Thanks for Everything" (1939).

With the onset of World War II, the team split up. Revel devoted much of his time to supporting the war effort, though he did find time to write some film scores with other lyricists. He helped organize the stage and film group that was the forerunner of the USO and the Hollywood Canteen. In addition, he edited and published two magazines: *At Ease* for hospitalized soldiers and *Vetville* for disabled GIs.

His film work during the period included scores for "Two Girls on Broadway" (1940), "Four Jacks and a Jill" (1941); "The Mayor of 44th Street" and "Ghost Catchers" (1944), and "The Stork Club" and "It Happened on Fifth Avenue" (1945). After the war, Revel turned out several record albums for use in therapeutic work, such as "Music out of the Moon" and "Music for Peace of Mind."

REVUE: a show consisting of songs, dances, and topical sketches. (See *Musical Comedy*.)

A revue was originally a form of burlesque in which recent events, especially plays of the past year, were reviewed by imitations of their salient features and chief actors. The revue became highly popular in Paris during the late nineteenth century. It was thought that American audiences would not like the topical satire of the French-style revue, but on May 12, 1894, "The Passing Show" opened on Broadway and became a hit. After a brief flurry of popularity, the form languished until it came back into vogue in 1907 with the first of the "Ziegfeld Follies." The 1911 "Revue of Revues" gave way to a new series of "Passing Shows." During the twenties, besides the "Follies," there were such gala revues as George White's "Scandals," "The Greenwich Village Follies," "The Music Box Revues," and the more intimate "Garrick Gaieties." In the late twenties, the sophisticated revue took over, leading to such successes as "The Little Show" (1929), "Three's a Crowd" (1930), "The Band Wagon" (1931), and "As Thousands Cheer" (1933).

After this period, the revue again fell out of fashion. Though revues continued to be staged, the yearly volume never came close to that of the earlier periods. Some of the successful revues of more recent years were "Call Me Mister" (1946), "Lend an Ear" (1948), and "New Faces of 1952." Some of the successful non-Broadway revues of the sixties were Los Angeles's "Billy Barnes" shows and Chicago's "Second City" series.

RHAPSODY IN BLUE: composition for piano and orchestra (1924). By George Gershwin.

In 1923, Paul Whiteman made the momentous decision to hold a jazz concert. His goal was to prove jazz, the new American idiom, worthy of consideration as a true art form. It was decided to hold the concert the next year at New York's Aeolian Hall on February 12, Lincoln's Birthday. Whiteman had met George Gershwin when both were working on George White's "Scandals." He asked Gershwin to write something for the concert. Busy with other musical chores, Gershwin at first declined.

Then, due to a reporter's mistake, the New York *Herald Tribune* in January, 1924, ran an item that Gershwin was composing the piece. Reading it caused Gershwin to have second thoughts.

While traveling to Boston for the premiere of his new show "Sweet Little Devil," the rhythm of the train gave him the idea for the general construction of the new composition. As reported by Isaac Goldberg in "George Gershwin" (New York; Simon and Schuster, 1931; revised edition, supplemented by Edith Garson, F. Ungar Publishing, 1958):

"I heard it as a sort of musical kaleidoscope of America—of our vast melting pot, of our unduplicated national pep, of our metropolitan madness.

Later, back in New York, with the concert only a few weeks away, the final pieces fell into place. Gershwin was at a party, entertaining, as he usually did, by playing the piano.

Well, there I was, rattling away without a thought of rhapsodies in blue or any other color. All at once I heard myself playing a theme that must have been haunting me inside, seeking outlet. No sooner had it oozed out of my fingers that I knew I had found it. . . . A week after my return from Boston I completed the Rhapsody in Blue.

Whiteman was ecstatic about it. The concert was an artistic (though not financial) success, and the climax of the program, played by Gershwin, was the rhapsody.

RHYTHM: the arrangement of tones within the pattern of the meter. (See also *Harmony, Measure, Time.*)

The time or meter of a composition tells how many beats there are to a measure and what the note value of each beat is. Rhythm is achieved by varying the accents within the meter.

RHYTHM-AND-BLUES: music recorded or performed by Negro artists primarily for Negro audiences. (This replaces the old, often resented term "race music.")

The phrase covers a wide range of different musical styles, from blues to offbeat jazz and rock 'n' roll.

Some observers have tried to exclude rock 'n' roll from the race-music category, attributing its development mainly to such singers as Elvis Presley. That rock 'n' roll is an amalgam of Negro and white rhythmic patterns is beyond dispute. The combination, however, occurred long before recent musical history. This can be attested to by anyone who frequented the small record studios on and around Broadway in the late nineteen-forties. Many small race labels used these studios to record their masters. Much of this music, by Negro groups, later became known as rock 'n' roll.

The difference between rhythm-and-blues and popular music in general often is nonexistent. Many records made originally for the Negro market gain general popularity. As a result, a list of national best-selling records and the separately listed rhythm-and-blues category often show duplications. The distinction is best made in reverse. Rhythm-and-blues numbers may spread to the general market, but popularly released songs won't get on the rhythm-and-blues list unless they are performed with the blues or jazz interpretation admired by the Negro audience.

RHYTHM SECTION: that part of a band which supplies the beat.

A band normally aligns its instruments to

supply three main components: melody, harmony, and rhythm. Melody and harmony are usually provided by combinations of brass and reed instruments and possibly such string instruments as the violin. (Brass instruments include the trumpet, French horn, trombone, and tuba; reeds include the clarinet and saxophone.)

The rhythm section can include percussion (piano, drums, bongos, gourds, etc.) and strings (double bass, guitar, or banjo). The makeup of the rhythm section depends on the musical arrangement and the size of the band. For example, the piano may be used as part of the rhythm section in some parts of an arrangement and provide melody or harmony in others. A big band may include most types of rhythm instruments in its makeup, while a small combo may depend on a double bass and/or piano.

RIO RITA: musical. Lyrics by Joseph McCarthy, music by Harry Tierney, book by Guy Bolton and Fred Thompson. New York opening: February 2, 1927, Ziegfeld Theatre. 494 performances.

Harry Tierney was a famous name in the American musical theater of the twenties. Today, few have ever heard of him, yet several of his songs live on in the popular repertoire. Born in Perth Amboy, New Jersey, on May 21, 1895, he became first a Tin Pan Alley composer and later a favorite of showman Florenz Ziegfeld. In 1919, he gained fame with the Broadway show "Irene," which included "Alice Blue Gown." For Ziegfeld, in 1923, he composed the score for Eddie Cantor's hit "Kid Boots." In 1927, he came through with his best-known effort for Ziegfeld's "Rio Rita." This musical marked both the pinnacle and the virtual end of Tierney's career. Tierney went to Hollywood to work on the movie version. In 1929, the New York bankers decreed that Hollywood cut back on musicals. Tierney went back to Broadway, but Ziegfeld's collapse and the change in musical tastes made it impossible for him to make any headway in the thirties. He died in New York on March 22, 1965.

"Rio Rita," which opened Ziegfeld's namesake theater, had a plot designed mainly as a background for lavish ballets and extravaganzas. Laid in Mexico, it deals with the efforts of Texas Rangers to track down a border bandit. Ranger Captain Jim leads his men across the Rio Grande to search for their man. There he meets the beautiful Rio Rita. Also in town are some American visitors to Mexico, including lawyer Ed Lovett and his friend Chick Bean, who supply comic relief. Lovett boasts to the Mexican girls that he's 'The Best Little Lover in Town."

Mexican General Esteban also loves Rio Rita. He meets her as she sings of her love for Jim ("Sweetheart"). He asks her to pretend that he is Jim and to sing the song of the Rio to him ("River Song"). Her heart still belongs to Jim, and when she sees him later, they sing of their love ("Rio Rita"). The rangers arrive to help seek the bandit ("March of the Rangers").

Rio Rita is made to believe that the man Jim is trying to capture is her brother. Esteban persuades her that Jim is just using her to trap the bandit; he succeeds and she breaks with Jim. Lovett sings to a girl named Dolly that his trip from Omaha has brought results ("I Can Speak Espagnol"). Jim speaks of his despair at losing Rita ("Following the Sun Around"). The search for the bandit continues. When the prey is cornered, it turns out that he is not Rita's brother. General Esteban graciously admits defeat, and the play closes on the "Wedding Scene" of Jim and Rita.

The original cast included J. Harold Murray, as Jim; Ethelind Terry, as Rio Rita; Vincent Serrano, as Esteban; Alf P. James, as the bandit; and Robert Woolsey and Bert Wheeler, as Lovett and Bean. Other songs were "Spanish Shawl," "The Kinkajou," "You're Always in My Arms," "If You're in Love, You'll Waltz," "Out on the Loose," "Come, Take a Trip," and "Roses."

ROBBINS, MARTY: singer, guitarist, composer. Born Glendale, Arizona.

When Marty Robbins was twelve, his family moved to Phoenix. Until he was nineteen, he seemed to have little inclination towards a career in music. But he enlisted in the Navy and, during a three-year hitch in the Pacific, taught himself the guitar and also began to compose songs. When he was discharged, he returned to Phoenix, where he began making guest singing appearances with a friend's band at a local nightclub. The crowd seemed to like him, and he was hired on a regular basis as vocalist and guitarist.

Marty's next step was to have his own radio show and then a television program called "Western Caravan." Most of his material was in the country-and-Western idiom, including blues, gospels, and Western ballads. Robbins appeared on "Grand Ole Opry," the number-one show in the country-and-Western field, first as a guest and in 1953 as a regular member.

He continued to compose and started to record for Columbia. In 1957, he scored his first major record success with "A White Sport Coat," which sold over a million copies. Then came such hits as "Big Iron," "El Paso," and "Devil Woman."

Marty's first album, in 1957, was "The Song of Robbins." Then came a Hawaiian album, "Song of the Islands." Other LPs were "Marty's Greatest Hits," "Gunfighter Ballads and Trail Songs," "Marty after Midnight," and "Devil Woman."

ROBERTA: musical. Lyrics and book by Otto Harbach, music by Jerome Kern. Adapted from Alice Duer Miller's novel "Gowns by Roberta." New York opening: November 18, 1933, New Amsterdam Theatre. 295 performances.

In spite of a pedestrian book, "Roberta" was a major success both on Broadway and as a Fred Astaire-Ginger Rogers movie vehicle. From it came some of Jerome Kern's most famous music, and the stage show also acted as a steppingstone to Hollywood for some of the screen's most illustrious male performers.

The plot, which revolved around a famous dress shop in Paris, was mainly a framework for Kern's music and a fashion show. All-American fullback John Kent is jilted by beautiful debutante Sophie Teale and, to forget, visits his Aunt Minnie in Paris. He is accompanied by a friend, crooner Huckleberry Haines. Aunt Minnie owns the famous dressmaking firm of Roberta's, and her chief designer is Stephanie, a Russian expatriate.

A highlight of the original show was the appearance of Fay Templeton in the brief part of Minnie. From 1885 through the nineteen-twenties, Fay Templeton was one of the names to be reckoned with in the musical theater. Today, the luster has dimmed, and she is mainly remembered by musical-comedy historians. In 1933, though, her greatness was still in everybody's memory, and her return to the stage from retirement for her last role was an event. In her main scene, early in the show, Minnie sings the great song "Yesterdays." Soon after, she expires in her chair. Before she does, Stephanie and the firm's doorman Ladislaw sing "The Touch of Your Hand."

Aunt Minnie leaves her shop to her nephew and Stephanie. The remainder of the plot consists mainly of their efforts to make the shop succeed. Though things are complicated for a time by Sophie Teale's arrival in Paris, John and Stephanie eventually become a twosome. It also turns out that Stephanie is really a Russian princess.

Perhaps the high spot of the show, in retrospect (the fact evaded first-night critics), was Stephanie's singing of "Smoke Gets in Your Eyes" to a guitar accompaniment in Act II. The song became a show stopper and today is one of Kern's most-played compositions. Strangely, it was not among those show numbers published in 1933. In the film version, Fred Astaire and Ginger Rogers performed one of their more famous dance routines to the song.

The original cast included Ray Middleton, as John; Tamara, as Stephanie; Bob Hope, as Huckleberry; Lyda Roberti; as Sophie; plus Sidney Greenstreet, as Minnie's friend Lord Delves; and, as a member of a band called "The California Collegians," Fred MacMurray. Another cast member whose name later glittered in Hollywood was dancer George Murphy. The score included "Let's Begin," "Madrigal," "You're Devastating," "Something Had To Happen," "I'll Be Hard To Handle" (words by Bernard Dougall), and "Hot Spot."

Two songs now firmly connected with "Roberta" were added for the film version: "I Won't Dance," for a Fred Astaire routine, and "Lovely To Look At," for a fashion-show scene. For the latter, Kern had Dorothy Fields and Jimmy McHugh as collaborators. Astaire was cast in the part originally played by Hope.

ROBERTSON, DON: composer, lyricist, instrumentalist. Born China, December 5, 1922.

One of the most successful of the post-World War II crop of young popular-music composers is Don Robertson. He has shown great versatility in turning out hit material in a wide range of categories, including popular ballads, special material for Elvis Presley, and country-and-Western songs.

Robertson's father, a physician, was head of the department of medicine at Peking Union Medical College. By the time Don was five, his family had moved back to the States, first to Boston, then to Chicago, where his father became a professor at the University of Chicago. Don began composing when he was seven but thought mainly of following in his father's footsteps. When he was about nine, he spent a summer vacation near the Carl Sandburg cottage. Robertson heard Sandburg sing cowboy songs to his own guitar accompaniment, and Sandburg taught Don some guitar chords.

In high school, Robertson also learned to play the trumpet and trombone and worked in local bands. Still, he entered premedical school after graduating from high school. He soon left to take a job as arranger at Chicago station WGN. In 1945, he went to California, where, for a time, he made demonstration records for publishers and song writers. In the early fifties, Robertson took a job as demonstration pianist at Capitol Records.

In 1952, he wrote a number of melodies and had lyricist Hal Blair add words. He made the rounds of the publishers with little success until he came to the firm of Hill and Range, who liked the material and placed three songs with Rosemary Clooney, Eddie Arnold, and Frankie Laine. Frankie Laine's record of "I Let Her Go" sold a hundred and ten thousand copies. Robertson's reputation in the industry was confirmed, and his songs were performed by many major popular and country-and-Western artists.

In 1954, he scored his first major hit with "I Really Don't Want to Know." Over fifty records have come out on this, with combined sales of several million. The same year, "I Don't Hurt Anymore" was the top-selling song in the country field. In 1955, Les Paul and Mary Ford won major attention with their version of "Hummingbird." In 1957, Hill and Range placed "I'm Counting on You" with Elvis Presley.

In 1959, "Please Help Me, I'm Falling" started out as a country-and-Western song, then found favor with popular singers, to bring another million-plus record to Robertson's list. After a lull of several years after 1957, Robertson began getting many requests from Elvis Presley for new material. Among the Presley pictures in which Robertson songs were featured were "Blue Hawaii" ("La Paloma") and "It Happened at the World's Fair" ("They Remind Me Too Much of You").

In late 1964, Don provided Lorne Green of the Bonanza TV show with "Ringo," which was one of the top singles of 1964–65.

ROCK 'N' ROLL: type of music, which became popular in the nineteen-fifties, characterized by a triplet beat in four-four time. Also, a dance step performed to this music.

Rock 'n' roll was performed by Negro entertainers primarily for Negro audiences for many years before it gained nationwide attention. Records of this type of music were part of the category known in the trade as "race records." (Rock 'n' roll was one of several variants grouped under the term.) The phrase "rock 'n' roll" was not coined until the early nineteen-fifties.

Rock 'n' roll was the result of a combination of music from two very diverse cultures in the United States: hillbilly music and Negro blues and spirituals. Authentic hillbilly music is directly traceable to Elizabethan music brought to this country by early Anglo-Saxon settlers, while the rhythms of blues and spirituals are related to centuries-old African music.

There have been many comments about the "poor quality" of rock 'n' roll. Whether or not this is true, there is much to be said for some facets of the style. The rhythmic patterns in particular are very interesting and will undoubtedly affect most areas of popular music in the future, whether or not rock 'n' roll continues as a highly popular form of entertainment.

RODGERS, JAMES FREDERICK (JIMMIE): singer, instrumentalist. Born Camas, Washington, September 18, 1933.

"Honeycomb" is the song that made Jimmie Rodgers nationally famous. He first heard it, performed by another singer, at the Unique Club in Nashville, Tennessee. Jimmie had recently won his first singing job at the club during his time off from the Air Force camp outside the city, where he was stationed. He hadn't intended to be a singer, but his service friends made him get up and sing one evening, and the audience liked his style so much that the management signed him. "Honeycomb" had gotten little coverage, so Jimmie arranged it, changed the lyrics to fit his style, and sang it wherever he performed after that.

After his four-year enlistment was up, Rodgers returned to his home town of Camas, Washington. His mother, a piano teacher, had given him music lessons as he grew up. He had majored in music at Clark College in Vancouver, Washington, but not with the idea of becoming an entertainer. His enlistment cut short his college career and also changed his ideas on music. First he learned to play the guitar while stationed in Korea; then came his Nashville engagement. When Jimmie returned to Camas, he joined a small band that worked many of the small nightclubs in the Portland, Oregon, area.

He decided to go it alone, singing and accompanying himself on the guitar and specializing in folk-type music. He was soon booked into the Fort Café in Vancouver, Washington, where he played for seventeen weeks. A fellow performer, Chuck Miller, who was working at a club across the street, heard Jimmie's act and urged him to go to New York and audition for Roulette Records. The artists-and-repertoire men at Roulette liked one number in particular—"Honeycomb" —and had Jimmie tape it for them. Jimmie went back to Camas. "Honeycomb" was played over and over by the Roulette executives. All agreed that it was a great rendition. Rodgers was called back to New York to make a commercial recording of the song in July, 1957, and soon "Honeycomb" was heard on nearly every radio station in the country.

Rodgers was in demand for appearances on the television shows of Ed Sullivan, Dinah Shore, Perry Como, and many others. A few months before, he had been thinking about quitting music and working in a paper mill to support his wife Coleen (they were married in January, 1957). Jimmie soon had a long series of hit records, many of them gold ones, including "Oh, Oh, I'm Falling in Love Again," "Kisses Sweeter than Wine," "Are You Really Mine?," "Bimbombey," "Woman from Liberia," and "I'm Goin' Home."

Besides guest appearances and recordings, Jimmie also had his own television show on NBC. In 1959, his life was reviewed on NBC's "This Is Your Life." Next came his first movie, "The Little Shepherd of Kingdom Come," for twentieth Century-Fox, in 1960. In 1962, Rodgers switched to Dot Records as both a performer and A&R chief for folk music. His first Dot records included "Rainbow at Midnight," "No One Will Ever Know," and "Face in the Crowd."

RODGERS, RICHARD CHARLES: composer. Born Hammels Station, New York, June 28, 1902. Won Pulitzer Prize Special Award for "Oklahoma!" (1943), Pulitzer Prize and New York Drama Critics' Award for "South Pacific" (1949); and Academy Award for Best Song of 1945 ("It Might as Well Be Spring").

Probably no single composer has affected the American musical theater as much as Richard Rodgers. In over forty years of brilliant, painstaking effort, Rodgers, with his distinguished collaborators Lorenz Hart and Oscar Hammerstein II, completely removed the last vestiges of the European operetta from the American stage and provided this country and the world with a new concept of the drama. The two main landmarks in the development of a true American musical form were Jerome Kern's "Show Boat" and Richard Rodgers's "Oklahoma!" Hammerstein, who wrote the lyrics for the first, was Rodgers's partner for the second.

Rodgers's parents were both musical. His mother was a pianist, and his father, a doctor, had a good voice and liked to sing. Young Rodgers soon showed an aptitude for music, playing tunes with one finger at four and with both hands by the time he was six. His father encouraged his son's musical tastes. Rodgers saw his first musical show when he was six. In grade and high school (New York's De Witt Clinton High School), Richard continued to play the piano, sometimes at school assemblies. At fourteen, while at a summer camp in Maine, he wrote his first song, "Campfire Days." In 1917, his older brother Mortimer arranged for him to write the songs for a show called "One Minute Please" presented by a boys' club at New York's Hotel Plaza.

In the summer of 1919, he met Lorenz Hart, a witty, cultured former Columbia student seven years his senior. The two hit it off right away, and when Rodgers entered Columbia University in the fall of that year, Hart wrote the lyrics to Rodgers's score for the Varsity Show "Fly with Me." Earlier in 1919, Rodgers and Hart had had their first song accepted for a Broadway show, "Any Old Place with You," presented in Lew Fields's production "A Lonely Romeo." Fields later was so impressed with the Rodgers and Hart Varsity Show that he took three songs from it and asked them to write several more for his 1920 production "Poor Little Ritz Girl."

For years after these early successes, no one on Broadway would accept their work. In 1922, the discouraged Rodgers forgot about songwriting and spent two years studying music theory at the Institute of Musical Art (which became the Juilliard School of Music). In 1924, with Herbert Fields, he and Hart wrote several songs for Lew Fields's Broadway show "The Melody Man." But the show was a failure and, in 1925, Rodgers considered dropping music and taking a job as a salesman for a children's-underwear firm. Then Rodgers and Hart were asked to write the score to a new revue, "The Garrick Gaieties." The show, which featured such songs as "Sentimental Me" and "Manhattan," was a tremendous success.

The 1926 "Gaieties" included their "Mountain Greenery." In rapid succession in the next few years, Rodgers and Hart wrote scores to a string of Broadway shows, including "The Girl Friend" and "Peggy-Ann" (1926), "A Connecticut Yankee" (1927), "Present Arms" (1928), "Spring Is Here" and "Heads Up" (1929), "Simple Simon" (1930), and "America's Sweetheart" (1931).

Richard Rodgers and Lorenz Hart run over a new composition in Hollywood in 1934.

After a relatively depressing few years (1930 to 1934) in Hollywood, Rodgers and Hart returned to Broadway with renewed vigor. (Their film output did include some great songs, though, such as "Mimi," "Isn't It Romantic," "Soon," "Lover," and "You Are Too Beautiful.") Starting with "Jumbo" in 1935, they provided sparkling scores to a series of Broadway successes, including "On Your Toes" (1936), "Babes in Arms" and "I'd Rather Be Right" (1937), "I Married an Angel" and "The Boys from Syracuse" (1938), "Too Many Girls" (1939), "Pal Joey" (1940), and "By Jupiter" (1942).

Brilliant but high-strung, Hart became more and more depressed and unpredictable. In 1943, he disappeared for two days. By the time his friends located him, extremely ill in a hotel room, he had contracted pneumonia, from which he died shortly after.

Rodgers turned to Oscar Hammerstein II, whom he had known since student days at Columbia. Writing in an almost completely different style, Rodgers went on to score the greatest triumph of his career up to that point with "Oklahoma!"

From then until Hammerstein's death in 1960, Rodgers and Hammerstein wrote a series of scores of high quality. In 1945, "Carousel" was a success, though not as long-lived at the box office as "Oklahoma!" The score is considered possibly Rodgers and Hammerstein's finest. During the same period, they wrote the score for a very successful movie, "State Fair." One of the songs, "It Might as Well Be Spring," won the Academy Award for Best Song of 1945.

Their next show, "Allegro," opened on Broadway on October 10, 1947, and ran for three hundred and fifteen performances. Though one of their relatively unsuccessful efforts, it included such standards as "A Fellow Needs a Girl," "Money Isn't Everything," "So Far," and "The Gentleman Is a Dope." In 1949, Rodgers and Hammerstein were off and running again with their smashing triumph "South Pacific." In 1951, they followed with "The King and I." (See *Carousel, The King and I, Oklahoma!,* and *South Pacific.*)

Their next two productions contained singable songs but were decidedly inferior to their earlier work. These were "Me and Juliet," which opened on May 28, 1953, and ran for three hundred and fifty-eight performances, and "Pipe Dream," which opened on November 30, 1955, and ran for two hundred and forty-six performances. The former contained "Marriage Type Love," "Keep it Gay," and "No Other Love," and the latter "Everybody's Got a Home but Me" and "All at Once You Love Her."

"Flower Drum Song" opened on December 1, 1958, and ran for six hundred and one performances. It rocketed a new singer, Pat Suzuki, to stardom and contained "You Are Beautiful," "Love, Look Away," and "I Enjoy Being a Girl." Rodgers and Hammerstein's last collaboration before the lyricist's death was "The Sound of Music" (see separate listing). Having lost his second great coworker, Rodgers showed his versatility by writing words as well as music for a new hit show, "No Strings" (see separate listing).

In 1965, Rodgers helped in the preparation of a new TV version of "Cinderella." (The old one had not been taped.) He had, meanwhile, found a new collaborater in young composer-lyricist Stephen Sondheim whom he had known since Sondheim's childhood. Their first effort, "Do I Hear a Waltz?" opened at the 46th St. Theatre on March 18, 1965.

ROMBERG, SIGMUND: composer. Born Nagy Kaniza, Hungary, July 29, 1887; died New York, New York, November 10, 1951.

Starting just before the turn of the century, a series of composers, mostly of European background, helped give birth to a true American musical theater. Before this, most American musical stage shows (apart from topical revues and vaudeville) were imported from Europe. Then such men as Victor Herbert, Gustave Kerker, Karl Hoschna, Rudolf Friml, and Sigmund Romberg, though still writing in the style of the operetta, provided original material in a peculiarly American vein. This type of show, however, was a transitional one to the more sophisticated work of Gershwin, Rodgers and Hart, and Cole Porter. The change in tastes caused some of the old-line composers to go out of style. But Romberg had the flexibility to write hit musicals even for the Broadway stage of the late forties.

Romberg showed musical ability at an early age, but his parents wanted him to go into something more sensible, like engineering. When he reached college age, they sent him to Vienna's Politechnische Hochschule. In Vienna he attended as many operettas as he could and became more convinced that he wanted to make his career in music. His parents tried to dissuade him by making him travel. But in 1909, on reaching New York, he found a job in a pencil factory at seven dollars a week and stayed on. He soon gained a job as a café pianist and moved from one job to another until, in 1912, he was conductor of the orchestra at Bustanoby's, a well-known restaurant. Music publisher Edward B. Marks suggested he try writing a turkey trot. Romberg wrote two which Marks published, "Some Smoke" and "Leg of Mutton."

The songs brought him to the attention of Broadway producers Lee and J. J. Shubert. In 1914, they brought Romberg in to write the score for a show called "The Whirl of the World." Romberg worked as a staff composer for the Shuberts for many years. He wrote for a wide range of productions, from revues to operettas to Al Jolson shows. The operettas included "The Blue Paradise" (1915), "Maytime" (1917), and "Blossom Time" (1921). In 1924, after three years of relatively hack assignments, Romberg got the chance to write the score for "The Student Prince in Heidelberg." He produced one of the greatest American operetta scores written to that time. "Golden Days," "Drinking Song," "Serenade," and "Deep in My Heart, Dear" are still popular favorites. The show opened on December 2, 1924, and ran for six hundred and eight performances.

Now an acknowledged master of operetta, Romberg turned out one hit after another over the next four years, including "The Desert Song" (1926), "My Maryland" (1927), "Rosalie" and "The New Moon" (1928). Some of the songs from these are "Romance," "The Desert Song," and "One Alone" ("The Desert Song"), "Your Land and My Land" ("My Maryland"), and "Softly, as in a Morning Sunrise," "Stouthearted Men," "One Kiss," and "Lover, Come Back to Me" ("The New Moon").

In the thirties and early forties, the change in popular tastes seemed to spell the end of major success for Romberg. Except for "Nina Rosa" in 1930 and "May Wine" in 1935, none of his shows had extended runs. But in 1945, working with Herbert and Dorothy Fields, he came up with a new hit, "Up in Central Park." At the time of his death, he was working on another musical, "The Girl in Pink Tights," which was produced posthumously in 1954 and had a mild success.

ROME, HAROLD JACOB: lyricist, composer. Born Hartford, Connecticut, May 27, 1908.

Harold Rome learned to play the piano in his childhood and, during his high-school years, performed with many dance bands. At Yale University, he joined the University Orchestra and traveled to Europe with it four times. After graduation, Rome entered Yale Law School, but soon switched to the School of Architecture. In 1934, with the depression at its height, he worked as an architectural draftsman and moonlighted by playing the piano at parties and writing songs.

As he was making more money in music than in architecture, he took a job on the entertainment staff at Green Mansions, the Adirondack resort. Back in New York, however, he got nowhere with music publishers. Then the International Ladies' Garment Workers' Union drama head Louis Schaffer heard Rome's melodies and asked him to work on a union musical revue. The result (which took a year and a half of painstaking effort) was "Pins and Needles" (1937). The show, though to the left of center, mercilessly satirized both Communism and Nazism. Its three editions ran for over a thousand performances. Following this success, Rome tried his hand at two more revues, "Sing Out the News" (1938) and "Let Freedom Sing" (1942), but both were failures (though the former contained "F.D.R. Jones").

Rome entered the Army in 1943. Towards the end of his Army career, he met Arnold Auerbach, a radio scriptwriter, and they began planning a revue about the return of soldiers to civilian life. The result, in 1946, was Rome's second smash revue, "Call Me Mister," which included "Along with Me," "The Red Ball Express," "The Face on the Dime," and "South America, Take It Away."

Rome continued to contribute to revues, though with limited success. "Michael Todd's Peep Show" (1950) had a mild success, with two hundred and seventy-eight performances, but "Alive and Kicking" and "Bless You All" (also 1950) were flops.

His first book musical was for producer Joshua Logan, who also wrote the libretto with Arthur Kober. "Wish You Were Here" dealt with love and laughter in a Catskill resort. The show opened on June 25, 1952, to poor reviews. Logan spent weeks reworking the book and turned the show into a solid hit that ran for two years. Rome's score included "Summer Afternoon," "Where Did the Night Go?," "Don José of Far Rockaway," and the title song. Rome went on to perhaps his greatest musical success, the major hit of 1954, "Fanny." (See separate listing.)

In 1959, Rome provided the words and music for the Western musical satire "Destry Rides Again." The show featured Andy Griffith and Dolores Gray, ran for four hundred and seventy-three performances. Some of the songs were "Hoop de Dingle," "Ballad of the Gun," "I Know Your Kind," "Anyone Would Love You," and "Are You Ready, Gyp Watson?"

In 1962, Rome clicked again with "I Can Get It For You Wholesale," based on Jerome Weidman's novel. The score included "When Gemini Meets Capricorn," "The Sound of Money," "Have I Told You Lately?," and "Miss Marmelstein." The last served as a major step on the road to stardom for a new young singer, Barbra Streisand.

ROSE, BILLY: producer, lyricist. Born New York, New York, September 6, 1899.

Billy Rose's career in show business reputedly began with an exercise in "scientific songwriting" in which he wrote his first song after doing extensive library research on the ingredients of a hit. From this, he constructed the wacky "Barney Google," which became one of the great novelty songs of the early twenties. Having clicked with his first songwriting attempt, he went on to success first in this field and later in flamboyant stage productions and financial affairs. His success in the last was such that in 1964 he was said to be one of the major stockholders in the American Telephone and Telegraph Company.

Rose was raised in New York. He won the title of New York amateur shorthand champion in 1916. A few years later, he became stenographer to Bernard Baruch, then on the War Industries Board in Washington. He became tired of stenography and decided to try songwriting. After "Barney Google," he found this much to his liking. Rose wrote lyrics for many of the twenties' greatest hits. He kept at this until the early thirties, turning out such lyrics as "That Old Gang of Mine," "I Found a Million Dollar Baby in a Five and Ten Cent Store," "Great Day," "Without a Song," "It's Only a Paper Moon," "Back in Your Own Back Yard," and "I've Got a Feeling I'm Falling."

By the late twenties, Rose was starting to turn his attention to bigger projects. In 1930, he produced the show "Crazy Quilt." Not long after, he opened his first theater restaurant, the Casino de Paris. In 1935, Rose decided to satisfy a life-long desire—to stage a gigantic production in the New York Hippodrome. The result was the 1936 extravaganza "Jumbo," which featured one of Rodgers and Hart's best scores, comedian Jimmy Durante, and a circus. The show was an artistic success but a financial failure. Rose continued his production work with the Casa Mañana show at the 1936–37 Fort Worth Exposition. In 1937, he turned out his first water spectacular with the musical "Aquacade" at the Great Lakes Exposition in Cleveland. He achieved a success with this production that he repeated at the 1939–40 San Francisco and New York World's Fairs. In 1938, he opened a new nightclub in New York, Billy Rose's Diamond Horseshoe, which remained a city showplace until 1951.

Rose's interest in the stage remained strong, resulting in his production of the hit show "Carmen Jones" in 1943. As still another facet of his personality, Rose showed that his ability with words had not diminished by writing the nationally syndicated column "Pitching Horseshoes" from 1946 to 1953.

ROSE, DAVID: composer, conductor, arranger. Born London, England, June 15, 1910.

That a good part of the airwaves is daily taken up with the driving rhythms of "rock 'n' roll tends to obscure the fact that the softer, more listenable music has greater staying power. The current *Schwann Long Playing Record Catalog* lists some thirty albums by David Rose, some of which had first appeared close to a decade before. While the rock-'n'-roll album will rise and fall in a few weeks, the albums of standards by such conductors as Rose remain in the inventory for years.

Rose was brought to the United States at the age of four. He grew up in Chicago, and showed musical aptitude at an early age. He studied music at the Chicago College of Music and became a pianist with a Chicago orchestra. Before long, he extended his career to arranging for a local radio station. By the late thirties, he had shifted his base of operations to the West Coast, where he became musical director of the West Coast Network. During World War II, Rose entered the Army Air Force and served as composer and director of the AAF show "Winged Victory."

After the war, Rose returned to Los Angeles and continued his work as composer, arranger, and conductor, appearing in concerts and on radio shows. Besides providing material for radio, he also worked on scores for movies. In addition to this, over the years, Rose composed much music for piano and for orchestra. His piano works include "Music for Moderns," "Da Easta Time," "Shadows," "Nostalgia," "Soprano's Nightmare," and "Sweet Spirit." His orchestral works include "Holiday for Strings," "Our Waltz," "Dance of the Spanish Onion," "Big Ben," "As Kreutzer Spins," and "Ensenada Escaped." Rose also has written songs, such as "One Love," "À Nous," and "Once upon a Lullaby."

Most of his records are by MGM. His albums include "Let's Fall in Love," "Lovers' Serenade," "Autumn Leaves," "Holiday for Strings," "Gigi," "Reflections in the Water," "Concert with a Beat," "Bonanza," "Box-Office Blockbusters," "The Stripper," "Cleopatra," and "David Rose's Very Best."

ROSS, JERRY: composer-lyricist. Born Bronx, New York, March 26, 1926, died New York, New York, November 11, 1955.

Jerry Ross was born to poor parents in the tenement area of the east Bronx. Like so many creative people born into such an environment, he had a driving urge to escape and succeed. His first opportunity came when he was ten and singing in a synagogue choir. Based on his singing ability, he was asked to join a Yiddish acting company, the East Bronx Theatre. By the time Ross was in high school, he had joined other such groups with more professional background. He lived in the Bronx, and the groups were in lower Manhattan, an hour's ride on the subway. After high school was over, he commuted downtown, returning home in the early hours of the morning. The resulting loss of sleep led to his contracting chronic bronchitis, which eventually led to his death.

Ross began to write songs while in high school and went on to take music courses at New York University. He worked summers in the Catskills, where his work came to the attention of singer Eddie Fisher. Fisher tried to interest publishers in Ross's work, but to no avail. In 1950, Ross met another struggling writer, Richard Adler. The two meshed perfectly, particularly since both liked to work interchangeably on words and music.

In 1951, they were recommended to song-writer-publisher Frank Loesser, who became their ardent sponsor. He was rewarded in 1953 with "Rags to Riches," which singer Tony Bennett turned into a million-selling hit. Some of the other songs Adler and Ross wrote during these years were "Teasin'," "The Newspaper Song," "Now Hear This," and "You're So Much a Part of Me."

Loesser began looking for broader fields for his young team. In 1953, this led to their signing for two shows, "John Murray Anderson's Almanac" and the George Abbott-Richard Bissell musical "The Pajama Game." They provided four songs for "Almanac" and the complete score for "Pajama Game." The latter was a sensational triumph. It immediately led to Abbott's requesting the team's services for "Damn Yankees," which was equally successful. (See *Pajama Game, The, and Damn Yankees.*) At this point, with Adler and Ross at the pinnacle of success, Ross died of his lung ailment at the age of twenty-nine.

ROYALTY: compensation paid to the owner of a copyright for the use of it.

Most popular-music writers do not receive a salary or a payment for their work but rather a royalty on each sheet of music and each record sold. Through such organizations as ASCAP and BMI, royalties are also exacted from nightclubs, theaters, radio stations, etc., for each performance of a composition.

Royalty agreements are not restricted to writers; any party holding a copyright on a work has the right to exact a royalty from any other party desiring to use the work. Most writers assign their copyrights to a publisher, who may exact a royalty from another publisher, record company, etc., for use of the copyright material.

There is a common misconception that a writer of a successful composition automatically makes a small fortune from it. Royalty rates generally are small, on the order of two cents on each record sold and three to five cents on each copy of sheet music. (Usually, the two cents a record is split between publisher and writer.) As the rate a publisher gives a writer is usually the same no matter how many collaborators work on the material, the one to five cents may be split several ways.

RUBY, HARRY: composer. Born New York, New York, January 27, 1895.

One of Tin Pan Alley's gifts to Hollywood,

Harry Ruby was one of the handful of song-writers who helped make the musical one of the pillars of the motion-picture industry. His contributions were recognized by the industry when his life story was reviewed in the movie "Three Little Words," released by Metro-Goldwyn-Mayer in 1950.

Ruby was raised in New York. After going to public grade school and a commercial high school, he tried his hand at business. He had managed to teach himself to play the piano as he was growing up. When he decided that a business career was not what he wanted, he got a job as staff pianist with the music-publishing firm of Gus Edwards. Ruby entered vaudeville for a while as pianist for the Messenger Boys Trio and the Bootblack Trio. He met vaudeville comedian and singer Bert Kalmar, who also was part owner of a music-publishing company. A lyricist, he had scored a mild success in 1911 with Ted Snyder on a song called "In the Land of Harmony."

Ruby became a staff pianist and song plugger for Kalmar's firm. Soon Ruby and Kalmar were collaborating. They wrote a song for Belle Baker, "He Sits Around," just before World War I. Over the next few years, their songs began to gain them much notice in Tin Pan Alley. In 1917, they wrote "When Those Sweet Hawaiian Babies Roll Their Eyes," and in 1920, "So Long, Oo Long" and, for Fannie Brice, "The Vamp from East Broadway." In 1923, they wrote the all-time standard "Who's Sorry Now?" Besides writing many individual hits, Ruby and Kalmar also wrote Broadway shows, beginning with "Helen of Troy, New York" in 1923. Later in the twenties, they wrote the scores for a number of successful musicals, including "The Ramblers" (1926), "Five O'Clock Girl" (1927), and "Good Boy" (music written with Herbert Stothart) and "Animal Crackers" (both in 1928). Otto Harbach, Oscar Hammerstein II, and Henry Myers wrote the book for "Good Boy." "Animal Crackers" helped pave the way to Hollywood for the Marx Brothers.

In 1928, Ruby and Kalmar moved to Hollywood. From then until Kalmar's death on September 18, 1947, they wrote songs for dozens of major Hollywood productions, in particular for movies by the comedy teams of the Marx Brothers and Wheeler and Woolsey. In 1930, they wrote the standard "Three Little Words" for the film "Check and Double Check." "Why Am I So Romantic?" appeared in the movie of "Animal Crackers." Some of the other films on which

Kalmar and Ruby worked were "The Cuckoos" (1930), "Horse Feathers" and "The Kid From Spain" (1932), "Duck Soup" (1933), "Hips Hips Hooray" (1934), "Bright Lights" (1935), and "Everybody Sing" (1938).

Ruby and Kalmar returned to Broadway in 1941 with the score for "High Kickers," starring Sophie Tucker and George Jessel. By the mid-forties, they were working on movie music again. In 1946, they wrote "Give Me the Simple Life" for "Wake Up and Dream" and the title song for "Do You Love Me?" Though Kalmar's death ended the partnership, one of their songs, "A Kiss To Build a Dream On," on which Oscar Hammerstein II collaborated on the lyrics, won an Academy Award nomination in 1951.

RUMBA: dance and dance rhythm of Cuban origin.

The rumba began in the poorer sections of Cuba as a form of sex pantomime. Other versions mimicked such prosaic occupations as riding a horse or mule or shoeing an animal. As the rumba became more popular with the rest of the island's population, it was modified and much of its suggestiveness toned down. The result was a variant called the "*son*." The *son*, which is slower in tempo, is the dance introduced in the United States in 1930 and which we know as the rumba.

The rhythm was introduced into this country through Moises Simons's song "El Manisero" ("The Peanut Vendor"). (On the original sheet music, it was described as a "fox-trot.")

Rumba music is in four-four time. The basic count is one, two, three, pause: a side step with one foot, feet together on next count, step forward with the first foot, then pause.

RYDELL, BOBBY: singer. Born Philadelphia, Pennsylvania, April 26, 1942.

One of the most promising teen-age stars of the early sixties, Bobby Rydell had earned a million dollars before he was twenty-one. His father, a factory foreman in Philadelphia, took his son to see famous name bands from the time Bobby was five. Bobby loved it and soon was picking up melodies and learning how to imitate band instruments. At the age of nine, he auditioned for Paul Whiteman's teen-age television show then originating in Philadelphia.

Though Bobby wasn't yet a teen-ager, he impressed Whiteman with his talent. Paul signed the boy as a regular member of the cast. It was Whiteman who suggested the name change from Robert Ridarelli to Bobby Rydell. After some

time with Whiteman, Bobby was old enough to join a teen-age rock-'n'-roll combo, Rocco and the Saints. Rydell played drums, and another young performer, Frankie Avalon, played trumpet. Avalon and Rydell doubled as vocalists.

Rydell told *Family Weekly* reporters Marya Saunders and Bob Gaines:

> While other kids were going to proms and basketball games, I was traveling hundreds of miles for record hops, sleeping in the back of an old car to save money, washing in garage rest rooms, eating meals at hot dog stands. While other kids were getting ready for high school graduation, I sat in dirty dressing rooms between performances in rock 'n' roll shows studying for exams I'd missed. Eventually I got my diploma, but it wasn't the same.

In 1960, Cameo Records gave him a date. One of the sides, "Kissin' Time," hit with the teen-age audience and gave Rydell his first gold record. Many other hits followed, such as "Wild One" and a rock-'n'-roll version of "Volare." Bobby appeared in rapid succession on most of the name network-television shows, from "The Ed Sullivan Show" to Dick Clark's "American Bandstand." He was a national celebrity at eighteen.

At nineteen, he was booked into New York's Copacabana nightclub. June 22, 1961, was a critical night in Bobby's life. If he clicked with the tough Copa audience, he was on his way to a steady career as an accepted performer. Failure could mean the oblivion that has befallen so many one-time teen-age idols. The wildly enthusiastic audience proved that Rydell was a performer and not a fad.

In 1963, Rydell, still a favorite singer with the high-school set, made his successful debut as a musical-comedy performer in the movie version of the hit stage show "Bye Bye Birdie."

ST. LOUIS BLUES: song (1914). Words and music by W. C. Handy.

It's impossible to think of a song that typifies the blues better than W. C. Handy's classic "St. Louis Blues." There were blues long before Handy, and there were blues after him; but he brought all the many years of his people's suffering to a point in this one song, and suddenly the blues had status.

William Christopher Handy, born in Florence, Alabama, on November 16, 1873, was from a

[207]

family of Methodist Episcopal ministers. Popular music was something to be avoided, and Handy was pointed from his early years toward the ministry. But he rebelled and turned to music. In 1912, he wrote "The Memphis Blues" and sold it to a white publisher for a few dollars (fifty dollars is the figure most often quoted). When the song succeeded, the impoverished Handy decided to write another one—now, hopefully, to make some money for its composer. The result was "St. Louis Blues."

He described writing the song in his autobiography, "Father of the Blues" (New York: Macmillan, 1941):

A flood of memories filled my mind. First there was a picture I had of myself, broke, unshaven, wanting even a decent meal, and standing before the lighted saloon in St. Louis without a shirt under my frayed coat. There was also from that same period a curious and dramatic little fragment that till now seemed to have little or no importance. While occupied with my own miseries during the sojourn, I had seen a woman whose pain seemed even greater. She had tried to take the edge off her grief by heavy drinking, but it hadn't worked. Stumbling along the poorly lighted street, she muttered as she walked, "My man's got a heart like a rock cast in the sea." . . . By the time I had finished all this heavy thinking and remembering, I figured it was time to get something down on paper, so I wrote "I hate to see de evenin' sun go down." If you ever had to sleep on the cobbles down by the river in St. Louis you'll understand the complaint.

Curiously, some of the song came straight out of his strict Episcopal upbringing. The final part of the melody was from an earlier song of Handy's, "Jogo Blues." This, in turn, Handy related, originated in the "come along" of church elder Lazarus Gardner while he was taking up the collection at the church of Handy's father.

Handy tried many publishers, and all rejected his new composition. Finally, he formed his own company with Harry H. Pace. (Earlier in his career, he had written a song with Pace.) The music was first printed in Memphis in 1914. Soon after, Handy moved to New York, where "St. Louis Blues" won the ear and the voice of Sophie Tucker. She began to plug it, and soon other performers were singing it. The first hit record came on Victor. Musicians have never ceased performing or recording "St. Louis Blues" from that day to this.

SAMBA: dance and dance rhythm of Brazilian origin.

Like South American dances, the samba in its original form was more sensuous than this country's tastes would allow. The ballroom version of the samba is toned down somewhat from its original style. Samba rhythm is much faster than the rumba and has been compared to the polka. It is in two-four time. The basic step involves a forward and backward rocking motion. The sequence is forward with the left foot, feet together, forward with the right, feet together, then the process repeated stepping backwards. The dance also features frequent breaks, in which the partners turn away from one another, move outward, then inward again, sometimes holding hands.

The samba comes close to being the national dance of Brazil. The form usually danced in Rio de Janeiro is the relatively complex samba-carioca. Much simpler sambas are danced in the rural areas. The samba recently combined with jazz to form the bossa nova. (See also *Bossa nova* and *Getz, Stan*.)

SCARLET RIBBONS: song (1949). Words by Jack Segal, music by Evelyn Danzig.

"Scarlet Ribbons" is a popular-music standard. It is also something of a folk-song classic, though it was written by two modern songwriters. Evelyn Danzig is not a full-time songwriter. She is the wife of Manuel M. Levine, formerly District Attorney of Nassau County, New York, and later a Justice of the Supreme Court of that state.

The song was finished in one afternoon in the Levine living room in Port Washington. Miss Danzig wrote the melody first. Jack Segal felt that it suggested a child praying or asking for something. He came up with the idea that the child was praying for ribbons and that scarlet was a pretty color connected with a child.

Mills Music accepted the song for publication and began showing it to various recording artists. The reception was excellent, and the first four records were made by major performers at the height of their careers (1949–50): Dinah Shore on Columbia, Jo Stafford on Decca, Juanita Hall (then starring in "South Pacific") on RCA Victor, and Dick Haymes on Decca. The singers were deeply affected by the song. (Dinah Shore, for instance, had to do many record takes because she would start crying in the middle each time.) But all four records failed. The song seemed too far out for most disc jockeys and much of the public of those years.

Though it was no longer heard on the radio, "Scarlet Ribbons" had been picked up by singers in many little clubs and coffeehouses—the forerunners of the current folk fad. The quality of the song was such that these performers were sure that the song came from a much older folk source.

As the song gained impetus, Mills's representatives went around once more to the record companies. The singers who had made the earlier recordings had changed firms, and no one was interested in rereleasing any of the old records. But other performers heard the song and liked it. Harry Belafonte's recording, which was almost his theme for several years, was a hit and helped establish the song as a popular-music and folk classic.

SCHWARTZ, ARTHUR: composer. Born Brooklyn, New York, November 25, 1900.

Arthur Schwartz attended public schools and Boys High School in Brooklyn and then New York University, where he received his bachelor-of-arts degree in 1920. He won a master-of-arts degree from Columbia in 1921 and a doctor of laws from Columbia in 1924. Also in 1924, he was admitted to the bar, fulfilling his father's fondest hopes. Although Arthur had shown musical ability in his early years, his father, a lawyer, was determined that Arthur follow the same profession. Thus the future composer had nothing in the way of a musical education other than a semester of harmony at NYU.

While attending law school, Schwartz had a song called "Alibi Baby" accepted by comedian W. C. Fields for the 1923 musical "Poppy." In 1924, he placed a song in Jerome Kern's "Dear Sir." In 1925, one was taken for "The Grand Street Follies." He also submitted some songs to George Gershwin during that year and was encouraged by him to go on with his musical efforts. In 1928, Schwartz decided to devote full time to music. The catalyst was his friend, lyricist Howard Dietz, who left the advertising business at the same time.

In 1929, their collaboration bore fruit with the success of the first "Little Show." This revue helped launch such noted performers as comedian Fred Allen and singer Libby Holman and provided the all-time hit "I Guess I'll Have to Change My Plan," sung by Clifton Webb. The

next two "Little Shows" were less successful. But in 1931, Schwartz and Dietz wrote the score for one of the most famous Broadway shows of that decade, "The Band Wagon." This featured the dancing of Fred and Adele Astaire—their last show together—and such songs as "Dancing in the Dark" and "I Love Louisa." In 1934, the team wrote the music for "Revenge with Music." The show was a failure, but from it came "You and the Night and the Music" and "If There Is Someone Lovelier than You."

In years after this, Schwartz and Dietz began to go separate ways. Schwartz wrote with other lyricists for Broadway and Hollywood and also became a producer. His production credits include "Hilda Crane" and "Inside U.S.A." on Broadway and such movies as "Cover Girl" and Cole Porter's biography "Night and Day." His motion-picture songs include "A Rainy Night in Rio," "Oh, But I Do," and "They're Either Too Young or Too Old." He also collaborated in writing a movie script, "Thank Your Lucky Stars," for which he also wrote the score. Schwartz also wrote the score for the first radio musical-comedy serial, "The Gibson Family."

In 1951, he scored one of his major Broadway triumphs with "A Tree Grows in Brooklyn." His lyricist was Dorothy Fields. Shirley Booth gave a sensational performance as Aunt Cissy on the stage as well as in the highly successful movie version. "Love Is the Reason" is the most famous song from a top score. In 1954, Schwartz and Fields repeated their triumph with "By the Beautiful Sea," again starring Shirley Booth.

The year 1963 saw a renewal of the Schwartz and Dietz partnership. This time they collaborated on a musical called "Jenny," based on a year in the life of actress Laurette Taylor and starring Mary Martin and Dennis O'Keefe.

SCORE: in popular music, the lyrics and music of a play or motion picture.

SECOND TIME AROUND, THE: song (1960). Words by Sammy Cahn, music by Jimmy Van Heusen.

"The Second Time Around" was written for a picture called "High Time," in which Bing Crosby plays a widower. He is involved with a Frenchwoman whose husband has died in the Resistance. Cahn and Van Heusen were asked to write a song about such a second-time romance. The working title, "The Second Time Around," came fairly easily, but the problem was to write a song flexible enough to fit the plot needs and yet appeal to people who might not know the picture. Cahn's words accomplished this.

After the song was accepted for the picture, the next question was record coverage. Frank Sinatra, Van Heusen, and Cahn were old friends. Frank came to Van Heusen with a request. Jimmy had written a song named for Sinatra's older daughter Nancy. Her younger sister Tina wanted one too. So Van Heusen wrote a song called "Tina." The same day he played this for Sinatra, he also played "The Second Time Around" and asked Sinatra to do it. Frank was enthusiastic about both songs and promptly recorded them to be released back-to-back. Sinatra's was the most popular recording of "The Second Time Around."

SEPTEMBER SONG: song (1938). Words by Maxwell Anderson, music by Kurt Weill.

"Knickerbocker Holiday," which was laid in Nieuw Amsterdam—the settlement that was to become New York City—required someone special to play the forceful, crotchety Peter Stuyvesant. Weill and Anderson decided on Walter Huston.

Huston had been known for years as a dramatic actor and is still thought of mainly that way. But he had made his initial stage success through music. He had been working as an engineer in 1909 when he met Bayonne Whipple. They began to develop a song-and-dance act. By the time they were married in 1914, they were a top vaudeville act, and remained so for close to fifteen years. Huston wrote some of their music himself, including "Why Bring That Up?" and "I Haven't Got the Do-Re-Mi."

It had been many years since Huston had sung, and his voice was far from what would be expected from a star. After he had accepted the part, Weill wired him: "What is the range of your voice?" The reply soon came: "No range. Regards."

Then Weill and Anderson got a cryptic request from Huston to listen to the next Bing Crosby show. Huston was a guest on the show and was asked to sing one of his old vaudeville songs. He did so in a "husky, toneless voice," but Weill and Anderson agreed that there was a tremendous appeal in the performance.

Anderson thought it over and said, "He ought to have something sad to sing, all by himself in the center of the stage." He went off for a half hour by himself and came back with the lyrics. Weill wrote the music almost as fast. (Essential

elements of anecdote from Leonard Paris: "Men and Melodies," New York: Thomas Y. Crowell, 1954.)

Huston's lament for his vanished youth and the little time left for love was the high point of the show. But "September Song" did not catch on with the public for some years. Nelson Eddy sang it a few years later in a movie, but there was little reaction. In 1946, a Bing Crosby recording became a best seller. Huston's less tuneful but compelling record slowly gained in popularity, however, and probably is heard more often than any other version.

SEVILLE, DAVID: composer, lyricist. Born Fresno, California, January 27, 1919.

The nonsense or novelty song has a long and honored history. Such folk songs as "Polly Wolly Doodle" and "Frog Came A-Courtin'" hark back to Elizabethan ballads. Gilbert and Sullivan and Stephen Foster in the nineteenth century added to the repertoire. The trend continues, with such songs as "The Music Goes Round and Round" in the thirties, "Mairzy Doats" in the forties, and "Witch Doctor" and "Alvin and the Chipmunks" in the late fifties and early sixties. The last two are by David Seville, one of the most successful novelty songwriters of recent times.

David Seville

[210]

Seville's original name was Ross Bagdasarian. According to an article he wrote for Liberty Records:

My father was a grape grower, and so it seemed logical (to my father) that I become a grape grower. At the age of 19, I decided that farming was a wonderful life—for my father. I had been going to the local college trying to find out how to be a grape grower, but I couldn't find any answers, so I left Fresno and went to New York and became an actor.

Ross's career was interrupted by four years in the Air Force.

After the war, I went back to Fresno, found a beautiful girl named Armen and married her. I decided by then that maybe my father had been right, so I went into the business of grape farming. After a full year of frustration, I harvested the grapes only to find the bottom had fallen out of the market. Armen and I ate a lot of grapes that year. Then we moved to Los Angeles.

We had $200, two children and an unpublished song called "Come On-A My House." I kept singing the song to anyone who would stand still long enough for the first chorus. Pretty soon, Columbia records heard about it and Rosemary Clooney recorded it. I started getting acting parts in pictures and while I was acting I was writing songs.

The success of "Come On-A My House" made Bagdasarian decide to concentrate on songwriting. In October, 1956, he wrote a song dedicated to his wife, "Armen's Theme." He felt he could use a simpler name and derived "David Seville" from the music. "The name seemed to fit the mood of the song. Anyway, it worked very nicely and I kept the name."

A key item in Seville's inventory was a tape recorder. "Since I can't read or write music, I whistle into tape machines." Early in 1958, he came up with a novelty song called "Witch Doctor," which uses the tape machine's capability of speeding up or slowing down the voice. The song was a hit. Later in the year, Seville experimented with a different set of taped voices. By recording his own voice at half speed, then playing it back at normal speed, he obtained the effect of a small animal singing. He assembled three half-speed voices, and the result was Alvin and the Chipmunks.

The Chipmunks' first recording, their "Christmas Song," was the hit of the season in December, 1958, and is now a standard Christmas event. In the years since, Chipmunk records scored several hits, Chipmunk toys graced coast-to-coast store counters, and, in the sixties, David Seville and the Chipmunks became network-television cartoon stars.

SHAW, ARTIE: band leader, clarinetist. Born New York, New York, May 23, 1910.

Artie Shaw was one of the best-known practicioners of big-band swing of the late thirties. Though he played many kinds of music, from slow dance ballads to modern jazz, Shaw's fame probably rests most on some of his recordings in the Latin vein.

He was born Arthur Arshawsky into a poor family on New York's lower East Side. He was interested in music by the time his family moved to New Haven, Connecticut, when he was eight. At ten, he had mastered the ukelele, and at thirteen, the saxophone. In his mid-teens, he started his first band, Shaw's Bellevue Ramblers, playing for dances after high-school basketball games. Local band leader Johnny Cavallero took note of Artie and got him to switch to still another instrument, the clarinet. By the time Shaw was nineteen, he was featured clarinetist with Irving Aaronson's Commanders, a well-known band of the twenties. During the thirties, Shaw became a staff musician with the Columbia Broadcasting System, playing everything from the classics to boogiewoogie. In 1936, he won notice for a program at Manhattan's Imperial Theatre in which he combined swing with a background of string instruments. Artie rapidly formed his own dance band, featuring his clarinet, which by 1938 was playing major radio shows and top nightclubs and was also turning out some of the best recordings of the era. From 1938 to 1940, the Shaw organization remained, in popularity polls, in the top ten of the band business. During this period, Artie took a Cole Porter song that had been generally ignored and turned out an instrumental version that swept the country. This became Shaw's most famous recording, and it helped make the song one of Porter's most-played numbers. The title: "Begin the Beguine."

In 1940, Shaw broke up his band and went to Mexico. But he cut short his temporary retirement when he found the Mexican music immensely inspiring. He came back to the States, formed a new big band, and recorded some of the numbers he particularly liked. One of these,

[211]

"Frenesi," soon won popularity to rival "Begin the Beguine." Another Latin song that won some attention was "Adios, Mariquita Linda." Shaw entered the Navy in World War II and formed a band that played in the front lines of battle. During one eleven-month tour of the Pacific, the band went through seventeen Japanese air attacks. Shaw won an *Esquire* magazine Armed Forces jazz poll as the most popular band leader.

Shaw continued in music after the war, but at a less hectic pace. His postwar activities included some recording, radio guest appearances, a few movie appearances, and performances as clarinet soloist with some of the nation's major symphony orchestras.

SHEARING, GEORGE: pianist, composer. Born London, England, August 13, 1919.

George Shearing was born totally blind into the large family of a poor English coal miner. Luckily, he had three main assets: talent, determination, and a sense of humor.

He went to the Shillington Street School for the Blind for eight years. He learned to read and write Braille but had no special music training. When he went on to the Linden Lodge School for the Blind at the age of twelve, his instructors encouraged his obvious musical ability. They urged him to go on to university, but, at sixteen, Shearing felt he had to help his family. He got a job at a local pub while continuing classical-music studies. About this time, some jazz recordings from the United States caught his attention. He liked the freshness of this music and began experimenting with his own compositions and arrangements.

George liked to wear a tuxedo at work, which the pub owner felt was too high-toned for his clientele. They argued, and George quit. One of his former Linden Lodge instructors got him a job with an all-blind band which toured England for nine months. As a result of the tour, Shearing received assignments to write arrangements for the British Broadcasting Corporation. Soon after, he made his first broadcast, on Arthur Arky's "Bandwagon." Though mainly known for his piano work, Shearing also is an accomplished accordionist and, at nineteen, he played both on the BBC to a growing audience.

At this stage of George's career, jazz critic and author Leonard Feather met Shearing when George sat in on a jam session in London which Feather was conducting. Soon a record date was set up with English Decca. George played the accordion, and Feather played the piano. The numbers were "Squeezin' the Blues" and "Blue Boogie." Shearing began to be more and more in demand in England. During World War II, in an air raid, he met his wife Trixie, who was an indispensable asset in Shearing's achieving recognition in the United States.

In 1946, after eight years of top billing in London, Shearing decided to try his hand at conquering American audiences. A two-month trip in early 1947 was reasonably successful. Back in London, Shearing received many offers for dates from American talent agencies. He returned with his wife in December, 1947. But the talent agencies found that the market had changed. Their excuse was that George was blind and had no gimmick. After much searching, he found a job as intermission pianist on New York's Fifty-second Street at the Three Deuces and Onyx clubs.

Discouraged, he returned to England for a record date (from which came several famous sides, including "I Only Have Eyes for You" and "You Are Too Beautiful"). But his wife stayed behind and finally won the ear of Irving Alexander, who was just opening his new Clique nightclub in New York. This time, first with a trio and soon with a quartet, Shearing caught on. The downstairs club, which later became Birdland, was soon crowded with avid listeners.

In 1949, MGM records signed his group, and their recording of "September in the Rain" was a hit. The quintet was rushed into feature spots at the important New York nightclub Café Society. After this came more and more well-received recordings and dates at nightclubs, college auditoriums, and jazz concerts. In March, 1955, Shearing left MGM and signed with Capitol Records. Here too he was consistently popular, and over two million of his Capitol albums were sold in the late fifties and early sixties. Shearing also made many appearances in schools and hospitals for blind children throughout the United States.

The now successful Shearing group often returned for engagements at the scene of their initial breakthrough. In 1952, Shearing immortalized the club in a new composition, "Lullaby of Birdland."

SHORE, FRANCES ROSE (DINAH): singer, television mistress of ceremonies. Born Winchester, Tennessee, March 1, 1920.

For many years, Dinah Shore's velvet tones

kept her at the top of many polls as best female vocalist. In those days, almost every one of her records sold in the hundreds of thousands, some in the millions. But record-buying habits change. By the late fifties, Dinah's records no longer headed national surveys. One of the most gracious of popular female vocalists, Dinah carved a new career as mistress of ceremonies of "The Dinah Shore Show," one of the highest-rated shows on television.

Dinah's family moved to Nashville when she was six. Even at that age, Dinah could sing many of the popular songs of the day. At ten, she made her first public appearance before her mother's Ladies Aid Society. After this, she sang publicly as often as she could in school recitals, amateur plays, and local affairs. Dinah started taking singing lessons in high school. Unfortunately, she also became a member of the high-school cheering squad. Her cheerleading caused a slight huskiness in her voice that displeased her teacher and made him suggest they stop the lessons.

Dinah gave up the lessons but kept on singing. She also began auditioning for local radio stations. Station WSM in Nashville soon put her on as a staff vocalist. In 1937, Dinah felt she was ready to go on to bigger and better things and headed for New York.

She auditioned for Tommy and Jimmy Dorsey and Benny Goodman, but they turned her down. She struggled for two bitter years but had next to nothing to show for it. On New Year's Eve, 1939, it looked like her luck had finally changed. She landed a twenty-five-dollar-a-week job singing in a Long Island nightclub. Dinah had only a dime to her name. In those days, the bus cost ten cents and the subway a nickel. Feeling elated, she decided to splurge on the more scenic bus trip. When she got home, she found a note canceling the job.

Drying her tears, she borrowed a nickel and called her parents in Nashville collect. Though they wanted her home, her determination impressed them enough to send her some money to fight on a little longer. Soon after, Xavier Cugat signed her for some records. Dinah also began to sing on local stations. Her work came to the attention of the radio networks, and she was picked as vocalist for the Chamber Music Society of Lower Basin Street. After a successful series with this group, Dinah moved on to become a star of "The Eddie Cantor Show." "Yes, My Darling Daughter," which she first sang on the show, became her first big hit.

Her popularity grew till she left the Cantor show and starred in her own radio spot. Dinah topped most popularity polls in the forties, winning such awards as Page One Songstress from the Newspaper Guild. Her engagements at top New York supper clubs were sellouts, and before too long, she was starring in movies as well. During the war, Dinah traveled to military bases throughout the world to entertain the Allied forces.

Her popularity as a record artist continued at its height through the forties and into the fifties. Some of her successes were "Bibbidi-Bobbidi-Boo," "Lavender Blue," "That Old Black Magic," "Baby, It's Cold Outside" (with Buddy Clark), "Dear Hearts and Gentle People," and "Buttons and Bows."

Dinah cut back on her singing activities for a while to devote time to raising her family. But the late fifties saw her back as a regular network-TV performer. The easy-going format plus Dinah's charm as hostess made the show a featured network program year after year. "The Dinah Shore Show" won many awards. Almost every singer whose records sold in the top brackets vied for the prestige to be gained from an appearance on Dinah's program.

During the 1963–64 season, she gave up her regular show. However, 1964–65 found her back on ABC-TV with a series of specials.

SHOW BOAT: musical. Lyrics and book by Oscar Hammerstein II, music by Jerome Kern. Lyrics to "Bill" by P. G. Wodehouse. Adapted from Edna Ferber's novel. New York opening: December 27, 1927, Ziegfeld Theatre. 572 performances.

In 1926, not too long after he had begun collaborating with young Oscar Hammerstein II, Jerome Kern sat down to read a book for relaxation, an event of major importance to the course of American musical theater. Soon no longer relaxed, he called Hammerstein's attention to his reading material, Edna Ferber's "Show Boat." Kern was sure that this would make a great musical, and Hammerstein agreed. Miss Ferber was dubious until Kern assured her that this would not be a girlie show but a true dramatic transposition. Kern transmitted his enthusiasm to Florenz Ziegfeld, and the "glorifier of the American girl" agreed to produce it. He also gave Kern and Hammerstein free rein to do it their way.

After several delays and a terrible period when

it seemed that Ziegfeld might drop the project, "Show Boat" opened. It was a year late. But it was worth the wait, for, in that interval, Kern and Hammerstein added "Ol' Man River."

Hammerstein recalled their work in his jacket notes for the Columbia recording of the 1946 revival. Once Kern got things started,

> During the next 14 months we kept writing, then rewriting and improving our adaptation. We had fallen hopelessly in love with it. We couldn't keep our hands off it. We acted out scenes together and planned the actual direction. . . . It is lucky we became so emotionally involved with Edna Ferber's characters, because love rendered us blind to all the dangers our friends saw in the undertaking. People seemed to go out of their way to discourage us. "How do you expect to make a musical play out of that?" they would ask. And they would look sorry for us.

The play was too long, and for weeks on the road they tried to cut it down.

> We never did reduce it to the time of other musical plays. . . . There seemed to be no way of simplifying this stubborn play. It was born big and it wants to stay that way.

As "Show Boat" begins, the showboat *Cotton Blossom* approaches the Natchez levee in the eighteen-eighties. The townspeople and the Negro workers on the levee sing their welcome. Cap'n Andy, proprieter of the boat, urges all to attend the show, which features leading lady Julie La Verne, handsome Steve Baker, and dancers Frank and Ellie. Accompanying Cap'n Andy on the boat are his sharp-tongued wife Parthy Ann Hawks and their daughter Magnolia. Among the colored help are Queenie and her boy friend Joe.

When the crowds have cleared, Gaylord Ravenal, a handsome river-boat gambler is seen on the levee. Ellie is attracted by his looks and drops her handkerchief. He isn't interested in her, though he wonders, "Where's the Mate for Me?" Magnolia appears on the upper deck of the *Cotton Blossom* and sees him. They are attracted to one another ("Make Believe"). Ravenal leaves, and Joe comes in. As Joe looks out over the Mississippi, he and the sweating stevedores sing of all the heartache and pain their race has endured in the New World ("Ol' Man River"). In the pantry, Julie and Queenie complain of their

men, but admit they still "Can't Help Lovin' Dat Man." Ellie makes another pass at Ravenal in front of a waterfront saloon. Again repulsed, she sings that "Life upon the Wicked Stage" isn't all it's cracked up to be.

Julie is discovered to be a mulatto and must leave the boat. Steve Baker, her sweetheart, goes with her. Magnolia is pressed into service as the new leading lady, and Ravenal comes aboard and wins the role of the leading man. Ellie tells Frank that, if all else fails, "I Might Fall Back on You." Soon Ravenal and Magnolia find they're in love ("You Are Love"). They marry and leave the *Cotton Blossom*.

The scene shifts to the 1893 Chicago World's Fair. Cap'n Andy and Parthy are there with Magnolia and Ravenal, and all sing "Why Do I Love You?" But Ravenal has slipped back into his gambling ways and the marriage is coming apart, though they soon have a daughter, Kim. Ravenal leaves Magnolia, who decides to earn a living as a singer. At the Trocadero Music Hall in New York in 1904, she again meets Julie. Julie sings her blues in "Bill." Thirteen years later, Magnolia and Kim return to Cap'n Andy, who has a new *Cotton Blossom*. Ravenal appears and asks forgiveness. Kim gives promise of being a new singing star in "Dance Away the Night."

The original cast included Charles Winninger, as Andy; Edna May Oliver, as Parthy; Howard Marsh, as Ravenal; Norma Terris, as Magnolia; Helen Morgan, as Julie; Sam White, as Frank; Eva Puck, as Ellie; and Jules Bledsoe, as Joe. (Paul Robeson debuted as Joe in the London version of "Show Boat.")

SILK STOCKINGS: musical. Lyrics and music by Cole Porter, book by George S. Kaufman, Leueen MacGrath, and Abe Burrows. Based on Melchior Lengyel's screenplay "Ninotchka." New York opening: February 24, 1955, Imperial Theatre. 478 performances.

"Silk Stockings" was Cole Porter's twenty-fifth Broadway score. It was also one of his best. As John Chapman wrote in the New York *Daily News:*

> . . . "Silk Stockings" is everything a musical should be. . . . It is handsome, slick, brisk, intelligent, witty and delightfully acted, and whenever the plot shows the merest sign of trying to take over more than its share, Cole Porter shoulders it aside with some of his best melodies, lyrics and rhythms.

In this razor-sharp satire of Russia and Hollywood, famous young Russian composer Peter Ilyitch Boroff comes to Paris for a concert and delays going home. He has fallen under the wing of brash American theatrical agent Steve Canfield, who is busy lining up such assignments for Boroff as writing the score for a motion-picture version of Tolstoi's "War and Peace." Three Russian agents, Bibinski, Brankov, and Ivanov, are sent to bring Boroff home. But they fall under the spell of the good life and are in no rush to go back either. As the show begins, the problems of getting Russians to return from Paris are reviewed in "Too Bad."

Chief Art Commissar Markovitch decides to take drastic measures. (As an example of the play's satire, at one point he orders an aide to look up some information in *Who's Still Who*.) He dispatches a grim, flat-heeled, fanatical female commissar, Ninotchka, to do the job. In Paris, she soon tangles with Canfield, who proves a worthy adversary.

Into the midst of this comes Hollywood film star Janice Dayton. A wild-eyed version of the sultry screen siren, she discloses that for many years she was a star in aquatic movies. She swam so much that her ears went bad. Now she must work "dry" and has come to Paris to independently produce her first nonwater picture, "War and Peace." She regales reporters at a news conference with a paean to one of the new entertainment wonders, "Stereophonic Sound." Later in the show, she turns a scene from "War and Peace" into a pseudo-striptease ("Josephine").

Ninotchka's stoic façade begins to yield to the delights of Western civilization ("Paris Loves Lovers"). Canfield shows his growing affection for her ("All of You" and "Silk Stockings"). Despite herself, Ninotchka becomes more soft and feminine. As she changes, the three other agents are assigned to follow her. Her sense of duty wins, and Ninotchka returns to Moscow with Boroff. But Canfield follows her and spirits the now converted Ninotchka out of Russia.

The original cast included Hildegarde Neff, as Ninotchka; Don Ameche, as Steve; Gretchen Wyler, as Janice; Philip Sterling as Boroff; David Opatoshu, as Bibinski; Henry Lascoe, as Ivanov; Leon Belasco, as Brankov; and George Tobias, as Commissar Markovitch. Other songs were "Without Love," "As on through the Seasons We Sail," "Siberia," and "Hail Bibinski."

SILVER BELLS: song (1952). Words by Ray Evans, music by Jay Livingston.

Jay Livingston and Ray Evans have the honor of writing several songs to sell a million copies of sheet music. One of these was "Silver Bells." But "Silver Bells" took several years to do it. "Every year in a two week period just before Christmas," they note, "Silver Bells sells a hundred thousand copies or better. In 1962, it passed the million mark."

The song was written for a picture, "The Lemon Drop Kid," based on a Damon Runyon story, that starred Bob Hope. In one scene, Hope was posing as a Santa Claus on a city street, and the studio wanted a song for him to sing. "When we were given the assignment," says Evans, "We felt definitely negative about it. A Christmas song was wanted and there were so many good ones, both traditional and recent (such as 'White Christmas'), that we thought, who needed another one? But we started to work on it, doubts or no doubts. We were digging for a title at home and there was some kind of little bell on the desk. We happened to glance at it, then said, 'Why not? Bells go with Christmas.' With this I got to work on the lyric and pretty soon we had the song finished."

A number of fairly successful records were released the first year. Two in particular helped push the song: one by Bing Crosby and Carol Richards and another by Margaret Whiting and Jimmy Wakely. These are still played at Christmas. The song often appears in new Christmas albums.

Why did the song succeed despite so much competition? Evans conjectures, "The main reason, it seems to us, is that this is the only song we can recall that's about Christmas in a big city with shop lights and shoppers and the rest. We were lucky—we only got that idea because that happened to be the locale of the picture."

SINATRA, FRANCIS ALBERT (FRANK): singer. Born Hoboken, New Jersey, December 12, 1917.

In 1942, Tommy Dorsey and his orchestra played a record-shattering engagement at New York's Paramount Theatre. Eager crowds—largely made up of high-school students—patiently stood in block-long lines waiting to get in. The Dorsey organization was a major attraction in those days of the name band, but the audiences came as much to see a young, lean, relatively new band vocalist named Frank

Frank Sinatra

Sinatra. When Frankie would start a song, girls sighed in unison and some swooned in the aisles. The sighing and swooning were fads that lasted only a short time, but Sinatra went on to become one of the greatest all-around entertainers in show business.

Frank was an only child. His father, Anthony Sinatra, was a fireman in Hoboken, and his mother often sang at social functions. Frank grew up in Hoboken and attended Demarest High School, where he helped organize the glee club and sang with the school-sponsored dance band. In 1933, he got a job on a delivery truck of the New Jersey *Observer*. He moved up to work as a copyboy, then as a cub sports writer. One evening in 1936, he took his fiancé, Nancy Barbato, to hear Bing Crosby sing in Jersey City. On the spur of the moment, he decided to quit the paper and become a singer.

He began singing with local bands. Then, with three instrumentalists, he formed the Hoboken Four, which won first prize on "The Major Bowes Original Amateur Hour" in 1937. By 1939, he was singing on eighteen radio shows a week in New York and Hoboken, but for no pay. The owner of the Rustic Cabin in Teaneck, New Jersey, heard a show and hired Frank as singer and head waiter at fifteen dollars a week. Harry James heard Frank there in 1939 and signed him to a two-year contract at seventy-five dollars a week. Soon after, Tommy Dorsey was driving from one engagement to another in the Midwest.

Turning on his radio, he heard a James record and was so impressed with the vocalist—Sinatra—that he determined to try to hire him. James let Frank out of his contract to accept Dorsey's offer of two hundred and fifty dollars a week.

With Dorsey, Sinatra made many hit records, including "I'll Never Smile Again," "Oh, Look at Me Now," "Violets for Your Furs," "Night and Day," and "This Love of Mine." He also developed his special vocal delivery by analyzing Dorsey's trombone phrasing. In late 1942, Frank left Dorsey to go out on his own. In 1943, he received a tumultuous welcome at New York's Paramount and was now an acknowledged star. From 1943 to 1945, he was a regular on the "Hit Parade." In 1943, he made "Higher and Higher," the first of a long series of movies. Other films he appeared in during the forties were "Anchors Aweigh" (1945), "Till the Clouds Roll By" (1947), and "The Kissing Bandit" and "On the Town" (1949). Through most of the forties, fifties, and into the sixties, despite changing styles of music, Sinatra's records were almost always among the best sellers.

The one exception was the early fifties, when several factors combined to force his popularity to low ebb. His record sales fell off, his movie roles stopped, and his throat began hemorrhaging. But Frank fought his way back the hard way by taking a screen test and a minimum salary to do the dramatic role of Maggio in the 1953 film "From Here to Eternity." The role won him an Academy Award, and from then on he scored success after success in all entertainment mediums to become one of the wealthiest performers in the world.

He put on the highly successful "Frank Sinatra Show" over the American Broadcasting Company television network during 1957–58. In later years, he made many starring guest appearances on such specials as "The Judy Garland Show." He appeared in one film after another, many of which he produced himself. Some of his movies of this period were "The Man with the Golden Arm" (1956), "The Tender Trap" (1955), "Johnny Concho" and "High Society" (1956), "The Joker Is Wild" and "The Pride and the Passion" (1957), "Can-Can" and "Oceans 11" (1960), and "Come Blow Your Horn" (1962). Some of his major record successes during the late fifties and sixties were "Come Fly with Me," "All the Way," "A Foggy Day," "The Girl That Got Away," "High Hopes," "Pocketful of Miracles," and "Love and Marriage."

SMOKE GETS IN YOUR EYES: song (1933). Words by Otto Harbach, music by Jerome Kern. (See also *Roberta*.)

Though "Smoke Gets in Your Eyes" was one of the prime reasons for "Roberta's" success, it was not written as a key part of the play. Rather, it was composed as a number to kill time between curtain changes.

Kern thought of a march he had written some time back as a theme for an unproduced radio series. He tried it out on the cast and production people at rehearsal. The reaction was negative. He was about to abandon it and do something else when he got the idea of trying it in a different, slow ballad tempo. This time, the effect was electric.

Once Kern finished a song, he usually refused to change it. He might, as he did on this occasion, change the tempo, but never a note of the final version.

Harbach took the music and began putting words to it. All went well until he came to the last line, "When a lovely flame dies." Musically there is an extra syllable in the phrase "lovely flame." This distorts the music, something that would normally displease Kern. Harbach struggled with this for hours, but a one-syllable word for "lovely" that would give the same meaning just wouldn't come. There were "fine flame," "bright flame," "hot flame," but these just didn't give the feeling the line had to convey. Finally he brought the lyric to Kern. The composer immediately noticed the distortion, but he had to agree that in this case it was justified. For one of the few times in his musical career, he deferred to the lyricist.

When Tamara sang "Smoke Gets in Your Eyes" in the show, it brought down the house. She had to give encore after encore. As recently as 1958, a new version of the song, by the Platters, sold a million records, mostly to people who had not yet been born when the song was first performed.

SOLITUDE: song (1934). Words by Irving Mills and Eddie DeLange, music by Duke Ellington.

Duke Ellington's music has a certain jazz-blues feel that no other writer has duplicated. "Solitude," is one of his most-performed compositions. As noted by Richard O. Boyer in his *New Yorker* magazine series (June and July, 1944) on Ellington, it was originally written as an instrumental.

[217]

Someone asked [Ellington] about Solitude and he said "I wrote it in Chicago in twenty minutes while waiting for a recording date. The other band, the one ahead of us, was late coming out and I wrote it holding a sheet of music paper against the wall. When we went in, it was the first thing we made. The sound engineer was half crying. It filled everybody up. To make people cry, that's music at its highest. My songs had a tendency in those days to be laments. There was always that melancholy in them. You look at the same melancholy again and again from a different perspective."

Lyrics were added by Ellington's long-time personal manager and music publisher Irving Mills, in collaboration with Eddie DeLange. The song won the twenty-five-hundred-dollar ASCAP award for the best popular song of 1934.

SOMETHING FOR THE BOYS: musical.
Lyrics and music by Cole Porter, book by Herbert and Dorothy Fields. New York opening: January 7, 1943, Alvin Theatre. 422 performances.

"Something for the Boys" won unanimous critical approval as a hilarious and tuneful showcase for the lusty antics of Ethel Merman. As Lewis Nichols wrote in the New York *Times*:

All season long the world has yearned hopefully for a big, fast, glittering musical comedy. It has it now, for . . . the fabulous Mike Todd brought in "Something for the Boys" and as it danced its way across the stage of the Alvin, it quite clearly was not only something for the boys, but for the girls as well.

The play is about three cousins who inherit a four-hundred-acre Texas ranch during World War II. The three, who meet for the first time when they are summoned to San Antonio, are Blossom Hart, a former chorus girl working in a defense plant; Harry Hart, who sells dolls and souvenir buttons on the sidewalk; and Chiquita Hart, a "shabby-genteel with a snooty voice" (Burton Rascoe, New York *World-Telegram*, January 8, 1943). They instantly take an intense dislike to each other, but when they learn of their inheritance, they patch up their differences in hopes of striking oil on the property. During Act I, they deliver a parody of Western songs in "When We're at Home on the Range."

When they arrive at the ranch, they find that their "mansion" looks like something out of "Tobacco Road." In addition, the ranch is next to Kelly Field Air Force Base, and, during a sham battle, it has been occupied by some soldiers from the base. The man in charge is Staff Sergeant Rocky Fulton, a band leader in civilian life. Blossom is wild about band leaders ("The Leader of a Big-Time Band"). She also expresses her feelings in the hit number of the show, "Hey, Good-Lookin'." To her dismay, she finds that Rocky is engaged to Melanie Walker, the stuck-up daughter of a Senator.

The Harts try to make something out of their inheritance by turning it into a boarding house for the wives of student flyers. The wives' feelings are expressed by one of their number, Mary-Frances ("I'm in Love with a Soldier Boy"). Blossom also turns part of the building into a defense plant employing the girls. Angry at the Harts, Melanie hints to the base colonel that the house is a brothel. Despite Rocky's involvement with Melanie, Blossom forgivingly sings that "He's a Right Guy."

The colonel arrives at the ranch and gets the wrong idea from seeing soldiers come out of one door while girls clad in towels go in another. (The soldiers had been shooting craps in a room rented them by Harry, and the girls were waiting to shower after finishing their defense work.) The colonel orders the place closed. One of the digressions during Act II is a wild and woolly song, "By the Mississinewah," performed by Blossom and Chiquita as two Indians from Indiana.

The day is saved when Blossom discovers that a filling in her tooth works as a radio. In an antic plane ride, she saves the crew with her tooth when the regular radio conks out. The Army wants the radios for defense, and Blossom gets Rocky.

The original cast included Ethel Merman, as Blossom; Paula Laurence, as Chiquita; Allen Jenkins, as Harry; Bill Johnson, as Rocky; Frances Mercer, as Melanie; and Betty Garrett, as Mary-Frances. The score included "Could It Be You?," "See That You're Born in Texas," "When My Baby Goes to Town," and "There's a Happy Land in the Sky."

SONDHEIM, STEPHEN: lyricist, composer, television scriptwriter. Born New York, New York, March 22, 1930.
In 1957, Stephen Sondheim achieved great

success as the lyricist of "West Side Story." In 1959, he scored again as lyricist for "Gypsy." Yet, Sondheim finds little joy in writing lyrics, though this gave him the opening he was looking for to the musical theater.

He was born into a wealthy New York family and attended private schools, including Ethical Culture, Fieldston, New York Military Academy, and George School. In 1945, while attending George School, in Newtown, Pennsylvania, Sondheim wrote music and book for a school show. He decided to get the opinion of Oscar Hammerstein II, a friend of his father's and a neighbor in Newtown.

Hammerstein told the boy that his work was worthless professionally. Then the great lyricist-librettist went over the work line by line, showing Stephen the do's and don'ts' from a Broadway standpoint. Sondheim continued to show him his efforts until Hammerstein's death.

Sondheim went on to major in music at Williams College. When he received his bachelor-of-arts degree, he continued his studies in composition and theory with Milton Babbitt at Princeton University. Unlike writing lyrics, Sondheim always enjoyed composing.

Through with schooling, Sondheim got started as a television scriptwriter. In 1953, he coauthored the "Topper" series. That same year, producer Lemuel Ayers asked Sondheim to write the score for a musical, "Saturday Night." Ayers died before the show could be produced. Later, when Martin Gabel was considering doing a musical version of James M. Cain's "Serenade," Sondheim played the "Saturday Night" score for Gabel and librettist Arthur Laurents. Nothing came of this project, and Sondheim kept on with his other work. In 1956, the Broadway play "Girls of Summer" had background music by Sondheim. That year, he also coauthored the "Last Word" TV series.

Sondheim ran into Arthur Laurents at a party. Laurents told him about his work on "West Side Story," and that the composer was Leonard Bernstein. Remembering "Saturday Night," Laurents asked if Sondheim would do the lyrics. Sondheim really didn't want to do just lyrics, but the lure of working with such people as Laurents, Bernstein, and Jerome Robbins was too much to resist. In spite of "West Side Story's" tremendous success, Sondheim swore he'd do no more lyricist-only work. But Laurents persuaded Sondheim to do "Gypsy"—and Stephen had a second hit.

Finally, persistence paid off. In 1962, "A Funny Thing Happened on the Way to the Forum," starring Zero Mostel, David Burns, Jack Gilford, and John Carradine, won critical raves. The long-running farce about ancient Rome featured words—and music—by Stephen Sondheim. His score included: "Comedy Tonight," "Love, I Hear," "Free," "Lovely," "Everybody Ought To Have a Maid," "That Dirty Old Man," "Bring Me My Bride," and "That'll Show Him."

Late 1964 found Sondheim once more working on lyrics for a book by Arthur Laurents. This was for a musical version of Laurents play, "The Time of the Cuckoo." Sondheim's collaborator was none other than Richard Rodgers. The new show, "Do I Hear a Waltz?" opened at the 46th St. Theatre on March 18, 1965.

SONG PLUGGER, SONG PLUGGING: song plugging means getting a song performed, mentioned in the press, or otherwise brought to public attention. The song plugger is the man who does this.

At one time, every popular-music publisher had several men called by this title. Today, song promotion is much subtler, and the old-time ruggedly individual song plugger has been replaced by organizations. There is still promotion, but it is hard to point to any one man or group of men who are doing it. There are, for instance, publicity departments that service the press and other media. There are professional departments to service the performer. There are marketing managers charged with nationwide advertising campaigns to promote a record or performer.

From the turn of the century well into the twenties, the song plugger was all these. He was the liaison between the publisher and the performer. A good song plugger had to have a thick skin, often be somewhat larcenous, ingenious, and wise in the ways of human behavior—which often meant the ways of the gutter. A plugger was a salesman, and before World War I, music was hawked like any other commodity. Many of the song pluggers had been traveling salesmen before entering the music field. In those days, with records just coming in and no radio or television, the music business depended on selling sheet music. The song plugger would get to know performers and talk them into doing new songs, partly through friendship, but more often by buying them gifts or giving them money or a part interest in the song. The plugger also had to go to the bars and music halls to make sure the song

[219]

was actually sung, helping out by planting people in the audience to sing along or applaud. He also might hand out to the audience small printed throwaway sheets with the lyrics.

This pattern changed when the publishers set up "professional parlors" to which the artists could come to hear and pick up new material. This caused the pluggers to become specialized. Inside pluggers at the parlors catered to the performers and played music for them on the piano; outside pluggers brought the performers into the parlors. The plugging game was the proving ground for many of the greatest popular composers. Among those who started as song pluggers were George Gershwin, Jerome Kern, and Richard Rodgers.

With the coming of records and radio, the picture changed again. Professional parlors went slowly out of existence, and as time went on and the disc jockey rose to prominence, the job of plugging passed from the publishers to the record companies (though the publishers still had to persuade the artists-and-repertoire men of the record firms to choose their songs to record; more directly, however, this was done without much in the way of old-time plugging). Much of plugging became mechanical, with songs popularized by juke boxes, promotional records for radio stations, trade-press advertising, etc. Contact still was required at various points in the cycle, however, and the disc jockey became the prime target of organizational plugging.

SOUND OF MUSIC, THE: musical. Lyrics by Oscar Hammerstein II, music by Richard Rodgers, book by Howard Lindsay and Russel Crouse. Suggested by Maria Augusta Trapp's book "The Trapp Family Singers." New York opening: November 16, 1959, Lunt-Fontanne Theatre. 1442 performances.

This musical tribute to the Trapp Family Singers did not get the same enthusiastic critical reception as earlier Rodgers and Hammerstein successes. But the public reception made this a smash hit, with the show's New York run trailing only "Oklahoma!" and "South Pacific" in number of performances of Rodgers and Hammerstein musicals. Certainly the score is one of the happiest, most melodic ever turned out for the American stage.

The setting is Austria in 1938. At the Nonnberg Abbey, young postulant Maria has strayed from her chores to sing her love for the beauties of nature ("The Sound of Music"). The kindly Mother Abbess has reluctantly decided that Maria should be released from her vows ("Maria"). She and Maria review the many things they have in common ("My Favorite Things") before the abbess sends Maria to become temporary governess for the large family of Count von Trapp. Maria warms to her task and soon teaches the Trapp children to sing ("Do-Re-Mi"). She also advises the oldest child, Liesl, in her first love for young Rolf Gruber. Liesl and Rolf discuss their plight ("Sixteen Going on Seventeen").

The captain arrives with his fiancée, wealthy Elsa Schraeder, and his good friend Max Detweiler. At first, he is surprised by his children's new love of song, particularly since he has not been too close to them since his wife's death. Elsa suggests a party, where the children sing good night to all ("So Long, Farewell"). As the days pass, Maria finds that she has fallen in love with the captain. She goes to the abbess, who advises her to have faith and courage ("Climb Ev'ry Mountain").

Meanwhile, as it becomes obvious that Hitler will annex Austria, Captain von Trapp falls out with Elsa and Max. The latter will bow to the new regime, as they advise von Trapp to do ("No Way To Stop It"). But Trapp refuses and, finding his new regard for Maria, marries her. Returning from their honeymoon to find that Germany has taken over and that even Rolf is now a Nazi, they decide to leave. To stall the Germans, who want Trapp to enter their employ, the captain and his family give a stage performance in which he sings his love for his homeland ("Edelweiss"). Max helps out by delaying the captain's Berlin escort while the Trapps hide in the abbey. Later, they make their way over to freedom in Switzerland.

The original cast included Mary Martin, as Maria; Patricia Neway, as the abbess; Theodore Bikel, as von Trapp; Kurt Kaszner, as Max; Marian Marlowe, as Elsa; Lauri Peters, as Liesl; and Brian Davies, as Rolf. Other songs were "The Lonely Goatherd," "How Can Love Survive?," "Laendler," "An Ordinary Couple," and "Processional."

For the movie version, released by 20th Century Fox in 1965, Rodgers wrote some new songs: "I Have Confidence in Me" and "Something Good." The cast included Julie Andrews as Maria; Christopher Plummer as von Trapp; Peggy Wood as the abbess; Dan Truhitte as Rolf; and Charmian Carr as Liesl.

The Sound of Music: Captain and Maria von Trapp, portrayed in the movie version by Christopher Plummer and Julie Andrews, lead their family in song at the Salzburg Festival.

SOUTH PACIFIC: musical. Lyrics by Oscar Hammerstein II, music by Richard Rodgers, book by Hammerstein and Joshua Logan. Adapted from James A. Michener's "Tales of the South Pacific." New York opening: April 7, 1949, Majestic Theatre. 1,925 performances.

Long before "South Pacific" reached Broadway, word had gotten around that this was something special. By opening night, there had been over five hundred thousand dollars in advance sales. Nor were the ticket holders disappointed. Rodgers and Hammerstein had come up with a show every bit as great as their original blockbuster "Oklahoma!" Said Brooks Atkinson in the New York *Times:* ". . . . a magnificent musical drama. . . . rhapsodically enjoyable." "Mary Martin," said *Life,* ". . . becomes in South Pacific one of the stage's really great ladies." Similar salutes were given costar Ezio Pinza. "South Pacific" was voted the best musical of the 1948–49 season by the New York Drama Critics' Circle.

The show is set in the islands of the South Pacific during World War II. In their island-hopping campaign, American forces have re-taken some formerly French-run islands from the Japanese and are preparing for the next phase of the struggle. "South Pacific" opens on the plantation of French planter Emile de Becque. Across the bay is another island, Bali Ha'i, off limits to American forces because the French planters have sent their women there for safe-keeping. Navy nurse Nellie Forbush is visiting Emile. As she tells him, she's "A Cockeyed Optimist." They met at a dance a few weeks before and were attracted to each other. Emile sings "Some Enchanted Evening."

Nellie leaves, and the scene shifts to the Navy Seabee-Marine encampment. The men greet "Bloody Mary," the wily old native woman who sells souvenirs and usually gets the better of fast-talking Seabee Luther Billis, who sets up many fast-buck deals among the troops. They look longingly at Bali Ha'i ("There Is Nothin' like a Dame").

[221]

Young Navy Lieutenant Joe Cable arrives. His mission is to go behind enemy lines to spy on Japanese movements. He hopes to get de Becque, who knows the key enemy-held island, to go with him. He and the base officers question Nellie about the planter, making her realize how little she knows about him. She decides, she tells the other nurses as she showers, "I'm Gonna Wash That Man Right outa My Hair." But when Emile comes and asks her to marry him, she accepts. Because of his love for Nellie, de Becque turns Cable down. Downcast, Cable is given time off, and Billis lures him to Bali Ha'i. There Bloody Mary introduces him to her beautiful young daughter Liat. He falls in love with Liat ("Younger than Springtime").

When Nellie finds that de Becque has two small half-Polynesian children, she rejects him. Emile agrees to go with Cable. He mourns his lost love ("This Nearly Was Mine"). On the enemy island, he and Cable send news that helps defeat the Japanese plans. Cable is killed, but Emile is found by American invasion forces. He returns to find Nellie waiting.

Besides Mary Martin, as Nellie, and Ezio Pinza, as de Becque, the original cast included Juanita Hall, as Bloody Mary; William Tabbert, as Cable; Myron McCormick, as Billis; and Betta St. John, as Liat. Other songs were "Dites-Moi," "Bali Ha'i," "A Wonderful Guy," "You've Got To Be Taught," "Honey Bun," and "Happy Talk."

The movie version by 20th Century Fox starred Mitzi Gaynor as Nellie; Rosanno Brazzi as de Becque (with dubbed in singing voice of Giorgio Tozzi); and Ray Walston as Luther.

SPEAK LOW: song (1942). Words by Ogden Nash, music by Kurt Weill.

One of the musical-comedy hits of the forties was "One Touch of Venus." The music was by a veteran composer, Kurt Weill, but the words were by a man who had never before written this type of material.

The lyricist was Ogden Nash, famous for many years as a writer of humorous verse. The chance to work with Weill came when Nash was in a psychological crisis. It was the summer of 1942, and the forty-year-old Nash had been turned down for military service. At the same time, he felt tired and typed with his role as a writer. When Weill's invitation to collaborate came, Nash seized on it as a way to resolve his dilemma.

Under Weill's patient hand, Nash gradually learned what was expected of him as a lyricist. He also was asked to work on the show's book with S. J. Perelman. Things seemed well underway when Mary Martin was approached to play the lead. She was tempted, but felt that something was missing. Weill decided that a song specially suited to her would turn the trick.

As Nash recalls in an article in *Family Weekly* ("Words To Fit the Music, April 5, 1964):

> Kurt knew his stars. He came to me with a new melody which gave me the spinal tingle that you get from "Begin the Beguine," "Old Black Magic," and Kurt's own "September Song." . . . "If we can find the right words for it, I think Mary would like to sing it," he said.
>
> So it was up to me. I was a novice, and in this particular crisis, the future of the show was in my hands—or in my skull.

Nash hummed the melody over and over. Days passed, but his goal seemed no closer. Words came, but they weren't the right ones. A vast, empty feeling of desperation began to flood over him. It was a feeling that can come to even the most experienced lyricist when the sheet of paper in front of him remains blank. To Nash, in the middle of his first major score, it was doubly discouraging.

Weill had been watching Nash's situation. One day, he came up to the younger man and quietly asked if Nash had read Shakespeare's "Much Ado about Nothing."

"No, why?" was the response.

"There is a line in it that might help you: 'Speak low, if you speak love.' Think of it."

Nash complied, and it wasn't long before the rest of the lyric fell into place. Mary Martin loved the song, and so did the first-night audience. "Speak Low" became one of the top standards in the annals of musical comedy.

STAFFORD, JO: singer. Born Coalinga, California.

One of the greatest popular singers of all time, Jo Stafford also holds the odd distinction of having introduced Europe to that great American institution the disc jockey. She did this in 1950 when she began a weekly radio show from Radio Luxembourg, at that time Europe's only commercial station.

Jo inherited some folk-music background from her mother, Anna York Stafford, who could play the five-string banjo and sing hill-country songs.

Jo was brought up in Long Beach, California, where she made her first public appearance at twelve, singing "Believe Me If All Those Endearing Young Charms" for a meeting of Jobs' Daughters. Soon after, she and her two sisters formed the Stafford Sisters Trio. They got their first radio job in 1935, singing with the Crockett Family of Kentucky over KNK, Hollywood. They soon had many more engagements, and Jo began doing solo numbers.

When one sister got married, breaking up the trio, Jo went on alone. She won a job with Tommy Dorsey as both a soloist and a member of the Pied Pipers vocal group. In 1944, she started what was to become a twenty-six-week stint on Johnny Mercer's radio show. Mercer also signed Jo to record for Capitol. Jo soon had her own radio shows, including the very popular "Supper Club," which was a network feature for four years, until 1949. In 1950, "The Jo Stafford Show" in Luxembourg was being beamed to all the major cities of Europe. During all these years, Jo turned out record after record, many of them all-time standards, first for Capitol (though she recorded with the Dorsey band on Victor), then on Columbia. Some of her better-known recordings are "Good Night, Irene," "Yes Indeed," "Georgia on My Mind," "Hey, Good-Lookin'" (with Frankie Laine), "It's No Secret," "Rag Mop," "You Belong to Me," and "Jambalaya."

STANDARD: a song that remains popular year after year.

Most "popular" music is popular for only a short time. In many instances, this period of hit status lasts only a few weeks. Thousands of songs are composed each year. Of these, only a few hundred become hits. And just a handful of the few hundred survive for any length of time. Those compositions which remain in favor with a large part of the public year in and year out are called "standards."

Not all standards achieve immediate success. A prime example is Cole Porter's "Begin the Beguine." This song first appeared as part of a Broadway musical that received little notice. After the show closed, a few orchestras and vocalists began to perform the song. As time went on, more and more attention was given the music until, quite some time after its initial release, "Begin the Beguine" became a popular favorite, then an all-time standard.

A few other examples of standards are typical: "Stardust," "Anything Goes," "Tea for Two,"

"Slaughter on Tenth Avenue," "Mack the Knife," "Ol' Man River," "Solitude," "Moon Indigo," "In the Mood," "People Will Say We're in Love," "All the Things You Are," "Rhapsody in Blue."

STAR DUST: song (1926). Words by Mitchell Parish, music by Hoagy Carmichael.

"Star Dust," one of the most durable, most played popular songs of all time, was written by a law student at the University of Indiana, Hoagy Carmichael. He was standing near the campus's "spooning wall," thinking of girls he'd known. He thought of one in particular, Dorothy. He'd been very fond of her, yet they had drifted apart. "Never be 21 again, so in love again, never feel the things I felt—the memory of love's refrain," Carmichael thought, and suddenly started humming the tune that was to become "Star Dust." He rushed to a piano at a local college candy shop to put it down.°

It took a long, hard, uphill fight before the song became successful. Carmichael practiced law briefly, but left the profession to play piano with bands. He gave copies of the song to several band leaders. Some of them played it at dances or nightclub dates, but the song remained generally unknown. In 1929, a copy of "Star Dust" was given by bandsman, Jean Goldkette to the then nationally famous orchestra leader Isham Jones. The song, originally an instrumental designed to a much faster jazz beat, had by now been slowed down to a ballad. The year before, Mitchell Parish had added words. Soon after receiving the music, Jones played "Star Dust" concert style on a nationwide radio program and also made a best-selling record. The song was finally on its way.

STARR, KAY: singer. Born Dougherty, Oklahoma, July 21, 1922.

Kay Starr made the unusual transition from hillbilly singer to jazz vocalist. She grew up in Dallas, Texas, and Memphis, Tennessee. By the time she was nine, she was winning amateur contests in Dallas, and, at eleven, she had her own show on Dallas station WRR.

When she was thirteen, her family moved to Memphis, where Kay got a job singing on station WREC. She was a staff vocalist on the station all through high school. At fifteen, she was singing on "Grand Ole Opry," the number-one country-and-Western program in the nation. But Kay also had shown that she could sing popular style

° "Star Dust Road," by Hoagy Carmichael.

[223]

and was asked to join Joe Venuti's band for a month during the summer. The same year saw Kay working with Bob Crosby and even appearing on a record date with Glenn Miller. At seventeen, after finishing high school, Kay joined Venuti for two years, then became featured vocalist with Charlie Barnet's band from 1943 to 1945.

Just when Kay Starr seemed set for stardom, her voice began to fail. Her doctor found that she had a throat infection, and she was not allowed to sing. Though she seemed finished at twenty-four, Kay refused to give up hope. She kept studying the music business, examining all kinds of songs to see which type would best suit her style. For well over a year, she couldn't sing a note. Then one day her doctor examined her and smiled—her throat had healed and she could go back to work. Kay found that her voice had become lower and huskier.

She signed with Capitol Records in 1946 as a solo vocalist and began turning out single records. The new quality of her voice caught on with the public. Her first hit record of the late forties was "I'm the Lonesomest Gal in Town." Over the next decade, she turned out many more best sellers, including her all-time success, "Wheel of Fortune." Some of the other records Kay scored with were "Angry," "Kay's Lament," "I'll Never Be Free," "Changing Partners," "If You Love Me," "Wabash Cannonball," and "Bonaparte's Retreat."

For several years in the mid-fifties, Kay cut down her musical activities to be closer to her daughter Kathy. As Kathy grew up, Kay began to return to music with regular engagements at Las Vegas and Lake Tahoe casinos and guest appearances on major television shows, including those of Ed Sullivan, Perry Como, and Dinah Shore. She also turned out several albums for Capitol in the sixties, including "Movin'!," "Movin' on Broadway," "One More Time," and "All Starr Hits!"

STREISAND, BARBRA: actress, singer. Born Brooklyn, New York, April 24, 1942.

In March, 1964, a twenty-one-year-old girl scored one of the greatest virtuoso triumphs of recent Broadway history. This was Barbra Streisand, portraying the late Fannie Brice in "Funny Girl." In a cover story, *Times* magazine said:

She is the sort that comes along once in a generation. She has more than mere technical versatility. The real force of her talent

Barbra Streisand

comes from an individual spirit that is unique, a kind of life force that makes her even more of a personality than a performer.

Miss Streisand began attending New York acting schools while still going to Brooklyn's Erasmus Hall High School. In her mid-teens, she completed several weeks in summer stock and began the grinding task of attending Broadway auditions. None of these paid off, but she then won a Greenwich Village nightclub talent contest. The Bon Soir and then the Blue Angel hired her. During her engagement at the Blue Angel, she appeared on Mike Wallace's "PM East" television show, and her name became known far beyond New York.

The Blue Angel provided still another turning point. Producer David Merrick watched her perform and signed her for a role in his forthcoming musical "I Can Get It for You Wholesale." As a timorous, spectacled secretary, Barbra sang a riotously funny song, "Miss Marmelstein," that stopped the show. Now she was in demand for starring appearances on most major TV shows and at nightclubs from coast to coast, from Basin Street East in New York to the Riviera in Las Vegas and the Cocoanut Grove in Hollywood.

In 1963, Columbia Records released her first solo album, "The Barbra Streisand Album." Within weeks, her diverse vocal stylings on the record, from blues to fast rhythm songs, were heard on every major radio station across the country. The record was soon among the top ten best-selling albums in the United States. While the album was still in this charmed circle, "The Second Barbra Streisand Album" was released and quickly joined the first one on the list. In 1964, "The Third Barbra Streisand Album" was released and became one of the five best sellers in the nation.

By now, the stage was set for Miss Streisand's next step up the Broadway ladder. Within two years after her brief role in "I Can Get It for You Wholesale," she had achieved star status. To re-create the vibrant nature of as gifted a person as Fannie Brice would tax the abilities of many a veteran actress. To Barbra Streisand, it came almost as second nature. Some of the critics found flaws in the overall production of "Funny Girl," but none could fault Miss Streisand. Her performance was hailed as one of the best of the season and the herald of greater things to come.

STRIKE UP THE BAND: musical. Lyrics by Ira Gershwin, music by George Gershwin, book by Morrie Ryskind and George S. Kaufman. New York opening: January 14, 1930, Times Square Theatre. 191 performances.

George S. Kaufman originally wrote "Strike Up the Band" as a satirical frontal attack on war. As first presented, the show ended with the United States preparing to attack Russia. The Philadelphia tryout in 1927 indicated that American audiences wouldn't accept the premise. Morrie Ryskind was called in two years later to rewrite the script, and the new version proved a great success. The later plot replaced Russia with Switzerland, and the comedy team of Bobby Clark and Paul McCullough was added in major roles.

The plot revolves around the antics of American chocolate tycoon H. J. Fletcher. He resents Swiss incursions on the American market and goes to Washington to try to gain a higher tariff on chocolates. The love interest of the play involves the on-and-off romance between his daughter Joan, and her boy friend Jim, who is suspicious of Mr. Fletcher's motives. The goings-on in Washington include the proposition by a Washington hostess, Mrs. Draper, of the administration's "unofficial spokesman," Colonel Holmes (Bobby Clark) ("If I Became the President").

Fletcher has trouble sleeping, and his doctor gives him a sleeping pill. The tycoon dreams that he is an American general leading a war against Switzerland because of the tariff. The wild antics of Clark and McCullough as members of the rival armies make a shambles of the war. The first-act finale featured the strident march music of Gershwin's title song. The war is won for the United States when the Swiss' secret password, a yodel, is discovered. Behind the scenes, the man behind the President works on a peace treaty. His goals include renaming Baluchistan Jugo-Slavia and partitioning Russia.

Fletcher is a national hero. But, as Jim has suggested to Joan, Fletcher has been using Grade B milk for his chocolate. When the papers unveil the scandal, Fletcher is ruined. Since it's only a dream, all ends happily as Jim and Joan are united.

The score included "Entrance of the Swiss Army," "Soon," "I've Got a Crush on You," "I Mean To Say," "A Typical Self-Made American," "Hangin' Around with You," "Mademoiselle in New Rochelle," and "The Unofficial Spokesman." Besides Clark and McCullough, the original cast included Dudley Clements, as Fletcher; Margaret Schilling, as Joan; Jerry Goff, as Jim; Victor Moore, as the President; Blanche Ring, as Mrs. Draper; and Red Nichols's band.

STROUSE, CHARLES: composer, pianist. Born New York, New York, June 7, 1928.

One of the most ecstatic welcomes given a new writing team was accorded by New York critics to Charles Strouse and Lee Adams for the score of "Bye Bye Birdie."

Strouse began taking piano lessons at the age of ten and decided when he was fifteen to take up music. He entered the Eastman School of Music at fifteen. During his early teens, Strouse had written some popular music, but he decided to major in classical composition. On graduating in 1947, he won two scholarships to Tanglewood, where he studied under Aaron Copland and had his pieces played by the orchestra. After this, he had a series of jobs in less serious music areas, including scoring and composing music for Twentieth Century-Fox newsreels, playing piano for Rosalie in "The Goldbergs" on television, and writing dance music for various mediums. He spent some time in Paris studying with Nadia Boulanger, and returned to the United States to study with Copland and David Diamond.

In 1950, Strouse went to a cocktail party, and met Lee Adams, then writing radio material for such shows as "Tex and Jinx." They got to talking about their varied interests and decided to get together the next day and work on a song or two. The result was something called "The Canasta Rhumba." They agree that this and several others following it were pretty terrible. After a while, they began to smooth out the rough spots and turn out popular songs that were salable. Some thirty of their numbers were published, including one called "The Mating Game" for a Debbie Reynolds movie. From 1953 to 1955, they worked as staff members at Green Mansions, a resort hotel, where they wrote variety shows, sketches, and even operas.

As Strouse and Adams became better known, they wrote special material for many top performers, including Carol Burnett, Jane Morgan, Dick Shawn, and Kaye Ballard. They also were able to place songs in eight revues, including "Shoestring Revue," "Shoestring '57," "Catch a Star," "Kaleidoscope," "The Littlest Revue," and two London shows, "From Here to There" and "Fresh Airs." Still, it was hard to earn a living from their collaboration, and both had to do other work. For Strouse, a good part of the time this meant working as a vocal coach, which he did almost until "Bye Bye Birdie" opened.

In 1958, word went around that Edward Padula was auditioning writing teams for a new musical about teen-age life in the United States. Strouse and Adams won in the third tryout round. They were hired at a hundred dollars a month and, within the first year, had written over forty possible songs for the show and played over seventy-five auditions for backers. After going through fifty-five songs, sixteen were selected for "Birdie." Of the first forty, only three were used: "One Boy," "The Telephone Hour," and "How Lovely To Be a Woman."

"Birdie" was a tremendous success, as was the 1963 movie. The next Strouse and Adams effort, "All-American," starring Ray Bolger, was a failure. The critics' complaints were less with the score than with the book. The year 1963 found Strouse and Adams hard at work on new show material. Strouse also continued working in serious music, on an opera and a piano concerto.

In 1964, Strouse and Adams gained their sec-

ond Broadway hit with the score for "Golden Boy" which starred Sammy Davis, Jr.

STYNE, JULE: composer, producer. Born London, England, December 31, 1905. Won Academy Award for Best Song of 1954 ("Three Coins in the Fountain").

It was a rare season on Broadway during the fifties and sixties that did not see the work of Jule Styne in one of his two roles: composer and producer. In 1959 came "Gypsy," starring Ethel Merman and with a score by Styne including "Let Me Entertain You" and "Some People." A few years before, it was "Bells Are Ringing," with Judy Holliday, that played to sellout audiences. And before that, Styne wrote the music for "Two on the Aisle," "Gentlemen Prefer Blondes," and "High Button Shoes."

As a producer, Styne was responsible in 1952 for Rodgers and Hart's "Pal Joey" receiving its long-deferred acclamation. In 1956, Styne was one of the producers at the extremely successful "Mr. Wonderful." Styne also produced the equally successful play "Will Success Spoil Rock Hunter?"

When Styne was eight, his family moved to Chicago. He started taking piano lessons early in life. He was a child prodigy and appeared with Detroit and Chicago symphony orchestras. At thirteen, he won a scholarship to Chicago Musical College. As he got older, Styne became less and less interested in classical music and more and more in popular. When he was twenty-six, he organized his own dance band. He became well-known in the field, and Hollywood hired him for a multitude of tasks: arranging, composing background music, and second vocal coach for Twentieth Century-Fox. His vocal chores included working with Shirley Temple and Alice Faye. Besides this he wrote songs for a number of movies with many of Hollywood's top lyricists. One of his first hits, with lyrics by Frank Loesser, was "I Don't Want To Walk without You." His composing went into high gear when he formed a close collaboration with lyricist Sammy Cahn in 1942. Fresh from several hit songs in New York, Cahn teamed up with Styne to write "I've Heard That Song Before." It was sung in a movie short by Frank Sinatra, then at the beginning of his career. They followed this up with a long list of songs for films, many of which are now standards. In 1944, there was "I'll Walk Alone"; in 1945, "It's Been a Long, Long Time" and "Let

It Snow! Let It Snow! Let It Snow!"; in 1946, "Give Me Five Minutes More." In 1947, they turned to Broadway with the hit score for "High Button Shoes," which included "Papa, Won't You Dance With Me?," "You're My Girl," and "I Still Get Jealous."

After "High Button Shoes," Cahn and Styne's paths began to diverge, with Styne concentrating more on Broadway and Cahn on Hollywood. Lee Robin was Styne's lyricist for "Gentlemen Prefer Blondes." Beginning in 1951 with "Two on the Aisle," Styne worked on a series of hit shows with lyricists Betty Comden and Adolph Green. These included part of the score for the Mary Martin-Cyril Ritchard version of "Peter Pan" (1954); "Bells Are Ringing" (1956); "Say, Darling" (1958); "Do Re Mi" (1960); and "Fade Out–Fade In" (1964). Some of Styne's compositions from these shows are: "Never-Never Land," "Mysterious Lady," and "Captain Hook's Waltz" ("Peter Pan"); "It's a Perfect Relationship," "Just in Time," "Long Before I Knew You," and "The Party's Over" ("Bells Are Ringing"); "It's the Second Time You Meet That Matters," "Dance Only with Me," and "Something's Always Happening on the River" ("Say, Darling"); and "I Know About Love," "Cry Like the Wind," "Adventure," and "Make Someone Happy" ("Do Re Mi"). "Bells Are Ringing," which starred Judy Holliday, provided Styne with his longest Broadway run to date, 924 performances.

With Stephen Sondheim, Styne turned out the score for the 1959 triumph, "Gypsy." (See separate listing.) During the '50s, he also found time for some occasional movie work, including the 1954 Academy Award winner, "Three Coins in the Fountain," which he wrote with his old partner, Sammy Cahn.

SUNNY: musical. Lyrics and book by Otto Harbach and Oscar Hammerstein II, music by Jerome Kern. New York opening: September 22, 1925, New Amsterdam Theatre. 517 performances.

"Sunny" was basically a showcase for the singing and dancing talents of Marilyn Miller, who had risen to stardom five years before in Jerome Kern's "Sally." More important, "Sunny" marked the first association of Kern and Oscar Hammerstein II and paved the way for their next collaboration, "Show Boat." Besides Marilyn Miller, "Sunny" also starred a number of well-

known comedians plus the dance team of Clifton Webb and Mary Hay. The comics included dancing comedian Jack Donahue, Joseph Cawthorn, and Esther Howard. There was also Cliff Edwards (Ukelele Ike). The plot, which took some weird turns, was tailored to meet the needs of the performers. As Hammerstein said (quoted by Stanley Green in "The World of Musical Comedy;" New York, Ziff-Davis, 1960), "Our job was to tell a story with a cast that had been assembled as if for a revue." Despite the inticacies of the plot, Miss Miller and a great score made the show a hit.

Sunny Peters is a bareback rider in a circus in England. At Southhampton, she is saluted by the soldiers of a New York regiment returned from World War I ("Sunny"). They have recognized her as the girl who entertained them in France during the war. Among them is young Tom Warren. Sunny and Tom fall in love ("Who?") Sunny had once been married to circus owner Jim Deming, who is attracted to Weenie Winters ("Let's Say Goodnight till It's Morning"). Tom and his unit are being shipped back to New York, and Sunny wants to return to America with him. To do this, she must first remarry Jim. Later, she and Jim sing of how things will be "When We Get Our Divorce." Sunny stows away on the ship carrying Tom home.

Besides Miss Miller, as Sunny, Jack Donahue played Jim, Paul Frawley was Tom, and Mary Hay was Weenie. Other numbers were "D'Ye Love Me?," "Hunt Ball," "The Chase," and "Two Little Bluebirds."

SWIM: In-place dance, derived from the Twist, featuring a swimming motion of the arms.

SWING: type of music associated with the big-band era. (See also *Big Band* and *Jazz*.)

Swing was a form of jazz, but whereas the jazz of the twenties was based on spontaneity and improvisation, swing was formalized and arranged. It came to the fore in the early thirties and more or less went out of vogue when the big-band era came to a close with the end of World War II. The word "swing" originally was simply slang for a fast-moving rendition. The term came to be applied to the big-band jazz of the thirties. One theory is that this mainly resulted from Duke Ellington's composition of 1931, "It Don't Mean a Thing (if it ain't got that swing)."

By 1935, big bands had become dominant in

[227]

popular music. Most played both dance music and swing. A few years later, some of the leading bands had given special concerts or theater performances devoted almost wholly to swing. In particular, Benny Goodman's famous Carnegie Hall concert in 1938 brought the popularity of swing to a coast-to-coast high. That same year, Goodman's engagement at New York's Paramount Theatre led to the highly publicized incident of the audience dancing in the aisles. Goodman won the nickname "King of Swing."

The arranger was an important factor in swing. Fletcher Henderson in the early days of swing played a leading role in bringing this form of jazz to prominence. He later had his own band and also became an arranger for Goodman. Some of the other major band leaders of the big-band swing era were Gene Krupa, Bunny Berigan, Artie Shaw, Earl "Fatha" Hines, Cab Calloway, Lionel Hampton, Count Basie, Duke Ellington, Tommy and Jimmy Dorsey, and Harry James. Probably the most sought-after records were those of the Goodman Carnegie Hall concerts.

Many swing numbers were jazz versions of popular songs, but some were written specifically as swing numbers, such as "In the Mood," "One O'Clock Jump," and "Three O'Clock Jump."

The dance performed to swing was the jitterbug, particularly the Lindy.

SWINGING ON A STAR: song (1944). Words by Johnny Burke, music by Jimmy Van Heusen.

One of Bing Crosby's best-known movie roles was that of the young parish priest Father O'Malley in "Going My Way." The movie's score, by Jimmy Van Heusen and Johnny Burke, had many notable numbers, including the title song, but the one most remembered is "Swinging on a Star."

In one scene, Father O'Malley has to teach the idea of the Ten Commandments to a group of tough slum children. It seemed like a good idea to use a song as part of the lecture, and Burke and Van Heusen were asked to write one. The song had to encompass the idea of the Ten Commandments in such a way that Crosby could appear to be giving it in their language. A group of embryo juvenile delinquents couldn't be expected to understand, much less warm up to, any high-flown phrases. This, Van Heusen notes, was the toughest problem he and Burke faced in their work on the film. They spent many hours trying out ideas, phrases, possible titles, but nothing seemed to work.

Then they were asked to dinner at Crosby's house. One of Bing's young sons began misbehaving during the meal, and Bing scolded him for being "stubborn as a mule." Burke immediately felt that this answered their song needs. The idea of someone being stubborn and not trying to better himself seemed just right. (The song begins, "A mule is an animal that's not very bright. . . .").

The next day, Burke and Van Heusen wrote the song, and the studio people and Crosby agreed it filled the bill. Both the picture and "Swinging on a Star" were highly successful. The movie won the Oscar for Best Picture of the Year, Bing Crosby won Best Actor honors, and "Swinging on a Star" won the Best Song of the Year award.

TAKING A CHANCE ON LOVE: song (1940). Words by John Latouche and Ted Fetter, music by Vernon Duke.

"Cabin in the Sky" was probably the high point of composer Vernon Duke's career. The hit song of the show and a major standard today, "Taking a Chance on Love," is proof that a songwriter must always resist the impulse to toss out his drawerful of unused melodies.

The song was the answer to an emergency. The out-of-town tryouts showed that the show had "first-act trouble." The act's finale was "inconclusive and a let-down." Something was needed to solve the problem and solve it fast, for one producer, with gallows humor, suggested the show be "closed before opening to cut costs." The song originally planned for this spot, Duke wrote in "Passport to Paris" (Boston: Little, Brown, 1955), "was a plaintive and rather offbeat lullaby, pretty enough, but carrying no 'sock'; it was in six-eight time, and few hits in the annals of our theater were ever written in that meter." The star, Ethel Waters, minced no words about how little she liked the number; she wanted some "meat and potatoes" instead.

Duke searched through his unpublished music. Three days before the opening, he found a song that seemed appropriate. It was called "Fooling Around with Love" and had been written with Ted Fetter some time before for a show George Abbott considered, then dropped. Duke played it for "Cabin in the Sky" lyricist John Latouche. Latouche liked it, but not the title. Fetter was called in, and, after an afternoon's work, the new lyrics, now titled "Taking a Chance on Love," resulted.

Duke wrote:

I took Ethel to the downstairs lounge at the Martin Beck, in between rehearsals, to play her the song, and she stopped me after the first eight bars with: "Mister, our troubles are over. That's it." . . . Johnny [Latouche] wrote four more choruses for the song, and he could easily have written another half dozen—ask anyone who was present at Cabin's opening, on October 26, 1940. If ever a song stopped the show, but cold, it was "Taking a Chance on Love." Ethel kept coming back, again and again, tears of happiness in her eyes, singing chorus after chorus; five reappearances—no more choruses. To the best of my recollection, she had to sing the last available one thrice.

TANGO: dance and dance rhythm of Argentine origin.

As did many popular dances and dance rhythms, the tango originated in the slums, in this case the Barrio de las Ranas area of Buenos Aires. It was originally called *"baile con corte,"* or "dance with a stop," and was extremely suggestive. A modified and less objectionable version was adapted by the more "refined" elements of the city. This newer dance was called the tango.

Just after the turn of the century, a Frenchman, Camille de Rhynal, was impressed with the tango during a trip to the Argentine. He decided to try to introduce it into Europe. It was still too improper for the genteel tastes of the Continent, and had to be cleaned up further before it could become a ballroom dance. Rhynal presented the new tango rhythm around 1907 in the south of France. By 1909, it was going strong in Paris. Rhynal himself, with Mindo Minty for a partner, won a major competition sponsored by a leading newspaper. The dance slowly spread throughout Europe and by 1914 had been taken back across the Atlantic and introduced into the United States.

In its early form, the tango involved many different and intricate steps. To permit more widespread performance, versions were developed with simpler step patterns. The music is slow, to go with gracious, gliding movements of the dance. The music on which today's tango is based is a *milongo,* a more subdued rhythm than the throbbing habanera beat used in Argentina. It is usually in four-four time. The steps are two slow, two quick, one slow. The quick step is twice as fast as the slow step. To compensate, less distance is covered in the quick step. There are many variations, such as dips, flareouts, and rocking steps.

In popular music, the tango rhythm, while not used too often, does occasionally account for very successful pieces, such as Leroy Anderson's "Blue Tango."

TEA FOR TWO: song (1924). Words by Irving Caesar, music by Vincent Youmans.

Fresh from his 1923 Broadway triumph "Wildflower," Vincent Youmans set his sights on a new musical comedy, one that was to prove the most successful of his career. The show, with book by Otto Harbach and Frank Mandel, was to arrive on Broadway in 1925 by way of Chicago and London and later give birth to seventeen road companies performing it all over the world. The name of the play was "No, No, Nanette."

In the pre-"Oklahoma!" days, music was not integrated with plot in most musical comedies. Instead, the book was prepared and certain points selected as good spots for songs. Usually the action was stopped to do the song. The authors of "No, No, Nanette" looked over their work and decided that a duet would be good for a particular situation. They asked Youmans to write the melody. The idea for it came to him while he was sitting in a lunchroom. He grabbed a piece of paper at his table and scribbled out the notes. Later, he whistled it to his coworkers as he accompanied himself on the piano, and it won their immediate approval.

The lyric was written by Irving Caesar, who was not a regular member of the production team. As the deadline for the opening approached, and Harbach was pressed for time, Caesar was asked to do two lyrics. The two he provided were the show stoppers. One was "I Want To Be Happy," the other "Tea for Two."

"Tea for Two" is one of the half dozen greatest songs Youmans ever wrote. It still gets more performances on radio and television than almost any other song ever written.

THEME: a recurrent melody that sets a tone for a dramatic performance; also called a "theme song."

Many movies have "title songs," which may or may not be theme songs. If a song is written to the words of the title and recurs often enough in the script to characterize the drama, it is also the theme. A performer or musical organization

[229]

may also use a theme song or melody as a musical signature.

THREE'S A CROWD: revue. Lyrics by Howard Dietz and others, music by Arthur Schwartz, Burton Lane, and others, sketches by Dietz, Groucho Marx, Fred Allen, Corey Ford, Laurence Schwab, and others. One song by Johnny Green, Edward Heyman, and Robert Sour. New York opening: October 15, 1930, Selwyn Theatre. 272 performances.

One of the brightest of the sophisticated revues popular in the late twenties and early thirties was "Three's a Crowd." Comedy was provided by the monologues of the great Fred Allen, the funniest of which was a takeoff on Admiral Byrd at the South Pole. Dancing chores were handled by Clifton Webb and Tamara Geva. Some of the sketches were on the risqué side. In one, a young woman enters a room in which a man is taking a bath. Apparently they are strangers, but she accidently looks into the bathtub and realizes that they are, indeed, old acquaintances.

Two great standards introduced by torch singer Libby Holman were show stoppers. One of these was sung by Miss Holman to a sailor whose back was to the audience. The sailor was Fred MacMurray, and the song, by Schwartz and Dietz, was "Something To Remember You By." The other hit song was by Johnny Green, Robert Sour, and Edward Heyman: "Body and Soul." Other Schwartz and Dietz songs were "The Moment I Saw You" and "Right at the Start of It."

THREEPENNY OPERA, THE (DIE DREI-GROSCHENOPER): musical. Lyrics and book by Bertolt Brecht, music by Kurt Weill. New York opening (with English translation of text by Marc Blitzstein): March 10, 1954, Theatre De Lys. 2,707 performances.

The off-Broadway revival of "The Threepenny Opera" met with tremendous enthusiasm from New York audiences. The play had originally been produced in the twenties in Germany, where it created a sensation. Within a year after its opening, it ran up over four thousand performances, first in Berlin and then in other cities. The show's book was adapted by German playwright Bertolt Brecht from John Gay's "Beggar's Opera" (written and produced in England in the eighteenth century). Brecht provided a libretto that was one of the most scathing satires ever turned out for the musical theater. Gay had exposed London's seamier side; Brecht turned the

material into a condemnation of life in postwar Germany and, by extension, the nonsocialist world in general. Nevertheless, taking Brecht's extreme left beliefs into account, the play does make much worthwhile social commentary. Apart from any political message, Kurt Weill's score is one of the best ever composed for the musical theater.

The play's main characters are J. J. Peachum, "King of the Beggars"; his daughter Polly; MacHeath, head of London's most feared gang of thieves; police commissioner John Brown; and his daughter Lucy. The rest of the cast includes and odd assortment of prostitutes, thieves, and beggars.

Polly marries MacHeath in a ceremony attended by Mack's gang and Police Commissioner Brown. The commissioner, who served with MacHeath in the army (which is satirized in "The Army Song"), is also being paid off by his old friend.

Polly then goes home and tells her father ("The Barbara Song"). Peachum is incensed and resolves to force the commissioner to jail MacHeath for his past crimes. Polly warns Mack. He is supposed to flee the city, but it is Thursday, his day to visit his favorite brothel. Peachum knows that MacHeath is a man of habit, and has gone to prostitute Ginny Jenny first and bribed her to turn Mack in. Mack is jailed, but he escapes because Lucy thinks that she is married to him.

Peachum is preparing to send his beggars out to disrupt the coronation of the queen unless he is paid off. Brown tries to talk him out of it, but is put off by Peachum's "Song of the Inadequacy of Human Behavior." Peachum makes a deal with Brown in return for Brown's retaking MacHeath. Despite his earlier experience, Mack returns to the brothel, and Jenny once more betrays him. He is sentenced to hang, but "A Mounted Messenger" appears from the queen ordering his release because of the coronation.

"Mack the Knife," the show's best-know song, is sung by a ballad singer in the prologue to Act I. Other songs were "Morning Anthem," "Jenny the Pirate's Bride," "The Wedding Song for Poorer People," "The Ballad of Sexual Slavery," "The Ballad of the Pleasant Life," "The Survival of Mankind," and "The Song of Solomon." In the 1954 revival, Jenny was played by Weill's widow Lotte Lenya, who performed the role in the original German cast.

[230]

TIME: the grouping of a piece's rhythmic structure into equal measures. (See also *Measure and Rhythm.*)

The time (or meter) of a composition usually is given by a number that looks like a fraction, such as 4/4, 3/4, or 1⅜. The number on top indicates the number of beats in a measure. The bottom number indicates the type of note to be played for each beat. For example, the number four on top indicates four beats to a measure; the number four on the bottom means that each beat is a quarter note.

The fox trot is in four-four, waltzes in three-four, and most marches in two-four.

TIN PAN ALLEY: the songwriting and music-publishing industry.

The term "Tin Pan Alley" came into currency at the beginning of the century. At one time, it stood for a place—Twenty-eighth Street and Sixth Avenue in New York—where, from the turn of the century to the twenties, the main music publishing firms were clustered. When the name was coined, the Alley's principal corporate inhabitants were Charles K. Harris, T. B. Harms, M. Witmark and Sons, Marks and Stern, and Shapiro, Bernstein and Von Tilzer. As time passed and the industry moved farther uptown, first to the area of Thirty-second Street and then to the Times Square section from Forty-second to Fiftieth Streets (and eventually to other parts of the city and other cities as well), the name "Tin Pan Alley" went with it.

The origin of "Tin Pan Alley" is arguable, though its reference to the many rehearsal pianos tinkling away in the old office-building cubby-holes of music row is plain enough. The most widely accepted story is related by Issac Goldberg in his book "Tin Pan Alley" (New York: John Day, 1930): In the first years of this century, composer and music publisher Harry Von Tilzer often was visited by newspaperman Monroe H. Rosenfeld of the New York *Herald.* Rosenfeld sometimes wrote articles about the goings-on in the music field. One day, he dropped into Von Tilzer's office to try to think of a title for an article he was writing about the area. Von Tilzer used to weave strips of newspaper through the strings of his office upright piano to give a tinny sound to the music. Rosenfeld sat for a while and listened to Von Tilzer play some popular numbers. The tinny effect made him suddenly shout, "I have it," and he coined the term "Tin Pan Alley" for his article title.

TIOMKIN, DIMITRI: composer, pianist. Born Ukraine, Russia, May 10, 1899. Won Academy Award for Best Score ("High Noon") and Best Song ("Do Not Forsake Me, Oh My Darlin'") of 1952, Best Score of 1954 ("The High and the Mighty") and 1958 ("The Old Man and the Sea").

"After two revolutions and many challenges," wrote Dimitri Tiomkin in his autobiography, "Please Don't Hate Me," "I met my nemesis, the English language." It is true that Tiomkin has won much attention for his unintentionally humorous declarations in Americanese. A review of his credentials, however, shows that while he may have trouble with English, he has little or none with the more universal language of music.

Tiomkin's father was an important physician and his mother a musician. His mother taught him the piano, and he showed enough talent for his parents to take him to St. Petersburg and enroll him in a children's piano class. For a time, after his father left the family and went to Germany, he returned to the Ukraine with his mother. When he reached thirteen, though, she moved to St. Petersburg and enrolled him in the conservatory. While attending school, he gave piano lessons and played in a movie theater. One of his pupils was the Negro favorite of a Russian

Dimitri Tiomkin

count, and from her he heard American ragtime for the first time.

He stayed in Russia for a while after the revolution. In 1919, after such incidents as almost being shot by mistake as a political prisoner, he decided to leave for Germany. In Berlin, he met violinist Efrem Zimbalist who, after hearing some of Tiomkin's American-style compositions, suggested he go to the United States. But Tiomkin stayed in Berlin to study under Ferrucio Busoni. After two and a half years, he debuted with the Berlin Philharmonic. While finding increased demands for his concerts, Tiomkin also wrote and sold light music such as waltzes and two-steps.

He went to Paris, where he formed a two-piano act with a friend named Raskov. In 1925, producer Morris Gest arranged a twelve-week cross-country tour of the United States for them. Once in America, Tiomkin's interest in popular music increased after he attended some of Paul Whiteman's jazz concerts. His love affair with the United States gained impetus from his marriage to ballerina Albertina Rasch, whom he met in New York. After several concerts in Town Hall and Carnegie Hall in New York, Tiomkin decided to gain a popular-music reputation by returning to Paris to give a Gershwin concert. The event was a great success and resulted in a nationwide recital tour of the United States.

Tiomkin was concentrating on concert work and composing such material as the "Mars Ballet" when his wife was asked to do choreography in Hollywood. She brought his ballet to the attention of the film producers and, over her husband's initial objections, talked him into writing for films. His first assignment, at the start of the thirties, was the score for Tolstoy's "Resurrection" for Universal Studios.

For a time, the Depression cut back on film activity, and Tiomkin returned to New York. It wasn't long before the early optimism of the New Deal reversed the picture, and this time he went back to Hollywood to stay. He was kept busy through the thirties working on scores and songs for such films as "Alice In Wonderland," "Lost Horizon," "Mr. Smith Goes to Washington," "You Can't Take It with You," and "The Great Waltz." His score for Frank Capra's "Battle of Britain" helped win plaudits for Capra from Winston Churchill.

After World War II, Tiomkin really hit his stride, winning four Academy Awards from 1952 to 1958 and writing a number of individual songs

that were national best sellers. Some of the films he provided music for were "High Noon," which won him two Oscars, "Duel in the Sun" "Giant," "Shadow of a Doubt," "The Story of Billy Mitchell," the screen score for "Carmen Jones," "Land of the Pharoahs," and "The Sundowners." During this period, he also provided the score and several songs for the movie "Friendly Persuasion." One of the songs from the latter was "Thee I Love," which sold one and a quarter million records for a young singer named Pat Boone.

Tiomkin won Oscars for scoring "The High and the Mighty" (1954) and "The Old Man and the Sea" (1958). In the 1960s, Tiomkin's name continued to appear on the list of Academy scoring nominations, for such films as: "The Alamo" (1960); "The Guns of Navarone" (1961); and "The Fall of the Roman Empire" (1964).

TO EACH HIS OWN: song (1946). Words and music by Jay Livingston and Ray Evans.

"To Each His Own" grew out of a publicity request by the New York office of Paramount Pictures. Paramount had completed a new picture, "To Each His Own." It was suggested that a song with the same title would draw attention to the picture. Paramount asked some of its name writers, but no one wanted the assignment; they felt that it would be impossible to write a worthwhile song to such a phrase.

In late 1945, Livingston and Evans were virtually unknown. They had recently been hired as staff writers at Paramount, and their work had consisted mostly of unimportant music for shorts and special features. Jay and Ray were given the assignment. They worked on it for three weeks and finally came up with what they felt was a good product.

"Luckily," Evans notes, "the head of Paramount's music department liked it. No one else did. Not only was the title strange-sounding to many in the music field, the song had a wide range." Jay and Ray and the musical director took it to just about every major record company and were turned down.

Paramount had its own music company, however. The music director got them to publish the song and, on the weight of this, got band leader Eddy Howard to make a record. Howard had made a reputation at Chicago's Aragon Ballroom but was not too well-known on the West Coast. In fact, Evans and Livingston had never heard of him, but a record was a record.

Howard's recording and a later one by Tony Martin sold over a million copies each. By 1964, over eight million records of "To Each His Own" had been sold. The song has become a standard, with several new recordings of it each year. In a day when sheet-music sales are usually almost negligible, "To Each His Own" has sold over a million copies.

TORMÉ, MELVIN HOWARD (MEL): singer, composer, lyricist. Born Chicago, Illinois, September 13, 1925.

Mel Tormé was raised in Chicago, attending elementary school and Hyde Park High School. He began to sing in vaudeville at an early age and was already making records by the time he was in high school. World War II was on, and Tormé interrupted his career to enter service in 1944. After his discharge, he returned to singing full time and was heard nationally on network radio shows as well as on records. He also wrote songs that were performed and recorded by other singing stars.

After a hiatus during the early fifties, he once more became a regular attraction on the night-club circuit, appearing at clubs in Las Vegas and at the Los Angeles Crescendo. His popularity, while not as flamboyant as during his teen-age days, was reflected in the fact that he had around twenty albums in circulation in 1964, including "At the Crescendo" (1958); "Back in Town," "Olé Tormé," and "Mel Tormé Swings Shubert Alley" (1960); "Swingin' on the Moon" and "Broadway Right Now!" (1961); "My Kind of Music," "I Dig Duke and the Count," and "At the Red Mill" (1962); and "Comin' Home Baby" (1963).

His own compositions include "Stranger in Town," "Abie's Irish Rose," "Christmas Song," "California Suite," and "Aint Gonna Be like That."

TREE GROWS IN BROOKLYN, A: musical. Lyrics by Dorothy Fields, music by Arthur Schwartz, book by Betty Smith and George Abbott. Based on Miss Smith's novel. New York opening: April 19, 1951, Alvin Theatre. 270 performances.

A tuneful, comic, yet poignant musical play, "A Tree Grows in Brooklyn" was adapted from Betty Smith's best-selling novel. As the show opens, it is a Saturday night around the turn of the century in Brooklyn's Williamsburg section. As the chorus sings, it is "Payday." Johnny

Nolan, a singer in a local quartet, is to meet his girl Hildy O'Dair and her friend Katie Rommely. Katie and Hildy switch hats, and Johnny sneaks up and kisses Katie by mistake. It is love at first sight, and soon Johnny walks off with Katie. Hildy's anger is assuaged by an introduction to Aloysius Moran, a power in the musicians' union, which Johnny aspires to join.

A few days later, Johnny calls on Katie, who lives with her sister Cissy. A warm-hearted, earthy woman, Cissy is living with the most durable of a long line of common-law husbands. Though his name is Oscar, she calls him Harry in honor of her first "husband," Harry Swanswine. Johnny is eager to show Katie his new union pin. He proposes to her, and they sing of their love ("Make the Man Love Me"). Now engaged, Johnny goes off to tell his friends that he's going to turn over a new leaf and go on the wagon ("I'm Like a New Broom"). But he gets drunk. The next day, with a hangover, Johnny meets Katie to pick out furniture as Katie sings joyously, "Look Who's Dancing."

A year passes, and the Nolans have a daughter, Francie. But Johnny can't stop drinking and is going downhill. Cissy has decided to adopt a baby and trick "Harry" into thinking it's his. Supposedly pregnant, she meets Hildy (now engaged to Aloysius) and tells her that "Love Is the Reason." Soon after, in a hilarious scene, son Oscar is "born."

Twelve years pass. Though her father can hardly hold a job and his hands tremble, Francie adores him. He's a well-meaning dreamer. His love for his daughter shows as he tells her she has a bad case of "Growing Pains." Cissy has arranged a meeting with her first love, Swanswine (as she sings earlier, "He's So Refined"), at Katie's. Swanswine's legal wife has died, and he wants to see Cissy again. When he arrives, Cissy realizes that she really loves her present "Harry." But "Harry" has seen Swanswine and gone away in anger.

Johnny by now is playing piano in Mae's brothel. She holds one of her recurrent piano raffles. Johnny wins. He has promised Francie a piano and is overjoyed, but Mae reneges and throws him out with only the piano stool. Deciding to make amends, he leaves home to work as a sandhog and is killed in a tunnel accident. He has left money with Cissy to buy Francie flowers for her public-school graduation. Meanwhile, Cissy, now really pregnant, wins "Harry" back. Some weeks later, a proud Katie looks at

[233]

her daughter's diploma. She is elated, for Francie is "only second generation in America and we got a school graduate with a diploma."

Shirley Booth, as Cissy, scored a major triumph in the original cast. Others in the cast were Johnny Johnston, as Johnny; Marcia Van Dyke, as Katie; Nat Frey, as "Harry"; Nomi Mitty, as Francie; Dody Heath, as Hildy; Ruth Amos, as Mae; and Albert Linville, as Swanswine. Other songs were "Mine 'Til Monday," "If You Haven't Got a Sweetheart," "I'll Buy You a Star," "That's How It Goes," "Is That My Prince?," and "Don't Be Afraid."

TWIST: type of dance.

The twist craze of the sixties originated in a 1958 song called "The Twist," by Atlanta-born country-and-Western artist Hank Ballard. In 1960, teen-age performer Chubby Checker began singing the song, and the twist soon became a favorite among high-school boys and girls in the United States and, later, other countries. In 1962, a new twist craze began among adults.

As Checker stated in *Ebony* magazine in January, 1961: "There are no basic steps in the Twist. You move chest, hips and arms from side to side and balance on the balls of the feet."

The origins of the twist go back far beyond Ballard's 1958 innovation. Similar steps were long performed in the Negro sections of major cities to rhythm-and-blues music. These probably go back to the fertility dances of native tribes. Dancer Geoffrey Holder (no friend of the twist) said in *Ebony* in February, 1962:

The oldest hootchy kootchy in the books has become the latest thing. Who would believe it? From the dawn of time, the classic way of showing male potency has been the same pelvic movement. In African fertility dances, you always find it naked, honest.

Later derivatives of the twist include such things as the frug, hully gully, swim, watusi, and La Bostela.

UP IN CENTRAL PARK: musical. Lyrics and book by Herbert and Dorothy Fields, music by Sigmund Romberg. New York opening: January 27, 1945, Century Theatre. 504 performances.

In 1945, it had been a good many years since Sigmund Romberg had scored a new success on Broadway. Many felt that he couldn't adjust to the new era of the American musical play. But Romberg proved them wrong with "Up in Central Park." In fact, he ended up with more praise

than the "young modern" writers of the book, the versatile Fields team. Otis L. Guernsey, Jr., wrote in the New York *Herald Tribune:*

. . . Romberg has contributed a lovely score. The book . . . doesn't match [the others'] efforts; nevertheless, two thirds of the show is charming enough to be worth 100 per cent of a ticket at the Century.

The run of "Up in Central Park" was the third longest on Broadway for a Romberg show; only "The Student Prince" and "The New Moon" ran longer.

The book deals with the smashing of the Boss Tweed's notorious New York political machine by the efforts of New York *Times* reporter John Matthews and *Harper's* magazine cartoonist Thomas Nast. The particular deals which lead to Tweed's downfall are those involved in the building of New York's Central Park in the eighteen-seventies. Matthew's efforts are complicated by his love for Rosie Moore, whose father is a subcontractor helping Tweed build the park at a thousand dollars a tree.

Rosie and her friend Bessie O'Cohane, whose father also works in the park, hope to make their way in show business up from the squalor of Twenty-third Street ("Up from the Gutter"). They like to go to Central Park, where, as Rosie sings, one of the attractions is the "Carousel in the Park." Rosie meets John Matthews. There are many obstacles in the path of their romance, but, as they sing, "It Doesn't Cost You Anything To Dream."

Boss Tweed and his Tammany henchman introduce themselves ("Boss Tweed"). At first, Tweed is contemptuous of the *Times* and *Harper's* exposés, for he has bought his way out of such situations before. While Tweed and his adversaries square off, Bessie's boy friend Joe Stewart is busy showing her some of the scenes of Central Park. One of the show's high spots, this leads into a series of scenes based on Currier and Ives prints, culminating in a ballet version of a skating scene in the park. Matthews continues looking for evidence against Tweed on the one hand and wooing Rosie on the other. As Matthews and Rosie tell each other, they'll be "Close as Pages in a Book."

Finally goaded by the exposures, Tweed storms into the *Times* office to try to bribe or frighten off his young pursuers. He fails. In the weeks that follow, they smash Tweed but also ruin Rosie's father. Angry at Matthews, Rosie agrees to marry City Comptroller Richard Connolly, who has promised to further her singing career. But she learns that Connolly is not only a fugitive from justice but a bigamist. Her marriage annulled, she can turn to Matthews. As the show ends, they meet at the bandstand on the Mall in Central Park.

The original cast included Noah Beery, as Tweed; Wilbur Evans, as Matthews; Maurice Burke, as Nast; Maureen Cannon, as Rosie; Betty Bruce, as Bessie; and Fred Barry, as Joe Stewart. The score included "When She Walks in the Room," "Rip Van Winkle," "The Fireman's Bride," "When the Party Give a Party," "Maypole Dance," "The Big Backyard," "April Snow," and "The Birds and the Bees."

VAGABOND KING, THE: operetta. Lyrics and book by Brian Hooker and W. H. Post, music by Rudolf Friml. Based on Justin Huntly McCarthy's play "If I Were King." New York opening: September 21, 1925, Casino Theatre. 511 performances.

With this swashbuckling romance, Rudolf Friml reached what probably was the pinnacle of his career in the American musical theater. It had what was perhaps his most brilliant score and was a worthy successor to his hit show of 1924, "Rose Marie."

The show revolved around fifteenth-century French poet François Villon, played in the original cast by Dennis King, one of the major matinee idols of the twenties. The story embellished somewhat the career of the real Villon. The poet, who lived from 1431 to about 1463, certainly was a rogue, often in trouble, several times banished, and once saved from hanging by amnesty of King Louis XI. He also had many troublesome amours, including one with a lady named Katherine de Vaucelles. He did not, however, lead a group of vagabonds to save Louis's throne.

In the show, Villon is the head of the vagabonds of Paris in the fourteen-sixties. The Duke of Burgundy is scheming to wrest the throne of France from Louis XI. Villon, who is loved by an earthy peasant girl, Huguette, also has an eye for ladies of high degree. Huguette is saluted in one of the melodic high spots of the score, the "Huguette Waltz." The king, who is aware of the power of the street mobs, in jest makes Villon king for twenty-four hours. One of Louis's goals is to humble the pride of a lady of the court, Katherine de Vaucelles. Villon is given the task of winning Katherine's hand in that twenty-four

hours or being hanged if he fails. As Villon presses his romantic suit, Katherine falls in love to such songs as "Only a Rose" and "Love Me Tonight." In the meantime, the Burgundians launch their attack and overwhelm the forces loyal to the king. In the stirring "Song of the Vagabonds," Villon rallies his army of rabble to turn back Burgundy and save the day. In the battle, Huguette gives her life to save Villon's. The king pardons Villon, who then marries Katherine.

In addition to Dennis King, the original cast included Jane Carroll, as Huguette, and Carolyn Thomson, as Katherine. Other songs were "A Flagon of Wine," "Some Day," "Tomorrow," "The Hunting Song," and "Nocturne." In the movie version of the fifties, Oreste starred as Villon, with Kathryn Grayson as Katherine. A number of new songs, by Johnny Burke and Friml, were added, including "Bon Jour" and "This Same Heart."

VALENTE, CATERINA: singer, actress. Born Paris, France, 1932.

In 1955, one of the major song hits in the United States was "Malagueña," sung by a young woman previously unfamiliar to the American public. The singer had an Italian name, the song was Cuban, and she sang it it in impeccable German. But languages are a forte of Caterina Valente, who can sing in English, German, French, Italian, Spanish, Swedish, and Japanese.

Her international outlook can be said to have been inherited. She was born in Paris to a Spanish father and Italian mother. Her parents were Italian citizens making their home in France. They were performers and took their family on tour with them throughout Europe and taught them the rudiments of show business. When Caterina was five, she made her debut as a singer and dancer in Stuttgart, Germany. Later, Caterina learned to accompany herself on the guitar.

At the start of World War II, the family was touring Germany. Since they were not German citizens and had been living in France, they were refused exit visas. They would not perform for the Nazis, and the family—which included Caterina, her two brothers, and a sister—were directed to do forced labor in Essen. By forging a telegram from another city in Germany, father Valente got them away from Essen. They remained in Breslau until the Russians took over the city.

After the war, Caterina toured for a while with

her family. In the early fifties, she tried to strike out on her own. She was turned down for a number of nightclub jobs in Paris. Then she auditioned for a radio singing job and lost out again. She later found out that the microphone was defective.

In 1952, she married a fellow vaudevillian, a German juggler named Eric Van Aro, and became a German citizen. He took an active interest in her singing, eventually devoting his full time to managing her career. In 1953, she finally got her solo chance as a singer in a circus. She was performing with her parents' dance troupe when the circus manager heard her singing while waiting for the next act. He asked her to perform for the audience and, at her husband's urging, she agreed. The audience loved it, and she was on the way to success.

Not long after, she auditioned for German jazz-band leader Kurt Edelhagen. He wanted someone to sing scat style à la Ella Fitzgerald. Accompanying herself on the guitar, Caterina delivered a rendition of "All of Me" that caused the band to burst into applause. She appeared with Edelhagen and also began to make records. Her first hit was a German version of Cole Porter's "I Love Paris." In 1955, came "Malagueña" and a flood of requests to appear in the United States. She was featured on "The Colgate Comedy Hour" and the next year returned to star at the Cotillion Room of New York's Hotel Pierre. She turned down American film bids because of European committments that included the internationally successful German musical "You Are Music." In 1957, she was featured in a French musical, "Casino de Paris." Following two more German films, she ranked as one of Europe's top movie stars.

In 1958, she was honored as Belgium's favorite singer with the decoration "Belgique Joyeuse 1900" and also won the award for light music from the International Committee in Florence. In December, 1958, she signed a worldwide recording contract with Teldec-Decca that required her to travel around the world twice a year to record in different nations. Her LP output includes "Continental Favorites" (1959), "Greatest in Any Language!" (1961), "German Evergreens" (1962), "Strictly U.S.A." (1963), and "I Happen To Like New York" (1964).

In 1964, she started a new phase of her career by signing for the Saturday-night television show "The Entertainers," on which she costarred with Carol Burnett, Bob Newhart, and Tessie O'Shea.

VALLEE, RUDY: singer, band leader, saxophonist, actor. Born Island Pond, Vermont, July 28, 1901.

Rudy Vallee was to the younger generations of the late twenties and early thirties what Frank Sinatra was to the teen-agers of the forties or Elvis Presley to those of the fifties and sixties. After years of fame as a vocalist, Vallee carved a new career for himself as a comedian, culminating in a brilliant success in the hit Broadway musical "How To Succeed in Business without Really Trying."

He was born Hubert Prior Vallée near the Canadian border. His family soon moved to Westbrook, Maine. At fifteen, Vallee quit high school to enlist in the Navy. His age was soon discovered, and he was sent home. In 1918, he became chief usher of the Strand Theatre in nearby Portland. A coworker gave him a saxophone, which Vallee taught himself to play, partly by listening to records of saxophonist Rudy Wiedoeft, whose first name Vallee adopted. By 1920, he was playing with the Strand orchestra. Rudy began college at the University of Maine in 1921 but soon changed to Yale. He continued playing to help pay his tuition. In 1923, Rudy took a nine-month vacation from Yale to work in London. There he picked up the song that became his theme, "My Time is Your Time."

After graduating from Yale in 1927, Rudy went at his music in earnest. By 1929, he was leading his own band, the Connecticut Yankees, at the Heigh-Ho Club in New York. That same year, he was given a contract to do a weekly show on station WNBC for Fleischmann's Yeast. Vallee remained a feature of network radio for ten years. In 1932, the show switched from straight band music to a variety hour, the first of its kind on radio. The Vallee show was the road to stardom for many performers. Rudy sang and made hits out of many songs that still are standards, including Maine's "Stein Song," Yale's "Whiffenpoof Song" (which he revised), "Good Night, Sweetheart," (of which he wrote the American version), "Lover, Come Back to Me," "Marie," and "Deep Night" (to which he wrote the lyrics). One of Rudy's first hits was a song he wrote himself, "I'm Just a Vagabond Lover."

"Vagabond Lover" was the title of Rudy's first starring movie in 1929. He made a number of movies during the thirties and forties, including "Second Fiddle" (1939), "Time Out for Rhythm" (1941), "Too Many Blondes" (1941), and "The Palm Beach Story" (1942), in which Vallee scored a major comedy success as stuffy millionaire John D. Hackensacker III. After a stint in the Coast Guard, Rudy returned to radio from 1944 to 1947. With the onslaught of television and the change in musical styles, Vallee's star paled. He began to concentrate more on comedy, appearing in a number of movies and in summer stock. In 1957, he played himself in the movie "The Helen Morgan Story." In October, 1961, Vallee appeared in "How to Succeed, etc." Said the New York *Herald Tribune:* "Rudy Vallee is very funny . . . in a tough-minded, high-minded, majestically incompetent way. . . . [He] is reflective, sober and preposterous."

In 1964, Vallee added still another laurel to his crown when he appeared as master of ceremonies in a well-received TV variety show, "On Broadway Tonight." The show went on as a summer replacement on CBS, but audience reaction was so favorable that it returned as a regular feature during the following winter.

VAN HEUSEN, JAMES (JIMMY): composer. Born Syracuse, New York, January 26, 1913. Won Emmy Award for Finest Musical Contribution of 1955 ("Love and Marriage"), Academy Award for Best Song of 1944 ("Swinging on a Star"), 1957 ("All the Way"), 1959 ("High Hopes"), and 1963 ("Call Me Irresponsible").

Van Heusen was born Edward Chester Babcock, which is still his legal name. On his father's side, he is said to be a descendant of Stephen Foster. He took to the piano at an early age and was composing by the time he was attending Syracuse's Central High School. One day, he sang Eddie Pola's novelty song "My Canary Has Circles under His Eyes" at a school assembly and was expelled. By the time Van Heusen was sixteen, he was an announcer on local radio station WSYR. He later had a program on WFBL on which he featured some of his own music. He attended Cazenovia Junior College for a while, received instruction in piano at Syracuse University, and studied voice under Howard Lyman from 1930 to 1932.

Van Heusen's next-door neighbors were the Arluck family, which included composer Harold Arlen. Jimmy and Harold's younger brother Jerry Arlen often collaborated. In 1933, Harold called them to New York to take over writing the Cotton Club show while he went off to Hollywood. The show failed, but Jimmy had his first published song, "Harlem Hospitality," which featured his new name.

While trying to crack Tin Pan Alley, Jimmy worked as a waiter and later as a freight-elevator operator. For several months, he wrote his songs on the elevator and plugged them in his free time. In 1934, one of his songs got him a job as a piano player at Santly Brothers music publishers. He worked for various firms as a pianist for several years. In 1938, working at Remick, he met Jimmy Dorsey, and they wrote Van Heusen's first hit, "It's the Dreamer in Me." Another Remick visitor was Frank Sinatra, with whom Van Heusen developed a close friendship. Band leader Eddie De Lange and Jimmy soon began working together. They wrote such songs as "Deep in a Dream," "Heaven Can Wait," "Can I Help It?," and "All This and Heaven Too." In 1939, they wrote the score for the extravaganza "Swingin' the Dream." Though the show failed, it contained a memorable song, "Darn That Dream."

Another important event occurred at Remick in 1939. Songwriter Johnny Burke, who had been working with James V. Monaco, came to New York on a visit. Van Heusen recalls, "He just came into the office to shoot the breeze. He said to me, 'Got any tunes?' I said, 'Sure.' So we went and wrote 'Oh! You Crazy Moon.' The next time he was in, we did 'Polka Dots and Moonbeams.' Soon after came 'Imagination.'" Thus started one of the major writing teams in Hollywood history. Moving to Hollywood, Van Heusen wrote hit after hit with Burke, including the scores to most of Bing Crosby's "Road" pictures. For "Road to Zanzibar" (1941) they provided such songs as "You Lucky People, You," "Birds of a Feather," and "African Etude." In 1944, for the Academy Award-winning "Going My Way," they wrote three great songs, "The Day after Forever," the Oscar-winning "Swinging on a Star," and the title song. They also wrote for such other movies as "Belle of the Yukon," "The Great John L.," "A Connecticut Yankee," and "Riding High." For the latter they provided "Sunshine Cake." In 1945, two of their songs were nominated for the Academy Award: "Aren't You Glad You're You?" and "Sleighride in July." In 1950, they scored one of their biggest successes with the score for "Mr. Music."

By the mid-fifties, Burke and Van Heusen were beginning to drift apart. After writing with several others, Van Heusen found a new partner in Sammy Cahn. In 1955, their score for the television version of "Our Town" (starring Frank Sinatra and Eva Marie Saint) won an Emmy.

[237]

That same year, their song "The Tender Trap" was an Oscar nominee. In the years that followed, they supplied a steady succession of hit songs, many of them for Frank Sinatra movies. In 1944, Van Heusen wrote "Nancy" in honor of Sinatra's older daughter. Sixteen years later, he wrote "Tina" for Sinatra's younger daughter.

The team of Van Heusen and Cahn won its first Oscar in 1957 for "All the Way," sung by Sinatra in "The Joker Is Wild." In 1958, for Frank's "Some Came Running," they wrote the Academy Award nominee "To Love and Be Loved." Their second Oscar arrived for "High Hopes," introduced by Sinatra in "A Hole in the Head." The next two years saw two more Van Heusen and Cahn songs win nominations, "The Second Time Around" (from "High Time") in 1960 and "Pocketful of Miracles" (from "Pocketful of Miracles") in 1961. They continued turning out scores for TV and movies. Their TV work included several Sinatra spectaculars. For Bing Crosby they wrote the music for such films as "Say One for Me" (1959) and "The Road to Hong Kong" (1962). For Yves Montand and Marilyn Monroe they wrote the title song and several others for "Let's Make Love" (1960). They continued to leave their mark on the Academy Awards with a nomination for "Pocketful of Miracles" (1961), an Oscar for "Call Me Irresponsible" (1963), and a double nomination for "My Kind of Town" and "Where Love Has Gone" (1964).

VAUGHAN, SARAH LOIS: singer, pianist. Born Newark, New Jersey, March 27, 1924.

"The Divine Sarah," as she has long been known to her fans, is not just a favorite with the public but also is a "musician's vocalist." Her song effects are achieved by a remarkable instrumentlike sense of phrasing and by subtle variations on the melody.

Sarah Vaughan made her first public appearance as a child, singing with the Mount Zion Baptist Church in Newark, New Jersey, where she grew up. She began taking piano lessons when she was seven, continuing her studies for some eight years afterward. She also learned to play the organ during those years. In 1943, she entered an amateur contest at the Apollo Theatre in New York's Harlem. First prize included a week's engagement with Earl Hines's orchestra. Sarah walked off with top honors and so impressed Hines and his band that she stayed on as vocalist and second pianist. Sarah was cofea-

tured with Billy Eckstine. Eckstine soon formed his own band, and Sarah joined him as a featured performer. She also began making records in December, 1944, for Continental.

With Eckstine she began to receive glowing tributes from music critics and fans. She decided to go out on her own. During 1945 and 1946, she received more and more favorable bookings as a soloist (except for a short engagement at New York's Copacabana with the John Kirby combo).

In the late forties, Sarah was well on her way to stardom. She was featured at major nightclubs in all the major cities. In 1947, she was selected by *Esquire* magazine as the new star of the year. She also won the first of many *Down Beat* polls. During one stay in 1949 at New York's Café Society, she met trumpeter George Treadwell. They were soon married, and George became Sarah's manager. He quickly won not only personal appearances for her but increasing television guest engagements. Sarah, who had been recording for Musicraft and MGM, switched to Columbia Records in 1949.

She won the top award from *Down Beat* from 1947 to 1952 and from *Metronome* from 1948 to 1953. Her popularity in Europe, as evidenced by her highly successful tours of England and France, became perhaps even greater than in this country.

Miss Vaughan's repertoire ranges from jazz through popular ballads to gospel songs. Some of her recordings include "The Lord's Prayer," "Trouble Is a Man," "After Hours," "Sometimes I Feel like a Motherless Child," and "What a Difference a Day Made."

VAUGHN, BILLY: band leader, arranger, musical director, composer. Born Glasgow, Kentucky, April 12, 1919.

A band leader who never publicly leads his band is a rarity. Rarer still is for the same leader to turn out million-selling records year after year. The man who has achieved this also won the first platinum record ever awarded, for a record that sold over three million copies. His name is Billy Vaughn.

His father was a fine country fiddler, and the rest of the family learned to perform on some type of instrument and play along with him. The older Vaughn was against his only son (Billy had three sisters) taking up music as a career. Instead, he wanted him to take over his successful barbershop in Glasgow. Billy went to Western Kentucky State Teachers College and attended barbering school in Louisville and a beauticians' school in Bowling Green.

Billy enlisted in the service in 1941 and served for four years. While stationed in Mississippi, he formed his own band, which played locally for dances and other functions. When he left the service, Billy decided to stay in the band business and formed his own combination. For some six years, they appeared in clubs and lounges throughout the South. At the same time, Vaughn began arranging and composing.

Back for a date in Bowling Green in the early fifties, he met singer Jimmy Sacca, and together they formed a vocal group, the Hilltoppers. Vaughn wrote a song called "Trying," and the group made a demonstration record of it. Local disc jockey Bill Stamps liked it, and in early 1952 he sent it to Dot Records, at that time located in Gallatin, Tennessee. Randy Wood, president of the young company (the man who also signed then newcomer Pat Boone), heard and liked it. He signed the group and not long after was rewarded with a gold record of "P.S. I Love You." After Vaughn had been with Dot for a year, Wood signed him as musical director. Billy wrote arrangements for the Fontaine Sisters, Pat Boone, and Gale Storm.

Vaughn formed his own recording orchestra. Shy by nature, Vaughn always disliked playing in public and insisted that the band be a studio one only. Almost from the start, Vaughn's records won nationwide acclaim. The band's hits included "Melody of Love," "Cimarron," "Blue Hawaii," "La Paloma," "Your Cheatin' Heart," and the platinum record of "Sail Along, Silvery Moon." The second platinum record ever awarded was won by Pat Boone; Billy arranged the number and conducted the orchestra for the recording session. In 1955 and again in 1958 (by which time Dot Records and Vaughn had moved to Hollywood), the country's disc jockeys voted Vaughn's band the most programed orchestra. Vaughn's fame spread to other parts of the world, and in March, 1959, he flew to Europe for the award of three gold records. "Sail Along, Silvery Moon" had sold over a million records in both Germany and Holland, as had "La Paloma" in Germany. Overall sales of Vaughn-conducted, -composed, -record, or -arranged compositions had topped twenty million by the beginning of the sixties.

VEE, BOBBY: singer. Born Fargo, North Dakota, April 30, 1943.

Bobby Vee

North Dakota has contributed more than its share of musical headliners—Peggy Lee, Lawrence Welk, and, more recently, teen-age favorite Bobby Vee. Born Bobby Velline, Vee was a star at seventeen and had achieved record sales of over six million by the time he was twenty.

Bobby's father, a chef, could play piano and violin, and his uncle was a good saxophonist. By the time Bobby began attending Central High School in Fargo, his older brothers Sidney, Jr., and Bill were accomplished guitarists and belonged to a fifteen-piece band that played for local functions. Bobby was allowed to sit in on practice sessions provided he would keep quiet. By the time he was fifteen, though, Vee had talked his brother Sid into teaching him to play the guitar. More important, he learned the words to a number of songs his brothers played.

In 1959, Buddy Holly, one of the better-known teen-age performers, was killed in a plane accident on his way to do a show in the Fargo area. The show's producers found out about the Central High outfit to which the Vellines belonged and asked them to fill in. The group bought them-

[239]

selves identical sweaters, called themselves "The Shadows," and selected young Bobby, the only one who knew many lyrics, as vocalist. The result was a rousing welcome from the twenty-five hundred persons at the affair. As a result, the Shadows were asked to go to Minneapolis for a record date, in which Bobby performed a song called "Susie Baby."

The record attracted attention, and the brothers followed up by writing and recording "Devil or Angel." The record sold seven hundred and fifty thousand copies. Now nationally known, Vee came on in succeeding years with a series of hit single records, including "More than I Can Say," "Stayin' In," "How Many Tears," and "Take Good Care of My Baby." His albums also did well. In 1963, Vee turned out a hit Liberty record called "The Night Has a Thousand Eyes." Besides signing an exclusive long-term contract with Liberty, Vee also made his movie debut in Twentieth Century-Fox's "Swinging Along." By the mid-sixties, he had appeared on most major network-television shows.

VERSE: the part of the lyric which acts as an introduction to the main body of the song, the chorus (See also *Chorus.*)

The verse is shorter than the chorus, ranging from a few measures to about twenty (the usual chorus has thirty-two). At one time, the verse was fairly lengthy, but the trend has been towards much shorter ones. In the forties, sixteen measures was fairly common; more recently, an eight-measure verse has been preferred. Many recent popular songs have no verses.

One exception to this trend is in the musical theater. The verse in a musical helps set the scene for the chorus and also provides a handy device for a smooth transition from spoken lines into a song. The verse also makes the song more flexible for use outside the show. The chorus can be written to be general enough so that, if it alone is performed, it can be enjoyed without any knowledge of the play.

VINTON, BOBBY: singer, band leader. Born Pittsburgh, Pennsylvania, April 16, c. 1941.

One of the favorites of the younger set in the sixties, Bobby Vinton doubles as singer and band leader. His father was also a band leader, and while growing up in Canonsburg, Pennsylvania (which also produced singer Perry Como), Bobby aspired someday to match the big-band sound with a band of his own. "I always wanted a big band with a young sound for young people. I

Bobby Vinton

was sure that kids of my generation wanted a full swinging group which would play even rock 'n' roll with a solid beat and rich voicing."

He formed his first band in high school and played for proms and parties. Soon he formed a new organization to play for Duquesne University students and teen-age dances in Pittsburgh. Bobby also began singing. In 1960, he prepared a series of tapes of his band and sent them to Epic Records in New York, which signed Vinton to an exclusive contract. Bobby's first album, "Dancing at the Hop" (1960), won him the rating from *Cash Box* magazine of one of the top four most promising bands. His second album, "Bobby Vinton Plays for His Lil' Darlin's" (1961), was equally successful. In 1962, Vinton organized a four-piece twist band, the Bachelors.

In 1962, Vinton also began to make records as a solo vocalist. "Roses Are Red" rapidly climbed to the top of the best-seller list and won both Vinton and Epic their first gold record. Bobby followed up in 1963 with such songs as "Trouble Is my Middle Name" and "Let's Kiss and Make Up."

WALLER, THOMAS (FATS): pianist, composer. Born New York, New York, May 21, 1904; died December 14, 1943, en route to N.Y.

Fats Waller was born in Harlem, the son of a preacher. His father made sure that Fats learned to play the piano and organ at an early age. Young Waller was given a good background in religious and classical music. It was not long before he played the organ for his father's services at Harlem's Abyssinian Baptist Church. While he was attending DeWitt Clinton High School, he took first prize in a contest for amateur pianists.

After graduating from high school, Waller decided to make music his career. He soon had his first job playing the organ on 135 Street at New York's Lincoln Theatre. By the mid-twenties, he had begun to establish a reputation as a jazz pianist of the first rank. At about the same time, some of his first songs were published, one of the earliest being the 1925 "Squeeze Me."

By the late twenties, Waller was in demand as a performer and composer. His songwriting included individual songs and material for shows. In 1928, he wrote for the Negro revue "Keep Shufflin'." The following year, he turned out two songs that have become standards, "I've Got a Feeling I'm Falling" (with Harry Link and lyrics by Billy Rose) and "Honeysuckle Rose." The same year provided Waller with the song that became his theme, "Ain't Misbehavin'." This was part of his contribution to the show "Hot Chocolates," which included his "Black and Blue." His Victor recording of "Ain't Misbehavin'" later became a best seller.

In the thirties, Waller concentrated more on performing and recording than on composing. His appearances included nightclub and hotel dates and radio shots. He did, however, keep his hand in composing with such numbers as the 1932 standard "Keepin' Out of Mischief Now." In 1943, he wrote the music for another show, "Early to Bed." Late in 1943, Waller passed away while on the Sante Fe Chief en route from California to New York.

WALTZ: dance and dance music of Austrian origin.

No type of music has so often been prematurely declared dead as the waltz. It has always been an important part of popular music, even at the height of rock 'n' roll or the twist fad. This should perhaps be qualified. The waltz as a source of popular music still has a secure place in our culture, but this cannot be said of the waltz as a dance, which has tended to fade out in favor of the fox trot (in fact, many people do a weird form of fox trot to waltz music) and faster dances.

The waltz, a graceful dance in three-quarter time, is sometimes thought to have come into existence full-blown in the romantic days of nineteenth-century Vienna. It is true that much waltz music of the twentieth century is based on the paths blazed by the Johann Strausses (father and son). But the origin of the waltz goes back at least several centuries. In the late sixteenth century, for instance, Austrian peasants danced the *Ländler* and the *Weller* (the *Weller* was also called the *Walzer-schliefer*, or "waltz-sliding dance"), which were forebears of the waltz. Paul Nettl in "The Story of Dance Music" (New York: Philosophical Library, 1947) notes that a famous composer of earlier days, Andreas Anton Schmelzer, provided many waltz airs for the seventeenth-century Austrian court. The first waltzes having a definite artistic musical form, he points out, were played for the ballrooms of the court about 1660. The "Age of the Waltz," though, did not start until the late eighteenth century, reaching its peak in Europe with the Strausses.

American popular music is studded with waltz tunes. Many of the best-selling popular pieces through the first two decades of this century were waltzes. During the World War I era, the United States went dance crazy, and the waltz enjoyed a vogue. But the dance craze ended after the war, and ragtime and jazz took away much of the public's interest.

Though the waltz declined, it remained popular. During the twenties, thirties, and into the forties, one of the most popular bands in the country was that led by Wayne King, "the American Waltz King." He composed many waltzes himself that became national favorites, the most successful of which also became his theme song, "The Waltz You Saved for Me." And as much as a quarter of all country-and-Western music is in waltz time.

WARING, FRED: choral conductor, band leader, arranger. Born Tyrone, Pennsylvania, June 9, 1900.

A great deal of credit for the growth of choral singing in popular music goes to Fred Waring. Starting with a dance band, Fred began experimenting with adding group singing until the Fred Waring Glee Club evolved. Not only did this become a radio favorite of the forties and fifties, it also produced many alumni who expanded this type of music, including Robert Shaw.

Waring began his musical career in his home town when, as a boy scout, he led the local drum-and-bugle corps. He formed a dance band of several members from this group to play at local affairs. Fred played the banjo. When he finished high school, he decided to study architectural engineering at Pennsylvania State College. He continued the band for weekend jobs, however. After trying many names, including the Banjazztra and Snap Orchestra, they settled on the Pennsylvanians.

The band made such a reputation that when Waring graduated, he was immediately in demand as an orchestra leader. During the twenties and thirties, the band played all over the country and also made a name on radio. By the thirties, Fred was also deeply involved in choral work. Besides founding the Glee Club, he also organized and trained choral groups for radio, symphony concerts, Broadway musicals, and educational projects.

The Fred Waring radio show was one of the most popular in the United States and Canada from the late forties well into the fifties. For five straight years, the show was named the best fifteen-minute program by American and Canadian critics. In 1951, it was voted the best daytime show as well.

During the sixties, Waring concentrated on turning out record albums with his Glee Club.

WARREN, HARRY: composer. Born Brooklyn, New York, December 24, 1893. Won Academy Award for Best Song of 1935 ("Lullaby of Broadway"), 1943 ("You'll Never Know"), and 1946 ("On the Atchison, Topeka and the Santa Fe").

Though not as well-known by the public as some of his more publicized contemporaries, Harry Warren's list of credits is as impressive as that of any composer in the business. Such songs as "Serenade in Blue," "Shuffle Off to Buffalo," "September in the Rain," "I Love My Baby," "You're My Everything," "Chattanooga Choo Choo," and "My Heart Tells Me" form just a small part of the catalogue of Warren hits.

Warren's family name had originally been Guaragna, and his father had emigrated from Calabria, Italy, in 1885. By the time Harry was born, his older sisters had changed the name to Warren. Harry took an early interest in music. He taught himself the accordion and also sang

Harry Warren

in the boys' choir at Our Lady of Loretto Church in Brooklyn.

Warren attended public schools in Brooklyn. At the age of fifteen, he left Commercial High School to play the snare drum in a carnival band. "Later," he recalls, "I bought myself a second-hand piano for seventy dollars and taught myself to play it."

Harry got a job at Vitagraph Studios in Brooklyn and worked his way up to assistant director. One of Harry's jobs was to play mood music while Corinne Griffiths, an early movie queen, acted. Warren began to get ideas for original compositions and started to think seriously about writing music. However, the United States entered World War I, and Harry enlisted in the Navy.

After the Armistice, Warren began writing songs. He made the usual calls on music publishers, but got nowhere. Switching tactics, he took a job as rehearsal pianist with the publishing firm of Stark and Cowan. In 1922, the firm published his first song, "Rose of the Rio Grande," a big instrumental hit of the twenties. Even better known is Harry's next published song, "I

Love My Baby," put out by Shapiro, Bernstein and Company. Two hits played and recorded in those years by Fred Waring were "Where Do You Work-a, John?" and "Way Down South in Heaven."

The next major step in Warren's career was a series of stage scores with Billy Rose.

The show was "Sweet and Low" in 1930. (By this time, Warren was a staff writer for Remick Music.) It contained such songs as "Cheerful Little Earful" and "Would You Like To Take a Walk?" Rose and Warren then collaborated on a show called "Crazy Quilt" (1931). Rose gave Warren the title "I Found a Million Dollar Baby," and Warren provided the melody for another all-time standard. He also wrote the music for an Ed Wynn show, "The Laugh Parade" (1931), which included "You're My Everything" and "Ooh, That Kiss."

Darryl F. Zanuck, then a producer with Warner Brothers, had decided that what his studio needed was to go in for musicals in a big way. He particularly liked the idea of turning a book he had just read, "Forty-Second Street," into a musical. His studio had a top lyricist in Al Dubin but no top composer to go with him. Edwin H. Morris, of Remick, a Warner-owned firm, recommended Warren. Within weeks, Warren was hard at work in Hollywood on his first movie score.

"Forty-Second Street" was a success in 1933, and Warren and Dubin were assigned to follow up with the music for "Gold Diggers of 1933." They wrote material for a great many more pictures in rapid succession, including "Roman Scandals," "Moulin Rouge," "Twenty Million Sweethearts," and "Sweet Music." Next came "Gold Diggers of 1935," which contained "Lullaby of Broadway." This won an Oscar (the first of Harry's three) for the Best Song of 1935.

Warren and Dubin's later movies included such songs as "She's a Latin from Manhattan," "Don't Give Up the Ship," "September in the Rain," "Remember Me," and "You Must Have Been a Beautiful Baby." By 1940, Harry had moved to Twentieth Century-Fox. His new lyricist was Mack Gordon. Among the many movies Gordon and Warren worked on were "Hello, Frisco, Hello," "Springtime in the Rockies," and "You'll Never Know" (from "Hello, Frisco, Hello") won the Academy Award for Best Song of 1943. They also worked on two Glenn Miller films, "Sun Valley Serenade" and "Orchestra Wives." For the first they wrote "Chattanooga

Choo Choo" and "I Know Why and So Do You," and for the second, "Kalamazoo" and "Serenade in Blue."

As World War II drew to a close, Warren moved to Metro-Goldwyn-Mayer. His main collaborator there was Johnny Mercer, with whom he wrote the scores for "The Harvey Girls" and "The Belle of New York." "The Harvey Girls" starred Judy Garland and included a rhythmic number called "On the Atchison, Topeka and the Sante Fe." This won Mercer and Warren the Academy Award for the Best Song of 1945.

In the years after World War II, competition from television forced the movie industry to abandon the lavish musical. Eventually, too, the contract-writer system was more or less ended. Warren remained under contract to MGM for a while, then switched to freelancing. Among the movies he worked on from the late forties until the sixties were "Diamond Horseshoe," "The Belle of New York," "The Rose Tattoo," "The Caddy," "An Affair to Remember," and "Cinderfella."

Harry continued to turn out hit songs both for the movies and for the general popular-music market. One of his songs of the fifties was "That's Amore," which was one of Dean Martin's greatest record hits, with sales exceeding three million copies.

Having written hundreds of all-time hit songs, Harry Warren is the first to admit that it's "hard to say how you write something. The easiest way is just to make up stories. But basically, for the professional songwriter, someone hires you to do it in most cases. Even then, though, it's a labor of love. But it is labor—though the writing may take a few minutes, you have to think about it for days and days before you put it down in final form."

WASHINGTON, NED: lyricist, librettist, master of ceremonies. Born Scranton, Pennsylvania, August 15, 1901. Won Academy Award for Best Song of 1940 ("When You Wish upon a Star") and 1952 ("Do Not Forsake Me, Oh My Darlin' ").

"Sauve," "dapper," and "debonair" are words that have been used to describe Ned Washington. His diplomatic bearing was given its due in 1950 when his home town appointed him "Scranton's Ambassador-at-Large." Despite outward appearances, a review of his lyrics shows a great flexibility, with words ranging from the highly sophisticated to the broadly comic. His efforts include the theme song for fellow Pennsylvanian Tommy Dorsey, "I'm Getting Sentimental over You," many of the warmest songs from Walt Disney movies, and the Oscar-winning Western ballad for the 1952 film "High Noon."

Washington attended Scranton Technical High and Charles Sumner School. Vaudeville was in its heyday during his youth, and he decided to make this his career after leaving school. He worked as a master of ceremonies and vaudeville agent and began writing special material and sketches for performers and, eventually, for Broadway shows. His Broadway efforts during the twenties and early thirties included "The Earl Carroll Vanities," "The Vanderbilt Revue," "Murder at the Vanities," "Tattle Tales," and "Blackbirds of 1934." He wrote a number of hit songs during the period, including the 1929 "London on a Rainy Night."

Like most of the top songwriters, he was snapped up by the movies with the advent of sound, eventually moving to Hollywood. One of his early efforts was the Marx Brothers' "Night at the Opera." He worked with most of the leading movie composers. In 1935, for example, he teamed with Burton Lane on the hit "You're My Thrill" for "Here Comes the Band." In 1940, he wrote "The Nearness of You" with Hoagy Carmichael for "Romance in the Dark." From the thirties through the sixties, he worked on many movies with many collaborators. Some of his other film credits include "My Foolish Heart," "I Walk Alone," "The Fabulous Dorseys," "The Show of Shows," "Mexicana," "Happy Go Lucky," and "Brazil."

His ability was recognized with Oscars for the best songs of 1940 and 1952. In addition, in 1940 he won the Box Office Blue Ribbon Award for the Best Song Lyrics of the Year. One of his Oscars was for "When You Wish upon a Star," from Disney's "Pinocchio." Some of his other efforts for Disney were "When I See an Elephant Fly" ("Dumbo") and "Jiminy Cricket" ("Pinocchio").

Among his many standards are "Can't We Talk it Over?," "Someday I'll Meet You Again," "I Don't Stand a Ghost of a Chance with You," "Smoke Rings," "Cosi Cosa," "Don't Call It Love," "Mad about You," and "Stella by Starlight."

WATUSI: In-place dance, derived from the Twist.

WEILL, KURT: composer. Born Dessau, Germany, March 2, 1900; died New York, New York, April 3, 1950.

When Bobby Darin or Louis Armstrong are heard beating out "Mack the Knife," the man he is really saluting is the late German-American composer Kurt Weill. The song is not new—it is from one of Weill's first outstanding successes, "The Threepenny Opera," produced in Germany in 1928.

Weill's father was a cantor, so it was not too surprising that Kurt proved to be musically gifted. His home town of Dessau possessed a royal court, that of the Duke of Anhalt. The conductor at the court was Weill's teacher. By the time Kurt was ten, he was earning money as an accompanist at the Duke's palace. In 1918, Weill entered the Berlin High School of Music. After graduating, he studied with composer-pianist Ferrucio Busoni.

Though he was a student of the classics, Weill earned money playing piano in a Berlin beer garden. His first opera, "The Protagonist," was written in 1924 to a surrealist text. The score was expressionistic and combined jazz and serious music. The piece was successfully produced in Dresden in 1926. His next attempt was "The Royal Palace" and included motion pictures as part of the play. Then came "The Czar Has Himself Photographed," which made further use of jazz and popular music. At this time, he began writing the music for "Mahagonny," a one-act sketch with a text by playwright Bertolt Brecht.

He and Brecht then decided on the more ambitious project of updating English poet John Gay's "Beggar's Opera," a musical eventually titled "Die Dreigroschenoper" ("The Threepenny Opera"). (See separate listing.) The show ran for almost five years in Berlin alone after its 1928 opening. All told, some four thousand performances were given in all parts of Germany.

Brecht and Weill then expanded their earlier one-act sketch into a three act play, "The Rise and Fall of the City of Mahagonny," a fantasy set in the American South (which neither of them had ever seen). It even included a song in English, "The Alabama Song." This was the beginning of the thirties. The Nazis started a riot at the play against Weill's liberal views, and the police had to put it down. Weill then started work on a new play, "The Lake of Silver." On February 19, 1933, the day after the show opened, the Reichstag burned, and Weill and his wife Lotte Lenya fled to Paris.

In 1935, Max Reinhardt brought Weill to this country to help put on the Jewish historical pageant "The Eternal Road." Weill's first musical success here was "Knickerbocker Holiday," which opened in 1938. (See separate listing.)

Then came an even greater success, "Lady in the Dark," in 1941. (See separate listing.) Two years later, "One Touch of Venus," with book by S. J. Perelman and Ogden Nash and lyrics by Nash, starred Mary Martin. "Speak Low," sung by Miss Martin, became a standard. In 1947, "Street Scene," based on Elmer Rice's drama, was premiered. The following year saw the first performance of "Down in the Valley," an American folk opera. In 1948, Weill collaborated with Alan Jay Lerner on "Love Life," which included "Green-Up Time," "Love Song," "Mr. Right," and "Here I'll Stay."

On October 30, 1949, "Lost in the Stars" premiered on Broadway. Based on Alan Paton's "Cry the Beloved Country," a story of racial strife in South Africa, it boasted some of Weill's most haunting music, including the title song. The show ran for a satisfying two hundred and seventy-three performances. Weill died during the show's run.

Lotte Lenya had been in retirement for many years when he died. She was persuaded to play in a special German version of "The Threepenny Opera" in a Weill memorial concert. In 1952, the work was presented in concert form under Leonard Bernstein's direction at Brandeis University.

Miss Lenya was beseiged with requests to permit production of the play in English. But she refused for many months because she "feared it would be overproduced." Finally, she accepted the bid of Stanley Chase and Carmen Capalbo. She also agreed to play Jenny again. The show opened in Marc Blitzstein's new and vibrant English translation off-Broadway at the Theater De Lys on March 10, 1954, and was cheered for twelve weeks by enraptured audiences. On September 20, 1955, it reopened at the same theater and ran for two thousand, six hundred and eleven performances, setting a record for an off-Broadway play.

WEISMAN, BENJAMIN (BEN): composer, pianist. Born Providence, Rhode Island, November 16, 1921.

The composer of many of Elvis Presley's hit songs, Ben Weisman arrived at popular-music success after a long apprenticeship that began with years of study in classical music. His father was a singer, and his mother's family had toured Europe as a vocal group. At five, Ben was a member of the boys' choir in a synagogue. When the Depression came, his father needed work and heard of a government-sponsored farm in Michigan. The family moved there, and at thirteen, Ben was helping round up cows on a ten-thousand-acre farm. His voice began to change, and he started studying piano. He progressed so rapidly that in a year he had completed the equivalent of a six-year course.

He then auditioned for a professor at the Chicago Musical University. The professor said that the boy had great talent and should go to New York to study. The family moved back east, and Weisman applied at Juilliard. He was a little too young, however, and studied instead on a scholarship for four years with Grace Castagnetta. In 1942, Ben joined the Army Air Force and after a short while was placed in the Air Force band. He learned to arrange for dance band and later accompanied such popular performers as Carole Landis and Al Jolson during camp performances.

Weisman stayed in popular music after his discharge. For a number of years, he worked as an accompanist, going on the road with a group called "The Smoothies" and later with Toni Arden and the Ames Brothers. After a while, he became tired of touring and begen thinking of writing popular music. In 1950, he teamed up with Fred Wise and Kay Twomey. One of the team knew Jean Aberbach, an owner of Hill and Range music publishers. In 1951, Aberbach signed Weisman and the others as staff writers. Soon Weisman had turned out such country-and-Western hits as "My Lips Are Sealed" and "Satisfaction Guaranteed."

Weisman was assigned to Elvis Presley in 1956. After studying his style, Ben turned out some twenty-five songs that Presley recorded. Almost all sold over a million records each. The songs included "Crawfish," "Wooden Heart," "Fame and Fortune," "Don't Leave Me Now" (from "Jailhouse Rock"), "Steppin' Out of Line," and "Rock-A-Hula Twist" (from "Blue Hawaii").

In the sixties, Ben began to freelance. He married and moved to Los Angeles in 1962. Here his new manager, Fred Raphael, introduced him to such lyricists as Dotty Wayne, Paul Francis Webster, and Sylvia Fine (Mrs. Danny Kaye). He and Dotty Wayne soon wrote "The Night Has a Thousand Eyes," which became one of the hits of 1962–63.

WELK, LAWRENCE: band leader, accordionist. Born Strasburg, North Dakota, March 11, 1903.

Lawrence Welk built a national reputation with "sweet" music when the rest of the entertainment picture was dominated by rock 'n' roll and the twist.

He was born on a farm. When his family emigrated to the United States from Alsace-Lorraine, they brought along few possessions. One was an old accordion, which Welk learned to play at an early age. By the time he was thirteen, he was playing it at local dances, church socials, and holiday celebrations. Lawrence helped out on the farm until he was twenty-one, when he decided to make music his career. After a few tours with local bands, he started his own group. In 1925, his six-man combo played the first of a long series of Midwest broadcasts on station WNAX, Yankton, South Dakota. By 1928, Welk was beginning to appear outside the Middle West. During one tour of the East, he played Pittsburgh. A friend heard the show and suggested to Welk that the music "has a bubbly, frothy quality, like champagne." Welk christened his style of playing "Champagne Music."

He moved his main base of operations to Chicago in the thirties. He worked out of Chicago until he was signed in 1951 for a short engagement at the Aragon Ballroom in Santa Monica, California. After his band returned to Chicago, the Aragon management asked Welk to return for six weeks. His work included a weekly television show. The arrangement lasted for eleven years, with Welk's show gradually reaching a wider and wider audience, until by 1953 it had become a mainstay on the American Broadcasting Company network. The show shifted to the Hollywood Palladium in July, 1961, under a lifetime contract for Welk to play for dancing every Friday and Saturday night. Not only did Welk's champagne music become a countrywide byword, the show also introduced many new TV performers, including Dixieland musician Pete Fountain, pianist Big Tiny Little, and, probably Welk's happiest discovery, the Lennon Sisters.

WEST SIDE STORY: musical. Lyrics by Stephen Sondheim, music by Leonard Bernstein, book by Arthur Laurents. New York opening: September 26, 1957, Winter Garden. 734 performances.

The transposition of Shakespeare's "Romeo and Juliet" to Broadway in "West Side Story" was more than an up-to-date recreation of a great love story. With Leonard Bernstein's versatile score and a book vibrant with the explosive problems of teen-age delinquency, "West Side Story" combined a poignant romance with a deeply moving, valid social commentary. And it did this while providing exciting entertainment on many levels, from wonderfully choreographed dance sequences to such melodic songs as "Maria." No wonder, then, that this was a smash hit on Broadway and a multiple Academy Award winner in the screen version.

"West Side Story" was several years in the making. The idea occurred to director-choreographer Jerome Robbins in 1949, and he soon interested Leonard Bernstein. The original concept, titled "East Side Story," was based on a romance between a Jewish girl and an Italian Catholic boy.

The plot of "West Side Story" revolves around the struggles of teen-age gangs in New York. The Jets, proud of their "Americanism," violently dislike the rival Sharks, made up of boys of Puerto Rican descent. In "Jet Song," Jet leader Riff promises to drive the Sharks, led by Bernardo, from the streets. He plans to begin his campaign at a local dance that night. Then Riff goes to enlist the aid of Tony, who helped found the Jets but has drifted away as he has grown older. Reluctantly, Tony agrees to go to the dance. He feels that "Something's Coming."

As the orchestra plays the "Dance at the Gym," the rival groups act out their feelings. But Tony meets Bernardo's sister Maria, just arrived from Puerto Rico to marry a boy named Chino, and falls in love with her ("Maria"). While the gangs go to Doc's drugstore to make plans for the coming rumble, Tony slips away to see Maria. In lieu of Juliet's balcony, the lovers meet on a tenement fire escape. They embrace and sing "Tonight." Tony promises to meet Maria the next day at the bridal shop where she works. As he leaves, Bernardo's girl Anita and two of her friends compare life in the United States and Puerto Rico ("America").

At the drugstore, Tony persuades the gang leaders to settle their grudge by a fist fight between two picked boys the next evening. When he sees Maria the next day, he promises to prevent a gang fight. That night, Tony intervenes, as he had promised Maria. But Bernardo shoves Tony and warns him to stay away from his sister. A knife fight begins ("The Rumble"). Riff is killed. Enraged, Tony kills Bernardo with Riff's knife. When a police whistle breaks it up, Chino vows to get Tony. He bursts in on Maria, who is joyfully singing "I Feel Pretty," to tell her the news. Though horrified, she cannot turn away Tony when he comes later. Anita's knock sends Tony back down the fire escape. Anita chides Maria for loving "A Boy like That," but Maria turns away Anita's wrath and gets Anita to agree to go to the Jets' headquarters and warn Tony of Chino's pursuit.

Anita goes, but the Jets taunt her unmercifully for being Puerto Rican. She, gives them the wrong news to tell Tony—that Chino has killed Maria. Tony rushes to Maria and is shot from ambush by Chino. Both gangs carry Tony's body away.

The original cast included Carol Lawrence, as Maria; Larry Kert, as Tony; Chita Rivera, as Anita; Mickey Calin, as Riff; and Ken Le Roy, as Bernardo. Other songs were "Cool," "One Hand, One Heart," "Somewhere," "Gee, Officer Krupke," and "I Had a Love." The movie version starred Natalie Wood, as Maria, and Richard Beymer, as Tony. Riff was played by Russ Tamblyn, Bernardo by George Chakiris, Anita by Rita Moreno, and Chino by José De Vega.

WESTON, PAUL: arranger, orchestra leader. Born Springfield, Massachusetts, March 12, 1912.

Though Paul Weston is known to the public for his many best-selling records, he has a more striking reputation with fellow recording artists as a maker of hits. Weston's arrangements have provided best-selling records for a long list of stars, from Tommy Dorsey's band to such vocalists as Jo Stafford (Mrs. Weston), Dinah Shore, and Dean Martin.

Weston began taking piano lessons at the age of eight and kept up his studies through high school. When he entered Dartmouth College in 1929, he learned to play the clarinet so that he could travel to football games with the college band. He organized a dance band to help pay his tuition, and also began to write musical scores.

After graduating, Weston concentrated on arranging. His work was soon featured by such name bands of the early thirties as those of Rudy Vallee, Phil Harris, and Joe Haymes. In 1936, he became chief arranger for Tommy Dorsey, a post he held for four years. In 1940, he decided to freelance and soon had more work than he could handle. Weston arranged and conducted many records of such singers as Dinah Shore and Ginny Simms. He did the same for several top radio shows, including "Duffy's Tavern," "Fibber McGee and Molly," and Johnny Mercer's program.

In October, 1943, Weston joined the new Capital Record company in Hollywood as an accompanist-arranger. After a few years, Weston turned out some instrumental recordings that met with such public acclaim that he was recognized as a star performer as well as a man behind the scenes. Some of Weston's arrangements for Capitol artists were "Laughing on the Outside" and "Adios, Muchachos" (Andy Russell), "Georgia on My Mind" and "Good Night, Irene" (Jo Stafford), and "Vieni Su" (Dean Martin). In the fifties, Weston switched to Columbia, with the same impressive results.

In 1957, Weston and four other Hollywood record executives were asked by the Hollywood Beautification Committee to help select recording artists' names for inscription in sidewalk plaques in the Hollywood and Vine area. Weston and the others thought that there should be a better way of honoring the industry's top performers. As a result, they organized the National Academy of the Recording Arts and Sciences. Weston was elected first president of the Hollywood chapter. After his term expired, Weston remained an officer of NARAS and, in 1963, was first vice-president of the national organization.

WHATEVER WILL BE, WILL BE (QUE SERA, SERA): song (1956). Words by Ray Evans, music by Jay Livingston.

"Whatever Will Be, Will Be" was the first song ever to be used in an Alfred Hitchcock film thriller. The heroine was singer Doris Day, and the script called for the use of a song as an important plot point. "The Man Who Knew Too Much" revolved around the kidnaping of a small boy, whose mother is played by Miss Day. The song provides the means by which she locates the child. The boy is too young to understand much in the way of spoken language, but there is a special song his mother has sung to him since he was a baby.

Evans and Livingston were given the task of

writing this song. "We almost always start out with a title and work from there," says Evans. "In this case, we looked over the script. It was a picture in a foreign locale—North Africa and England. We talked it over and decided something Continental was in order. We keep lists of titles; we always put down anything that seems interesting for future reference. Glancing down the list, we saw 'Whatever will be, will be.' This seemed to make sense. It was a phrase used in many different languages and also sounded like a good mother-child song."

With this as a point of departure, Evans and Livingston wrote the song in short order, and it was accepted by Hitchcock. The song is sung all the way through the movie. At the end of the picture, the song is performed for something like five minutes as the mother frantically searches for her child.

The record was released at the same time as the picture. "[It] took off right away. It was a big surprise to us, since this was the height of rock and roll." The record, Evans recalls, was a hit not just in the United States, but internationally. "All kids love it, and we think that's why it was so successful. In France alone, thirty-nine records were turned out by different performers. The philosophy appeals to the young as well as the old, and the theme is expressed in just about every philosophy." "Que Sera Sera" won the Academy Award for the Best Song of 1956.

WHITEMAN, PAUL: band leader, musical director. Born Denver, Colorado, March 28, 1891.

Paul Whiteman is one of the giants of popular music. During the twenties and thirties, his bands made music and recording history. Some of the most lasting compositions to evolve from the popular music of those decades were commissioned by Whiteman, and many of the most famous names in the field were alumni of his organizations.

Whiteman's father was supervisor of music in Denver public schools and is credited by some with starting the first high-school orchestra. Whiteman's mother and sister were singers. For a time, though, Paul rebelled against music. When his mother gave him a violin to begin lessons with, he smashed it and had to mow lawns for weeks to earn the money to replace it. When he reached high school, though, he played with the school orchestra. While still in his teens, he joined the Denver Symphony as first violist. He continued as a classical musician after gradua-

tion, later joining the San Francisco People's Symphony, with which he appeared at the 1915 San Francisco World's Fair.

Paul was smitten, however, with the new jazz. He quit the symphony to play at Tait's Café in San Francisco and, in 1919, started his own band, which has been called the first dance orchestra. That same year, Whiteman took his band to Los Angeles, where top movie stars, including Charlie Chaplin and Douglas Fairbanks, became his fans.

His fame, particularly word of his new style of music, "symphonic jazz," spread to the East. With a nine-piece group, he introduced his fast-paced versions of the classics at the Ambassador Hotel in Atlantic City. He received a sensational welcome, and Victor signed him to a record contract. In short order, he turned out one of the biggest-selling records in history, a jazz version of "Meditation" from the opera "Thaïs." The cycle was completed with a triumphal performance at the Palais Royale, a famed Broadway club of the twenties.

From here on, Whiteman was a fixture of the nation's popular music. He was asked to organize Whiteman bands at clubs and hotels across the world. By 1924, fifty-two such bands were playing in North America and Europe. Whiteman also played for "George White's Scandals" in the early twenties and for "The Ziegfeld Follies" in the late twenties.

In 1923, Whiteman received a tremendous ovation from an audience in London which included the Prince of Wales and many members of royalty. When he returned to the United States, he announced his plans to hold a jazz concert on Lincoln's Birthday, 1924, at Aeolian Hall in New York. He commissioned Victor Herbert and George Gershwin to create new works for the event. For Gershwin, the result was "Rhapsody in Blue." In 1925, Whiteman also played Gershwin's one-act jazz operetta "135th Street" at Carnegie Hall.

Whiteman continued to experiment with new musical approaches throughout his career. One of his arrangements even included typewriters. Besides Gershwin works, Whiteman also introduced Deems Taylor's suite "Circus Days" and Ferde Grofé's "Grand Canyon Suite." His band rosters over the years included some of the brightest names in musical history: Bix Beiderbecke, the Dorsey Brothers, Red Nichols, Jack Teagarden, Henry Bargy, Henry Busse, and Lennie Hayton. Other famous alumni include

Bing Crosby, Dinah Shore, Mildred Bailey, Morton Downey, and Ferde Grofé.

WHERE'S CHARLEY?: musical. Lyrics and music by Frank Loesser, book by George Abbott. Based on Brandon Thomas's play "Charley's Aunt." New York opening: October 11, 1948, St. James Theatre. 792 performances.

On the basis that old things are often best, the young production team of Cy Feuer and Ernest Martin gained the rights, after World War II, for a musical version of the famous English farce "Charley's Aunt." Written in 1892, the farce had an initial London run of four years and has been performed in some part of the world just about every year since. In 1940, it had a highly successful revival on Broadway starring José Ferrer.

Feuer and Martin asked the experienced George Abbott to handle libretto and direction. For the score, they called in a newcomer to Broadway (though a well-known songwriter in Hollywood), Frank Loesser. The reviews were somewhat mixed. Said Richard Watts, Jr., in the New York *Post*: "We saw Mr. Bolger in his customary fine form, and that is always a treat, but I found his surroundings strangely dreary." But the public liked the show, and it became a hit. "Where's Charley?" started Feuer and Martin on a string of five straight Broadway triumphs and also pointed Loesser towards such successes as "Guys and Dolls" and "The Most Happy Fella."

The musical takes place at Oxford. Two students, Charley Wykeham and Jack Chesney, are eager to invite their girls, Amy Spettigue and Kitty Verdun, to tea at their quarters so that they can propose. The girls' guardian, crotchety Stephen Spettigue, who is against their seeing Charley and Jack, is sending Amy and Kitty to Scotland in a few days. The girls won't come unless there's a chaperone. Since Charley's aunt, Donna Lucia D'Alvadorez, is due from Brazil that day, they decide that she'll fill this role. Donna Lucia is an Englishwoman whose millionaire Brazilian husband has recently died.

Then Jack Chesney's father, Sir Francis Chesney, comes with bad news. Sir Francis inherited some family debts, and Jack will have to leave school and get a job. Jack suggests that Sir Francis solve this by wooing rich Donna Lucia.

Later a telegram comes saying that she will be delayed. In desperation, the students decide to have Charley impersonate his aunt, juggling things so he can occasionally switch back to regular clothes to woo Amy. The girls arrive. Sir Francis returns and tries to make love to the pseudo-Donna Lucia. Mr. Spettigue storms in to take his niece and ward away. But when he finds that Charley's "aunt" is the rich lady from Brazil ("Pernambuco"—where the nuts come from), he vies with Sir Francis for her hand.

Jack manages to get Kitty alone. ("My Darling, My Darling"). Charley, in one of his quick changes to male attire, sings "Once in Love with Amy." The problem of gaining Spettigue's approval still remains. Luckily, Charley's real aunt appears. Sensing what's taking place, she poses as Mrs. Beverly Smythe. She soon realizes that Sir Francis is a man she was quite fond of years before. She helps get Spettigue's approval and also reveals her identity to Sir Francis, her husband-to-be. All ends happily as Jack Chesney leads the ensemble in singing the finale, "At the Red Rose Cotillion."

The original cast included Ray Bolger, as Charley; Allyn McLerie, as Amy; Byron Palmer, as Jack; Doretta Morrow, as Kitty; Paul England, as Sir Francis; Jane Lawrence, as Donna Lucia; and Horace Cooper, as Spettigue. The score included "The New Ashmolean Marching Society and Students Conservatory Band," "Make a Miracle," "The Woman in His Room," and "Lovelier than Ever."

WILDCAT: musical. Lyrics by Carolyn Leigh, music by Cy Coleman, book by N. Richard Nash. New York opening: December 16, 1960, Alvin Theatre. 171 performances.

The problem with tailoring a book for a particular star is that the star's withdrawal can bring a premature end to the show's run. Such was the case with "Wildcat." The score, however, which brought the team of Carolyn Leigh and Cy Coleman to Broadway prominence, compares in freshness and melody with most recent productions. Leigh and Coleman received more critical acclaim for their next effort, "Little Me," but "Wildcat" has provided the more enduring music for records, radio, and television.

The show opens with tht arrival of Wildcat "Wildy" Jackson in the town of Centavo City in 1912. An oil strike has been made ("Oil"), and Wildy, a tough-talking but really very feminine girl, wants to get in on it. Her aim is to help her lame younger sister Janie. She exhorts Janie to keep fighting ("Hey, Look Me Over"). Wildy falsely leads people to believe that she has oil leases and talks handsome drill boss Joe Dynamite into being her foreman. She and her sister move into a rooming house run by Countess Emily O'Brien. The countess asks Wildy to name her dearest wish. In reply, Wildy sings of her hopes for Janie ("That's What I Want for Janie").

On learning that ten likely acres for oil are owned by an old hermit named Sookie, Wildy decides to charm him into giving her a lease on them. She proves her toughness to Sookie by starting a brawl among Joe's drilling crew. As she and Sookie sing to each other, each likes to do "What Takes My Fancy." She gets the lease, but Joe doesn't believe that oil is there. He tells Wildy off ("You're a Liar"). To try to win Joe back, Wildy promises she'll be all woman ("Give a Little Whistle).

When Joe still balks, Wildy angrily tells the sheriff that Joe is a fugitive, having killed a man in El Paso. After Joe's arrest, she gets the sheriff to parole him in her custody so the crew can start work. Soon after, at a fiesta Joe organizes, he makes fun of Wildy's attempt at a party dress, and she is deeply hurt. A helpful Mexican smoothes things over ("El Sombrero"). The next day, drilling starts to the work song "Corduroy Road."

Then Joe finds that the man in El Paso didn't die. Realizing that Wildy has tricked him, he decides to leave. After the crew disperses, he goes back to get his equipment and finds that Wildy has gone dejectedly to throw the dynamite in the well hole. Fearing that she'll kill herself, he drags her away just in time. Now they embrace as the explosion, naturally, brings in a gusher.

The original cast included Lucille Ball, as Wildy; Keith Andes, as Joe; Paula Stewart, as Janie; Edith King, as the countess; and Don Tomkins, as Sookie. Other songs were "Wildcat," "You've Come Home," "One Day We Dance," "Tall Hope," and "Tippy, Tippy Toes."

WILLIAMS, ANDY: singer, actor. Born Wall Lake, Iowa, November 3, 1932.

Comedienne Kay Thompson was responsible for Andy Williams's initial success. Andy and his three older brothers met Miss Thompson in California, where they had gone after a series of radio shows in the Midwest. Though only in his mid-teens, Andy already had a lot of show-business experience.

When Andy was a boy, the local church had no choir, so Andy's father organized his own—

Andy Williams

Mr. and Mrs. Williams and their sons Bob, Dick, Don, and Andy. When the family moved to Des Moines, the boys sang on their own radio program. They went on to radio work in Chicago and Cincinnati, after which they headed west.

The Williams brothers and Miss Thompson commanded top billing at nightclubs in this country and Europe for six years. After the group broke up, Andy's brothers, tired of traveling, settled down with their families. Andy decided to make a stab at going it alone. Steve Allen's "Tonight" show gave Andy a good showcase. Then Andy replaced Pat Boone on his weekly "Chevy Showroom."

In 1956, Eddie Heywood wrote "Canadian Sunset" as an instrumental. Words were added, and Andy made a best-selling record of the song. In 1959, Andy turned out "Hawaiian Wedding Song," which was voted one of the best records of the year in a disc-jockey poll. In the fall of the same year, the Variety Club of America honored him as Personality of the Year, an award won by such other performers as Al Jolson, Steve Allen, and Jack Paar.

Andy's excellent stage presence, his easy-going, natural manner, made him a good choice to MC his own hour-long television specials, "Music from Shubert Alley" and "The Man in the Moon." In 1962–63, he followed this up with his own hour-long weekly show. For 1964–65, he slowed the pace down again, going back to a series of special shows. One of the songs he was sure to sing was "Moon River," which won a gold record for Andy in 1961 and an Academy Award for its writers, Henry Mancini and Johnny Mercer. In 1962, Williams recorded the next Mancini-Mercer Award winner, "Days of Wine and Roses," as both a single and part of an album. The album was a best seller during the spring of 1963, as was Williams's recording of "Can't Get Used To Losin' You."

WILLIAMS, ROGER: pianist, arranger. Born Omaha, Nebraska, October, 1926.

Roger Williams, born Louis Weertz, was the son of a Lutheran minister. His mother had been a music teacher and director of the symphony orchestra at Emporia State College in Kansas. When Roger was a few months old, his family moved to Des Moines, Iowa, where his father became senior pastor of St. John's Church. Roger could play the piano by ear before he was three and wrote his first composition when he was about four. By the time he was eight, he could play a dozen instruments.

In North High School in Des Moines, Roger not only conducted the school orchestra and choir but also was a basketball player and boxer. When he graduated in 1943, he tried to enlist but was rejected because of hay fever. Hearing that the California climate might help, he moved to Los Angeles, where he continued his music studies under Philip Tronitz. His hay fever was arrested, and he was accepted by the Navy. He was sent to study engineering at Idaho State College and was assigned from time to time to entertain service men.

During a course in gunnery, his hand was crushed by the breech of a gun. At first, it seemed that he might lose the hand, but the Navy surgeon at the base operated brilliantly and saved it. Roger painstakingly worked for months on exercises to restore the strength of his fingers. By the time he was discharged in November, 1945, he had succeeded and was able to study the piano again in Des Moines. For a time, he also had his own radio show and a number of concert dates in the Midwest. In 1949, he returned to Idaho State to complete his bachelor-of-science degree. In 1950, he went on to Drake University in Des Moines to obtain his master of arts in music. He later gained a doctorate in music and one in humane letters.

In 1952, he entered New York's Juilliard School of Music. At one class, jazz pianist Teddy Wilson heard him and urged him to continue in the popular field. Williams did, studying with jazz musician Lennie Tristano. This led to a winning appearance on "Arthur Godfrey's Talent Scouts." Roger also won a thousand dollars on "Chance of a Lifetime" soon after this.

Roger still found it hard to get work. In the mid-fifties, he was playing only occasionally in New York cocktail lounges when he was heard by Dave Kapp, of Kapp Records. Kapp liked Williams's style and gave him a record contract. His first album for Kapp, "The Boy Next Door," was mildly successful.

Then came Roger's big break. He was present at a recording session for another performer. She finished a half hour early, so Kapp asked Williams if he wanted to rehearse anything. Kapp had suggested that Roger make an arrangement of "Autumn Leaves." Williams played it. All present agreed this was too good to let pass, and a record was cut. Six weeks later, the record was number one in the country. Requests for guest appearances poured in from major television shows, including Ed Sullivan's. With this success under his belt, Roger turned out a series of records that sold well in the millions. Some of his best-selling albums are "Roger Williams' Greatest Hits," "Roger Williams—Mr. Piano," "Maria," and "Yellow Bird." Besides continued TV appearances, Williams played over two hundred concerts in the United States and Canada in the late fifties and early sixties.

WILLSON, MEREDITH: composer, lyricist, librettist, conductor, arranger, author. Born Mason City, Iowa, May 18, 1902.

Meredith Willson, long one of radio's most respected musical directors, took a good many years to get around to his first Broadway show. When he did, he drew on memories of his home town. The result was a new career as a major musical-comedy composer at a time when many men are thinking of retirement.

Though Willson's mother gave piano lessons, he became a piccolo player and flutist. Meredith played piccolo in his high-school band. After finishing high school, he went to New York to

Meredith Willson plays for his wife, Rini, and librettist Richard Morris.

over the years, became enthusiastic about the idea of a musical on this theme. Three years later, Willson began writing what was to become "The Music Man" (see separate listing). He interested producers Feuer and Martin in it (they suggested the title), and they said that they would work on it after they produced "Silk Stockings." They lost interest, however, and Willson had to spend many months and rewrite the book thirty-two times (in the end, he called in playwright Frank Lacey to help him) before Kermit Bloomgarden agreed to do it on Broadway. The show opened in 1957 to thunderous praise.

In 1960, Willson's second straight hit, "The Unsinkable Molly Brown," starring Tammy Grimes, opened on Broadway. Willson wrote the score and Richard Morris the book. The musical numbers included "I Ain't Down Yet," "Belly Up to the Bar, Boys," "Bon Jour," "I'll Never Say No," "If I Knew," "Chick-a-Pen," "Keep-a-Hoppin'," "Leadville Johnny Brown," "Up Where the People Are," and "Dolce Far Niente." The show opened at the Winter Garden on November 3, 1960, and ran for five hundred and thirty-two performances. In 1963, Willson wrote the book and score for "Here's Love," based on the movie "The Miracle on 34th Street" (see separate listing).

WILSON, NANCY: singer. Born Chillicothe, Ohio, February 20, 1937.

Nancy Wilson has a satin-smooth, effortless voice and can sing the gamut from shy-little-girl songs to throaty blues, encompassing jazz and sophisticated love songs on the way. She is considered by many as heiress apparent to Ella Fitzgerald. She placed second to Ella as Best Female Vocalist in the 1963 *Down Beat* poll.

The oldest of six children, Nancy spent most of her growing-up years in Columbus, Ohio, where she attended West High School. In 1952, while still going to high school, she had her own twice-a-week show on television station WTVN.

Nancy entered Central State College in Wilberforce, Ohio, in 1954, but the lure of show business was too strong. She toured as vocalist with Rusty Bryant's band for two and a half years, and then returned to Columbus.

In 1959, Nancy decided to try her luck in New York, working weekdays as a typist in the New York Institute of Technology and singing at clubs on weekends. Cannonball Adderley was also in town, and Nancy called him. (She had impressed him when she joined his band in a number when

study at the Institute of Musical Art (now the Juilliard School of Music). At nineteen, he became first flutist in John Philip Sousa's band. He joined the New York Philharmonic after three years with Sousa. In 1929, Willson joined station KFRC in San Francisco as musical director for the northwestern section of the American Broadcasting Company. From there he moved to the National Broadcasting Company. Soon Willson was working on some of radio's major shows.

He composed serious music and popular songs in his spare time. His first symphony, "San Francisco," was composed in 1937. Among his song hits were "You and I," "I See the Moon," and "May the Good Lord Bless and Keep You." As time went on, Willson also began writing humorous books dealing with his musical experiences, including "And There I Stood With My Piccolo," "Eggs I Have Laid," and "But He Doesn't Know the Territory."

Whenever he had an attentive audience, Willson loved to reminisce about his small-town boyhood. At one such session, Frank Loesser, one of the people with whom he had worked

Nancy Wilson

they were appearing in Columbus.) He brought her to the attention of his manager, John Levy, who got her a contract with Capitol Records. In 1960, her first album, "Like in Love," appeared. Her popularity began to build.

She became a favorite of top jazzmen, and some of the greatest shared record dates with her. With George Shearing, for example, she turned out the albums "The Swingin's Mutual" (1961) and "Hello, Young Lovers" (1962). She and Adderley teamed up in the 1962 hit jazz album "Nancy Wilson/Cannonball Adderley." In 1963, she really hit her stride with a series of best-selling albums, including "Broadway—My Way," "Hollywood—My Way," and "Yesterday's Love Songs, Today's Blues." The first of these stayed on the best-seller lists for almost a year; the last became one of the five best-selling albums in the United States a little over a month after release. At the beginning of 1964, Nancy provided still another top-rated album, "Something Wonderful." In 1965, she came up with a best-selling single, "Don't Come Running Back to Me."

WONDERFUL TOWN: musical. Lyrics by Betty Comden and Adolph Green, music by Leonard Bernstein, book by Joseph Fields and Jerome Chodorov. Based on Fields and Chodo-rov's play "My Sister Eileen," which was based on Ruth McKenney's stories. New York opening: February 25, 1953, Winter Garden. 559 performances.

"Wonderful Town" featured what was probably Leonard Bernstein's most singable score before "West Side Story." It also had some of Comden and Green's wittiest lyrics. New York *Times* critic Brooks Atkinson wrote:

Miss [Rosalind] Russell is a full-fledged clown in a tumultuous musical show that is more literate than a lot of serious dramas. . . . the source of all the pleasures is the book that Joseph Fields and Jerome Chodorov have written out of the material of their 1940 comedy, My Sister Eileen.

The plot revolves about the arrival in New York's Greenwich Village of two small-town girls from Ohio: Ruth, who wants to become a writer, and her attractive sister Eileen, who yearns for a stage career. They're inveigled by landlord Appopolous into taking a small basement flat which has a barred, unshaded street-level window through which passers-by can peer. After they've paid their rent, a sharp boom from below indicates that for a good part of the time they will have to listen to blasting for a new subway. Frightened and homesick, they sing "Ohio." Upstairs live Helen and Wreck, a professional football player, who hope to get married but are afraid to ask for the permission of Helen's wealthy mother. Wreck is suddenly ensconced in Ruth and Eileen's kitchen because of a visit by Helen's mother.

Naïve and very feminine, Eileen soon has many men doing her bidding, while intelligent, wise-cracking Eileen is very much alone, as she laments in "One Hundred Easy Ways (To Lose a Man)." But Ruth storms the *Manhatter* magazine office and succeeds in leaving her manuscripts with associate editor Bob Baker. He and the other editors warn her, "Go back where you came from" ("What a Waste"). Baker would like to meet "A Quiet Girl." After a series of misadventures, including a hilarious sequence with a group of Brazilian, non-English-speaking cadets ("Conga!"), all ends well. A front-page story about Eileen, resulting from her arrest due to the wild conga party, leads to an engagement at Speedy Valenti's Village nightclub. Baker and Ruth find that they're in love, and Helen's mother approves Helen's now necessary marriage to Wreck.

Besides Rosalind Russell, as Ruth, the original cast included Edith Adams, as Eileen; Jordan Bentley, as Wreck; Michele Burke, as Helen; Henry Lascoe, as Appopolous; and George Gaynes, as Baker. Lyricists Comden and Green also appeared in several very funny sketches. Other songs were "A Little Bit in Love," "It's Love," and "The Wrong Note Rag."

YOU'RE JUST IN LOVE: song (1950). Words and music by Irving Berlin.

In her autobiography "Who Could Ask for Anything More," as told to Pete Martin (Doubleday, Garden City, New York: 1955), Ethel Merman discusses the hit number of Irving Berlin's 1950 stage success "Call Me Madam," in which she starred:

> You'd think a man who's written several hundred hit songs and more in his lifetime . . . wouldn't be a worry wart. If you think that, you don't know our Irving. He practically bit his fingernails to his armpits trying to think up a comedy song for "Call Me Madam." He kept saying, "I had so many good comedy songs in 'Annie Get Your Gun,' but I don't have one in this show."
>
> I comforted him by saying, "Maybe a new one wouldn't fit into the story anyhow." Then, in New Haven, during the tryout, in just two days time, he wrote the biggest hit of the show, "You're not Sick, You're Just in Love." I sang it with Russell Nype and it was a smash. We put it in the opening night in Boston.

Though the song is a ballad, Miss Merman notes: "What with all the encores Russell Nype and I gave it and the pieces of business we thought out, it worked itself into a comedy song too.

YOU'LL NEVER KNOW: song (1943). Words by Mack Gordon, music by Harry Warren.

In 1943, Harry Warren and Mack Gordon were assigned to write music for a nostalgic scene in a Twentieth Century-Fox film, "Hello, Frisco, Hello," set in San Francisco in the last century. They wanted to write a song that would meet the needs of the script and yet not be tied in the public's mind to a nineteenth-century setting.

Warren and Gordon were asked to entertain soldiers at an Army camp in Santa Ana, California. As they drove to the base, they talked

about what kind of ballad to write for the picture. Gordon thought about the soldiers they were going to entertain, who were far away from home. "If we could get a song," he mused, "—where a girl was singing to someone far away—without mentioning any special place—that might do the trick." By the time Warren and Gordon had reached Santa Ana, Gordon had come up with a few lines for "You'll Never Know." Warren started composing the melody when they returned to Hollywood. In a few days, the song was ready.

"When we wrote the song," Warren recalls, "we liked it. We thought it was a nice, old-fashioned ballad for what it was for. But we started to get a feeling something special had happened a few days later when we were at a cocktail party at the house of the film's producer, Bill Perlberg. He called us over and said, 'Play the song you just wrote.' We did and everyone liked it so much, we got the first idea it might be a hit. Alice Faye sang it in the picture, and it sold over a million copies of sheet music."

The song won the Academy Award for the Best Song of 1943, adding a second Oscar to the one Warren won in 1935 with Al Dubin for "Lullaby of Broadway."

YOUMANS, VINCENT: Composer. Born New York, New York, September 27, 1898; died Denver, Colorado, April 5, 1946.

Vincent Youmans started playing the piano at the age of four. His father, a successful hatter, provided good classical teachers for his son but drew the line at music being anything more than a hobby. Youmans's parents wanted their son to become an engineer. Vincent was sent to the best private schools and enrolled in engineering at Yale in 1915. But Youmans decided against engineering, quit school, and became a clerk in a Wall Street brokerage in 1916. When the United States entered World War I, he enlisted in the Navy and was assigned to Great Lakes Training Station, where he helped produce musicals to entertain the trainees. He began writing music for the shows and became more interested in this than in anything he had done before.

After his discharge, Vincent went to New York and found a job as a staff pianist at the music-publishing firm of T. B. Harms. A fellow worker there was George Gershwin, who recommended Youmans to young producer Alex Aarons. Youmans worked a great deal with Victor Herbert rehearsing operetta singers, experience that was to prove invaluable as he became more interested in musical comedy.

In 1921, in collaboration with Paul Lannin, Youmans wrote the score for "Two Little Girls in Blue," which ran for two hundred and twenty-six performances on Broadway. The lyricist was Ira Gershwin, writing under the name of Arthur Francis. Youmans followed this up with a series of hit shows, including "Wildflower" (1923); "No, No, Nanette" ('24; N.Y. opening, '25), and "Hit the Deck" (1927), and a series of "distinguished failures." "No, No, Nanette" included such standards as "Tea for Two" and "I Want To Be Happy." "Hit the Deck" boasted "Some-

times I'm Happy" and "Hallelujah!" The less successful or unsuccessful shows, added some of the most outstanding songs of today's musical repertoire, including "More than You Know," "Drums in My Heart," and "Rise 'n' Shine." In 1933, Youmans wrote the score for the Ginger Rogers-Fred Astaire movie "Flying Down to Rio," which included "Carioca," "Orchids in the Moonlight," and the title song.

That year, he contracted tuberculosis and retired to a sanitarium in Denver, Colorado. He recovered somewhat, lived in New Orleans for some years, but then took a turn for the worse. He returned to Colorado, where he died at the age of forty-seven.

Special Articles

Tape Recorder Tips

by VERN BUSHWAY

Tape Recorder Design Engineer
Mincom Division of Minnesota Mining & Mfg. Co.

T his book deals with music—the people who make it and the music itself. But music is something you must hear to appreciate. The equipment you use for this—tape recorder, radio or record player—has a great deal to do with what you get out of music. Small flaws in the equipment or in the way it is set up can make the difference between your hearing a true rendition of the original performance or a very poor copy. Some ideas of how to get the most out of tape recording equipment are given here. Similar information on radio and records will be found in the article on stereophonic sound.

The first part of this article gives a general review of how a tape recorder works. The second half provides hints on how to choose or adjust a recorder to get the best performance.

The basic steps in recording sound on tape and later playing back the sound from the tape are shown in Figure 1. The basic principle is that there is a definite relationship between the nature of a sound wave and that of an alternating current electrical wave. Sound travels through the air in waves, alternately compressing and expanding the air molecules. If you could "see" a sound wave, it would look like the series of ripples that spread in a still pond after a stone has been tossed in the water. The shape of the sound waves—the spacing between the alternates hills and valleys and the speed of the wave (sound cycles per second)—determine whether the sound is soft or loud, or its pitch. Another word for the wave speed in cycles-per-second is *frequency*.

An electrical alternating current also takes the form of a wave with similar peaks and valleys. It starts at zero, rises to a maximum of voltage, then decreases past zero to a point equal in value to the maximum point but in the opposite or "negative" direction. The cycle is then repeated. The louder is the sound, the higher is the peak or the lower the valley for both the sound and electrical wave. Also, as the pitch of a tone changes, the number of cycles that occur in a second changes. The relationship between sound and current waves is a direct one—if the sound causes the air to vibrate, say, 40 times a second, the electric current will have a value of 40 cycles per second.

What happens in recording is that the sound is directed into a microphone. The

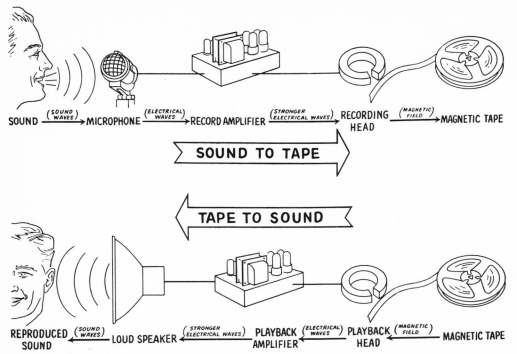

SOUND $\xrightarrow{\text{(SOUND WAVES)}}$ MICROPHONE $\xrightarrow{\text{(ELECTRICAL WAVES)}}$ RECORD AMPLIFIER $\xrightarrow{\text{(STRONGER ELECTRICAL WAVES)}}$ RECORDING HEAD $\xrightarrow{\text{(MAGNETIC FIELD)}}$ MAGNETIC TAPE

> SOUND TO TAPE

< TAPE TO SOUND

REPRODUCED SOUND $\xleftarrow{\text{(SOUND WAVES)}}$ LOUD SPEAKER $\xleftarrow{\text{(STRONGER ELECTRICAL WAVES)}}$ PLAYBACK AMPLIFIER $\xleftarrow{\text{(ELECTRICAL WAVES)}}$ PLAYBACK HEAD $\xleftarrow{\text{(MAGNETIC FIELD)}}$ MAGNETIC TAPE

FIGURE 1: These simplified sketches show (top) how sound is recorded on tape and (bottom) how it is then played back from the tape.

microphone sets up a current wave in the electrical wiring. This electrical signal is originally weak, so special electronic systems known as amplifiers must increase the signal strength to a proper level for the next step in the process. This next step is to store the equivalent of the original sound for playback later. Storage is accomplished in the tape recorder through use of the principles of magnetism.

One of these principles is that an electric current can induce a magnetic field in certain materials that have the property of being able to be magnetized. For the recorder, this requires the use of two different types of magnetic material. One kind is used to make the magnetic recording head. This head must have the property of being easily magnetized when an electric current flows around it, but immediately losing its magnetism when the current stops. The recording head is a magnet bent into a curved shape as shown in Figure 2. As the Figure shows, the electrical wiring of the recorder leads from the amplifier system into a coil of wire around the head.

When an electrical current flows through the coil, it "induces" or causes the head to become magnetized. When the current stops, the head becomes demagnetized. When the current reverses, the poles of the head become reversed; i.e., the north pole becomes the south pole and vice versa. In addition, the strength of the magnetic field grows stronger or weaker as the electric current becomes stronger or weaker.

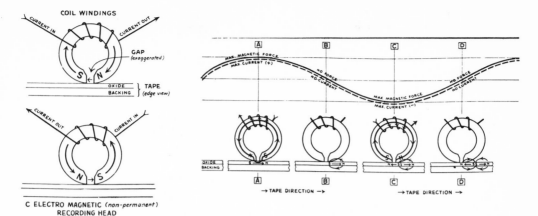

FIGURE 2: These diagrams give a detailed picture of the way a magnetic recording head works. The two sketches at the left show how the changes in direction of the alternating electric current changes the magnetic properties of the recording head. At right, a typical recording sequence is shown with the current and magnetic force changing from zero to a maximum, then back through zero to be a minimum, and so on. As the second and fourth diagrams of the recording head show, when current and magnetic force are zero, no forces are acting on the tape.

The second kind of magnetic material must have the property of keeping its magnetism, once it has been magnetized, "permanently." By "permanently magnetized," we mean the material, once magnetized, will remain so unless another external magnetic field is applied to demagnetize the material. This second type of material is coated onto the plastic base of the recording tape. (It forms the 'dull' side of the tape.)

Now let's see how the recording head stores the sound information on the tape. The key item is the air gap between the north and south poles of the bent magnet head. When the head has been magnetized by an electric current, the magnetic lines of force want to form a circle. It's easier to go through the tape coating than the air gap and this is the way they go. Of course, the current is also alternating. As the tape goes by the head, then, a whole series of small bar magnets, alternately north and south, are induced in the tape coating (Figure 3). The spacing and the properties of these little magnets depends on

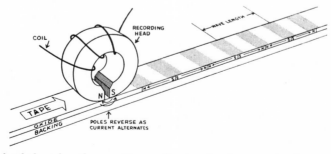

FIGURE 3: This sketch shows how the magnetic recording tape lays down a series of very small magnets on the oxide coating of the tape. (Tape magnet sizes are greatly exagerrated.)

[261]

the original nature of the sound patterns. If the air originally vibrated 40 times a second, then 40 south and 40 north little magnet sections would be produced on the tape every second it passes under the recording head. If the original signal was 60 cps, then 60 north and 60 south magnets would be produced, and so on.

Once the desired music has been recorded on the tape, the next step is playback. (See Figure 4.) Generally speaking, playback is the opposite of recording. The now-

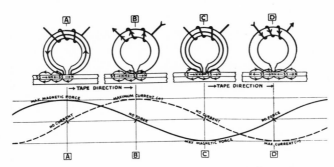

FIGURE 4: These sketches show a typical sequence in playback in which the magnetic pattern on the tape sets up a corresponding pattern in the electrical current flowing in the wire coil.

magnetized tape passes under the playback head. In some sets, the same head is used for both recording and playback, in others a different head is provided for each operation. The continuous alternation between little north and south magnets on the tape sets up a similar magnetic field in the head. This, in turn, causes a current to flow in the coil. The current then goes to the amplifier which increases the signal strength. The signal is re-layed to the loudspeaker, causing the air to vibrate to give sound waves equivalent to the patterns stored on the tape.

The tape will remain magnetized, as we have noted, until something is done to "erase" it. The erasing operation simply involves using an erasing head to send magnetic forces through the tape that realign the tape's atomic particles to an unmagnetized state.

This, then, is a very simple description of how a tape recorder works. Now let's see what you can do to make sure your recorder gives you as faithful sound reproduction as possible. The first consideration, if you're starting from scratch, is how to tell a good unit. In general, you get what you pay for. A really good set is more expensive than an ordinary one. The key consideration in recorder performance is what is known as the "signal to noise ratio." All this means is the amount of static, or unwanted noise, you get in relation to the desired sound signal.

In poorer recorders, the main source of unwanted noise is usually the amplifier. A cheap amplifier does not have the necessary electronic parts to prevent interference from such things as the living room lights, electrical alternating motors in washing machines, etc. In this case, you would hear a humming noise that masked all other noise source. There isn't much you can do about this if you decide to buy a set for as little money as possible. The only thing to do in this case is just listen to several types of sets and see which seems to give the best sound.

On the other hand, a good recorder should eliminate this 60 cycle alternating current hum. If you are looking for a quality set, there are two types of noise you should watch for: tape hiss and vacuum tube noise. Vacuum tubes cause a sound something like "shhhhh." Tape hiss is a sort of hissing noise caused by the physical movement of particles in the magnetic coating as they are affected by the magnetized head. In some cases, the limiting factor on a vacuum tube amplifier is 60 cycle hum. If you hear this instead of the "shhhh" sound, you know the amplifier is not all it should be. Taking the set as a whole, the most important thing to listen for is tape hiss. Tape hiss can't be eliminated, but it will be easily masked by other, more detrimental noise sources. Thus if you hear tape hiss, you know it's a good set, if not, then the electronics are poor and thus the signal to noise ratio.

Other important considerations in selecting an audio recorder are *flutter* and *wow*. These are noise effects due to the mechanical design of the tape transport. In both cases, you can only detect these things by carefully listening to the equipment. If you hear a violin note and it seems to vary in pitch, this is caused by wow. Flutter would cause the note to change frequency and have a "fuzzy" sound. With a pure tone, flutter effects are like getting a picture out of focus.

Once you've selected your recorder, the next question is how to set it up properly. Each recorder has its own alignment procedures and these instructions should be followed. The following short discussion of how to achieve very precise alignment is for the reader with a knowledge of electronics. For those without this background, it would be best just to follow equipment instructions and skip to the latter part of the article for some hints on proper set operation.

As far as professional alignment of a tape recorder is concerned, normally the equipment is set up for a one per cent harmonic distortion point. The first step in doing this is to run the input gain to the recorder to where it "saturates" the tape; that is, to where the tape can't take any more information. To find this point, you would connect a V-U meter or a voltmeter on the output and find where the signal not only stops increasing, but start to decrease. By then backing the signal off 12 db°, you will be at the one per cent point. This can be read off directly if a V-U meter is used.

As far as operation is concerned, one important point is to keep the recording-playback heads clean. Any dirt on the head surface will oppose the passage of magnetic force and so degrade the signal. To clean the heads, just take a swab or 'Q' tip, dip it in alcohol, and brush the head surface. Equally as important is to buy good quality recording tape. Some tapes are available at very low prices, but a cheap tape can clog the recording head due to particles of its magnetic coating flaking off on the head. A poor tape won't stand as many plays and also will give poor high frequency response.

° The letters db stand for decibels. The intensity of sound is measured in decibels, just as the strength of an electrical current is measured in volts.

When you're recording, the microphone should be at least 18 inches from the subject's mouth, otherwise distortion will occur. In addition, if very good quality is desired, it may be advisable to discard the microphone that comes with the recorder. The better the microphone, the better the frequency response. Voice alone has a very narrow range of only a few thousand cycles per second. Music, however, has a very wide range. Thus to do a good job of music recording, a microphone with as wide a range as possible is desired. The microphone should have a high frequency response, as close to 10–15 kc as possible. It should also have as low a response as possible. Most microphones go down to about 200 cps and 5 kc. A good low frequency response, however, is closer to 30–40 cps.

Another critical point most people overlook is that the recording heads can become magnetized. If this happens, you can ruin very high quality tapes. Say you buy an expensive new stereo tape with beautiful 'highs' (high frequency responses up to, say, 15 kc). If you play it on a recorder with a magnetized head, the head will erase these highs right off. Each time the tape is played after this with the same head, more and more of the quality is ruined.

One thing particularly important to keep in mind is to prevent operating the recorder in such a way that the head becomes permanently magnetized. To prevent such an occurrence, remember *never* to turn off the recorder while it's on "recording." If you do, a large line current surge in the recording amplifier puts a big "spike" on the head in one direction which can cause permanent magnetization.

Assuming that you avoid permanent magnetization, it's still a good idea to do something from time to time to make sure the head is demagnetized. This can be done with a hand degausser, which costs about $4–5. If you should get one, though, make sure you are shown exactly how to use it. This involves initially holding it some distance from the head, slowly bringing the instrument in towards the head at a constant rate, going around the head very slowly, then slowly moving the degausser away.

Another key consideration for good recording is the physical condition of the head. For instance, with use, the head wears and the air gap size and the angle the head makes with the tape will change. This will cause a loss in high frequency response. Unless you have some background in electronics and the design of recording heads, it would be best occasionally to have the head checked and aligned by a good maintenance service.

For those with experience, the following procedure is usually followed for alignment. A spring device or azimuth screw is generally provided to shift the head from side to side. You want the head to be at right angles to the tape. To do this, record a 15 kc signal about 10–15 db down from normal operating level and adjust the position of the head for maximum output at this frequency.

A good tape recorder can give you many years of first class musical enjoyment. However, it is not something you can simply push a button on year after year and forget about. Like any other mechanical device, you must give it the care, periodic checkup and cleaning it requires.

Stereophonic Sound

by W. P. Hopper, Jr.

Senior Project Engineer
Packard-Bell Home Products Division

Certainly the main innovation in the field of sound reproduction in recent years has been the introduction and continuing development of stereophonic sound. (This article will discuss "stereo" mainly in connection with FM radio and records. For a detailed review of music on tape, see the article on Magnetic Tape Recording.) The word *stereophonic* is derived from two Greek words. The word *stereo* can be translated as "solid" and the word *phonic* as "sound." A closer approximation to the meaning of stereophonic, rather than "solid sound," is "truthful sound." That is, reproduction of material that is as faithful to the original sound as possible.

In music, the basic goal of stereo is to provide the listener with normal depth of sound a person's ears give him when he hears an actual performance. The fact that a person has two ears means that he can hear sound from two slightly different angles. The slight variation in position results in each ear gaining a different impression of the music. When these two impressions are combined in the brain, the result is a sense of direction and depth not provided by each ear alone.

In the past, a performance was recorded (or broadcast) *monaurally*. That is, it was copied by electronic equipment located in one position only. When monaural sound is played back or transmitted to a listener, it does not have the depth or directivity of the original performance. The sounds do not have the richness and feeling they should have. In stereo, however, two or more channels are used to record and play back the music instead of one. In the recording or radio studio, the musical sounds are first directed to two or more microphones. The microphones are carefully placed to receive the sound at the proper angles. These angles are selected so the sound picked up by the microphones will come as close as possible to what the ears would normally hear. The sound is then recorded or transmitted on two different channels. In the case of radio, two different signals would then be sent out from the station. These signals would activate two different sets of speakers in the home set.

In recording, the original signals would be recorded on opposite sides of the record grooves. The sounds on the record remain separate and are transmitted through the two speaker sets when the record is played at home. The blending of the sounds for radio or recording is finally done by the hearing system of the individual.

Of course, all important in what a listener actually hears is the question of set selection. A poor stereo set, or one improperly installed, will not provide sound that faithfully reproduces the original. There are some simple tests that can be used to gain some comparison of the merits of different equipment in the store. But, with all that, a major part of the decision will always depend simply on how good the music sounds to a person's ears.

One test is to see how easy it is to locate different stereo stations. With a good set, it should be easy to tune in on a given station. It shouldn't be necessary to keep turning the dial back and forth a number of times before finding the correct setting. This depends partly on whether or not the store has an outside antenna. Even without this, however, with the equipment on stereo, background noise should not be too noticeable if the set is well designed. With a good antenna installation, any marked noise or background hiss indicates poor stereo design. Other tests can be applied by a buyer with a little more technical awareness. For example, some stations transmit what are known as SCA (Subsidiary Communication Authorization) signals. That is, the station has been licensed by the Federal Communication Commission to send out a second, third or even fourth signal along with its normal programing. These signals are in the form of background music sold to subscribers, such as stores, restaurants, etc. Normally, no trace of this signal should be found on a good home stereo receiver. Therefore, the first step is to find out which stations have SCA authority. After locating such a station on the dial, the treble should be turned to maximum in the monaural position. After listening to the background noise level, switch the decoder into operation. There should be little or no change. On the other hand, if the system is poor, the SCA signal will be heard in the form of a high pitched beep or whistling noise in the background.

A second check is to find a station on which the announcer is talking "on one side." That is, in some cases an announcer will be positioned so that the sound of his voice is transmitted on just one of the two stereo channels. The balance control should then be turned to shut off the "strong" side. Then listen to the signal on the "weak" side. If it's relatively loud and distorted, then the set has inadequate channel separation. Conversely, if it's necessary to turn the volume all the way up to hear anything on the weak side, and the sound obtained is in the form of a distorted whisper, then the equipment is providing good separation.

Another test is to tune in on a stereo station that has a very strong signal. Then remove the antenna and either turn on a fluorescent light or listen for ignition noise from passing automobiles. While these things are going on, switch the set from monaural to stereo. If there is no interference from these outside sources in monaural, but there is in stereo, the set has poor stereo properties.

A final check would be to wait for a piece of music with muted brass, or any chimes or cymbals of high amplitudes. While the music is on, switch from monaural to stereo. If more distortion is evident in stereo, then the receiver is a poor one.

[266]

It should be stressed that the location of a set in the home, as well as the size and condition of the room it will be installed in, greatly affect the way a set will sound. This is one reason a set can sound very different in the home than it does in the store. Drapes, furniture, glass panels, all will affect the signal. Drapes absorb sound whereas glass tends to reflect it. Thus if a set was placed so that a large set of drapes was on one wall and a glass panel on the other, the listener might not get the properly balanced stereo signal. (In this case, just opening the drapes when the set is playing might solve the problem.)

The best approach is to pick out a set that seems best in the store and have it delivered to the home on a trial basis. If it doesn't sound as it should in the home, and there seems no way to change its position or the room arrangement to get good response, it could be exchanged for a set better adapted to the particular home.

In general, the best arrangement for maximum enjoyment is a perfect triangle with speakers at two angles and the listener at the third. However, since room conditions do affect the stereo, it's an advantage to have a set with speakers that can be angularly adjusted. Again, proper adjustment is basically a hearing test. The speakers must be moved until the listener seems to get full response from both sides, but as a "curtain of sound" rather than separate responses from two sources.

As far as speakers are concerned, each source should consist of a set of two speakers or more. A single speaker practical for response over a wide range of frequencies is difficult to design because of distortion problems originating in the mechanics of speaker parts. For good response, a minimum of two speakers per side is needed: one to carry bass and low mid-range frequencies and another to carry upper mid-range and highs. There are two ways to mount the speakers, either separately with one on top of the other, or with one speaker mounted inside the other. There's no particular advantage to the second, or co-axial method, except that the set takes less space. For good reception, the treble speaker should be fairly high off the floor—almost at eye level when a person is in normal seated position.

For noise free reception, just as for TV, an outside antenna is very important. A TV antenna, it should be noted, may not receive signals well for stereo FM. Most TV antennas are deliberately designed with a 'hole' in reception properties in the FM frequencies to prevent interference. The FM antenna should be one made specially for directional FM reception. Omnidirectional or turnstile antennas are not recommended for maximum stereo performance. A good FM antenna is not expensive. Once installed, the antenna should be oriented either in the direction of the listener's favorite station or fitted with a rotator so that the largest number of stations can be obained clearly.

Set ventilation is something that need be considered only in special cases. A normal floor set poses no problems. But if the stereo is mounted into a wall, provisions must be made for adequate ventilation.

As far as record players (or, for that matter, stereo tape recorders) are concerned, the general rules set forth above for speaker installation and sound fidelity still apply. It is, of course, important that the records be kept clean. They should be handled only by the edges or the label and, when not in use, returned to the record jacket. In addition, the grooves should be cleaned periodically. Record brushes and fluids both seem to do a good job.

The stylus should be checked every so often for worn or chipped spots. The diamond needle is considered to be the standard in the industry at present, since it lasts longer and causes less record wear. The other needle that is widely used is the sapphire. There is no difference in sound reproduction between a good diamond and a good sapphire needle. The diamond costs more than the sapphire, but, on the other hand, last about three times (or more) as long.

Most high fidelity stores have strobe discs on which the speed of the turntable can be tested. If the set is running too fast, the strobe shows on pattern and if the speed is too slow, another. Generally speaking, the step pulley arrangement used in most record changers is more or less foolproof as far as playing too fast is concerned. They can run too slow if the parts are binding somewhere. Most service manuals tell how to clean the idler wheel and the other key parts to prevent dirt or other foreign material from causing this to happen.

The Popular Song

by HAL LEVY

Instructor in Popular Songwriting
University of California at Los Angeles

The popular song, like the art song, aria, hymn or anthem, is a combination of inter-dependent words and music which, when sung, communicates idea and emotion. The difference is that a popular song appeals to a wider range of people. It may be an experience shared by a group of sophisticated adults enjoying an evening of musical theatre or it may be the ten-cent decision of a pre-teenager standing in front of a malt-shop jukebox. It may be folk music, country music, blues, jazz, songs of foreign origins or influence—calypso, beguine, tango, rhumba, bossa nova. It may be a part of that mainstream of American "pop" music—the ballads, rhythm songs and novelty songs of Tin Pan Alley.

In all cases, however, the basic requirements of a song remain constant. The lyric must be written with the full understanding that it has no life of its own, that it is only fifty per cent of a song, that it must complement the music, that it is meant to be sung and must therefore be singable. The music must be written with the same problems and goals in mind—that the lyric is essential to its completeness and that the human voice, not some instrument, is essential to its presentation.

This is not to say that one cannot enjoy reading Oscar Hammerstein's book of song lyrics; it means only that Hammerstein was such an artist and craftsman that his lyrics often could stand alone. So, too, with music. Many songs survive by notes not words, for the abstractions of music seem less vulnerable to changing times and tastes than do the specifics of language.

Whatever the destiny of a song, however, the elements of creation remain the same. Every song must have an idea, an emotion, a point of view, a form, a rhythmic basis, a melody, a quality of sound, a style, and it must be singable. Every song does have these elements. The only variables are qualitative and depend on the writers.

That a song should have an idea is, perhaps, obvious. That the idea should be origi-nal and/or strong, provocative, interesting, beautiful, etc. is apparently not so obvious. Or at least not so easy to come by.

The emotion most common to songs is romantic love, but joy, sorrow, anger, religious faith and other emotions also find expression. These emotions are amplified by the basic device of singing, a device that encourages exaggeration in language and then heightens that exaggeration by the addition of music. The singing of a song is a highly-charged, non-realistic performance which we are not only willing but delighted to accept. Stage, radio, home record player, jukebox—the medium doesn't matter. We enjoy being moved by a song.

A point of view is a quality acknowledged in a show song, often ignored in a non-show song. But no matter how aware or unaware the lyricist may be, there is always an "I" who is singing the song, some kind of person with some kind of background, some kind of manner, something on his mind. There is also always a "you" in a song (except in a soliloquy), a "you" who is, perhaps, being addressed, or an impersonal third-person-plural audience that is just being sung at.

In addition to the point of view, a song writer must consider the matter of identification, the relating of listener to singer. Depending on the nature of the song and the sex of the singer, the listener might identify with the singer and project himself into the singer's role, or he might identify with the theoretical person to whom the singer is singing. Either way, this is a large part of the vicarious enjoyment the listener gains from a good song well sung.

One of the things that, early in the development of a song, must be considered and decided upon is form. It is as essential to a song as it is to any work of art. It is part of the game and technique of writing, part of the enjoyment of listening, and its values are as numerous as its variations.

The composer, of course, is concerned with musical form, and it might be assumed that the lyricist is concerned with literary form. Such is not the case. The lyricist, no less than the composer, must think in musical terms. He is not writing a "kind of poetry" or a "kind of verse," he is writing a lyric—words to be joined with music and then sung. Like it or not, the lyricist must write not lines of lyrics but measures (or bars) of lyrics. He must write words that make four bars of musical sense, and then write more words that make more bars of musical sense, until finally, at the end of thirty-two or thirty-eight or forty-eight bars, he has written the lyrics for what might become a song.

The finished song will have an over-all form, but meanwhile, enroute, the lyricist deals in smaller forms: the phrase (the smallest combination of notes and syllables), the theme (a combination of phrases—a major musical-lyrical statement), and the stanza (eight bars, twelve bars, sixteen bars—a combination of themes and development that becomes a major section of a song). All of these smaller forms are a combination of rhythm and melody—the pulsating beat of the song plus the melody line with its close relationship to the strong and weak beats of the measure.

Every lyrical-musical phrase, beginning with the initial one in the song, can be treated in one of the same three ways. Being a statement it can be repeated, it can be developed, or it can give way to a new statement. This is a choice that must be made at the end of every phrase, every theme, every stanza. It is by the exercise of this choice that a stanza (in effect a small song) is built, and it is the way a complete song is built.

Musical forms are almost limitless in their variety, but there are certain ones which have become relatively common. This is not to demean their worth; indeed the principal reason for their popularity is undoubtedly their proved effectiveness.

The simplest, most ancient, and still the most used in the folk field, is the verse-chorus song—ABABAB ad infinitum. (A word here about A and B. They are simply an accepted way of designating different stanza forms. Hence an ABABAB song would have two different kinds of stanzas alternating regularly.) This ABABAB form has proved to be the best for narrative songs, in which the story is told in the verses (the A stanzas), the chorus (the B stanzas) being used for everyone to "jine in" on something simple and repetitive. This kind of song was probably used by the earliest of singing storytellers and is still a favorite at camp meetings, group sings, hootenannys and the like.

Perhaps the most common form in "pop" music is the AABA song—an initial stanza, repeated, then a different or "B" stanza, then back to the original. Given the time limitation of a popular song, this form seems to be happily suited to developing or "proving" the kind of small story that is possible. The first "A" stanza is a statement; the second "A" is a repetition with some degree of amplification or development; the "B" is called a "bridge" or "release" and is the stanza which gives a second dimension or climax to the story; the final "A" provides either climax or denouement, depending on what happens in the release.

It is not true that pop songs must be thirty-two bars long. Indeed, it can be argued that a thirty-two bar song has a tiresome predictability about it and should be avoided, and that any other number of bars, capably handled, is preferable. There is, however, a reason for the high frequency of thirty-two bar songs, namely that the music of Western civilization is, for the most part, based on four-bar units. Usually it takes at least two such four-bar units to make a satisfactory stanza. This, plus the preference for four-stanza songs (AABA and ABAB/ABAC), creates an eight-times-four situation, or thirty-two bars.

The ABAB or ABAC song mentioned above is second only to AABA form in popularity. But whereas the AABA song progresses steadily through its four stanzas and gives one a feeling of unity, the ABAB and ABAC songs are binary songs, cut in half in both content and feel. At the end of the first AB there is a sense of completion and the sense of starting the second and final half of the song. Even the AB has a half-and-half, question-and-answer, antecedent-consequent quality. It is in the nature of the content and the nature of the form. ABAB and ABAC, it develops, are the best ways of telling a certain kind of story, a different kind of story than can be told in AABA.

There are innumerable other forms, but they all seem somehow to be based on these three most common ones. The fact is, any form will work, as long as it works. Which is not meant to be nonsense, but simply recognition of the truth that form does follow function, and that it can be created.

The rhythmic bases of songs were touched on when we started talking about form.

And, to be sure, rhythm is an integral part of form. But it is too basic, too important, not to be given its own paragraph. The primary aspect of rhythm is beat, that sense of pulsation that comes with repeated downbeats, that persistent and satisfying phenomenon that has been called the "heartbeat" of the song. Corny but true. It is the peg upon which the entire song hangs, musically and lyrically. Once started, it cannot stop. It is security and satisfaction. It *is* the heartbeat.

The beat is often not so much heard as felt. It is like the string bass in the rhythm section of a dance band. There is, however, another rhythmic element—the rhythm patterns that, with change of tone, constitute the melodic line. These are the combinations of whole notes and half notes and quarter notes and eighth notes and triplets and rests that are wedded to the syllables of words and the punctuation of phrases. Although "the wedding of words and music" is an oft-repeated phrase and a highly desirable condition, it must be admitted that not all songs are happily married. All too often a lyricist puts words to a melody without knowing or caring that the rhythm of the language is not matching the rhythm of the music. Similarly, a composer will often set a lyric, unaware that he is forcing words into awkward, illegitimate rhythms. Either way, the shattered language rhythms create nonsense, distort meanings, limit communication, deprive the song of its full emotional potential.

To a somewhat lesser extent, the same problems exist in the matter of melody. Melody is obviously more the province of the composer than the lyricist, but to ignore the melody of language is to invite disaster. Language does have melody; it is called inflection. And to the highest possible degree the melodies of language and music should be integrated. The principal reason for this is that the sound of our language is something we know and like and respond to. So when a line of lyric is sung with the same general melody (inflection) that we are used to in speech, we enjoy the familiarity and can respond to the way it has been expanded, exaggerated, emotionalized. If, however, the music does not mirror the melody of the language (or vice versa) then we are apt to be displeased with the result. This is not to say that every time a word inflection goes up the music should go up. Such a one-to-one correlation is neither possible nor desirable. But the relationship of inflection and melody should be acknowledged and used.

Sound is something that will happen, no matter what the writers write. But good sound, the right sound, is something they have to make happen. A composer has twelve notes to use, and the number of ways in which he can use them has yet to approach its limits. Beyond the melody line he has the harmonic structure and again a vast array of sounds to choose and create. But sound is not his domain alone. True, the singer will be singing the composer's notes (if the composer is lucky) and the accompanying instruments will be playing his harmonies. But the singer will be singing words, and those words have sounds, and those sounds are at the command of the lyricist.

A song often has an overall lyrical sound, but this likely is the result of many individual and specifically chosen sounds. They may be abstract sounds—"Hey and a ho and a hey nonino" or "Zip-a-dee-doo-dah." They may be rhymes—masculine, feminine, triple, internal, good, bad, loud, soft, trite, bright. They may be alliterations, consonance, assonance. But sounds, no less than anything else, have to be controlled. They can help nail down a form, they can attract attention, they can delight, they can relate to the music, they can help unify a song. They can also do all the opposites. It's up to the lyricist. He must be able to hear the sound of his writing.

If the idea is what you write, then style is how you write it. Victor Herbert, Jerome Kern and George Gershwin wrote differently. Leonard Bernstein, Harold Arlen and Richard Rodgers write differently. And although each show might have a different need, although each collaborator might have a different influence, it can be said that composers do have a style, a way of writing. It may result from conscious or unconscious determinants, but the fact remains, composers can be analyzed to determine their melodic lines, their forms, their harmonic structures, etc.

No less can a lyricist be analyzed. It may be the way with a rhyme of a Larry Hart or a Yip Harburg. It may be the idiomatic humor of a Johnny Mercer or an Ira Gershwin. It may be the simplicity of an Irving Berlin. It may be the semantic purity of an Oscar Hammerstein or the literary sophistication of a Cole Porter, a Frank Loesser or an Alan Lerner. They all work with words, they plumb their own idioms, they create their own characters, they bend and mold the language to their needs, and the result is lyrics, their lyrics—writing with a style. To be sure, lyrics no less than music can be dissected and understood, can even be imitated. But style, though it may be admired in others, cannot be acquired from others. To be most artful and effective, style must be found within oneself, developed by oneself.

If a song makes sense or gives pleasure when read, that's nice. If a song turns out to be interesting to instrumentalists and orchestras, that's very nice. Even the lyricist will enjoy the increased royalties and performance money. But a song, that specially integrated combination of words and music, can find its moment of truth only in the voice of a singer.

Songwriters, it must follow, must then know something about the human voice, the capabilities of singers, and how best to guarantee their song the most successful presentation possible. The composer will worry about range; a one-octave singer can't sing a two-octave song. And he'll worry about awkward intervals and spaces to breathe. The lyricist will worry about open-throated vowels for high notes, short vowels and lots of consonants for up-tempo songs, long and sweet-sounding vowels for ballads, a choice of words and juxtaposition of words that will provide for easy enunciation.

From the musical and lyrical idea, all the way to the singer, a song develops. It has all the problems and qualities mentioned here, and as many more unmentioned. Anyone can write a song and almost everyone does. But it is an art and a craft, with few artists and few craftsmen.

What is a song? The answer lies not here. It lies in the works of the men we've noted, all of them and others, too. They had a song in their heart, a talent in their head, and they knew how to wear out a pencil.

[273]

Appendix

National Academy of Recording Arts & Sciences

1958 Award Winners*

Category #1. RECORD OF THE YEAR
"Nel Blu Dipinto Di Blu" (Volare)—Domenico Modugno

Category #2. ALBUM OF THE YEAR
"The Music from 'Peter Gunn'"—Henry Mancini

Category #3. SONG OF THE YEAR
"Nel Blu Dipinto Di Blu" (Volare)—Domenico Modugno

Category #4. BEST VOCAL PERFORMANCE, FEMALE
"Ella Fitzgerald Sings the Irving Berlin Song Book"—Ella Fitzgerald

Category #5. BEST VOCAL PERFORMANCE, MALE
"Catch a Falling Star"—Perry Como

Category #6. BEST PERFORMANCE BY AN ORCHESTRA
"Billy May's Big Fat Brass"—Billy May

Category #7. BEST PERFORMANCE BY A DANCE BAND
"Basie"—Count Basie

Category #8. BEST PERFORMANCE BY A VOCAL GROUP OR CHORUS
"That Old Black Magic"—Louis Prima and Keely Smith

Category #9. BEST JAZZ PERFORMANCE, INDIVIDUAL
"Ella Fitzgerald Sings the Duke Ellington Song Book"—Ella Fitzgerald

Category #10. BEST JAZZ PERFORMANCE, GROUP
"Basie"—Count Basie

Category #11. BEST COMEDY PERFORMANCE
"The Chipmunk Song"—David Seville

* Non-popular categories included for completeness.

[277]

Category #12. BEST COUNTRY & WESTERN PERFORMANCE
"Tom Dooley"—The Kingston Trio

Category #13. BEST RHYTHM & BLUES PERFORMANCE
"Tequila"—The Champs

Category #14. BEST ARRANGEMENT
"The Music from 'Peter Gunn'"—Henry Mancini
Arranged by Henry Mancini

Category #15. BEST ENGINEERED RECORD, CLASSICAL
"Duets with a Spanish Guitar"—Laurindo Almeida & Salli Terri
Engineer: Sherwood Hall, III

Category #16. BEST ENGINEERED RECORD, OTHER THAN CLASSICAL
"The Chipmunk Song"—David Seville
Engineer: Ted Keep

Category #17. BEST ALBUM COVER
"Only The Lonely"—Frank Sinatra
Art Director: Frank Sinatra

Category #18. BEST MUSICAL COMPOSITION FIRST RECORDED AND
RELEASED IN 1958 (OVER FIVE MINUTES' DURATION)
"Cross Country Suite"—Composed by Nelson Riddle

Category #19. BEST ORIGINAL CAST ALBUM, BROADWAY OR TV
"The Music Man" by Meredith Willson—Original Broadway Cast

Category #20. BEST SOUND TRACK ALBUM, DRAMATIC PICTURE
SCORE OR ORIGINAL CAST
"Gigi"—Original Cast Motion Picture Sound Track

Category #21. BEST PERFORMANCE, DOCUMENTARY OR SPOKEN WORD
"The Best of The Stan Freberg Shows"—Stan Freberg

Category #22. BEST RECORDING FOR CHILDREN
"The Chipmunk Song"—David Seville

Category #23. BEST CLASSICAL PERFORMANCE, ORCHESTRAL
"Gaiete Parisienne"—Felix Slatkin conducting the
Hollywood Bowl Symphony Orchestra

Category #24. BEST CLASSICAL PERFORMANCE—INSTRUMENTAL
(WITH CONCERTO SCALE ACCOMPANIMENT)
Tchaikovsky: Concerto No. 1, in B-Flat Minor, Op. 23
Van Cliburn, Pianist; Symphony Orchestra under
the direction of Kiril Kondrashin

Category #25. BEST CLASSICAL PERFORMANCE—INSTRUMENTALIST
(OTHER THAN CONCERTO SCALE ACCOMPANIMENT)
"Segovia Golden Jubilee"—Andres Segovia

Category #26. BEST CLASSICAL PERFORMANCE—CHAMBER MUSIC
(INCLUDING CHAMBER ORCHESTRA)
Beethoven Quartet 130—Hollywood String Quartet

Category #27. BEST CLASSICAL PERFORMANCE—VOCAL SOLOIST
(WITH OR WITHOUT ORCHESTRA)
"Operatic Recital"—Renata Tebaldi

Category #28. BEST CLASSICAL PERFORMANCE—OPERATIC OR CHORAL
"Virtuoso"—Roger Wagner Chorale

1959 Award Winners

Category #1. RECORD OF THE YEAR
"Mack The Knife"—Bobby Darin

Category #2. ALBUM OF THE YEAR
"Come Dance With Me"—Frank Sinatra

Category #3. SONG OF THE YEAR
"The Battle of New Orleans"—Jimmy Driftwood, composer

Category #4. BEST VOCAL PERFORMANCE, FEMALE
"But Not For Me"—Ella Fitzgerald

Category #5. BEST VOCAL PERFORMANCE, MALE
"Come Dance With Me"—Frank Sinatra

Category #6. BEST PERFORMANCE BY A DANCE BAND
"Anatomy of a Murder"—Duke Ellington

Category #7. BEST PERFORMANCE BY AN ORCHESTRA
"Like Young"—David Rose and his Orchestra with André Previn

Category #8. BEST PERFORMANCE BY A CHORUS
"Battle Hymn of the Republic"—Mormon Tabernacle Choir

Category #9. BEST JAZZ PERFORMANCE, SOLOIST
"Ella Swings Lightly"—Ella Fitzgerald, Vocal

Category #10. BEST JAZZ PERFORMANCE—ORCHESTRA
"I Dig Chicks"—Jonah Jones

Category #11. BEST CLASSICAL PERFORMANCE—ORCHESTRA
Debussy: Images for Orchestra—Boston Symphony Orchestra,
Charles Munch, Conductor.

Category #12. BEST CLASSICAL PERFORMANCE—CHAMBER MUSIC
(INCLUDING CHAMBER ORCHESTRA)
Beethoven: Sonata No. 21, in C, Op. 53 ("Waldstein");
Sonata No. 18, in E-Flat, Op. 31, No. 3
Arthur Rubinstein, Pianist

Category #13. BEST CLASSICAL PERFORMANCE—CONCERTO OR
INSTRUMENTAL SOLOIST (WITH FULL ORCHESTRAL
ACCOMPANIMENT)
Rachmaninoff Piano Concerto #3—Van Cliburn, Pianist,
Kiril Kondrashin conducting the Symphony of the Air

Category #14. BEST CLASSICAL PERFORMANCE—INSTRUMENTAL
SOLOIST (OTHER THAN FULL ORCHESTRAL ACCOMPANIMENT)
Beethoven: Sonata No. 21, in C, Op. 53 ("Waldstein")
Sonata No. 18, in E-Flat, Op. 31, No. 3
Arthur Rubinstein, Pianist

Category #15. BEST CLASSICAL PERFORMANCE—VOCAL SOLOIST
(WITH OR WITHOUT ORCHESTRA)
Bjoerling in Opera—Jussi Bjoerling

Category #16. BEST CLASSICAL PERFORMANCE—OPERA CAST OR
CHORAL
Mozart: "The Marriage of Figaro"—Della Casa, Peters,
Elias, London, Tozzi,—Vienna State Opera Chorus,
Vienna Philharmonic Orchestra,
Erich Leinsdorf, conducting.

Category #17. BEST MUSICAL COMPOSITION FIRST RECORDED AND
RELEASED IN 1959 (MORE THAN FIVE MINUTES' DURATION)
"Anatomy of a Murder"—Composed by Duke Ellington

Category #18. BEST SOUND TRACK ALBUM—BACKGROUND SCORE FROM
MOTION PICTURE OR TELEVISION
"Anatomy of a Murder" (Motion Picture)—Duke Ellington

Category #19. BEST SOUND TRACK ALBUM, ORIGINAL CAST—
MOTION PICTURE OR TELEVISION
"Porgy and Bess"—With Motion Picture Cast, and music
conducted by André Previn and Ken Darby

Category #20. BEST BROADWAY SHOW ALBUM
TIE: "Gypsy"—Ethel Merman and Broadway Show Cast;
Musical Director Milton Rosenstock

"Redhead"—Gwen Verdon, Richard Kiley and Broadway
cast; music directed by Jay Blackton.

Category #21. BEST COMEDY PERFORMANCE—SPOKEN WORD
"Inside Shelley Berman"—Shelley Berman

Category #22. BEST COMEDY PERFORMANCE—MUSICAL
"The Battle of Kookamonga"—Homer and Jethro

Category #23. BEST PERFORMANCE—DOCUMENTARY OR SPOKEN WORD
(OTHER THAN COMEDY)
"A Lincoln Portrait"—Carl Sandburg

Category #24. BEST PERFORMANCE BY "TOP 40" ARTIST
"Midnight Flyer"—Nat King Cole

Category #25. BEST COUNTRY AND WESTERN PERFORMANCE
"The Battle of New Orleans"—Johnny Horton

Category #26. BEST RHYTHM AND BLUES PERFORMANCE
"What a Diff'rence a Day Makes"—Dinah Washington

Category #27. BEST PERFORMANCE—FOLK
"The Kingston Trio at Large"—The Kingston Trio

Category #28. BEST RECORDING FOR CHILDREN
"Peter and the Wolf"—Peter Ustinov, Narrator

Category #29. BEST ARRANGEMENT
"Come Dance with Me"—Frank Sinatra
Arranged by Billy May

Category #30. BEST ENGINEERING CONTRIBUTION—CLASSICAL
RECORDING
"Victory At Sea, Vol. I"—Robert Russell Bennett, Conductor,
and the RCA Victor Symphony Orchestra
Engineer: Lewis W. Layton

Category #31. BEST ENGINEERING CONTRIBUTION—NOVELTY
RECORDING
"Alvin's Harmonica"—David Seville
Engineer: Ted Keep

Category #32. BEST ENGINEERING CONTRIBUTION—OTHER THAN
CLASSICAL OR NOVELTY
"Belafonte at Carnegie Hall"—Harry Belafonte
Engineer: Robert Simpson

Category #33. BEST ALBUM COVER
Shostakovich Symphony #5—Howard Mitchell conducting
the National Symphony Orchestra
Art Director: Robert M. Jones

Catgory #34. BEST NEW ARTIST OF 1959
BOBBY DARIN

Special National Trustees Awards
for Artists & Repertoire Contribution

1. RECORD OF THE YEAR:
"Mack The Knife"—Bobby Darin
A & R Producer: Ahmet Ertegun

2. ALBUM OF THE YEAR:
"Come Dance With Me"—Frank Sinatra
A & R Producer: Dave Cavanaugh

1960 Award Winners

Category #1. RECORD OF THE YEAR
"Theme from a Summer Place"—Percy Faith

Category #2. ALBUM OF THE YEAR
"Button Down Mind"—Bob Newhart

Category #3. SONG OF THE YEAR
"Theme from Exodus"—Ernest Gold, composer

Category #4. BEST VOCAL PERFORMANCE SINGLE RECORD OR
TRACK—FEMALE
"Mack the Knife"—Ella Fitzgerald

Category #5. BEST VOCAL PERFORMANCE—ALBUM—FEMALE
"Mack the Knife"—Ella in Berlin—Ella Fitzgerald

Category #6. BEST VOCAL PERFORMANCE SINGLE RECORD OR
TRACK—MALE
"Georgia On My Mind"—Ray Charles

[282]

Category #7. BEST VOCAL PERFORMANCE ALBUM MALE
"GENIUS OF RAY CHARLES"—Ray Charles

Category #8. BEST ARRANGEMENT
"MR. LUCKY"—Henry Mancini

Category #9. BEST PERFORMANCE BY A BAND FOR DANCING
"DANCE WITH BASIE"—Count Basie

Category #10. BEST PERFORMANCE BY AN ORCHESTRA
"MR. LUCKY"—Henry Mancini

Category #11. BEST PERFORMANCE BY A VOCAL GROUP
"WE GOT US"—Eydie Gorme/Steve Lawrence

Category #12. BEST PERFORMANCE BY A CHORUS
"SONGS OF THE COWBOY"—Norman Luboff Choir

Category #13. BEST JAZZ PERFORMANCE SOLO OR SMALL GROUP
"WEST SIDE STORY"—André Previn

Category #14. BEST JAZZ PERFORMANCE LARGE GROUP
"BLUES AND THE BEAT"—Henry Mancini

Category #15. BEST CLASSICAL PERFORMANCE ORCHESTRA
"BARTOK: MUSIC FOR STRINGS, PERCUSSION AND CELESTE"—Chicago Symphony,
Fritz Reiner, Conductor

Category #16. BEST CLASSICAL PERFORMANCE VOCAL OR
INSTRUMENTAL CHAMBER MUSIC
"CONVERSATIONS WITH THE GUITAR"—Laurindo Almeida

Category #17. BEST CLASSICAL PERFORMANCE CONCERTO OR
INSTRUMENTAL SOLOIST
"BRAHMS PIANO CONCERTO #2," Sviatoslav Richter, pianist, Erich Leinsdorf
conducting Chicago Symphony Orchestra

Category #18. BEST CLASSICAL PERFORMANCE INSTRUMENTAL SOLOIST
OR DUO (OTHER THAN WITH ORCHESTRAL ACCOMPANIMENT)
"THE SPANISH GUITARS OF LAURINDO ALMEIDA"—Laurindo Almeida

Category #19. BEST CLASSICAL PERFORMANCE VOCAL SOLOIST
"LEONTYNE PRICE RECITAL"—Leontyne Price

Category #20. BEST CLASSICAL OPERA PRODUCTION
"TURANDOT"—Tebaldi, Nilsson, Bjoerling, Tozzi—The Rome Opera House
Chorus and Orchestra, Erich Leinsdorf, conducting

Category #21. BEST CLASSICAL PERFORMANCE CHORAL (INCLUDING ORATORIO)

"The Messiah"—Sir Thomas Beecham conducting the Royal Philharmonic Orchestra and Chorus

Category #22. BEST CONTEMPORARY CLASSICAL COMPOSITION—First released from September 1, 1959 to November 30, 1960

"Tender Land Suite": Aaron Copland conducting Boston Symphony Orchestra

Category #23. BEST SOUND TRACK ALBUM OR RECORDING OF MUSIC SCORE FROM MOTION PICTURE OR TELEVISION

"Exodus"—Ernest Gold (Motion Picture)

Category #24. BEST SOUND TRACK ALBUM OR RECORDING OF ORIGINAL CAST FROM MOTION PICTURE OR TELEVISION

"Can Can"—Frank Sinatra, Original Music by Cole Porter (Motion Picture)

Category #25. BEST SHOW ALBUM (ORIGINAL CAST)

"The Sound of Music"—Mary Martin and the Original Broadway Cast

Category #26. BEST COMEDY PERFORMANCE (SPOKEN WORD)

"Button Down Mind Strikes Back"—Bob Newhart

Category #27. BEST COMEDY PERFORMANCE (MUSICAL)

"Jonathan and Darlene Edwards in Paris"—Jonathan and Darlene Edwards (Jo Stafford & Paul Weston)

Category #28. BEST PERFORMANCE—DOCUMENTARY OR SPOKEN WORD (OTHER THAN COMEDY)

"F. D. R. Speaks"—Franklin D. Roosevelt

Category #29. BEST PERFORMANCE BY A POP SINGLE ARTIST

"Georgia On My Mind"—Ray Charles

Category #30. BEST COUNTRY AND WESTERN PERFORMANCE

"El Paso"—Marty Robbins

Category #31. BEST RHYTHM AND BLUES PERFORMANCE

"Let the Good Times Roll"—Ray Charles

Category #32. BEST PERFORMANCE—FOLK

"Swing Dat Hammer"—Harry Belafonte

Category #33. BEST ALBUM CREATED FOR CHILDREN

"Let's All Sing with the Chipmunks"—David Seville (Ross Bagdasarian)

Category #34. BEST ENGINEERING CONTRIBUTION CLASSICAL RECORDS

"Spanish Guitars of Laurindo Almeida"—Laurindo Almeida
Engineer: Hugh Davies

Category #35. BEST ENGINEERING CONTRIBUTION POPULAR
      RECORDING
      "The Gershwin Song Book"—Ella Fitzgerald
        Engineer: Luis P. Valentin

Category #36. BEST ENGINEERING CONTRIBUTION NOVELTY
      "The Old Payola Roll Blues"—Stan Freberg
        Engineer: John Kraus

Category #37. BEST ALBUM COVER
      "Latin Ala Lee"—Peggy Lee
        Art Director: Marvin Schwartz

Category #38. BEST NEW ARTIST OF 1960 (Not released under own name
      prior to September 1, 1959)
      BOB NEWHART

Category #39. BEST JAZZ COMPOSITION OF MORE THAN FIVE MINUTES
      DURATION
      "Sketches of Spain"—Miles Davis and Gil Evans

Special National Trustees Awards for Artists & Repertoire Contribution

1. RECORD OF THE YEAR:
      "Theme from a Summer Place"—Percy Faith
      A & R Producer, Ernest Altschuler

2. ALBUM OF THE YEAR:
      "Button Down Mind"—Bob Newhart
      A & R Producer, George Avakian

1961 Award Winners

1. RECORD OF THE YEAR:
      "Moon River"—Henry Mancini
      A & R Producer, Dick Pierce

2. ALBUM OF THE YEAR (other than classical):
      "Judy at Carnegie Hall"—Judy Garland
      A & R Producer, Andrew Wiswell

3. ALBUM OF THE YEAR—CLASSICAL:
   "Stravinsky Conducts, 1960: Le Sacre du Printemps; Petrouchka"—
   Igor Stravinsky
   A & R Producer, John McClure

4. SONG OF THE YEAR:
   "Moon River"—Composers, Henry Mancini and Johnny Mercer

5. BEST INSTRUMENTAL THEME OR INSTRUMENTAL VERSION
   OF SONG:
   "African Waltz"—Composer, Galt MacDermott

6. BEST SOLO VOCAL PERFORMANCE—FEMALE:
   "Judy at Carnegie Hall"—Judy Garland

7. BEST SOLO VOCAL PERFORMANCE—MALE:
   "Lollipops and Roses"—Jack Jones

8. BEST JAZZ PERFORMANCE—SOLOIST OR SMALL GROUP (instrumental):
   "André Previn Plays Harold Arlen"—André Previn

9. BEST JAZZ PERFORMANCE—LARGE GROUP (instrumental):
   "West Side Story"—Stan Kenton

10. BEST ORIGINAL JAZZ COMPOSITION:
    "African Waltz"—Composer, Galt MacDermott

11. BEST PERFORMANCE BY AN ORCHESTRA—FOR DANCING:
    "Lazy River"—Si Zentner

12. BEST PERFORMANCE BY AN ORCHESTRA—FOR OTHER THAN
    DANCING:
    "Breakfast at Tiffany's"—Henry Mancini

13. BEST ARRANGEMENT:
    "Moon River"—Arranger, Henry Mancini

14. BEST PERFORMANCE BY A VOCAL GROUP:
    "High Flying"—Lambert, Hendricks and Ross

15. BEST PERFORMANCE BY A CHORUS:
    "Great Band with Great Voices"—Johnny Mann Singers

16. BEST SOUND TRACK ALBUM OR RECORDING OF SCORE FROM
    MOTION PICTURE OR TELEVISION:
    "Breakfast at Tiffany's" (motion picture)—Henry Mancini

17. BEST SOUND TRACK ALBUM OR RECORDING OF ORIGINAL CAST FROM MOTION PICTURE OR TELEVISION:
    "West Side Story"—Conductor and Co-music Director, Johnny Green; Co-music Directors, Saul Chaplin, Sid Ramin, and Irwin Kostal

18. BEST ORIGINAL CAST SHOW ALBUM:
    "How to Succeed in Business Without Really Trying"—Composer, Frank Loesser

19. BEST COMEDY PERFORMANCE:
    "An Evening with Mike Nichols and Elaine May"—Mike Nichols and Elaine May

20. BEST DOCUMENTARY OR SPOKEN WORD RECORDING (other than comedy):
    "Humor in Music"—Leonard Bernstein

21. BEST ENGINEERING CONTRIBUTION—POPULAR RECORDING:
    "Judy at Carnegie Hall"—Engineer, Robert Arnold

22. BEST ENGINEERING CONTRIBUTION—NOVELTY RECORDING:
    "Stan Freberg Presents the United States of America"—Engineer, John Kraus

23. BEST ALBUM COVER (other than classical):
    "Judy at Carnegie Hall"—Art Director, Marvin Schwartz

24. BEST RECORDING FOR CHILDREN:
    "Prokofiev: Peter and the Wolf"—Leonard Bernstein

25. BEST ROCK AND ROLL RECORDING:
    "Let's Twist Again"—Chubby Checker

26. BEST COUNTRY AND WESTERN RECORDING:
    "Big Bad John"—Jimmy Dean

27. BEST RHYTHM AND BLUES RECORDING:
    "Hit the Road Jack"—Ray Charles

28. BEST FOLK RECORDING:
    "Belafonte Folk Singers at Home and Abroad"—Belafonte Folk Singers

29. BEST GOSPEL OR OTHER RELIGIOUS RECORDING:
    "Everytime I Feel the Spirit"—Mahalia Jackson

30. BEST NEW ARTIST OF 1961:
    PETER NERO

31. BEST CLASSICAL PERFORMANCE—ORCHESTRA:
    "Ravel: Daphnis et Chloé"—Conductor, Charles Munch

32. BEST CLASSICAL PERFORMANCE—CHAMBER MUSIC:
    "Beethoven: Serenade, Opus 8"—Jascha Heifetz, William Primrose, and
    Gregor Piatigorsky

33. BEST CLASSICAL PERFORMANCE—INSTRUMENTAL SOLOIST
    (with orchestra):
    "Bartok: Concerto No. 1 for Violin and Orchestra"—Isaac Stern

34. BEST CLASSICAL PERFORMANCE—INSTRUMENTAL SOLOIST OR
    DUO WITHOUT ORCHESTRA:
    "Reverie for Spanish Guitar"—Laurindo Almeida

35. BEST OPERA RECORDING:
    "Puccini: Madame Butterfly"—Conductor, Gabriele Santini

36. BEST CLASSICAL PERFORMANCE—CHORAL (other than opera):
    "Bach: B Minor Mass"—Robert Shaw

37. BEST CLASSICAL PERFORMANCE—VOCAL SOLOIST (with or without
    orchestra):
    "Art of the Prima Donna"—Joan Sutherland

38. BEST CONTEMPORARY CLASSICAL COMPOSITION:
    "Discantus"—Composer, Laurindo Almeida
    "Movements for Piano and Orchestra"—Composer, Igor Stravinsky

39. BEST ENGINEERING CONTRIBUTION—CLASSICAL RECORDING:
    "Ravel: Daphnis et Chloé"—Conductor, Charles Munch; Engineer,
    Lewis W. Layton

40. BEST ALBUM COVER—CLASSICAL:
    "Puccini: Madame Butterfly"—Art Director, Marvin Schwartz

1962 Award Winners

1. RECORD OF THE YEAR:
    "I Left My Heart in San Francisco"—Tony Bennett
    A & R Producer, Ernie Altschuler

2. ALBUM OF THE YEAR (other than classical):
    "The First Family"—Vaughn Meader
    A & R Producers, Bob Booker and Earle Doud

[288]

3. ALBUM OF THE YEAR—CLASSICAL:
   "Columbia Records Presents Vladimir Horowitz"—Vladimir Horowitz
   A & R Producer, Tom Frost

4. SONG OF THE YEAR:
   "What Kind of Fool Am I"—Composers, Leslie Bricusse and Anthony
   Newley

5. BEST INSTRUMENTAL THEME:
   "A Taste of Honey"—Composers, Bobby Scott and Ric Marlow

6. BEST SOLO VOCAL PERFORMANCE—FEMALE:
   "Ella Swings Brightly with Nelson Riddle"—Ella Fitzgerald

7. BEST SOLO VOCAL PERFORMANCE—MALE:
   "I Left My Heart in San Francisco"—Tony Bennett

8. BEST JAZZ PERFORMANCE—SOLOIST OR SMALL GROUP (instrumental):
   "Desafinado"—Stan Getz

9. BEST JAZZ PERFORMANCE—LARGE GROUP (instrumental):
   "Adventures in Jazz"—Stan Kenton

10. BEST ORIGINAL JAZZ COMPOSITION:
    "Cast Your Fate to the Winds"—Composer, Vince Guaraldi

11. BEST PERFORMANCE BY AN ORCHESTRA—FOR DANCING:
    "Fly Me to the Moon Bossa Nova"—Joe Harnell

12. BEST PERFORMANCE BY AN ORCHESTRA OR INSTRUMENTALIST
    WITH ORCHESTRA—PRIMARILY NOT JAZZ OR FOR DANCING:
    "The Colorful Peter Nero"—Peter Nero

13. BEST INSTRUMENTAL ARRANGEMENT:
    "Baby Elephant Walk"—Arranger, Henry Mancini

14. BEST BACKGROUND ARRANGEMENT:
    "I Left My Heart in San Francisco"—Arranger, Marty Manning

15. BEST PERFORMANCE BY A VOCAL GROUP:
    "If I Had a Hammer"—Peter, Paul and Mary

16. BEST PERFORMANCE BY A CHORUS:
    "Presenting the New Christy Minstrels"—The New Christy Minstrels

17. BEST ORIGINAL CAST SHOW ALBUM:
    "No Strings"—Composer, Richard Rodgers

18. BEST CLASSICAL PERFORMANCE—ORCHESTRA:
     "STRAVINSKY: THE FIREBIRD BALLET"—Igor Stravinsky conducting the
     Columbia Symphony Orchestra

19. BEST CLASSICAL PERFORMANCE—CHAMBER MUSIC:
     "THE HEIFETZ-PIATIGORSKY CONCERTS"—Jascha Heifetz, Gregor Piatigorsky,
     and William Primrose

20. BEST CLASSICAL PERFORMANCE—INSTRUMENTAL SOLOIST OR
     SOLOISTS WITH ORCHESTRA:
     "STRAVINSKY: CONCERTO IN D FOR VIOLIN"—Isaac Stern, Violin (Igor
     Stravinsky conducting Columbia Symphony Orchestra)

21. BEST CLASSICAL PERFORMANCE—INSTRUMENTAL SOLOIST OR
     DUO (WITHOUT ORCHESTRA):
     "COLUMBIA RECORDS PRESENTS VLADIMIR HOROWITZ"—Vladimir Horowitz

22. BEST OPERA RECORDING:
     "VERDI: AIDA"—Georg Solti conducting Rome Opera House Orchestra
     and Chorus
     Principal Soloists: Leontyne Price, Jon Vickers, Rita Gorr, Robert Merrill,
     and Giorgio Tozzi

23. BEST CLASSICAL PERFORMANCE—CHORAL (other than opera):
     "BACH: ST. MATTHEW PASSION"—Philharmonic Choir, Wilhelm Pitz, Choral
     Director; Otto Klemperer conducing the Philharmonic Orchestra

24. BEST CLASSICAL PERFORMANCE—VOCAL SOLOIST WITH OR
     WITHOUT ORCHESTRA:
     "WAGNER: GOTTERDAMERUNG—BRUNNHILDE'S IMMOLATION SCENE/
     WESENDONCK SONGS"—Eileen Farrell, soprano

25. BEST CLASSICAL COMPOSITION BY CONTEMPORARY COMPOSER:
     "THE FLOOD"—Composer, Igor Stravinsky

26. BEST ENGINEERING CONTRIBUTION—CLASSICAL RECORDING:
     "R. STRAUSS: ALSO SPRACH ZARATHUSTRA"—Fritz Reiner conducting Chicago
     Symphony. Engineer, Lewis W. Layton

27. BEST ALBUM COVER—CLASSICAL:
     "THE INTIMATE BACH"—Art Director, Marvin Schwartz

28. BEST COMEDY PERFORMANCE:
     "THE FIRST FAMILY"—Vaughn Meader

29. BEST DOCUMENTARY OR SPOKEN WORD RECORDING (other than comedy):
   "The Story-teller: A Session with Charles Laughton"—Charles Laughton (posthumously)

30. BEST ENGINEERING CONTRIBUTION—OTHER THAN NOVELTY AND OTHER THAN CLASSICAL:
   "Hatari!"—Engineer, Al Schmitt

31. BEST ENGINEERING CONTRIBUTION—NOVELTY:
   "The Civil War, Vol. I"—Engineer, Robert Fine

32. BEST ALBUM COVER (other than classical):
   "Lena . . . Lovely and Alive"—Art Director, Robert Jones

33. BEST RECORDING FOR CHILDREN:
   "Saint-Saens: Carnival of the Animals/Britten: Young Person's Guide to the Orchestra"—Leonard Bernstein

34. BEST ROCK AND ROLL RECORDING:
   "Alley Cat"—Bent Fabric

35. BEST COUNTRY AND WESTERN RECORDING:
   "Funny Way of Laughin' "—Burl Ives

36. BEST RHYTHM AND BLUES RECORDING:
   "I Can't Stop Loving You"—Ray Charles

37. BEST FOLK RECORDING:
   "If I Had a Hammer"—Peter, Paul and Mary

38. BEST GOSPEL OR OTHER RELIGIOUS RECORDING:
   "Great Songs of Love and Faith"—Mahalia Jackson

39. BEST NEW ARTIST OF 1962:
   ROBERT GOULET

1963 Award Winners

1. RECORD OF THE YEAR:
   "The Days of Wine and Roses"—Henry Mancini
   A & R Producer, Steve Sholes

2. ALBUM OF THE YEAR (OTHER THAN CLASSICAL):
   "The Barbra Streisand Album"—Barbra Streisand
   A & R Producer, Mike Berniker

3. ALBUM OF THE YEAR—CLASSICAL:
   "Britten: War Requiem"—Benjamin Britten conductor London Symphony Orchestra & Chorus. Vocal soloists: Galina Vishnevskaya, Peter Pears, Dietrich Fischer-Dieskau. Bach Choir, David Willcocks, director. Highgate School Choir, Edward Chapman, director.
   A & R Director, John Culshaw

4. SONG OF THE YEAR:
   "The Days of Wine and Roses"—Composers, Henry Mancini, Johnny Mercer

5. BEST INSTRUMENTAL THEME:
   "More (Theme from "Mondo Cane")"—Norman Newell, Nino Oliviero, Riz Ortolani, Composers

6. BEST VOCAL PERFORMANCE—FEMALE:
   "The Barbra Streisand Album"—Barbra Streisand

7. BEST VOCAL PERFORMANCE—MALE:
   "Wives and Lovers"—Jack Jones

8. BEST INSTRUMENTAL JAZZ PERFORMANCE—SOLOIST OR SMALL GROUP:
   "Conversations with Myself"—Bill Evans, soloist

9. BEST INSTRUMENTAL JAZZ PERFORMANCE—LARGE GROUP:
   "Encore: Woody Herman, 1963"—Woody Herman

10. BEST ORIGINAL JAZZ COMPOSITION:
    "Gravy Waltz"—Composers, Steve Allen, Ray Brown

11. BEST PERFORMANCE BY AN ORCHESTRA—FOR DANCING:
    "This Time by Basie! Hits of the 50's and 60's"—Count Basie

12. BEST PERFORMANCE BY AN ORCHESTRA OR INSTRUMENTALIST WITH ORCHESTRA—PRIMARILY NOT JAZZ OR FOR DANCING:
    "Java"—Al Hirt

13. BEST INSTRUMENTAL ARRANGEMENT:
    "I Can't Stop Loving You"—Count Basie—Arranger, Quincy Jones

14. BEST BACKGROUND ARRANGEMENT:
    "The Days of Wine and Roses"—Henry Mancini—Arranger, Henry Mancini

15. BEST PERFORMANCE BY A VOCAL GROUP:
    "Blowin' in the Wind"—Peter, Paul and Mary

16. BEST PERFORMANCE BY A CHORUS:
    "Bach's Greatest Hits"—The Swingle Singers

17. BEST ORIGINAL SCORE FROM A MOTION PICTURE OR TELEVISION SHOW:
"Tom Jones"—Composer, John Addison

18. BEST SCORE FROM AN ORIGINAL CAST SHOW ALBUM:
"She Loves Me"—Composers, Jerry Bock and Sheldon Harnick
A & R Producer, Arnold Maxin

19. BEST CLASSICAL PERFORMANCE—ORCHESTRA:
"Bartok: Concerto for Orchestra"—Erich Leinsdorf conducting the Boston Symphony Orchestra

20. BEST CLASSICAL PERFORMANCE—CHAMBER MUSIC:
"Evening of Elizabethan Music"—Julian Bream Consort

21. BEST CLASSICAL PERFORMANCE—INSTRUMENTAL SOLOIST OR SOLOISTS (WITH ORCHESTRA):
"Tchaikovsky: Concerto No. 1 in B-Flat Minor for Piano & Orchestra"—Artur Rubinstein

22. BEST CLASSICAL PERFORMANCE—INSTRUMENTAL SOLOIST OR DUO (WITHOUT ORCHESTRA):
"The Sound of Horowitz"—(Works of Schumann, Scarlatti, Schubert, Scriabin)—Vladimir Horowitz

23. BEST OPERA RECORDING:
"Puccini: Madama Butterfly"—Erich Leinsdorf conducting the RCA Italiana Orchestra & Chorus. Principal soloists, Leontyne Price, Richard Tucker, Rosalind Elias
A & R Producer, Richard Mohr

24. BEST CLASSICAL PERFORMANCE—CHORAL (OTHER THAN OPERA):
"Britten: War Requiem"—Bach Choir, David Willcocks, Director. Highgate School Choir, Edward Chapman, Director. Benjamin Britten conducting the London Symphony Orchestra and Chorus

25. BEST CLASSICAL PERFORMANCE—VOCAL SOLOIST (WITH OR WITHOUT ORCHESTRA):
"Great Scenes from Gershwin's Porgy & Bess"—Leontyne Price

26. BEST CLASSICAL COMPOSITION BY CONTEMPORARY COMPOSER:
"War Requiem"—Composer, Benjamin Britten

27. BEST ENGINEERED RECORDING—CLASSICAL:
"Puccini: Madama Butterfly"—Erich Leinsdorf conducting the RCA Italiana Orchestra & Chorus. Principal soloists, Leontyne Price, Richard Tucker, Rosalind Elias. Engineer, Lewis Layton

28. BEST ALBUM COVER—CLASSICAL:
"Puccini: Madama Butterfly"—Erich Leinsdorf conducting the RCA Italiana Orchestra & Chorus. Principal soloists, Leontyne Price, Richard Tucker, Rosalind Elias. Art Director, Robert Jones

29. MOST PROMISING NEW CLASSICAL RECORDING ARTIST:
ANDRE WATTS (Pianist)

30. BEST COMEDY PERFORMANCE:
"Hello Muddah, Hello Faddah"—Allan Sherman

31. BEST DOCUMENTARY, SPOKEN WORD OR DRAMA RECORDING (OTHER THAN COMEDY):
"Who's Afraid of Virginia Woolf?"—Original cast, Uta Hagen, Arthur Hill, George Grizzard with Melinda Dillon—Winner, Edward Albee

32. BEST ENGINEERED RECORDING—OTHER THAN CLASSICAL:
"Charade"—Henry Mancini Orchestra and Chorus—Engineer, James Malloy

33. BEST ENGINEERED RECORDING—SPECIAL OR NOVEL EFFECTS:
"Civil War Vol. II"—Frederick Fennell—Engineer, Robert Fine

34. BEST ALBUM COVER—OTHER THAN CLASSICAL:
"The Barbra Streisand Album"—Barbra Streisand, Art Director, John Berg

35. BEST ALBUM NOTES:
"The Ellington Era"—Duke Ellington—Stanley Dance, Leonard Feather, Annotators

36. BEST RECORDING FOR CHILDREN:
"Bernstein Conducts for Young People"—Leonard Bernstein, conductor New York Philharmonic

37. BEST ROCK AND ROLL RECORDING:
"Deep Purple"—Nino Tempo & April Stevens

38. BEST COUNTRY AND WESTERN RECORDING:
"Detroit City"—Bobby Bare

39. BEST RHYTHM AND BLUES RECORDING:
"Busted"—Ray Charles

40. BEST FOLK RECORDING:
"Blowin' in the Wind"—Peter, Paul and Mary

41. BEST GOSPEL OR OTHER RELIGIOUS RECORDING (MUSICAL):
"Dominique"—Soeur Sourire (The Singing Nun)

42. BEST NEW ARTIST OF 1963:
    SWINGLE SINGERS

Winners of the 1964 Achievement Awards

1. RECORD OF THE YEAR:
   "The Girl from Ipanema"—Stan Getz and Astrud Gilberto
   A & R Producer, Creed Taylor

2. ALBUM OF THE YEAR—NON-CLASSICAL:
   "Getz/Gilberto"—Stan Getz, Joao Gilberto
   A & R Producer, Creed Taylor

3. ALBUM OF THE YEAR—CLASSICAL:
   "Bernstein: Symphony No. 3 ("Kaddish")"—Leonard Bernstein, conductor,
   the New York Philharmonic Orchestra
   A & R Producer, John McClure

4. SONG OF THE YEAR:
   "Hello, Dolly!"—Composer, Jerry Herman

5. BEST INSTRUMENTAL COMPOSITION (OTHER THAN JAZZ):
   "The Pink Panther Theme"—Composer, Henry Mancini

6. BEST VOCAL PERFORMANCE—FEMALE:
   "People"—Barbra Streisand

7. BEST VOCAL PERFORMANCE—MALE:
   "Hello, Dolly!"—Louis Armstrong

8. BEST INSTRUMENTAL JAZZ PERFORMANCE—SMALL GROUP OR
   SOLOIST WITH SMALL GROUP:
   "Getz/Gilberto"—Stan Getz

9. BEST INSTRUMENTAL JAZZ PERFORMANCE—LARGE GROUP OR
   SOLOIST WITH LARGE GROUP:
   "Guitar from Ipanema"—Laurindo Almeida

10. BEST ORIGINAL JAZZ COMPOSITION:
    "The Cat"—Composer, Lalo Schifrin

11. BEST INSTRUMENTAL PERFORMANCE—NON-JAZZ:
    "Pink Panther"—Henry Mancini

12. BEST INSTRUMENTAL ARRANGEMENT:
    "Pink Panther"—Henry Mancini—Arranger, Henry Mancini

13. BEST ACCOMPANIMENT ARRANGEMENT FOR VOCALIST/S OR
    INSTRUMENTALIST/S:
    "People"—Barbra Streisand—Arranger, Peter Matz

14. BEST PERFORMANCE BY A VOCAL GROUP:
    "A Hard Day's Night"—The Beatles

15. BEST PERFORMANCE BY A CHORUS:
    "The Swingle Singers Going Baroque"—The Swingle Singers

16. BEST ORIGINAL SCORE WRITTEN FOR A MOTION PICTURE OR
    TELEVISION SHOW:
    "Mary Poppins"—Composers, Richard M. and Robert Sherman

17. BEST SCORE FROM AN ORIGINAL CAST SHOW ALBUM:
    "Funny Girl"—Composers, Jule Styne and Bob Merrill
    A & R Producer, Richard Jones

18. BEST COMEDY PERFORMANCE:
    "I Started Out as a Child"—Bill Cosby

19. BEST DOCUMENTARY, SPOKEN WORD OR DRAMA RECORDING
    (OTHER THAN COMEDY):
    "BBC Tribute to John F. Kennedy"—"That Was the Week That Was" Cast

20. BEST ENGINEERED RECORDING:
    "Getz/Gilberto"—Stan Getz, Joao Gilberto—Engineer, Phil Ramone

21. BEST ENGINEERED RECORDING—SPECIAL OR NOVEL EFFECTS:
    "The Chipmunks Sing the Beatles"—The Chipmunks—Engineer, Dave
    Hassinger

22. BEST ALBUM COVER:
    "People"—Barbra Streisand—Art Director, Robert Cato; Photographer, Don
    Bronstein

23. BEST RECORDING FOR CHILDREN:
    "Mary Poppins"—Julie Andrews, Dick Van Dyke, and original cast

24. BEST ROCK AND ROLL RECORDING:
    "Downtown"—Petula Clark

25. BEST RHYTHM AND BLUES RECORDING:
    "How Glad I Am"—Nancy Wilson

26. BEST FOLK RECORDING:
    "We'll Sing in the Sunshine"—Gale Garnett

27. BEST GOSPEL OR OTHER RELIGIOUS RECORDING (MUSICAL):
"GREAT GOSPEL SONGS"—Tennessee Ernie Ford

28. BEST NEW ARTIST OF 1964:
THE BEATLES

29. BEST COUNTRY & WESTERN SINGLE:
"DANG ME"—Roger Miller
A & R Producer, Jerry Kennedy

30. BEST COUNTRY & WESTERN ALBUM:
"DANG ME/CHUG-A-LUG"—Roger Miller
A & R Producer, Jerry Kennedy

31. BEST COUNTRY & WESTERN VOCAL PERFORMANCE—FEMALE:
"HERE COMES MY BABY" (single)—Dottie West

32. BEST COUNTRY & WESTERN VOCAL PERFORMANCE—MALE:
"DANG ME" (single)—Roger Miller

33. BEST COUNTRY & WESTERN SONG:
"DANG ME"—Composer, Roger Miller

34. BEST NEW COUNTRY & WESTERN ARTIST OF 1964:
ROGER MILLER

35. BEST ALBUM NOTES:
"MEXICO (LEGACY COLLECTION)"—Carlos Chavez—Annotators, Stanton
Catlin, Carleton Beals

36. BEST PERFORMANCE—ORCHESTRA:
"MAHLER: SYMPHONY NO. 5 IN C SHARP MINOR/BERG: "WOZZECK"
EXCERPTS"—Phyllis Curtin—Erich Leinsdorf conducting the Boston
Symphony Orchestra

37. BEST CHAMBER PERFORMANCE—INSTRUMENTAL:
"BEETHOVEN: TRIO NO. 1 IN E FLAT, OP. 1, NO. 1"—Heifetz-Piatigorsky
Concerts with Jacob Lateiner, piano

38. BEST CHAMBER MUSIC PERFORMANCE—VOCAL:
"IT WAS A LOVER AND HIS LASS (MORLEY, BYRD & OTHERS)"—New York Pro
Musica, Noah Greenberg conductor

39. BEST PERFORMANCE—INSTRUMENTAL SOLOIST OR SOLOISTS
(WITH ORCHESTRA):
"PROKOFIEFF: CONCERTO NO. 1 IN D MAJOR FOR VIOLIN"—Isaac Stern
(Eugene Ormandy conducting Philadelphia Orchestra)

40. BEST PERFORMANCE—INSTRUMENTAL SOLOIST (WITHOUT ORCHESTRA):
"Vladimir Horowitz Plays Beethoven, Debussy, Chopin (Beethoven: Sonata No. 8 "Pathetique"; Debussy: Preludes; Chopin: Etudes & Scherzos 1 thru 4)"—Vladimir Horowitz

41. BEST OPERA RECORDING:
"Bizet: Carmen"—Herbert von Karajan conducting Vienna Philharmonic Orchestra & Chorus—Principal Soloists: Leontyne Price, Franco Corelli, Robert Merrill, Mirella Freni

42. BEST CHORAL PERFORMANCE (OTHER THAN OPERA):
"Britten: A Ceremony of Carols"—The Robert Shaw Chorale—Robert Shaw Conductor

43. BEST VOCAL SOLOIST PERFORMANCE (WITH OR WITHOUT ORCHESTRA):
"Berlioz: Nuits D'ete (Song Cycle)/Falla: El Amor Brujo"—Leontyne Price (Fritz Reiner conducting Chicago Symphony)

44. BEST COMPOSITION BY A CONTEMPORARY COMPOSER:
"Piano Concerto"—Composer, Samuel Barber

45. BEST ENGINEERED RECORDING:
"Britten: Young Person's Guide to the Orchestra"—Carlo Maria Giulini conducting Philharmonia Orchestra—Engineer, Douglas Larter

46. BEST ALBUM COVER:
"Saint-Saens: Carnival of the Animals/Britten: Young Person's Guide to the Orchestra"—Arthur Fiedler conducting Boston Pops—Art Director, Robert Jones—Graphic Artist, Jan Balet

47. MOST PROMISING NEW RECORDING ARTIST:
MARILYN HORNE (Mezzo-Soprano)

Musicals Awarded Pulitzer Prize for Drama

Season	Show
1931–32	Of Thee I Sing
1949–50	South Pacific
1959–60	Fiorello!
1961–62	How to Succeed in Business Without Really Trying

Academy Award Nominations and Winners

Music—Best Song

1934°° SEVENTH YEAR

CARIOCA from "Flying Down To Rio," RKO Radio.
>Music: Vincent Youmans.
>Lyrics: Edward Eliscu and Gus Kahn.

°CONTINENTAL from "The Gay Divorcee," RKO Radio.
>Music: Con Conrad.
>Lyrics: Herb Magidson.

LOVE IN BLOOM from "She Loves Me Not," Paramount.
>Music: Ralph Rainger.
>Lyrics: Leo Robin.

1935 EIGHTH YEAR

CHEEK TO CHEEK from "Top Hat," RKO Radio.
>Music and Lyrics: Irving Berlin.

LOVELY TO LOOK AT from "Roberta," RKO Radio.
>Music: Jerome Kern.
>Lyrics: Dorothy Fields and Jimmy McHugh.

°LULLABY OF BROADWAY from "Gold Diggers of 1935," Warner Bros.
>Music: Harry Warren.
>Lyrics: Al Dubin.

1936 NINTH YEAR

DID I REMEMBER from "Suzy," Metro-Goldwyn-Mayer.
>Music: Walter Donaldson.
>Lyrics: Harold Adamson.

I'VE GOT YOU UNDER MY SKIN from "Born to Dance," Metro-Goldwyn-Mayer.
>Music and Lyrics: Cole Porter.

° Denotes winner.
°° Awards for Best Song started in 1934.

A Melody From the Sky from "Trail of the Lonesome Pine," Paramount.
    Music: Louis Alter.
    Lyrics: Sidney Mitchell.
Pennies From Heaven from "Pennies From Heaven," Columbia.
    Music: Arthur Johnston.
    Lyrics: Johnny Burke.
*The Way You Look Tonight from "Swing Time," RKO Radio.
    Music: Jerome Kern.
    Lyrics: Dorothy Fields.
When Did You Leave Heaven from "Sing Baby Sing," 20th Century-Fox.
    Music: Richard A. Whiting.
    Lyrics: Walter Bullock.

1937   TENTH YEAR
Remember Me from "Mr. Dodd Takes the Air," Warner Bros.
    Music: Harry Warren.
    Lyrics: Al Dubin.
*Sweet Leilani from "Waikiki Wedding," Paramount.
    Music and Lyrics: Harry Owens.
That Old Feeling from "Vogues of 1938," Wanger, UA.
    Music: Sammy Fain.
    Lyrics: Lew Brown.
They Can't Take That Away From Me from "Shall We Dance," RKO Radio.
    Music: George Gershwin.
    Lyrics: Ira Gershwin.
Whispers in the Dark from "Artists and Models," Paramount.
    Music: Frederick Hollander.
    Lyrics: Leo Robin.

1938   ELEVENTH YEAR
Always and Always from "Mannequin," Metro-Goldwyn-Mayer.
    Music: Edward Ward.
    Lyrics: Chet Forrest and Bob Wright.
Change Partners and Dance With Me from "Carefree," RKO Radio.
    Music and Lyrics: Irving Berlin.
Cowboy and the Lady from "The Cowboy and the Lady," Goldwyn, UA.
    Music: Lionel Newman.
    Lyrics: Arthur Quenzer.
Dust from "Under Western Stars," Republic.
    Music and Lyrics: Johnny Marvin.
Jeepers Creepers from "Going Places," Warner Bros.
    Music: Harry Warren.
    Lyrics: Johnny Mercer.

MERRILY WE LIVE from "Merrily We Live," Roach, M-G-M.
    Music: Phil Craig.
    Lyrics: Arthur Quenzer.
A MIST OVER THE MOON from "The Lady Objects," Columbia.
    Music: Ben Oakland.
    Lyrics: Oscar Hammerstein II.
MY OWN from "That Certain Age," Universal.
    Music: Jimmy McHugh.
    Lyrics: Harold Adamson.
NOW IT CAN BE TOLD from "Alexander's Ragtime Band," 20th Century-Fox.
    Music and Lyrics: Irving Berlin.
*THANKS FOR THE MEMORY from "Big Broadcast of 1938," Paramount.
    Music: Ralph Rainger.
    Lyrics: Leo Robin.

1939   TWELFTH YEAR
FAITHFUL FOREVER from "Gulliver's Travels," Paramount.
    Music: Ralph Rainger.
    Lyrics: Leo Robin.
I POURED MY HEART INTO A SONG from "Second Fiddle," 20th Century-Fox.
    Music and Lyrics: Irving Berlin.
*OVER THE RAINBOW from "The Wizard of Oz," Metro-Goldwyn-Mayer.
    Music: Harold Arlen.
    Lyrics: E. Y. Harburg.
WISHING from "Love Affair," RKO Radio.
    Music and Lyrics: Buddy de Sylva.

1940   THIRTEENTH YEAR
DOWN ARGENTINE WAY from "Down Argentine Way," 20th Century-Fox.
    Music: Harry Warren.
    Lyrics: Mack Gordon.
I'D KNOW YOU ANYWHERE from "You'll Find Out," RKO Radio.
    Music: Jimmy McHugh.
    Lyrics: Johnny Mercer.
IT'S A BLUE WORLD from "Music in My Heart," Columbia.
    Music and Lyrics: Chet Forrest and Bob Wright.
LOVE OF MY LIFE from "Second Chorus," Paramount.
    Music: Artie Shaw.
    Lyrics: Johnny Mercer.
ONLY FOREVER from "Rhythm on the River," Paramount.
    Music: James Monaco.
    Lyrics: John Burke.

OUR LOVE AFFAIR from "Strike Up the Band," Metro-Goldwyn-Mayer.
    Music and Lyrics: Roger Edens and Georgie Stoll.
WALTZING IN THE CLOUDS from "Spring Parade," Universal.
    Music: Robert Stolz.
    Lyrics: Gus Kahn.
*WHEN YOU WISH UPON A STAR from "Pinocchio," Disney, RKO Radio.
    Music: Leigh Harline.
    Lyrics: Ned Washington.
WHO AM I? from "Hit Parade of 1941," Republic.
    Music: Jule Styne.
    Lyrics: Walter Bullock.

1941   FOURTEENTH YEAR
BABY MINE from "Dumbo," Disney, RKO Radio.
    Music: Frank Churchill.
    Lyrics: Ned Washington.
BE HONEST WITH ME from "Ridin' on a Rainbow," Republic.
    Music and Lyrics: Gene Autry and Fred Rose.
BLUES IN THE NIGHT from "Blues in the Night," Warner Bros.
    Music: Harold Arlen.
    Lyrics: Johnny Mercer.
BOOGIE WOOGIE BUGLE BOY OF COMPANY B from "Buck Privates," Universal.
    Music: Hugh Prince.
    Lyrics: Don Raye.
CHATTANOOGA CHOO CHOO from "Sun Valley Serenade," 20th Century-Fox.
    Music: Harry Warren.
    Lyrics: Mack Gordon.
DOLORES from "Las Vegas Nights," Paramount.
    Music: Lou Alter.
    Lyrics: Frank Loesser.
*THE LAST TIME I SAW PARIS from "Lady Be Good," Metro-Goldwyn-Mayer.
    Music: Jerome Kern.
    Lyrics: Oscar Hammerstein II.
OUT OF THE SILENCE from "All-American Co-Ed," Roach, UA.
    Music and Lyrics: Lloyd B. Norlind.
SINCE I KISSED MY BABY GOODBYE from "You'll Never Get Rich," Columbia.
    Music and Lyrics: Cole Porter.

1942   FIFTEENTH YEAR
ALWAYS IN MY HEART from "Always In My Heart," Warner Bros.
    Music: Ernesto Lecuona.
    Lyrics: Kim Gannon.

[303]

DEARLY BELOVED from "You Were Never Lovelier," Columbia.
    Music: Jerome Kern.
    Lyrics: Johnny Mercer.
HOW ABOUT YOU? from "Babes On Broadway," Metro-Goldwyn-Mayer.
    Music: Burton Lane.
    Lyrics: Ralph Freed.
IT SEEMS I HEARD THAT SONG BEFORE from "Youth On Parade," Republic.
    Music: Jule Styne.
    Lyrics: Sammy Cahn.
I'VE GOT A GAL IN KALAMAZOO from "Orchestra Wives," 20th Century-Fox.
    Music: Harry Warren.
    Lyrics: Mack Gordon.
LOVE IS A SONG from "Bambi," Disney, RKO Radio.
    Music: Frank Churchill.
    Lyrics: Larry Morey.
PENNIES FOR PEPPINO from "Flying with Music," Roach, UA.
    Music: Edward Ward.
    Lyrics: Chet Forrest and Bob Wright.
PIG FOOT PETE from "Hellzapoppin'," Universal.
    Music: Gene de Paul.
    Lyrics: Don Raye.
THERE'S A BREEZE ON LAKE LOUISE from "The Mayor of 44th Street," RKO Radio.
    Music: Harry Revel.
    Lyrics: Mort Greene.
*WHITE CHRISTMAS from "Holiday Inn," Paramount.
    Music and Lyrics: Irving Berlin.

1943   SIXTEENTH YEAR
BLACK MAGIC from "Star Spangled Rhythm," Paramount.
    Music: Harold Arlen.
    Lyrics: Johnny Mercer.
CHANGE OF HEART from "Hit Parade of 1943," Republic.
    Music: Jule Styne.
    Lyrics: Harold Adamson.
HAPPINESS IS A THING CALLED JOE from "Cabin in the Sky," Metro-Goldwyn-Mayer.
    Music: Harold Arlen.
    Lyrics: E. Y. Harburg.
MY SHINING HOUR from "The Sky's the Limit," RKO Radio.
    Music: Harold Arlen.
    Lyrics: Johnny Mercer.

Saludos Amigos from "Saludos Amigos," Disney, RKO Radio.
 Music: Charles Wolcott.
 Lyrics: Ned Washington.
Say a Prayer for the Boys Over There from "Her's to Hold," Universal.
 Music: Jimmy McHugh.
 Lyrics: Herb Magidson.
They're Either Too Young or Too Old from "Thank Your Lucky Stars," Warner
 Bros.
 Music: Arthur Schwartz.
 Lyrics: Frank Loesser.
We Mustn't Say Goodbye from "Stage Door Canteen," Lesser, UA.
 Music: James Monaco.
 Lyrics: Al Dubin.
You'd Be So Nice To Come Home To from "Something to Shout About," Columbia.
 Music and Lyrics: Cole Porter.
*You'll Never Know from "Hello, Frisco, Hello," 20th Century-Fox.
 Music: Harry Warren.
 Lyrics: Mack Gordon.

1944   SEVENTEENTH YEAR
I Couldn't Sleep a Wink Last Night from "Higher and Higher," RKO Radio.
 Music: Jimmy McHugh.
 Lyrics: Harold Adamson.
I'll Walk Alone from "Follow the Boys," Universal.
 Music: Jule Styne.
 Lyrics: Sammy Cahn.
I'm Making Believe from "Sweet and Lowdown," 20th Century-Fox.
 Music: James V. Monaco.
 Lyrics: Mack Gordon.
Long Ago and Far Away from "Cover Girl," Columbia.
 Music: Jerome Kern.
 Lyrics: Ira Gershwin.
Now I Know from "Up in Arms," Avalon, RKO Radio.
 Music: Harold Arlen.
 Lyrics: Ted Koehler.
Remember Me to Carolina from "Minstrel Man," PRC.
 Music: Harry Revel.
 Lyrics: Paul Webster.
Rio de Janeiro from "Brazil," Republic.
 Music: Ary Barroso.
 Lyrics: Ned Washington.

SILVER SHADOWS AND GOLDEN DREAMS from "Lady Let's Dance," Monogram.
    Music: Lew Pollack.
    Lyrics: Charles Newman.
SWEET DREAMS SWEETHEART from "Hollywood Canteen," Warner Bros.
    Music: M. K. Jerome.
    Lyrics: Ted Koehler.
*SWINGING ON A STAR from "Going My Way," Paramount.
    Music: James Van Heusen.
    Lyrics: Johnny Burke.
TOO MUCH IN LOVE from "Song of the Open Road," Rogers, UA.
    Music: Walter Kent.
    Lyrics: Kim Gannon.
THE TROLLEY SONG from "Meet Me in St. Louis," Metro-Goldwyn-Mayer.
    Music and Lyrics: Ralph Blane and Hugh Martin.

1945   EIGHTEENTH YEAR
ACCENTUATE THE POSITIVE from "Here Come the Waves," Paramount.
    Music: Harold Arlen.
    Lyrics: Johnny Mercer.
ANYWHERE from "Tonight and Every Night," Columbia.
    Music: Jule Styne.
    Lyrics: Sammy Cahn.
AREN'T YOU GLAD YOU'RE YOU from "The Bells of St. Mary's," Rainbow, RKO Radio.
    Music: James Van Heusen.
    Lyrics: Johnny Burke.
CAT AND CANARY from "Why Girls Leave Home," PRC.
    Music: Jay Livingston.
    Lyrics: Ray Evans.
ENDLESSLY from "Earl Carroll Vanities," Republic.
    Music: Walter Kent.
    Lyrics: Kim Gannon.
I FALL IN LOVE TOO EASILY from "Anchors Aweigh," Metro-Goldwyn-Mayer.
    Music: Jule Styne.
    Lyrics: Sammy Cahn.
I'LL BUY THAT DREAM from "Sing Your Way Home," RKO Radio.
    Music: Allie Wrubel.
    Lyrics: Herb Magidson.
*IT MIGHT AS WELL BE SPRING from "State Fair," 20th Century-Fox.
    Music: Richard Rodgers.
    Lyrics: Oscar Hammerstein II.
LINDA from "G. I. Joe," Cowan, UA.
    Music and Lyrics: Ann Ronell.

Love Letters from "Love Letters," Wallis, Paramount.
    Music: Victor Young.
    Lyrics: Edward Heyman.
More and More from "Can't Help Singing," Universal.
    Music: Jerome Kern.
    Lyrics: E. Y. Harburg.
Sleighride in July from "Bell of the Yukon," International, RKO Radio.
    Music: James Van Heusen.
    Lyrics: Johnny Burke.
So in Love from "Wonder Man," Beverly Prods., RKO Radio.
    Music: David Rose.
    Lyrics: Leo Robin.
Some Sunday Morning from "San Antonio," Warner Bros.
    Music: Ray Heindorf and M. K. Jerome.
    Lyrics: Ted Koehler.

1946 NINETEENTH YEAR

All Through the Day from "Centennial Summer," 20th Century-Fox.
    Music: Jerome Kern.
    Lyrics: Oscar Hammerstein II.
I Can't Begin to Tell You from "The Dolly Sisters," 20th Century-Fox.
    Music: James Monaco.
    Lyrics: Mack Gordon.
Ole Buttermilk Sky from "Canyon Passage," Wanger, Universal.
    Music: Hoagy Carmichael.
    Lyrics: Jack Brooks.
*On the Atchison, Topeka and Santa Fe from "The Harvey Girls," Metro-
    Goldwyn-Mayer.
    Music: Harry Warren.
    Lyrics: Johnny Mercer.
You Keep Coming Back Like a Song from "Blue Skies," Paramount.
    Music and Lyrics: Irving Berlin.

1947 TWENTIETH YEAR

A Gal in Calico from "The Time, Place and the Girl," Warner Bros.
    Music: Arthur Schwartz.
    Lyrics: Leo Robin.
I Wish I Didn't Love You So from "The Perils of Pauline," Paramount.
    Music and Lyrics: Frank Loesser.
Pass That Peace Pipe from "Good News," Metro-Goldwyn-Mayer.
    Music and Lyrics: Ralph Blane, Hugh Martin and Roger Edens.

You Do from "Mother Wore Tights," 20th Century-Fox.
> Music: Josef Myrow.
> Lyrics: Mack Gordon.

*Zip-A-Dee-Doo-Dah from "Song of the South," Disney-RKO Radio.
> Music: Allie Wrubel.
> Lyrics: Ray Gilbert.

1948   TWENTY-FIRST YEAR

*Buttons and Bows from "The Paleface," Paramount.
> Music and Lyrics: Jay Livingston and Ray Evans.

For Every Man There's a Woman from "Casbah," Marston Pictures, U-I.
> Music: Harold Arlen.
> Lyrics: Leo Robin.

It's Magic from "Romance on the High Seas," Curtiz, Warner Bros.
> Music: Jule Styne.
> Lyrics: Sammy Cahn.

This is the Moment from "That Lady in Ermine," 20th Century-Fox.
> Music: Frederick Hollander.
> Lyrics: Leo Robin.

The Woody Woodpecker Song from "Wet Blanket Policy," Walter Lantz, UA (Cartoon).
> Music and Lyrics: Ramey Idriss and George Tibbles.

1949   TWENTY-SECOND YEAR

*Baby, It's Cold Outside from "Neptune's Daughter," Metro-Goldwyn-Mayer.
> Music and Lyrics: Frank Loesser.

It's a Great Feeling from "It's a Great Feeling," Warner Bros.
> Music: Jule Styne.
> Lyrics: Sammy Cahn.

Lavender Blue from "So Dear to My Heart," Disney-RKO Radio.
> Music: Eliot Daniel.
> Lyrics: Larry Morey.

My Foolish Heart from "My Foolish Heart," Goldwyn-RKO Radio.
> Music: Victor Young.
> Lyrics: Ned Washington.

Through a Long and Sleepless Night from "Come to the Stable," 20th Century-Fox.
> Music: Alfred Newman.
> Lyrics: Mack Gordon.

1950   TWENTY-THIRD YEAR

Be My Love from "The Toast of New Orleans," Metro-Goldwyn-Mayer.
> Music: Nicholas Brodszky.
> Lyrics: Sammy Cahn.

Bibbidy-Bobbidi-Boo from "Cinderella," Disney, RKO Radio.
    Music and Lyrics: Mack David, Al Hoffman and Jerry Livingston.
°Mona Lisa from "Captain Carey, USA," Paramount.
    Music and Lyrics: Ray Evans and Jay Livingston.
Mule Train from "Singing Guns," Polomar Pictures, Republic.
    Music and Lyrics: Fred Glickman, Hy Heath and Johnny Lange.
Wilhelmina from "Wabash Avenue," 20th Century-Fox.
    Music: Josef Myrow.
    Lyrics: Mack Gordon.

1951   TWENTY-FOURTH YEAR
°In the Cool, Cool, Cool of the Evening from "Here Comes the Groom,"
    Paramount.
    Music: Hoagy Carmichael.
    Lyrics: Johnny Mercer.
A Kiss to Build a Dream On from "The Strip," Metro-Goldwyn-Mayer.
    Music and Lyrics: Bert Kalmar, Harry Ruby and Oscar Hammerstein II.
Never from "Golden Girl," 20th Century-Fox.
    Music: Lionel Newman.
    Lyrics: Eliot Daniel.
Too Late Now from "Royal Wedding," Metro-Goldwyn-Mayer.
    Music: Burton Lane.
    Lyrics: Alan Jay Lerner.
Wonder Why from "Rich, Young and Pretty," Metro-Goldwyn-Mayer.
    Music: Nicholas Brodszky.
    Lyrics: Sammy Cahn.

1952   TWENTY-FIFTH YEAR
Am I in Love from "Son of Paleface," Paramount.
    Music and Lyrics: Jack Brooks.
Because You're Mine from "Because You're Mine," Metro-Goldwyn-Mayer.
    Music: Nicholas Brodszky.
    Lyrics: Sammy Cahn.
°High Noon (Do Not Forsake Me, Oh My Darlin') from "High Noon,"
    Kramer, UA.
    Music: Dimitri Tiomkin.
    Lyrics: Ned Washington.
Thumbelina from "Hans Christian Andersen," Goldwyn, RKO Radio.
    Music and Lyrics: Frank Loesser.
Zing a Little Zong from "Just for You," Paramount.
    Music: Harry Warren.
    Lyrics: Leo Robin.

1953   TWENTY-SIXTH YEAR

THE MOON IS BLUE from "The Moon is Blue," Preminger-Herbert Prod., UA.
  Music: Herschel Burke Gilbert.
  Lyrics: Sylvia Fine.
MY FLAMING HEART from "Small Town Girl," Metro-Goldwyn-Mayer.
  Music: Nicholas Brodszky.
  Lyrics: Leo Robin.
SADIE THOMPSON'S SONG (BLUE PACIFIC BLUES) from "Miss Sadie Thompson,"
    Beckworth, Columbia.
  Music: Lester Lee.
  Lyrics: Ned Washington.
°SECRET LOVE from "Calamity Jane," Warner Bros.
  Music: Sammy Fain.
  Lyrics: Paul Francis Webster.
THAT'S AMORE from "The Caddy," York Pictures, Paramount.
  Music: Harry Warren.
  Lyrics: Jack Brooks.

1954   TWENTY-SEVENTH YEAR

COUNT YOUR BLESSINGS INSTEAD OF SHEEP from "White Christmas," Paramount.
  Music and Lyrics: Irving Berlin.
THE HIGH AND THE MIGHTY from "The High and the Mighty," Wayne-Fellows
    Prods., Inc., Warner Bros.
  Music: Dimitri Tiomkin.
  Lyrics: Ned Washington.
HOLD MY HAND from "Susan Slept Here," RKO Radio.
  Music and Lyrics: Jack Lawrence and Richard Myers.
THE MAN THAT GOT AWAY from "A Star is Born," A Transcona Enterprises Prod.,
    Warner Bros.
  Music: Harold Arlen.
  Lyrics: Ira Gershwin.
°THREE COINS IN THE FOUNTAIN from "Three Coins in the Fountain,"
    20th Century-Fox.
  Music: Jule Styne.
  Lyrics: Sammy Cahn.

1955   TWENTY-EIGHTH YEAR

I'LL NEVER STOP LOVING YOU from "Love Me or Leave Me," Metro-Goldwyn-Mayer.
  Music: Nicholas Brodszky.
  Lyrics: Sammy Cahn.

*LOVE IS A MANY-SPLENDORED THING from "Love is a Many-Splendored Thing," 20th Century-Fox.
   Music: Sammy Fain.
   Lyrics: Paul Francis Webster.
SOMETHING'S GOTTA GIVE from "Daddy Long Legs," 20th Century-Fox.
   Music and Lyrics: Johnny Mercer.
(LOVE IS) THE TENDER TRAP from "The Tender Trap," Metro-Goldwyn-Mayer.
   Music: James Van Heusen.
   Lyrics: Sammy Cahn.
UNCHAINED MELODY from "Unchained," Hall Bartlett Prods., Inc., Warner Bros.
   Music: Alex North.
   Lyrics: Hy Zaret.

1956   TWENTY-NINTH YEAR
FRIENDLY PERSUASION (THEE I LOVE) from "Friendly Persuasion," Allied Artists.
   Music: Dimitri Tiomkin.
   Lyrics: Paul Francis Webster.
JULIE from "Julie," Arwin Prods., M-G-M.
   Music: Leith Stevens.
   Lyrics: Tom Adair.
TRUE LOVE from "High Society," Sol C. Siegel Prod., M-G-M.
   Music and Lyrics: Cole Porter.
*WHATEVER WILL BE, WILL BE (QUE SERA, SERA) from "The Man Who Knew Too Much," Filwite Prods., Inc., Paramount.
   Music and Lyrics: Jay Livingston and Ray Evans.
WRITTEN ON THE WIND from "Written on the Wind," Universal-International.
   Music: Victor Young.
   Lyrics: Sammy Cahn.

1957   THIRTIETH YEAR
AN AFFAIR TO REMEMBER from "An Affair to Remember," Jerry Wald Prod., Inc., 20th Century-Fox.
   Music: Harry Warren.
   Lyrics: Harold Adamson and Leo McCarey.
*ALL THE WAY from "The Joker is Wild," A.M.B.L. Prod., Paramount.
   Music: James Van Heusen.
   Lyrics: Sammy Cahn.
APRIL LOVE from "April Love," 20th Century-Fox.
   Music: Sammy Fain.
   Lyrics: Paul Francis Webster.

Tammy from "Tammy and the Bachelor," Universal-International.
    Music and Lyrics: Ray Evans and Jay Livingston.
Wild is the Wind from "Wild is the Wind," A Hal Wallis Prod., Paramount.
    Music: Dimitri Tiomkin.
    Lyrics: Ned Washington.

1958   THIRTY-FIRST YEAR

Almost in Your Arms (Love Song from "Houseboat") from "Houseboat,"
    Paramount and Scribe, Paramount.
    Music and Lyrics: Jay Livingston and Ray Evans.
A Certain Smile from "A Certain Smile," 20th Century-Fox.
    Music: Sammy Fain.
    Lyrics: Paul Francis Webster.
*Gigi from "Gigi," Arthur Freed Prods., Inc., M-G-M.
    Music: Frederick Loewe.
    Lyrics: Alan Jay Lerner.
To Love and Be Loved from "Some Came Running," Sol C. Siegel Prods., Inc.,
    M-G-M.
    Music: James Van Heusen.
    Lyrics: Sammy Cahn.
A Very Precious Love from "Marjorie Morningstar," Beachwold Pictures,
    Warner Bros.
    Music: Sammy Fain.
    Lyrics: Paul Francis Webster.

1959   THIRTY-SECOND YEAR

The Best of Everything from "The Best of Everything," Company of Artists, Inc.,
    20th Century-Fox.
    Music: Alfred Newman.
    Lyrics: Sammy Cahn.
The Five Pennies from "The Five Pennies," Dena Prod., Paramount.
    Music and Lyrics: Sylvia Fine.
The Hanging Tree from "The Hanging Tree," Baroda Prods., Inc., Warner Bros.
    Music: Jerry Livingston.
    Lyrics: Mack David.
*High Hopes from "A Hole in the Head," Sincap Prods., UA.
    Music: James Van Heusen.
    Lyrics: Sammy Cahn.
Strange Are the Ways of Love from "The Young Land," C. V. Whitney Pictures,
    Inc., Columbia.
    Music: Dimitri Tiomkin.
    Lyrics: Ned Washington.

1960   THIRTY-THIRD YEAR

THE FACTS OF LIFE from "The Facts of Life," Panama & Frank Prod., UA.
  Music and Lyrics: Johnny Mercer.
FARAWAY PART OF TOWN from "Pepe," G. S.-Posa Films International Prod.,
    Columbia.
  Music: Andre Previn.
  Lyrics: Dory Langdon.
THE GREEN LEAVES OF SUMMER from "The Alamo," Batjac Prod., UA.
  Music: Dimitri Tiomkin.
  Lyrics: Paul Francis Webster.
*NEVER ON SUNDAY from "Never on Sunday," Melinafilm Prod., Lopert Pictures
    Corp. (Greek).
  Music and Lyrics: Manos Hadjidakis.
THE SECOND TIME AROUND from "High Time," Bing Crosby Prods., 20th Century-Fox.
  Music: James Van Heusen.
  Lyrics: Sammy Cahn.

1961   THIRTY-FOURTH YEAR

BACHELOR IN PARADISE from "Bachelor in Paradise," Ted Richmond Prod., M-G-M.
  Music: Henry Mancini.
  Lyrics: Mack David.
LOVE THEME FROM EL CID (The Falcon and the Dove) from "El Cid," Samuel
    Bronston Prod. in association with Dear Film Prod., Allied Artists.
  Music: Miklos Rozsa.
  Lyrics: Paul Francis Webster.
*MOON RIVER from "Breakfast at Tiffany's," Jurow-Shepherd Prod., Paramount.
  Music: Henry Mancini.
  Lyrics: Johnny Mercer.
POCKETFUL OF MIRACLES from "Pocketful of Miracles," Franton Prod., UA.
  Music: James Van Heusen.
  Lyrics: Sammy Cahn.
TOWN WITHOUT PITY from "Town Without Pity," Mirisch Company in association
    with Gloria Films, UA.
  Music: Dimitri Tiomkin.
  Lyrics: Ned Washington.

1962   THIRTY-FIFTH YEAR

*DAYS OF WINE AND ROSES from "Days of Wine and Roses," Martin Manulis-Jalem
    Prod., Warner Bros.
  Music: Henry Mancini.
  Lyrics: Johnny Mercer.

Love Song From Mutiny on the Bounty (Follow Me) from "Mutiny on the Bounty," Arcola Prod., M-G-M.
  Music: Bronislau Kaper.
  Lyrics: Paul Francis Webster.
Song From Two for the Seesaw (Second Chance) from "Two for the Seesaw," Mirisch-Argyle-Talbot Prod. in association with Seven Arts Productions, UA.
  Music: Andre Previn.
  Lyrics: Dory Langdon.
Tender is the Night from "Tender is the Night," 20th Century-Fox.
  Music: Sammy Fain.
  Lyrics: Paul Francis Webster.
Walk on the Wild Side from "Walk on the Wild Side," Famous Artists Prods., Columbia.
  Music: Elmer Bernstein.
  Lyrics: Mack David.

1963   THIRTY-SIXTH YEAR
*Call Me Irresponsible from "Papa's Delicate Condition," Amro Prods., Paramount.
  Music: James Van Heusen.
  Lyrics: Sammy Cahn.
Charade from "Charade," Universal-Stanley Donen Prod., Universal.
  Music: Henry Mancini.
  Lyrics: Johnny Mercer.
It's a Mad, Mad, Mad, Mad World from "It's a Mad, Mad, Mad, Mad World," Casey Prod., UA.
  Music: Ernest Gold.
  Lyrics: Mack David.
More from "Mondo Cane," Cineriz Prod., Times Film.
  Music: Riz Ortolani and Nino Oliviero.
  Lyrics: Norman Newell.
So Little Time from "55 Days at Peking," Samuel Bronston Prod., Allied Artists.
  Music: Dimitri Tiomkin.
  Lyrics: Paul Francis Webster.

1964   THIRTY-SEVENTH YEAR
*Chim Chim Cher-ee from "Mary Poppins," Walt Disney Productions, Buena Vista Distribution Co.
  Music and Lyrics: Richard M. Sherman and Robert B. Sherman.
Dear Heart from "Dear Heart," A W. B.-Out-of-Towners Production, Warner Bros.
  Music: Henry Mancini.
  Lyrics: Jay Livingston and Ray Evans.

HUSH . . . HUSH, SWEET CHARLOTTE from "Hush . . . Hush, Sweet Charlotte," An
    Associates & Aldrich Production, 20th Century-Fox.
    Music: Frank DeVol.
    Lyrics: Mack David.
MY KIND OF TOWN from "Robin and the 7 Hoods," A P-C Production, Warner Bros.
    Music· James Van Heusen.
    Lyri′ s: Sammy Cahn.
WHERE LOVE HAS GONE from "Where Love Has Gone," A Paramount-Embassy
    Pictures Production, Paramount.
    Music: James Van Heusen.
    Lyrics: Sammy Cahn.

Music—Scoring Awards

(NOTE: During the years 1934 through 1937, this was a *Music Department Achievement* and the
Award was presented to the departmental head instead of to the composer.)

1934 SEVENTH YEAR
(Best Score)
THE GAY DIVORCEE, RKO Radio Studio Music Dept.; Max Steiner, Head.
    Score: Kenneth Webb and Samuel Hoffenstein.
THE LOST PATROL, RKO Radio Studio Music Dept.; Max Steiner, Head.
    Score: Max Steiner.
*ONE NIGHT OF LOVE, Columbia Studio Music Dept.; Louis Silvers, Head.
    Thematic music: Victor Schertzinger and Gus Kahn.

1935 EIGHTH YEAR
(Best Score)
*THE INFORMER, RKO Radio Studio Music Dept.; Max Steiner, Head.
    Score: Max Steiner.
MUTINY ON THE BOUNTY, Metro-Goldwyn-Mayer Studio Music Dept.; Nat W.
    Finston, Head.
    Score: Herbert Stothart.
PETER IBBETSON, Paramount Studio Music Dept.; Irvin Talbot, Head.
    Score: Ernst Toch.

1936 NINTH YEAR
(Best Score)
*ANTHONY ADVERSE, Warner Bros. Studio Music Dept.; Leo Forbstein, Head.
    Score: Erich Wolfgang Korngold.
THE CHARGE OF THE LIGHT BRIGADE, Warner Bros. Studio Music Dept.; Leo
    Forbstein, Head.
    Score: Max Steiner.

THE GARDEN OF ALLAH, Selznick International Pictures Music Dept.; Max Steiner, Head.
>Score: Max Steiner.
THE GENERAL DIED AT DAWN, Paramount Studio Music Dept.; Boris Morros, Head.
>Score: Werner Janssen.
WINTERSET, RKO Radio Studio Music Dept.; Nathaniel Shilkret, Head.
>Score: Nathaniel Shilkret.

1937   TENTH YEAR
(Best Score)
HURRICANE, Samuel Goldwyn Studio Music Dept.; Alfred Newman, Head.
>Score: Alfred Newman.
IN OLD CHICAGO, 20th Century-Fox Studio Music Dept.; Louis Silvers, Head.
>Score: No composer credit.
THE LIFE OF EMILE ZOLA, Warner Bros. Studio Music Dept.; Leo Forbstein, Head.
>Score: Max Steiner.
LOST HORIZON, Columbia Studio Music Dept.; Morris Stoloff, Head.
>Score: Dimitri Tiomkin.
MAKE A WISH, Principal Productions; Dr. Hugo Riesenfeld, Musical Director.
>Score: Dr. Hugo Riesenfeld.
MAYTIME, Metro-Goldwyn-Mayer Studio Music Dept.; Nat W. Finston, Head.
>Score: Herbert Stothart.
°ONE HUNDRED MEN AND A GIRL, Universal Studio Music Dept.; Charles Previn, Head.
>Score: No composer credit.
PORTIA ON TRIAL, Republic Studio Music Dept.; Alberto Colombo, Head.
>Score: Alberto Colombo.
THE PRISONER OF ZENDA, Selznick International Pictures Music Dept.; Alfred Newman, Musical Director.
>Score: Alfred Newman.
QUALITY STREET, RKO Radio Studio Music Dept.; Roy Webb, Musical Director.
>Score: Roy Webb.
SNOW WHITE AND THE SEVEN DWARFS, Walt Disney Studio Music Dept.; Leigh Harline, Head.
>Score: Frank Churchill, Leigh Harline and Paul J. Smith.
SOMETHING TO SING ABOUT, Grand National Studio Music Dept.; C. Bakaleinikoff, Musical Director.
>Score: Victor Schertzinger.
SOULS AT SEA, Paramount Studio Music Dept.; Boris Morros, Head.
>Score: W. Franke Harling and Milan Roder.
WAY OUT WEST, Hal Roach Studio Music Dept.; Marvin Hatley, Head.
>Score: Marvin Hatley.

1938 ELEVENTH YEAR
(Best Score)
*ALEXANDER'S RAGTIME BAND, 20th Century-Fox. Alfred Newman.
CAREFREE, RKO Radio. Victor Baravalle.
GIRLS SCHOOL, Columbia. Morris Stoloff and Gregory Stone.
GOLDWYN FOLLIES, Goldwyn, UA. Alfred Newman.
JEZEBEL, Warner Bros. Max Steiner.
MAD ABOUT MUSIC, Universal. Charles Previn and Frank Skinner.
STORM OVER BENGAL, Republic. Cy Feuer.
SWEETHEARTS, Metro-Goldwyn-Mayer. Herbert Stothart.
THERE GOES MY HEART, Hal Roach, UA. Marvin Hatley.
TROPIC HOLIDAY, Paramount. Boris Morros.
THE YOUNG IN HEART, Selznick, UA. Franz Waxman.

(Original Score)
*THE ADVENTURES OF ROBIN HOOD, Warner Bros. Erich Wolfgang Korngold.
ARMY GIRL, Republic. Victor Young.
BLOCKADE, Walter Wanger, UA. Werner Janssen.
BLOCKHEADS, Hal Roach, UA. Marvin Hatley.
BREAKING THE ICE, RKO Radio. Victor Young.
THE COWBOY AND THE LADY, Goldwyn, UA. Alfred Newman.
IF I WERE KING, Paramount. Richard Hageman.
MARIE ANTOINETTE, Metro-Goldwyn-Mayer. Herbert Stothart.
PACIFIC LINER, RKO Radio. Russell Bennett.
SUEZ, 20th Century-Fox. Louis Silvers.
THE YOUNG IN HEART, Selznick, UA. Franz Waxman.

1939 TWELFTH YEAR
(Best Score)
BABES IN ARMS, Metro-Goldwyn-Mayer. Roger Edens and George E. Stoll.
FIRST LOVE, Universal. Charles Previn.
THE GREAT VICTOR HERBERT, Paramount. Phil Boutelje and Arthur Lange.
THE HUNCHBACK OF NOTRE DAME, RKO Radio. Alfred Newman.
INTERMEZZO, Selznick, UA. Lou Forbes.
MR. SMITH GOES TO WASHINGTON, Columbia. Dimitri Tiomkin.
OF MICE AND MEN, Roach, UA. Aaron Copland.
THE PRIVATE LIVES OF ELIZABETH AND ESSEX, Warner Bros. Erich Wolfgang
    Korngold.
SHE MARRIED A COP, Republic. Cy Feuer.
*STAGECOACH, Walter Wanger, UA. Richard Hageman, Frank Harling, John Leipold
    and Leo Shuken.
SWANEE RIVER, 20th Century-Fox. Louis Silvers.

[317]

THEY SHALL HAVE MUSIC, Goldwyn, UA. Alfred Newman.
WAY DOWN SOUTH, Lesser, RKO Radio. Victor Young.

(Original Score)
DARK VICTORY, Warner Bros. Max Steiner.
ETERNALLY YOURS, Walter Wanger, UA. Werner Janssen.
GOLDEN BOY, Columbia. Victor Young.
GONE WITH THE WIND, Selznick, M-G-M. Max Steiner.
GULLIVER'S TRAVELS, Paramount. Victor Young.
THE MAN IN THE IRON MASK, Small, UA. Lud Gluskin and Lucien Moraweck.
MAN OF CONQUEST, Republic. Victor Young.
NURSE EDITH CAVELL, RKO Radio. Anthony Collins.
OF MICE AND MEN, Roach, UA. Aaron Copland.
THE RAINS CAME, 20th Century-Fox. Alfred Newman.
*THE WIZARD OF OZ, Metro-Goldwyn-Mayer. Herbert Stothart.
WUTHERING HEIGHTS, Goldwyn, UA. Alfred Newman.

1940   THIRTEENTH YEAR
(Best Score)
ARISE, MY LOVE, Paramount. Victor Young.
HIT PARADE OF 1941, Republic. Cy Feuer.
IRENE, Imperadio, RKO Radio. Anthony Collins.
OUR TOWN, Sol Lesser, UA. Aaron Copland.
THE SEA HAWK, Warner Bros. Erich Wolfgang Korngold.
SECOND CHORUS, Paramount. Artie Shaw.
SPRING PARADE, Universal. Charles Previn.
STRIKE UP THE BAND, Metro-Goldwyn-Mayer. Georgie Stoll and Roger Edens.
*TIN PAN ALLEY, 20th Century-Fox. Alfred Newman.

(Original Score)
ARIZONA, Columbia. Victor Young.
THE DARK COMMAND, Republic. Victor Young.
THE FIGHT FOR LIFE, U.S. Government-Columbia. Louis Gruenberg.
THE GREAT DICTATOR, Chaplin, UA. Meredith Willson.
THE HOUSE OF SEVEN GABLES, Universal. Frank Skinner.
THE HOWARDS OF VIRGINIA, Columbia. Richard Hageman.
THE LETTER, Warner Bros. Max Steiner.
THE LONG VOYAGE HOME, Argosy-Wanger, UA. Richard Hageman.
THE MARK OF ZORRO, 20th Century-Fox. Alfred Newman.
MY FAVORITE WIFE, RKO Radio. Roy Webb.
NORTH WEST MOUNTED POLICE, Paramount. Victor Young.
ONE MILLION B.C., Hal Roach, UA. Werner Heymann.

OUR TOWN, Sol Lesser, UA. Aaron Copland.
*PINOCCHIO, Disney, RKO Radio. Leigh Harline, Paul J. Smith and Ned Washington.
REBECCA, Selznick, UA. Franz Waxman.
THE THIEF OF BAGDAD, Korda, UA. Miklos Rozsa.
WATERLOO BRIDGE, Metro-Goldwyn-Mayer. Herbert Stothart.

1941 FOURTEENTH YEAR
(Scoring of a Dramatic Picture)
*ALL THAT MONEY CAN BUY, RKO Radio. Bernard Herrmann.
BACK STREET, Universal. Frank Skinner.
BALL OF FIRE, Goldwyn, RKO Radio. Alfred Newman.
CHEERS FOR MISS BISHOP, Rowland, UA. Edward Ward.
CITIZEN KANE, Mercury, RKO Radio. Bernard Herrmann.
DR. JEKYLL AND MR. HYDE, Metro-Goldwyn-Mayer. Franz Waxman.
HOLD BACK THE DAWN, Paramount. Victor Young.
HOW GREEN WAS MY VALLEY, 20th Century-Fox. Alfred Newman.
KING OF THE ZOMBIES, Monogram. Edward Kay.
LADIES IN RETIREMENT, Columbia. Morris Stoloff and Ernst Toch.
THE LITTLE FOXES, Goldwyn, RKO Radio. Meredith Willson.
LYDIA, Korda, UA. Miklos Rozsa.
MERCY ISLAND, Republic. Cy Feuer and Walter Scharf.
SERGEANT YORK, Warner Bros. Max Steiner.
SO ENDS OUR NIGHT, Loew-Lewin, UA. Louis Gruenberg.
SUNDOWN, Walter Wanger, UA. Miklos Rozsa.
SUSPICION, RKO Radio. Franz Waxman.
TANKS A MILLION, Roach, UA. Edward Ward.
THAT UNCERTAIN FEELING, Lubitsch, UA. Werner Heymann.
THIS WOMAN IS MINE, Universal. Richard Hageman.

(Scoring of a Musical Picture)
ALL AMERICAN CO-ED, Roach, UA. Edward Ward.
BIRTH OF THE BLUES, Paramount. Robert Emmett Dolan.
BUCK PRIVATES, Universal. Charles Previn.
THE CHOCOLATE SOLDIER, Metro-Goldwyn-Mayer. Herbert Stothart and Bronislau Kaper.
*DUMBO, Disney, RKO Radio. Frank Churchill and Oliver Wallace.
ICE-CAPADES, Republic. Cy Feuer.
THE STRAWBERRY BLONDE, Warner Bros. Heinz Roemheld.
SUN VALLEY SERENADE, 20th Century-Fox. Emil Newman.
SUNNY, RKO Radio. Anthony Collins.
YOU'LL NEVER GET RICH, Columbia. Morris Stoloff.

1942   FIFTEENTH YEAR
(Scoring of a Dramatic or Comedy Picture)
ARABIAN NIGHTS, Universal. Frank Skinner.
BAMBI, Disney, RKO Radio. Frank Churchill and Edward Plumb.
THE BLACK SWAN, 20th Century-Fox. Alfred Newman.
THE CORSICAN BROTHERS, Small, UA. Dimitri Tiomkin.
FLYING TIGERS, Republic. Victor Young.
THE GOLD RUSH, Chaplin, UA. Max Terr.
I MARRIED A WITCH, Cinema Guild, UA. Roy Webb.
JOAN OF PARIS, RKO Radio. Roy Webb.
JUNGLE BOOK, Korda, UA. Miklos Rozsa.
KLONDIKE FURY, Monogram. Edward Kay.
*NOW, VOYAGER, Warner Bros. Max Steiner.
THE PRIDE OF THE YANKEES, Goldwyn, RKO Radio. Leigh Harline.
RANDOM HARVEST, Metro-Goldwyn-Mayer. Herbert Stothart.
THE SHANGHAI GESTURE, Arnold, UA. Richard Hageman.
SILVER QUEEN, Sherman, UA. Victor Young.
TAKE A LETTER, DARLING, Paramount. Victor Young.
THE TALK OF THE TOWN, Columbia. Frederick Hollander and Morris Stoloff.
TO BE OR NOT TO BE, Lubitsch, UA. Werner Heymann.

(Scoring of a Musical Picture)
FLYING WITH MUSIC, Roach, UA. Edward Ward.
FOR ME AND MY GAL, Metro-Goldwyn-Mayer. Roger Edens and Georgie Stoll.
HOLIDAY INN, Paramount. Robert Emmett Dolan.
IT STARTED WITH EVE, Universal. Charles Previn and Hans Salter.
JOHNNY DOUGHBOY, Republic. Walter Scharf.
MY GAL SAL, 20th Century-Fox. Alfred Newman.
*YANKEE DOODLE DANDY, Warner Bros. Ray Heindorf and Heinz Roemheld.
YOU WERE NEVER LOVELIER, Columbia. Leigh Harline.

1943   SIXTEENTH YEAR
(Scoring of a Dramatic or Comedy Picture)
THE AMAZING MRS. HOLLIDAY, Universal. Hans J. Salter and Frank Skinner.
CASABLANCA, Warner Bros. Max Steiner.
THE COMMANDOS STRIKE AT DAWN, Columbia. Louis Gruenberg and Morris Stoloff.
THE FALLEN SPARROW, RKO Radio. C. Bakaleinikoff and Roy Webb.
FOR WHOM THE BELL TOLLS, Paramount. Victor Young.
HANGMEN ALSO DIE, Arnold, UA. Hanns Eisler.
HI DIDDLE DIDDLE, Stone, UA. Phil Boutelje.
IN OLD OKLAHOMA, Republic. Walter Scharf.
JOHNNY COME LATELY, Cagney, UA. Leigh Harline.

THE KANSAN, Sherman, UA. Gerard Carbonara.

LADY OF BURLESQUE, Stromberg, UA. Arthur Lange.

MADAME CURIE, Metro-Goldwyn-Mayer. Herbert Stothart.

THE MOON AND SIXPENCE, Loew-Lewin, UA. Dimitri Tiomkin.

THE NORTH STAR, Goldwyn, RKO Radio. Aaron Copland.

*THE SONG OF BERNADETTE, 20th Century-Fox. Alfred Newman.

VICTORY THROUGH AIR POWER, Disney, UA. Edward H. Plumb, Paul J. Smith and Oliver G. Wallace.

(Scoring of a Musical Picture)

CONEY ISLAND, 20th Century-Fox. Alfred Newman.

HIT PARADE OF 1943, Republic. Walter Scharf.

THE PHANTOM OF THE OPERA, Universal. Edward Ward.

SALUDOS AMIGOS, Disney, RKO Radio. Edward H. Plumb, Paul J. Smith and Charles Wolcott.

THE SKY'S THE LIMIT, RKO Radio. Leigh Harline.

SOMETHING TO SHOUT ABOUT, Columbia. Morris Stoloff.

STAGE DOOR CANTEEN, Lesser, UA. Frederic E. Rich.

STAR SPANGLED RHYTHM, Paramount. Robert Emmett Dolan.

*THIS IS THE ARMY, Warner Bros. Ray Heindorf.

THOUSANDS CHEER, Metro-Goldwyn-Mayer. Herbert Stothart.

1944   SEVENTEENTH YEAR

(Scoring of a Dramatic or Comedy Picture)

ADDRESS UNKNOWN, Columbia. Morris Stoloff and Ernst Toch.

THE ADVENTURES OF MARK TWAIN, Warner Bros. Max Steiner.

THE BRIDGE OF SAN LUIS REY, Bogeaus, UA. Dimitri Tiomkin.

CASANOVA BROWN, International, RKO Radio. Arthur Lange.

CHRISTMAS HOLIDAY, Universal. H. J. Salter.

DOUBLE INDEMNITY, Paramount. Miklos Rozsa.

THE FIGHTING SEABEES, Republic. Walter Scharf and Roy Webb.

THE HAIRY APE, Levey, UA. Michel Michelet and Edward Paul.

IT HAPPENED TOMORROW, Arnold, UA. Robert Stolz.

JACK LONDON, Bronston, UA. Frederic E. Rich.

KISMET, Metro-Goldwyn-Mayer. Herbert Stothart.

NONE BUT THE LONELY HEART, RKO Radio. C. Bakaleinikoff and Hanns Eisler.

THE PRINCESS AND THE PIRATE, Regent, RKO Radio. David Rose.

*SINCE YOU WENT AWAY, Selznick, UA. Max Steiner.

SUMMER STORM, Angelus, UA. Karl Hajos.

THREE RUSSIAN GIRLS, R & F Prods., UA. Franke Harling.

UP IN MABEL'S ROOM, Small, UA. Edward Paul.

VOICE IN THE WIND, Ripley-Monter, UA. Michel Michelet.

WILSON, 20th Century-Fox. Alfred Newman.
WOMAN OF THE TOWN, Sherman, UA. Miklos Rozsa.

(Scoring of a Musical Picture)
BRAZIL, Republic. Walter Scharf.
*COVER GIRL, Columbia. Carmen Dragon and Morris Stoloff.
HIGHER AND HIGHER, RKO Radio. C. Bakaleinikoff.
HOLLYWOOD CANTEEN, Warner Bros. Ray Heindorf.
IRISH EYES ARE SMILING, 20th Century-Fox. Alfred Newman.
KNICKERBOCKER HOLIDAY, RCA, UA. Werner R. Heymann and Kurt Weill.
LADY IN THE DARK, Paramount. Robert Emmett Dolan.
LADY LET'S DANCE, Monogram. Edward Kay.
MEET ME IN ST. LOUIS, Metro-Goldwyn-Mayer. Georgie Stoll.
THE MERRY MONAHANS, Universal. H. J. Salter.
MINSTREL MAN, PRC. Leo Erdody and Ferdie Grofe.
SENSATIONS OF 1945, Stone, UA. Mahlon Merrick.
SONG OF THE OPEN ROAD, Rogers, UA. Charles Previn.
UP IN ARMS, Avalon, RKO Radio. Louis Forbes and Ray Heindorf.

1945   EIGHTEENTH YEAR
(Scoring of a Dramatic or Comedy Picture)
THE BELLS OF ST. MARY'S, Rainbow, RKO Radio. Robert Emmett Dolan.
BREWSTER'S MILLIONS, Small, UA. Lou Forbes.
CAPTAIN KIDD, Bogeaus, UA. Werner Janssen.
ENCHANTED COTTAGE, RKO Radio. Roy Webb.
FLAME OF THE BARBARY COAST, Republic. Dale Butts and Morton Scott.
G. I. HONEYMOON, Monogram. Edward J. Kay.
G. I. JOE, Cowan, UA. Louis Applebaum and Ann Ronell.
GUEST IN THE HOUSE, Guest in the House, Inc., UA. Werner Janssen.
GUEST WIFE, Greentree Prods., UA. Daniele Amfitheatrof.
THE KEYS OF THE KINGDOM, 20th Century-Fox. Alfred Newman.
THE LOST WEEKEND, Paramount. Miklos Rozsa.
LOVE LETTERS, Wallis, Paramount. Victor Young.
MAN WHO WALKED ALONE, PRC. Karl Hajos.
OBJECTIVE-BURMA, Warner Bros. Franz Waxman.
PARIS-UNDERGROUND, Bennett, UA. Alexander Tansman.
A SONG TO REMEMBER, Columbia. Miklos Rozsa and Morris Stoloff.
THE SOUTHERNER, Loew-Hakim, UA. Werner Janssen.
*SPELLBOUND, Selznick, UA. Miklos Rozsa.
THIS LOVE OF OURS, Universal. H. J. Salter.
VALLEY OF DECISION, Metro-Goldwyn-Mayer. Herbert Stothart.
WOMAN IN THE WINDOW, International, RKO Radio. Hugo Friedhofer and Arthur
    Lange.

(Scoring of a Musical Picture)

*ANCHORS AWEIGH, Metro-Goldwyn-Mayer. Georgie Stoll.

BELLE OF THE YUKON, International, RKO Radio. Arthur Lange.

CAN'T HELP SINGING, Universal. Jerome Kern and H. J. Salter.

HITCHHIKE TO HAPPINESS, Republic. Morton Scott.

INCENDIARY BLONDE, Paramount. Robert Emmett Dolan.

RHAPSODY IN BLUE, Warner Bros. Ray Heindorf and Max Steiner.

STATE FAIR, 20th Century-Fox. Charles Henderson and Alfred Newman.

SUNBONNET SUE, Monogram. Edward J. Kay.

THREE CABALLEROS, Disney-RKO Radio. Edward Plumb, Paul J. Smith and
    Charles Wolcott.

TONIGHT AND EVERY NIGHT, Columbia. Marlin Skiles and Morris Stoloff.

WHY GIRLS LEAVE HOME, PRC. Walter Greene.

WONDER MAN, Beverly, RKO Radio. Lou Forbes and Ray Heindorf.

1946   NINETEENTH YEAR

(Scoring of a Dramatic or Comedy Picture)

ANNA AND THE KING OF SIAM, 20th Century-Fox. Bernard Herrmann.

*THE BEST YEARS OF OUR LIVES, Goldwyn, RKO Radio. Hugo Friedhofer.

HENRY V, Rank, UA (British). William Walton.

HUMORESQUE, Warner Bros. Franz Waxman.

THE KILLERS, Universal. Miklos Rozsa.

(Scoring of a Musical Picture)

BLUE SKIES, Paramount. Robert Emmett Dolan.

CENTENNIAL SUMMER, 20th Century-Fox. Alfred Newman.

THE HARVEY GIRLS, Metro-Goldwyn-Mayer. Lennie Hayton.

*THE JOLSON STORY, Columbia. Morris Stoloff.

NIGHT AND DAY, Warner Bros. Ray Heindorf and Max Steiner.

1947   TWENTIETH YEAR

(Scoring of a Dramatic or Comedy Picture)

THE BISHOP'S WIFE, Goldwyn, RKO Radio. Hugo Friedhofer.

CAPTAIN FROM CASTILE, 20th Century-Fox. Alfred Newman.

*A DOUBLE LIFE, Kanin, U-I. Miklos Rozsa.

FOREVER AMBER, 20th Century-Fox. David Raksin.

LIFE WITH FATHER, Warner Bros. Max Steiner.

(Scoring of a Musical Picture)

FIESTA, Metro-Goldwyn-Mayer. Johnny Green.

*MOTHER WORE TIGHTS, 20th Century-Fox. Alfred Newman.

MY WILD IRISH ROSE, Warner Bros. Ray Heindorf and Max Steiner.

ROAD TO RIO, Hope-Crosby, Paramount. Robert Emmett Dolan.

Song of the South, Disney, RKO Radio. Daniele Amfitheatrof, Paul J. Smith and
    Charles Wolcott.

1948   TWENTY-FIRST YEAR
(Scoring of a Dramatic or Comedy Picture)
Hamlet, Rank-Two Cities, U-I (British). William Walton.
Joan of Arc, Sierra Pictures, RKO Radio. Hugo Friedhofer.
Johnny Belinda, Warner Bros. Max Steiner.
*The Red Shoes, Rank-Archers-Eagle-Lion (British). Brian Easdale.
The Snake Pit, 20th Century-Fox. Alfred Newman.

(Scoring of a Musical Picture)
*Easter Parade, Metro-Goldwyn-Mayer. Johnny Green and Roger Edens.
The Emperor Waltz, Paramount. Victor Young.
The Pirate, Metro-Goldwyn-Mayer. Lennie Hayton.
Romance on the High Seas, Curtiz, Warner Bros. Ray Heindorf.
When My Baby Smiles at Me, 20th Century-Fox. Alfred Newman.

1949   TWENTY-SECOND YEAR
(Scoring of a Dramatic or Comedy Picture)
Beyond the Forest, Warner Bros. Max Steiner.
Champion, Screen Plays Corp., UA. Dimitri Tiomkin.
*The Heiress, Paramount. Aaron Copland.

(Scoring of a Musical Picture)
Jolson Sings Again, Sidney Buchman, Columbia. Morris Stoloff and George Duning.
Look for the Silver Lining, Warner Bros. Ray Heindorf.
*On the Town, Metro-Goldwyn-Mayer. Roger Edens and Lennie Hayton.

1950   TWENTY-THIRD YEAR
(Scoring of a Dramatic or Comedy Picture)
All About Eve, 20th Century-Fox. Alfred Newman.
The Flame and the Arrow, Norma-F.R., Warner Bros. Max Steiner.
No Sad Songs for Me, Columbia. George Duning.
Samson and Delilah, Paramount. Victor Young.
*Sunset Boulevard, Paramount. Franz Waxman.

(Scoring of a Musical Picture)
*Annie Get Your Gun, Metro-Goldwyn-Mayer. Adolph Deutsch and Roger Edens.
Cinderella, Disney, RKO Radio. Oliver Wallace and Paul J. Smith.
I'll Get By, 20th Century-Fox. Lionel Newman.
Three Little Words, Metro-Goldwyn-Mayer. Andre Previn.
The West Point Story, Warner Bros. Ray Heindorf.

1951   TWENTY-FOURTH YEAR
(Scoring of a Dramatic or Comedy Picture)
DAVID AND BATHSHEBA, 20th Century-Fox. Alfred Newman.
DEATH OF A SALESMAN, Kramer, Columbia. Alex North.
*A PLACE IN THE SUN, Paramount. Franz Waxman.
QUO VADIS, Metro-Goldwyn-Mayer. Miklos Rozsa.
A STREETCAR NAMED DESIRE, Charles K. Feldman Prods., Warner Bros. Alex North.

(Scoring of a Musical Picture)
ALICE IN WONDERLAND, Disney, RKO Radio. Oliver Wallace.
*AN AMERICAN IN PARIS, Metro-Goldwyn-Mayer. Johnny Green and Saul Chaplin.
THE GREAT CARUSO, Metro-Goldwyn-Mayer. Peter Herman Adler and Johnny Green.
ON THE RIVIERA, 20th Century-Fox. Alfred Newman.
SHOW BOAT, Metro-Goldwyn-Mayer. Adolph Deutsch and Conrad Salinger.

1952   TWENTY-FIFTH YEAR
(Scoring of a Dramatic or Comedy Picture)
*HIGH NOON, Kramer, UA. Dimitri Tiomkin.
IVANHOE, Metro-Goldwyn-Mayer. Miklos Rozsa.
MIRACLE OF FATIMA, Warner Bros. Max Steiner.
THE THIEF, Fran Prods., UA. Herschel Burke Gilbert.
VIVA ZAPATA!, 20th Century-Fox. Alex North.

(Scoring of a Musical Picture)
HANS CHRISTIAN ANDERSEN, Goldwyn, RKO Radio. Walter Scharf.
THE JAZZ SINGER, Warner Bros. Ray Heindorf and Max Steiner.
THE MEDIUM, Transfilm-Lopert (Italian). Gian-Carlo Menotti.
SINGIN' IN THE RAIN, Metro-Goldwyn-Mayer. Lennie Hayton.
*WITH A SONG IN MY HEART, 20th Century-Fox. Alfred Newman.

1953   TWENTY-SIXTH YEAR
(Scoring of a Dramatic or Comedy Picture)
ABOVE AND BEYOND, Metro-Goldwyn-Mayer. Hugo Friedhofer.
FROM HERE TO ETERNITY, Columbia. Morris Stoloff and George Duning.
JULIUS CAESAR, Metro-Goldwyn-Mayer. Miklos Rozsa.
*LILI, Metro-Goldwyn-Mayer. Bronislau Kaper.
THIS IS CINERAMA, Cinerama Prods. Corp. Louis Forbes.

(Scoring of a Musical Picture)
THE BANDWAGON, Metro-Goldwyn-Mayer. Adolph Deutsch.
CALAMITY JANE, Warner Bros. Ray Heindorf.
*CALL ME MADAM, 20th Century-Fox. Alfred Newman.
5,000 FINGERS OF DR. T., Kramer-Columbia. Frederick Hollander and Morris Stoloff.
KISS ME KATE, Metro-Goldwyn-Mayer. Andre Previn and Saul Chaplin.

1954   TWENTY-SEVENTH YEAR

(Scoring of a Dramatic or Comedy Picture)

THE CAINE MUTINY, A Stanley Kramer Prod., Columbia. Max Steiner.

GENEVIEVE, A J. Arthur Rank Presentation-Sirius Prods. Ltd., U-I (British). Muir Mathieson.

*THE HIGH AND THE MIGHTY, Wayne-Fellows Prods., Inc., Warner Bros. Dimitri Tiomkin.

ON THE WATERFRONT, Horizon-American Corp., Columbia. Leonard Bernstein.

THE SILVER CHALICE, A Victor Saville Prod., Warner Bros. Franz Waxman.

(Scoring of a Musical Picture)

CARMEN JONES, Otto Preminger, 20th Century-Fox. Herschel Burke Gilbert.

THE GLENN MILLER STORY, Universal-International. Joseph Gershenson and Henry Mancini.

*SEVEN BRIDES FOR SEVEN BROTHERS, Metro-Goldwyn-Mayer. Adolph Deutsch and Saul Chaplin.

A STAR IS BORN, A Transcona Enterprises Prod., Warner Bros. Ray Heindorf.

THERE'S NO BUSINESS LIKE SHOW BUSINESS, 20th Century-Fox. Alfred Newman and Lionel Newman.

1955   TWENTY-EIGHTH YEAR

(Scoring of a Dramatic or Comedy Picture)

BATTLE CRY, Warner Bros. Max Steiner.

*LOVE IS A MANY-SPLENDORED THING, 20th Century-Fox. Alfred Newman.

THE MAN WITH THE GOLDEN ARM, Otto Preminger Prod., UA. Elmer Bernstein.

PICNIC, Columbia. George Duning.

THE ROSE TATTOO, Hal Wallis, Paramount. Alex North.

(Scoring of a Musical Picture)

DADDY LONG LEGS, 20th Century-Fox. Alfred Newman.

GUYS AND DOLLS, Samuel Goldwyn Prods., Inc., M-G-M. Jay Blackton and Cyril J. Mockridge.

IT'S ALWAYS FAIR WEATHER, Metro-Goldwyn-Mayer. Andre Previn.

LOVE ME OR LEAVE ME, Metro-Goldwyn-Mayer. Percy Faith and George Stoll.

*OKLAHOMA!, Rodgers & Hammerstein Pictures, Inc., Magna Theatre Corp. Robert Russell Bennett, Jay Blackton and Adolph Deutsch.

1956   TWENTY-NINTH YEAR

(Scoring of a Dramatic or Comedy Picture)

ANASTASIA, 20th Century-Fox. Alfred Newman.

*AROUND THE WORLD IN 80 DAYS, The Michael Todd Co., Inc., UA. Victor Young.

BETWEEN HEAVEN AND HELL, 20th Century-Fox. Hugo Friedhofer.

GIANT, Giant Prod., Warner Bros. Dimitri Tiomkin.

THE RAINMAKER, A Hal Wallis Prod., Paramount. Alex North.

(Scoring of a Musical Picture)

THE BEST THINGS IN LIFE ARE FREE, 20th Century-Fox. Lionel Newman.

THE EDDY DUCHIN STORY, Columbia. Morris Stoloff and George Duning.

HIGH SOCIETY, Sol C. Siegel Prod., M-G-M. Johnny Green and Saul Chaplin.

*THE KING AND I, 20th Century-Fox. Alfred Newman and Ken Darby.

MEET ME IN LAS VEGAS, Metro-Goldwyn-Mayer. George Stoll and Johnny Green.

1957 THIRTIETH YEAR

NOTE: Rules changed this year to One Award for Music Scoring instead of separate Awards for Scoring Dramatic or Comedy Picture and Scoring of a Musical Picture.

AN AFFAIR TO REMEMBER, (Dramatic or Comedy), Jerry Wald Prods., Inc.,
    20th Century-Fox. Hugo Friedhofer.

BOY ON A DOLPHIN, (Dramatic or Comedy), 20th Century-Fox. Hugo Friedhofer.

*THE BRIDGE ON THE RIVER KWAI, (Dramatic or Comedy), A Horizon Picture,
    Columbia, Malcolm Arnold.

PERRI, (Dramatic or Comedy), Walt Disney Prods., Buena Vista Film Dist. Co., Inc.
    Paul Smith.

RAINTREE COUNTY, (Dramatic or Comedy), Metro-Goldwyn-Mayer. Johnny Green.

1958 THIRTY-FIRST YEAR

NOTE: Rules changed this year to Two Awards—One Award for Scoring of a Dramatic or Comedy Picture, and One Award for Scoring of a Musical Picture.

(Scoring of a Dramatic or Comedy Picture)

THE BIG COUNTRY, Anthony-Worldwide Prods., UA. Jerome Moross.

*THE OLD MAN AND THE SEA, Leland Hayward, Warner Bros. Dimitri Tiomkin.

SEPARATE TABLES, Clifton Prods., Inc., UA. David Raksin.

WHITE WILDERNESS, Walt Disney Prods., Buena Vista Film Dist. Co., Inc. Oliver
    Wallace.

THE YOUNG LIONS, 20th Century-Fox. Hugo Friedhofer.

(Scoring of a Musical Picture)

THE BOLSHOI BALLET, A Rank Organization Presentation-Harmony Film, Rank Film
    Distributors of America, Inc. (British). Yuri Faier and G. Rozhdestvensky.

DAMN YANKEES, Warner Bros. Ray Heindorf.

*GIGI, Arthur Freed Prods., Inc., M-G-M. Andre Previn.

MARDI GRAS, Jerry Wald Prods., Inc., 20th Century-Fox. Lionel Newman.

SOUTH PACIFIC, South Pacific Enterprises, Inc., Magna Theatre Corp. Alfred Newman
    and Ken Darby.

1959 THIRTY-SECOND YEAR

(Scoring of a Dramatic or Comedy Picture)

*BEN-HUR, Metro-Goldwyn-Mayer. Miklos Rozsa.

THE DIARY OF ANNE FRANK, 20th Century-Fox. Alfred Newman.

THE NUN'S STORY, Warner Bros. Franz Waxman.
ON THE BEACH, Lomitas Prods., Inc., UA. Ernest Gold.
PILLOW TALK, Arwin Prods., Inc., U-I. Frank DeVol.

(Scoring of a Musical Picture)
THE FIVE PENNIES, Dena Prod., Paramount. Leith Stevens.
LI'L ABNER, Panama and Frank, Paramount. Nelson Riddle and Joseph J. Lilley.
*PORGY AND BESS, Samuel Goldwyn Prods., Columbia. Andre Previn and Ken Darby.
SAY ONE FOR ME, Bing Crosby Prods., 20th Century-Fox. Lionel Newman.
SLEEPING BEAUTY, Walt Disney Prods., Buena Vista Film Dist. Co., Inc.
George Bruns.

1960   THIRTY-THIRD YEAR
(Scoring of a Dramatic or Comedy Picture)
THE ALAMO, Batjac Prod., UA. Dimitri Tiomkin.
ELMER GANTRY, Burt Lancaster-Richard Brooks Prod., UA. Andre Previn.
*EXODUS, Carlyle-Alpina S. A. Prod., UA. Ernest Gold.
THE MAGNIFICENT SEVEN, Mirisch-Alpha Prod., UA. Elmer Bernstein.
SPARTACUS, Bryna Prods., Inc., U-I. Alex North.

(Scoring of a Musical Picture)
BELLS ARE RINGING, Arthur Freed Prod., M-G-M. Andre Previn.
CAN-CAN, Suffolk-Cummings Prods., 20th Century-Fox. Nelson Riddle.
LET'S MAKE LOVE, Company of Artists, Inc., 20th Century-Fox. Lionel Newman and
Earle H. Hagen.
PEPE, G. S.-Posa Films International Prod., Columbia. Johnny Green.
*SONG WITHOUT END (The Story of Franz Liszt), Goetz-Vidor Pictures Prod.,
Columbia. Morris Stoloff and Harry Sukman.

1961   THIRTY-FOURTH YEAR
(Scoring of a Dramatic or Comedy Picture)
*BREAKFAST AT TIFFANY'S, Jurow-Shepherd Prod., Paramount. Henry Mancini.
EL CID, Samuel Bronston Prod. in association with Dear Film Prod., Allied Artists,
Miklos Rozsa.
FANNY, Mansfield Prod., Warner Bros. Morris Stoloff and Harry Sukman.
THE GUNS OF NAVARONE, Carl Foreman Prod., Columbia. Dimitri Tiomkin.
SUMMER AND SMOKE, Hal Wallis Prod., Paramount. Elmer Bernstein.

(Scoring of a Musical Picture)
BABES IN TOYLAND, Walt Disney Prods., Buena Vista Dist. Co., Inc. George Bruns.
FLOWER DRUM SONG, Universal-International-Ross Hunter Prod. in association with
Joseph Fields, U-I. Alfred Newman and Ken Darby.

[328]

KHOVANSHCHINA, Mosfilm Studios, Artkino Pictures (Russian). Dimitri Shostakovich.
PARIS BLUES, Pennebaker, Inc., UA. Duke Ellington.
°WEST SIDE STORY, Mirisch Pictures, Inc. and B and P Enterprises, Inc., UA.
    Saul Chaplin, Johnny Green, Sid Ramin and Irwin Kostal.

1962 THIRTY-FIFTH YEAR
(NOTE: Title of Awards changed)

(Music Score—substantially original)
FREUD, Universal-International-John Huston Prod., U-I. Jerry Goldsmith.
°LAWRENCE OF ARABIA, Horizon Pictures (G.B.), Ltd.-Sam Spiegel-David Lean Prod.,
    Columbia. Maurice Jarre.
MUTINY ON THE BOUNTY, Arcola Prod., M-G-M. Bronislau Kaper.
TARAS BULBA, Harold Hecht Prod., UA. Franz Waxman.
TO KILL A MOCKINGBIRD, Universal-International-Pakula-Mulligan-Brentwood Prod.,
    U-I. Elmer Bernstein.

(Scoring of Music—adaptation or treatment)
Billy Rose's JUMBO, Euterpe-Arwin Prod., M-G-M. George Stoll.
GIGOT, Seven Arts Prods., 20th Century-Fox. Michel Magne.
GYPSY, Warner Bros. Frank Perkins.
°Meredith Willson's THE MUSIC MAN, Warner Bros. Ray Heindorf.
THE WONDERFUL WORLD OF THE BROTHERS GRIMM, Metro-Goldwyn-Mayer &
    Cinerama. Leigh Harline.

1963 THIRTY-SIXTH YEAR
(Music Score—substantially original)
CLEOPATRA, 20th Century-Fox Ltd.-MCL Films S.A.-WALWA Films S.A. Prod.,
    20th Century-Fox. Alex North.
55 DAYS AT PEKING, Samuel Bronston Prod., Allied Artists. Dimitri Tiomkin.
HOW THE WEST WAS WON, Metro-Goldwyn-Mayer & Cinerama. Alfred Newman
    and Ken Darby.
IT'S A MAD, MAD, MAD, MAD WORLD, Casey Prod., UA. Ernest Gold.
°TOM JONES, Woodfall Prod., UA-Lopert Pictures. John Addison.

(Scoring of Music—adaptation or treatment)
BYE BYE BIRDIE, Kohlmar-Sidney Prod., Columbia. John Green.
°IRMA LA DOUCE, Mirisch-Phalanx Prod., UA. Andre Previn.
A NEW KIND OF LOVE, Llenroc Prods., Paramount. Leith Stevens.
SUNDAYS AND CYBELE, Terra-Fides-Orsay-Films Trocadero Prod., Columbia.
    Maurice Jarre.
THE SWORD IN THE STONE, Walt Disney Prods., Buena Vista Distribution Co.
    George Bruns.

[329]

1964   THIRTY-SEVENTH YEAR

Best Music Score—substantially original:

(For which only the composer shall be eligible)

BECKET, A Hal Wallis Production, Paramount. Laurence Rosenthal.

THE FALL OF THE ROMAN EMPIRE, A Bronston-Roma Production, Paramount. Dimitri Tiomkin.

HUSH . . . HUSH, SWEET CHARLOTTE, An Associates & Aldrich Production, 20th Century-Fox. Frank DeVol.

MARY POPPINS, Walt Disney Productions, Buena Vista Distribution Co. Richard M. Sherman and Robert B. Sherman.

THE PINK PANTHER, A Mirisch-G-E Production, United Artists. Henry Mancini.

Best Scoring of Music—adaptation or treatment:

(For which only the adapter and/or music director shall be eligible)

A HARD DAY'S NIGHT, A Walter Shenson Production, United Artists. George Martin.

MARY POPPINS, Walt Disney Productions, Buena Vista Distribution Co. Irwin Kostal.

MY FAIR LADY, Warner Bros. Andre Previn.

ROBIN AND THE 7 HOODS, A P-C Production, Warner Bros. Nelson Riddle.

THE UNSINKABLE MOLLY BROWN, A Marten Production, Metro-Goldwyn-Mayer. Robert Armbruster, Leo Arnaud, Jack Elliott, Jack Hayes, Calvin Jackson and Leo Shuken.

RIAA* Gold Record Awards

Date Awarded	Company	Selection	Artist
1958			
March 14	RCA Victor	Catch a Falling Star (S)	Perry Como
July 8	Capitol	Oklahoma	Gordon MacRae
July 8	Capitol	He's Got the Whole World in His Hands (S)	Laurie London
Aug. 11	RCA Victor	Hard Headed Woman (S)	Elvis Presley
Aug. 18	RCA Victor	Patricia (S)	Perez Prado
1959			
Jan. 21	Capitol	Tom Dooley (S)	Kingston Trio
Feb. 20	Capitol	Hymns	Ernie Ford
June 1	Columbia	Johnny's Greatest Hits	Johnny Mathis
Nov. 16	Capitol	Music Man	Original Cast
Nov. 16	Columbia	Sing Along with Mitch	Mitch Miller
Dec. 18	RCA Victor	South Pacific	Rodgers & Hammerstein
Dec. 31	RCA Victor	Peter Gunn	Henry Mancini
1960			
Jan. 19	RCA Victor	Student Prince	Mario Lanza
Feb. 17	RCA Victor	60 Years of Music	Honoring 30 Great Artists
Feb. 17	RCA Victor	Elvis	Elvis Presley
Feb. 12	Dot	Pat's Great Hits	Pat Boone
April 18	Capitol	Kingston Trio at Large	Kingston Trio
April 18	Capitol	Kingston Trio	Kingston Trio
April 21	Columbia	More Sing Along with Mitch	Mitch Miller

*Record Industry Association of America
(S) indicates a single record as opposed to an album.

Gold Record Awards (continued)

Date Awarded	Company	Selection	Artist
April 21	Columbia	Heavenly	Johnny Mathis
May 5	Columbia	Warm	Johnny Mathis
Oct. 24	Capitol	Love is the Thing	Nat King Cole
Oct. 24	Capitol	Here We Go Again	Kingston Trio
Oct. 24	Capitol	From the Hungry i	Kingston Trio
Dec. 7	Columbia	Sound of Music	Original Cast
Dec. 7	Columbia	Merry Christmas	Johnny Mathis
Dec. 7	Columbia	Christmas Sing Along	Mitch Miller
Dec. 7	Columbia	Still More! Sing Along	Mitch Miller
1961			
Feb. 14	Dot	Calcutta (S)	Lawrence Welk
March 16	Dot	Calcutta Album	Lawrence Welk
June 22	Capitol	Come Dance with Me	Frank Sinatra
June 22	Capitol	Sold Out	Kingston Trio
June 28	RCA Victor	Glenn Miller Story	Glenn Miller Orchestra
Sept. 18	London	Christmas Carols	Montovani
Sept. 18	London	Theatre Land	Montovani
Sept. 18	London	Film Encores Vol. I	Montovani
Sept. 18	London	Gems Forever	Montovani
Sept. 18	London	Strauss Waltzes	Montovani
Oct. 10	Capitol	Spirituals	Ernie Ford
Oct. 17	RCA Victor	Elvis' Golden Records	Elvis Presley
Oct. 16	RCA Victor	Belafonte at Carnegie Hall	Harry Belafonte
Nov. 22	RCA Victor	Tchaikovsky Concerto	Van Cliburn
Dec. 14	Columbia	Big Bad John (S)	Jimmy Dean
Dec. 7	Mercury	Encore—Golden Hits	The Platters
Dec. 21	RCA Victor	Blue Hawaii	Elvis Presley
1962			
Jan. 9	RCA Victor	The Lion Sleeps (S)	The Tokens
Jan. 12	Columbia	Holiday Sing Along with Mitch	Mitch Miller
Jan. 12	Columbia	Party Sing Along with Mitch	Mitch Miller
Jan. 12	Columbia	More Johnny's Greatest Hits	Johnny Mathis
Jan. 12	Columbia	West Side Story	Original Cast
Feb. 9	Columbia	Camelot	Original Cast
Feb. 9	Columbia	Flower Drum Song	Original Cast

Gold Record Awards (continued)

Date Awarded	Company	Selection	Artist
Feb. 16	Dot	Theme from a Summer Place	Billy Vaughn
Feb. 16	Dot	Blue Hawaii	Billy Vaughn
Feb. 16	Dot	Sail Along Silvery Moon	Billy Vaughn
March 1	Warner Bros.	Bob Newhart Button Down Mind	Bob Newhart
March 8	Columbia	Saturday Night Sing Along with Mitch	Mitch Miller
March 7	Columbia	Memories Sing Along with Mitch	Mitch Miller
March 7	Columbia	Sentimental Sing Along with Mitch	Mitch Miller
March 12	Capitol	Star Carol	Ernie Ford
March 22	Capitol	Nearer the Cross	Ernie Ford
March 30	RCA Victor	Can't Help Falling in Love (S)	Elvis Presley
June 21	Capitol	Frank Sinatra Sings for Only the Lonely	Frank Sinatra
June 21	Capitol	Nice 'n' Easy	Frank Sinatra
June 21	Capitol	Songs for Swingin' Lovers	Frank Sinatra
June 27	Capitol	String Along	Kingston Trio
June 27	Capitol	Music, Martinis and Memories	Jackie Gleason
June 27	Capitol	Music for Lovers Only	Jackie Gleason
June 27	Capitol	Judy at Carnegie Hall	Judy Garland
July 6	Columbia	Happy Times Sing Along	Mitch Miller
July 20	Columbia	Memories Are Made of This	Ray Conniff
July 20	Columbia	Concert in Rhythm	Ray Conniff
July 19	Columbia	'S Marvelous	Ray Conniff
July 19	ABC Paramount	I Can't Stop Loving You (S)	Ray Charles
July 19	ABC Paramount	Modern Sounds in Country & Western Music	Ray Charles
Aug. 13	Epic	Roses Are Red (S)	Bobby Vinton
Aug. 31	Columbia	Theme From a Summer Place (S)	Percy Faith
Oct. 30	RCA Victor	Breakfast at Tiffany's	Henry Mancini
Nov. 7	Capitol	This is Sinatra	Frank Sinatra
Dec. 4	Columbia	Bouquet	Percy Faith Strings
Dec. 4	Columbia	So Much in Love	Ray Conniff
Dec. 4	Columbia	Faithfully	Johnny Mathis
Dec. 4	Columbia	Swing Softly	Johnny Mathis
Dec. 4	Columbia	Open Fire, Two Guitars	Johnny Mathis

Gold Record Awards (continued)

Date Awarded	Company	Selection	Artist
Dec. 10	Warner Bros.	Peter, Paul and Mary	Peter, Paul and Mary
Dec. 10	Warner Bros.	My Son the Folk Singer	Allan Sherman
Dec. 18	Cadence	The First Family	Vaughn Meader
1963			
Jan. 7	Columbia	West Side Story	Original Soundtrack
Jan. 7	Columbia	Glorious Sound of Christmas	Eugene Ormandy— Philadelphia Orchestra
Feb. 5	Mercury	1812 Overture—Tschaikovsky	Antal Dorati and the Minneapolis Symphony
Feb. 26	Mercury	Hey Paula (S)	Paul and Paula
March 12	RCA Victor	Exodus	Original Soundtrack
March 12	RCA Victor	Calypso	Harry Belafonte
March 12	RCA Victor	G. I. Blues	Elvis Presley
March 12	RCA Victor	Season's Greetings from Perry Como	Perry Como
March 22	Columbia	Viva	Percy Faith
March 27	Warner Bros.	The Music Man	Soundtrack
April 19	Columbia	Time Out	Dave Brubeck Quartet
July 11	Columbia	I Left my Heart in San Francisco	Tony Bennett
Aug. 13	RCA Victor	Elvis' Christmas Album	Elvis Presley
Aug. 13	RCA Victor	Girls, Girls, Girls	Elvis Presley
Aug. 13	RCA Victor	Belafonte Returns to Carnegie Hall	Harry Belafonte
Aug. 13	RCA Victor	Belafonte	Harry Belafonte
Aug. 23	RCA Victor	Jump-Up-Calypso	Harry Belafonte
Aug. 27	Warner	Moving	Peter, Paul & Mary
Sept. 3	London	Exodus	Montovani
Sept. 19	Columbia	Days of Wine & Roses	Andy Williams
Oct. 14	Columbia	Moon River and Other Great Movie Themes	Andy Williams
Oct. 21	Columbia	Handel's Messiah	Eugene Ormandy Philadelphia Orchestra
Oct. 21	Columbia	Christmas with Conniff	Ray Conniff
Oct. 21	Columbia	The Lord's Prayer	Mormon Tabernacle Choir
Oct. 21	Columbia	Porgy and Bess	Original Sound Track
Nov. 6	Columbia	Folk Song Sing Along	Mitch Miller

Gold Record Awards (continued)

Date Awarded	Company	Selection	Artist
Nov. 13	Warner	In the Wind	Peter, Paul & Mary
Nov. 29	Dot	Sugar Shack (S)	Jim Gilmer and the Fireballs
Dec. 17	(Philips) Mercury	Singing Nun	Soeur Sourire
1964			
Jan. 8	Columbia	My Fair Lady	Original Cast
Jan. 15	Premier Albums	John Fitzgerald Kennedy A Memorial Album	
Jan. 15	Capitol	Carousel	Motion Picture Sound Track
Jan. 15	Capitol	The King and I	Motion Picture Sound Track
Jan. 15	Capitol	Ramblin' Rose	Nat King Cole
Feb. 3	Capitol	Meet The Beatles!	The Beatles
Feb. 3	Capitol	I Want to Hold Your Hand (S)	The Beatles
March 31	Capitol	Can't Buy Me Love (S)	The Beatles
April 4	RCA Victor	Honey In The Horn	Al Hirt
April 13	Capitol	The Beatles' Second Album	The Beatles
May 12	Columbia	The Second Barbra Streisand Album	Barbra Streisand
June 2	RCA Victor	Hello, Dolly!	Original Cast
Aug. 10	Kapp	Hello, Dolly!	Louis Armstrong
Aug. 17	Columbia	The Wonderful World of Andy Williams	Andy Williams
Aug. 19	Reprise	Everybody Loves Somebody (S)	Dean Martin
Aug. 19	RCA Victor	Christmas Hymns and Carols	Robert Shaw
Aug. 19	RCA Victor	Victory At Sea, Volume I	Robert Russell Bennett
Aug. 24	Philips	Rag Doll (S)	The 4 Seasons
Aug. 24	Capitol	Something New	The Beatles
Aug. 25	Capitol	A Hard Day's Night (S)	The Beatles
Sept. 4	Capitol	The Best of the Kingston Trio	Kingston Trio
Sept. 4	Capitol	Unforgettable	Nat King Cole
Oct. 16	Columbia	Ramblin"	New Christy Minstrels
Oct. 16	Columbia	The Barbra Streisand Album	Barbra Streisand

Gold Record Awards (continued)

Date Awarded	Company	Selection	Artist
Sept. 21	Capitol	Funny Girl	Original Cast
Oct. 30	Monument	Oh, Pretty Woman (S)	Roy Orbison
Nov. 2	Columbia	Johnny Horton's Greatest Hits	Johnny Horton
Dec. 16	RCA Victor	Cotton Candy	Al Hirt
Dec. 18	Columbia	The Andy Williams Christmas Album	Andy Williams
Dec. 18	Columbia	Call Me Irresponsible	Andy Williams
Dec. 18	Columbia	My Fair Lady	Movie Soundtrack
Dec. 31	Capitol	I Feel Fine (S)	The Beatles
Dec. 31	Capitol	Beatles' 65	The Beatles
Dec. 31	Capitol	The Beatles' Story	The Beatles
Dec. 31	Vista	Mary Poppins	Movie Soundtrack
1965			
Jan. 21	Epic	Glad All Over	The Dave Clark Five
Jan. 21	Warner Bros.	Peter, Paul and Mary In Concert	Peter, Paul and Mary
Jan. 29	Reprise	Everybody Loves Somebody	Dean Martin
Feb. 11	Columbia	Wonderland of Golden Hits	Andre Kostelanetz
Feb. 11	Columbia	Barbra Streisand/The Third Album	Barbra Streisand
Feb. 11	Columbia	Ring of Fire	Johnny Cash
Feb. 18	Capitol	Beach Boys In Concert	The Beach Boys
Feb. 18	Capitol	All Summer Long	The Beach Boys
Feb. 20	RCA Victor	Sugar Lips	Al Hirt
March 1	Warner Bros.	Downtown (S)	Petula Clark
March 23	Columbia	People	Barbra Streisand
March 30	RCA Victor	The Sound of Music	Movie Soundtrack
April 26	Warner Bros.	Trini Lopez at P. J.'s	Trini Lopez
May 19	Smash	King of the Road (S)	Roger Miller
June 16	MGM-Verve	Gilberto	Stan Getz
June 16	MGM	Mrs. Brown You've Got a Lovely Daughter (S)	Herman's Hermits
July 1	Capitol	Beatles VI	The Beatles
July 19	London	(I Can't Get No) Satisfaction (S)	The Rolling Stones
July 30	Columbia	Dear Heart	Andy Williams
Aug. 5	MGM	Wooly Bully (S)	Sam the Sham and The Pharaohs

Gold Record Awards (continued)

Date Awarded	Company	Selection	Artist
Aug. 23	Capitol	Help!	The Beatles
Aug. 31	MGM	I'm Henry VIII, I am (S)	Herman's Hermits
Aug. 31	MGM	Introducing Herman's Hermits (S)	Herman's Hermits
Aug. 31	MGM	Herman's Hermits on Tour (S)	Herman's Hermits
Sept. 1	Mercury	More Encore of Golden Hits	The Platters
Sept. 1	Smash	Return of Roger Miller	Roger Miller

Discography

Discography

The first part of the Discography lists long-play albums of performers and composers discussed in the book. The goal is not to present an exhaustive survey but to list the most popular or most representative records. Only general records dealing with a composer's work are listed in Part One; musical-comedy albums are listed in Part Two.

When a single manufacturer's catalogue number is given, the record is available in monaural only. When two numbers are given or where (S) precedes the number, the record is available in monaural and stereo. When there are two numbers, the second is the stereo version. (D) stands for Duophonic. As of mid-1964, the records are available from dealers.

Record-company abbreviations: ABC (ABC-Paramount), Audio Fi (Audio Fidelity), Buena (Buena Vista), Cad (Cadence), Camd (Camden), Cap (Capitol), Col (Columbia), Cor (Coral), Dec (Decca), Har (Harmony), Imper (Imperial), Jub (Jubilee), Lib (Liberty), Lon (London), Mer (Mercury), Pre (Premier), Rich (Richmond), Rou (Roulette), U Artists (United Artists), Vic (RCA Victor), Voc (Vocalion), At (Atlantic).

Part One.   *Performers and Composers*

ALLEN, STEVE   Dot 3473, 25473 "12 Golden Hits." Dot 3519, 25519 "Piano Greats." Dot 3515, 25515 "Gravy Waltz" (with Don Trenner Orch.).

ANDERSON, LEROY   Dec 8121 "Anderson Pops Concert Orch." Dec 4335, 74335 "Anderson Orch." Vic LM-2638, LSC 2638 "Music of Leroy Anderson" (by Boston Pops).

ANDREWS, JULIE   Col OL-5090, OS-2015 "My Fair Lady." Col CL-1712, CS-8512 "Broadway's Fair Julie." Buena (S)4026 "Mary Poppins" (movie soundtrack).

ANDREWS SISTERS   Cap (D)T-1924 "Hits of the Andrews Sisters." Dot 3406, 25406 "Greatest Hits," Vol. 1. Dot 3543, 25543 "Greatest Hits," Vol. 2.

ANKA, PAUL   ABC (S)371 "Instrumental Hits." ABC (S)420 "Diana." Vic LPM-2691, LSP-2691 "21 Golden Hits."

ANNETTE   Buena 3301 "Annette." Buena 3302 "Annette Sings Anka." Buena 3304 "Italianette." Buena (S)3316 "Beach Party."

ANTHONY, RAY   Cap (S)T-723 "Dream Dancing." Cap T-1477 "Hits of Ray Anthony." Cap (S)T-1608 "Dream Dancing Medley."

[341]

ARLEN, HAROLD   Verve 4057/8, 64057/8 "Songbook" (Ella Fitzgerald, 2 records). Col CL-1559, CS-8359 "String of Arlen" (Tony Bennett).

ARMSTRONG, LOUIS   Dec 4137, 74137 "Golden Favorites." Dec 8284 "Jazz Classics." Dec 4330, 74330 "Satchmo—Autobiography." Verve 8569, 68569 "Essential Louis Armstrong." Col CL-851/4 "Louis Armstrong Story" (4 records).

BAXTER, LES   Cap (S)T-868 "Ports of Pleasure." Cap (S)T-1388 "Baxter's Best." Cap (S)T-1846 "Quiet Village."

BEATLES   Cap (S)T-2047 "Meet the Beatles." Cap (S)T-2080 "Beatles' Second Album."

BELAFONTE, HARRY   Vic LOC-6009, LSO-6009 "At the Greek Theatre." Vic LOC-6006, LSO-6006 "At Carnegie Hall." Vic LPM-2695, LSP-2695 "Streets I Have Walked." Vic LPM-2574, LSP-2574 "Many Moods." Vic LPM-1248, LSP-1248 "Calypso."

BENNETT, TONY   Col C2L-23, C2S-823 "At Carnegie Hall" (2 records). Col C1-2141, CS-8941 "Many Moods of Tony." Col CL-2175, CS-8975 "When Lights Are Low." Col CL-1229, CS-8652 "Greatest Hits."

BERLIN, IRVING   Verve 4019-2 (4030/1), 64019-2 (64030/1) "Songbook" (Ella Fitzgerald, 2 records).

BERNSTEIN, LEONARD   Command 855, 855SD "Music of Leonard Bernstein." Col ML-5651, MS-6251 "'West Side Story' Ballet Music." Vic LPM-2710, LSP-2710 "Peter Nero—In Person" (includes music from "West Side Story").

BOONE, PAT   Dot 3071, 25071 "Pat's Great Hits," Vol. 1. Dot 3261, 2561 "Pat's Great Hits," Vol. 2. Dot 3455, 25455 "Golden Hits." Dot 3534, 25334 "Tie Me Kangaroo Down."

BREWER, TERESA   Voc 3693 "Teresa Brewer." Cor 57027 "Music, Music, Music." Philips 200062, 600062 "Greatest Hits."

BROWN, NACIO HERB   MMO-1017 "Music of Nacio Herb Brown" (Music Minus One).

CALLOWAY, CAB   Cor 57408, 757408 "Blues." Pre (S)2013 "Hi-de-hi-de-ho."

CANTOR, EDDIE   Audio Fi 702 "Date with Eddie Cantor." Camd CAL-870, CAS-870 "Sings Ida . . . and His Other Hits."

CARMICHAEL, HOAGY   Dec 8588 "Stardust Road."

CHARLES, RAY   ABC 415, S-415 "Greatest Hits." At 2-900 (8063/4) "Ray Charles Story" (Vol. I and II). At 8083 "Ray Charles Story, Vol. 3."

CHECKER, CHUBBY   Cameo P-7001 "Twist." Cameo P-7008, PS-7008 "Twistin' round the World." Cameo P-7022 "Biggest Hits." Cameo P-7020, PS-7020 "Limbo Party."

CHEVALIER, MAURICE   Cap T-10360 "The Young Chevalier." MGM (S)4205 "Very Best." MGM (S)4015P "Sings Lerner & Loewe." MGM (S)4120 "Paris to Broadway."

CLOONEY, ROSEMARY   Col CL-1230 "Rosie's Greatest Hits." Vic LPM-2565, LSP-2565 "Rosemary Clooney." Reprise 6088, 9-6088 "Love."

COLE, NAT "KING"   Cap (S)WCL-1613 ([S]W-1926/8) "Nat 'King' Cole Story" (3 records). Cap T-357 "Unforgettable." Cap (S)W-824 "Love Is the Thing." Cap (S)W-1724 "Swingin' Side of Nat 'King' Cole."

COMO, PERRY   Vic LPM-1885, LSP-1885 "When You Come to the End of a Perfect Day." Vic LPM-1971, LSP-1971 "Saturday Night." Vic LPM-1981, LSP-1981 "Golden Records." Camd 582 "Dreamer's Holiday."

CONNIFF, RAY   Col CL-925 "'S Wonderful." Col CL-1074, CS-8037 "'S Marvelous." Col CL-2150, CS-8950 "Speak to Me of Love."

COOKE, SAM   Keen 2001 "Songs of Sam Cooke." Vic LPM-2625, LSP-2625 "Sam Cooke's Best." Vic LPM-2673, LSP-2673 "Mr. Soul." Vic LPM-2709, LSP-2709 "Night Beat."

CROSBY, BING   Dec 8269 "Blue Hawaii." Har 7094 "Crosby Classics." MGM (S)3882 "Bing and Satchmo." Dec DX-151 "Musical Autobiography" (5 records). Dec 4257 "Swinging on a Star." MGM 4129 "Great Standards."

CROSBY, BOB   Dec 8061 "Crosby and Bob Cats." Dot 3278, 25278 "Great Hits." Cap (D)T-1556 "Hits."

CUGAT, XAVIER   Mer 20870, 60870 "Best of Cugat." Mer 20065 "Cugat's Favorites." Col CL-1094, CS-8055 "Cugat Cavalcade."

DAMONE, VIC   Cap (S)T-1646 "Linger Awhile." Cap (S)T-1748 "Lively Ones." Col CL-1912, CS-8712 "Young and Lively."

DARIN, BOBBY   Cap (S)T-1791 "Oh! Look at Me Now." Cap (S)T-1866 "You're the Reason I'm Livin'." Cap (S)T-1942 "18 Yellow Roses."

DAVIS, SAMMY, JR.   Dec 4153, 74153 "Mr. Entertainment." Dec 8854, 78854 "Porgy and Bess." Reprise 6063/2, 9-6063/2 "At the Cocoanut Grove" (2 records). Reprise 6096, 9-6096 "Treasury of Hits."

DAY, DORIS   Col CL-1210, CS-8635 "Greatest Hits." Col CL-2131, CS-8931 "Love Him." Col OL-5960, OS-2360 "Annie Get Your Gun."

DENNIS, MATT   Kapp 1024 "Matt Dennis Plays and Sings." Jub (S)1105 "Welcome Matt Dennis."

DENNY, MARTIN   Lib 3141, 7141 "Enchanted Sea." Lib 3034, 7034 "Exotica," Vol. 1. Lib 3077, 7006 "Exotica," Vol. 2. Lib 3116, 7116 "Exotica," Vol. 3. Lib 3237, 7237 "Taste of Honey."

DOMINO, FATS   Imper 9103 "Sings Million Record Hits." Imper 9062 "12,000,000 Records." ABC (S)455 "Here Comes Fats Domino."

DORSEY, JIMMY   Dec 8609 "Great Jimmy Dorsey." Dot 3437, 25437 "So Rare."

DORSEY, TOMMY   Col C2L-8 "Fabulous Dorseys" (2 records). Colpix (S)401 "Great T.D." Vic LPM-6003 "That Sentimental Gentleman" (2 records). Vic LPM-1423/3 "Tribute to Dorsey" (2 records).

ELLINGTON, DUKE   Col C3L-27 "Ellington Era," Vol. 1 (3 records). Col CL-1245, CS-8072 "Newport 1958." Cap (D)T-1602 "Best of Ellington."

EVERLY BROTHERS   Cad 3025 "Best of the Everly Brothers." Warner Brothers (S)1471 "Golden Hits."

FAITH, PERCY   Col CL-1493, CS-8637 "Greatest Hits." Col CL-2023, CS-8823 "Themes for Lovers." Col CL-2024, CS-8824 "Shangri-La!" Col CL-2167, CS-8967 "More Themes for Young Lovers."

[343]

FITZGERALD, ELLA   Verve 4010/4 "Sings Duke Ellington" (4 records). Dec DX-156 "Best of Ella" (2 records). Dec 8149 "Lullabies of Birdland." Verve 4003 "Ella and Louis." Dec 4129 "Golden Favorites." (See Arlen, Berlin, Gershwin, Porter, and Rodgers and Hart for "Song Books.")

FORD, "TENNESSEE" ERNIE   Cap (S)T-756 "Hymns." Cap (S)T-818 "Spirituals." Cap T-1380 "16 Tons." Cap (D)T-700 "This Lusty Land." Cap (S)T-1227 "Gather 'Round."

FRANCIS, CONNIE   MGM 3793 "Greatest Hits." MGM 3686 "Who's Sorry Now?" MGM (S)3794 "Rock 'n' Roll Million Sellers." MGM (S)4167 "Very Best."

FRIML, RUDOLF   Westminster 6069, 15008 "Friml Plays Friml." Col CL-1630, CS-8430 "Night with Friml" (Frank DeVol).

GARLAND, JUDY   Cap (S)WBO-1569 "Judy at Carnegie Hall" (2 records). Cap (S)T-1999 "Hits." Dec 8190 "Greatest Performances." MGM 4005 "Judy Garland Story," Vol. 2. MGM 3989 "Star Years."

GERSHWIN, GEORGE   Distinguished 107 "Gershwin Piano Recital." Verve 29-5 (4024/8), 629-5 (64024/8) "Song Books" (Ella Fitzgerald, 5 records). Col C2L-1 "Album of Gershwin" (Percy Faith, 2 records). Cor 57021 "Great Gershwin" (Paul Whiteman).

GETZ, STAN   Verve 8432, 68432 "Jazz Samba." Verve 8494, 68494 "Big Band Bossa Nova." Prestige (S)7256 "Greatest Hits."

GOODMAN, BENNY   Vic LPM-2698, LSP-2698 "Together Again!" Vic LOC-6008, LSO-6008 "In Moscow" (2 records). Col CL-814/6 "Carnegie Hall Jazz Concert" (3 records). Col CL-817/19 "King of Swing" (3 records). Vic LPM-1226 "Trio-Quartet-Quintet." Vic LPT-6703 "Golden Age of Swing" (5 records).

GORME, EYDIE   Col CL-2012, CS-8812 "Blame it on Bossa Nova." Col CL-2120, CS-8920 "Gorme Country Style." ABC 192 "Eydie Swings the Blues."

GOULD, MORTON   Vic LM-1994, LSC-1994 "Jungle Drums." Vic LM-2633, LSC-2633 "Love Walked In." Vic LM-2682, LSC-2682 "Good Night Sweetheart." Vic LM-2768, LSC-2768 "More Jungle Drums."

GOULET, ROBERT   Col OL-6050, OS-2450 "Loves Manhattan." Col CL-1676, CS-8476 "Always You." Col CL-1826, CS-8626 "Two of Us."

GRANT, EARL   Dec 4165, 74165 "Ebb Tide." Dec 4231, 74231 "Beyond the Reef." Dec 4299, 74299 "At Basin Street East." Dec 4454, 74454 "Fly Me to the Moon."

HAMPTON, LIONEL   Verve 8112 "Flying Home." Verve 8106 "Airmail Special." Dec 8088 "All American Award Concert." Dec 4296, 74296 "Golden Favorites." Audio Fi 1913, 5913 "Hamp's Big Band."

HERBERT, VICTOR   Col C2L-10, C2S-801 "Album of Victor Herbert" (Percy Faith, 2 records). Col CL-765 "Music of Victor Herbert" (Andre Kostelanetz). Lon 3122, 165 "Music of Herbert and Romberg" (Mantovani). Vic LM-2515, LSC-2515 "Music of Victor Herbert" (Robert Shaw Chorale).

HERMAN, WOODY   Cap (D)T-1554 "Hits." Dec 8133 "Woodchoppers Ball." Philips 200065, 600065 "Woody Herman—1963." Atlantic 1328 "Monterey Jazz Festival." Jazzland 17, 917 "Fourth Herd."

[344]

HERMAN'S HERMITTS   MGM E/SE-4295 "Herman's Hermits on Tour."

HEYWOOD, EDDIE   Lib 3250, 7250 "Golden Encores." Lib 3210, 7210 "Greatest." Vic LPM-1529, LSP-1529 "Canadian Sunset."

HORNE, LENA   Charter (S)101 "Sings Your Requests." Vic LPM-2465, LSP-2465 "On the Blue Side." Vic LPM-2364, LSP-2364 "At the Sands." Vic LOC-1028, LSO-1028 "At the Waldorf."

IVES, BURL   Dec 4361, 74361 "Burl." Dec DX-167 "Best of Burl Ives" (2 records). U Artists 3117, 6117 "Sings Berlin." Col CL-628 "Wayfaring Stranger."

JAMES, HARRY   MGM (S)4058 "Solid Gold Trumpet." Cap (D)T-1515 "Hits." Har 7191 "Songs That Sold a Million." Har 7159 "Great Vocalists." Cap (S)T-1093 "Harry's Choice." Col CL-655 "All Time Favorites."

JOLSON, AL   Dec DX-169 "Best" (2 records). Dec 9063 "Immortal Al Jolson." Dec 9034/8 "Al Jolson Story" (5 records).

JONES, JACK   Kapp 1337, 3337 "She Loves Me." Kapp 1259, 3259 "This Was My Love." Kapp 1265, 3265 "I've Got a Lot of Living to Do." Kapp 1328, 3328 "Call Me Irresponsible," "Hits."

KENTON, STAN   Cap (S)W-724 "In Hi Fi." Cap W-736 "City of Glass." Cap (S)TBO-1327 "Road Show." Cap (S)T-1609 "West Side Story." Cap (S)T-1844 "Adventures in Time."

KERN, JEROME   Col CL-776 "Music of Jerome Kern" (Andre Kostelanetz). Col CL-1386, CS-8181 "Night with Kern" (Percy Faith).

KING, WAYNE   Dec 4309, 74309 "Golden Favorites." Dec 8951, 78951 "Lady Esther Serenade." Vic LPN 1186 "Waltzes You Saved for Me."

KINGSTON TRIO   Cap T-996 "Kingston Trio." Cap (S)T-1658 "College Concert." Cap (S)T-1705 "Best."

KOSTELANETZ, ANDRE   Col ML-5607, MS-6207 "Kostelanetz Festival." Col CL-1827, CS-8627 "Broadway's Greatest." CL-2039, CS-8839 "Wonderland of Hits."

LAINE, FRANKIE   Col CL-1962, CS-8762 "Wanderlust." Col CL-1231, CS-8636 "Greatest Hits." Mer 20587, 60587 "Golden Hits."

LAWRENCE, STEVE   Col CL-2121, CS-8921 "Academy Award Losers." Col CL-2021, CS-8821 "Steve and Eydie at the Movies."

LEE, BRENDA   Dec 4216, 74216 "Sincerely." Dec 4082, 74082 "This Is Brenda Lee." Dec 4039, 74039 "Brenda Lee."

LEE, PEGGY   Cap (S)T-1290 "Latin à la Lee!" Cap (S)T-1520 "Basin Street East." Cap (S)T-1049 "Things Are Swingin'." Cap (S)T-1057 "I'm a Woman." Har 7005 "Peggy Lee Sings with Benny Goodman."

LERNER, ALAN JAY & LOEWE, FREDERICK   Vic LPM-6005, LSP-6005 "An Evening with Lerner and Loewe" (2 records). MGM-3781, S-3781 "Lerner and Loewe."

LOESSER, FRANK   MGM 3449 "Songs by Young and Loesser" (by Joni James).

LOMBARDO, GUY   Cap (D)T-739 "Medley," Vol. 1. Cap (S)T-1244 "Medley," Vol. 2. Cap (S)T-1598 "Medley," Vol. 3. Dec DX-154 "Sweetest Music This Side of Heaven" (4 records). Dec 1836 "Enjoy Yourself."

LONDON, JULIE   Lib 3006, 7027 "Julie is Her Name." Lib 3291, 7291 "Julie's Golden Greats." Lib 3105, 7105 "London by Night."

MANCINI, HENRY   Vic LPM-2755, LSP-2755 "Charade." Vic LPM-2360, LSP-2360 "Mr. Lucky Goes Latin." Vic LPM-2147, LSP-2147 "Blues and the Beat." Vic LPM-1956, LSP-1956 "Peter Gunn."

MARTIN, DEAN   Cap T-401 "Dean Martin Sings." Cap (D)T-1047 "This Is Dean Martin." Cap (S)T-1659 "Dino." Reprise 6054, 9-6054 "Dino Latino."

MARTIN, FREDDY   Cap (S)T-1582 "Hits." Cap (S)T-2018 "Tonight We Love." Cap (S)T-2098 "Best of New Favorites."

MARTIN, MARY   Col ML-4751 "Anything Goes"; "Band Wagon." Cap W-913 "Annie Get Your Gun." Col OL-4180, OS-2040 "South Pacific." Vic LOC-1019, LSO-1019 "Peter Pan." Col KOL-5450, KOS-2020 "Sound of Music."

MARTIN, TONY   Dot 3466, 25466 "Fly Me to the Moon." Mer 20644, 60644 "Golden Hits." Dot 3360, 25360 "Greatest Hits."

MATHIS, JOHNNY   Col CL-1133, CS-8634 "Greatest Hits." Col CL-1351, CS-8152 "Heavenly." Col CL-2098, CS-8898 "Romantically." Col CL-1028 "Wonderful, Wonderful." Col CL-2016, CS-8816 "Newest Hits."

McHUGH, JIMMY   Dec 8423 "Songs of Jimmy McHugh" (by Russ Morgan).

MERCER, JOHNNY   Cap T-1858 "Best." Cap (D)W-1984 "Frank Sinatra Sings the Select Mercer."

MERMAN, ETHEL   Reprise 6062, 9-6062 "In Vegas." Reprise 6032, 9-6032 "Her Greatest." Dec DX-153 (8178/9) "Musical Autobiography" (2 records). Dec 9018, 79018 "Annie Get Your Gun." Dec 9022, 79022 "Call Me Madam."

MILLER, GLENN   Vic LPT-6700 "Glenn Miller Limited Edition" (5 records). Vic LPM-1506 "Carnegie Hall Concert." Vic LPM-1192, LSP-1192 "Glenn Miller Story." 20th Century-Fox (S)3020/1 "Original Soundtracks" (2 records).

MILLER, MITCH   Col CL-1160, CS-8004 "Sing Along with Mitch." Col CL-1544, CS-8638 "Greatest Hits." Col CL-2063, CS-8863 "Hymn Sing Along."

MILLS BROTHERS   Dot 3157, 25157 "Great Hits," Vol. 1. Dot 3308, 25308 "Great Hits," Vol. 2. Dot 3338, 25338 "Yellow Bird." Dec 4084 "Old Golden Favorites."

NELSON, RICK   Imper 9048 "Ricky Nelson," Vol. 1. Imper 9050 "Ricky Nelson," Vol. 2. Imper 9061 "Sings Again." Dec 4419, 74419 "For Your Sweet Love."

NERO, PETER   Vic LPM-2383, LSP-2383 "New Piano in Town." Vic LPM-2536, LSP-2536 "For the Nero-Minded." Vic LPM-2710, LSP-2710 "In Person." Vic LPM-2853, LSP-2853 "Reflections."

PAGE, PATTI   Col CL-2132, CS-8932 "Love after Midnight." Col CL-2049, CS-8849 "Say Wonderful Things." Mer 20495 "Golden Hits," Vol. 1. Mer 20794, 60794 "Golden Hits," Vol. 2. Mer 20138, 60049 "Waltz Queen."

PETER, PAUL AND MARY   Warner Brothers (S)1507 "In the Wind." Warner Brothers (S)1473 "Moving." Warner Brothers (S)1449 "Peter, Paul and Mary."

PIAF, EDITH   Cap TBL 2193 "Piaf" (3 records). Cap (S)T-10348 "Piaf and Sarapo at the Bobino." Col CL-898 "Vie en Rose." Cap (S)T-10328 "Chansons."

PORTER, COLE   Verve 4001-2 "Song Book" (Ella Fitzgerald, 2 records). Col CL-729 "Music of Cole Porter" (Andre Kostelanetz). Vic LM-2559, LSC-2559 "Kern and Porter" (Morton Gould).

PRESLEY, ELVIS   Vic LPM-1707, LSP-1707 "Golden Records," Vol. 1. Vic LPM-2075, LSP-2075 "Golden Records," Vol. 2. Vic LPM-2765, LSP-2765 "Golden Records," Vol. 3. Vic LPM-2426, LSP-2426 "Blue Hawaii." Vic LPM-2256, LSP-2256 "G.I. Blues." Vic LPM-1382, LSP-1382 "Elvis." Vic LPM-1254, LSP-1254 "Blue Suede."

PREVIN, ANDRÉ   Col CL-2158, CS-8959 "Sound Stage!" Col CL-2034, CS-8834 "In Hollywood." Col CL-2018, CS-8818 "Four To Go."

PRIMA, LOUIS   Cap T-1531 "Hits of Louis and Keely." Dot 3262, 25262 "Greatest Hits."

REESE, DELLA   Vic LPM-2872, LSP-2782 "Basin Street East." Vic LPM-2419, LSP-2419 "Classic Della." Jub 1116 "And That Reminds Me."

ROBBINS, MARTY   Col CL-1918, CS-8718 "Devil Woman." Col CL-1325, CS-8639 "Greatest Hits." Col CL-1855, CS-8655 "Portrait of Marty."

RODGERS, JIMMIE   Rou (S)25033 "Number One Ballads." Rou (S)25179 "15 Million Sellers." Dot 3525, 25525 "Honeycomb."

RODGERS, RICHARD   Vic LPM-2513, LSP-2513 "Music of Rodgers" (Melachrino). Vic LM-2294, LSC-2294 "Slaughter on 10th Avenue" (Boston Pops).

RODGERS, RICHARD, AND HAMMERSTEIN, OSCAR, II   MGM (S)3817 "Rodgers and Hammerstein" (Cyril Ornadel). Cad 3005 "Andy Williams Sings Rodgers and Hammerstein."

RODGERS, RICHARD, AND HART, LORENZ   Cap (D)W-1825 "Frank Sinatra Sings Rodgers and Hart." Verve 4002-2 (4022/3), 64022/3 "Rodgers and Hart" (Ella Fitzgerald, 2 records). U Artists 3273, 6273 "Melodies of Rodgers and Hart."

ROMBERG, SIGMUND   Rich 20086, 30086 "Best of Herbert and Romberg" (Frank Chacksfield). Col CL-1302, CS-8108 "Night with Romberg" (Percy Faith). Vic LPM-2106, LSP-2106 "Music of Romberg" (Melachrino).

ROSE, DAVID   MGM 3592, S-3592 "Autumn Leaves." MGM 3748, S-3748 "Plays David Rose." MGM 3215 "Holiday for Strings." MGM 4062, S-4062 "The Stripper."

RYDELL, BOBBY   Cameo (S)1040 "All the Hits," Vol. 2. Cameo 1009 "Biggest Hits," Vol. 1. Cameo 1028 "Biggest Hits," Vol. 2. Cameo (S)1011 "At the Copa."

SEVILLE, DAVID   Lib 3209, 7209 "Alvin Show." Lib 3170, 7170 "Around the World with the Chipmunks." Lib 3229, 7229 "Chipmunk Songbook."

SHAW, ARTIE   Vic LPM-1648 "Reissued by Request." Camd (S)465 "Great Artie Shaw." Vic LPM-1241 "Gramercy Five."

SHEARING, GEORGE   Cap (D)T-648 "Shearing Spell." Cap (S)T-1038 "Burnished Brass." Cap (S)T-1187 "On Stage!" Cap (S)T-1472 "Shearing Touch." Cap (S)T-1992 "Jazz Concert."

SHORE, DINAH   Cap (S)T-1704 "Fabulous Hits." Har 7239 "Lavender Blue."

SINATRA, FRANK   Cap (D)T-2036 "Great Hits." Reprise 1010, 9-1010 "Sinatra's Sinatra." Cap (S)WCO-1762 "Great Years" (3 records). Reprise 1004, 9-1004 "Sinatra and Strings." Reprise 1003, 9-1003 "I Remember Tommy." Cap (S)W-1053

"Only the Lonely." Cap (S)W-1069 "Come Dance with Me." Vic LPM-1569 "Frankie and Tommy Dorsey."

STAFFORD, JO   Cap (S)T-1921 "Hits." Col CL-1228 "Greatest Hits."

STARR, KAY   Cap T-1358 "One More Time." Cap (D)T-415 "Hits."

STREISAND, BARBRA   Col CL-2007, CS-8007 "Barbra Streisand Album." Col CL-2054, CS-8854 "Second Barbra Streisand Album." Col CL-2154, CS-8954 "Third Barbra Streisand Album."

TIOMKIN, DIMITRI   Cor 57006 "Movie Themes."

TORME, MELVIN HOWARD   Beth 6020 "At the Crescendo." Verve 8440, 68440 "My Kind of Music." Col CL-2318, CS-9118, "That's All."

VALENTE, CATERINA   Dec 8852 "Schlagerparade." Lon 91267, 99025 "German Evergreens." Lon 3307 "Strictly U.S.A."

VALLEE, RUDY   Dec 4242, 74242 "Stein Songs." Reg 6029 "Let's Do It."

VAUGHAN, SARAH   Mer 20645, 60645 "Golden Hits." Mer 20316, 60002 "Best of Berlin" (with Billy Eckstine). Mer 12123 "All Time Favorites." Rou (S)52060 "Divine One."

VAUGHN, BILLY   Dot 3540, 25540 "Number One Hits." Dot 3288, 25288 "Great Golden Hits." Dot 3276, 25276 "Theme from 'A Summer Place.'" Dot 3165, 25165 "Blue Hawaii." Dot 3100, 25100 "Sail Along, Silv'ry Moon."

VEE, BOBBY   Lib 3285, 7285 "Night Has a Thousand Eyes." Lib 3245, 7245 "Golden Greats." Lib 3181, 7181 "Bobby Vee."

VINTON, BOBBY   Epic LN-24020, BN-26020 "Roses Are Red." Epic LN-24081, BN-26081 "There, I've Said It Again." Epic LN-24068, BN-26068 "Blue Velvet."

WALLER, THOMAS "FATS"   Vic LPM-1246 "Aint Misbehavin'." Vic LPM-1502 "Handful of Keys." Cap T-10258 "In London." Rich 20082 "Music of Fats Waller" (by Ted Heath).

WARING, FRED   Cap (S)T-936 "All Through the Night." Cap (S)T-1389/90 "Broadway Cavalcade" (2 records). Cap (S)T-1610 "The Meaning of Christmas."

WILLIAMS, ANDY   Col CL-1809, CS-8609 "Moon River." Col CL-2171, CS-8971 "Call Me Irresponsible." Col CL-2015, CS-8815 "Days of Wine and Roses."

WILLIAMS, ROGER   Kapp 1063 "Almost Paradise." Kapp 1260, 3260 "Greatest Hits." Kapp (S)1112 "Near You." Kapp 1290, 3290 "Mr. Piano."

WILSON, NANCY   Cap (S)T-2082 "Today, Tomorrow, Forever." Cap (S)T-2012 "Yesterday's Love Songs . . . Today's Blues." Cap (S)T-1934 "Hollywood—My Way." Cap (S)T-1828 "Broadway—My Way."

Part Two.   *Musicals*

The musicals listed in the Discography are discussed in the book. Most are covered in individual items including plot synopses. Original-cast members, songs in the score, etc., can usually be found by referring to these items. Only records generally available from dealers at this writing are included.

ALLEGRO   This original cast reissue (1965), Vic LOC-1099, LSO-1099 (e), features John Battles, Lisa Kirk and Annamary Dickey.

ANNIE GET YOUR GUN   The original-cast album, Dec 9018, 19018, stars Ethel Merman. Col OL-5960, OS-2360 features Doris Day and Robert Goulet. MGM 3768 offers Betty Hutton and Howard Keel in excerpts; the record is filled out with extracts from "Three Little Words." Cap W-913, with Mary Martin and John Raitt, is on a par with the original-cast recording.

ANYTHING GOES   Dec 8318 stars Bing Crosby and Donald O'Connor. Col ML-4751 pairs excerpts with pieces from "The Band Wagon," both with Mary Martin and Fred Astaire.

BABES IN ARMS   Mary Martin helps recreate this first rate Rodgers and Hart score in COL OL-7070, OS-2570.

BABES IN TOYLAND   Kenny Baker sings selections in Dec 8458; extracts from "The Red Mill" complete the disc. Buena (S)4022 offers Annette and Tommy Sands in the movie soundtrack.

BAND WAGON, THE   For Col ML-4751, see "Anything Goes." MGM 3051 stars Fred Astaire.

BOYS FROM SYRACUSE, THE   Cap (S)TAO-1933 is an excellent recording of the 1963 off-Broadway revival. Col OL-7080, OS-2580 features Jack Cassidy and Bibi Osterwald.

BRIGADOON   The original-cast album, Vic LOC-1001, LSO-1001, is still probably the best. Vic LPM-6005, LSP-6005, a two-record set, offers Jan Peerce and Robert Merrill; selections from "Gigi," "My Fair Lady," and "Paint Your Wagon" complete this Lerner and Loewe album. The Peerce and Merrill version of "Brigadoon" can be also had on Vic LPM-2275, LSP-2275. Col CL-1132 features Shirley Jones and Jack Cassidy. MGM 3135 is the movie soundtrack.

BYE BYE BIRDIE   Col OL/KOL-5510, OS/KOS-2025 is the original-cast recording. Mercury 13000, 17000 has the original London cast. Vic LOC-1081, LSO-1081 is the movie soundtrack.

CALL ME MADAM   Irving Berlin and Ethel Merman are at their best in the original-cast recording, Dec 9022, 79022.

CAMELOT   Julie Andrews, Richard Burton, and Robert Goulet grace the original-cast recording, Col OL-5620, OS-2031, of this melodious score.

CAN-CAN   Cap W-452 is the original-cast recording. Cap (S)W-1301, the movie soundtrack, includes several Cole Porter songs not in the original.

CARNIVAL!   MGM (S)3946OC features Anna Maria Alberghetti in the original cast.

CAROUSEL   John Raitt, Jan Clayton, and Jean Darling are in the original-cast recording, Dec 9020, 79020. Shirley Jones and Gordon MacRae are in the soundtrack recording, Cap (S)W-694. Alfred Drake and Roberta Peters sing on Command 843, 843-SD. Robert Merrill and Patrice Munsel sing on Vic LPM-1048.

DAMN YANKEES   Vic LOC-1021 is the original-cast recording. Vic LOC-1047, LSO-1047 is the soundtrack. Both feature Ray Walston and Gwen Verdon; the soundtrack has Tab Hunter in the role played by Stephen Douglass in the original.

FANNY   Vic LOC-1015 is the original-cast recording. Warner Brothers (S)1416 is the movie version.

FINIAN'S RAINBOW   The original-cast album, Col OL-4602, OS-2080, stars Ella Logan and David Wayne. The recording of the 1960 Broadway revival, Vic LOC-1057, LSO-1057, stars Jeannie Carson and Howard Morris.

FIORELLO!   Tom Bosley plays La Guardia in the original-cast recording, Cap (S)WAO-1321.

FLOWER DRUM SONG   Col OL-5350, OS-2009 is the original-cast recording. Dec 9098, 79098 is the soundtrack.

FUNNY GIRL   Barbra Streisand gives a stellar performance in the original-cast recording, Cap (S)VAS-2059.

FIDDLER ON THE ROOF   Zero Mostel stars in the original-cast version of the top 1964–65 hit. Vic LOC-1093, LSO-1093.

FUNNY THING HAPPENED ON THE WAY TO THE FORUM, A   Zero Mostel and the rest of the original cast have a romp on Cap (S)WAO-1717.

GENTLEMEN PREFER BLONDES   Carol Channing and Yvonne Adair star in the original-cast recording, Col OL-4290, OS-2310.

GIRL CRAZY   Col CL-822 features Mary Martin.

GUYS AND DOLLS   Dec 9023, 79023 is the original-cast recording of this excellent score.

GYPSY   The original-cast recording, Col OL-5420, OS-2017, stars Ethel Merman. The soundtrack recording, Warner Brothers (S)B-1480, features Rosalind Russell and Natalie Wood.

HELLO, DOLLY!   Carol Channing has a perfect showcase in the original-cast recording, Vic LOCD-1087, LSOD-1087.

HERE'S LOVE   Col KOL-6000, KOS-2400 is the original-cast recording.

HIGH BUTTON SHOES   The original cast recording, with Phil Silvers and Nanette Fabray, was reissued in 1965—Vic LOC-1107, LSO-1107 (e).

HOW TO SUCCEED IN BUSINESS WITHOUT REALLY TRYING   The original-cast recording, Vic LOC-1066, LSO-1066, stars Robert Morse and Rudy Vallee.

IRMA LA DOUCE   Col OL-5560, OS-2029 is the Broadway-cast recording. U Artists 4109, 5109 is the soundtrack.

JUMBO   Doris Day and Jimmy Durante appear in the movie version, Col OL-5860, OS-2260.

KING AND I, THE   Dec 9008, 79008 is the original-cast recording. Cap (S)W-740 is the soundtrack. Yul Brynner plays the king in both.

KISMET   The original-cast recording, Col OL-4850, OS-2060, has Alfred Drake and Doretta Morrow. MGM 3281 features Howard Keel, Ann Blyth, and Vic Damone.

KISS ME, KATE   Col OL-4140, OS-2300 is the original-cast recording. A later recording, Cap (S)TAO-1267, features the same principals (Patricia Morison, Alfred Drake,

Lisa Kirk, and Harold Lang). MGM 3077 offers Kathryn Grayson and Howard Keel. Col CL-1768, CS-8568 has Earl Wrightson and Virginia Mayo.

LITTLE MARY SUNSHINE   Eileen Brennan stars in the original-cast recording, Cap (S)WAO-1240, of this off-Broadway success.

LITTLE ME   The original-cast recording, Vic LOC-1078, LSO-1078, features Sid Caesar.

MILK AND HONEY   Molly Picon stars in the original-cast recording, Vic LOC-1065, LSO-1065.

MOST HAPPY FELLA, THE   Col O3L-240 (three records) is the complete musical. Col OL-5118, OS-2330 gives the songs only. Both are with the original cast.

MR. PRESIDENT   Col KOL-5870, KOS-2270 is the original-cast recording of a score that is tuneful but not up to Irving Berlin's best.

MUSIC MAN, THE   Robert Preston stars in two excellent versions: Cap (S)W-990 (original cast) and Warner Brothers (S)B-1459 (soundtrack).

MY FAIR LADY   The original-cast recording, Col OL-5090, OS-2015, stars Julie Andrews and Rex Harrison. Jan Peerce and Robert Merrill sing in Vic LPM-6005, LSP-6005 (a two-record set completed by extracts from other Lerner and Loewe hits—"Gigi," "Paint Your Wagon," and "Brigadoon") and in Vic LPM-2274, LSP-2274. Col WL-155 is the Spanish version.

NEW MOON, THE   Cap (S)W-1966, featuring Gordon MacRae, Dorothy Kirsten, and the Roger Wagner Chorale, is almost the complete score. Cap T-219 offers MacRae in excerpts from "The New Moon" and "The Vagabond King."

NO STRINGS   Cap (S)O-1695 is the original-cast recording of the first show for which Richard Rodgers wrote both words and music.

OH, KAY!   Col CL-1050 is a 1957 recording of a 1926 show that included some of Gershwin's best songs.

OKLAHOMA! The original-cast recording, Dec 9017, 79017, stars Alfred Drake, Joan Roberts, and Celeste Holm. The soundtrack recording, Cap (S)WAO-595, stars Gordon MacRae and Shirley Jones. Col CL-828, CS-8739 features Nelson Eddy and Kaye Ballard.

OLIVER!   The Broadway cast of this English musical, on Vic LOCD-2004, LSOD-2004, stars Georgia Brown, of the original London company. Cap (S)T-1784 offers Stanley Holloway and Alma Cogan.

ON THE TOWN   Col OL-5540, OS-2028 features original-cast members Betty Comden and Adolph Green, who also wrote the book and lyrics. Dec 8030 stars Mary Martin and has excerpts from "Lute Song" on the other side.

ON YOUR TOES   Dec 9015 is a recording of the 1954 Broadway revival, featuring Vera Zorina, Bobby Van, and Elaine Stritch.

110 IN THE SHADE   The original-cast album, Vic LOC-1085, LSO-1085, stars Inga Swenson, Robert Horton, and Stephen Douglass.

PAINT YOUR WAGON   Vic LOC-1006 is the original-cast album. Jan Peerce and Robert Merrill sing in Vic LPM-6005, LSP-6005 (a two-record set of Lerner and Loewe completed by parts of "Gigi," "My Fair Lady," and "Brigadoon") and in Vic LPM-2274, LSP-2274.

PAJAMA GAME, THE   Col OL-4840, the original-cast album, stars Janis Paige, John Raitt, and Eddie Foy. Doris Day replaces Miss Paige in the movie version, Col OL-5210.

PAL JOEY   Col OL-4364 offers the cast of the 1950 revival, starring Harold Lang, Vivienne Segal, and Helen Gallagher. Cap (D)W-912 is the soundtrack.

PETER PAN   Mary Martin and Cyril Ritchard star in Vic LOC-1019, LSO-1019, which offers the original cast of the Broadway and television versions.

PORGY AND BESS   Col OSL-162 and Bethlehem EXLP-1, three records each, are complete versions. Selections may be had in Dec 9024, 79024 (original cast), Vic LOP-1507, LSO-1507 (Lena Horne and Harry Belafonte), and Vic LM-2679, LSC-2679 (Leontyne Price and William Warfield). Col OL-5410, OS-2016 is the movie version.

ROBERTA   Dec 8007 stars Kitty Carlisle and Alfred Drake. Cap T-384, starring Gordon MacRae, offers excerpts from "The Desert Song" on the other side.

SHE LOVES ME   MGM (S)4118OC, a two-record set, is the original-cast recording.

SHOW BOAT   Col OL-4058 is a recording of the 1946 Broadway revival, with Jan Clayton, Carol Bruce, Charles Fredericks, and Kenneth Spencer. Col OL-5820, OS-2220 stars John Raitt, Barbara Cook, and William Warfield. Vic LOP-1505, LSO-1505 features Howard Keel and Anne Jeffreys. Vic LM-2008 offers Robert Merrill, Patrice Munsel, and Risë Stevens.

SILK STOCKINGS   One of Cole Porter's best scores is delivered with gusto by Don Ameche, Hildegarde Neff and Gretchen Wyler in the original cast recording, reissued in 1965, Vic LOC-1102, LSO-1102 (e).

SOUND OF MUSIC, THE   Col KOL-5450, KOS-2020 is the original-cast recording, starring Mary Martin and Theodore Bikel. Warner Brothers (S)1377 features the Trapp Family Singers. Movie soundtrack version, starring Julie Andrews, includes some new material by Richard Rodgers—Vic LOCD-2005, LSOD-2005.

SOUTH PACIFIC   The original-cast album, Col OL-4180, OS-2040, with Mary Martin and Ezio Pinza, is hard to beat. Vic LOC-1032, LSO-1032 is the soundtrack.

TAKE ME ALONG   Jackie Gleason, Walter Pidgeon, Eileen Herlie, and Robert Morse star in the original-cast recording, Vic LOC-1050, LSO-1050.

THREEPENNY OPERA, THE   Lon 76004 is the original movie version. Vic LOC-1086, LSO-1086 is the '64 soundtrack with Sammy Davis as the Streetsinger.

TREE GROWS IN BROOKLYN, A   Col OL-4405 is the original cast version.

UNSINKABLE MOLLY BROWN, THE   Tammy Grimes scores as the heroine in the original-cast recording, Cap (S)WAO-1509. MGM (S)4232 is the movie soundtrack, with Debbie Reynolds.

UP IN CENTRAL PARK   Dec 8016 has excerpts from this show on one side, selections from "The Red Mill" on the other.

VAGABOND KING, THE   Vic LM-2509, LSC-2509 features Mario Lanza. The other contenders are excerpts: Dec 8362 (with Alfred Drake) teams up with "The Student Prince"; Cap T-219 reverses to "The New Moon."

WEST SIDE STORY   Col OL-5320, OS-2001 is the original-cast recording. Col OL-5670, OS-2070 is the movie version. Both are excellent.

WILDCAT   Vic LOC-1060, LSO-1060, the original-cast recording, stars Lucille Ball.

WONDERFUL TOWN   Dec 9010, 79010 is the original-cast recording. Columbia OL-5360, OS-2008 is the television soundtrack. Rosalind Russell stars in both.

Bibliography

Bibliography

General

Blum, Daniel (ed.). *Theatre World*. Philadelphia: Chilton Books, annual.

Boone, Pat. *Twixt Twelve and Twenty*. Englewood Cliffs, New Jersey: Prentice-Hall, 1955.

Burton, Jack. *Tin Pan Alley Blue Book*. New York: Century House, 1958. Revised, expanded edition in two volumes, 1962.

————. *Blue Book of Broadway Musicals*. New York: Century House, 1952.

Chujoy, Anatole. *The Dance Encyclopedia*. New York: A. S. Barnes, 1949.

Current Biography New York: H. W. Wilson, various years.

Delauney, Charles. *New Hot Discography*. New York: Criterion, 1948.

Ewen, David. *Complete Book of the American Musical Theater*. New York: Henry Holt, 1958.

————. *Men of Popular Music*. New York: Ziff-Davis, 1941.

————. *Panorama of American Popular Music*. Englewood Cliffs, New Jersey: Prentice-Hall, 1957.

————. *Songs of America*. New York: Ziff-Davis, 1947.

————. *The Story of the American Musical Theater*. Philadelphia: Chilton Books, 1961.

Feather, Leonard. *The Encyclopedia of Jazz*. New York: Horizon Press, 1955. Revised edition, 1962.

Field, James J. *American Popular Music, 1875–1950*. Philadelphia: Musical Americana, 1956.

40 Years of Hit Tunes (1918–58). New York: ASCAP, 1958.

Gleason, Ralph J. (ed.). *Jam Session: An Anthology of Jazz*. New York: G. P. Putnam's Sons, 1958.

Goffin, Robert. *Jazz*. New York: Doubleday, 1944.

Goldberg, Isaac. *Tin Pan Alley*. New York: John Day, 1930.

Goodman, Benny, and Kolodin, Irving. *The Kingdom of Swing*. New York: Stackpole Sons, 1939.

Green, Stanley. *The World of Musical Comedy*. New York: Ziff-Davis, 1960.

Grove's Dictionary of Music and Musicians. New York: St. Martin's Press, 1961.

Handy, W. C., and Niles, E. A. *Blues*. New York: A. & C. Boni, 1926.

Hobson, Wilder. *American Jazz Music*. New York: W. W. Norton, 1939.

Hughes, Langston. *The First Book of Jazz*. New York: Franklin Watts, 1955.

Lewine, Richard, and Simon, Alfred. *Encyclopedia of Theatre Music*. New York: Random House, 1961.

Marks, E. B. (with A. J. Liebling). *They All Sang*. New York: Viking Press, 1934.

Mattfeld, Julius (compiler). *Variety Music Cavalcade*. Englewood Cliffs, New Jersey: Prentice-Hall, 1952. Revised edition, 1962.

McNamara, Daniel I. *The ASCAP Biographical Dictionary of Composers, Authors and Publishers*. New York: Thomas Y. Crowell, 1946. Revised edition, 1952.

Miller, Paul E. *Esquire Jazz Book*. Smith and Durrell, 1942.

————. *Miller's Yearbook of Popular Music*. New York: Pem Classics, 1943.

Musician's Guide. New York: Music Information Services.

Nettl, Paul. *The Story of Dance Music*. New York: Philosophical Library, 1947.

Panassié, Hugues. *Hot Jazz*. New York: M. Witmark and Sons, 1936.

————. *The Real Jazz*. Smith and Durrell, 1942.

Panassié, Hugues, and Gautier, Madeline. *Guide to Jazz*. Boston: Houghton-Mifflin, 1956.

Paris, Leonard A. *Men and Melodies*. New York: Thomas Y. Crowell, 1954.

Rodgers and Hammerstein Fact Books. New York: Rodgers and Hammerstein, 1955. Supplement, 1960.

Sargent, Winthrop. *Jazz: Hot and Hybrid*. New York: E. P. Dutton, 1946.

Smith, Cecil. *Musical Comedy in America*. New York: Theatre Arts Books, 1950.

Spaeth, Sigmund. *A History of Popular Music*. New York: Random House, 1948.

————. *The Importance of Music*. New York: Fleet Publishing, 1963.

30 Years of Hollywood Music (1928–58). New York: ASCAP, 1959.

Witmark, Isadore, and Goldberg, Isaac. *From Ragtime to Swingtime*. Lee Furman, 1939.

Biography

Armitage, Merle, *et al. George Gershwin*. New York: Longmans, Green, 1938.

Armstrong, Louis. *Swing That Music*. New York: Longmans, Green, 1936.

————. *Satchmo: My Life in New Orleans*. Englewood Cliffs, New Jersey: Prentice-Hall, 1954.

Astaire, Fred. *Steps in Time*. New York: Harper and Brothers, 1959.

Cantor, Eddie (with David Freeman). *My Life Is in Your Hands*. New York: Harper and Brothers, 1928. Revised edition, New York: Blue Ribbon Books, 1932.

Cantor, Eddie (with Jane Kesner Ardmore). *Take My Life*. New York: Doubleday, 1957.

Carmichael, Hoagy. *The Stardust Road*. New York: Rinehart, 1946.

Cugat, Xavier. *Rumba Is My Life*. New York: Didier, 1948.

Duke, Vernon. *Passport to Paris*. Boston: Little, Brown, 1955.

Ewen, David. *The Story of George Gershwin*. New York: Henry Holt, 1943.

————. *A Journey to Greatness: The Life and Music of George Gershwin*. New York: Henry Holt, 1956.

                    . *Richard Rodgers*. New York: Henry Holt, 1957.

                    . *The World of Jerome Kern*. New York: Henry Holt, 1960.

Ford, Tennessee Ernie. *This Is My Song, This Is My Story*. Englewood Cliffs, New Jersey: Prentice-Hall, 1963.

Gammond, Peter. *Duke Ellington: His Life and Music*. London: Phoenix House, 1958.

Green, Stanley. *The Rodgers and Hammerstein Story*. New York: John Day, 1963.

Goldberg, Isaac. *George Gershwin*. New York: Simon and Schuster, 1931.

Handy, W. C. (edited by Arna Bontemps). *Father of the Blues: An Autobiography*. New York: Macmillan, 1941.

Horricks, Raymond. *Count Basie and His Orchestra*. London: Victor Gollancs, 1957.

Ives, Burl. *Wayfarin' Stranger*. New York: McGraw-Hill, 1948.

Jablonski, Edward. *Harold Arlen: Happy with the Blues*. Garden City, New York: Doubleday, 1961.

Levant, Oscar. *A Smattering of Ignorance*. New York: Doubleday, Doran, 1940.

Merman, Eethel (as told to Pete Martin). *Who Could Ask for Anything More*. Garden City, New York: Doubleday, 1955.

Shaw, Artie. *The Trouble with Cinderella*. New York: Farrar, Straus and Young, 1952.

Taylor, Deems. *Some Enchanted Evenings: The Story of Rodgers and Hammerstein*. New York: Harper and Brothers, 1953.

Tiomkin, Dmitri. *Please Don't Hate Me*. New York: Doubleday, 1959.

Ulanov, Barry. *Duke Ellington*. Creative Age Press, 1946.

                    . *The Incredible Crosby*. New York: McGraw-Hill, 1948.

Waters, Ethel (with Charles Samuels). *His Eye Is on the Sparrow*. New York: Doubleday, 1958.

Waters, Edward N. *Victor Herbert: A Life in Music*. New York: The Macmillan Co., 1955.

Willson, Meredith. *And There I Stood with My Piccolo*. New York: Henry Holt, 1955.

                    . *Eggs I Have Laid*. New York: Henry Holt, 1955.

                    . *But He Doesn't Know the Territory*. New York: G. P. Putnam's Sons, 1959.

Woollcott, Alexander. *The Story of Irving Berlin*. New York: G. P. Putnam's Sons, 1925.

Songwriting Methods

Eisler, Hanns. *Composing for the Films*. London: Dennis Dobson, 1937.

Ellington, Duke. *Piano Method for the Blues*. New York: Robbins Music, 1943.

Garland, Wallace Graydon. *Popular Songwriting Methods*. New York: American Music Guild, 1942.

Gershwin, Ira. *Lyrics on Several Occasions*. New York: Alfred A. Knopf, 1959.

Hammerstein, Oscar, II. *Lyrics*. New York: Simon and Schuster, 1949.

Korb, Arthur. *How To Write Songs That Sell*. New York: Greenberg, 1949.

Miller, Glenn. *Method for Orchestral Arranging*. New York: Mutual Music Society, 1943.